S0-AAD-472

Human Development

ACROSS THE LIFESPAN

FOURTH EDITION

Human Development
ACROSS THE LIFESPAN

John S. Dacey
Boston College

John F. Travers
Boston College

Boston   Burr Ridge, IL   Dubuque, IA   Madison, WI   New York   San Francisco   St. Louis
Bangkok Bogotá Caracas Lisbon London Madrid
Mexico City Milan New Delhi Seoul Singapore Sydney Taipei Toronto

McGraw-Hill College

A Division of The McGraw·Hill Companies

HUMAN DEVELOPMENT ACROSS THE LIFESPAN, FOURTH EDITION

Copyright © 1999 by The McGraw-Hill Companies, Inc. All rights reserved. Previous edition © 1996 Times Mirror Higher Education Group, Inc. All rights reserved. Printed in the United States of America. Except as permitted under the United States Copyright Act of 1976, no part of this publication may be reproduced or distributed in any form or by any means, or stored in a data base or retrieval system, without the prior written permission of the publisher.

✿ This book is printed on recycled, acid-free paper containing 10% postconsumer waste.

4 5 6 7 8 9 0 QPD/QPD 9 3 2 1 0

ISBN 0–697–36429–1

Editorial director: *Jane E. Vaicunas*
Executive editor: *Mickey Cox*
Developmental editor: *Sharon Geary*
Marketing manager: *James Rozsa*
Senior project manager: *Kay J. Brimeyer*
Production supervisor: *Sandra Hahn*
Freelance design coordinator: *Mary L. Christianson*
Senior photo research coordinator: *Carrie K. Burger*
Art editor: *Joyce Watters*
Supplement coordinator: *Audrey A. Reiter*
Compositor: *ElectraGraphics, Inc.*
Typeface: *10/12 Garamond*
Printer: *Quebecor Printing Book Group/Dubuque, IA*

Freelance designer: *Diane Beasley*
Cover photograph: *Telegraph/FPG International*

The credits section for this book begins on page 565 and is considered an extension of the copyright page.

Library of Congress Cataloging-in-Publication Data

Dacey, John S.
    Human development across the lifespan / John Dacey, John Travers.
— 4ᵗʰ ed.
    p.   cm.
    Rev. ed. of : Human development. 3ʳᵈ ed. © 1996.
    Includes bibliographical references and indexes.
    ISBN 0–697–36429–1 (alk. paper)
    1. Developmental psychology.   I. Dacey, John S.   Human
development.   II. Travers, John F.   III. Title
    BF713.D33   1999
    155—dc21   98–19632
                                                            CIP

www.mhhe.com

*This book is dedicated with deep affection
to the two people who have helped us the most—
Linda Schulman and Barbara Travers,
our wives.*

Brief Contents

Contents

PART V
Middle Childhood

PART VI
Adolescence

PART VII
Early Adulthood

CHAPTER 13

Physical and Cognitive Development in Early Adulthood   *343*

CHAPTER 14

Psychosocial Development in Early Adulthood   *369*

PART VIII
Middle Adulthood

CHAPTER 15

Physical and Cognitive Development in Middle Adulthood   *401*

CHAPTER 16

Psychosocial Development in Middle Adulthood   *427*

PART IX
Late Adulthood

CHAPTER 17

Physical and Cognitive Development in Late Adulthood   455

CHAPTER 18

Psychosocial Development in Late Adulthood   483

CHAPTER 19

Dying and Spirituality   *503*

An Applied View

A Sociocultural View

What's Your View?

As we move into the twenty-first century, our society has clearly adopted a belief that all individuals should have the opportunity to develop their potential to the fullest. One way of achieving this goal is to know as much as possible about human development—how we change from the helplessness of infancy to the competence of adulthood to the wisdom of old age.

Perhaps the human saga is not written as clearly as we would like. As Thomas Jefferson once noted, although the human condition is not open to complete scrutiny, it is, nevertheless, susceptible to considerable improvement. Clues providing insights into the riddle of human development are beginning to multiply. Genetic discoveries are occurring at a rate that can only be described as breathtaking: the gene that causes cystic fibrosis has been identified; genetic markers that point to a family disposition for breast cancer are known; the march to identify all the human genes (The Human Genome Project) continues unabated.

As the population of our nation continues to change, we have become more sensitive to the influence that culture exerts on development. We recognize that all children do not learn in the same manner; all cultures do not view adolescence from the same perspective; not all cultures place the same value on work. Never before has it been so clear that development results from the interaction of heredity and environment and that neglect of either side of our equation can only lead to damaging misinterpretations.

Basic Themes of Human Development Across the Lifespan

Reflecting the exciting changes that are taking place in our knowledge of human development, we have woven our narrative around several integrating themes: the biopsychosocial model, the cultural context of development, the roles of age and gender, and applications to daily living. We return to these themes in each chapter as a means of making more meaningful the basic knowledge of human development.

The Biopsychosocial Approach

The biopsychosocial approach will help you to integrate the wealth of information that you will find in the pages to come. By thinking of lifespan development as the product of the interaction of biological, psychological, and social forces, you will better appreciate the complexity of development. For example, biological influences on development range from the role of genes in development to adult health concerns; psychological influences include all aspects of cognitive and personality development; social influences refer to such powerful forces as family, school, peers, and the media. The biopsychosocial approach helps to explain how the interaction of these forces is the key to understanding human development.

Contextual Influences on Development

Our goal in urging you to adopt a sociocultural perspective is to help you develop a greater understanding of those who seem "different." If you adopt this perspective, you will come to realize that different people have different worldviews that decisively influence their thinking. People from different cultures do not all think alike and, as we will stress, these differences are assets. Recognizing how diverse people are in their thinking and behavior will help you to identify and comprehend variations in how individuals are raised, how they think, and how they become functioning members of their culture.

In various places throughout the book, we will be discussing the four major tenets of the contextual model: the relative plasticity of life; the historical embeddedness of all development; the diversity of development; and the bidirectionality of the causes of all human behavior. Since we feel so strongly about the importance of these factors, you will find a discussion of sociocultural issues in each chapter. We also open several sections of the book with a sociocultural perspective on the issues to be discussed.

The Roles of Age and Gender

Inasmuch as this book is organized chronologically, we will, of course, be explaining the influence of age in every chapter. In some ways, the effects of age are quite apparent and in other ways these effects are subtle and complex. As concern about gender equity has received more publicity, the stereotypes about males and females are slowly eroding. If people are treated according to stereotypical characteristics, then their potential is immediately limited. Although gender stereotyping is only one part of the gender story, it illustrates the importance of the relationship between gender and development. For example, children at an early age construct social categories from the world around them, attach certain characteristics to these categories, and label the categories. This process may be positive because it helps to organize the world; it may also be negative if the characteristics associated with the category are limiting—"girls just can't do math." We'll examine how this theme plays out, both positively and negatively, throughout the lifespan.

Applications to Daily Living

The study of lifespan development is an exciting, rapidly changing, and highly relevant subject that can shed light on the developmental changes that you witness in yourself and see in your friends and family members of all ages. To help you put the theories and research of this book into a meaningful framework, we have written several "An Applied View" boxes for each chapter. These range from the appeal of street gangs for some children to the role of television in a child's life to an adolescent's search for identity to problems that the adult children of alcoholics encounter.

We have also included boxes that ask you to interact with the text's material. Called "What's Your View?," these boxes are intended to have you think about and act on topics you have just read about and discussed. What does your knowledge and your experience tell you about these matters? We are not presenting answers in these boxes. Rather we hope you apply your best judgment to the questions raised.

Major Changes in the Fourth Edition

Thanks to suggestions from students who used the third edition of our text and the insightful comments of reviewers, we have made the following substantial changes in the fourth edition.

- A major change from the previous edition was the incorporation of a student study guide throughout the text. After each major section of a chapter, we provided a set of between four and seven fill-in-the blank questions, together with the correct answers. These are meant to offer immediate review of material as you read through the chapter. At the end of each chapter, we provided a set of 15 to 20 multiple-choice questions and their answers so that you may review your knowledge of the entire chapter. Professors may well use some of each type of questions on their tests, so the questions are not only reviews, but also may be previews of "coming attractions." In this edition, we have incorporated

many suggested improvements (and some corrections) to this feature.

- Another major change involves the removal of two chapters: the chapter on general theories of adolescent development and the chapter on the transition to adulthood and the effect of stress on adults. This was done to make the book fit better with the typical semester class meeting schedule, again at the suggestion of many reviewers. Coverage of the most essential topics in those chapters has been moved to appropriate sections of several other chapters. Special care has been taken to ensure that discussion of these topics is as up-to-date as possible.

- We have decided not only to incorporate more research on cultural diversity as a regular part of the text, but also to continue to highlight some of this material in our new "A Sociocultural View" boxes. We have changed the name of these boxes from "A Multicultural View" because we feel that in addition to highlighting cultural diversity, we need to feature research on age, gender, and other social factors that are associated with controversial developments. We have added new boxes containing what we consider to be information of particularly high quality.

- We have integrated the biopsychosocial approach even more in this edition, explaining its relevance at least once in every chapter.

- Because we believe that the vignettes that open each chapter in our book set the tone for that chapter, we have continued our efforts to improve these vignettes or to replace them with better ones.

- Earlier in this preface we mentioned that development is a lifelong process, which implies that lifespan psychology books must constantly change to accommodate fresh insights into the developmental process. To meet this challenge, we have:

  1. Introduced a section in Chapter One in which we want you to "think about lifespan" from the viewpoint of several different perspectives. By focusing your thinking in this way, we think you can better understand the importance of the biopsychosocial concept, of which we hope you'll find a helpful explanatory theme throughout the book.

  2. Expanded the discussion of Vygotsky and his important ideas concerning the role of context in development. You'll also find a more extensive analysis of his basic developmental concepts plus a more intense examination of his views on language development.

  3. Continued to monitor and present the latest genetic research and combined this with a

careful overview of the most recent contributions of The Human Genome Project.

4. Broadened our discussion of the latest trends to include both national and international proceedings as a result of the current and continually growing interest in adoption.

5. Included a detailed consideration of the self concept and the development of self and self control due to the widespread interest in and concerns about the meaning of self-esteem in our society.

6. Felt ourselves intrigued by the artistic ability all children demonstrate, its appearance, development, and abrupt termination, all of which we discuss in this latest edition.

7. Introduced a new section on nutrition and obesity, which we believe has particular relevance for children in today's society.

8. Continued to expand on and strengthen such key developmental topics as gender development, emotional development, and attachment.

9. Added information on symptoms of eating disorders and suicide ideation.

10. Presented new studies on teen sexuality, including innovations in sex education.

11. Completely revised our section on several aspects of personality development in Chapters 14, 16, and 18.

12. Included new data on menopause and the risks of hormone replacement therapy.

13. Updated findings on physical development in old age, especially sensory abilities.

14. Added recent research on the processes of memory, including the newest work on CREB's.

15. Revised aspects of the section on grieving.

16. Conducted an especially thorough updating of references in general. All but the most classic of older references have been removed, and nearly 600 new references have been added to this edition.

Teaching—Learning Features of the Fourth Edition

You will enjoy and learn from this book to the extent that its topics, organization, and clarity make its contents meaningful to you. Helping you to master the book's contents in as uncomplicated a manner as possible has been the most important pedagogical goal of our work. To accomplish this task, we have built a number of features into each chapter:

• Chapter Outlines. The major topics of each chapter are presented initially so that you may quickly find the subject you need. An outline helps you to retain material (a memory aid) and is an efficient method for reviewing content.

• Opening Vignette. Each chapter opens with a vignette that illustrates the chapter's content. These vignettes are intended to demonstrate how the topics described in the chapter actually work in the daily lives of human beings, young and old.

• List of Objectives. Following the introductory section of each chapter, we present a carefully formulated list of objectives to guide your reading. When you finish reading the chapter return to the objectives and test yourself to see if you can respond to their intent; that is, can you analyze, can you apply, can you identify, can you define, can you describe?

• View Boxes. We have designed our boxes to expand on the material under discussion and to do so in a manner calculated to aid student retention. The view boxes are of three types:

1. What's Your View? Here we present controversial issues and you are asked to give your opinion after you have studied the facts.

2. An Applied View. Here you will see how the topics under discussion apply to an actual situation, in settings such as a classroom or a medical facility.

3. A Sociocultural View. Here we analyze the contributions of different cultures to individual development, as well as research on newly discovered influences of aging, gender, and other social factors.

• Conclusion. At the end of each chapter you will find a brief concluding statement that summarizes the main themes of the chapter. This statement provides you with a quick check of the purpose of the chapter and the content covered.

• Chapter Highlights. Immediately following the brief concluding section is a more detailed number of summary statements that are grouped according to the major topics of the chapter. This section should help you to review the chapter quickly and thoroughly. Turn to the chapter's table of contents and then check against the chapter highlights to determine how successful you are in recalling the pertinent material of the chapter.

• Key Terms. You will find at the end of each chapter a list of those terms that are essential to understanding the ideas and suggestions of that chapter. These terms are highlighted and explained in the context of the chapter. We urge you to spend time mastering the meaning of each of these terms and relate them to the context in which they appear.

- What Do You Think? Following the Key Terms, you will find a series of questions intended to have you demonstrate your knowledge of the chapter's content, not only by applying the material to different situations but also by asking you to be creative in answering the question or solving the problem.

- Suggested Readings. Interspersed in appropriate places throughout the text, you will find an annotated list of four or five books or journal articles that we think are particularly well suited to supplement the contents of the chapter. These references are not necessarily textbooks; they may not deal specifically with either education or psychology. We believe, however, that they shed an illuminating light upon the chapter's material.

- Student Study Guide. As we mentioned earlier, we have decided to include the student study guide in the body of the text as one means of making the material as meaningful as possible and to aid retention.

Supplementary Materials

*The supplements listed here may accompany **Dacey/ Travers Human Development across the Lifespan 4e.** Please contact your local McGraw-Hill representative for details concerning policies, prices, and availability as some restrictions may apply.*

For the Instructor:

Instructor's Manual and Test Bank
by Judith E. Robinson

The Instructor's Manual to accompany the fourth edition of Human Development Across the Lifespan has been revised and expanded to include new teaching ideas and features available for instructors. Instructors who are new to the course, as well as those who are experienced instructors, will benefit from the helpful organization and support the Instructor's Manual lends to the main text. Features in this edition of the Instructor's Manual include, for each chapter, a summary outline, learning objectives, key terms, lecture suggestions, classroom or student activities, and questions for review and discussion. In addition, we have included supplementary resources for both video/film and website use for the human development instructor. The summary outline and learning objectives closely follow the text and highlight the important concepts and topics from each chapter. The learning objectives are also used in the test bank to help instructors select supporting questions. Key terms from the text are listed to show which terms need to be emphasized within lectures. Complete lecture suggestions that give entertaining, yet educational, ideas on how to enliven classroom discussion of the text material are provided as well. In addition, classroom activities serve to provide hands-on suggestions for applying course material to students' every day lives in and out of the classroom. Questions for review and discussion are available for each chapter to aid instructors in promoting class participation and/or as essay question assignments. The website addresses provided in each chapter can be reached directly, or more conveniently through the McGraw-Hill Developmental Website, *www.mhhe.com/developmental,* where related sites are hot linked.

The Test Bank portion of the Instructor's Manual/ Test Bank provides instructors with a resource of over 1,400 test questions specifically related to the main text. This expanded testing tool includes 75 multiple choice questions for each chapter, including answers, from which to develop test materials. The answers are correlated to the corresponding learning objective that the question tests. In addition, each test item is identified by type as either factual, conceptual, or applied for easier test development.

Computerized Test Bank
by Judith E. Robinson

This computerized test bank contains all of the questions in the print version and is available in both Macintosh and Windows platforms. These questions can be rearranged and customized using Microtest III, a powerful yet easy to use test generating program by Chariot Software Group. Professors may choose questions, instructions, headings, and even fonts. Tests may be personalized by adding or importing instructors' own questions to those already in the test bank.

The McGraw-Hill Developmental Psychology Image Database Overhead Transparencies and CD-ROM

This set of 200 full-color images was developed using the best selection of our human development art and tables and is available in both a print overhead transparency set as well as in a CD-ROM format with a fully functioning editing feature. These images have been selected to correspond with the instructor's manual. Plus, instructors can add their own lecture notes to the CD-ROM as well as organize the images to correspond to their particular classroom needs.

Videocases in Human Development

This four-tape set of videos features spontaneous, unrehearsed interviews on topics in human development. Each videotape features excerpts from real people as they talk about personal issues that have particular significance to them. Videocases in Human Development are the perfect supplement for the professor who wants to expose students to the real-life issues that face people at every developmental stage of life. Video One: Prenatal Issues; Video Two: Childhood Issues; Video Three: Adolescent Issues; Video Four: Adulthood Issues. Topics covered include alternative parenting, biracial adoption, ADD, homelessness, homosexual teens, substance abuse, and aging and sexuality. An Instructor's Manual is included and provides an overview of each tape along with follow up discussion questions.

Web Site

Please visit our developmental web site for additional information on this title as well as text-specific resources and web links for both instructors and students. Our web site address is *www.mhhe.com/developmental.*

The AIDS Booklet

The fourth edition by Frank D. Cox of Santa Barbara City College is a brief but comprehensive introduction to acquired immune deficiency syndrome, which is caused by HIV (human immunodeficiency virus) and related viruses.

Annual Editions—Human Development 1998/1999

Published by Dushkin/McGraw-Hill, is a collection of 45 articles on topics related to the latest research and thinking in human development. These editions are updated annually and contain helpful features including a topic guide, an annotated table of contents, and unit overviews, a topical index. Instructor's guide containing testing materials is available.

Sources: Notable Selections in Human Development

A collection of over 40 articles, book excerpts, and research studies that have shaped the study of human development and our contemporary understanding of it. The selections are organized topically around major areas of study within human development. Each selection is preceded by a headnote that establishes the relevance of the article or study and provides biographical information on the author.

Taking Sides:

A debate-style reader designed to introduce students to controversial viewpoints on the fields most crucial issues. Each issue is carefully framed for the student, and the pro and con essays represent the arguments of leading scholars and commentators in their fields. Instructor's guide containing testing materials is available.

For the Student:

The Critical Thinker

Richard Mayer and Fiona Goodchild of the University of California, Santa Barbara, use excerpts from introductory psychology textbooks to show students how to think critically about psychology.

Guide to Life-Span Development for Future Educators

Guide to Life-Span Development for Future Nurses

New course supplements that helps students apply the concepts of human development to education. The supplement contains information, exercises, and sample tests designed to help students prepare for certification and understand human development from a professional perspective.

Acknowledgements

This book was produced through the cooperation of many people at McGraw-Hill Publishers. We would especially like to thank our editors, Mickey Cox, Sharon Geary, and Kay Brimeyer. Their commitment to turning out the best possible book is greatly appreciated. We would also like to thank our graduate assistants, who contributed significantly to this edition with their ideas and criticism: Biz Bracher, Lisa Davidson, and Andrea Krasker. Finally we would like to acknowledge the excellent contribution of the following reviewers:

- Pat Lefler, *Lexington Community College*

- Suzanne E. Cortez, *Northern Kentucky University*

- Leslie Minor-Evans, *Central Oregon Community College*

- Joanne Stephenson, *Union University*

- Karen H. Nelson, *Austin College*

- Gary Creasey, *Illinois State University*

* Ellen Pastorino, *Gainsville College*

- Susan K. Beck, *Wallace State College*

- Patricia Guth, *Westmoreland Co. Community College*

- M. L. Corbin Sicoli, *Cabrini College*

- A Douglas McKenzie, *San Antonio College*

- Thomas Faase, *St. Norbert College*

- Anna Maria Myers, *Polk Community College*

To the Student

Owner's Manual: A Guide to Content Features

Chapter Outline

Outlines at the beginning of each chapter show what material will be covered.

List of Objectives

A carefully formulated list of objectives is presented after each chapter introduction to help guide your reading. After reading each chapter, you can use the objectives as a way to test your knowledge and to review the material.

Ellen and Kevin were delighted. The parents of a 3-year-old boy, they were now looking forward to their second child. Kevin, having shared in the birth of their first child, was calmer but even more excited as he looked forward to the events of this pregnancy and birth. Ellen, a healthy 31-year-old, was experiencing all the signs of a normal pregnancy. The morning sickness abated at 12 weeks. She felt movement at 17 weeks, and an ultrasound at 20 weeks showed normal development. Weight gain, blood glucose levels, blood pressure, and AFP (alphafetoprotein) test results were all within acceptable ranges.

Since this was Ellen's second pregnancy, she felt more comfortable with her changing body. Visits to the obstetrician were pleasant and uneventful. At 28 weeks, loosening ligaments caused her pelvis to irritate the sciatic nerve at the base of the spine. Her obstetrician recommended Tylenol, a heating pad, and rest. He also recommended a visit to an orthopedist to confirm the treatment. Ellen refused to take any medication and decided not to bother with a second opinion. Since she felt she could tolerate the pain for the 12 weeks until delivery, she would not be X-rayed or take even a mild painkiller. She rationalized that the back pain was acceptable because it accompanied a normal pregnancy.

At 31 weeks, Ellen noticed episodes of unusual movement and became concerned. A week later, fearing that the baby might be in distress, she called the obstetrician to describe the jabs, pokes, and excessive movements she was experiencing. The doctor immediately scheduled a biophysical profile: an eight-point check of the internal organs and another ultrasound.

Ellen nervously gulped the required 32 ounces of water an hour before the examination. Arriving at a glistening new medical center, she was quickly escorted to an examining room. The technician was both professional and serious as he looked for a problem (increasing Ellen's anxiety). The examination included a thorough check of the baby's heart chambers, a type of EKG (electrocardiogram) measurement, and an assessment of blood flow—all displayed in vibrant colors. The cord, internal organs, position of the baby, and body weight were all evaluated. Ellen was able to listen to the baby's heartbeat while watching the heart chambers function.

Later that day, Ellen's obstetrician called to tell her the results: no apparent medical problems, just an unusually active baby. Ellen and Kevin sagged with relief. They also received a bonus: a reassuring ultrasound image of their unborn child's face—in living color! ☺

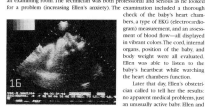

Ultrasound is frequently used when questions arise about a pregnancy. Soundwaves directed onto the uterus bounce off the bones and tissues of the fetus and are formed into an image.

Opening Vignette

Each chapter opens with a vignette that illustrates the chapter's content and demonstrates how chapter material actually works in our daily lives.

Ellen's journey through the nine months of her pregnancy is quite typical: normal prenatal development accompanied by occasional worrisome moments. Given current concern about the quality of life for a woman and her developing child, we can understand the importance placed on prenatal development. In fact, today's acceptance of the impact that these nine months have on an individual's future has led to greater emphasis on *prepregnancy* care. If you think about this for a moment, it makes considerable sense because some women don't realize they're pregnant for two or three months. By then, rapid growth has occurred (as we'll see, such growth is particularly true of the central nervous system) with the potential for serious damage if elements such as alcohol and drugs have been abused.

In this Chapter, we'll first explore the prenatal world, that nine-month period that provides nourishment and protection and serves as a springboard for birth. Next we'll turn to those agents that can influence prenatal development. These are both physical and psychological and can be either positive or negative. We'll then look at birth itself, the completion of a journey that has involved remarkable development. For various reasons, some fetuses can't endure this nine-month journey, so our final focus in this Chapter will be the special case of these early, or premature, births. In the past few years, great advances—technological, medical, and psychological—have resulted in an increasing number of premature babies surviving.

When you finish reading this Chapter, you should be able to

- Describe the periods of prenatal development.
- Analyze the major features of each period.
- Indicate the times of greatest sensitivity to insult.
- Identify dangerous maternal diseases.
- Distinguish those drugs that can cause permanent damage during prenatal development.
- Assess the potential of fetal surgery.
- Discriminate the various stages of the birth process.
- Designate the possible causes of prematurity.

The Prenatal World

Although it may be difficult to imagine, you are the product of one cell, the zygote, or fertilized egg. Once the union of sperm and egg took place, in only a matter of hours (about 24–30) that one cell began to divide rapidly. The initial phase of the event occurred in a very protected world—the prenatal environment.

Once the egg is released from the ovary, it passes into the fallopian tube. Fertilization occurs in the first part of the fallopian tube, about three days after the egg has entered the tube. The fertilized egg must now pass through the remainder of the fallopian tube to reach the uterus, a journey of about three to four days to travel five or six inches. During its passage through the fallopian tube, the zygote receives all of its nourishment from the tube. Figure 4.1 illustrates passage into the uterus and **implantation.**

Implantation seems to occur in three phases:

1. **Apposition,** during which the fertilized egg, now called a **blastocyst,** comes to rest against the uterine wall.

2. **Adhesion,** during which the prepared surface of the uterus and the outer surface of the fertilized egg, now called the **trophoblast,** touch and actually "stick together."

3. **Invasion,** during which the trophoblast digs in and begins to bury itself in the uterine lining.

An Applied View

These boxed features give examples to show how the material you are learning can be applied to real life situations, such as in a classroom or medical facility.

What's Your View?

Controversial issues related to developmental psychology are presented in these boxes for you to read and think over.

An Applied View — How Well Do Parents Know What Their Teens Are Doing?

The Who's Who organization recently (1997) surveyed 3,370 teenagers 16- to 18-year-olds, all of whom have an "A" or a "B" average and are planning to attend college. Because these students are among the highest achievers in the United States one might assume that their parents would be reasonably well aware of their activities. As the chart below reveals, there are some serious discrepancies.

There are at least three important questions that are posed by these data: Why is there such a great distance between what the teens say they do and what their parents believe? Might these "good students" be underreporting their actual activities? As you will see in ot her chapters of this book, in some cases these students' rates of behavior are lower than for more ordinary students, and in some cases higher—why do you suppose this is so?

Do You Think that Your Child . . .	Parental Myth	Teen Reality
Has contemplated suicide?	9%	26%
Has cheated on a test?	37%	76%
Has had sex?	9%	19%
Has friends with drug problems?	12%	36%
Has driven a car while drunk?	3%	10%
Has worries about pregnancy?	22%	46%

Source: Who's Who Special Report, 1997.

The Effects of Divorce

A smoothly functioning family can provide support and nurturance to an adolescent during times of stress (Young & others, 1997). But when the family is itself in a state of disarray, such as during a divorce, not only is the support weakened, but the family often becomes a source of stress (Fergusson & Lynskey, 1996).

Divorce has become commonplace in American society. Even with slight decreases in the divorce rate in recent years, more than one million divorces still occur every year, which is roughly half the number of marriages performed during the same time (U. S. Bureau of Census, 1996). Divorce tends to occur most in families with a newborn, and second most in families with an adolescent present. Estimates suggest that divorce affects as much as one-third to one-half of the adolescent population.

What, then, are the effects of divorce on the development of the adolescent? Unfortunately, conclusions are often based as much on speculation as on research findings, due to problems in the research. Divorcing parents often refuse to let

several young adults who will bear the brunt of the cost for elderly transportation, and some older adults who will be isolated without it.

What's Your View? — What Should Happen When the Elderly Lose Their License?

By 2020, up to one out of every five Americans will be 65 or older, and the vast majority will possess a driver's license. This is of concern because statistics show that accidents caused by drivers over the age of 75 equal or surpass those of teenagers, who have been considered the most dangerous group of drivers. A number of states are moving to monitor older drivers more aggressively. However, in those cases where a license is denied or revoked, the drivers may find themselves stranded without crucial transportation (Harvard Health Letter, 1991).

Hearing

Decline in hearing ability may be a more serious problem than decline in vision. However, we seem to be much less willing to wear hearing aids than we are to wear glasses, perhaps because we rely on vision more.

Most people hear fairly well until late adulthood, but men seem to lose some of their acuity for higher pitches during their middle years (Marshall, 1981). This difference may occur mostly in men who are exposed to greater amounts of noise in their occupations and in traveling to and from their jobs.

Smell

Some atrophy of olfactory fibers in the nose occurs with age. When artificial amplifiers are added, however, the ability of the older people to recognize foods by smell is greatly improved.

Taste

Studying the effects of aging on the sense of taste is difficult because taste itself is so dependent on smell. About 95 percent of taste derives from olfactory nerves. It is clear, however, that there is decline in tasting ability among the elderly (Cowart & others, 1994). Whereas young adults have an average of 250 taste buds, elderly adults have an average of no more than 100.

Touch

The tactile sense also declines somewhat after the age of 65 (Turner & Helms, 1989), but the evidence for this comes strictly from the reports of the elderly. Until scientific studies are performed, this finding must be accepted with caution.

Other Body Systems

Included in the category of body systems are the skeletal system, skin, teeth, hair, and locomotion (ability to move about).

Skeletal System

Although the skeleton is fully formed by age 24, changes in stature can occur because of the shrinking of the discs between spinal vertebrae (Mazess, 1982). As mentioned earlier, collagen changes. Frequently this causes bone tissue to shrink (Twomey & others, 1983). Thus the bones become more brittle. Because the entire skeletal system becomes tighter and stiffer, the aged frequently have a small loss of

A number of factors can cause the body to become shorter and stiffer with age.

A Sociocultural View

Analysis on the contributions of different cultures has been integrated throughout the 4th edition of *Human Development Across the Lifespan*. Highlights include new research on aging, gender, and other social factors.

A Sociocultural View — The Gender-Role Training of Western Men

Judith Jordan (cited in Bergman, 1991) stated:
I used to think that what we have here is just Western culture—competitive, individualistic, self-sufficient. But the cross-cultural data suggests that this country is off the scale—that we are so far into the individualistic, competitive ethic, and that, in fact, we continue to socialize males to be soldiers—whether on the battlefield or in industry—and you don't socialize soldiers to be empathic, listening, caring people. I think, ultimately, the individualistic ethic is starting to fail in terms of ecological and economic success in the world, and it will push the system to move into some new paradigms, and I feel some hope about that.

The well-being of young American men has been found to be influenced by closeness to child and wife, adjustment to the husband role, and the number of close friends (Julian & others, 1992). If Jordan is right that men are socialized to be soldiers and dread close relationships, this would indicate that the emotional health of American men is endangered by their gender-role training. If they are not taught to be caretakers of relational processes in the way women are, then they will have difficulty being emotionally close to their wives and children, and thus their personal well-being will suffer. What's your opinion? What new paradigms for men might Ms. Jordan be referring to?

An insightful book on this topic is Robert Bly's *Iron John.* Reading, MA:Addison-Wesley. A teacher of both poetry and philosophy, Bly combines the two in this fascinating tale of a journey with the self. Among other insights, he explores the modern young man's grief over his inability to become close to his father.

Yearn to understand first and to be understood second.

employment in factories. The second, which began in the 1960s with "no-fault" divorce, led to the proliferation of single-parent families, about 90 percent of which are headed by females.

With each of these events, much of the teaching and appreciation that boys used to get from their ever-present fathers was lost. Mothers have tried to make up for this loss, but because of deep-seated gender differences, only another male can induct a boy into adulthood successfully (see Chapter 13). Bly believed that only those young men who achieve a mentor relationship with some other older man are likely to attain a mature personality. This man may be an uncle, one of the father's friends, or some older man at work. Without such a person, the young man will not be brave enough to confront himself, and he will sink into a defensive, self-deluding lifestyle. Bly also suggested that because the typical conflicts that exist between sons and fathers are absent in the mentor relationship, the mentor actually can be more helpful to the young man.

Levinson found that after each man selects a dream, mentor relationship, occupation, and love relationship, at around age 30 (plus or minus two years) he comes to reexamine his feelings about the four major tasks. Important decisions are made at this time, such as an alteration of the dream, a change in mentor, a change in occupation, and sometimes a change in marital status. For some, this transitional period proves to be very smooth. In most cases, however, it challenges the very foundations of life itself. Although he often keeps it to himself, the typical male at this stage undergoes a seriously disturbing period of self-doubt. Fortunately, most emerge from these doubts with a clearer understanding of their strengths and weaknesses, and a clearer view of what they wish to make of themselves.

Thus, for Levinson, the transition from late adolescence to early adulthood (and also for the years to come) tends to proceed in stages as orderly as those we have seen in the earlier stages of life. More variation occurs as we grow older, because we are controlled less and less by our genetic inheritance and more and more by the environment in which we find ourselves, and by our own individual decisions. This growing independence from our genes and our early experiences is reflected clearly in these two theories. Even if we have had a hard childhood, with alcoholic parents and traumatic accidents, we should be developing the ability to be in charge of our lives. As we grow older, we have the opportunity, and indeed the responsi-

Suggested Readings

An integrated list of books or journal articles to supplement the chapter reading can be found in the margins of each chapter.

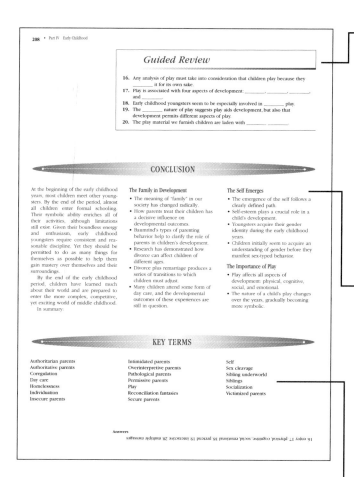

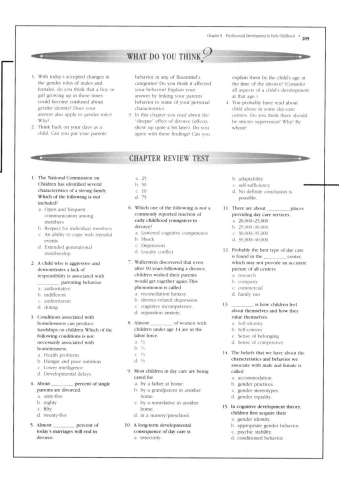

Student Study Guide

To help you fully learn the material, the fourth edition of this text includes a built-in student study guide. (Students need not buy a separate study guide—it is part of the book!) The student study guide is composed of:

- Chapter opening learning objectives

* In-chapter guided reviews featuring fill-in-the-blank questions

- End of chapter multiple-choice sample tests

Chapter Highlights

Each chapter conclusion is followed by a series of summary statements. These highlights are grouped according to chapter topic and help you review the chapter quickly and thoroughly.

Key Terms

Because key terms are essential to your ability to understand material, they are highlighted and explained in the context of each chapter, listed at the end of each chapter, and are defined again in a glossary at the end of the book.

What Do You think?

Following the Key Terms, you will find a series of questions challenging you to demonstrate your knowledge of the chapter's content.

PART I

Life is like playing a violin in public and learning the instrument as one goes on.

Samuel Butler

The year was 1955.

During those 365 days, the psychologists Emmy Werner and Ruth Smith (1995) began to collect data on every child born on the island of Kauai, a part of the Hawaiian chain. That year a total of 837 children were born.

Amazingly, Werner and Smith studied 505 of these children from their prenatal days until they were in their early thirties. (The drop in the number of children studied was due to some of the children dying, some moving to other islands, and some moving to the U.S. mainland.)

Of these 505 children, one in three was born with the threat of serious developmental difficulties, such as the effects of a difficult birth or an environment that triggered formidable challenges. Some faced the prospect of a life of grinding poverty. Others were exposed to divorce, desertion, alcoholism, or mental illness.

Two out of three children in this vulnerable group were exposed to four or more of these risk factors. And yet, one in three of these high-risk children developed into a confident, competent young adult.

How can we explain this phenomenon? What developmental forces were at work that enabled certain children to overcome dramatically difficult obstacles, and yet permitted others to succumb? In a sense, the children of Kauai provide us with a window through which we can view the events that shape the lifespan, the biological, psychological, and environmental interactions that make us what we are. ✪

Lifespan psychology studies the changes in our lives that occur from conception to death. If you think about your own life—starting school, perhaps going off to college, beginning a job, getting married, having a child—you begin to appreciate the complexity of development. It's usually difficult, however, to look at ourselves objectively, so let's examine the life of an outstanding individual—Colin Powell—whose rise to fame and power offers an insightful view into what is meant by lifespan development.

Powell, whom America came to know quite well as chairman of the Joint Chiefs of Staff, was born in Harlem on April 5, 1937, the son of Jamaican immigrant parents. He gained confidence and self-esteem from the care, love, and attention that he received from his family. His parents valued education and he quickly realized the importance of learning. As a young African American, Powell decided that opportunities were greater in the army than in the corporate world.

In Colin Powell's life we see the impact of those forces that so powerfully affect development: family, peers, and experiences.

A product of the ROTC program at the City College of New York, Powell soon demonstrated those leadership qualities that would mark him as an outstanding soldier. In 1963, as a second lieutenant and newly married, Powell was sent to Vietnam. Wounded in action there, he showed the bravery and the compassion for his colleagues that have been constant themes in his career. Returning to the United States, he obtained a master's degree in business administration and in 1972 was selected as a White House Fellow.

During the following years, Powell served in various parts of the world, gradually attaining the rank of Major General. He was recalled to the White House to be military adviser to the Secretary of Defense in 1982, then in 1986 returned to the army. In 1987 he was asked to be National Security Adviser to the president, and in 1989 he became chairman of the Joint Chiefs of Staff. During these years, he became the first African American to attain the rank of a four-star general.

Powell's rise to the top military post in the United States confounded many who thought that only West Point graduates could ascend to such heights. His courage in Vietnam, however, resulted in six medals (including the Purple Heart and a Bronze Star) and earned him the respect and admiration of President George Bush, who recommended his appointment. During the Gulf War, Powell played a pivotal role in determining strategy and in advising the president.

As you examine the paths that Colin Powell chose in his life, you can begin to identify those themes that make studying the human lifespan so fascinating. You can see how his family was a powerful and positive influence throughout his early years. Later, his wife, Alma Johnson, and their three children provided vital support. His decision to make the army a career led to international experiences and a network of friends who would help shape his future. These developmental milestones in Colin Powell's life served to make him the person he is today, but at the same time it is possible to discern behaviors that have been remarkably persistent throughout his lifespan: courage, compassion for others, and devotion to family and country.

In our work, we'll trace the significant changes that occur at various times in the lifespan, emphasizing that the potential for development is a constant in our lives, from youth to old age! Although these changes may not be as dramatic as those we have just traced in Colin Powell's life, they are important to us as individuals making our own progress throughout our lifespans. Let's turn our attention now to the importance of biopsychosocial interactions as a means of guiding your reading and integrating the many and varied paths of development.

You would enjoy reading Colin Powell's autobiography, *My American Journey,* published in 1995 by Random House.

The Importance of Biopsychosocial Interactions

Before beginning our work on analyzing the lifespan, we'll first discuss the importance of **biopsychosocial interactions** in human development. If you think of lifespan development as the product of the interaction of biological, psychological, and social forces, you can better understand and appreciate the complexity of development. Keeping these interactions in mind, which are more apparent in the childhood years, also provides a guide to explore cross-cultural and sociocultural issues that greatly enrich our understanding of human development (Garcia Coll & others, 1996).

If you examine Table 1.1 carefully, you'll note several characteristics listed for the biological, psychological, and social aspects of interactions. These certainly aren't exhaustive but indicate several developmental features that affect growth during the lifespan. More importantly, however, we would like you to think about the interactions that occur among the three categories and how these interactions affect development. To give a simple example, genetic damage (biological) may negatively affect cognitive development (psychological), and lead to poor peer relationships (social).

TABLE 1.1 ELEMENTS OF BIOPSYCHOSOCIAL INTERACTIONS

Bio	Psycho	Social
Genetics	Cognitive development	Attachment
Fertilization	Information processing	Relationships
Pregnancy	Problem solving	Reciprocal interactions
Birth	Perceptual development	School
Physical development	Language development	Peers
Motor development	Moral development	Television
Puberty	Self-efficacy	Stress
Menstruation	Personality	Marriage
Disease	Body image	Family

Let's consider Laura, a 5-year-old who entered first grade in September. Laura is unhappy, and most mornings she pleads that she is too sick to go to school. She is having difficulty with her school work and her teacher reports that she disrupts the class by interrupting others and wandering around the room. Because of Laura's classroom behavior, she is unpopular with the other children in the class. After complaining of headaches, Laura is examined by the school nurse, who finds that she needs glasses. Laura's life now changes positively. Here is an example of how a physical problem can affect psychological development (learning and reading) as well as social development (popularity with classmates).

We believe that by recognizing the significance of biopsychosocial interactions, you'll better understand and remember the material of any chapter. This perspective also helps to emphasize those social-cultural features that so powerfully influence development through the lifespan.

With these ideas in mind, then, we'll first explore the meaning of lifespan development in this chapter and attempt to indicate its importance to you by illustrating how peaks and valleys come into all of our lives. Although we all chart an individual course, we can still identify many similarities in our lives. We walk, we talk, we attend school, and we search for a satisfying career. Yet within this sameness, we all have and choose different experiences that shine a unique light on our journey through the lifespan.

Following this discussion, we would like you to think about various aspects of development, particularly how different viewpoints affect the way you interpret developmental change. Then we turn to several issues that are crucial in any analysis of a person's passage through the lifespan. Finally, we'll examine those research techniques that will help you to assess and interpret the issues, theories, and studies you'll meet in the coming pages.

When you finish reading this chapter, you should be able to

- Use biopsychosocial interactions as a means of interpreting and recalling developmental data.

- Define lifespan development.

- Describe how different perspectives on development influence a person's understanding of developmental change.

- Identify major developmental issues.

- Apply your knowledge of lifespan techniques to the studies you read.

These photos (a–e) show Bill Clinton at various stages of his lifespan.

The Meaning of Lifespan Psychology

Lifespan development is the study of human development from conception to death. As such, it is important to you personally because it helps you to understand your own behavior once you have grasped its main ideas. Studying lifespan development should also provide you with insights into the behavior of others and, because of this, you should achieve better personal and professional relationships with those around you (Strough & others, 1996). To help you fulfill this objective, we have included *What's Your View?*, *A Sociocultural View,* and *Applied View* boxes.

As you can tell from the brief discussion at the Chapter's opening, development is a lifelong process. Psychologists now realize that development, once thought to end at childhood, or possibly adolescence, is a process that continues from conception to death. Today we realize that the changes of adulthood—maturity and aging—are as developmental as those of any other period. By analyzing the various developmental periods—infancy, early childhood, middle childhood, adolescence, and adulthood—researchers are trying to discover the features of each period and to uncover the mechanisms by which we move from one stage of life to the next.

For purposes of research and speculation, we'll divide the lifespan into segments, while recalling that each segment is part of a whole. In this book, we divide the lifespan as follows:

Prenatal—conception to birth
Infancy—birth to 2 years
Early childhood—2 to 5 years
Middle childhood—6 to 11 years
Adolescence—12 to 18 years
Early adulthood—19 to 34 years
Middle adulthood—35 to 64 years
Later adulthood—65+

As you continue your reading, remember that development does not proceed randomly. It is tightly linked to what psychologists call context; that is, the circumstances in which an individual develops. Context is such an important feature of development that we will return to it frequently throughout this book because to understand development as fully as possible, you must also understand its context.

Culture and Development

As our nation changes, we're all interacting with others from quite different backgrounds. How we respond to others who seem different can have a serious impact on achievement in school, success in work, and harmonious relationships with others. Americans pride themselves on living in a culturally diverse nation that encourages newcomers to share their way of life. Even under the best of conditions, however, immigrants can experience difficulties: language, customs, acceptance, job opportunities. The receiving country also must adapt. Schools, churches, markets, and politics all must change accordingly.

Children from different cultures bring their differences with them; thus, their different customs may influence the relationships they form. For example, the way in which they interact with others may differ, which may puzzle others; their learning styles may vary, which can affect their classroom achievement. Many immigrant children, who have fled war and poverty, carry emotional scars. As you can well imagine, all of these conditions have developmental consequences.

For example, a white female elementary school teacher in the United States recently gave her students a math problem: If there are four blackbirds sitting in a tree and you shoot one of them with a slingshot, how many are left? A white student quickly answers, "Three." An African immigrant student answered with equal confidence, "Zero." The teacher was puzzled, thinking that the new student either had misunderstood the wording or had a math problem. Actually the immigrant student reasoned that if you shoot one bird, the others will fly away (Wing, 1992). Here is a good example of the need to understand the backgrounds of our changing population.

We think it's important to recognize the contributions a particular culture makes to the development of its children. Think of culture as the customs, values, and traditions inherent in one's environment. Different cultures have different developmental expectations for their children. Asian children, for example, are encouraged to avoid emotional displays, a characteristic that does not necessarily apply to Asian-American children (Sue & Sue, 1991). We also urge you to remember that the biology + environment = development equation plays out within the confines of a particular culture. Consequently, understanding children's behavior demands an understanding of their cultures.

To help you grasp the significance of culture in development you should remember that there are three answers to this question: How well do you understand the cultures of your friends, or the individuals you're working with, or your neighbors?

1. You understand at a *superficial* level; that is, you know the facts that make up a person's cultural history.

2. You understand at an *intermediate* level; that is, you understand the central behaviors at the core of a person's social life. Language usage is a good example here. Does a child's culture tolerate, even encourage, calling out, which could be a major problem for teachers not familiar with the acceptable behaviors of this child's culture.

3. You understand at a *significant* level; that is, you grasp the values, beliefs, and norms that structure a person's view of the world and how to behave in that world. In other words, you change psychologically as a result of interactions with a different culture (Casas & Pytluk, 1995).

Consequently, as we begin our work of studying lifespan development we want to impress on you the need to be aware that "different does not mean deficient."

Merging Cultures

You can now more readily appreciate how members of any one group—Irish-American, Italian American, African American—use standards from their own cultural backgrounds to form opinions about those from other cultures. If you understand why those from other groups behave as they do, you are less inclined to conclude that "different means deficient." For example, when meeting someone from another culture, if we understand at a superficial level, we are initially struck by differences of behavior, speech, clothing, and food. If these differences aren't too sharp, we may accept them; if the differences are quite distinct, we judge them unfavorably. Remember, however, if you were a member of their group, you would probably behave just as they do (Triandis, 1990).

Taking the time and making the effort to understand these differences will move our relationships with others to a level of mutual understanding in all settings. As an illustration, think of the changing American classrooms, where children and teachers from many different cultures are now coming together. Many minority children have had to make major adjustments to the dominant culture in the classroom (Chen & others, 1997). Teachers who are aware of the differences between the home culture and that of the school can do much to ensure that these children succeed academically and personally to achieve their potential.

A good example of this kind of endeavor can be seen in Kim's (1990) description of Hawaiian children's school experiences. Many Hawaiian children achieve at the lowest academic level and are labeled as lazy and disruptive by some teachers. Yet these same children are remarkably responsible at home—cooking, cleaning, taking care of their brothers and sisters. They demonstrate considerable initiative and a high performance level. When something needs to be done, they get together and make a group effort to do whatever is necessary. When they find themselves in an individualistic, competitive classroom, however, their performance suffers.

In a series of experiments, teachers were encouraged to model desired behaviors and not assign specific tasks to students. By the end of the academic year, the students would begin the day by examining the schedules of their learning centers and then divide themselves into groups that assigned tasks to individual members, obtained materials, and used worksheets. Although their achievement scores improved significantly, once the students were returned to regular classrooms for the fourth grade, a familiar pattern of problems appeared (Kim, 1990).

The classroom is not the only location in which cultures merge. The business world now has people of various cultures working side by side and also has those designated as minorities assuming leadership positions in which members of the dominant culture report to them. As companies become more global and as the number of international markets increases steadily, the workplace is beginning to

Chart Your Own Lifespan

Endeavoring to illustrate how important knowledge of the lifespan is to each of us, Sugarman (1986) has devised a simple exercise that you can do quickly. Using a blank sheet of paper, assume that the left edge of the page represents the beginning of your life and the right edge where you are today. Now draw a line across the page that indicates the peaks and valleys that you have experienced so far.

For example, the chart for one of the authors of this book is shown below. In this chart, the first valley was a financial reversal for the author's parents. The first peak represents happy and productive high school years, followed by entry into teaching, and then marriage a few years later. The deep valley was a serious accident followed by years of recuperation and then the birth of children and the publication of a first book. You can see that it looks like a temperature chart. Try it for yourself.

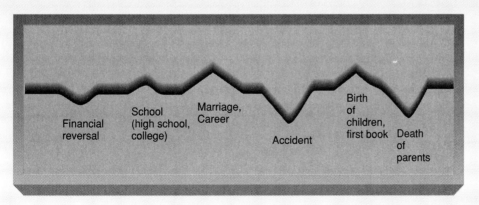

Sugarman (1986) suggested that when you finish, sit back and ask yourself these questions:

- Are there more peaks than valleys?
- Is there a definite shape to my chart?
- Would I identify my peaks and valleys as major or minor?
- What caused the peaks and valleys?

- Could I have done anything to make the peaks higher and the valleys more shallow?
- What happened during the plateaus?
- What's my view of these highs and lows in my life?

You have drawn a picture of your lifespan and the questions that you have just answered are actually the subject matter of lifespan development.

resemble the classroom as a meeting place of cultures. As your parents and grand-parents age, they'll contact and form friendships with older individuals from diverse backgrounds (Brislin, 1990).

Our goal in urging you to adopt a multicultural perspective is to help you develop a greater understanding of those who seem different, that is, reach a level of significant understanding. If you adopt this perspective, you will come to realize that different people have different world views that decisively influence their thinking (Shweder, 1991). People from different cultures do not all think alike. Recognizing how diverse people are in their thinking and behavior will help you to identify and comprehend variations in people's backgrounds and how they become functioning members of their culture. In this way, you will work, play, or study more congenially with others, thus fostering more positive relations in our society. And yet, cross-cultural awareness should also make us aware that we are all alike in important ways. It's mainly in our behavior, the manner in which we deal with the demands of our environments, that we differ.

Guided Review

1. The biopsychosocial model illustrates the interaction of _____ and _____ in development.
2. The values, beliefs, and behaviors that characterize a large group of people refer to that group's _____.
3 Understanding children's development demands an understanding of their _____ context.
4. You react to a culture at the _____, _____, or _____ levels of understanding.
5. People use the standards of their _____ to judge other people.
6. Kim's study of Hawaiian schoolchildren indicated that classroom _____ negatively affected their performance.

Thinking About Lifespan Development

John Smith, age 17, won a four-year all-paid scholarship at a prestigious eastern university, capping a brilliant elementary and secondary school career. At graduation, those in attendance were buzzing about his spectacular performance.

"What do you expect; his father is brilliant, you know. The apple doesn't fall far from the tree."

"His family must have helped him. His brother went through the same program two years ago."

"I never knew a teenager to study so hard. He was always at his books."

As you begin to consider the possible paths that lifespan development takes and the forces that shape its direction, you may examine all the information you're about to acquire from a particular perspective. That is, you may think that once parents pass along their genes to their children, development is fixed on an unchanging path, as in the explanation of John Smith's success—biology gives you all the answers. Or you may believe that the environment John was born into determines development, the second explanation—the environment furnishes all you need to

Answers

1. heredity, environment 2. culture 3. cultural 4. superficial, intermediate, significant 5. culture 6. competition

know about development. Perhaps you believe that how you interact with the environment explains everything you need to know about development, the third explanation—learning gives all the answers. Or you may even think that a combination of all these perspectives provides deeper insight into development—some type of interaction holds the clues of growth.

Since these beliefs about biology, environment, and contextualism have at times attracted considerable support, let's briefly examine each of them.

A Biological Perspective

The chief claim of those adhering to a biological explanation of development points to the critical role of the genes, which establish the rate and nature of development. In other words, maturation occurs according to a predetermined biological timetable.

Biological explanations of development gradually lost their appeal in the 1960s and 1970s, only to reemerge in the 1980s and 1990s with the enormous explosion of genetic knowledge, as seen in the *Human Genome Project* with its goal of mapping all the human genes. (See Chapter 3 for a more detailed discussion.) Consequently, today we recognize biology's contributions to all aspects of development.

An Environmental Perspective

The environment acts in ways that we are only beginning to comprehend. Thanks to the systems analysis of Uri Bronfenbrenner (1978, 1989), we now realize that there are many environments acting on us. Bronfenbrenner visualized the environment as a set of nested structures, each inside the next. He identified the deepest level of the environment that affects development as the **microsystem** (for example, the home or school).

The next level moves beyond the immediate setting and necessitates examining the relations between immediate settings in which the person actually participates, which is the **mesosystem** (the relationship among microsystems). A good example is seen in a child's school achievement. Those children who are fortunate enough to be in a family that maintains close and warm relationships with the school can be expected to do well in their classroom work.

The **exosystem,** Bronfenbrenner's next level, is an environment in which you are not actually present, but which nevertheless affects development. For example, let's assume that a working couple has a child in a private school. One of them loses a good paying position. The result is that the next year their child has to go to a different school. The child's environment changes radically through forces at work in an unrelated environment.

The **macrosystem,** Bronfenbrenner's final level, is the blueprint of any society, which is a kind of masterplan for human development within that society. Think for a moment about the differences that people in the mainland Chinese society have encountered when compared to the experiences of American citizens.

But these systems also interact; they don't remain isolated from each other. Consider the youngster whose father has just lost his job (changes in the exosystem), which then cause the family to move to another location with different friends and schools for the child (changes in the micro- and mesosystems). You can see how a system analysis helps to emphasize the significance of context to development.

The Developmental Contextualism Perspective

Finally, we know today that heredity and environment produce their results in a complex, interactive manner. To complicate our analysis even more, however, we are constantly interacting with the environment to produce developmental changes. Consequently, any single perspective lacks the sophistication to explain the hidden depths of development. Remember, we've had nine months of development following conception, so we immediately begin to shape the reactions of those around us; that is, our behavior causes parents and siblings to respond in a unique fashion. As a result, a more detailed and multifaceted perspective than just heredity or just environment is needed.

Once this need was recognized, the idea of **reciprocal interactions** became a powerful explanatory tool in the hands of developmental psychologists. Reciprocal interactions mean that we respond to those around us in a way that causes them to change; their responses to us then change, which in turn produces new changes in us. It's an unending process that doesn't rely exclusively on either heredity or environment but rather uses the interactions between the two to describe and explain developmental changes. By stressing the complexity of developmental analysis, those adhering to a reciprocal interaction perspective have made it clear that there are no simple cause-and-effect explanations of development. All of us, children, adolescents, and adults, experience a constant state of reorganization as we move through the life cycle.

Developmental contextualism, popularized by Richard Lerner (1991), is the current version of this perspective. Developmental contextualism focuses not only on the interactions between heredity and environment but also incorporates recent research relating to **cultural constructivism,** which means that you use the particular environment around you to construct your own worldview.

Developmental contextualism begins with the idea that all of our characteristics, psychological as well as biological, function by a reciprocal interaction with the environment, called the *context*. Context is an inclusive term that attempts to portray environmental complexity by identifying four major forces of our development:

1. The *physical setting,* such as the home, classroom, workplace.

2. *Social influences,* such as our family, peers, significant others.

3. *Our personal characteristics,* such as physical appearance, temperament, language fluency.

4. The *influence of time,* that is, change brought about by the sheer chronology of our lives; to put it simply, the longer we're able to survive, the more changes we experience with their inescapable and inevitable consequences for our development.

These forces are illustrated in Figure 1.1.

Exchanges between individuals and their contexts are the basic change processes in development. Consequently, the crucial element in our development is the changing relationship between our complexity and a multilayered context. If you think about this deceptively simple statement, you can appreciate the need to study development, not from any single perspective, like biology or environment but from a more sophisticated analytical appraisal.

For example, consider what happens when you interact with your environment. Your genes provide a blueprint that is passed on to the cells, tissues, and organs of your body, influencing the growth of such widely divergent growth features as your brain development and temperament (to name only two). On the other hand, the intricate and involved layers of the context, ranging from your family to your peers to your wider social sphere, simultaneously weave their networks of influence. Simple explanations? Hardly. What is needed is a developmental perspective equally as intricate as the behavior it attempts to clarify.

An easy-to-obtain and brief, but careful analysis of developmental contextualism by Richard Lerner can be found in *Developmental Psychology,* January 1991, volume 27(1), 27–32.

Issues in Lifespan Development

In lifespan psychology, as in any discipline, several issues or themes appear with sufficient frequency to warrant special mention. Here we'll discuss several issues

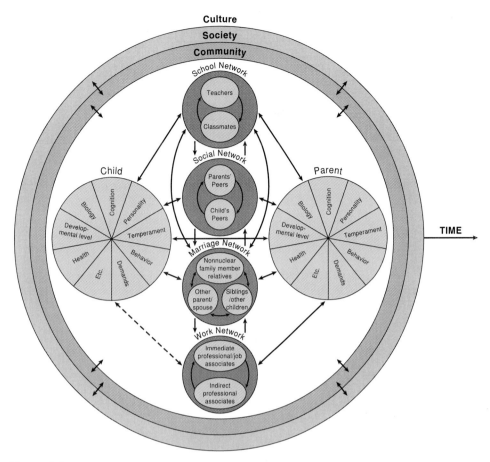

Figure 1.1

A developmental contextual model of person–context interaction (Lerner, 1984, 1986).

The Effects of Early Experience: Lasting or Temporary?

As an example of a youth who got off to a rocky start but selected his own environments, consider the early school problems of Winston Churchill. Coming from a family environment in which he was emotionally neglected, Churchill constructed a reality that enabled him to overcome these early disadvantages. Beginning school at 7 years of age, he immediately set his own agenda: He refused to learn anything he wasn't interested in; he was rebellious and troublesome; he waged a constant battle with authority.

At the bottom of his class, Churchill maintained this pattern through his years at Harrow, the famous British prep school. As one of his biographers, William Manchester, writes:

Churchillian stubbornness, which would become the bane of Britain's enemies, was the despair of

his teachers. He refused to learn unless it suited him. He was placed in what today would be called a remedial reading class, where slow boys were taught English. He stared out the window. Math, Greek, and French were beneath his contempt. (Manchester, 1983, p.157)

These words describe one of the world's greatest leaders, a statesman who led the English people through the darkest days of World War II and ultimately triumphed. Yet by today's standards he probably would be labeled a difficult child "with a behavior disorder." Churchill's path to greatness, his brilliant mind, his troubled early years, his rebellious youth, and his dogged perseverance all combine to paint a clear picture of how biopsychosocial interactions shaped his lifespan.

Guided Review

7. Those adhering to a biological perspective on development believe that _____ proceeds by a predetermined biological timetable.
8. The outstanding proponent of a systems analysis of development is _____ _____.
9. Changes in you that cause changes in me are called _____ _____.
10. An individual's context includes _____ _____, _____ _____, _____ _____, and _____ _____ _____ _____.

We pride ourselves on being a nation of immigrants, a country that welcomes newcomers with the promise of unrestricted opportunity. To achieve this objective during a time of increasing immigration demands consideration and tolerance for those of different color, nationality, and beliefs.

that affect your understanding of development and that appear repeatedly throughout the book.

Gender and Development

A sociocultural issue that has attracted the attention of developmental psychologists is that of gender development. Let's begin by defining terms that we can use in a consistent manner. Developmental psychologists, responding to Unger's plea (Unger & Crawford, 1996), have urged that we use the terms sex and gender more carefully. In this new context, sex refers to biological maleness or femaleness (for example, the sex chromosomes), whereas gender suggests psychosocial aspects of maleness and femaleness (for example, changing gender roles).

Definitions

Although no absolute distinction is possible—we can't completely separate our ideas about gender from a person's body—this distinction will help us to focus on the major forces contributing to the acquisition of gender identity while preserving the integrity of the biopsychosocial model. Within this framework, we can now distinguish among gender identity, gender stereotypes, and gender roles.

- **Gender identity** is a conviction that one belongs to the sex of birth.

- **Gender stereotypes** reflect those beliefs about the characteristics associated with male or female.

- **Gender role** refers to culturally acceptable sexual behavior.

Studies of gender development have focused on theoretical explanations, research into gender similarities and differences, and gender stereotypes. We'll analyze these topics throughout our work, but here it is instructive to mention a few signs that indicate the changing status of women in our society.

As concern about gender equity has received more publicity, stereotypes about males and females are slowly eroding. If, despite this trend, however, people are treated according to stereotypical characteristics, then their potential is immediately limited. Although gender stereotyping is only one part of gender development, it illustrates the importance of the relationship between gender and development. At an early age, children construct social categories from the world around them, attach certain characteristics to these categories, and then label the categories. This process may be positive since it helps children to organize their world. It may also be negative, if the characteristics associated with a particular category are limiting—"girls just can't do math" (Serbin & others, 1993).

Answers

One of the first categories children form is sex-related; there is a neat division in their minds between male and female. Children then move from the observable physical differences between the sexes and begin to acquire gender knowledge about the behavior expected of males and females. Although its content varies according to the source of this knowledge, gender role stereotyping has commenced, and attitudes toward gender are being shaped. As Serbin and her colleagues (1993) noted, despite the societal changes we have seen in acceptable gender roles, gender role stereotypes have remained relatively stable. Although gender stereotyping is only one part of gender development, it illustrates the importance of the relationship between gender and development.

Continuity versus Discontinuity

We can summarize the issue of continuity versus discontinuity as follows: Do developmental changes appear as the result of a slow but steady progression (continuity) or as the result of abrupt changes and stages (discontinuity)? As a rather dramatic illustration, consider the phenomenon known as attachment in infancy. Sometime after 6 months of age, babies begin to show a decided preference for a particular adult, usually the mother. We then say that the infant has attached to the mother. During any time of stress—anxiety, illness, appearance of strangers—the baby will move to the preferred adult. With regard to continuity or discontinuity, does attachment appear suddenly as completely new and different behavior, or do subtle clues signal its arrival? (For an excellent overview of this topic, see Robins & Rutter, 1990.)

Continuities and discontinuities appear in all our lives because the term development implies change. Puberty, leaving home, marriage, and career all serve to shape psychological functioning. Continuities will occur, however, because our initial experiences, our early learning, and our temperaments remain with us. The form of the behavior may change over the years but the underlying processes may remain the same. For example, the conduct disorders of childhood (stealing, fighting, truancy) may become the violence of adulthood (theft, wife abuse, child abuse, murder, personality disorders). Surface dissimilarities may be evident in the types of behavior, but the processes that cause both kinds of behavior may be identical, thus arguing for continuity in development.

We must explain, however, those periods in our lives that seem to be quite different from those that preceded them; for example, walking and talking. We also negotiate transitions at appropriate times in our lives, such as leaving home, beginning a career, getting married, adjusting to the birth of children. It's not just a matter of "doing these things," because the circumstances surrounding them also have important developmental effects. What is the "right" age to get married? Is it a positive occasion and not something that "should" be done? The reality of these events has caused other developmental psychologists to see development as mainly discontinuous. Most developmental psychologists now believe that both continuity and discontinuity characterize development.

Stability versus Change

Whether children's early experiences (either positive or negative) affect them throughout their lifespan is a question that today intrigues developmental psychologists. If a child suffers emotional or physical neglect, abuse, or malnutrition, does it mean the child is scarred for life? Or if a child has been encouraged to adopt a caring attitude toward others, will such positive behavior persevere? If you answer yes, you believe in **stability;** if your answer is no, then you accept the likelihood of change. We know, for example, that human beings show amazing **resiliency,** which testifies to our ability to change; recall the Werner & Smith study (1995) mentioned at the beginning of the Chapter. Yet resiliency has its limits, which testifies to the lingering effects of stability. Most developmental psychologists would argue for the presence of both stability and change throughout our lives.

Nature versus Nurture

An enduring issue in developmental psychology has been—which exercises a greater influence on development, our inborn tendencies (nature) or our surrounding world (nurture)? The issue today is often framed in a slightly different way—which is more decisive for our development, our genes or our environment? Again, most developmental psychologists lean toward an interplay between these two forces in shaping development. We (the authors) would argue strongly that the *interaction* between genes and environment explain the individual developmental paths each of us follows through our lifespans. Our belief is that human beings, using their genetic heritages, interact with their environment, not as passive recipients but as active shapers of their destinies. We'll discuss this idea in greater length throughout our work, especially in Chapter 6.

These issues help to identify lifespan psychology as a dynamic discipline, one with great theoretical and practical implications. But, as fascinating as these issues are, we can't forget the integrated nature of development. With these ideas in mind to help you interpret developmental data, we turn now to those research techniques that developmental psychologists use in resolving questions about the lifespan.

Guided Review

11. Although newcomers to any society must adapt to that country, those in the _____ country must also adjust.
12. Today's immigrants attempt to maintain their _____ identity.
13. The term gender implies _____ aspects of maleness and femaleness.
14. When children believe they belong to the sex of their birth, this is called _____ _____.
15. _____ _____ refers to culturally acceptable sexual behavior.
16. A belief in _____ is to hold the opinion that early experiences in a child's life continue to exert influence throughout the lifespan.
17. Those who believe that developmental changes occur because of a slow and steady progression believe in _____.

Developmental Research

Having identified several key developmental issues and theoretical viewpoints, we must now ask—how can we obtain reliable data about these topics so that we can better understand them?

Today we use many approaches to understanding human behavior. Each has its strengths and weaknesses; none is completely reliable. Most developmental psychologists employ one of three data collection methods: descriptive studies, manipulative experiments, and naturalistic experiments. In the first type, information is gathered on subjects without manipulating them in any way. In the second two, an experiment is performed before the information is gathered.

Developmental psychologists also use one of four time variable designs: **one-time, one-group studies; longitudinal studies; cross-sectional studies;** and a

Answers

11. receiving 12. cultural 13. psychological 14. gender identity 15. gender role 16. stability 17. continuity

When Are Research References Too Old?

Probably for the rest of your career, you will be reading research—articles, chapters in books, monographs, and so on. When should you decide that a reference is too old to be credible any longer? As with so many aspects of social science, the answer is "It all depends." Guidelines exist, however, so let's try to understand them by looking at several references. Before reading our decision, you might try to guess what a good judgment would be.

As many as one-third of adolescents receive less than 70 percent of their minimum daily requirement for the most common minerals such as calcium and iron (U.S. Department of Health, Education, and Welfare, 1972).

Since eating habits of adolescents are likely to change with the times (depending, among other things, on the economic condition of the country), this statistic is unreliable because more than 20 years have passed since the data were collected.

Although the average number of homosexuals who are contracting AIDS each year is decreasing, they are still the most vulnerable group (U.S. National Center for Health Statistics, 1990).

This study is much more recent, but it too is suspect because we know that the AIDS epidemic is changing very rapidly. In fact, heterosexual females are now experiencing the greatest rate of increase per capita.

Noise-induced hearing loss is recognized as the second most common cause of irreversible hearing loss in older persons (Surjan & others, 1973).

Here is another study that is quite dated, but because there is no known reason to believe that aging factors have changed much over the years, if the study was well designed, we may still accept the results.

The major crisis in the first year and one-half of human life is the establishment of basic trust (Erikson, 1963).

This statement is not a research finding but rather represents Erikson's belief as reflected in his psychosocial theory of human development. As such, it is accurate because that is exactly what Erikson said.

Can you think of other factors that influence the timeliness of research references? Can you think of other criteria for judging them?

combination of the last two, called **sequential studies.** Each type of study varies according to the effect of time on the results.

Data Collection Techniques

The three data collection techniques are described in the following sections.

Descriptive Studies

Descriptive studies are quite common. Most are numerically descriptive; for example, how many 12-year-olds versus 17-year-olds think the government is doing a good job? How much money does the average 40-year-old woman have to spend per week? How many pregnant teenage girls were or were not using birth control? How happily or unhappily does the average 66-year-old man view his sex life? Some studies ask people their opinions about themselves (called self-report studies) or other people. These studies may use interviews or questionnaires. Other studies describe people simply by counting the number and types of their behaviors (called observational studies). A third type of study, case studies, presents data on an individual or individuals in great detail, in order to make generalizations about a particular age group.

An example of the case study approach is Mack and Hickler's *Vivienne: The Life and Suicide of an Adolescent Girl* (1982). After Vivienne's death, the researchers obtained the family's permission to read her diary, poems, and letters. They also interviewed her relatives, friends, and teachers to shed light on her thinking as she came closer and closer to committing this tragic act. Although their findings may explain the suicide of only this one person, the researchers' hope was to discover the variables that caused such a decision. A more recent case study approach is of the biographical type. For example, Gardner (1997) closely examined the biographies of four eminent persons: Wolfgang Mozart, Sigmund Freud, Virginia Woolf, and Mahatma Gandhi. From these four cases, he built a new theory about creative innovation.

Descriptive studies have the advantage of generating a great deal of data. Because the sequence of events is not under the observer's control, however, causes and effects cannot be determined. That is, just because two variables are associated does not mean that one causes the other.

Typically, the association between variables is established through a statistical technique known as correlation. This technique provides a numerical evaluation of how great the degree of association is between any two variables. For instance, height and weight are associated with each other, but not perfectly. The taller people are, the more they weigh, but this is not always true; the correlation between height and weight for a typical sample of people is moderately high. Although there is a definite association, we would not say the height causes weight, or vice versa—they are simply correlated. We examine the correlation between variables to see how high they are. If high, we may want to set up experiments to further examine the relationship.

Manipulative Experiments

In the quest for the causes of behavior, psychologists have designed many **manipulative experiments.** In these, the investigators attempt to keep all variables (all the factors that can affect a particular outcome) constant except one, which they carefully manipulate; this is called a **treatment.** If differences occur in the results of the experiment, they can be attributed to the variable that was manipulated in the treatment. The experimental subjects must respond to some test the investigator selects to determine the effect of the treatment. Figure 1.2 illustrates this procedure.

In the Figure, E is the experimental group and C is the control group, which receives no special treatment; x stands for the treatment; and the lowercase b and a refer to measurements done before and after the experiment. The two groups must have no differences between them, either before or during the experiment (except the treatment). Otherwise, the results remain questionable.

An example would be a study in which sixth and seventh grade inner-city students were taught relaxation techniques as part of a conflict prevention program (Dacey, deSalvatore, & Robinson, 1996). Most students benefitted from the instruction, but boys were much more apt to use the physiological relaxation technique taught in the program, whereas girls were more likely to employ the cognitive method that was taught.

Though manipulative experiments often can lead us to discover what causes what in life, they have some problems. How do you know your results are reliable? Was the treatment similar to normal conditions? Do subjects see themselves as special because you picked them and thus react atypically? For these reasons, researchers may turn to naturalistic experiments.

Naturalistic Experiments

In **naturalistic experiments,** the researcher acts solely as an observer and does as little as possible to disturb the environment. "Nature" performs the experiment, and

Figure 1.2

The classic experiment

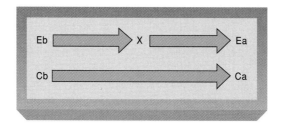

the researcher acts as a recorder of the results. (Note: Do not confuse these experiments with descriptive studies that are done in a natural setting, such as a park; those are not experiments.) An example is the study of the effects of the Northeast blizzard of 1978 by Nuttall and Nuttall (1980). These researchers compared the reactions of those people whose homes were destroyed with the reactions of people whose homes suffered only minor damage.

Only with a naturalistic experiment do we have any chance of discovering causes and effects in real-life settings. The main problems with this technique are that it requires great patience and objectivity, and it is impossible to meet the strict requirements of a true scientific experiment.

Time Variable Designs

In the following sections, we'll describe the four **time variable designs.**

One-Time, One-Group Studies

As the name implies, **one-time, one-group studies** are those that are carried out only once on one group of subjects. Thus investigating causes and effects is impossible because the sequence of events cannot be known.

Longitudinal Studies

The **longitudinal study,** which makes several observations of the same individuals at two or more times in their lives, can answer important questions. Examples are determining the long-term effects of learning on behavior; the stability of habits and intelligence; and the factors involved in memory.

A good example of a longitudinal growth study is that of Werner and Smith (1992), who investigated the long-term effects of birth problems. They found that even when the problems were of a serious nature, some children proved to be remarkably resilient.

The chief advantage of the longitudinal method is that it permits the discovery of lasting habits and of the periods in which they appear. A second advantage is the possibility of tracing those adult behaviors that have changed since early childhood. Longitudinal research, however, has many problems. It is expensive and often hard to maintain because of changes in availability of researchers and subjects. Changes in the environment can also distort the results. For example, if you began in 1960 to study changes in political attitudes of youths from 10 to 20 years of age, you would probably have concluded that adolescents become more and more radical as they grow older. But the war in Vietnam would surely have had much to do with this finding. The results of the same study done between 1970 and 1980 would probably not show this trend toward the radical.

Cross-Sectional Studies

Cross-sectional studies compare groups of individuals of various ages at the same time to investigate the effects of aging. For example, if you want to know how creative thinking changes or grows during adolescence, you could administer creativity tests to groups of 10-, 12-, 14-, 16-, and 18-year-olds and check on the differences of the average scores of the five groups. Jaquish and Ripple (1980) did just this, but their subjects ranged in age from 10 to 84!

As with each of the other research designs, a problem occurs with this method. Although careful selection can minimize the effects of cultural change, it is possible that the differences you may find may be due to differences in age cohort, rather than maturation. Age cohorts are groups of people born at about the same time. Each cohort has had different experiences throughout its history, and this can affect the results as well as the actual differences in age. Figure 1.3 compares the longitudinal and cross-sectional approaches.

Figure 1.3

Comparison of the longitudinal
and cross-sectional approaches

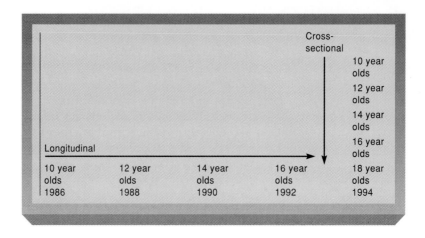

Sequential (Longitudinal/Cross-Sectional) Studies

When a cross-sectional study is done at several times with the same groups of individuals (such as administering creativity tests to the same five groups of youth,
but at three different points in their lives), the problems mentioned before can be
alleviated. Table 1.2 illustrates such a study. Although this type of research is complicated and expensive, it may be the only type that is capable of answering important questions in the complex and fast-changing times in which we live.

Table 1.3 shows how each of the data collection methods may be combined

---

TABLE 1.2   ILLUSTRATION OF A LONGITUDINAL/CROSS-SECTIONAL STUDY

Creativity Test			
Test 1 March 4, 1999	Test 2 March 4, 2001	Test 3 March 4, 2003	
Group A (12 years old)	Group A (14 years old)	Group A (16 years old)	Mean Score Group A
Group B (14 years old)	Group B (16 years old)	Group B (18 years old)	Mean Score Group B
Group C (16 years old)	Group C (18 years old)	Group C (20 years old)	Mean Score Group C
Mean Score 1999	Mean Score 2001	Mean Score 2003	

**TABLE 1.3   RELATIONSHIPS OF DATA COLLECTION TECHNIQUES
AND TIME VARIABLE DESIGNS**

Data Collection Techniques			
Time Variable Designs	Descriptive	Manipulated	Naturalistic
One-time, one-group	_____	_____	_____
Longitudinal	_____	_____	_____
Cross-sectional	_____	_____	_____
Sequential	_____	_____	_____

An Applied View

Understanding the Research Article

As you continue your reading and work in lifespan development, your instructor will undoubtedly ask you to review pertinent articles that shed light on the topic you're studying. Many of these articles present the results of an experiment that reflects the scientific method.

The typical research article contains four sections: the introduction, the Method section, the Results section, and Discussion, (Moore, 1983). We'll review each of these sections using a well-designed study—The Effects of Early Education on Children's Competence in Elementary School, published in Evaluation Review (Bronson & others, 1984)—to illustrate each of the four sections.

1. **The Introduction** The introductory section states the purpose of the article (usually as an attempt to solve a problem) and predicts the outcome of the study (usually in the form of hypotheses). The introduction section also contains a review of the literature. In the introductory section of the article by Bronson and her associates, the researchers state that their intent is to coordinate the effects of early education programs on the performance of pupils in elementary school. They concisely review the pertinent research and suggest a means of evaluating competence.

2. **The Method Section** The method section informs the reader about the subjects in the experiment (Who were they? How many? How were they chosen?), describes any tests that were used, and summarizes the steps

taken to carry out the study. In the study by Bronson and her associates, the subjects were 169 second-grade children who has been in an early education program and 169 other children who had not been in the preschool program. The outcome measure was a classroom observation instrument. The authors then explained in considerable detail how they observed the pupils.

3. **The Results Section** In the results section, the results gathered on the subjects is presented, together with the statistics that help us to interpret the data. In the article we are using, the authors present their data in several clear tables and show differences between the two groups using appropriate statistics.

4. **Discussion** Finally, the authors of any research article will discuss the importance of what they found (or did not find) and relate their findings to theory and previous research. In the Bronson article, the authors report that the pupils who had experienced any early education program showed significantly greater competence in the second grade. The authors conclude by noting the value of these programs in reducing classroom behavior problems and improving pupils' competence.

Don't be intimidated by research articles. Look for the important features and determine how the results could help you to understand people's behavior at a particular age.

with each of the time variable designs. For each of the cells in this table, a number of actual studies could serve as examples. Can you see where each study mentioned in this section would go?

To conclude this section, Figure 1.4 compares the various research techniques. By controlled, we mean the degree to which the investigator can control the relevant variables. By inclusive, we mean the degree to which all relevant information is included in the data.

Figure 1.4

A comparison of research techniques

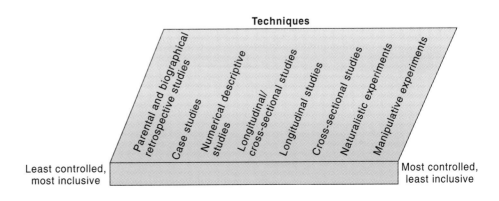

Guided Review

18. In a manipulative experiment, the experimenter attempts to keep all the variables constant except one, which is called the _____.
19. A study that observes the same individuals two or more times in their lives is known as a _____ study.
20. Comparing groups of individuals of various ages at the same time is an example of _____ research.
21. The typical research article contains four sections: _____, _____, _____, and _____.

NOTE TO OUR READERS

At the end of each of the first ten Chapters (just before the Conclusion), we'll present a table that contains the developmental milestones of the topic we're discussing. As our discussion begins to focus on adolescence and adulthood, the identification of universal norms or milestones becomes increasingly complex, even confusing, hence our reluctance to pursue this technique beyond middle childhood.

To illustrate these forthcoming tables, let's turn to the popular and widespread use of developmental tasks as a tool to understand human growth. The developmental task concept has a long and illustrious tradition in psychology but, alas, times change and key developmental tasks need updating. For example, to fully participate in a modern society, individuals must be technologically competent and computer literate. As an illustration of attempts to update developmental tasks, let's turn to the work of Furnham and Weir (1996).

Analyzing lay theories of development (what the average person thinks about development), these researchers stressed the significance of lay theories because they are the partial causes of and consequence of social behavior. Furnham (an English psychologist) and Weir (an American psychologist) surveyed respondents in an effort to discover if adults have realistic expectations about the ages at which children can perform simple, everyday tasks. Their general findings were that adults tend to underestimate the ages at which older children (9–15 years) can successfully perform tasks and overestimate the ages at which younger children (2–4 years) can. Table 1.4 presents some examples of their findings.

Findings such as these contain significant implications. If adults expect a child to behave in a certain way because of age, and their behavior doesn't

TABLE 1.4 SOME DEVELOPMENTAL TASKS OF THE LIFESPAN

Task	Subjects' Estimates (years)	Norm (years)
Walk alone for twenty yards	2.07	2
Point to nose, eyes, mouth	2.33	3
Repeat a sentence of six syllables	4.44	3
Know left from right by showing correct hand	4.87	6
Know the number of toes and fingers without looking	4.95	7
Recite the days of the week in correct order	5.07	9
Name in correct order the months of the year	5.95	10
Tell simple jokes	6.30	10
Repeat seven digits	6.56	12
Classify fruit from vegetables	7.69	12

Answers

18. treatment 19. longitudinal 20. cross-sectional 21. introduction, method, results, discussion

"measure up," then definite consequences can follow. For example, the respondents in this study believed that children recognize an emotion like disgust at 7.27 years of age while in reality a child doesn't acquire this ability until 10 years of age. Consequently, a mother, believing she showed her disgust with something her son did, may punish the child because he didn't respond correctly. If the child doesn't understand why he was punished (particularly if this happens frequently), the relationship between the two could be negatively affected.

CONCLUSION

In this Chapter we have presented a model of development—the biopsychosocial model—that forms the structure of the book. We urge you to use this model to help you grasp and retain the material and meaning of the various Chapters. We have also identified the various age groups that constitute the lifespan and that are the focus of this book. Lifespan study can aid us in adjusting to a society in which rapid change seems to be an inevitable process. By acquiring insights into your own development and recognizing the developmental characteristics of people of differing ages, you can hope to have more harmonious relationships with others. Also, as a result of reading about the strengths and weaknesses of different research methods, you should be more analytical and critical of the studies that are presented.

In summary:

The Meaning of Lifespan Psychology

- As psychologists realized that development did not cease at adolescence but continued into adulthood and old age, lifespan psychology assumed an important place in developmental psychology.
- Reciprocal interactions is a valuable concept in understanding development.
- The timing of experiences as well as the transitions during the lifespan help us to gain insights into developmental processes.

- Today we are aware of the significance of context in development.

Thinking About Lifespan Development

- A biological perspective on development emphasizes the controlling impact the genes have on development.
- A systems analysis of development focuses attention on the complexity of the environment.
- The environment provides the settings for learning to exercise its role in development.
- The need for more sophisticated perspectives on development has highlighted the place of reciprocal interactions in development.
- Developmental contextualism has proven to be an enlightening and compelling framework for developmental analysis.

Issues in Lifespan Development

- Any analysis of lifespan development must address key developmental issues, such as the importance of culture and development, if it is to present a complete picture of development.
- Many psychologists believe that development occurs as a steady progression of small accomplishments (for example, most infants begin to move on the floor by pulling themselves on their stomachs; they then move to a

position on their hands and knees and move much more quickly, which is an example of continuous development); other psychologists believe that development occurs in spurts or stages, such as the marked difference between crawling and walking, which is an example of discontinuity.
- The controversy over stability versus change continues to divide developmental psychologists.
- Sensitive periods seem to exist; that is, there are times in our lives when we acquire new behaviors more easily than at other times.

Developmental Research

- To explain the various ages and stages of development, we must use the best data available to enrich our insights and to provide a thoughtful perspective on the lifespan.
- Good data demand careful research methods, otherwise we would be constantly suspicious of our conclusions.
- The most widely used research techniques include descriptive studies, manipulative experiments, and naturalistic experiments.
- Developmental psychologists also use four time variable designs one-time, one-group; longitudinal studies; cross-sectional studies; and sequential studies.

KEY TERMS

Biopsychosocial interactions
Cross-sectional studies
Cultural constructivism
Descriptive studies
Developmental contextualism
Gender identity
Gender role

Gender stereotypes
Longitudinal studies
Manipulative experiments
Macrosystem
Mesosystem
Microsystem
Naturalistic experiments

One-time, one-group studies
Reciprocal interaction
Resiliency
Sequential studies
Stability
Time variable designs
Treatment

WHAT DO YOU THINK?

1. We urged you to refer to the biopsychosocial model as you continue your reading of the text. Can you explain its potential value? Now think of an example in your own life, or in the life of a family member, and describe how biological, psychological, and social factors interacted to produce a particular effect. Do you think the model helped you to explain that person's behavior?

2. We presented several issues that thread their way through lifespan studies; for example, culture and development, gender and development, the role of sensitive periods, continuity versus discontinuity, stability versus change. Why do you think these are issues? Examine each one separately and defend your reasons for stating that they have strong developmental implications.

3. Throughout the Chapter, we have stressed the important role that context plays in development. What do you think of this emphasis? Although this is only the first Chapter of your reading, recall your own life and think about the influence (both positive and negative) that those around you have had. Use these personal experiences in your answer.

CHAPTER REVIEW TEST

1. A model that uses the interaction of biological, psychological, and social influences to explain development is the
   a. psychoanalytic.
   b. cognitive.
   c. biopsychosocial.
   d. behavioral.

2. When one person's reactions bring about change in the behavior of another person, this is called
   a. transfer.
   b. reciprocal interactions.
   c. accommodation.
   d. psychosocial crisis.

3. The resurgence of interest in biological explanations of development is due to
   a. government subsidies.
   b. the influence of learning theorists.
   c. recent genetic research.
   d. studies of prenatal development.

4. Who believed that a system analysis of development was most fruitful?
   a. Watson
   b. Piaget
   c. Gesell
   d. Bronfenbrenner

5. When we refer to the values, beliefs, and characteristics of a people, we are referring to
   a. culture.
   b. race.
   c. ethnicity.
   d. customs.

6. One of the most prominent believers in a contextual perspective on development was
   a. Lerner.
   b. Hall.
   c. Piaget.
   d. Skinner.

7. More complex explanations of development depend on the idea of
   a. genes.
   b. reciprocal interactions.
   c. naturalistic research.
   d. stimulus-response experiments.

8. If you believe that a child carries the scars of childhood abuse for life, you believe in
   a. equal potential.
   b. stability.
   c. continuity.
   d. resiliency.

9. A more detailed form of reciprocal interactions as an explanation of development is known as
   a. behavioral analysis.
   b. information processing.
   c. developmental contextualism.
   d. operant conditioning.

10. When you believe that you belong to the sex of your birth, you have acquired
    a. gender identity.
    b. gender stereotypes.
    c. gender role.
    d. equality.

11. Beliefs about the characteristics associated with males and females is called
    a. gender identity.
    b. gender stereotype.
    c. gender role.
    d. equality.

12. Descriptive studies
    a. determine cause and effect.
    b. manipulate variables.
    c. require experimenter control.
    d. generate considerable data.

13. When an experimenter keeps all variables constant but one, that one is called
    a. determined.
    b. predicted.
    c. descriptive.
    d. treatment.

14. An example of a cross-sectional study is
    a. comparing individuals of various ages at the same time.
    b. continued observations of the same individuals.
    c. careful description by the researcher.
    d. one that requires no manipulation.

15. The typical research article contains four sections. Which item is not included in a research article?
    a. introduction
    b. method
    c. results
    d. author biography

Answers

Ellen Marie Cotter was born on February 17, 1931, in Boston. The daughter of middle-class parents, she seemed a normal, healthy, and happy baby. It was not until she was 5 years old that she began to exhibit behavior that bothered her parents. From having an outgoing, cheerful personality, Ellen slowly started to withdraw until she refused to speak to anyone but her parents. She also had a disturbing tendency to sit and stare out the window.

Deeply bothered, her parents decided to do everything they could to help their child, no matter what the financial sacrifice might be. Their family doctor, Dr. John Patterson, finding no physical causes of her problem, mentioned that he had heard of a new technique for treating psychological problems, called psychoanalysis. The leader of the psychoanalytic movement, an individual by the name of Sigmund Freud, believed that a person's behavior was a clue to inner thoughts and feelings. Ellen's parents seized on this and wanted to know more about it: What was involved in psychoanalysis? Who were the leading proponents of the movement? Where was the movement located?

Their doctor, a well-read man of his times, told them as much as he knew about Freud. When Ellen's parents said they were willing to take her to Vienna, regardless of the expense, Dr. Patterson said that Freud was almost 80 years old and in poor health but that he had a very kind habit of writing thoughtful replies to the letters of strangers, especially if the problem interested him.

The Cotters decided to contact Freud and sent him a detailed description of their daughter's condition. Dr. Patterson also suggested that they tell Freud as much as possible about the early years of Ellen's life because Freud was particularly fascinated by the effect of early experiences. After sending off their lengthy letter, the Cotters anxiously awaited each day's mail. Much to their amazement and delight, about three months later an envelope postmarked Vienna arrived at their home.

In his reply, Freud, although declaring his inability to conduct therapy under the circumstances, wrote that the Cotters should examine certain conditions in their daughter's life very carefully. He told them to search for any signs of anxiety, which can be extremely painful for a child and could actually produce some of the symptoms they had described. He pointed out that small children suffered from many anxieties that can radically affect their behavior.

Pleased with this professional and caring reply, Ellen's parents spent hours trying to identify anything that might have caused her any anxiety. They could only think of one episode: The previous summer while on a train trip Ellen had become separated from them while they were storing their luggage. She had stepped from the train thinking she had seen her father standing on the platform and then thought the train was leaving without her. The Cotters decided they would redouble their efforts to provide a sense of security for their daughter.

Six years passed, and in the summer of 1937, Ellen's father, an excellent salesman, was asked by his company to travel to Switzerland to train the staff of the company's newly opened office. Both parents thought the trip, especially the ocean voyage, would be enjoyable for Ellen. They were to be in Switzerland for only four weeks, but soon after their arrival they heard stories about a remarkable Swiss psychologist, Jean Piaget. A relatively young man of 41, Piaget was then at the peak of his experimental career. Through their Swiss contacts, the Cotters arranged to meet Piaget and discuss their daughter's problem with him. Arriving at Piaget's hotel overlooking beautiful Lake Geneva, the Cotters were immediately taken with him. As the father of three daughters, Piaget was quite sympathetic about Ellen's problems. Although Piaget emphasized that his focus on children's cognitive development had left him little time to study emotional development, after hearing the Cotters' story, he made some insightful comments.

He told them that children of Ellen's age had a natural tendency to relate everything to themselves (e.g., "The moon follows me around"), which he thought was normal. No matter what happened, children believed it was about them; they felt responsible. The term he used to describe this phase of development was egocentric. Piaget said that something might have happened—he didn't know what—for which Ellen blamed herself. The Cotters deeply appreciated the window into cognitive development Piaget had opened for them and thanked him profusely. Piaget, with his customary courtesy, asked them to keep him informed of Ellen's progress.

On the boat trip home, the parents discussed what Piaget had said and decided that both Freud's and Piaget's ideas were helpful. But they wondered whether they themselves could do anything specific. Ellen's father rather casually remarked that he had read recently about a young psychologist by the name of B. F. Skinner who believed that behavior was powerfully influenced by carefully planned reinforcements. That is, if people selected the behaviors they think are appropriate, and reinforced those behaviors, they will continue to appear. Ellen's parents decided they would reinforce those behaviors that were directed toward social development in an effort to encourage Ellen to interact with others.

Both parents agreed that although it had been a lengthy journey from the United States to Vienna to Switzerland and then back to the United States, they had learned much about human behavior and could now offer some realistic help to their daughter. ✪

In the scenario just described, three (of the seven theorists you'll read about in this Chapter) historical figures were introduced to illustrate how theory "works" in practice. At this point you may say, "I don't need theory; just give me the facts." Unfortunately, the facts alone don't tell the whole story. How many of us can see a beautiful building in a pile of bricks or a stunning painting in jars of paint? Always needed is some focus, some structure to give meaning to the facts. In lifespan development that focus is found in theory, the perspective that leads us, sometimes clearly, sometimes grudgingly, to understanding. Not that you must become a fervent disciple of any one theory; you undoubtedly will use theories as most of us do, selecting and applying what seems best suited to the facts before you, which is our intent as we present some of the major developmental theorists in this Chapter.

For many people, the word *theory* means someone's guess about why something happens the way it does. In this book, we use the word differently. We believe that theories do not stand alone; they are related to other aspects of science. Although we cannot give you the one final answer on how we develop—no one can do that—we can, however, introduce you to the best current thinking in the study of human development.

In this Chapter, you'll see how theories help to explain human development by examining seven important developmental theorists: Sigmund Freud, Erik Erikson, Abraham Maslow, Jean Piaget, Lev Vygotsky, B.F. Skinner, and Albert Bandura. When you finish reading this chapter, you should be able to

• Describe the purposes of theory making and the relationships of theory to other aspects of science.

• Itemize Freud's stages of development, together with his concepts of the functions and constructs of the human psyche.

- Compare and contrast Erik Erikson's eight stages of psychosocial crisis.

- Identify and apply the basic needs in Abraham Maslow's hierarchy of needs.

- Define Piaget's four stages of cognitive development, as well as explain the roles played by the two central processes of organization and adaptation.

- Describe the input and significance of culture in development.

- Explain the role of reinforcement, punishment, and extinction in Skinner's behavioral theory.

- Apply Bandura's theory of observational learning to specific situations.

- Discuss these issues from an applied, a multicultural, and your own point of view.

The Psychoanalytic Approach

On a beautiful spring day in 1885 Sigmund Freud sat down and wrote a startling letter to his fiancee. Telling her that he had just about completed a massive task—destroying his notes, letters, and manuscripts of the past fourteen years, a destructive act that he would repeat several times in his lifetime—Freud revealed his mistrust of future biographers. Yet, in spite of his efforts, the autobiographical nature of much of his published works and his vast correspondence left a lasting legacy. In fact, we can safely say in more than 100 years of psychological research, it is impossible to think of anyone who has played a larger role than Sigmund Freud. Even his most severe critics admit that his theory on the development of personality is a milestone in the social sciences. In fact, many people mistakenly think **psychoanalytic theory,** the name he gave to his theory, is the same as psychology.

Let's begin by examining Freud's ideas about the structure of the mind.

Structures of the Mind

Dr. Sigmund Freud was a medical doctor who proposed the psychoanalytic theory of development.

Freud divided the mind into three structures: the **id,** the **ego,** and the **superego,** which appear at different stages of the young child's development. They are empowered by the libido, Freud's term for psychic energy, which is similar to the physical energy that fuels bodily functions. The characteristics of the three structures of the mind are as follows:

- *The id.*   This structure, the only one present at birth, contains all of our basic instincts, such as our need for food, drink, dry clothes, and nurturance. It is the simplest of the structures, operating only in the pursuit of bodily pleasures.

- *The ego.*   The ego is the central part of our personality, the (usually) rational part that does all the planning and keeps us in touch with reality. It begins to develop from the moment of birth. Freud believed that the stronger the ego becomes, the more realistic, and usually the more successful, a person is likely to be.

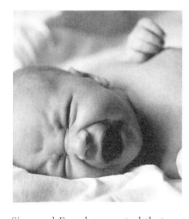

Sigmund Freud suggested that babies react to needful feelings such as hunger in several steps. First they become aware of the need, then they cry; next they imagine that the need has been met, and then they fall back to sleep. Slowly they learn that imagination is no substitute for real satisfaction of a need.

- *The superego.*   Throughout infancy, we gain an increasingly clearer conception of what the world is like. Toward the end of the first year our parents and others begin to teach us what they believe is right and wrong and expect us to begin to behave according to the principles they espouse.

Now starts the never-ending battle between the desires of the id and the demands of the superego. The main job of the ego is to strive unceasingly for compromises between these two "bullies."

Freud also believed that an array of defense mechanisms keeps important information in the unconscious mind from awareness, an attempt to decrease anxiety in the conflict between the id and the ego (Gay, 1988). These mechanisms are unconscious attempts to prevent awareness of unpleasant or unacceptable ideas. The psychic censor, a function of the mind, stands guard over these unconscious thoughts by using defense mechanisms to block awareness. Table 2.1 describes some of the most common defense mechanisms.

The Developing Personality

For Freud, development means moving through five instinctive stages of life, each of which he assigns to a specific age range. Each stage is discrete from the others and has a major function, which is based on a pleasure center. Unless this pleasure center is stimulated appropriately (not too much, not too little), the person becomes fixated (remains at that stage) and is unable to become a fully mature person. Here are the five stages.

- The **oral stage** (0 to 1 1/2 years old). The oral cavity (mouth, lips, tongue, gums) is the pleasure center. Its function is to obtain an appropriate amount of sucking, eating, biting, and talking.

- The **anal stage** (1 1/2 to 3 years old). The anus is the pleasure center. The function here is successful toilet training.

- The **phallic stage** (3 to 5 years old). The glans of the penis and the clitoris are the pleasure centers in this stage and in the two remaining stages. The major function of this stage is the healthy development of sexual interest, which is achieved through masturbation and unconscious sexual desire for the parent of the opposite sex. Resolution of the conflicts caused by this desire (called the Oedipal conflict in males and the Electra conflict in females) is the goal.

- The **latency stage** (5 to 12 years old). During this stage, sexual desire becomes dormant, which is especially true for males through the defense mechanism of introjection (see table 2.1). Boys refuse to kiss or hug their mothers and treat female age-mates with disdain. Because our society is more tolerant of the daughter's attraction to her father, the Electra complex is less resolved and girls' sexual feelings may be less repressed during this stage.

- The **genital stage** (12 years old and older). At this stage a surge of sexual hormones occurs in both genders, which brings about an unconscious recurrence of the phallic stage. Normally, however, youths have learned that

Maturity is a high price to pay for growing up.
Tom Stoppard

TABLE 2.1 SOME COMMON DEFENSE MECHANISMS

Repression   Unconsciously forgetting experiences that are painful to remember. Example: failure to remember an incident of sexual abuse

Compensation   Attempting to make up for an unconsciously perceived inadequacy by excelling at something else. Example: learning to play the guitar if unable to make the soccer team

Rationalization   Coming to believe that a condition that was contrary to your desires is actually what you had wanted all along. Example: being glad a trip was canceled, because "it would have been boring anyway"

Introjection   Adopting the standards and values of someone you are afraid to disagree with. Example: joining a gang

Regression   Reverting to behaviors that were previously successful when current behavior is unsuccessful. Example: crying about getting a low grade in school with the unconscious hope that the teacher will change the grade

Displacement   When afraid to express your feelings toward one person (e.g., anger at your teacher), expressing them to someone less powerful, such as your sister

desire for one's parents is taboo, and so they set about establishing relationships with members of the opposite sex who are their own age. If fixation occurs at any stage, anxiety results, and defense mechanisms will be used to deal with it.

📖 Clark, Ronald W. (1980). *Freud: The man and the cause.* New York: Random House. If you're interested in learning more about Freud and the psychoanalytic movement, this is one of the most judicious and even-handed books written about the father of psychoanalysis.

Guided Review

1. For Freud, the best way to understand the human being is through the _____.
2. Unconscious attempts to avoid awareness of unpleasant ideas are called _____.
3. The structure of the mind containing our basic instincts is called _____.
4. When a person attempts to excel at one thing because of feeling inadequate in another, this is called _____.
5. Reverting to behaviors of an earlier age is called _____.
6. In the developing personality, when pleasure is derived from such behaviors as sucking, this is the _____ stage.

The Psychosocial Crises Approach

Influenced by Freud, but searching for a different perspective, Erik Erikson, the chief proponent of a psychosocial theory of development (as opposed to Freud's psychosexual) wrote *Childhood and Society* (1963), a perceptive and at times poetic description of human life. Erikson's view of human development flowed from his extensive study of people living in an impressive variety of cultures: Germans, East Indians, the Sioux of South Dakota, the Yuroks of California, and wealthy adolescents in the northeastern United States (Erikson, 1959, 1968). His ideas also stem from intensive studies of historical figures such as Martin Luther (Erikson, 1958) and Mahatma Gandhi (Erikson, 1969), which led him to see human development as the interaction between genes and the environment.

According to Erikson, human life progresses through a series of eight stages. Each of these stages is marked by a crisis that needs to be resolved so that the individual can move on. Erikson used the term *crisis* in a medical sense; that is, it is like an acute period during illness, at the end of which the patient takes a turn for the worse or better. Table 2.2 gives an overview of his psychosocial theory.

Erikson's Eight Psychosocial Stages

Psychologist Erik Erikson is best known for his theory of psychosocial crises.

Let us look at each stage more closely.

1. *Basic trust versus mistrust* (birth to 1½ years old). In the first stage, which is by far the most important, infants should develop a sense of basic trust. For Erikson, trust has an unusually broad meaning. To the trusting infant, it is not so much that the world is a safe and happy place but rather that it is an orderly, predictable place; that is, infants learn about causes and effects. Trust flourishes with warmth, care, and also discipline.

2. *Autonomy versus shame and doubt* (1½ to 3 years old). When children are about 1½ years old, they should move into the second stage, characterized by the crisis of autonomy versus shame and doubt. Children begin to gain control over their bodies and is the usual age at which toilet training is begun. Erikson agreed with other psychoanalysts about the importance of

Answers

toilet training and believed that the sources of generosity and creativity lie in this experience. Toilet training is not the only accomplishment of the period, because children of this age usually start learning to be self-governing in all of their behaviors.

3. *Initiative versus guilt* (3 to 5 years old). The third crisis, initiative versus guilt, begins when children are about 3 years old. Building on the ability to control themselves, children now learn to have some influence over others in the family and to successfully manipulate their surroundings. They should not merely react, they should initiate. If parents and others make children feel incompetent, however, they develop a generalized feeling of guilt about themselves.

4. *Industry versus inferiority* (5 to 12 years old). The fourth stage corresponds closely to the child's elementary school years. Now the task is to go beyond imitating ideal models and to learn the basic technology of the culture. Children expand their horizons beyond the family and begin to explore the neighborhood. Their play becomes more purposeful, and they seek knowledge to complete the tasks that they set for themselves. A sense of accomplishment in making and building should prevail, otherwise children may develop a lasting sense of inferiority.

5. *Identity and repudiation versus identity confusion* (12 to 18 years old). The main task of the adolescent is to achieve a state of identity. Erikson, who originated the term **identity crisis,** used the word in a special way. In addition to thinking of identity as the general picture one has of oneself, Erikson referred to it as a state toward which one strives. If you are in a state of identity, the various aspects of your self-image would be in agreement with each other; they would be identical. Ideally, a person in the state of identity has no internal conflicts whatsoever.

6. *Intimacy and solidarity versus isolation* (18 to 25 years old). In the sixth stage, intimacy with others should develop. Erikson is speaking here of far more than sexual intimacy. He is talking about the essential ability to relate one's deepest hopes and fears to another person, and to accept in turn another person's need for intimacy.

7. *Generativity versus stagnation* (25 to 65 years old). Generativity means the ability to be useful to ourselves and to society. As in the industry stage,

TABLE 2.2 ERIK ERIKSON'S PSYCHOSOCIAL THEORY OF DEVELOPMENT

Age (years)	Psychosocial Stage	Psychosocial Crisis	Strength	Environmental Influence
1	Infancy	Trust vs. mistrust	Hope	Maternal
2–3	Early childhood	Autonomy vs. shame, doubt	Willpower	Both parents or adult substitutes
4–5	Preschool, nursery school	Initiative vs. guilt	Purpose	Parents, family, friends
6–11	Middle childhood	Industry vs. inferiority	Competence	School
12–18	Adolescence	Identity vs. identity confusion	Fidelity	Peers
18–35	Young adulthood	Intimacy vs. isolation	Love	Partners: spouse/lover friends
35–65	Middle age	Generativity vs. stagnation	Care	Family, society
Over 65	Old age	Integrity vs. despair	Wisdom	All humans

Adapted from *Childhood and Society* by Erik H. Erikson, with the permission of W.W. Norton & Company, Inc. Copyright 1950, ©1963 by W.W. Norton & Company, Inc., renewed © 1978, 1991 by Erik H. Erikson.

According to Erikson, a sense of intimacy with another person of the opposite gender should develop between the ages of 18 and 25. If it does not, a sense of isolation results.

Live so that when your children think of fairness and integrity, they think of you.

H. J. Brown

Erikson, Erik. (1958). *Young man Luther.* New York: Norton. Martin Luther was the main force behind the Protestant Reformation. In Erikson's penetrating analysis of the causes behind Luther's actions, we have a wonderfully clear example of Erikson's ideas about adolescence in general and negative identity in particular.

the goal here is to be productive and creative, thus leading to a sense of personal fulfillment. Furthermore, a sense of trying to make the world a better place for the young in general, and for one's own children in particular, emerges. In this stage many people become mentors to younger individuals, sharing their knowledge and philosophy of life. When people fail in generativity, they begin to stagnate, to become bored and self-indulgent, unable to contribute to society's welfare. Such adults often act as if they are their own child.

8. *Integrity versus despair* (65 years old and older). When people look back over their lives and feel they have made the wrong decisions, or more commonly, that they have too frequently failed to make any decision at all, they see life as lacking integration. They feel despair at the impossibility of "having just one more chance to make things right." They often hide their terror of death by appearing contemptuous of humanity in general, and of those of their own religion or race in particular. They feel disgust for themselves.

To the extent that individuals have been successful in resolving the first seven crises, they achieve a sense of personal integrity. Adults who have a sense of integrity accept their lives as having been well spent. They feel a kinship with people of other cultures and of previous and future generations. They have a sense of having helped to create a more dignified life for humankind. They have gained wisdom.

Guided Review

7. Each of Erikson's stages is highlighted by a _____ that must be resolved before passage to the next stage.
8. At each stage the individual is pressured by _____ needs and the demands of _____.
9. In Erikson's first stage, it is critical for infants to learn that their world is a _____ place.
10. During Erikson's fifth stage, which occurs during or after adolescence, it is frequently necessary to resolve an _____ _____.

Answers

7. crisis 8. internal, society 9. predictable 10. identity crisis

The Humanistic Approach

Another way to understand lifespan changes is to identify those needs that must be satisfied if personal goals are to be achieved. To help you recognize the role that needs play in our lives, we'll turn to the work of Abraham Maslow and his needs hierarchy.

Maslow and Needs Satisfaction

How many times have you heard the question, "Do you feel self-actualized?" (or a similar question), which reflects one of Maslow's most famous concepts, that of self-actualization. For Maslow, **self-actualization** means that we use our abilities to the limit of our potentialities (Maslow et al., 1987). If people are convinced that they should—and can—fulfill their promise, they are then on the path to self-actualization. Self-actualization is a growth concept, and individuals move toward this goal (physical and psychological health) as they satisfy their basic needs. Growth toward self-actualization requires the satisfaction of a hierarchy of needs. Maslow's theory identifies five basic needs: physiological, safety, love and belonging, esteem, and self-actualization. (See Figure 2.1.)

The Hierarchy of Needs

In the hierarchy of needs, those needs at the base of the hierarchy are assumed to be more basic relative to the needs above them in the hierarchy.

- **Physiological needs,** such as hunger and sleep, are dominant and are the basis of motivation. Unless they are satisfied, everything else recedes. For example, students who frequently do not eat breakfast or suffer from poor nutrition generally become lethargic and withdrawn; their learning potential is severely lowered. Adolescents, who can be extremely sensitive about their weight, are particularly prone to this behavior.

- **Safety needs** represent the importance of security, protection, stability, freedom from fear and anxiety, and the need for structure and limits. For example, individuals who are afraid of school, of peers, of a superior, or of a parent's reaction have their safety needs threatened and their well-being can be affected.

- **Love and belongingness needs** refers to the need for family and friends. Healthy, motivated people wish to avoid feelings of loneliness and isolation. People who feel alone, not part of the group, or who lack any sense of belongingness usually have poor relationships with others, which can then affect their achievement in life.

- **Esteem needs** refer to the reactions of others to us as individuals and also to our opinion of ourselves. We want a favorable judgment from others, which

Figure 2.1

Maslow's hierarchy of needs

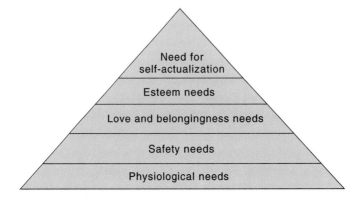

should be based on honest achievement. Our own sense of competence combines with the reactions of others to produce a sense of self-esteem. Consequently, we must acquire competence and find the opportunities that permit us to achieve and to secure reinforcement, both from others and from our own sense of satisfaction in what we have done.

• By **self-actualization needs,** Maslow was referring to that tendency, in spite of the lower needs being satisfied, to feel unfulfilled unless we are doing what we think we are capable of doing. As Maslow noted (Maslow et al., 1987), musicians must make music, artists must paint, and writers must write. The form that needs take isn't important: One person may desire to be a great parent; another may desire to be an outstanding athlete. Regardless of professions, "what human beings can be, they must be" (Maslow et al., 1987, p.22).

Closely allied to these basic needs are cognitive needs (the desire to know and understand) and aesthetic needs. But as Maslow noted, we must be careful not to make too sharp a distinction between these and the basic needs; they are tightly interrelated (Maslow et al., 1987). As you can see, Maslow's remarkably perceptive analysis furnishes us with rich general insights into human behavior, especially those needs that lead to developmental changes during the lifespan.

Guided Review

11. Using our potential as fully as possible is an example of _____.
12. Basic to Maslow's theory is the satisfaction of basic _____.
13. When Maslow referred to safety needs, he meant _____ as well as physical security.
14. The satisfaction of esteem needs depends on honest _____.
15. Human beings have a need for _____ and _____.

The Cognitive Developmental Approach

Have you ever been in a restaurant and wondered why some babies try to find the toy they knocked off their tray, while others made no attempt to retrieve it or even look for it? This apparently simple behavior and other things that babies say and do fascinated the Swiss psychologist, Jean Piaget. Born in Neuchatel, Switzerland in 1896, Piaget's training as a biologist had a major impact on his thinking about cognitive development. His fascination with the processes that led children to make incorrect answers in reasoning tests caused him to turn his attention to the analysis of children's developing intelligence. (Many believe Piaget's influence was due to his overarching theory of cognitive development, which also was responsible for the resurgence of interest in cognitive studies. For an excellent discussion of this topic, see Bjorklund, 1997.)

Jean Piaget's Theory

Whereas Freud was concerned with the structures of the personality, Jean Piaget (1896–1980) sought to understand the *cognitive structures* of the intellect (1953, 1966; Flavell, 1963). Beginning his scholarly career at the age of 11(!), Piaget

Jean Piaget was among the first to study normal intellectual development.

Answers

11. self-actualization 12. needs 13. psychological 14. achievement 15. love, belongingness

published numerous papers on birds, shellfish, and other topics of natural history. As a result, the diligent Swiss was offered the curator's position at the Geneva Natural History Museum. He was only 15 at the time and turned the offer down to finish high school. He received his Ph.D. in biology at the age of 21 and wrote more than 50 books during his lifetime.

According to Piaget, thinking is composed of numerous operations that enable the individual to manipulate the environment. Operations are mental, internalized actions. They are similar to programs in a computer. Programs enable the computer to manipulate the data fed into it in various ways. Mental operations do the same. In fact, mental operations allow people to take things apart and reassemble them without actually touching the object. To continue the metaphor, schemes are like files used in computer programs. How did Piaget explain these accomplishments?

Key Concepts in Piaget's Theory

Stages. After many years of observing children of all ages, Piaget believed that intelligence matures through the growth of increasingly effective **cognitive structures.** These structures can best be defined as the blueprints that enable us to organize and adapt to our world. Piaget believed that cognitive development means that we form more sophisticated cognitive structures as we pass through four stages: the *sensorimotor stage* (birth to 2 years old); the *preoperational stage* (2 to 7 years old); the *concrete operational stage* (7 to 11 years old); and the *formal operational stage* (11 years old and up). Thus, Piaget believed that cognitive functioning begins as responses to concrete phenomena—babies know only what they can touch, taste, or see. Our ability to use symbols and to think abstractly increases with each subsequent stage until we are able to manipulate abstract concepts and consider hypothetical alternatives. Piaget's stages of cognitive development are illustrated in Table 2.3.

Functional Invariants. Piaget stated that we inherit a method of intellectual functioning that enables us to respond to our environment by forming cognitive structures. He suggested that two psychological mechanisms, **adaptation** and **organization,** are responsible for the development of our cognitive structures. Because we use these same two mechanisms constantly throughout our lives, Piaget named them **functional invariants.**

Piaget believed that adaptation consists of **assimilation** and **accommodation.** When we assimilate something, we incorporate it; we take it in. Think of eating. We take food into the structure of our mouths and change it to fit the shape of our mouths, throats, and digestive tract. We take objects, concepts, and events into our minds similarly: We incorporate them into our mental structures, changing them to fit the structures as we change the food to fit our physical structures. For example, you are now studying Piaget's views on cognitive development. These ideas are unique and will require effort to understand them. You are attempting to

TABLE 2.3 PIAGET'S STAGES OF COGNITIVE DEVELOPMENT		
Stage	**Age**	**MajorFeatures**
Sensorimotor	Birth to 2 years	Infants use their bodies to form cognitive structures
Preoperational	2 to 7 years	
Concrete operational	7 to 11 years	Use of symbols; rapid language growth
		Can reason about physical objects
Formal operational	11+ years	Abstract thinking leads to reasoning with symbols

comprehend them by using the cognitive structures you now possess. You are assimilating Piaget's ideas; that is, you are mentally taking them in and shaping them to fit your cognitive structures.

But we also change as a result of assimilation; that is, we accommodate to what we have taken in. The food we eat produces biochemical changes; the stimuli we incorporate into our minds produce mental changes. *We change what we take in; we are also changed by it.* For example, not only are you taking in Piaget's ideas, but they are also changing your views on intelligence and cognitive development. The change in your cognitive structures will produce corresponding behavioral changes; this is the process of accommodation.

Thus, the adaptive process is the heart of Piaget's explanation of learning. As we try to "fit" new material into existing cognitive structures, we try to strike a balance between assimilation and accommodation, a process that is called **equilibration.** For example, we all make mistakes but by continued interaction with the environment, we correct these mistakes and change our cognitive structures (we have accommodated).

But our mental life doesn't consist of random activities; it is organized. The cognitive structures that we form enable us to engage in ever more complex thinking. Physical structures can again provide an analogy for Piaget's ideas on organization. To read this text you are balancing it, turning the pages, and moving your eyes. All of these physical structures are organized so that you can read. Likewise, for you to understand this material, your appropriate cognitive structures are organized so that they can assimilate and accommodate.

Schemes. Organization and adaptation are inseparable; they are two complementary processes of a single mechanism. Every intellectual act is related to other similar acts, which introduces Piaget's notion of schemes. **Schemes** are organized patterns of thought and action, that is, they are the cognitive structures and behavior that make up an organized unit. Schemes help us to adapt to our environment and may be best thought of as the inner representation of our activities and experiences. A scheme is named by its activity: the grasping scheme, the sucking scheme, the kicking or throwing scheme.

To give you an idea of how schemes develop, consider a baby reaching out and touching something, say a blanket. The child immediately begins to learn about the material (e.g., its heaviness, its size); the child is forming a cognitive structure about the blanket. When the child combines knowledge about the blanket with the act of reaching for it, Piaget called this behavior a scheme—in this case, the grasping scheme.

How do these schemes "work" in Piaget's theory? If you think of his theory in this way it may help: Stimuli come from the environment and are filtered through the functional invariants. The functional invariants, adaptation and organization, use the stimuli to form new structures or change existing structures. For example, you may have had your own idea of what intelligence is, but now you change your structures relating to intelligence because of your new knowledge about Piaget. Your content or behavior now changes because of the changes in your cognitive structures. The process is as follows.

Environment
(filtered through)
the Functional Invariants
(produce)
Cognitive Structures
(which combine with behavior to form)
Schemes

Piaget has been criticized for not stressing the role and impact of social interactions in cognitive development, which brings us to the work of Lev Vygotsky.

The Cultural Framework Approach

Lev Vygotsky placed great emphasis on the role of social processes in intellectual development.

Recently several American psychologists went to Rwanda to help with the massive psychological problems caused by the heart-rending violence of the past few years (Seppa, 1996). They found that traditional Western therapeutic methods, such as individualized therapy, were useless. Successful programs in Africa demand methods that help restore social supports and relationships. They also discovered that urging patients to "talk it out" simply did not work. Using song, dance, and story-telling,which their patients found natural and comforting, proved to be more successful.

Incidents such as this testify to the value of the work of the Russian psychologist Lev Vygotsky (1896–1934), who has attracted considerable attention because of his emphasis on social processes. Born in Russia in 1896, Vygotsky was educated at Moscow University and quickly turned his attention to educational psychology, developmental psychology, and psychopathology. For Vygotsky, the clues to understanding mental development are in children's social processes; that is, cognitive growth depends on children's interactions with those around them. The adults around children interact with them in a way that emphasizes those things that a culture values.

Although his career was abruptly terminated by his death from tuberculosis in 1934, his work today, because of its cultural emphasis, is more popular now than it was when he died. In contrast to Piaget who, as we have seen, believed that children function as "little scientists," Vygotsky turned to social interactions to explain children's cognitive development.

Lev Vygotsky's Theory

Just as we carefully laid the foundation to help you understand the key concepts in Piaget's theory before reading about his developmental stages, we'll use the same technique here. If you understand Vygotsky's basic ideas, you'll be able to grasp how his theory "works." In this way you'll fully appreciate the richness and practicality of his ideas.

Vygotsky believed that he had devised a unique idea of development, one that identified dual paths of cognitive development: elementary processes that are basically biological, and psychological processes that are essentially sociocultural (Vygotsky, 1978). Children's behaviors emerge from the intertwining of these two paths. For example, brain development provides the physiological basis for the appearance of external or egocentric speech, which gradually becomes the inner speech children use to guide their behavior.

Three fundamental themes run through Vygotsky's work: the unique manner in which he identified and used the concept of development, the social origin of mind, and the role of speech in cognitive development.

1. Vygotsky's *concept of development* is at the heart of his theory. He thought that elementary biological processes are qualitatively transformed into higher psychological functioning by developmental processes. In other words, such behaviors as speech, thought, and learning are all explained by development. Let's concentrate on speech for a moment.

    Think of the "noises" that babies make in their speech development—crying, cooing, babbling—all of which are accompanied by physical movement. Children gradually begin to point at objects and adults tell them the name—ball, cup, milk. First words come, children start to string words together, talk aloud, and, finally, use speech much the way adults do. Instead of seeing a series of independent accomplishments, Vygotsky viewed these changes as *a series of transformations brought about by developmental processes*. He thought developmental psychologists focused too often on the *products* of development (babbling, pointing, words, etc.) rather than the *processes* that caused them.

> **It follows then that we need to concentrate not on the product of development, but on the very processes by which higher forms are established (Vygotsky, 1978, p. 64).**

He was the first to admit that we lack definite knowledge about these processes, but they should be the focus of developmental research.

2. Vygotsky believed that to understand cognitive development, we must examine *the social and cultural processes* shaping children (Wertsch & Tulviste, 1992). But how do these processes affect cognitive development? He argued (1978) that any function in a child's cultural development appears twice, on two planes: first, in an interpsychological category (social exchanges with others), and, second, within the child as an intrapsychological category (using inner speech to guide behavior).

   The question now is: What happens to transform external activity to internal activity? For Vygotsky, the answer is to be found in the process of *internalization*. As he stated, the transformation of an interpersonal process (egocentric speech) into an intrapersonal process (inner speech) is the result of a long series of developmental events (Vygotsky, 1978, p. 57). He termed this internalization process "the distinguishing feature of human psychology," the barest outline of which is known.

3. Although Vygotsky lacked hard data to explain this belief, he believed that speech is one of the most powerful tools humans use to progress developmentally.

> . . . the most significant moment in the course of intellectual development, which gives birth to the purely human forms of practical and abstract intelligence, occurs when speech and practical activity, two previously completely independent lines of development, converge (Vygotsky, 1978, p. 24).

Let's now turn to one of Vygotsky's most famous ideas, the notion of the *Zone of Proximal Development*.

The Zone of Proximal Development

Commenting on the relationship between learning and development, Vygotsky (1978) noted that learning, in some way, must be matched with a pupil's developmental level, which is too frequently identified by an intelligence test score. Vygotsky believed that we cannot be content with the results of intelligence testing, which only identifies a student's developmental level at the time of testing.

For example, after administering a Stanford-Binet Intelligence test, we find that a pupil's IQ on this test is 110, which would be that student's current level of mental development. We then assume that the pupil can only work at this level. Vygotsky argued, however, that with a little help, pupils might be able to do work that they could not do on their own.

We know that pupils who have the same IQ are quite different in other respects. Motivation, interest, health, and a host of other conditions produce different achievement levels. For example, our student with an IQ of 110 may be able to deal effectively with materials of various levels of difficulty. That is, when working alone, he might be able to do only addition problems but can solve subtraction problems with his teacher's help.

To explain this phenomenon, Vygotsky introduced his notion of the **zone of proximal development.** He defined the zone of proximal development as the

An Applied View

Literary Lunches

Another example of the value of Vygotsky's zone of proximal development can be seen in a phenomenon called *Literary Lunches*. This idea, which is becoming quite popular across the country, has teachers inviting several senior citizens to read the same book as middle school students. Then both students and adults meet for lunch to discuss the book. The seniors help the students to grasp the more subtle themes in the story, while the students help the seniors to realize that most of the students in our schools are good people with ideas of their own. The understanding of both groups is extended and enriched by their interactions.

In one class recently, both groups had read the enormously popular *Nothing but the Truth* by Avi, the author of many outstanding books for young people. In this story, the conflict between a student and teacher has community-wide ramifications that hurts everyone involved. This story led to an animated discussion of character development in which the students gained a greater perspective of the forces working on adults, and the seniors acquired a more sympathetic idea of the pressures on students—Vygotsky's zone of proximal development in action.

distance between a child's actual developmental level, as determined by independent problem solving, and the higher level of potential development as determined by problem solving under adult guidance or in collaboration with more capable peers (Vygotsky, 1978). It is the difference between what children can do independently and what they can do with help.

These ideas of Vygotsky lead to the notion of **scaffolding.** Think of scaffolding as a way of helping children move from initial difficulties with a topic to a point where, with help, they perform the task independently. Picture a child learning to play tennis. She volleys fairly well, but has difficulty serving. Watching her, you notice that when she tosses the ball into the air and starts to swing, her grip slips slightly. You mention this to her and suggest that she change her grip. She tries, but still has difficulty. You remind her of the proper finger placement; she continues to practice; gradually it all comes together, and you fade gracefully into the background.

Scaffolding applies to children's school work as well. Let's assume that a mother approaches her son's math teacher. Worried about her son's math, trying to help, but feeling uncomfortable with anything mathematical, she accurately concludes she couldn't fake math skills she doesn't have. So the teacher suggests that she show her son how important math is in the consulting work she does part-time, in keeping score in the tennis games she loves, in shopping, and in anything the mother can think of that makes math relevant. The teacher could also suggest that she shop for books and computer software for math games that require problem-solving and logical-thinking skills and play them with her son.

While all of this is going on, the teacher urges the mother to constantly tell her son, "You're not bad in math; you just need to catch-up on a few things." In this case, the teacher and the mother, while not forcing anything on the child, provide support (a scaffold) that will gradually be withdrawn.

As Vygotsky noted (1978), instruction is effective only when it proceeds ahead of development. That is, teaching awakens those functions that are already maturing and that are in the zone of proximal development. Although teaching and learning are not identical to development, they can act to stimulate developmental processes.

Finally, Table 2.4 will help you to identify the most significant differences between Vygotsky and Piaget.

TABLE 2.4. KEY DIFFERENCES BETWEEN PIAGET AND VYGOTSKY

	Piaget	Vygotsky
Perspective	Individual child constructs view of world by forming cognitive structures—"the little scientist"	Child's cognitive development progresses by social interactions with others ("social origins of mind")
Basic psychological mechanism	Equilibration—child acts to regain equilibrium between current level of cognitive structures and external stimuli	Social interaction, which encourages development through the guidance of skillful adults
Language	Emerges as cognitive structures develop	Language begins as preintellectual speech and gradually develops into a sophisticated form of inner speech; one of the main forces responsible for cognitive development
Learning	Assimilation and accommodation lead to equilibration	Learning results from the interaction of two processes: biological elementary processes (such as brain development), plus sociocultural interactions
Problem solving	Child independently searches for data needed to change cognitive structures, thus enabling child to reach solution	Two aspects of problem solving: (1) key role of speech to guide "planful" behavior; (2) joint efforts with others

Guided Review

16. Piaget's major concern was with the development of _____ _____.
17. Vygotsky differed from Piaget in that he was more interested in the role that _____ _____ played in cognitive development.
18. Piaget believed that cognitive development occurred by passage through cognitive _____.
19. _____ are mental, internalized actions.
20. Vygotsky believed that for learning to be effective, it must be matched with a pupil's _____ level.
21. The difference between a child's actual developmental level and the level of potential development is what Vygotsky called the _____ _____ _____.

The Behavioral Approach

Our final approach to human development takes us into the world of behavioral theory. Two of its best-known proponents are B.F. Skinner, famous for his insights into the role of reinforcement, and Albert Bandura, who called our attention to the power of modeling in development.

Skinner and Operant Conditioning

B.F. Skinner (1904–1990) received his doctorate from Harvard and after teaching for several years at the Universities of Minnesota and Indiana, he returned to Harvard.

Answers

16. cognitive structures 17. social interactions 18. stages 19. Operations 20. developmental 21. zone of proximal development

Convinced of the importance of reinforcement, Skinner developed an explanation of learning that stressed the consequences of behavior. What happens after we do something is all-important. Reinforcement has proven to be a powerful tool in the developing, shaping, and control of behavior, both in and out of the classroom.

Skinner's Views

Harvard psychologist B. F. Skinner is identified with operant conditioning.

Skinner has been in the forefront of psychological and educational endeavors for the past several decades. Innovative, practical, tellingly prophetic, and witty, Skinner's work has had a lasting impact. In several major publications—*The Behavior of Organisms* (1938), *Science and Human Behavior* (1953), *Verbal Behavior* (1957), *The Technology of Teaching* (1968), *Beyond Freedom and Dignity* (1971), *About Behaviorism* (1974)—and in a steady flow of articles, Skinner reported his experiments and developed and clarified his theory. He never avoided the challenge of applying his findings to practical affairs. Psychology, education, religion, psychotherapy, and other subjects have all felt the force of Skinner's thought.

In his theory, called **operant conditioning** (also called **instrumental conditioning**), Skinner demonstrated that the environment has a much greater influence on learning and behavior than previously realized. Skinner argued that the environment (parents, teachers, peers) reacts to our behavior and either reinforces or eliminates that behavior. Consequently, the environment holds the key to understanding behavior.

Skinner argued that if the environment reinforces a certain behavior, it's more likely to result the next time that stimulus occurs. Thus, if the teacher asks a particular question again, the student is more likely to give the right answer, because that response was reinforced. If the response is punished, the response is less likely in the future. If the response is simply ignored, it also becomes less likely in the future. Each of these three concepts—**reinforcement, punishment,** and no response (which Skinner calls **extinction**)—needs further explanation.

Skinner preferred the term reinforcement to reward. Defining reinforcement as anything that makes a response more likely to happen in the future, Skinner iden-

---

An Applied View — *Who Can Find the Raisin?*

Probably the best way to understand Skinner's view of behaviorism is to apply its principles to teaching someone. For this suggested activity, you need two cups, a raisin, and two squares of paper of different colors, big enough to cover the cups.

For 1- to 2-year-olds, you must start very simply. Follow these steps:

1. Place a raisin in one of the cups and cover that cup with a large square of either color.

2. Cover the empty cup with the large square of the other color. Do this so that the child cannot see what you are doing.

3. Ask the child to guess which cup the raisin is in by pointing to one of the squares. If the child gets the right one, he or she wins the prize. If not, say, "Too bad. Maybe you'll get it next time. Let's try again."

4. Now, out of the child's sight, switch the positions of the cups, but cover the cup with the raisin with the same square. Do this until the child regularly guesses correctly. This is called continuous reinforcement. Generally speaking, the older the child, the quicker the learning.

5. Now cut out two large circles, each a different color, and repeat steps 1 through 4 using circles instead of squares. Does the child learn more quickly this time?

For older children, the game can be made more and more complex. Use a greater variety of shape combinations, and use three or even four cups. Finally, try to get the child to verbalize what he or she thinks is the principle behind this activity. Perhaps the child could even invent another way of doing it! As you perform this experiment, you will gain insights into the behaviorist ideas of reinforcement and extinction.

Do what you can, with what you have, with where you are.
Theodore Roosevelt

Skinner, B.F. (1948). *Walden Two.* New York: Macmillan. Many students find it hard to see how Skinner's behaviorism would function in everyday life. In this novel, we see how a community based on his principles would operate. In fact, for a while at least, several such communities really existed. Reading *Walden Two* will provide you practical insights into Skinner's work.

tified two kinds of reinforcement. **Positive reinforcement** refers to any event that, when it occurs after a response, makes that response more likely to happen in the future. **Negative reinforcement** is any event that, when it ceases to occur after a response, makes that response more likely to happen in the future. Notice that both types of reinforcement make a response more likely to happen. Giving your daughter candy for doing the right thing would be positive reinforcement. Ceasing to twist your brother's arm when he gives you back your pen would be negative reinforcement.

What does operant conditioning have to do with development? In Skinner's opinion, human development is the result of the continuous flow of learning that comes about from the operant conditioning we receive from the environment every day. For Skinner, development is a continuous, incremental sequence of conditioned acts that fulfill children's needs as quickly and completely as possible. Ideally, then, the demands of normal living are introduced at a controlled rate that helps a child to master them without acquiring negative feelings (Thomas, 1992).

These ideas about change in human behavior have been enhanced by the ideas of Albert Bandura and his associates. They extend the behaviorist view to cover social behavior.

Bandura and Social Cognitive Learning

Albert Bandura, one of the chief architects of social learning theory, has stressed the potent influence of **modeling** on personality development (Bandura, 1997). He called this **observational learning.** In a famous statement on **social (cognitive) learning theory,** Bandura and Walters (1963) cited evidence to show that learning occurs through observing others, even when the observers do not imitate the model's responses at that time and get no reinforcement. For Bandura, observational learning means that the information we get from observing other people, things, and events influences the way we act.

Social learning theory has particular relevance for development. As Bandura and Walters noted, children often do not do what adults tell them to do but rather what they see adults do. If Bandura's assumptions are correct, adults can be a potent force in shaping the behavior of children because of what they do.

The importance of models is seen in Bandura's interpretation of what happens as a result of observing others:

- By observing others, children may acquire new responses, including socially appropriate behaviors.

- Observation of models may strengthen or weaken existing responses.

- Observation of a model may cause the reappearance of responses that were apparently forgotten.

- If children witness undesirable behavior that is either rewarded or goes unpunished, undesirable behavior may result. The reverse is also true.

Bandura, Ross, and Ross (1963) studied the relative effects of live models, filmed human aggression, and filmed cartoon aggression on preschool children's aggressive behavior. The filmed human adult models displayed aggression toward an inflated doll; in the filmed cartoon aggression, a cartoon character displayed the same aggression.

Later, all the children who observed the aggression were more aggressive than youngsters in a control group. Filmed models were as effective as live models in transmitting aggression. The research suggests that competent models are more readily imitated than models who lack these qualities (Bandura & Walters, 1963). You can see, then, how modeling can be a powerful force in development. (For a more detailed account of how recent research supports these conclusions, see Chapter 10.)

TABLE 2.5. COMPARING THEORIES OF DEVELOPMENT

	Psychoanalytic	Psychosocial	Humanistic	Cognitive	Cultural	Behavioral
Major Figures	Freud	Erikson	Maslow	Piaget	Vygotsky	Skinner, Bandura
Major ideas	Passage through the psychosexual stages	Passage through the psychosocial stages	Satisfaction of basic needs	Development of cognitive structures through stages of cognitive development	Social processes embedded within a culture influence development	Power of operant conditioning; role of modeling in development
Essential features	Id, ego, superego; psychosexual stages	Psychosocial crises; psychosocial stages	Hierarchy of needs	Formation of cognitive structures; stages of cognitive development	Social processes; zone of proximal development	Reinforcement of responses; observational learning; modeling
Source of Developmental Problems	Conflict during development leads to fixation, regression, and personality problems	Inadequate resolution of psychosocial crises	Satisfaction of needs incomplete; movement toward self-actualization frustrated	Weak formation of cognitive structures	Environmental support lacking or insufficient	Lack of reinforcement, incorrect pairing of stimuli and responses
Goal	Sexually mature individual	A sense of personal integrity	Fulfilling individual potential	Satisfactory formation and use of cognitive structures	Recognition and use of social processes to guide development	The acquisition of conditioned acts to fulfill needs

Table 2.5 summarizes several features of the six categories of theorists discussed in this chapter.

Now that you have completed reading about the major developmental theorists, we would like you to analyze the information in the following case study and interpret it according to a theory (or theories) you have just read about. For example, let's assume you use Maslow's theory. You'd want to mention the hierarchy of needs: Were Thomas' needs being met? Could anything be done about it? How would that affect Thomas' feeling about himself? Another of your classmates may believe that Erikson's work is more applicable. Discuss and compare the various interpretations. There are no right or wrong answers, rather we would like you and your classmates to discuss your various interpretations and actually see how theory guides your analysis of behavior.

I. Background Information

A. *Thomas: eight years old*
   White
   Public school
   First grade (not promoted)
   Sixth of six children

B. *Home Conditions*
The mother is forty-two years old, separated from her husband, and almost totally blind. Four of the six children live with her in a low-income section of the city. The oldest son and a married daughter do not reside in the home.

II. The Problem

Thomas, bothered by asthma, exhibits frequent temper tantrums and is failing the first grade for the second time.

III. History

Thomas is the youngest of six children; his birth was accompanied by marital and family problems. The pregnancy was unplanned and unwanted, and the father left home before the child was born. Thomas was born prematurely, had immediate difficulty with breathing, and was put in a respirator for twenty days before coming home.

Feeding, motor development, and verbal development were all normal, but he manifested considerable separation anxiety; that is, he cried excessively when his mother left him alone. He still shows signs of this behavior at eight years of age, although less frequently. The mother states that he is "fidgety" (cannot remain still) and that he worries about his small size.

IV. Impressions

After several interviews with both the boy and his mother, the case worker commented that both mother and child display clear signs of anxiety. A definite theme of aggression and violence runs through Thomas's conversation. Teachers report that he exhibits little motivation and bothers other children in class. He has a very short attention span and shows increasing aggressiveness.

The interviewer reported that the mother seeks constant reassurance and experiences great difficulty with the disciplining of her children. The interviewer stated that the combination of an insecure mother and an unhappy, aggressive son whom she is finding difficult to control points to serious developmental problems for Thomas.

V. Summary

Thomas continues to do very poorly in school. He wants love from and dependence on his mother, yet simultaneously seeks independence and escape from his mother's control. This conflict produces ambivalent feelings toward his mother. That is, he displays considerable anger toward his mother for trying to control him; he bitterly resents his father's absence.

Instead of expressing his anger, he remains passive, especially in school, which is the primary cause of his poor scholastic performance. Thomas' behavior resolves his conflict, however, since he can remain with his mother but also strike back at her with his school failure.

Guided Review

22. Skinner's view of learning is referred to as _____ or _____ conditioning.
23. This explanation of learning depends heavily on the role of the _____.
24. When a response is _____, it is more likely to reoccur.
25. Bandura's social learning theory, also called observational learning, stresses the role of _____ in learning.

CONCLUSION

In this chapter, we introduced you to several interpretations of development that will help you to understand and integrate developmental data. Although we might have chosen many theories to include in this chapter (some of which we'll discuss later), those we have presented here have played or are playing major roles in our understanding of human development. You have much to remember, but we'll be coming back again and again to these seminal ideas

Answers

22. operant, instrumental 23. environment 24. reinforced 25. modeling

to help you to gain a firm understanding of them.

In summary:

The Psychoanalytic Approach

- Freud considered the unconscious mind to be the key to understanding human beings.
- Important information in the unconscious mind is kept hidden through an array of defense mechanisms.
- The mind is divided into three constructs: the id, the ego, and the superego, each of which appears at different stages of a child's development.
- Personality development is divided into five instinctive stages of life—oral, anal, phallic, latency, and genital—each stage serving a major function.
- Failure to pass through a stage of development results in fixation, which halts a person from becoming fully mature.

The Psychosocial Crises Approach

- Erikson believed that human life progresses through eight "psychosocial" stages, each one marked by a crisis and its resolution.

- Although the ages at which one goes through each stage vary, the sequence of stages is fixed. Stages may overlap, however.
- A human being must experience each crisis before proceeding to the next stage. Inadequate resolution of the crisis at any stage hinders development.

The Humanistic Approach

- Maslow believed that progress toward fulfillment of an individual's potential depended on needs satisfaction.
- Maslow identified five basic needs in his needs hierarchy.

The Cognitive Developmental Approach

- Piaget focused on the development of the cognitive structures of the intellect during childhood and adolescence.
- Organization and adaptation play key roles in the formation of structures.
- Piaget believed that cognitive growth occurred in four discrete stages: sensorimotor, preoperational, concrete operational, and formal operational.

The Cultural Framework Approach

- Lev Vygotsky, a leading commentator on the role of culture in development, emphasized the significance of social processes to bring about satisfactory growth.
- Vygotsky believed that the capacity to learn depends on abilities of the child's teachers as well as on the child's abilities.
- The difference between the child's ability to learn independently and to learn with help is called the zone of proximal development.

The Behavioral Approach

- Skinner believed that the consequences of behavior are critical.
- Skinner's paradigm involves three steps: a stimulus occurs in the environment; a response is made in the presence of that stimulus; and the response is reinforced, punished, or extinguished.
- Bandura has extended Skinner's work to the area of social learning, which he calls observational learning.

KEY TERMS

Accommodation
Adaptation
Anal stage
Assimilation
Cognitive structures
Ego
Equilibration
Esteem needs
Extinction
Functional invariants
Genital stage
Id

Identity crisis
Instrumental conditioning
Latency stage
Love and belongingness needs
Modeling
Negative reinforcement
Observational learning
Operant conditioning
Oral stage
Organization
Phallic stage
Physiological needs

Positive reinforcement
Psychoanalytic theory
Punishment
Reinforcement
Safety needs
Scaffolding
Schemes
Self-actualization
Self-actualization needs
Social (cognitive) learning theory
Superego
Zone of proximal development

WHAT DO YOU THINK?

1. What is your reaction to the statement, "The truth or falseness of a theory has little to do with its usefulness"?
2. Some people say that in his concept of human development, Freud emphasized sexuality too much. What do you think?

3. Which is better, assimilation or accommodation? If you could do only one, which would it be? Why?
4. Skinner criticized the other theorists in this Chapter for believing they can describe what goes on in the human mind. After

all, he said, no one has ever looked inside one. What's your position?
5. Is it possible for a person to be deeply intimate with another person and still be in a state of identity confusion?

CHAPTER REVIEW TEST

1. Freud's structure of the mind included
   a. cognitive structures.
   b. safety needs.
   c. ego.
   d. reinforcing elements.

2. The id is that structure of the mind that is present
   a. at birth.
   b. through experience.
   c. by internal representations.
   d. through crisis resolution.

3. Freud believed that development entailed moving through psychosexual stages. Difficulty at any stage can cause a person to become
   a. fixated.
   b. operational.
   c. negatively reinforced.
   d. displaced.

4. Ideas that are rejected by the conscious mind are kept from consciousness by
   a. the ego.
   b. fear reactions.
   c. the superego.
   d. defense mechanisms.

5. Jimmy was told by his teacher that he could not go on a field trip with the class because of his misbehavior. Jimmy said he was glad; the trips are "no fun any way." Jimmy's defense mechanism is called
   a. regression.
   b. compensation.
   c. rationalization.
   d. displacement.

6. One-year-old Jane has already learned that her mother will be there when Jane needs her. This predictable world helps a child to develop
   a. creativity.
   b. intimacy.
   c. generativity.
   d. trust.

7. The psychosocial crisis of industry versus inferiority must be resolved during
   a. the school years.
   b. early childhood.
   c. adolescence.
   d. adulthood.

8. When we analyze our personal sense of competence and combine it with the opinion of others, we are attempting to satisfy our need for
   a. belongingness.
   b. self-actualization.
   c. esteem.
   d. security.

9. Maslow has arranged his theory of needs satisfaction in the form of a
   a. spiral.
   b. hierarchy.
   c. stage sequence.
   d. plateau.

10. Piaget's theory of cognitive development focused on the formation and development of
    a. zones of proximal development.
    b. reinforcement schedules.
    c. cognitive structures.
    d. modeling strategies.

11. Piaget placed considerable emphasis on operations, which he viewed as
    a. reflexes.
    b. age-appropriate responses.
    c. internalized actions.
    d. interactions.

12. Although both Piaget and Vygotsky devoted their lives to studying cognitive development, Vygotsky placed greater emphasis on
    a. cognitive structures.
    b. social interactions.
    c. sensitive periods.
    d. observational learning.

13. Skinner carefully analyzed the role of reinforcement in development and distinguished it from
    a. cognitive structures.
    b. reward.
    c. operations.
    d. needs.

14. In operant conditioning, the environment acts as the major source of
    a. operations.
    b. cognitive structures.
    c. defense mechanisms.
    d. reinforcement.

15. The great value of observational learning is that a person need not overtly react to learn
    a. mental operations.
    b. new responses.
    c. ego identity.
    d. schedule of reinforcements.

Answers

1. c 2. a 3. a 4. d 5. c 6. d 7. a 8. c 9. b 10. c 11. c 12. b 13. b 14. d 15. b

PART **II**

Beginnings

*My mother
groan'd!
My father wept.
Into the dangerous
world I leapt.*

William Blake

CHAPTER 3 *The Biological Basis of Development*

On October 6, 1998, Frank and Ellen Smith arrived at Dr. James Otis's office a few minutes early for their appointment. Married for seven years, they had been unable to conceive and had found that their problem was caused by male infertility, in this case, a low sperm count. As they attempted to learn more about their problem, they discovered that they were not alone; estimates are that one in six heterosexual couples has a fertility problem.

Other couples whom they had met in their search for a solution had recommended Dr. Otis as a physician who was sympathetic, knowledgeable, and successful in using DI—donor insemination. (Currently, close to 100,000 women in the United States will use DI each year.) Frank and Ellen chose this procedure because the screening process in accepting sperm for freezing lowers the risk of sexually transmitted diseases (STDs) and also provides detailed information about the donor: race, ethnic background, blood type, hair and eye color, physical characteristics, and personal background information.

The Smiths found that Dr. Otis was exactly as he had been described. Unhurried and calm, he told the couple just what would be expected of them. He also stressed that he received sperm from a large, nationally known, respected sperm bank. He explained that freezing techniques had improved in the last few years. Cryobiology, the study of how best to freeze living tissue, had made great strides by adding chemicals such as glycerol to liquid nitrogen at a temperature of –190°C. This technique protects cells and tissues by preventing any damage that could be caused by the formation of ice crystals.

Frank and Ellen felt reassured by their discussion with Dr. Otis. They couldn't afford the time and money required for adoption, but from their reading they had decided their chances of conceiving through donor insemination were good. Healthy couples with no other problems have a 70 to 80 percent success rate within one year. This figure compares with a natural conception rate of 85 to 90 percent for fertile couples.

The Smiths were also pleased that Dr. Otis had so carefully explained the procedure to them. After carefully tracking a woman's menstrual cycle and searching for accurate clues to the time of ovulation by examining her vaginal mucus and urine, the physician injects the semen through the cervix with a needleless syringe.

Their hopes and expectations were justified. Ellen conceived on the couple's fourth attempt and later gave birth to a healthy baby boy. ✪

In 1902 a murder was committed that shocked even the sophisticated residents of Paris. The brutality of the crime and the cleverness of the murderer suggested that its solution would be difficult, if not impossible. Yet using the latest technology of those times, the famous French detective, Alfonse Bertillon, quickly identified the killer. You have probably guessed by now that the murderer left his fingerprint at the scene of the crime, which was the evidence that convicted him. Eighty-three years later, near Leicester, England, the killer of two young girls was arrested and convicted because of genetic material found at the site of the crime. The "DNA" fingerprint discovered, because of its uniqueness, was considered to be a statement of personal identity. These two incidents are telling testimony both to the rapid advancement of biological research and to the importance of biological data in our lives (Jones, 1993).

Any journey begins with the first step. For students of the lifespan, this means the time when development commences—when sperm joins with egg, uniting the mother's genetic endowment with that of the father. As you can tell from the Chapter's opening, today's technology gives couples a bewildering array of reproductive choices. In this Chapter, you will explore a world so tiny that it is almost impossible to imagine. You will read about some great biological discoveries of the past century and about recent breakthroughs that have led scientists to the origins of life itself.

In this Chapter you'll read about the fertilization process, during which the sperm and egg unite. Today, however, we can no longer refer to "the union of sperm and egg." We must ask additional questions: Whose sperm? Whose egg? Where did the union occur? Was it in the woman's body? Which woman will carry the fertilized egg? You can see, then, that fertilization is a process filled with the potential for conflict and controversy because of new techniques that enable fertilization to occur outside of a woman's body.

Sometime in your life you probably have said, "Oh, I've inherited that trait." That's the easy answer. How did you inherit that characteristic? Do you remember that DNA you heard about in your science classes? Here you'll learn that the discovery of DNA involved some of the world's greatest biologists in a race to be the first to find the "secret of life." Today scientists are engaged in a struggle to "map the human genome" in *The Human Genome Project,* which is an endeavor to identify our genetic endowment—the 50,000 to 100,000 genes that lie in the nucleus of every cell. Once these genes are identified and located, efforts can be made to combat up to 3,000 genetic diseases! Perhaps equally as exciting is the attempt to identify "susceptibility" genes, which do not of themselves cause disease but make certain individuals susceptible to such diseases as breast cancer, colon cancer, and Alzheimer's.

Our characteristics, however, don't just appear; they're passed on from generation to generation. Following our discussion of genes, we'll trace the manner in which hereditary traits are transmitted. Unfortunately, we are all too well aware that occasionally the transmission of traits produces abnormalities, which we also discuss. Finally, no discussion of human heredity is complete without acknowledging the ethical issues that have arisen because of these new developments. Answers still elude us, but at least we can ask several critical questions: Should scientists be allowed to implant specific genes to satisfy a couple's preferences? Should society determine that certain types of genes be implanted to ensure "desirable" products? No easy questions, these, but you can be sure that they will arise in the future.

When you finish reading this Chapter, you should be able to

- Recall that development results from the interaction of heredity and environment.

- Identify the essential elements in the reproductive process.

- Distinguish between internal and external fertilization.

- List the steps that lead to ovulation.

- Describe how the genetic process functions.

- Formulate questions relating to the sensitive nature of the new reproductive technology.

The Fertilization Process

The fusion of two specialized cells, the sperm and the egg (or ovum), mark the beginning of development and the zygote (the fertilized ovum) immediately begins to divide. This fertilized ovum contains all of the genetic material that the organism will ever possess. During the initial phase of development following fertilization, distinguishing the male from the female is almost impossible.

The Beginnings

Any discussion of fertilization today must account for the advances that both research and technology have made available. Consequently, our discussion will include **external fertilization** techniques, such as in vitro fertilization (the famous "test-tube" babies). Table 3.1 contains a glossary of many terms you will find in this discussion. Be sure to refer to it when you meet an unfamiliar term. Otherwise, the amazing richness of the genetic world can escape you.

In our analysis of genetic material and its impact on our lives, we'll attempt to follow the manner in which we receive genes from our parents so our story begins with the male's sperm and the female's egg.

TABLE 3.1 A GENETIC GLOSSARY

Acrosome: Area at the tip of the sperm that contains the chemicals enabling the sperm to penetrate the egg's surface.

Allele: Alternate forms of a specific gene; there are genes for blue eyes and brown eyes.

Autosome: Chromosomes other than the sex chromosomes.

Chromosome: Stringlike bodies that carry the genes; they are present in all of the body's cells.

DNA: Deoxyribonucleic acid, the chemical structure of the gene.

Dominance: The tendency of a gene to be expressed in a trait, even when joined with a gene whose expression differs; brown eyes will appear when genes for blue and brown eyes are paired.

Fertilization: The union of sperm and egg to form the fertilized ovum or zygote.

Gametes: The mature sex cells; either sperms or eggs.

Genes: The ultimate hereditary determiners; they are composed of the chemical molecule deoxyribonucleic acid (DNA).

Gene locus: The specific location of a gene on the chromosome.

Genotype: The genetic composition of an individual.

Heterozygous: The gene pairs for a trait differ; a person who is heterozygous for eye color has a gene for brown eyes and one for blue eyes.

Homozygous: The gene pairs for a trait are similar; the eye color genes are the same.

Meiosis: Cell division in which each daughter cell receives one-half of the chromosomes of the parent cell. For humans this maintains the number of chromosomes (46) at fertilization.

Mitosis: Cell division in which each daughter cell receives the same number of chromosomes as the parent cell.

Mutation: A change in the structure of a gene.

Phenotype: The observable expression of a gene.

Recessive: A gene whose trait is not expressed unless paired with another recessive gene; both parents contribute genes for blue eyes.

Sex chromosome: Those chromosomes that determine sex; in humans they are the 23d pair, with an XX combination producing a female, and an XY combination producing a male.

Sex-linkage: Genes on the sex chromosome that produce traits other than sex.

Trisomy: Three chromosomes are present rather than the customary pair; Down syndrome is caused by three chromosomes at the 21st pairing.

Zygote: The fertilized egg.

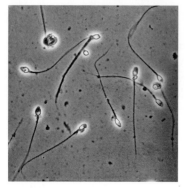

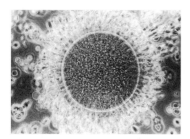

(a)

(b)

The sperm (a), in its search for the egg (b), carries the 23 chromosomes from the male.

The Sperm

Certain cells are destined to become the sperm and eggs. The chief characteristics of the sperm are its tightly packed tip (the acrosome), containing 23 chromosomes, a short neck region, and a tail to propel it in its search for the egg (Wolpert, 1991). Sperm are so tiny that estimates are that the number of sperm equal to the world's population could fit in a thimble. Sperm remain capable of fertilizing an egg for about 24 to 48 hours after ejaculation (Moore & Persaud, 1998). Of the 200 million sperm that enter the vagina, only about 200 survive the journey to the woman's fallopian tubes, where fertilization occurs.

The major purpose of a male's reproductive organs is to manufacture, store, and deliver sperm. The sperm has as its sole objective the delivery of its DNA to the egg. Males, at birth, have in their testes those cells that will eventually produce sperm. At puberty, a meiotic division occurs in which the number of chromosomes is halved and actual sperm are formed. Simultaneously, the pituitary gland stimulates the hormonal production that results in the male secondary sex characteristics: pubic hair, a beard, and a deep voice.

The Ovum (Egg)

The egg is larger than the sperm, about the size of the period at the end of this sentence. The egg is round and its surface is about the consistency of stiff jelly. You may find it hard to believe, but a whale and a mouse come from eggs of about the same size. In fact, the eggs of all mammals are about the same size and appearance. When females are born, they already have primal eggs. From 1 to 2 million eggs have been formed in the ovaries. Since only one mature egg is required each month for about 35 years, the number present far exceeds the need. Eggs are usually fertilized about 12 hours after they are discharged from the surface of the ovary or they die within 12 to 24 hours (Moore & Persaud, 1998). From this brief discussion, you can identify the major differences between eggs and sperm. Eggs are massive compared to sperm; eggs are well-equipped with cytoplasm, while sperm has very little.

The Menstrual Cycle

The pituitary gland secretes a hormone that stimulates the ripening of eggs, and after two weeks one egg, which has ripened more than the others, is discharged from the ovary's surface (Curtis & Barnes, 1994). (Figure 3.1 illustrates the relationship of the ovum to the ovary, the fallopian tubes, and the uterus.) This process, called *ovulation,* triggers a chemical reaction that inhibits the ripening of further eggs. It also prepares the uterine lining for a potential fertilized ovum.

Figure 3.1

The relationship of ovary, egg, fallopian tube, and uterus.

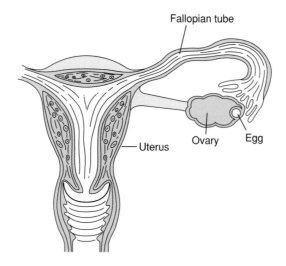

If fertilization does not occur, the prepared uterine lining is shed in menstruation and the entire process begins again. During each menstrual cycle many eggs are discarded. As a woman approaches the end of her egg-producing years, these last ova have been present for as many as 40 years. This may explain why the children of older women are more susceptible to genetic defects. The eggs have been exposed to environmental hazards (such as radiation) too long to escape damage (Jones, 1993; Moore & Persaud, 1998).

Implantation

When the egg is discharged from the ovary's surface (a process called **ovulation),** it is enveloped by one of the **fallopian tubes.** The diameter of each fallopian tube is about that of a human hair, but it almost unfailingly ensnares the egg and provides a passageway to the uterus. If fertilization occurs, it takes place soon after the egg enters the fallopian tube. Figure 3.2 illustrates the fertilization process.

Fusion of the two cells is quickly followed by the first cell division. As the fertilized egg, now called the **zygote,** travels toward **implantation** within the uterus, cell division continues. The cells multiply rapidly and after about seven days reach the uterine wall. The fertilized egg is now called a **blastocyst.** The journey is pictured in Figure 3.3.

Although individuals may change in the course of their lives, their hereditary properties do not change. The zygote (the fertilized egg), containing all 46 chromosomes, represents the "blueprint" for our physical and mental makeup. Under ordinary circumstances, environmental conditions leave the 46 chromosomes

Figure 3.2

Fertilization of the egg. The sperm, carrying its 23 chromosomes, penetrates the egg, with its 23 chromosomes. The nuclei of sperm and egg fuse, resulting in 46 chromosomes.

Figure 3.3

From ovulation to implantation.

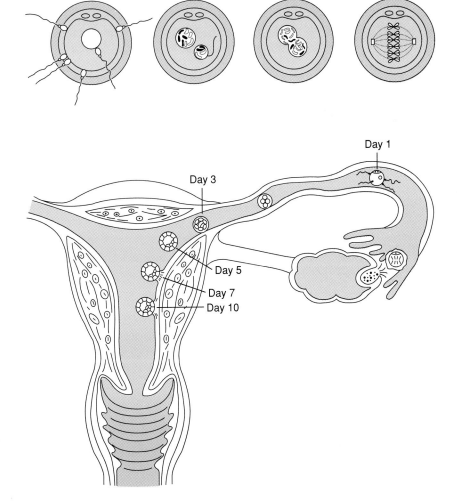

unaltered. (We know today that environmental agents such as drugs, viruses, or radiation may cause genetic damage.)

Once fertilization occurs, the zygote is not yet free from risk. Let's use a figure easy to work with and assume that 100 eggs are exposed to sperm. Here is the estimated mortality rate from fertilization to birth:

84 are fertilized
69 are implanted
42 survive one week
37 survive seven weeks
31 survive to birth

Thus, nature's toll results in about a 70 percent mortality rate.

Twins

Occasionally, and for reasons that still elude us, twins are born. Most twins occur when a woman's ovaries release two ripened eggs (rather than one) and both are fertilized by separate sperm. These twins are called **nonidentical,** or **dizygotic.** Their genes are no more alike than those of siblings born of the same parents but at different times.

Less frequently, twins develop from a single fertilized egg that divided after conception. Interestingly, identical twins usually do not result when the fertilized egg initially divides into two cells; separation occurs later when the dividing egg consists of several hundred cells (Wolpert, 1991). This process leads to **identical,** or **monozygotic,** twins whose genes are identical; that is, they share the same genotype (Bouchard, 1994).

Monozygotic twins are born with remarkable consistency, about 3 or 4 per thousand births, regardless of race. The rate of nonidentical (dizygotic) twin births, however, varies considerably from country to country. For example, in the United States about 8 to 10 pairs of dizygotic twins are born per 1,000 live births. The rate is about the same in Great Britain and other European countries. In Asia about 2 or 3 pairs of dizygotic twins are born per 1,000 live births. In Africa, about 20 pairs of dizygotic twins are born per 1,000 live births (Jones, 1993; Lytton, Singh, & Gallagher, 1995).

Infertility

Although the fertilization process just described is the normal process for most women, there are exceptions. For some couples, **infertility,** for whatever reason, is a serious problem. Today hundreds of thousands of childless couples desperately desire children. These couples share a growing problem in our society: infertility.

Causes of Infertility

Estimates are that about one in six American couples meet the criteria for infertility: an inability to achieve pregnancy after two years. Several reasons have been offered for this increased rate. In males, the number and quality of sperm is often suspected; rarely are structural or hormonal abnormalities the culprit. For example, the number of **sexually transmitted diseases (STDs),** especially chlamydia (usually a silent infection that may lurk in a woman's pelvic organs) show a marked acceleration. These, in turn, can lead to **pelvic inflammatory disease (PID),** which then can cause infertility. Also, a growing number of women are delaying child bearing until their thirties or later. Older women are more likely to become infertile if they have had abdominal surgery or if they experience **endometriosis,** a condition that increases with age. (Endometriosis is the growth of endometrial tissue outside of the uterus.) **Intrauterine devices (IUDs)** were popular through the 1970s. Although discredited because of the hazards they introduce, especially the risk of infection, they still are responsible for some problems seen today. Here is a summary of the most common infertility problems (Marrs, 1997).

- Ovulation and/or sperm problems   40 percent
- Sperm/mucus interaction   15 percent
- Fallopian tubes and/or uterus   15 percent
- Pelvic environment   15 percent
- Unexplained   15 percent

   Simply because a woman does not become pregnant within a specific time does not necessarily indicate infertility. Couples should wait for two years before suspecting infertility if a woman is in her twenties, one year if she is between 30 and 35, and six months if she is over 35. Even if a couple finds that they are indeed infertile, they needn't abandon their hopes of parenthood. Many reproductive techniques are available today. The new technologies we are about to discuss offer couples new hope. Hundreds of in vitro fertilization centers and sperm banks now exist around the country.

Sperm Banks

Today more than 400 sperm banks operate in the United States. Sixteen cryobanks store and sell frozen sperm, which are frozen in liquid nitrogen at $-190°C$ and remain potent for years. As we mentioned in the Chapter's opening, much of the appeal of this technique lies in the screening processes used, which are intended to reduce the possibility of sexually transmitted diseases. Safety is obviously a serious consideration and *The American Association of Tissue Banks* has recently formulated rules for sperm banks (Marrs et al., 1997).

Assisted Reproduction

Although you are probably most familiar with in vitro fertilization, another process, **artificial insemination by donor (AID),** is by far the most widely used procedure. Many new forms of **assisted reproductions technologies (ART)** are now available (Marrs & others, 1997):

- **In vitro fertilization,** in which fertilization of egg with sperm occurs in dish
- **Gamete intrafallopian transfer (GIFT),** in which sperm and egg are placed in the fallopian tube with the intent of achieving fertilization in a more natural environment (also known as embryo transfer)
- **Zygote intrafallopian transfer (ZIFT),** in which the fertilized egg is transferred to the fallopian tube
- **Sperm** and **egg donation,** in which males and females either donate or sell their sperms and eggs
- **Cryopreservation,** which refers to freezing embryos for future use
- **Surrogate motherhood,** in which one woman carries another woman's embryo for nine months

Consequently, today a child may have as many as five parents:

- A sperm donor (father or other male)
- An egg donor (mother or other female)
- A surrogate mother
- The couple who raises the child

In Vitro Fertilization (IVF)

In vitro fertilization (IVF) is the external fertilization technique you are probably most familiar with. The steps in IVF are as follows (Curtis & Barnes, 1994):

1. The woman is usually treated with hormones to stimulate maturation of eggs in the ovary, and she is observed closely to determine the timing of ovulation (i.e., the time at which the egg leaves the surface of the ovary).

2. The physician makes an incision in the abdomen and inserts a laparoscope (a thin tubular lens through which the physician can see the ovary) to remove mature eggs.

3. The egg is placed in a solution containing blood serum and nutrients.

4. **Capacitation** takes place—this is a process in which a layer surrounding the sperm is removed so that it may penetrate the egg.

5. Sperm are added to the solution; fertilization occurs.

6. The fertilized egg is transferred to a fresh supporting solution.

7. Fertilized eggs (usually three) are inserted into the uterus.

8. The fertilized egg is implanted in the uterine lining.

During this period, the woman is being treated to prepare her body to receive the fertilized egg. For example, the lining of the uterus must be spongy or porous enough to hold the zygote. The fertilized egg must be inserted at the time it would normally reach the uterine cavity. About 27,000 IVF procedures are done every year in the United States with an estimated success rate of about 20 percent (Curtis & Barnes, 1994; Marrs & others, 1997).

Adoption

For many couples who remain childless in spite of several attempts at external fertilization, **adoption** (to take a child of other parents voluntarily as one's own) offers a viable option. Today's traditional middle to upper-middle class white couples who decide to adopt face competition from single adults, older adults, and homosexual adults. Because single parenthood is widely accepted today, more single women are keeping their children. The increasing use of contraception and the legality of abortion have also caused a sharp reduction in the number of available children, leading to heightened interest in adopting children from other nations. Nevertheless, more children are available for adoption than is commonly thought, but they fall into several categories: older children, minority children, and handicapped children. Although these children are available for immediate adoption, the waiting period for healthy white infants may run into years (Brodzinsky, Lang, & Smith, 1995).

Adoption procedures were formerly closed **(closed adoption)** and the biological parents were completely removed from the life of their child once the child was surrendered for adoption. The bonds between birth parent(s) and child were legally and permanently severed; the child's history was sealed by the court. These procedures were done with the best intentions, but it was if the child had no genetic past. Supposedly the natural parents and the adoptive couple were saved from emotional upset. Many biological mothers, however, reported in later interviews that they never recovered from the grieving process.

Today, however, when a pregnant woman approaches an adoption agency, she gets what she wants. She can insist that her child be raised by a couple with specific characteristics: nationality, religion, income, number in family. She can ask to see her child several times a year, perhaps take the youngster on a vacation, and telephone the child frequently. The adoption agency will try to meet these demands. This process is called **open adoption,** and although many adoptive couples dislike the arrangement, they really have no choice. Thus we see a new definition of adoption: the process of accepting the responsibility of raising an individual who has two sets of parents.

When couples choose to adopt, they should carefully consider the age of the child. They may find one age group more appealing than others. Each developmental period—infancy, early childhood, middle childhood, adolescence—has its own strengths and weaknesses that you should consider as a potential adoptive

A Sociocultural View

Foreign Adoption—An Odyssey

Recently, friends of ours, Steve and Nancy, decided to adopt a Romanian infant girl of 15 months. Their story is both touching and moving, as well as a detailed chronicle of what's involved in the process.

The young couple examined the pros and cons of both domestic and foreign adoptions and ultimately decided on a foreign adoption. They felt there were too many complications with most domestic adoptions, less certain outcomes of adoption and often very lengthy waits. The downside of an international adoption is that generally the children are older and often spend a year or more in an orphanage.

The adoption agency they worked with was certified by the Romanian government. The agency had a Romanian husband-and-wife team working to identify adoptable children and assist with negotiating the process in Romania and also helping the adoptive parents once in Romania. The son of this couple works for the agency in the USA and communicates regularly with his parents.

Steve and Nancy were told that they must use one of the certified agencies in order to adopt. They also needed to follow Massachusetts laws for a detailed home study, including criminal background checks. In addition they had to apply to the Immigration and Naturalization Services (INS) for approval. They were also checked by the FBI. The only input they had to the adoption process was to specify a child as young as possible; the agency matches children and parents. On a second adoption, however, prospective parents are allowed to specify the sex.

They found that going through the Romanian system was a difficult process. They were told about the infant Katie in June 1996 and anticipated going to Romania the following September to get her. (Katie is from Iasi, near the Ukrainian border.) The home study done on Steve and Nancy plus their INS paperwork were submitted to the Romanian Adoption Review Committee, which approved them as adoptive parents. The birth parent(s) must also give their permission for the child to be adopted.

Once the adoption committee approves both parents and children, the paperwork goes back to the local courts for finalization. Next, a hearing is held followed by an appeal period. Ultimately the adoption paperwork was completed in early January. They had to wait three weeks for

Katie's passport and then went back to Romania to bring her home.

At the orphanage, Steve and Nancy were able to see only the main entry way and a small room off to the side. They were told that this orphanage was the best in the country. Supposedly, the director was well educated, with degrees in early childhood education. The orphanage seemed bright and clean, and the children are taken outside to play, which is very unusual in Romania. There were Disney characters on the wall and Polaroid pictures of the children visiting with their version of Santa Claus. They couldn't learn much about the children's diet or stimulation other than the information that Katie had oranges and in all likelihood bananas. They also learned little about staffing conditions (ratio of staff to children, education of staff, etc.).

When they brought Katie home in late January, she was almost 15 months old. She was slightly anemic when she arrived, but an iron-based formula quickly corrected the problem. Today Katie is an excellent eater and enjoys almost everything except fruit juices. She adjusted quickly to her new parents and their home. She had no difficulty with eating or sleeping, nor was she irritable. The only problem was a viral infection that lasted for about 5 weeks. The social worker visited about 3 weeks after they arrived home and again at the 2+ month mark. In that time she noticed how much more interactive Katie had become. They recently had their final home study visit, and the social worker was very pleased with Katie's development.

Katie will be 22 months old on September 4 and is a normal toddler. She's very active, has good motor skills, is beginning to exhibit a temper when she does not get her own way, and tests Steve and Nancy to see how much she can get away with—very normal reactions for an almost 2-year-old. The only problem seems to be a language delay, but comprehension seems to be normal. A speech pathologist has recommended a re-evaluation in 4 months, with the belief that her language skills will explode before then. She is now mimicking much of what Steve and Nancy say to her, thus it would appear that she will swiftly overcome this language delay.

In summary, Katie came into a warm, loving environment, has adjusted well, and seems on the way to a normal and happy childhood.

parent. They should also realize that once children know they are adopted and understand what that means, the relationship with their adoptive parents inevitably changes. This "moment of truth" affects both parents and children. For example, children must cope with the idea of being relinquished, which is not an easy task. Parents must accept the idea that their children will want to know more about their biological parents, which is a natural concern.

> As a means of ensuring the physical and emotional well-being of children, adoption has proven to be an unqualified success. Adopted children fare significantly better than children reared in institutional environments or in foster care (Brodzinsky, Lang, & Smith, 1995).

Guided Review

1. _____ is the process uniting sperm and egg.
2. A fertilized egg is known as a _____.
3. The _____ gland secretes hormones that stimulate the ovaries to ripen and release an egg each month.
4. The most well-known example of an external fertilization technique is _____ _____ fertilization.
5. The most popular external fertilization technique is _____.
6. Estimates are that _____ in _____ American couples are infertile.
7. A form of adoption that today is becoming more popular is _____ adoption.

Heredity at Work

The original cell, the possessor of 46 chromosomes, begins to divide rapidly after fertilization, until the infant has billions of cells at birth. The cells soon begin to specialize: some become muscle, some bone, some skin, some blood, and some nerve cells. These are the somatic, or body, cells. The process of division by which these cells multiply is called **mitosis** (see Figure 3.4). In a mitotic division, the number of chromosomes in each cell remains the same.

A second type of cell is also differentiated: the germ, or sex, cell that ultimately becomes either sperm or egg. These reproductive cells likewise divide by the process of mitosis until the age of puberty. But then a remarkable phenomenon occurs—another type of division called **meiosis,** or reduction division (see Figure 3.5). Each sex cell, instead of receiving 46 chromosomes upon division, now receives 23.

Mitosis is basically a division of cells in which each chromosome is duplicated so that each cell receives a copy of each chromosome of the parent cell. What is doubled in mitotic division is the amount of deoxyribonucleic acid (DNA), the chief component of the genes. Meiosis, which occurs only in germ cell reproduction, is responsible both for the shuffling of hereditary characteristics received from each parent and for their random appearance in offspring. During the reduction division, the chromosomes separate longitudinally so that 23 go to one cell and 23 to another.

For the male, reduction division begins to occur just before puberty. For the female, the process differs slightly. Since she is required to produce only one mature egg a month, there is no provision for an indefinitely large number of eggs, as there

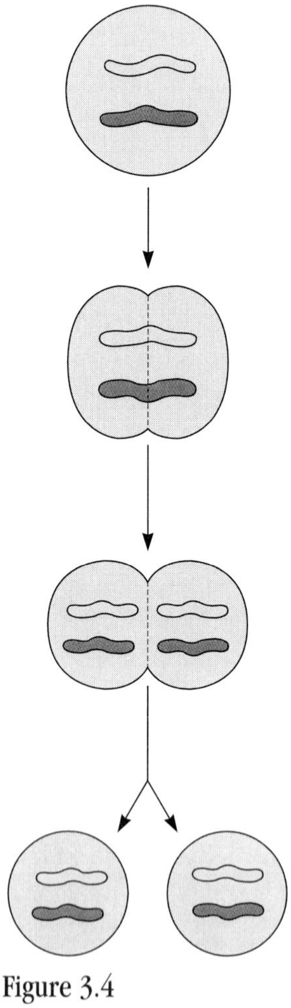

Figure 3.4

A mitotic division is a cell division in which each daughter cell receives the same number of chromosomes as the parent cell—46.

Answers

1. Fertilization 2. zygote 3. pituitary 4. in vitro 5. AID 6. one, six 7. open

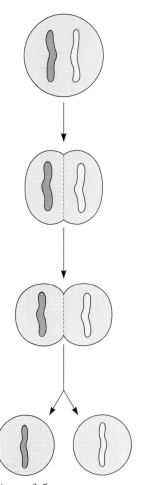

Figure 3.5

A meiotic division is a cell division in which each daughter cell receives one half of the chromosomes of the parent cell—23.

Watson, J. (1968). *The double helix*. Boston: Atheneum. This book has become a scientific classic. It is James Watson's personal, colorful look at the discovery of DNA and is guaranteed to hold your attention. If you are the least bit intimidated by the thought of reading about your genetic heritage, this book should eliminate your concerns. (Available in paperback.)

is for sperm. A woman normally sheds only 300 to 400 mature ova in her lifetime, whereas the normal male in a single ejaculation emits hundreds of millions of sperm.

At birth the female's ovaries contain tiny clusters of all the eggs that will mature in later years. Just before puberty, the final phases of the reduction division occur, and mature eggs are formed. It is as if there is a lengthy waiting period, from birth until about the age of 12 or 13, before the process is finally completed. The 23 chromosomes with their hereditary content are present at birth but must await the passage of time before biological maturity occurs in the female.

Now that we have traced the process by which fertilization occurs and discovered what is passed from parents to child, we still need to know "why I am who I am." This brings us to the discovery of DNA, one of this century's greatest achievements.

DNA: Structure and Function

We know that each chromosome contains thousands of genes and that each of these thousands of genes has a role in the growth and development of each human being (Cohen, 1997). The amazing chemical compound **DNA** is the chemical key to the life force in humans, animals, and plants and is the molecular basis of the genes. Each cell in your body contains about 6 feet of DNA, and, if all the DNA in your cells were stretched out, it would reach to the moon and back 8 thousand times (Jones, 1993). Genes not only perform certain duties within the cell but also join with other genes to reproduce both themselves and the whole chromosome (see Figure 3.6).

Each gene follows the instructions encoded in its DNA and sends these instructions, as chemical messages, into the surrounding cell. The cell then produces certain substances or performs certain functions according to instructions (Rensberger, 1996). These new products then interact with the genes to form new substances. The process continues to build the millions of cells needed for various bodily structures (Curtis & Barnes, 1994).

Examine Figure 3.6 and note how the strands intertwine. The strands, similar to the sides of a ladder, are connected by chemical rings: adenine (A), guanine (G), cytosine (C), and thymine (T). The letters are not randomly connected: A joins with T, G with C. If a code were written as AGCTTGA, it must appear as:

A G C T T G A
T C G A A C T

Thus, one sequence determines the other.

A remarkable feature of DNA is its ability to reproduce itself and ensure that each daughter cell receives identical information. During mitosis the DNA splits as readily as a person unzips a jacket (Curtis & Barnes, 1997). Each single strand grows a new mate, A to T and G to C, until the double-helix model is reproduced in each daughter cell.

> The DNA in a human cell is distributed over 46 chromosomes in a tangle like you wouldn't believe. Replication starts at hundreds or thousands of sites, at precisely defined moments in the cell's reproductive cycle. Billions of chemical units in the DNA thread must be copied exactly, exactly once. No more, no less. Any foul-up can be damaging or fatal. The imagination falters before the complexity of the process (Raymo, 1996).

The four letter possibilities, AT, TA, GC, and CG, seem to limit genetic variation. But when we consider that each DNA molecule is quite lengthy, involving thousands, perhaps millions of chemical steps (TA, GC, AT, CG, AT, CG, TA), the possible combinations seem limitless. Recent estimates indicate that there may be as many as three thousand million DNA letters involved (Jones, 1993). The differences

Figure 3.6

The DNA double helix. (a) The overall structure that gave DNA its famous name. (b) A closer examination reveals that the sides of the spiral are connected by chemicals similar to the rungs of a ladder.

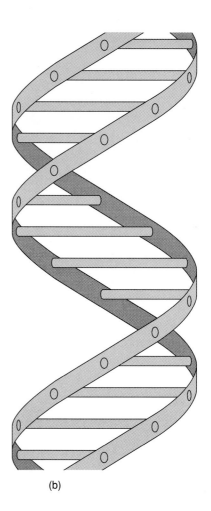

(a)

(b)

in the DNA patterns account for the individual genetic differences among humans and for differences between species.

Guided Review

8. Cell division in which each daughter cell receives the same number of chromosomes as the parent cell is called _____.

9. A reduction division, in which the number of chromosomes is halved is called _____.

10. The chemical key to life is _____.

11. The amount of _____ is doubled in each mitotic division.

12. A remarkable feature of DNA is its ability to _____ itself.

13. In genetic coding, A is linked with ____ and G is linked with ____.

Chromosomes and Genes

Genes that control a particular trait, say for a cleft chin, can have alternate forms called alleles (Rensberger, 1996). If two alleles are identical (either for cleft or non cleft), the person is homozygous for the trait (cleft). If the alleles are different, then the organism is heterozygous (Cole & Cole, 1996). As genetic research continued,

Answers

8. mitosis 9. meiosis 10. DNA 11. DNA 12. reproduce 13. T, C

however, studies showed that the patterns of inheritance were not quite as simple and direct as originally thought. The effects of any gene are influenced not only by the alleles of that trait, but also by other genes and also by the environment. We now know that most traits result from the interaction of many genes, and also that most genes influence more than a single trait (Curtis & Barnes, 1994). When many genes interact to produce a particular trait, the process is called polygenic inheritance. Abrupt changes in genes are possible, a phenomenon called mutations. Think of mutations as inherited accidents, which may have adverse effects on any individual, but rarely affects evolutionary change (Jones, 1993).

After the sperm and egg unite, the new cell (the potential individual) possesses 23 pairs of chromosomes, or 46 chromosomes, which represents our total biological heritage. One member of each pair of chromosomes has been contributed by the father and one by the mother. Each pair, except the 23rd, is remarkably alike. The 23d pair defines the individual's sex: an XX combination indicates a female; XY indicates a male. The sperm actually determines sex, since it alone can carry a Y chromosome. Thus there are two kinds of sperm: the X chromosome carrier and the Y chromosome carrier. Figure 3.7 illustrates the chromosomal arrangement of a typical male and female.

Genetic Information

How much information is contained in this biological heritage? Each chromosome contains the equivalent of about 3 billion letters. Since the average word contains six letters, each chromosome incorporates information equal to about 500 million words. At about 300 words per typical printed page, this translates into the equivalent of about 2 million pages. The average book consists of about 500 pages. Thus the information in one human chromosome corresponds to that in 4,000 books.

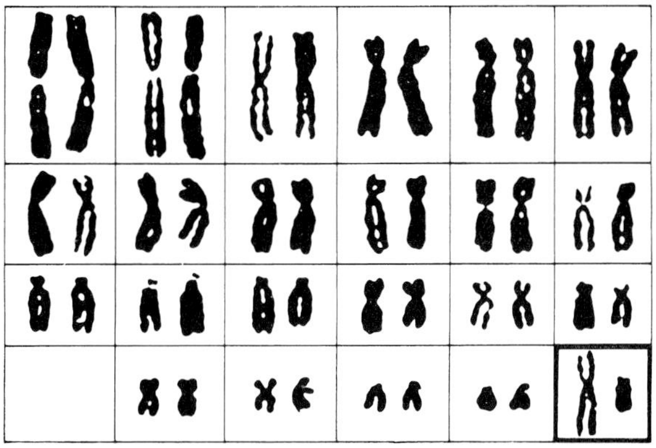

Figure 3.7

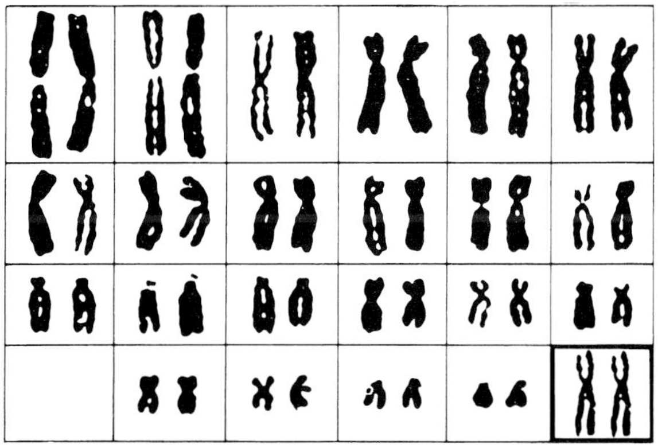

(a) At the top is the chromosome structure of a male, and (b) at the bottom is the chromosome structure of a female. The 23d pair is shown in the bottom right box of each figure; notice that the Y chromosome of the male is smaller. To obtain this chromosomal picture, a cell is removed from the individual's body, usually from the inside of the mouth. The chromosomes are magnified extensively and then photographed.

(a)

(b)

The strong resemblance of these family members to each other is testimony to the role of heredity in our makeup.

To avoid any misunderstanding, however, we want to reemphasize that development results from the interaction of heredity and environment. It's the process by which our **genotype** (our genetic heritage) is expressed as a **phenotype** (our observable characteristics). Genes always function in an environment, and environmental circumstances affect the way the genes express themselves.

Male–Female Differences

By a process of division, each cell in the body will have a replica of all 46 chromosomes. The size of the elements involved is almost bewildering. We have commented on the size of the sperm—so small that it can only be seen microscopically. The head of the sperm, which is about one-twelfth of its total length, contains the 23 chromosomes. The Y carrier is smaller than the X, which contains more genetic material. The Y carrier is also lighter and speedier and can reach the egg more quickly. But it is also more vulnerable.

Consequently, the male, from conception, is the more fragile of the two sexes. Estimates are that 160 males are conceived for every 100 females. However, so many males are spontaneously aborted that only 105 males are born for every 100 females. A similar pattern appears in neonatal life and continues throughout development, until women finally outnumber men, reversing the original ratio. Consequently, certain conclusions follow:

• Structurally and functionally, females resist disease better than males.

• The male is more subject to hereditary disease and defect.

• Environmental elements expose the male to greater hazards.

• Females are born with and retain a biological superiority over males.

The significance of the chromosomes lies in the material they contain—the genes. Each gene is located at a particular spot on the chromosome, called the *gene locus*. The genes, whose chemical structure is DNA, account for all inherited characteristics, from hair and eye color to skin shade, even the tendency toward baldness.

Aside from performing their cellular duties, the genes also reproduce themselves. Each gene constructs an exact duplicate of itself, so that when a cell divides, the chromosomes and genes also divide and each cell retains identical genetic material. As the cells divide, however, they do not remain identical. Specialization appears and different kinds of cells are formed at different locations.

> Genes are often presented to nonscientific audiences as the factors that determine eye color, skin color, height, and other fundamentally trivial attributes. They do, but the role of genes is far more profound. They also determine that a human being has two legs and can talk. They ensure that the head sits atop the neck and that the heart pumps rhythmically. They give us an opposable thumb and a large brain. . . . In other words, genes govern— or at least have a powerful say in—everything from the molecules in cells to the design and workings of the whole body (Rensberger, 1996, pp. 85-86).

Examples of Chromosomal Disorders

The study of chromosomes is called **cytogenetics** and thanks to new research techniques that enlarge prints of the chromosomes 2,000 to 3,000 times, our knowledge has increased tremendously. Although the chance of a chromosomal error in pregnancy is small, the risk increases with the age of the woman. Increasing age of the father may also be a factor, though less significant (Feinbloom, 1993). A discussion of chromosomal disorders follows.

Down syndrome is caused by a deviation on the 21st pair of chromosomes; the individual may have 47 chromosomes. This defect was discovered in 1866 by a

Down syndrome is caused by a deviation on the 21st pair of chromosomes. These children have distinctive facial features and are usually motorically and mentally retarded.

British doctor, Langdon Down, and produces distinctive facial features, small hands, a large tongue, and possible functional difficulties such as mental retardation, heart defects, and an added risk of leukemia.

The appearance of Down syndrome is closely related to the mother's age: Chances of giving birth to a child with Down syndrome are about 1 in 750 between the ages of 30 and 35; 1 in 300 between 35 and 39; and 1 in 80 between 40 and 45. After 45 years the incidence jumps to 1 in 40 births. Under age 30 the ratio is only 1 in 1,500 births. Recent evidence suggests that in one-third of the cases, the extra chromosome may come from the father (Blackman, 1997).

Although the exact cause of Down syndrome remains a mystery, the answer may lie in the female egg production mechanism, which results in eggs remaining in the ovary for 40 or 50 years. The longer they are in the ovary, the greater the possibility of damage. No treatment exists for Down syndrome other than good medical supervision and special education. These individuals usually are cheerful, perhaps slightly stubborn, with a good sense of mimicry and rhythm. Since the severity of the defect varies, institutionalization of the child is no longer immediately recommended. Some youngsters develop better in the home, especially if the parents believe they can cope successfully.

Other disorders relate to the sex chromosomes. If you recall, the 23d pair of chromosomes are the sex chromosomes, XX for females, XY for males. Estimates are that 1 in every 1,200 females and 1 in every 400 males has some disorder in the sex chromosomes. Occasionally a male will possess an XXY pattern rather than the normal XY. This is called **Klinefelter syndrome** (named after Dr. Harry Klinefelter in 1942), a disorder that may cause small testicles, reduced body hair, possible infertility, and language impairment. Klinefelter's occurs in about 1 in 1,000 male births; the condition may be helped by injections of testosterone (Bock,1993). Another pattern that appears in males is XYY, which may cause larger size and increased aggression (about 1 in 1,000 male births). Heated controversy and inconclusive results have surrounded the study of the "super male."

Females occasionally possess an XO pattern (lack of a chromosome) rather than XX. This is called **Turner syndrome** and is characterized by short stature, poorly developed secondary sex features (such as breast size), and usually sterility (about 1 in 2,500 female births).

Examples of Genetic Disorders

This section discusses the incidence and characteristics of several specific genetic disorders. Even as this is being written, thanks to the Human Genome Project, new genetic discoveries are being announced daily. (For an excellent analysis of genetic disorders, see McKusick, 1992.)

Jews of Eastern European origin are struck hardest by **Tay-Sachs disease,** which causes death by the age of 4 or 5. At birth the afflicted children appear normal, but development slows by the age of 6 months, and mental and motor deterioration begins. About 1 in every 25 to 30 Jews of Eastern European origin carries the defective gene, which is recessive; thus danger arises when two carriers marry. The disease results from a gene failing to produce an enzyme that breaks down fatty materials in the brain and nervous system. The result is that fat accumulates and destroys nerve cells, causing loss of coordination, blindness, and finally death. Today there are reliable genetic tests to identify carriers, and amniocentesis (see Chapter 4) can detect the genetic status of a fetus of carrier parents (Cherry, 1992).

Sickle-cell anemia, which mainly afflicts those of African descent, appeared thousands of years ago in equatorial Africa and increased resistance to malaria. Estimates are that 10 percent of the African American population in the United States carry the sickle-cell trait. Thus, two carriers of the defective gene who marry have a one in four chance of producing a child with sickle-cell anemia.

The problem is that the red blood cells of the afflicted person are distorted and pointed. Because of the cells' shape, they encounter difficulty in passing through

Hemophilia is an example of sex-linked inheritance, which affected several of the royal families of Europe (such as the Romanovs, pictured here).

the blood vessels. They tend to pile up and clump, producing oxygen starvation accompanied by considerable pain. The body then acts to eliminate these cells, and anemia results.

In the population of the United States, **cystic fibrosis (CF)** is the most severe genetic disease of childhood, affecting about 1 in 1,200 children. About 1 in 30 individuals is a carrier. The disease causes a malfunction of the exocrine glands, the glands that secrete tears, sweat, mucus, and saliva. Breathing is difficult because of the thickness of the mucus. The secreted sweat is extremely salty, often producing heat exhaustion. Cystic fibrosis kills more children than any other genetic disease.

Cystic fibrosis has been deadly for several reasons: Its causes remained unknown, and carriers could not be detected. Thus until a child manifested the breathing and digestive problems characteristic of the disease, identification was impossible. The CF gene now has been identified, however, and new research offers hope. Discovery of the CF gene has made possible the detection of carriers, a tremendous legacy of the Human Genome Project.

Phenylketonuria (PKU) results from the body's failure to break down the amino acid phenylalanine, which then accumulates, affects the nervous system, and causes mental retardation. Most states now require infants to be tested at birth. If PKU is present, the infants are placed on a special diet that has been remarkably successful.

But this success has produced future problems. Women treated successfully as infants may give birth to retarded children because of a toxic uterine environment. Thus at the first signs of pregnancy, these women must return to a special diet. The "cured" phenylketonuric still carries the faulty genes.

Spina bifida (failure of the spinal column to close completely) is an example of a genetic defect caused by the interaction of several genes with possible environmental involvement. During the first few weeks following fertilization, the mesoderm sends a chemical signal to the ectoderm that causes the beginnings of the nervous system. The process is as follows:

1. The chemical signal is sent from the mesoderm to the ectoderm.

2. A tube (the neural tube) begins to form, from which the brain and spinal cord develop.

3. Nerve cells are formed within the tube and begin to move to other parts of the developing brain.

4. These neurons now begin to form connections with other neurons.

5. Some of the neurons that don't connect with other neurons die.

If the neural tube does not close, spina bifida results, which can cause mental retardation. Studies have shown that if women take extra folic acid when they're pregnant, the number of cases of spina bifida decreases (Blackman, 1997).

Disorders also occur because of what is known as **sex-linked inheritance.** If you recall, the X chromosome is substantially larger than the Y (about three times as large). Therefore the female carries more genes on the 23d chromosome than the male. This difference helps to explain sex linkage. Think back now to the difference between dominant and recessive traits. If a dominant and recessive gene appear together, the dominant trait is expressed. An individual must have two recessive genes for the recessive trait (say, blue eyes) to appear. But on the 23d set of chromosomes, nothing on the Y chromosome offsets the effects of a gene on the X chromosome.

Perhaps the most widely known of these sex-linked characteristics is **hemophilia,** a condition in which the blood of hemophiliacs does not clot properly. Several of the royal families of Europe were particularly prone to this condition. Another sex-linked trait attributed to the X chromosome is **color blindness.** The X chromosome contains the gene for color vision and if it is faulty, nothing on the Y chromosome counterbalances the defect.

In 1970 a condition called **fragile X syndrome** was discovered. In this disorder, the end of the X chromosome looks ready to break off. Recent research points to a genetic abnormality as the cause, which offers promise of greater insights into symptoms of the problem (Feinbloom, 1993). Although fragile X seems to cause no physical problems, about 80 percent of these boys are mentally retarded. Fragile X appears in about 1 in 2,000 live births.

These are the more frequent chromosomal and genetic diseases, which are summarized in Table 3.2. (Other diseases also have, or are suspected of having, a strong genetic origin: diabetes, epilepsy, heart disorders, cancer, arthritis, and some mental illnesses.)

To end this part of our work on a more optimistic note, let's turn our attention to the promising and exciting discoveries of the Human Genome Project.

The Human Genome Project

On August 24, 1989, Pete Rose was banished from baseball. For baseball fans, that was the news of the day. In fact, it was headline news around the country. That same day, another announcement far more important for human health appeared in most news outlets, but with far less fanfare. Researchers had found the gene that caused cystic fibrosis (CF).

The CF gene discovery came as part of the **Human Genome Project,** an undertaking comparable to the Manhattan Project that resulted in the atomic bomb and the Apollo Project that produced the first moon landings. The Human Genome

TABLE 3.2   CHROMOSOMAL AND GENETIC DISORDERS

Chromosomal Disorders		
Name	Effects	Incidence
Down syndrome	47 chromosomes; distinctive facial features, mental retardation, possible physical problems	Varies with age; older women more susceptible (under 30—1 in 1,500 births; 35–39—1 in 300 births)
Klinefelter syndrome	XXY chromosomal patterns in males; possible infertility, possible psychological problems	About 1 in 1,000 male births
Turner syndrome	One X chromosome missing in female (XO), lack of secondary sex characteristics, infertile	About 1 in 2,500 female births
XYY syndrome	XYY chromosomal pattern in males; tend to be large, normal intelligence and behavior	About 1 in 1,000 male births
Genetic Disorders		
Tay-Sachs disease	Failure to break down fatty material in central nervous system; results in blindness, mental retardation, and death (usually by 4 or 5 years of age)	One in 25 Jews of Eastern European origin is a carrier
Sickle-cell anemia	Blood disorder produces anemia and considerable pain; caused by sickle shape of red blood cells	About 1 in 10 African Americans is a carrier
Cystic fibrosis	Body produces excessive mucus, causing problems in the lungs and digestive tract; may be fatal, suspect gene recently identified	About 1 in 2,000 births
Phenylketonuria (PKU)	Body fails to break down amino acid (phenylalanine); results in mental retardation, treated by special diet	About 1 in 15,000 births
Spina bifida	Neural tube problem in which the developing spinal column does not close properly; may cause partial paralysis and mental retardation	About 1 in 1,000 births (depending on geographical area)

Project is nothing less than an attempt to identify and map the 50,000 to 100,000 genes that constitute our genetic makeup. It is a project, international in scope, that will take about 15 years and cost at least 3 billion dollars to identify the 3 billion genetic letters that make up our genetic material (Cohen, 1997)!

It's been an elusive goal, which is understandable when you realize that genes make up only 3 percent of DNA. (Scientists call the remaining 97 percent "evolutionary junk.") Actually, efforts to map the human gene extend as far back as 1911 when scientists concluded that the gene for color blindness must be on the X chromosome. Here's a brief chronology detailing only a few of the major steps leading to the establishment of the Human Genome Project (Cook-Deegan, 1995; Bodmer & McKie, 1995; Cooper, 1994).

1911—Color blindness linked to the X chromosome
1943—DNA determined to be the major agent in heredity
1953—DNA structure discovered
1968—First mapping of a human disease trait on a chromosome
1970—Enzymes used as a cutting tool on DNA
1983—Genes for Huntington's disease and muscular dystrophy *located*
1989—Gene for cystic fibrosis *discovered*
1990—Human Genome Project officially begins
1993—Gene for Huntington's disease *discovered*

That's only part of the story, of course. Once defective genes are identified, work can begin on the diseases and problems they cause. For example, once the gene that causes cystic fibrosis was discovered, research began on its treatment and the drug *pulmozyme* is now in use. A gene that causes certain forms of cancer is now under attack by the drug *amonafide*. Forms of hypertension, schizophrenia, and Alzheimer's have also been targeted by an emerging drug therapy (Cohen, 1997).

Several exciting discoveries have already been made: The first preliminary, comprehensive map of all human chromosomes has been accomplished (Angier, 1993); the genes responsible for cystic fibrosis and Huntington's disease have been identified, as well as the breast cancer susceptibility genes (BRCA1, BRCA2); genetic defects have been identified only days after fertilization (Rensberger, 1996).

Detecting disease, however, is only one objective of the Human Genome Project. As David Baltimore (1994, p. 78) noted:

> But the Genome Project is something quite different (than searching for the causes of disease) because it will allow us to to examine human variability, for example, variations in mathematical ability or in what we call intelligence. Those variations are caused by the interactions of many genes. And certainly, the best way that biologists have to unravel which genes are involved in complex traits is to find a set of markers that are linked to the disease and then find the genes associated with those markers. In other words, we need the linkage maps and the physical maps that will be generated by the Human Genome Project.

And yet, the difficulty of the task that remains can't be discounted. Although there are hundreds of diseases caused by a single gene, for thousands of others the contribution is much more obscure. For example, some diseases need an environmental trigger (which may be the case for schizophrenia), whereas in other diseases more than one gene may have to be faulty (Bodmer & McKie, 1995).

Studies of genetic susceptibility will undoubtedly follow the same pattern. The genes that make people susceptible to certain diseases do not, of themselves, cause disease. Rather, the combination of a particular environment with a particular gene are the two needed ingredients. Once the mechanisms that cause a susceptibility gene to spring into action are more fully understood, such preventative measures as screening techniques and drug therapy will save many lives.

Unfortunately, this explosion of knowledge is also leading to uncertain, even dangerous, consequences. For example, if a family member is susceptible to a particular disease, do insurance companies have the legal right to deny this person, and perhaps the entire family, health insurance? Where are the lines drawn between public and private interests? How private/public is a person's medical history? Grappling with this and similar issues has led the National Institutes of Health and the Department of Energy to join forces and create a program for studying the ethical, legal, and social implications of the Human Genome Project—the ELSI program.

Cook-Deegan, R. (1995). *The gene wars: Science, politics, and the human genome.* New York: Norton. You will find this an excellent, readable account of the Human Genome Project. The personal histories are especially appealing.

Will "it's genetic" continue to mean "we can't do anything about it" in cocktail party prattle? Will genetics continue as the stalking horse for racist ideology and ethnic prejudice? Surely we can move beyond these vacuous ideologies to a richer understanding that embraces both genetic and environmental in the complex dance of life. The interesting question is not whether it is nature or nurture, but how they interact (Cook-Deegan, 1995, p. 351).

Guided Review

14. The genetic composition of an individual is referred to as the _____, whereas the observed expression of a gene is called the _____.
15. In assessing function, it is necessary to recall that there are _____ types of sperm, the _____ _____ carrier and the _____ _____ carrier.
16. The ____ carrier is the lighter and speedier of the sex chromosomes.
17. Down syndrome is perhaps the best-known _____ disorder.
18. _____ anemia and _____ disease are examples of genetic disorders.

Heredity *and* Environment

As you have read this Chapter, the amazing biological advances in studies of human development probably fascinated you. You may be tempted to believe that biology holds clues to most of the secrets of development. Remember, however, the environmental role in development. In a remarkable long-term study (mentioned in Chapter 1), Emmy Werner and Ruth Smith (1992) studied all of the children (837) born on the island of Kauai in 1955. (Kauai is an island in the Hawaiian chain.) What's unusual about this study is that the authors studied 505 of these children from their prenatal days until they were 31–32 years of age. (The drop in numbers from the original 837 was due to some of the subjects dying and some moving to other islands or to mainland U.S.A.)

To give you an idea of the wealth of information contained in this study, the following summary shows how all of the 505 subjects were studied intensely at various intervals during a 30-year period.

Total number of live births (1955)	837
Subjects examined at age 2 (pediatric and psychological exams)	734
Subjects examined at age 2 and 10	698
Subjects examined at age 18	614
Subjects examined at age 31–32	505

Answers

14. genotype, phenotype 15. two, X chromosome, Y chromosome 16. Y 17. chromosomal 18. Sickle-cell, Tay-Sachs

Of the 505 individuals followed over the 30+ year span, one in three was born with the odds stacked dramatically against them. They either experienced birth problems, grew up in poverty, or were members of dysfunctional families (desertion, divorce, alcoholism, mental illness). Two out of three children in this particularly vulnerable group encountered four or more risk factors before they were 2 years old and developed serious learning and/or behavior problems.

Nevertheless, one of three of these high-risk children developed into a competent, confident young adult by the age of 18. How can we explain this phenomenon? What was at work in these children that let them overcome daunting adversity?

Werner discovered several protective factors that helped the children to overcome their difficulties: a child's temperament (active, low excitability), a high degree of sociability, alertness, and concentration. Families of competent children had four or fewer children, with at least two years between each child. The competent children also established a bond with someone who gave them positive attention (a grandparent, uncle, or older sibling). These relationships helped the children to find meaning in their lives and gave them a belief that they could control their destinies. In their thirties, these individuals were leading satisfactory adult lives.

> **There is no single set of qualities or circumstances that characterizes all such resilient children. But psychologists are finding that they stand apart from their more vulnerable siblings almost from birth. They seem to be endowed with innate characteristics that insulate them from the turmoil and pain of their families and allow them to reach out to some adult—a grandparent, teacher, or family friend—who can lend crucial emotional support. (Werner & Smith, 1992)**

A good way to conclude our work in this Chapter is to remember that genetic action results from genes interacting with environmental experiences. A good example of this conclusion can be found in the work of Robert Plomin and his associates (1995), who investigated genetic effects on the family environment. Noting that children don't passively accept environmental influences, these researchers pointed out that children select, modify, and even create their environments. Also, if you recall from the findings of Werner and Smith (1992), the ultimate outcomes of children's difficulties were determined by the environment into which they were born—heredity interacting with environment.

Guided Review

19. Werner's study is a sharp reminder that development is explained by the _____ of genes and the environment.
20. Mapping the human genes is the goal of the _____ _____ _____.

CONCLUSION

In this chapter we explored the biological basis of our uniqueness. We considered not only the power and beauty of nature in establishing our genetic endowment but also the growing influence of technology. The genes the mother and father provide unite to produce a new and different human being. Yet this new life still shows many of the

Answers

characteristics of both parents. We saw how this newness and sameness has challenged researchers for decades.

Beginning with the discoveries of Mendel and still continuing, the secrets of hereditary transmission remain at the forefront of scientific endeavor, especially given the impetus of the Human Genome Project. Today's work, building on our knowledge of DNA, provides hope for the future while simultaneously raising legal and ethical questions that have yet to be resolved.

In summary:

The Fertilization Process

- Knowledge of hormonal control of the menstrual cycle is crucial for understanding fertilization.
- The study of twins, especially monozygotic twins, has long fascinated psychologists.
- The increasing number of infertile couples has led to a growing demand for external fertilization.
- The most widely used external fertilization technique is AID (artificial insemination by donor).
- The success rate of external fertilization procedures has improved with increasing knowledge.
- Today's adoption procedures include both closed and open adoption.

Heredity at Work

- Mitosis and meiosis are the means of cell division.
- DNA is the chemical key to life.
- Understanding how traits are transmitted requires a knowledge of the workings of dominant and recessive genes.

Chromosomes and Genes

- The Human Genome Project is an endeavor to map all of the genes.
- Chromosomal defects include: Down syndrome, Klinefelter syndrome, and Turner syndrome.
- Genetic defects include: Tay-Sachs, sickle-cell anemia, cystic fibrosis, phenylketonuria, and spina bifida.

Heredity and Environment

- Development can only be explained in light of the interactions between genes and the environment.
- The exact nature of the dynamic interactions between genes and the environment still eludes us.

KEY TERMS

Adoption
Artificial insemination by donor (AID)
Assisted reproductive technologies (ART)
Blastocyst
Capacitation
Color blindness
Closed adoption
Cryopreservation
Cystic fibrosis (CF)
Cytogenetics
Dizygotic
DNA
Down syndrome
Egg donation
Endometriosis

External fertilization
Fallopian tubes
Fragile X syndrome
Gamete intrafallopian transfer (GIFT)
Genotype
Hemophilia
Human Genome Project
Identical
Implantation
Infertility
Intrauterine devices (IUDs)
In vitro fertilization (IVF)
Klinefelter syndrome
Meiosis
Mitosis
Monozygotic

Nonidentical
Open adoption
Ovulation
Pelvic inflammatory disease (PID)
Phenotype
Phenylketonuria (PKU)
Sex-linked inheritance
Sexually transmitted diseases (STDs)
Sickle-cell anemia
Sperm donation
Spina bifida
Surrogate motherhood
Tay-Sachs disease
Turner syndrome
Zygote
Zygote intrafallopian transfer (ZIFT)

WHAT DO YOU THINK?

1. You may have begun your work in lifespan psychology with the idea that either heredity or environment was all-important. Do you still think that way? Or do you believe that one may be somewhat more important than the other? Does the biopsychosocial model help you to answer these questions?
2. Several controversies have occurred lately about surrogate mothers and the children they bear. Do you have any strong feelings about surrogacy? Can you defend it? Regardless of your personal feelings, can you present what you see as the pros and cons of surrogacy?
3. In your reading, perhaps you noticed that the process of in vitro fertilization depended on research findings from studies of the menstrual cycle. Can you explain this, paying particular attention to the administering of hormones and the timing of their administration?
4. James Watson and Francis Crick received a Nobel Prize for their discovery of the double-helix structure of DNA. Why is the discovery of DNA so important in our lives? Can you think of anything you have read about in the newspapers or seen on television that derives from this discovery?

CHAPTER REVIEW TEST

1. From ovulation to implantation takes about
   a. seven days.
   b. two weeks.
   c. one month.
   d. nine months.

2. The union of sperm and egg is a process known as
   a. mitosis.
   b. fertilization.
   c. meiosis.
   d. mutation.

3. In vitro fertilization takes place
   a. in the fallopian tube.
   b. in the uterus.
   c. outside the woman's body.
   d. in the ovary.

4. Which of the following is not a female secondary sex characteristic?
   a. higher voice
   b. wider hips
   c. breasts
   d. thick hair

5. The process by which eggs are ripened and released is called
   a. ovulation.
   b. mitosis.
   c. fertilization.
   d. implantation.

6. Each sex cell carries a total of _____ chromosomes.
   a. 23
   b. 24
   c. 47
   d. 46

7. _____ twins are likely to occur when a woman's ovaries release two ripened eggs that are fertilized by separate sperm.
   a. Nonidentical
   b. Identical
   c. Siamese
   d. Monozygotic

8. Which factor is not thought to be a cause of infertility in men?
   a. influenza
   b. low sperm count
   c. defective sperm
   d. genetic disease

9. Which of the following statements is true?
   a. XX indicates male.
   b. XY indicates male.
   c. XO indicates male.
   d. X—indicates male.

10. Which of the following is an example of a genetic disorder?
    a. Sickle-cell anemia
    b. Turner syndrome
    c. Klinefelter syndrome
    d. Down syndrome

11. When a natural mother relinquishes her child, but retains input into the process of adoption, it's called _____ adoption.
    a. closed
    b. foreign
    c. selected
    d. open

12. Which of the following is an example of a chromosomal disorder?
    a. Spina bifida
    b. Chronic disease syndrome
    c. Phenylketonuria
    d. Turner syndrome

13. _____ is the most widely used external fertilization technique.
    a. IVF
    b. AID
    c. SART
    d. PID

14. Which combination is not possible?
    a. AT
    b. TA

c. GT
d. GC

15. DNA possesses the remarkable ability to _____ itself.
    a. accommodate
    b. reproduce
    c. assimilate
    d. disengage

16. Which of the following populations is more likely than others to be afflicted with sickle-cell anemia?
    a. Eastern Europeans
    b. African Americans
    c. Asians
    d. Hispanics

17. Down syndrome is caused by
    a. the body's failure to break down amino acids.
    b. the fragile X syndrome.
    c. a deviation on the 21st pair of chromosomes.
    d. an XO pattern.

18. An example of sex-linked inheritance includes
    a. PKU.
    b. neural tube defects.
    c. Tay-Sachs disease.
    d. hemophilia.

19. The Human Genome Project is an endeavor to identify and map
    a. certain substances within cells.
    b. all human genes.
    c. cell divisions.
    d. nucleotides within DNA.

20. Which of the following is not suspected of having a strong genetic origin?
    a. Polio
    b. Epilepsy
    c. Diabetes
    d. Cancer

Answers

1. a 2. b 3. c 4. d 5. a 6. a 7. a 8. a 9. b 10. a 11. d 12. d 13. a 14. c 15. b 16. b 17. c 18. d 19. b 20. a

Ellen and Kevin were delighted. The parents of a 3-year-old boy, they were now looking forward to their second child. Kevin, having shared in the birth of their first child, was calmer but even more excited as he looked forward to the events of this pregnancy and birth. Ellen, a healthy 31-year-old, was experiencing all the signs of a normal pregnancy. The morning sickness abated at 12 weeks. She felt movement at 17 weeks, and an ultrasound at 20 weeks showed normal development. Weight gain, blood glucose levels, blood pressure, and AFP (alphafetoprotein) test results were all within acceptable ranges.

Since this was Ellen's second pregnancy, she felt more comfortable with her changing body. Visits to the obstetrician were pleasant and uneventful. At 28 weeks, loosening ligaments caused her pelvis to irritate the sciatic nerve at the base of the spine. Her obstetrician recommended Tylenol, a heating pad, and rest. He also recommended a visit to an orthopedist to confirm the treatment. Ellen refused to take any medication and decided not to bother with a second opinion. Since she felt she could tolerate the pain for the 12 weeks until delivery, she would not be X-rayed or take even a mild painkiller. She rationalized that the back pain was acceptable because it accompanied a normal pregnancy.

At 31 weeks, Ellen noticed episodes of unusual movement and became concerned. A week later, fearing that the baby might be in distress, she called the obstetrician to describe the jabs, pokes, and excessive movements she was experiencing. The doctor immediately scheduled a biophysical profile: an eight-point check of the internal organs and another ultrasound.

Ellen nervously gulped the required 32 ounces of water an hour before the examination. Arriving at a glistening new medical center, she was quickly escorted to an examining room. The technician was both professional and serious as he looked for a problem (increasing Ellen's anxiety). The examination included a thorough check of the baby's heart chambers, a type of EKG (electrocardiogram) measurement, and an assessment of blood flow—all displayed in vibrant colors. The cord, internal organs, position of the baby, and body weight were all evaluated. Ellen was able to listen to the baby's heartbeat while watching the heart chambers function.

Later that day, Ellen's obstetrician called to tell her the results: no apparent medical problems, just an unusually active baby. Ellen and Kevin sagged with relief. They also received a bonus: a reassuring ultrasound image of their unborn child's face—in living color! ✪

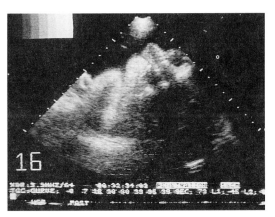

Ultrasound is frequently used when questions arise about a pregnancy. Soundwaves directed onto the uterus bounce off the bones and tissues of the fetus and are formed into an image.

Ellen's journey through the nine months of her pregnancy is quite typical: normal prenatal development accompanied by occasional worrisome moments. Given current concern about the quality of life for a woman and her developing child, we can understand the importance placed on prenatal development. In fact, today's acceptance of the impact that these nine months have on an individual's future has led to greater emphasis on *prepregnancy* care. If you think about this for a moment, it makes considerable sense because some women don't realize they're pregnant for two or three months. By then, rapid growth has occurred (as we'll see, such growth is particulary true of the central nervous system) with the potential for serious damage if elements such as alcohol and drugs have been abused.

In this Chapter, we'll first explore the prenatal world, that nine-month period that provides nourishment and protection and serves as a springboard for birth. Next we'll turn to those agents that can influence prenatal development. These are both physical and psychological and can be either positive or negative. We'll then look at birth itself, the completion of a journey that has involved remarkable development. For various reasons, some fetuses can't endure this nine-month journey, so our final focus in this Chapter will be the special case of these early, or premature, births. In the past few years, great advances—technological, medical, and psychological—have resulted in an increasing number of premature babies surviving.

When you finish reading this Chapter, you should be able to

- Describe the periods of prenatal development.

- Analyze the major features of each period.

- Indicate the times of greatest sensitivity to insult.

- Identify dangerous maternal diseases.

- Distinguish those drugs that can cause permanent damage during prenatal development.

- Assess the potential of fetal surgery.

- Discriminate the various stages of the birth process.

- Designate the possible causes of prematurity.

The Prenatal World

Although it may be difficult to imagine, you are the product of one cell, the zygote, or fertilized egg. Once the union of sperm and egg took place, in only a matter of hours (about 24–30) that one cell began to divide rapidly. The initial phase of the event occurred in a very protected world—the prenatal environment.

Once the egg is released from the ovary, it passes into the fallopian tube. Fertilization occurs in the first part of the fallopian tube, about three days after the egg has entered the tube. The fertilized egg must now pass through the remainder of the fallopian tube to reach the uterus, a journey of about three to four days to travel five or six inches. During its passage through the fallopian tube, the zygote receives all of its nourishment from the tube. Figure 4.1 illustrates passage into the uterus and **implantation.**

Implantation seems to occur in three phases:

1. **Apposition,** during which the fertilized egg, now called a **blastocyst,** comes to rest against the uterine wall.

2. **Adhesion,** during which the prepared surface of the uterus and the outer surface of the fertilized egg, now called the **trophoblast,** touch and actually "stick together."

3. **Invasion,** during which the trophoblast digs in and begins to bury itself in the uterine lining.

Figure 4.1

Passage of the zygote into the uterus

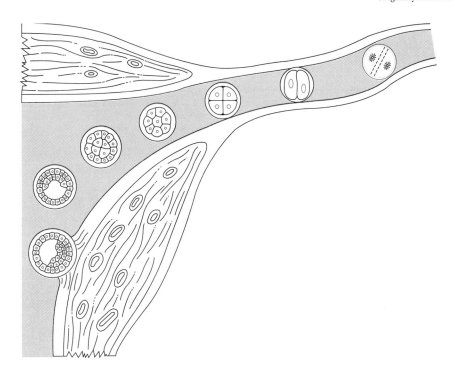

During the prenatal months, we can identify three fairly distinct stages of development: germinal, embryonic, and fetal.

The Germinal Period

The **germinal period** extends through the first two weeks. The passage through the fallopian tube takes three to four days and then the fertilized egg floats in the uterine cavity for about three more days before beginning implantation (Moore & Persaud, 1998). The zygote is now 1 week old and called a blastocyst. During the second week, the blastocyst becomes firmly implanted in the wall of the uterus. From its outer layer of cells, the **placenta,** an **umbilical cord,** and the **amniotic sac** begin to develop. The inner cell layer develops into the embryo itself. Figure 4.2 illustrates the developmental significance of the blastocyst.

The placenta and the umbilical cord serve critical functions during development. The placenta supplies the embryo with all its needs, carries off all its wastes, and protects it from danger. The placenta has two separate sets of blood vessels, one going to and from the baby through the umbilical cord, the other going to and from the mother through the arteries and veins supplying the placenta.

We can summarize the first two weeks following conception as follows:

Week 1: The zygote moves through the fallopian tube to the uterus with continued cell division.
Week 2: The blastocyst adheres to the uterine wall and begins to form the placenta, umbilical cord, and amniotic sac.

The Embryonic Period

In the **embryonic period,** from the third through the eighth week, a recognizable human being emerges. The nervous system develops rapidly, which suggests that the embryo at this time is quite sensitive to any obstructions to its growth. Our earlier discussion of sensitive periods as a time when certain experiences have a significant impact on the developing organism is clearly supported during the embryonic period. With the rapid formation of many different organ systems, any negative agent (drugs, disease) can have long-lasting effects.

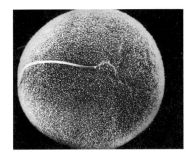

Fertilization through the embryonic period: The moment of fertilization

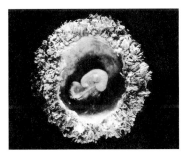

This 4-week-old embryo now has a beating heart, body buds are beginning to emerge, and the eye region is becoming discernible.

Figure 4.2

During the second week, the blastocyst becomes firmly implanted in the wall of the uterus and the placenta, umbilical cord, and embryo itself begin to form from its outer layer of cells.

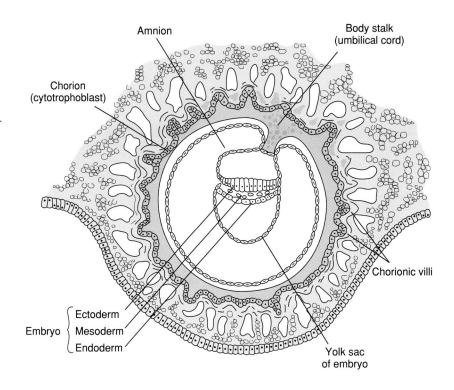

In an astonishing display of nature's power, the brain evidences a rate of growth and development that almost defies belief. And yet, if you stop and think about it, this tremendous growth surge is vital for survival, given the control the brain exercises over such critical functions as breathing. Estimates are that in a relatively brief time during brain maturation, at least 100 million (some estimates run as high as 200 million) brain cells are formed and mature.

The beginning of this amazing phenomenon (about the third prenatal week) lies in a process called *neural induction* when a chemical signal is sent from the mesoderm to the ectoderm thus signalling the onset of nervous system development. Nerve cells proliferate rapidly in the *neural tube* but quickly leave this area and commence a sometimes tortuous journey to the region of the brain where they will become functional. This phase, called *cell migration,* begins during the seventh prenatal week. Each of these nerve cells, now called *neurons,* will make connections (called synapses) with 10,000 to 200,000 other neurons (Huttenlocher, 1994).

While this building process is going on, recent discoveries (Shatz, 1996) suggest that the developing brain's electrical activity helps to shape the structure of the brain. In other words, the brain's early electrical activity isn't just a by-product of the building process but is an integral part of shaping the brain's physical makeup.

Perhaps the most remarkable change in the embryo is **cellular differentiation.** Three distinct layers are being formed: the **ectoderm,** which will give rise to skin, hair, nails, teeth, and the nervous system; the **mesoderm,** which will give rise to muscles, skeleton, and the circulatory and excretory systems; and the **endoderm,** which will give rise to lungs, liver, and pancreas. (See Figure 4.3 for details.)

Usually by the completion of the fourth week, the heart begins to beat—the embryo's first movement. The accompanying photographs show that during the fifth week eyes and ears begin to emerge, body buds give clear evidence of becoming arms and legs, and the head area is the largest part of the rapidly growing embryo.

During the sixth and seventh weeks, fingers begin to appear on the hands, the outline of toes is seen, and the beginnings of the spinal cord are visible. In the germinal period, the number and differentiation of cells rapidly increase; in the embryonic period, the organs are formed, a process called **organogenesis** (Sadler, 1995).

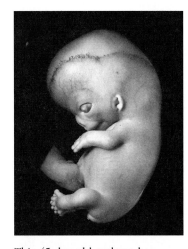

This 45-day-old embryo has visible arms and legs, with the beginnings of toes and fingers. It is possible to detect eyes and ears in the rapidly growing head area.

Figure 4.3

Development from the three layers of the blastocyst

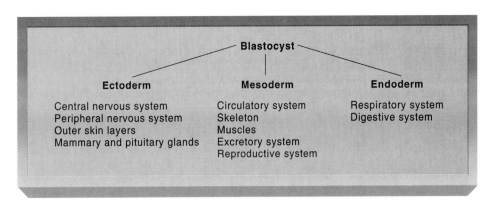

```
                        Blastocyst
           ┌───────────────┼───────────────┐
        Ectoderm        Mesoderm        Endoderm

  Central nervous system    Circulatory system    Respiratory system
  Peripheral nervous system Skeleton              Digestive system
  Outer skin layers         Muscles
  Mammary and pituitary glands  Excretory system
                            Reproductive system
```

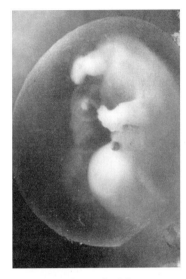

Coming to the end of the embryonic period, this 7-week-old embryo has begun to assume a more human appearance. It is now about 1 inch in length with discernible eyes, ears, nose, mouth, arms, and legs.

After eight weeks, 95 percent of the body parts are formed and general body movements are detected. During these weeks embryonic tissue is particularly sensitive to any foreign agents during differentiation, especially beginning at the third or fourth week of the pregnancy. We can summarize the embryonic period as follows:

Weeks 3+: Rapid development of nervous system
Week 4: Heart beats
Week 5: Eyes and ears begin to emerge, body buds for arms and legs
Week 6 and 7: Fingers and toes, beginning of spinal cord
Week 8: About 95 percent of body parts differentiated—arms, legs, beating heart, nervous system

The embryonic period can be hazardous for the newly formed organism. Estimates are that about 30 percent of all embryos are aborted at this time without the mother's knowledge; about 90 percent of all embryos with chromosomal abnormalities are spontaneously aborted.

At the end of this period, a discernible human being with arms, legs, a beating heart, and a nervous system exists. It is receiving nourishment and discharging waste through the umbilical cord, which leads to the placenta. The placenta itself never actually joins with the uterus but exchanges nourishment and waste products through the walls of the blood vessels (Moore & Persaud, 1998). The future mother begins to experience some of the noticeable effects of pregnancy: the need to urinate more frequently, morning sickness, and increasing fullness of breasts.

The Fetal Period

The **fetal period** extends from the beginning of the third month to birth. During this time, the fetus grows rapidly both in height and weight. The sex organs appear during the third month, and it is possible to determine the baby's sex. Visible sexual differentiation begins, and the nervous system continues to increase in size and complexity.

By the fourth month, the fetus is about 8 to 10 inches in length and weighs about 6 to 8 ounces. The fourth to the fifth month is usually the peak growth period. During this time, the mother begins to feel movement. The fetus now swallows, digests, and discharges urine. Growth is rapid during the fourth month to accommodate an increasing oxygen demand (Nilsson & others, 1993). The fetus produces specialized cells: red blood cells to transport oxygen and white blood cells to combat disease.

The fetus is now active—sucking, turning its head, and pushing with hands and feet—and the mother is acutely aware of the life within her. Figure 4.4 represents the fetus in the fourth month.

By the end of the fifth month, the baby is 10 to 12 inches long and weighs about a pound. The fetus sleeps and wakes like the newborn does, even

Figure 4.4

The fetus at 4½ months—a time of rapid growth and considerable activity.

manifesting a favorite sleep position. Rapid growth continues in the sixth month, with the fetus gaining another 2 inches and 1 pound, but slows during the seventh month. Viability, the ability to survive if born, is attained. After six months very few new nerve and muscle cells appear, since at birth the nervous system must be fully functioning to ensure automatic breathing.

Fetal Surgery

As amazing as it may sound, surgeons can operate on a fetus. Fetal surgery has saved several lives and with continued refinement promises a healthy future for many babies. Three types of fetal surgery have received considerable attention.

First, to cure a condition in which the brain ventricles fill with fluid and expand (called *fetal hydrocephalus*), surgeons now operate within the womb. They must pierce the woman's abdomen and uterine wall and penetrate the fetal skull. They then insert a tube (catheter) into the brain to drain this region until birth. Unless this condition is treated, fluid presses against the walls (membranes) of the fetal brain ventricles and can cause mental retardation or even death.

In a second type of fetal surgery to correct a blocked urinary tract in the fetus (called *fetal hydronephosis*), the surgeon removes the fetus from the womb, operates, and then returns the fetus to the uterus. The surgeon then adds either saline solution (salt water) or amniotic fluid that has been saved and warmed and, finally, sews the uterus. This surgery could not be accomplished unless drugs preventing labor were available. If the condition is not corrected, the lungs of the fetus cannot develop. The blocked urinary tract causes urine to stay in the bladder, which can actually burst. Or urine can back up into the kidneys, causing serious damage. The major problem is that the fetus stops producing amniotic fluid, which is mainly fetal urine. The fetus swallows amniotic fluid, which causes the lungs to grow. Without the amniotic fluid, the lungs don't grow; and at birth, the fetus simply can't breathe.

Finally, to correct a condition in which the fetus has a hole in its diaphragm (the muscle separating the abdomen from the chest cavity), surgeons make an incision across the uterus and cut into the fetal chest and abdomen. (This condition is called *diaphragmatic hernia*.) Surgeons push back into the abdomen any abdominal organs that might have moved through the hole in the diaphragm into the chest cavity. They then close the hole. Without this surgery, the abdominal organs that have pushed into the chest cavity restrict the growth of the lungs and eventually the fetus cannot breathe.

Kolata, G. (1990). *The baby doctors*. New York: Dell. You should find this book fascinating, a riveting account of the types of surgery now being performed on fetuses and newborns.

Development of the Senses

During the two final fetal months, organ development prepares the fetus for the shock of leaving the sheltered uterine world. The senses are ready to function; some, in fact, are already functioning. For example, the fetus is able to hear sound—the silent world of the fetus is a myth—and responds to auditory stimuli. The fetus hears many environmental sounds—voices, stomach rumblings, and the pulsing of the mother's blood (Niijhuis,1992). Our senses seem to develop as follows.

- *Touch*. Touch refers to the reaction to pressure, temperature, and pain, and seems to produce a generalized response. The sense of touch becomes functional by the beginnng of the third month (Blass & Ciaramitaro, 1994).

- *Taste*. Taste buds appear as early as the third fetal month and seem to be more widely distributed in fetal life than in adult life. Initially taste buds appear on the tonsils, palate, and part of the esophagus. In the adult, taste cells are restricted to the tongue. Although the mechanism for taste is present before birth, the presence of the amniotic fluid limits the taste response until after birth (Smith & Blass, 1996).

- *Smell*. Like taste, the neurological basis for smell appears before birth, thus there exists the possiblity of response (Cole & Cole, 1996). But since the nasal

Prenatal Learning: Fact or Fiction?

As an example of the importance of these prenatal days, consider this question: Is it fact or fantasy to think that **prenatal learning** is a possibility? Although we cannot as yet answer this question with certainty, several clues will help us.

One of the leading centers of research into fetal life is at the University of North Carolina. Here, Anthony De-Casper and his colleagues are attempting to piece together the puzzle of fetal learning in a series of experiments. For example, they had infants suck on a nipple attached to a tape recorder. Fast sucking activated a recording of their mothers' voices, and slower sucking produced another woman's voice. The babies showed a preference for their mothers' voices, as indicated by fast sucking.

Taking these results one step further, DeCasper asked a group of pregnant women to read a children's story aloud twice a day for six weeks before their expected delivery day. At birth the infants' patterns showed that they preferred the familiar story to one they had never heard (DeCasper & others, 1994). Obviously, some fetal "learning" had occurred. Results are sufficiently promising to stimulate continued research. (For a discussion of this phenomenon across species, see Smotherman & Robinson, 1996).

cavity is filled with amniotic fluid, it is not likely that the sense of smell functions before birth. Premature infants, in the last month, can smell substances when air enters the nasal cavity.

- *Hearing.* As previously noted, most fetuses can hear sound by the fourth month. The auditory mechanism is well developed structurally in later fetal life, but since the middle ear is filled with fluid, the fetus cannot respond to sounds of normal intensity. Strong auditory stimuli, however, produce a response (Berk, 1997).

- *Vision.* There is general agreement that the absence of adequate retinal stimulation eliminates the possibility of true sight during prenatal life. By the end of pregnancy, the uterus and the mother's abdominal wall may be stretched so thin that light filters through, exposing the fetus to some light and dark contrast. Visual development begins in the second week following fertilization and continues until after birth. At birth, the eye is sufficiently developed to differentiate light and dark (Brazelton & Nugent, 1995).

What does all of this mean? The foundation of the nervous system forms in the first few weeks following conception; by six weeks, the reflexes are active and electrical brain-wave patterns appear. Touching the fetal forehead as early as nine weeks causes the fetus to turn away, and if the soles of its feet are stroked, the toes curl up. The entire body is sensitive to touch. By mid-pregnancy, the inner ear is fully developed, and the fetus reacts with movement to external sound.

During amniocentesis, the fetal heart rate changes and movement increases, suggesting that the fetus has sensed tactile stimulation. Muscular development of the eyes enables the fetus to move its eyes during sleep or to change its position. From about the 16th week, the fetus is sensitive to any light that penetrates the uterine wall and the amniotic fluid. Toward the end of pregnancy, a bright light pointed at the mother's abdomen causes the fetus to move. The fetus begins to swallow amniotic fluid early in the pregnancy and demonstrates taste by turning toward and swallowing more of a sweet substance injected into the amniotic fluid.

This description of fetal life leads to an inevitable conclusion: Given adequate conditions, the fetus at birth is equipped to deal effectively with the transition from its sheltered environment to the extrauterine world.

We can summarize these developments as follows:

Third month: Sex organs appear
Fourth month: Rapid growth, red blood cells, white blood cells; active sucking
Fifth month: Hears sound, sleeps, 10 to 12 inches long, 1 pound
Sixth month: Rapid growth, 12 to 14 inches, 2 pounds
Seventh month: Growth slows, viability attained
Eighth and ninth months: Preparation for birth; senses ready to function, brain is 25 percent of adult weight

At the end of the ninth month, the fetus (just before birth) is about 20 inches long, weighs about 7 pounds, 6 ounces, and its brain at birth is 20 to 25 percent of its adult weight. Table 4.1 summarizes the course of prenatal development.

TABLE 4.1 PRENATAL DEVELOPMENT	
Name	**Development**
Zygote	Fertilization (union of sperm and egg) Cleavage at about 30 hours
Blastocyst	Rapid cell division Implantation (about sixth or seventh day)
Embryo	Begins at third week Central nervous system grows rapidly Heart begins to beat at about 28 days Digestive organs form during the second month Muscular system appears during the second month Sex differentiation occurs at about seven weeks 95% of body parts differentiated at the end of the eighth week
Fetus	Organs begin to function from 8 to 12 weeks Rapid growth during fourth month Viability at about 27 weeks

Guided Review

1. The fertilized egg passes through the _____ _____ on its way to the uterus.
2. Apposition, adhesion, and invasion are the three phases of _____.
3. The embryonic period extends from the _____ to the _____ week of development.
4. The three distinct layers during the embryonic period are the _____ , the _____ , and the _____.
5. The period beginning with the third month of pregnancy and extending to birth is known as the _____ period.
6. The peak growth period in prenatal development is during the _____ and _____ months.
7. For fetal surgery to be successful, _____ must be prevented.

Influences on Prenatal Development

When we speak of "environmental influences" on children, we usually think of the time beginning at birth. But remember: At birth an infant has already had 9 months of prenatal living, with all of this period's positive and negative features. Many

Answers

1. fallopian tube 2. implantation 3. third, eighth 4. ectoderm, mesoderm, endoderm 5. fetal 6. fourth, fifth 7. labor

women today experience the benefits of the latest research about prenatal care. Diet, exercise, and rest are all carefully programmed to the needs of the individual woman. Where women, especially pregnant teenagers, lack such treatment, the rates of prenatal loss, stillbirths, and neonatal (just after birth) mortality are substantially higher.

In spite of this care, some children still experience problems, which introduces the concept of **developmental risk.** Developmental risk is a term used to identify those children whose well-being is in jeopardy. Such risks incorporate a continuum of biological and environmental conditions. These range from the very serious (genetic defects) to the less serious (mild oxygen deprivation at birth). What now seems clear is that the earlier the damage (a toxic drug or maternal infection), the greater the chance of negative long-term effects.

If you recall our earlier discussion of sensitive periods (see Chap. 1), times of rapid growth (especially during the embryonic period with the accelerated development of the central nervous system) are also times of particular susceptibility. Risks, however, that arise just before, during, and after birth show the most serious consequences during infancy and early childhood and gradually recede during the school years. Specifically, what causes a child to be developmentally at risk?

Teratogens

With regard to developmental risk, our major concern here is with those substances that exercise their influence in the prenatal environment, a time of increased sensitivity. Teratogenic agents, which are any agents that cause abnormalities, especially demand our attention (Moore & Persaud, 1998). **Teratogens** that can cause birth defects are drugs, chemicals, infections, pollutants, or a mother's physical state, such as diabetes. Table 4.2 summarizes several of the more common teratogenic agents and the times of greatest potential risk. By examining table 4.2, you can see that these teratogenic agents fall into two classes: infectious diseases and different types of chemicals.

TABLE 4.2 TERATOGENS, THEIR EFFECTS, AND TIME OF RISK

Agent	Possible Effects	Time of Risk
Alcohol	Fetal alcohol syndrome (FAS), growth retardation, cognitive deficits	Throughout pregnancy
Aspirin	Bleeding problems	Last month, at birth
Cigarettes	Prematurity, lung problems	After 20 weeks
DES	Cancer of female reproductive system	From 3 to 20 weeks
LSD	Isolated abnormalities	Before conception
Lead	Death, anemia, mental retardation	Throughout pregnancy
Marijuana	Unknown long-term effects, early neurological problems	Throughout pregnancy
Thalidomide	Fetal death, physical and mental abnormalities	The first month
Cocaine	Spontaneous abortion, neurological problems	Throughout pregnancy
AIDS	Growth failure, low birth weight, developmental delay, death from infection	Before conception, throughout pregnancy, during delivery, during breast feeding
Rubella	Mental retardation, physical problems, possible death	First three months, may have effects during later months
Syphilis	Death, congenital syphilis, prematurity	From five months on
CMV	Retardation, deafness, blindness	Uncertain, perhaps 4 to 24 weeks
Herpes simplex	CNS damage, prematurity	Potential risk throughout pregnancy and at birth

Infectious Diseases

Some diseases that are potentially harmful to the developing fetus and that are acquired either before or during birth are grouped together as the STORCH diseases (Blackman, 1997): **S**yphilis, **T**oxoplasmosis, **O**ther infections, **R**ubella, **C**ytomegalovirus, and **H**erpes.

Syphilis. **Syphilis** is sexually transmitted and, if untreated, may affect the fetus. It makes no difference whether the mother contracted the disease during pregnancy or many years before. If the condition remains untreated, about 50 percent of the infected fetuses will die any time during or after the second trimester. Of those who survive, serious problems such as blindness, mental retardation, and deafness may affect them. Given the advances in antibiotic treatments, the incidence of congenital syphilis has steadily decreased.

Toxoplasmosis. **Toxoplasmosis** is caused by a protozoan (a single-celled microorganism) that is transmitted by many animals, especially cats, or occasionally from raw meat or uncooked fish (Cherry, 1992). Because the infection is usually undetected, the woman may pass the organism to the fetus. The results include both spontaneous abortions and premature deliveries. Low birth weight, a large liver and spleen, and anemia characterize the disease. Serious long-term consequences include mental retardation, blindness, and cerebral palsy. The incidence of toxoplasmosis is about 1 or 2 per 1,000 live births.

Other Infections. This category includes such diseases as influenza, chicken pox, and several rare viruses.

Rubella (German measles). When pregnant women hear the name **German measles** (the technical term is **rubella**), warning signals are raised, and with good reason. Women who contract this disease may give birth to a baby with a serious defect: congenital heart disorder, cataracts, deafness, or mental retardation. The risk is especially high if the disease appears early in the pregnancy, when a spontaneous abortion may result. The infection appears in less than 1 per 1,000 live births.

Any woman who has had German measles as a child cannot assume she is immune, so a pregnant woman should take the precaution of a blood test. The American Medical Association recommends that any woman of child-bearing age who has not been vaccinated for German measles be immunized. These women should then avoid becoming pregnant for at least three months.

Cytomegalovirus (CMV). **Cytomegalovirus (CMV)** is the most common STORCH infection, with an incidence of 10 to 20 per 1,000 live births. CMV is a disease that can cause damage ranging from mental retardation to blindness, deafness, and even death. One of the major difficulties in combating this disease is that it remains unrecognized in pregnant women. Consequently, we do not know the difference in outcome between early and late infection.

Herpes Simplex. In the adult, type I **herpes simplex** virus usually appears in the mouth, whereas type II herpes appears in the genital area. If the disease is passed on to the fetus (usually during the passage through the birth canal), a child develops symptoms during the first week following birth. The central nervous system seems to be particularly susceptible to this disease, with serious long-term consequences. The incidence is less than 1 per 1,000 live births.

The Special Case of AIDS

The final infection we wish to discuss is **AIDS (acquired immune deficiency syndrome).** To give you some idea of the seriousness of the problem, consider these facts (Altman, 1994).

The effects of teratogens: Mothers may pass the AIDS virus to their babies during pregnancy, delivery, and through breast milk. While babies of AIDS-infected mothers may not necessarily receive the virus, those who do are likely to succumb by 5 or 6 years of age.

- About 5.5 million women of child-bearing age (worldwide) are infected with HIV (human immunodeficiency virus).

- 200,000 babies will be born this year with HIV.

- In the United States, 7,000 to 8,000 women infected with HIV will give birth this year.

- Of these births, 2,000 will have HIV.

- One in four babies born to HIV-infected mothers will develop AIDS.

Statistics showing that only one in four babies born of mothers infected with HIV develops AIDS have long puzzled investigators. Studies have shown that these figures are directly related to the amount of the virus that the mother is carrying (Altman, 1994). That is, the more extensive the infection, the greater the chance that the baby will be born with the virus. Consequently, treatment with zidovudine (ZVD, formerly called azidothymidine or AZT) or other treatments early in the pregnancy may help to prevent the transmission of the virus (Fox, 1997).

An infected mother can pass HIV to the fetus during pregnancy, during delivery, and after birth, occasionally through breast milk. Through 1991, 1 million children worldwide had been born infected with HIV infection. These figures help to explain the growing and intensifying movement to provide schoolchildren with AIDS education as soon as they can grasp the concepts involved.

We know today that AIDS is a disorder that cripples the body's disease-fighting mechanisms, and that the virus causing it can lie dormant for years (Curtis & Barnes, 1994). What triggers full-blown AIDS remains unknown, but remember that AIDS is the end stage of the infection and is not in itself a disease.

With regard to the fetus, estimates are that an infected mother transmits HIV from 30 percent to 50 percent of the time. Thus, 50 to 70 percent of these fetuses remain unaffected. When the virus is transmitted, a condition called *AIDS embryopathy* may develop. This causes growth retardation, small head size (microcephaly), flat nose, and widespread, upward-slanted eyes, among other characteristics. Also associated with AIDS are higher rates of preterm disease, low birth weight, and miscarriage.

For those fetuses who become infected, AIDS has a shorter incubation period than for adults. Symptoms may appear as early as six months after birth and include weight loss, fever, diarrhea, and chronic infections. Once symptoms appear, babies rarely survive more than five to eight months (Hochhauser & Rothenberger, 1992).

Chemicals

Many women of child-bearing age in the United States use one or more of the following drugs: alcohol, cocaine, marijuana, or nicotine. Fifteen percent of these women use drugs with sufficient frequency to cause damage to a fetus during pregnancy. Estimates are that 30 to 40 percent of pregnant women smoke; 60 to 90 percent use analgesics during pregnancy; 20 to 30 percent use sedatives; and an undetermined number continue to use illicit drugs (Stimmel, 1991). Also, a number of women continue to use drugs before they realize they are pregnant.

Prescription drugs such as **thalidomide** have also produced tragic consequences. During the early 1960s, this drug was popular in West Germany as a sleeping pill and an antinausea measure that produced no adverse reactions in women. In 1962 physicians noticed a sizable increase in children born with either partial or no limbs. In some cases, feet and hands were directly attached to the body. Other outcomes were deafness, blindness, and occasionally, mental retardation. In tracing the cause of the outbreak, investigators discovered that the mothers of these children had taken thalidomide early in their pregnancies.

DES (diethylstilbestrol) is another example of a teratogenic drug. In the late 1940s and 1950s, DES (a synthetic hormone) was administered to pregnant women, supposedly to prevent miscarriage. Researchers found that the daughters of the

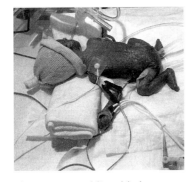

This cocaine-addicted baby was born prematurely and suffers from such behavior disturbances as tremulousness, irritability, and muscular rigidity.

women who had received this treatment were more susceptible to vaginal and cervical cancer. These daughters also experienced more miscarriages when pregnant than would be expected. Recent suspicions have arisen about the sons of DES women; they seem to have more abnormalities of their reproductive systems.

As knowledge of the damaging effect of these agents spreads, women have grown more cautious once they realize they are pregnant. We know now that these agents pass through the placenta and affect the growing embryo and fetus. We also know that certain prenatal periods are more susceptible to damage than others; for example, the embryonic period. Figure 4.5 illustrates times of greater and lesser vulnerability.

To keep a pregnancy as safe as possible, a woman should begin by avoiding the obvious hazards.

Smoking. Smoking negatively affects everything about the reproduction process: fertility, conception, possible spontaneous abortion, fetal development, labor and delivery, and a child's maturation. Smoking is probably the most common environmental hazard in pregnancy, and it results in a smaller than normal fetus. Babies of smoking mothers may have breathing difficulties and low resistance to infection, and they seem to suffer long-lasting effects after birth.

Maternal smoking produces a condition called intrauterine growth retardation (IUGR). The birth weight of neonates whose mothers smoked during pregnancy is about 200 grams less than normal. Those infants whose mothers stopped smoking

Figure 4.5

Teratogens and the timing of their effects on prenatal development. The danger of structural defects caused by teratogens is greatest early in embryonic development. This is the period of organogenesis, which lasts for several months. Damage caused by teratogens during this period is represented by the dark-colored bars. Later assaults by teratogens typically occur during the fetal period and, instead of structural damage, are more likely to stunt growth or cause problems of organ function.

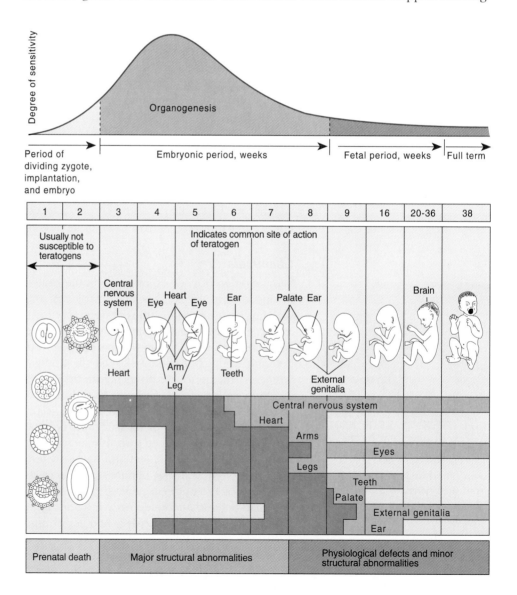

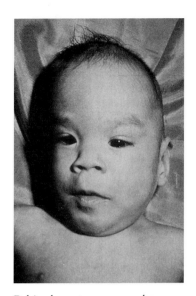

Babies born to women who drank heavily during their pregnancies may manifest distinctive characteristics such as those shown in this photo.

before the 16th week showed the greatest improvement in their birth weights (Moore & Persaud, 1998).

Alcohol. Women who consume alcohol daily during their pregnancy can produce damage in their babies, especially a condition called **fetal alcohol syndrome (FAS),** which has four clusters of clinical features (Feinbloom, 1993; Moore & Persaud, 1998):

- Psychological functioning, as a result of central nervous system abnormalities, which may include mild to moderate retardation, irritability, hyperactivity, and possible learning disabilities

- Growth factors, both prenatal and postnatal growth retardation

- Physical features such as a small head, widely spaced eyes, thin upper lip, and possible defects in limbs, joints, face, and heart

- Structural effects, which may include major malformations such as heart and genitourinary defects

Almost all drugs (including aspirin), unnecessary medication, and risky chemicals at work or at home—should be avoided. Most pregnant women today are also cautious about the amount of caffeine and sweeteners they use. For example, the FDA has cautioned pregnant women to moderate their consumption of caffeine-containing foods and beverages. These simple precautions will eliminate danger for most women.

Maternal Influences

Among the significant influences on prenatal development are maternal nutrition and maternal emotions.

Maternal Nutrition

Because the fetus depends on its mother for nourishment, most women today are keenly aware of the need to have a proper diet that will help them give birth to a healthy, happy baby. If the nutrients supplied by the mother are too low, a condition called IUGR (intrauterine growth retardation) may occur, which can be associated with problems after birth. But a pregnant woman can't "eat for two." A rule of thumb to remember is this: For a sedentary pregnancy, add about 300 extra calories; for an active pregnancy, add about 500 extra calories. When you consider the rapidity of prenatal growth (especially from two to seven months), you can understand the importance of a mother's diet, both for her and the child she is carrying (Sears & Sears, 1994).

Women of child-bearing age who wish to have children need to evaluate their weight and nutritional habits well before pregnancy. In this way they can establish good eating habits and attempt to maintain normal weight for their size. The manner in which the weight is gained is important: 1½ to 3 pounds during the first three months, and then 1 pound every nine days is recommended (Cherry, 1992). Such planning will help women to accommodate the recommended 25 pounds that they will gain during their pregnancy. How much weight to gain is always an important question for pregnant women. Most doctors believe a weight gain of 25 to 30 pounds is acceptable.

A pregnant teenager may need more calories than an adult woman. A weight gain of up to 35 pounds may be necessary for her to produce a baby of normal weight. Here we see one of the problems of teenage pregnancy: A young girl is still growing and needs additional calories for herself. If she resists this need because of a concern for appearance or a desire to shield her pregnancy, the fetus may not receive enough nourishment (Alexander & Korenbrot, 1995).

The woman's physician will usually recommend supplements to her regular diet, such as additional protein, iron, calcium, sodium, fiber, folic acid, and vitamins.

We have previously mentioned the dangers of alcohol, cigarette smoking, and caffeine.

The effects of drugs, disease, and diet, although dramatic, are not the only influences on prenatal development. How a woman feels about her pregnancy is also highly significant.

Maternal Emotions

Most pregnant women experience a wide range of emotions that are typically not sufficiently intense to affect the fetus. Seriously stressed mothers often have babies who are restless, irritable, and have feeding problems or bowel difficulties. (For an excellent discussion of the antecedents of infant temperament, see DiPietro & others, 1996.) Although the fetus is not perfectly insulated from the mother's stress, unless the stress that the mother experiences is unusually severe and prolonged, the effects on the fetus are usually of short duration (Marrs & others, 1997).

No direct evidence is available that indicates a mother's emotions affect prenatal growth. Nevertheless, data continue to accumulate suggesting that a woman under stress releases hormones that may influence prenatal development. Although a definite link between maternal emotions and prenatal growth and even later neonatal behavior is still lacking, a pattern of events can be traced.

Women adjust to pregnancy differently. They develop a capacity for mothering during pregnancy that enables them to accomplish four major tasks (Rubin, 1995).

1. *Keep herself and her child healthy and safe during pregnancy, labor, and birth*. For example, a woman comes to realize that her unborn child depends on her for nourishment and she becomes much more aware of the value of a proper diet to help her give birth to a healthy, happy baby. Physicians usually recommend supplements such as additional protein, iron, calcium, sodium, fiber, and vitamins and stress the avoidance of alcohol, cigarettes, even coffee, tea, and soft drinks.

2. *Ensure that her family is ready to give her baby a warm welcome, which suggests that emotions are alive and well during pregnancy*. Most women report that delight, anxiety, worry, and irritability are common and that mood swings are characteristic, especially during the first trimester when so much is happening (hormonal changes, increased fatigue, cravings, sickness). Feelings range from delight at the pregnancy to fear of pain during delivery, which usually diminish during the second trimester. But worry and anxiety may increase during the third trimester as sleep becomes difficult and birth draws near.

3. *Begin the attachment process with her unborn child*. During pregnancy a woman comes to accept this new life and then develops more intense feelings as she senses the baby stirring within her. For example, current technology such as ultrasound also enhances attachment. Rubin (1995) noted that several women stated some of the most enjoyable moments of their pregnancies were when they showed friends ultrasound images of their babies. You can see what's happening here: The movement, the pictures, and the acceptance of new life all combine to strengthen feelings of attachment.

4. *Learn to give of herself*. One of the most difficult tasks for many women is to accept the changes in their bodies during pregnancy. They reconcile themselves to these changes when they conclude that what they lose in physical apearance (the effects of the pregnancy) was offset by what they gain in this new relationship. They report a sense of inner peace that lasts into the third trimester when fears about the delivery begin to occupy their thoughts, together with questions about being a good mother.

Rubin's conclusions: The maternal role is characterized by enduring love, self-denial, and empathy. Once the baby is born, mothers commence a lengthy series of interactions that strengthen (or weaken) their attachment to their children.

Different Attitudes Towards Pregnancy

Pregnancy is seen quite differently by different cultures. You have just read a typical American view of the issues surrounding a woman during the prenatal months. Physical matters, such as the need for proper diet and exercise, are stressed. For example, women are warned about any deficiencies in vitamins and minerals (especially iodine and iron). Psychological matters, such as emotional health, were also mentioned as important influences on prenatal development. These concerns are typical of most Western societies, and they are real concerns when you realize that approximately an estimated half-million women throughout the world die each year as a result of pregnancy and childbirth (Konner, 1991).

For example, in a study of 996 Swiss women, conditions surrounding pregnancy were quite similar (Fricker, Hinderman, & Bruppacher, 1995). Sixty-two percent of the women reported that they didn't feel any stress during their pregnancy, and over 60 percent reported no unusual emotional strain. About 30 percent of the women smoked, but that figure dropped to 18 percent during the last trimester. (Most of the women stated that they were aware of the negative effects of smoking during pregnancy.) About 50 percent abstained from alcohol during these months, while the other 50 percent reported light usage (occasional glasses of wine).

None of the women used hard drugs; 3 percent reported using marijuana. Their consumption of coffee and tea varied only slightly. All of the women received some type of prenatal care. Interestingly, this group had a low rate of cesarean sections (6.8 percent). All in all this is a familiar story, with the exception of the number of cesarean sections, which increases to more than 20 percent in the United States.

Turning to another part of the world, in Nepal, land-locked between India and China and closed to outside influence, women don't feel fulfilled unless they become pregnant, which reflects Hindu religious beliefs. Their status as one of the least-developed countries in the world is reflected by the staggering death rate for children—40 to 50 percent of children die before they reach the age of 5 years (Escarce, 1995).

As you might imagine, pregnant women in Nepal are thought of quite differently than in Western society. (Again, remember that cultural differences are not cultural "deficiencies.") Nutritional considerations focus on feeding the pregnant woman more of her usual diet. Many pregnant women continue to work in the fields, often doing strenuous chores, such as carrying heavy loads.

After the fifth month, she is not allowed in temple; after the eighth month, she may not cook for others or touch water they are to drink. Pregnancy is closely linked to menstruation in the minds of the Nepalese because they commonly believe that it is the blood that would have been lost in menstruation that causes the child to grow. Ironically, the infant isn't considered impure.

Many of the worldwide perspectives on pregancy have their roots in ancient rituals. For example, in Korea many of the pregnancy riruals follow the Tae Kyo rules for safe and easy childbirth and to protect the infant from misfortune. In Southeast Asian cultures, pregnancy is not considered an illnesss, so prenatal care may be neglected. The Buddhist belief in reincarnation captures the notion that pregnancy is a way of bringing back to life dead relatives. Rural Turkish culture sees pregnancy as part of divine creation, in which a man's godlike power and authority is based on his power to generate life (Fox, 1997; Olds, London, & Ladewig, 1996; Pritham & Sammons, 1993).

Any discussion of cultural differences, however, must also consider *variations within cultures*. For example, a third-generation Chinese family may have quite different values and beliefs than a traditional Chinese family that has absorbed American culture.

Cherry, S. (1992). *Understanding pregnancy and childbirth*. New York: Collier. This popular book, available in paperback, has been a best-seller for several years. It carefully presents detailed information about pregnancy and birth.

Nevertheless, prenatal problems arise, and today's diagnostic techniques often enable early detection of these difficulties.

Diagnosing Fetal Problems

Some women have a greater chance of developing difficulties during pregnancy or delivering a child with problems. To cope with these conditions, the rapidly expanding field of fetal diagnosis not only identifies problems but also offers means of treatment. About 1 percent of infants suffer from some genetic defect, whereas another 0.5 percent suffer from defective chromosomes. As a result, prenatal testing is steadily becoming more common, especially for older women.

For example, children born with cystic fibrosis or sickle-cell anemia acquire these diseases from parents who are both carriers. Tests are now available to determine whether a person is a carrier of a particular genetic disease. If both potential partners are carriers, the chances of children acquiring the disease can be calculated. Among the diagnostic tools now available are the following.

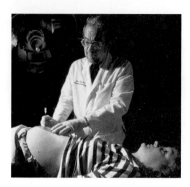

Here a pregnant woman is undergoing amniocentesis. Amniotic fluid is withdrawn and analyzed to determine sex and any chromosomal abnormalities. Amniocentesis may be done from the 15th week onward.

Amniocentesis

Probably the technique you have heard most about is **amniocentesis,** which entails inserting a needle through the mother's abdomen, piercing the amniotic sac, and withdrawing a sample of the amniotic fluid. (Amniocentesis may be done from the 15th week of pregnancy on.) The fluid sample provides information about the child's sex and almost 70 chromosomal abnormalities.

Alpha-Fetoprotein (AFP) Test

Occasionally, AFP (a protein produced by a baby's liver) escapes from the spinal fluid in those fetuses with neural tube problems. It then passes into the mother's bloodstream. Spina bifida babies (see Chap. 3) show a raised level of AFP, which may be detected in the mother's blood by a test called MSAFP (maternal serum alpha fetoprotein).

Fetoscopy

In a **fetoscopy,** a tiny instrument called a fetoscope is inserted into the amniotic cavity, making it possible to see the fetus. If the view is clear, defects of hands and legs are visible. (Fetoscopy is usually performed after the 16th week.) Today, doctors avoid fetoscopy if possible because of potential injury to the fetus and use a relatively new method for obtaining fetal blood: percutaneous umbilical blood sampling. A needle is inserted through the abdomen and uterus into the blood vessels of the umbilical cord. Not only can this aid genetic diagnosis, it also permits blood transfusions to the fetus (Nightingale & Goodman, 1990).

Chorionic Villi Sampling (CVS)

The outer layer of the embryo is almost covered with chorionic villi, fingerlike projections that reach into the uterine lining. A catheter (small tube) is inserted through the vagina to the villi, and a small section is suctioned into the tube. **Chorionic villi sampling (CVS)** is an excellent test to determine the fetus's genetic structure and may be performed beginning at 8 weeks, usually between 8 and 12 weeks.

Ultrasound

Ultrasound is a procedure that uses sound waves to produce an image that enables a physician to detect structural abnormalities. Useful pictures can be obtained as early as 7 weeks. Ultrasound is frequently used in conjunction with other techniques such as amniocentesis and fetoscopy (Sadler, 1995).

Guided Review

8. _____ _____ is the term used to describe children whose well-being is in jeopardy.
9. The acronym _____ indicates some of the potentially harmful diseases that can affect the developing fetus.
10. A harmful agent that can cause abnormalities in the developing fetus is called a _____.
11. _____ is the most common environmental hazard in pregnancy and can result in a smaller than normal fetus.
12. Amniocentesis can be used after the _____ week of pregnancy.
13. A comprehensive test to determine the fetus's genetic structure is _____ _____ _____.

Answers

8. developmental risk 9. STORCH 10. teratogen 11. smoking 12. 15th 13. chorionic villi sampling

The Birth Process

The odyssey that began approximately nine months earlier reaches its climax at birth. In spite of what you may have heard, no one knows exactly what causes labor to begin or why it begins about 280 days after the first day of the last menstrual period. Before this moment arrives, the mother has to make certain decisions. Does she, for example, ask the physician to use an anesthetic, or does she want natural childbirth? Both methods have their advantages and disadvantages. Does she want the father with her during labor and birth (Sears & Sears, 1994)?

Natural childbirth provides an unforgettable experience for the mother (and often the father, a common practice today), but it is hard, painful work. The use of analgesics prevents much of the birth pain, but women today are sensitive to the possibility that any drug may affect the baby adversely, decreasing alertness and activity for days after birth (Brazelton & Nugent, 1995).

Stages in the Birth Process

A woman usually becomes aware of the beginning of labor by one or more of these signs:

- The passage of blood from the vagina

- The passage of amniotic fluid from the ruptured amniotic sac through the vagina

- Uterine contractions and accompanying discomfort

The first two clues are certain signs that labor has begun; other pains (false labor) are occasionally mistaken for signs of true labor. Three further stages of labor can also be distinguished:

1. *Stage One: Dilation.* The neck of the uterus (the cervix) dilates to about four inches in diameter. Dilation is the process responsible for labor pains and may last for 12 or 13 hours, or even longer.

   Think of the baby at this stage as enclosed in a plastic cylinder. It is upside down in the mother's abdomen, with the bottom of the cylinder under the mother's rib and the tip buried deep in her pelvis. The cervix is about one-half inch long and almost closed. Before the next stage, expulsion, occurs, the diameter of the cervix must be stretched to a diameter of four inches. (The comedienne Carol Burnett has said that the only way you can imagine this feeling is if you pulled your upper lip over your head!)

2. *Stage Two: Expulsion.* With the cervix fully dilated, the fetus no longer meets resistance and the uterine contractions drive it through the birth canal. Uterine pressure at this stage is estimated to be 60 pounds. Once the cervix is fully open, the baby passes through the birth canal. This expulsion phase should be completed about two hours after the cervix becomes fully dilated for those giving birth for the first time, about half that time for women who have previously given birth (Olds, London, & Ladewig, 1996). This is the phase when most fathers, if they are present, become exultant. They describe the appearance of the head of the baby (called the *crowning*) as an unforgettable experience.

   Note that the times for expulsion (90 minutes and 30–45 minutes) are averages. If this second stage of labor is prolonged—with no evidence of a problem—surgical intervention remains unnecessary. Occasionally, women spend five or six hours (or more) in a normal first birth.

3. *Stage Three: The Afterbirth.* In the **afterbirth** stage, the placenta and other membranes are discharged. This stage is measured from the birth of the

baby to the delivery of the placenta and may last only a few minutes. If the spontaneous delivery of the placenta is delayed, it may be removed manually. Figure 4.6 illustrates the birth process.

When a pregnancy ends spontaneously before the 20th week, a spontaneous abortion, commonly called a **miscarriage** has occurred. After the 20th week, the spontaneous end of a pregnancy is called a **stillbirth** if the baby is born dead, or a premature birth if the baby survives. Occasionally a pregnancy occurs outside of the uterus. In an **ectopic pregnancy,** the fertilized egg attempts to develop outside the uterus, usually in one of the fallopian tubes, sometimes referred to as a *tubal pregnancy.* About 1 in every 200 pregnancies is ectopic.

Figure 4.6

Stages in the birth process

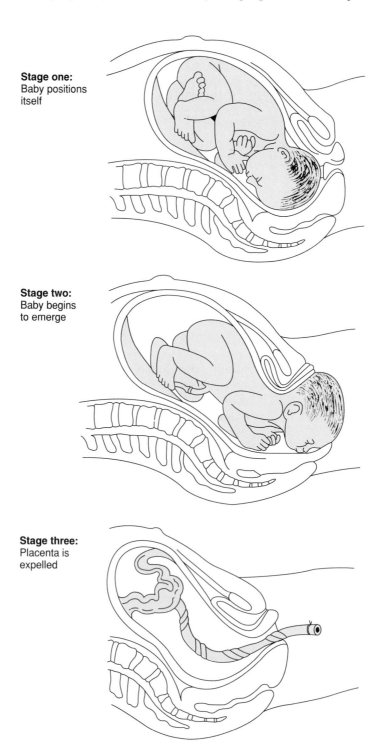

Stage one:
Baby positions
itself

Stage two:
Baby begins
to emerge

Stage three:
Placenta is
expelled

Many women feel "down" after giving birth. This is fairly common and is now thought to be a normal part of pregnancy and birth for some women. Called **postnatal depression,** this condition may have several causes: hormonal changes after birth, a sense of anticlimax after completing something she has anticipated for so many months, sheer fatigue, and tension about care of the baby (especially after a first birth). These feelings of depression usually leave quickly, but if they persist longer than two or three weeks help should be sought. The danger here is that untreated depression may intensify, causing more lasting problems for both mother and child.

For most women, the birth process, as painful as it may be, proceeds normally. Occasionally, however, problems arise.

Birth Complications

Birth can sometimes be exceptionally difficult, even dangerous. The following are a few of the more common complications.

Forceps Delivery

Occasionally, for safety, the physician will withdraw the baby with forceps during the first phase of birth. A **forceps delivery** presents some danger of rupturing blood vessels or causing brain damage but, with new guidelines, forceps delivery is considered quite safe. For example, forceps are not used unless the cervix is completely dilated and the head is within 2 inches of the mouth of the vagina (Cherry, 1992).

A decision about a forceps delivery depends on two conditions: those involving the fetus and those related to the mother. Is the fetus in distress? Is the baby in the correct position? Has the mother sufficient strength for the final push? Specifically, a forceps delivery may be called for when the woman has been in the second stage of labor for several hours or when an emergency arises for either the mother (shock, exhaustion) or the fetus (clear signs of fetal distress such as a slowing heart rate).

Breech Birth

During the last month of pregnancy, most babies move into a headdown (vertex) position. Most babies who don't turn during this time will be in **breech birth** presentation position. It's almost as if the baby were sitting in the uterus, head up and feet and buttocks down. Several conditions can contribute to a breech presentation: more than one fetus in the uterus, an abnormally shaped uterus, a placenta partially (or even fully) covering the uterine opening, and prematurity.

About four out of every hundred babies are born feet first, or buttocks first, while one out of a hundred is in a crosswise position (transverse presentation). These breech births can be worrisome because the baby must be carefully guided through the birth canal. Care must be taken to avoid squeezing the umbilical cord, thus restricting the flow of oxygen to the baby (Feinbloom, 1993). In spite of these concerns, most breech babies are born well and healthy. The major concern is with premature babies who, given the size of their heads in proportion to the rest of their bodies, often require a cesarean birth.

Cesarean Section

If for some reason the child cannot come through the birth canal, surgery is performed to deliver the baby through the abdomen, in a procedure called **cesarean section.** For example, a cesarean may produce a healthier baby than does prolonged labor and difficult birth. Among the conditions suggesting a cesarean include: a pelvis too small for a safe vaginal delivery, an abnormal presentation position, and previous cesareans that increase the possibility of uterine rupture (Cherry, 1992).

Although now fairly safe, this operation is considered major surgery and is not recommended unless necessary. More than 20 percent of all live births are cesarean, a figure many consider to be excessive. Today many women attempt a vaginal delivery following a cesarean if the conditions that caused the original cesarean are no longer a concern and if only one fetus is present. The success rate for a natural delivery after having had a cesarean is from 60 percent to 80 percent.

Prematurity

About seven out of every hundred births are premature, occurring less than 37 weeks after conception. Fortunately, today it is possible to simulate womb conditions so that the correct temperature and humidity, bacteria control, and easily digestible food can be provided for the child. Still, prematurity presents real dangers, ranging from mental deficiency to death. (We'll shortly discuss this topic in more detail.)

Anoxia (Lack of Oxygen)

If anything should happen during the birth process that interrupts the flow of oxygen to the fetus, brain damage or death can result. A substantial need for oxygen exists during birth because pressure on the fetal head can cause some rupturing of the blood vessels in the brain. After the umbilical cord is cut, delay in lung breathing can also produce **anoxia.** Failure here can cause death or brain damage. Controversy surrounds infants who have experienced anoxia, survived, but show evidence of mental dullness. Whether the damage is permanent is difficult to predict (Niijhuis, 1992).

The Rh Factor

Rh factor refers to a possible incompatibility between the blood types of mother and child. If the mother is Rh-negative and the child Rh-positive, miscarriage or even infant death can result. During birth some of the baby's blood inevitably enters the mother's bloodstream. The mother then develops antibodies to destroy fetal red blood cells. This usually happens after the baby is born, so the first baby may escape unharmed. During later pregnancies, however, these antibodies may pass into the fetus's blood and start to destroy the red blood cells of an Rh-positive baby.

Estimates are that about 10 percent of marriages are between Rh-negative women and Rh-positive men. Today, a protective vaccine (RhoGam) has almost eliminated the possibility of Rh incompatibility when Rh-negative women are identified. In a case where the first baby's blood causes the mother to produce antibodies, exchange blood transfusions may be given to the baby while still in the uterus.

Childbirth Strategies

Most babies escape complications and experience little if any birth difficulty. To help the newly born child adjust to a new environment, Leboyer (1975) believed that we must stop "torturing the innocent." Traditionally, newborns encounter a cold, bright world that turns them upside down and slaps them. Leboyer advocated a calmer environment. He suggests extinguishing all lights in the delivery room except a small night light and making the room silent at the time of birth. Immediately after birth the child is placed not on a cold metal scale, but on the mother's abdomen, a natural resting place. After several minutes, the child is transferred to a basin of warm water. Leboyer claimed that this process eases the shock of birth and that babies are almost instantly calm and happy.

Another technique, called **prepared childbirth,** or the Lamaze method after French obstetrician Fernand Lamaze, has become extremely popular with the medical profession. For several sessions women are informed about the physiology of childbirth and instructed in breathing exercises. The technique is intended to relieve fear and pain by relaxation procedures.

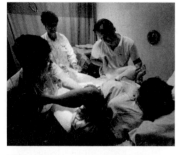

The presence of the father during birth can be a source of physical and psychological support for the mother. Fathers present during birth describe it as an "unforgettable experience."

A range of birth options is now available to couples. Some, for example, are choosing home births under the guidance of midwives, who are trained delivery specialists. Midwives assist with about 50 percent of all nonhospital deliveries. Some hospitals are providing birthing rooms, which have a more relaxed and homelike atmosphere than the typical delivery room and may provide birthing beds or birthing chairs for greater comfort (Tapley & Todd, 1988). Still, between 95 and 99 percent of all births occur in hospitals.

The Special Case of Prematurity

The average duration of pregnancy is 280 days. Occasionally, however, some babies are born early; they are premature or preterm, often called "preemies." Formerly these babies had high mortality rates, but with today's sophisticated technology their chances of survival are much greater. Before we discuss the condition of these babies and the reasons for their early appearance, let's establish some pertinent facts.

Facts about Prematures

In 1961 the World Health Organization (WHO) redefined **prematurity** to include those infants born before 37 weeks gestation with a birth weight of 1,500 grams (about 3 pounds) or less. Thus two criteria were suggested: immaturity and low birth weight.

Within this definition, two additional classifications are possible:

- Infants born before 37 weeks whose weight is appropriate for their age; these are called preterm AGA—appropriate for gestational age.

- Those born before 37 weeks whose weight is low for their age; these are called preterm SGA—small for gestational age.

A third classification has recently been proposed—very low birth weight (VLBW), which is defined as below 1,500 grams (about 3 pounds).

Causes of Prematurity

About 250,000 of all infants born in the United States can be classified as premature. Although it is still impossible to predict which women will begin labor prematurely, prematurity has been linked to certain conditions. For example, *once a woman has given birth prematurely,* the risk of prematurity in the next pregnancy is about 25 percent. *Multiple births* (a growing phenomenon due to the increasing use of fertility drugs) also produce babies whose birth weights are lower than that of a single baby. *Age* also has been identified as a correlate of prematurity. If the mother is under 17 or over 35, the risk is substantially increased.

Other causes frequently linked to prematurity include *low socioeconomic status (SES).* In underdeveloped countries as many as one infant in four is born prematurely. In the United States more premature babies are born to poor than affluent women. *Smoking* remains a significant factor in any discussion of prematurity, as does *alcohol.* Alcohol also increases the likelihood of prematurity. About 60 percent of American women drink. For those taking 10 drinks per week while pregnant, the chance of having a low-birth-weight baby doubles. Other causes of prematurity include maternal infection, cervical problems, high blood pressure, unusual stress, diabetes, and heart disease. Even when all of these causes are enumerated, explaining exactly what happened in any given pregnancy still is difficult, if not impossible (Witter, 1993).

Though these children may differ from full-term babies in the early days of their development, most of these differences eventually disappear. Most prematures reach developmental levels similar to those of full-term babies. The only difference is that it takes premature babies a little longer to get there (Fox, 1997).

For example, Beckwith and her colleagues (1990) studied 55 infants born at a

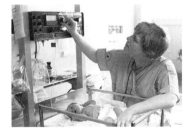

With advances in the treatment of prematures (temperature control, nutrition), the outlook for these babies has greatly improved. Psychological insights into the development of prematures have led to the conclusion that parental support and stimulation are needed during the baby's hospitalization to ensure that attachment proceeds as normally as possible.

Guidelines for Parents of Prematures

Although the new technology designed for prematures is marvelous, these babies need to sense parental love. In what has become a classic discussion of the treatment of prematures, Helen Harrison (1983) has proposed several guidelines that parents of prematures can use, even with the technological nature of the premature nursery.

- *Try to understand the baby.* Begin by observing carefully, learning what upsets and soothes. How does the baby respond to different types of stimulation? How long does it take to calm the baby after some upset? What kinds of clues are being given to signal discomfort (changes in skin color, muscular reaction, breathing rate)?

- *Use as much body contact as possible.* Since these babies came into the world early, they often seem physically insecure (when compared to the normal infant after birth). Touching the baby with the whole hand on back or chest and stomach often relaxes the premature. Massaging both relaxes and shows affection.

- *Talk to the baby.* Studies have repeatedly shown that prematures, while seemingly unresponsive, show better rates of development when exposed to the mother's voice as often as possible.

When the premature infant can be taken from the incubator and given to the parent, a delicate moment has arrived. Some parents find it difficult to react positively to a premature; they feel guilty, occasionally harbor feelings of rejection, and must fight to accept the situation. They are simply overwhelmed. Usually this reaction passes quickly. On the occasion of this initial contact, parents should have been well prepared for holding a baby that is still entangled in wires and tubes.

gestational age of 37 weeks or less and with a birth weight of 5½ pounds or less. Despite birth complications and accompanying problems (respiratory difficulties, for example), the children showed intellectual development within the normal range: At the age of 12, the children had an average IQ of 108, with a range of 77 to 134. Thus they survived birth complication and developed free of any major handicaps, although 25 percent exhibited learning problems. The authors attributed the causes of learning problems versus no learning problems to differences in neurobehavioral functioning (ability to organize their behavior, visual attention) and supportive home environments.

One conclusion seems inevitable: The younger and smaller the infant, the greater the risk for later difficulties. Although we can't predict the developmental outcome of these babies with a high degree of certainty, we would agree with the following statement.

Avery, M. C. & G. Litwack (1983). *Born early.* New York: Little, Brown. Vital data, good writing, and a positive outlook make this an excellent introduction to the topic of prematurity. It's become a classic in the premature literature.

Low birth weight children represent a heterogeneous group of term and preterm infants with varying degrees of social and medical risk. Adverse outcomes include a broad spectrum of conditions ranging from normal growth and development to severe developmental abnormalities. Although the vast majority of low birth weight children function within the normal range, they have higher rates of subnormal growth, health conditions, and inferior neurodevelopmental outcomes than do normal birth weight children (Hack, Klein, & Taylor, 1995, p. 191).

Guided Review

14. Labor usually begins _____ days after the first day of the last menstrual period.
15. The spontaneous end of pregnancy is called a _____ if it occurs before the 20th week.
16. A fertilized egg that develops in a fallopian tube is called an _____ pregnancy.
17. _____ _____ can cause a woman to feel a little "down" for a few days following delivery.
18. Births occurring less than 37 weeks after conception are said to be _____.
19. Lamaze's method is also referred to as _____ _____.
20. The _____ _____ _____ has identified the criteria for prematurity.

CONCLUSION

In this Chapter, you have seen how a human being begins its journey through the lifespan. Nature's detailed choreography of prenatal development provides a remarkably complex yet elegantly simple means of ensuring the survival of generations. Once conception occurs, uniting the genetic contribution of both mother and father, the developmental process is under way, sheltered for the first nine months in the protective cocoon of the womb.

For some, the process is interrupted and the uterine stay is shortened. Today these prematures, thanks to technological advances, have a heightened chance of survival and of normal physical and psychological development.

In summary:

The Prenatal World

- Once fertilization has occurred, implantation occurs in three stages.

- The germinal period is the time when the fertilized egg passes through the fallopian tube.
- The embryonic period is a time of rapid development and great sensitivity.
- The fetal period is a time of preparation for life outside the womb.
- The senses develop during the prenatal months and are ready to function at birth.

Influences on Prenatal Development

- Developmental risk is a term that applies to those children whose welfare is in jeopardy.
- Teratogens are those agents that cause abnormalities.
- Infectious diseases and chemical agents are the two basic classes of teratogens.

- Today AIDS is recognized as a potential danger for newborns.
- Maternal nutrition and emotions are important influences during pregnancy.
- Advancing technology has provided diagnostic tools for the detection of many fetal problems.

The Birth Process

- Birth occurs as a series of stages.
- Complications can develop during the birth process.
- Childbirth strategies are evolving that are designed to ease the transition from womb to world.
- Today the outlook for prematures is much more optimistic than in previous times.

KEY TERMS

Adhesion
Afterbirth
AIDS (acquired immune deficiency syndrome)
Amniocentesis
Amniotic sac
Anoxia (lack of oxygen)
Apposition
Blastocyst
Breech birth

Cellular differentiation
Cesarean section
Chorionic villi sampling (CVS)
Cytomegalovirus (CMV)
DES (Diethylstilbestrol)
Developmental risk
Ectoderm
Ectopic pregnancy
Embryonic period
Endoderm

Fetal alcohol syndrome (FAS)
Fetal period
Fetoscopy
Forceps Delivery
German measles (rubella)
Germinal period
Herpes Simplex
Implantation
Invasion
Mesoderm

Answers

14. 280 15. miscarriage 16. ectopic 17. postnatal depression 18. premature 19. prepared childbirth 20. World Health Organization

Miscarriage
Organogenesis
Placenta
Postnatal depression
Prematurity
Prenatal learning

Prepared childbirth
Rh Factor
Stillbirth
Syphilis
Teratogens
Thalidomide

Toxoplasmosis
Trophoblast
Ultrasound
Umbilical cord

WHAT DO YOU THINK?

1. Considerable discussion has occurred recently about the possibility of prenatal learning. Where do you stand on this issue? Be sure to support your opinion with facts from this Chapter.

2. You probably have heard how careful women must be when they are pregnant. They are worried about such things as smoking and drinking. Do you think we have become too nervous and timid about these dangers? Why?

3. Turn back to table 4.2. From your own knowledge (relatives and friends, for example), indicate which of these teratogens you think are most common. Select one and explain why you think it is a common threat and what could be done to help prevent it. (Lead paint is a good example.)

4. Significant medical and ethical questions surround such techniques as fetal surgery. Assume that a physician does not inform a woman that her fetus is a good candidate for fetal surgery. The baby is stillborn. Is the doctor guilty of malpractice or any crime? Can you think of other examples?

CHAPTER REVIEW TEST

1. It takes a fertilized egg about _____ _____ to travel through the fallopian tube to the uterus.
   a. 3 days
   b. 14 days
   c. 30 days
   d. 9 months

2. It then takes another _____ _____ days for the fertilized egg to implant.
   a. 3 days
   b. 7 days
   c. 14 days
   d. 30 days

3. The first two weeks following fertilization are called the _____ period.
   a. embryonic
   b. fetal
   c. germinal
   d. pregnancy

4. A _____ is a one-week-old zygote.
   a. fetus
   b. embryo
   c. blastocyst
   d. trophoblast

5. During the _____ period the nervous system develops rapidly.
   a. embryonic
   b. fetal
   c. gestational
   d. germinal

6. Which system does not develop from the mesoderm?
   a. muscular
   b. skeletal
   c. circulatory
   d. respiratory

7. Development is most vulnerable to outside agents during the _____ period.
   a. embryonic
   b. germinal
   c. fetal
   d. sensitive

8. The peak growth period for the fetus is during the _____ and _____ months.
   a. first, second
   b. fourth, fifth
   c. sixth, seventh
   d. eighth, ninth

9. Red blood cells transport _____ and white blood cells to combat disease.
   a. oxygen
   b. amniotic fluid
   c. teratogens
   d. villi

10. Which of the following statements is true?
    a. The earlier the damage, the greater the chance of negative long-term effects.
    b. The fetus is safe from all harm while in the womb.
    c. Babies are usually born on the day predicted.
    d. A fetus hears no sound until birth.

11. Toxoplasmosis is
    a. a sexually transmitted disease.
    b. a virus capable of causing deafness or cataracts.
    c. a disease capable of causing mental retardation or death.
    d. a problem caused by the genetic makeup of the father.

12. Which of the following will not result from exposure to rubella?
    a. congenital heart disorder
    b. mental retardation
    c. deafness
    d. nearsightedness

13. _____ is not a STORCH infection.
    a. RDS
    b. CMV
    c. Herpes simplex
    d. Toxoplasmosis

14. It is almost impossible for a mother to pass the AIDS virus to her baby through
    a. delivery.
    b. handling.
    c. pregnancy.
    d. breast milk.

15. It is recommended that pregnant women add _____ calories to their regular diets.
    a. 300
    b. 1,200
    c. 2,400
    d. 100

16. A woman's emotions can affect her pregnancy indirectly by a release of her
    a. villi.
    b. teratogens.
    c. hormones.
    d. Rh factor.

17. _____ is a technique in which a needle is inserted through a pregnant woman's abdomen and into the amniotic sac in order to obtain a fluid sample.
    a. Ultrasound
    b. Chorionic villi sampling
    c. Amniocentesis
    d. Non-stress test

18. Which statement about prematurity is *not* true?
    a. it is associated with vitamin therapy
    b. it is associated with low SES
    c. it is associated with multiple births
    d. it is associated with cigarette use

19. _____ was a pioneer in the technique of prepared childbirth.
    a. Leboyer
    b. Lamaze
    c. DeCasper
    d. Salk

20. Mental retardation, hyperactivity, and primary growth retardation can be symptoms of
    a. fetal alcohol syndrome (FAS).
    b. Rh factor.
    c. prematurity.
    d. anoxia.

21. Premature babies of very low birth weight are
    a. not normally at severe risk.
    b. not permitted visits by their parents.
    c. more likely to develop cerebral palsy.
    d. more likely to have problems later in life.

Answers

1.a 2.a 3.c 4.c 5.a 6.d 7.a 8.b 9.a 10.a 11.c 12.d 13.d 14.b 15.a 16.c 17.c 18.a 19.b 20.a 21.d

PART **III**

Infancy

Newborn babies are beautifully programmed to fit their parents' fantasies and to reward the work of pregnancy.

T. Berry Brazelton

CHAPTER 5

Physical and Cognitive Development in Infancy

L iz gazed at the infant girl in her arms. Although she had carried this tiny creature within her for nine months, it was still a stranger. Would it be an easy baby? Who would she really look like? Would she do well in school? Of course she would be smart! As these thoughts flashed through her mind, she remembered a course in child psychology she had taken. How had the instructor referred to a newborn? Neonate; yes, that was it. She had read the books on what to expect: feedings, sleep patterns, possible illnesses. But what really was a neonate? What was an infant? Catching herself in these musings, she began to laugh. ✺

Liz certainly was not the first person to speculate about infancy. It is interesting to trace several of these speculations, since they offer insights into the remarkable changes that have occurred in our interpretation of infancy. Do you remember Shakespeare's character Jaques in *As You Like It*? In his speech about the seven ages of our lives, he describes an infant in the first age as "mewling and puking in the nurse's arms."

Freud's description of infancy as richly laden with sexual experiences presented a far different view, one that met with fierce opposition. Noting that it is a serious error to believe that children have no sexual life and that sexuality only begins at puberty, Freud argued that "from the very first children have a copious sexual life." They direct their first sexual lusts and their curiosity to those who are nearest and for other reasons dearest to them—parents, brothers, and sisters.

John Watson, one of America's early behaviorists, had discovered the writings of Pavlov on classical conditioning and believed that conditioning answered all of

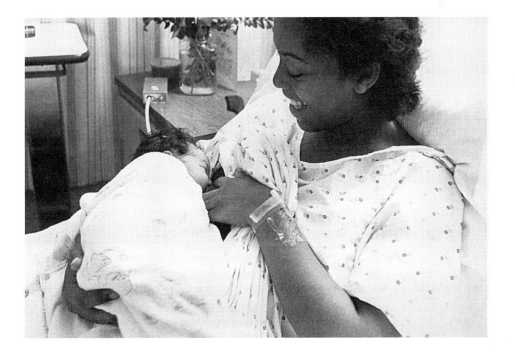

our questions about human behavior. Under Pavlov's influence, Watson viewed infants as a source of potential stimulus-response connections. He believed that if you turn your attention to an infant early enough, you can make that infant into anything you want—it's all a matter of conditioning. His famous statement about infancy is worth repeating here.

> Give me a dozen healthy infants and my own specified world to bring them up in and I'll guarantee to take any one at random and train him to become any type of specialist I might select—doctor, lawyer, artist, merchant-chief and, yes, even beggar-man and thief, regardless of his talents, penchants, tendencies, abilities, vocations, and race of his ancestors. (Watson, 1924, p. 104)

Piaget's view of infancy differed radically from Watson's. Rather than seeing children as small sponges waiting for something to be poured into them, Piaget believed that children actively construct their own views of the world during these early years. One of the first psychologists to question the apparently passive state of infants, Piaget argued that infants are much more competent than originally thought and they actually construct their own view of the world, a view that changes with age (Piaget, 1967). During these years children build the cognitive structures that are the foundation of their intelligence.

To help you understand an infant's world, in this Chapter you'll examine the methods used to assess the well-being of infants following birth. Then you'll trace various aspects of infant development: physical, motor, perceptual, cognitive, language, and social/emotional. You'll also begin to discern the issues and themes discussed in Chapter 1. For example, stability is particularly important in any discussion of infancy. Do the events that occur in infancy leave an indelible mark that lasts a lifetime?

When you finish reading this Chapter, you should be able to

- Describe those abilities that infants begin to demonstrate at birth.

- Analyze the brain's role in development.

- Identify critical neonatal reflexes that enhance survival and enable neonates to adapt to their environment.

- Distinguish the typical clues that signal normal physical and cognitive development.

- Appraise an infant's cognitive development by observing behavior in a variety of situations.

- Evaluate an infant's language development using the key signs of language acquisition.

Physical and Motor Development

Infancy is a time of rapid physical and nervous system development, accomplishments that ensure an infant's survival and ability to cope with its world. The typical newborn weighs about 7½ pounds and is about 20 inches in length. In one year after its birth, an infant's length increases by one-half and its weight almost triples. Infancy sees exciting changes in psychomotor development. For example, think how excited parents are at their baby's first step.

As their baby's growing physical competence becomes observable, parents begin to treat their child differently, recognizing greater individuality and maturity. Different parenting practices now spring into action and these varied practices reflect the culture into which a child is born. The manner in which Balinese mothers carry their children affect children's motor development; infants in Ghana show superior motor abilities due to their considerable physical freedom; the expectations of Jamaican mothers cause their infants to sit and walk relatively early (Bornstein, 1995). In other words, different families in different cultures go about parenting in different ways.

> All cultures recognize infancy as a stage of development. Our "newborn" and "infant" are for the Chagga of Tanganyika "mnangu "(the incomplete one) and "mkoku" (one who fills lap). For us, a child is an infant until she talks, and becomes a toddler when he walks; for the Alor of the Lesser Sundra Islands, the first stage of infancy lasts from birth to the first smile, and the second stage from the smile to the time when the child can sit alone or begins to crawl. (Bornstein, 1995, p.5)

Growing children experience changes in shape and body composition, in the distribution of tissues, and in their developing motor skills, and these changes then influence cognitive, psychosocial, and emotional development (Field, 1990). For example, the infant's head at birth is about a quarter of the body's total length, but in the adult it is about one-seventh of body length. Different tissues (muscles, nerves) also grow at different rates, and total growth represents a complex series of changes. The basis of this rapidly unfolding and complex process is, of course, the brain.

Brain Development

The adult human brain weighs about 3 to 4 pounds and contains about 100–200 billion neurons. As we have seen, nervous system development begins during the embryonic period when neurons reproduce at the rate of about 250,000 per minute. During infancy, connections among the neurons begin to increase notably (as much

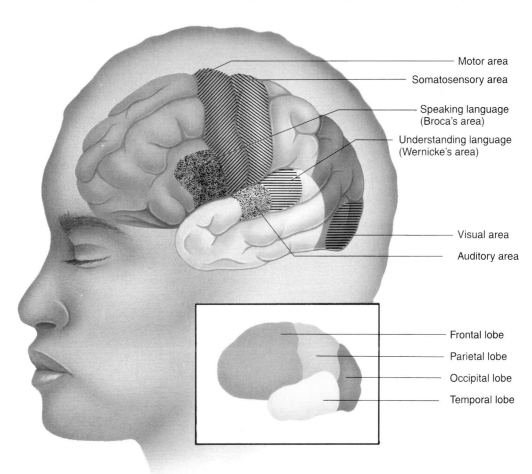

Motor area
Somatosensory area
Speaking language (Broca's area)
Understanding language (Wernicke's area)
Visual area
Auditory area

Frontal lobe
Parietal lobe
Occipital lobe
Temporal lobe

Figure 5.1

Brain development

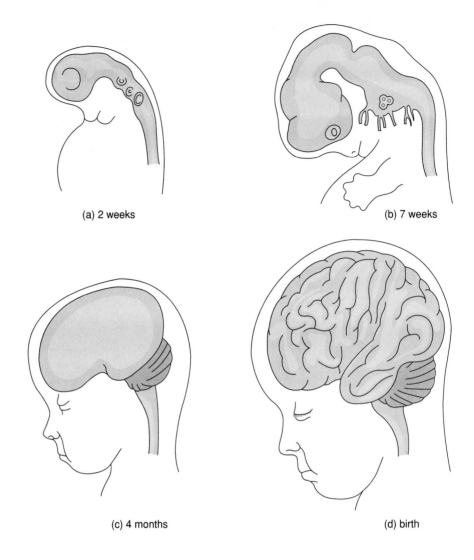

(a) 2 weeks

(b) 7 weeks

(c) 4 months

(d) birth

as 100 to 1,000 connections for each of the billions of neurons). This amazing complexity provides the biological basis for cognitive development (Fischbach, 1992). Estimates are that the baby's brain at birth is about a quarter of its adult size. At 6 months it's about 50 percent of its adult weight, 60 percent at 1 year, 75 percent at 2½ years, 90 percent at 6 years, and 95 percent at 10 years. The developmental pattern is seen in Figure 5.1.

At birth, the baby's experiences add a new dimension to the brain's wiring process. For example, the range of a baby's pleasant and unpleasant experiences begin to shape an infant's emotional life; the degree to which parents talk to their babies, the more complex will be their wiring for language; when babies have the opportunity to interact with appropriate toys and objects, the more refined their circuitry for motor control becomes.

Two patterns of development are apparent in the first two years following birth. The first relates to the brain's functional areas. For example, the motor area is the most advanced (for survival purposes) followed in descending order by the sensory area, the visual area, and the auditory area. The association areas—the areas devoted to thinking and reasoning—are the slowest to develop. By two-years-of-age, development in the sensory area slows and the association area shows signs of rapid development (Tanner, 1989).

Each of the brain's four lobes (frontal, parietal, temporal, and occipital) exercises specialized functions. For example, the frontal lobe contains the motor area for control of all the skeletal muscles; the parietal lobe seems to be the controlling center for the body's sense areas; the temporal lobe manages auditory functions; the occipital lobe analyzes visual information. Brain structures for thinking are

TABLE 5.1 NEONATAL REFLEXES

Name of Reflex	How Elicited	Description of Response
Plantar grasp	Press thumbs against the balls of the infant's foot	Toes tend to curl
Babinski	Gently stroke lateral side of sole of foot	Toes spread in an outward and upward manner
Babkin	Press palm of hand while infant lies on back	Mouth opens; eyes close
Rooting	Gently touch cheek of infant with light finger pressure	Head turns toward finger in effort to suck
Sucking	Mouth contacts nipple of breast or bottle	Mouth and tongue used to manipulate (suck) nipple
Moro	Loud noise or sudden dropping of infant	Stretches arms and legs and then hugs self; cries
Grasping	Object or finger is placed in infant's palm	Fingers curl around object
Tonic neck reflex	Place infant flat on back	Infant assumes fencer position: turns head and extends arm and leg in same direction as head
Stepping	Support infant in upright position; soles of feet brush surface	Infant attempts regular progression of steps

diffused throughout the cortical area, which makes considerable sense when you think (!!!) about answering a question. You listen to the question (auditory area); you respond by speaking (motor area); you search your memory.

At birth, of course, the infant must assume those life-sustaining functions that the mother provided for nine months, which leads us to an analysis of the important role that native reflexes play.

Neonatal Reflexes

When a stimulus repeatedly elicits the same response, that behavior is usually called a **reflex.** Popular examples include the eye blink and the knee jerk. All of the activities needed to sustain life's functions are present at birth (breathing, sucking, swallowing, elimination). These reflexes serve a definite purpose: The gag reflex enables infants to spit up mucus; the eye blink protects the eyes from excessive light; an antismothering reflex facilitates breathing.

In an attempt to rank an infant's reflexes in order of importance, Harris and Liebert (1992) note that the most crucial reflexes are those associated with breathing. Breathing patterns are not fully established at birth, and sometimes infants briefly stop breathing. These periods are called **apnea,** and although there is some concern that apnea may be associated with sudden infant death, these periods are quite common in all infants. Usually they last for about 2 to 5 seconds; episodes that extend from about 10 to 20 seconds may suggest the possibility of a problem. Sneezing and coughing are both reflexes that help to clear air passages.

Next in importance are those reflexes associated with feeding. Infants suck and swallow during the prenatal period and continue at birth. They also demonstrate the rooting reflex, in which they'll turn toward a nipple or a finger placed on the cheek and attempt to get it into the mouth. Table 5.1 describes some of the more important neonatal reflexes.

Newborn Abilities

In the days immediately following birth until about two weeks to one month, the infant is called a **neonate.** During this period, babies immediately begin to use their abilities to adapt to their environment. Among the most significant of these are the following:

Sample photographs of a model's happy, surprised, and sad expressions, and an infant's corresponding expressions.

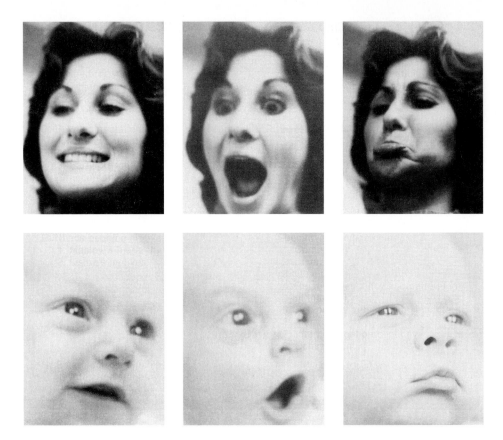

- *Infants display clear signs of imitative behavior at 7 to 10 days.* (Try this: Stick out your tongue at a baby who is about 10 days old. What happens? The baby will stick its tongue out at you!) Here neonates are telling us that they have the ability to imitate almost immediately after birth, an ability that should alert parents to immediately demonstrate desirable behavior for their children to learn and imitate.

  Infants' imitation of such tongue movements as just described is well established in babies as young as a few hours to more than six weeks of age (Jones, 1996). The evidence is clear, but interpretations vary. Some researchers, such as Jones (1996), argue that this type of behavior is more exploratory than imitative. Other researchers believe that the baby's behavior is innate, ready to be used when activated by adults (Abravanel & DeYoung, 1991). (This belief attributes the baby's response to *innate releasing mechanisms* in all humans.)

- *Infants can see at birth* and, if you capture their attention with an appropriate object (such as a small, red rubber ball held at about 10 inches from the face), they will track it as you move the ball from side to side. Infants react to color at between 2 and 4 months; depth perception appears at about 4 to 5 months (Brazelton & Nugent, 1995).

- *Infants not only can hear at birth (and prenatally), but they also can perceive the direction of the sound.* In a famous yet simple experiment, Michael Wertheimer (1962) sounded a clicker (similar to those children play with) from different sides of a delivery room only 10 minutes after an infant's birth. The infant not only reacted to the noise, but attempted to turn in the direction of the sound, indicating that children immediately tune into their environment and *understand* how they are being spoken to, either lovingly or harshly, which affects their reactions to those around them (Olds, London, & Ladewig, 1996).

- *Infants are active seekers of stimulation.* Infants want—actually need—people, sounds, and physical contact to stimulate their cognitive development and to give them a feeling of security in their world. Remember that infants are

Before continuing your reading, try to decide how competent you think a newborn baby is. In one view, infants are empty, unresponsive beings merely waiting for things to be done to and for them. They become active, healthy babies only because of maturation and the actions of those around them.

In another view, newborns are seen as amazingly competent and capable of much more than is now expected of them. Adherents of this belief view infants as "Super Babies," capable of prodigious accomplishments from birth, if not before. Consequently, from the first months of an infant's life, infants need some form of education.

In a third view, infants are seen as neither passive objects nor as superbabies, designed for instant greatness. Newborn babies are seen as bringing abilities with them into the world, a cluster of competencies that enables them to survive but also permits them to engage in a wider range of activities than was previously suspected (Brazelton & Nugent, 1995). Babies "tune into" their environments—they react to the tone of an adult's voice, they

sense how they're being handled (gently or roughly)—and are quite skillful in detecting the moods of those around them. Adherents of this view advise: Let them be babies, using the natural methods that have proven successful: love, attention, and warmth.

The expectations that parents have for their babies determine how they treat their babies and these expectations have important physical, cognitive, and psychosocial consequences. Ask your parents to think back on their child-bearing days and try to recall how competent they thought babies were. Ask them if it made any difference in how they treated you. If you have brothers or sisters or friends with children, ask them what they expected a newborn baby would be like?

Combining their practical outlook on infancy with what you have read, decide which of the above three views of infancy you think is most realistic. Which will most help infants to fulfill their potential? What's your view? (Note: After you have read this Chapter, return to this box and see if you would answer the question in the same way.)

engaged in a subtle, though powerful battle to establish control over their bodies. For example, they are struggling to regulate their bodily functions such as eating, breathing, and heart rate. But for brief moments, perhaps for only 15 or 20 seconds, they stop these efforts and pay close attention to the environment in a search for stimulation. This happens even when they are hungry.

One of the authors takes students to Boston's Children Hospital for observation visits, and attempts to find a nurse bottle-feeding an infant. Watching what happens when someone moves into the baby's field of vision, they are surprised at the baby's reaction. *The baby stops sucking and stares intently at that person's face!* Not for long, but long enough to interrupt feeding. Now you may not be too impressed with this, but think about it. An infant's hunger drive is extremely powerful, yet momentarily, the need for stimulation is even stronger, indicating that infants show a willingness, even a need, to interact with other human beings.

- *Infants, using these abilities, begin their efforts to master the developmental tasks of the first two years:* learning to take solid foods, learning to talk, learning to walk.

Neonatal Assessment Techniques

Although all infants are born with these reflexes and abilities, not all possess them to the same degree. For example, some neonates demonstrate much weaker reflex action than others, a condition that affects their chances of surviving. Consequently, efforts to develop reliable measures of early behavior, called *neonatal assessment,* have increased sharply.

Three basic classifications of neonatal tests are used to assess infant reflexes and behavior: *the Apgar scale, neurological assessment,* and *behavioral assessment.*

1. *The Apgar.* In 1953 Virginia Apgar proposed a scale to evaluate a newborn's basic life signs. The **Apgar** is administered one minute after

TABLE 5.2 PHYSICAL GROWTH—INFANCY		
Age (months)	**Height (in.)**	**Weight (lb.)**
3	24	13–14
6	26	17–18
9	28	20–22
12	29.5	22–24
18	32	25–26
24	34	27–29

birth and repeated at three-, five-, and ten-minute intervals. Using five life signs—heart rate, respiratory effort, muscle tone, reflex irritability, and skin color—an observer evaluates the infant by a three-point scale. Each of the five dimensions receives a score of 0, 1, or 2. (0 indicates severe problems, whereas 2 suggests an absence of major difficulties.)

2. *Neurological Assessment.* The **neurological assessment** is used for three purposes:

- Identification of any neurological problem
- Constant monitoring of a neurological problem
- Prognosis about some neurological problem

   Each of these purposes requires testing the infant's reflexes, which is critical for neurological evaluation and basic for all infant tests.

3. *Behavioral Assessment.* The **Brazelton Neonatal Behavioral Assessment Scale** (named after T. Berry Brazelton) has become a significant worldwide tool for infant assessment. Brazelton and Nugent (1995) believe that the baby's state of consciousness (sleepy, drowsy, alert, fussy) is the single most important element in the examination.

   Although the Brazelton tests the reflexes we have just discussed, its major emphasis is on how the infant interacts with its environment. In other words, it also permits us to examine the infant's behavior, which, as we have mentioned, is sensitive to cultural differences. (For an excellent discussion of the role of culture in the origins of individual differences in neonatal behavior, see Nugent and others, 1995).

All three of these assessment techniques provide clues about the infant's ability to function on its own. Tests such as these, plus careful observation, have given us much greater insight into infant development. These tests have also helped us to realize that infants are much more competent than we previously suspected.

To summarize, then, we can say that infant growth occurs at a rate unequaled in any other developmental period, with the possible exception of adolescence. If you recall, the average weight at birth is about 7 pounds and length is about 20 inches. Table 5.2 illustrates height and weight increases during infancy.

Given the rapid development of the brain and the survival value of the reflexes, we should expect motor development to proceed rapidly, which is just what happens.

Motor Development

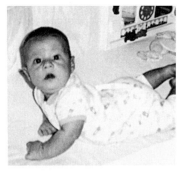

Note the steady development of body control in this picture, especially the head and upper body. Control of the lower body and legs follows by several months.

One of the key markers that parents use to measure their child's development is motor development: Is she sitting up on time? Shouldn't she be crawling by now? I wonder if she'll ever walk. Why can't she hold her head steady? Since motor development occurs in a head-to-feet direction (called *cephalocaudal*), as opposed to a *proximodistal* direction (from the center of the body to the extremities), an in-

An Applied View

Toilet Training—Easy or Difficult?

By the end of their child's infancy period, most parents begin to think about toilet training. One important fact to remember is that voluntary control of the sphincter muscles, which are the muscles that control elimination, does not occur until about the 18th month. (For some children, control is not possible until about 30 months.) Attempting to train children before they are ready can only cause anxiety and stress for the child and frustration for the parents (Brazelton, 1990).

Children really can't be trained; they learn when to use the toilet. It is not something parents do to a child; rather, parents help the child without feelings of tension and fear. Certain signs of readiness can alert parents that they can initiate the process.

- Necessary muscle control does not occur until well into the second year.
- A child must be able to communicate, either by words or gesture, the need to use the bathroom.
- At about 2 years, almost all children want to use the toilet, to become more "grown-up," and to rid themselves of the discomfort of wet or soiled diapers.

Parents should try to obtain equipment that the child feels most comfortable with—either a chair that sits on the floor or one that fits over the toilet seat. Here are estimates for ages of control:

- Most children start training at from 24–30 months.
- The average age of daytime control was 28.5 months.
- The average age of nighttime control was 33.3 months. (Girls attain nighttime control about two and a half months before boys.)

Most parents expect their children to be toilet trained by the end of infancy, usually sometime between 2 and 3 years of age. Physiologically, most children are ready to learn control; socially it is desirable; psychologically it may be traumatic unless parents are careful. If youngsters are punished for a behavior that they find difficult to master, their perception of the environment is affected, which may produce feelings of insecurity. The common sense of most adults results in a combination of firmness and understanding, thus helping youngsters master a key developmental task.

---

fant's ability to control its head signals advancing motor development. Here are several important characteristics of motor control.

Head Control

The most obvious initial head movements are from side to side, although the 1-month-old infant occasionally lifts its head when in a prone position. Four-month-old infants can hold their heads steady while sitting and will lift their head and shoulders to a 90-degree angle when on their abdomens. By the age of 6 months, most youngsters can balance their heads quite well.

Locomotion: Crawling and Creeping

Crawling and creeping are two distinct developmental phases. In **crawling,** the infant's abdomen touches the floor and the weight of the head and shoulders rests on the elbows. Locomotion is mainly by arm action. The legs usually drag, although some youngsters push with their legs. Most youngsters can crawl after age 7 months.

Creeping is more advanced than crawling, since movement is on hands and knees and the trunk does not touch the ground. After age 9 months, most youngsters can creep.

Most descriptions of crawling and creeping are quite uniform. The progression is from propulsion on the abdomen to quick, accurate movements on hands and knees, but the sequence is endlessly varied. Youngsters adopt a bewildering diversity of positions and movements that can only loosely be grouped together.

Locomotion: Standing and Walking

After about age 7 months, infants when held will support most of their weight on their legs. Coordination of arm and leg movements enables babies to pull themselves up and grope toward control of leg movements. The first steps are a propul-

Most youngsters somewhere in the 7 to 9 month period begin to pull themselves up to a standing position. Their legs are now strong enough to support them while standing.

TABLE 5.3 MILESTONES IN MOTOR DEVELOPMENT

Age	Head Control	Grasping	Sitting	Creeping, Crawling	Standing, Walking
1–3 months	Can lift head and chest while prone	Grasps objects, briefly holds objects, carries objects to mouth	Sits awkwardly with support		
4–8 months	Holds head steady while sitting, balances head	Develops skillful use of thumb	Transition from sitting with slight support to brief periods without support		
8–12 months	Has established head control	Coordinates hand activities, handedness begins to appear	Good trunk control, sits alone steadily	Crawling movements appear at about 7 months (trunk touches floor)	Can stand and take steps holding on to something; by 12 months will pull self up
12–14 months		Handedness pronounced, holds crayon, marks lines	Can sit from standing position	Creeping (trunk raised from floor) begins at 9–10 months and continues until steady walking	Stands alone; begins to walk alone
18 months					Begins to run

sive, lunging forward. Gradually a smooth, speedy, and versatile gait emerges. The world now belongs to the infant.

Once babies begin to walk, their attention darts from one thing to another, thus quickening their perceptual development (our next topic). Tremendous energy and mobility, coupled with a growing curiosity, push infants to search for the boundaries of their world. It is an exciting time for youngsters but a watchful time for parents, since they must draw the line between encouraging curiosity and initiative and protecting the child from personal injury. The task is not easy. It is, however, a problem for all aspects of development: What separates unreasonable restraint from reasonable freedom?

Table 5.3 summarizes milestones in motor development.

Neonatal Problems

Not all infants enter the world unscathed. Occasionally the developmental sequence that we have just discussed does not run smoothly. Among the most prominent of possible problems are the following.

Failure to Thrive

The weight and height of **failure-to-thrive (FTT)** infants consistently remain far below normal. They are estimated to be in the bottom 3 percent of height and weight measures. They account for about 3 percent of pediatric hospital admissions.

There are two types of FTT, organic and nonorganic. *Organic FTT* accounts for 30 percent of FTT cases, and the problem is usually some gastrointestinal disease, occasionally a problem with the nervous system. *Nonorganic FTT,* much more difficult to diagnose and treat, lacks a physical cause. Consequently, researchers have looked to the environment and identified problems such as poverty, neglect, and often ignorance of good parenting practices. The seriousness of this problem is evident from the outlook for FTT infants: Almost 50 percent of them will continue to experience physical, cognitive, and behavioral problems (Blackman, 1997).

Sudden Infant Death Syndrome

Discussion of the survival value of reflexes introduces one of the most perplexing problems facing both parents and researchers, **sudden infant death syndrome (SIDS).** An estimated 4,000 infants 2 to 4 months old die each year from SIDS. There is little warning, although almost all cases are preceded by mild cold symptoms and usually occur in late winter or early spring.

SIDS rarely occurs before age 1 month or after age 1 year; most victims are between 2 and 4 months old. Deaths peak between November and March. Boys are more vulnerable than girls, in this case by a 3-to-2 margin (Donner, 1997).

SIDS is particularly devastating for parents because of the lack of warning. These infants are apparently normal. Parents put them in a crib for a nap or for the night and return later to find them dead (hence the common name, "crib death"). You can imagine the effect this has on parents, particularly the feelings of guilt: What did I do wrong? Why didn't I look in earlier? Why didn't I see that something was wrong? Today, special centers have been established to counsel grieving parents.

Although no definite answers to the SIDS dilemma have yet been found, current research points to a respiratory problem. Control of breathing resides in the brain stem, and autopsies have indicated that the SIDS infant may not have received sufficient oxygen while in the womb, a condition known as *fetal hypoxia.* Consequently, parents are being urged to be extremely cautious when their babies are sleeping: Keep them on their back as much as possible (Klonof-Cohen, 1997).

A startling twist in the analysis of SIDS deaths has recently led researchers to attribute *some* of these deaths to child abuse. One possible cause is called *Munchausen by proxy,* where a parent deliberately injures or kills a child to attract attention. (Munchausen by proxy is a variant of adult Munchausen in which victims inflict harm on themselves, again to seek attention and sympathy.) Remember, however, in the vast majority of SIDS cases (estimates range from 95–98%), the parents are blameless (Firstman & Talan, 1997). This bizarre finding will undoubtedly lead to more detailed studies.

Sleeping Disorders

Most sleeping disorders are less serious than FTT or SIDS. Nevertheless, infant sleeping problems negatively affect growth and trouble parents. As Ferber (1985, p. 15) stated:

> The most frequent calls I receive at the Center for Pediatric Sleep Disorders at Children's Hospital in Boston are from a parent or parents whose children are sleeping poorly. When the parent on the phone begins by telling me "I am at the end of my rope" or "We are at our wits' end" I can almost predict what will be said next.

Ferber went on to explain that typically the parent has a child between the ages of 5 months and 4 years who does not sleep readily at night and wakes repeatedly. Parents become tired, frustrated, and often angry. Frequently the relationship between the parents becomes tense.

Usually a sleeping disorder has nothing to do with parenting. Also, usually nothing is wrong with the child, either physically or mentally. Occasionally problems do exist; for example, a bladder infection or, with an older child, emotional factors causing night terrors. A sleep problem is not normal and should not be waited out.

Neonates sleep more than they do anything else (usually from 14 to 15 hours per day) and have three sleep patterns: light or restless, periodic, and deep. Little, if any, activity occurs during deep sleep (about 25 percent of sleep). Neonates are mostly light sleepers and have the brain-wave patterns associated with dreaming (although infants probably do not dream).

Some internal clock seems to regulate sleep patterns, with most deep sleep spells lasting approximately 20 minutes. At the end of the second week, a consistent and predictable pattern emerges. Neonates sleep in short stretches, about seven or eight per day. The pattern soon reverses itself, and infants assume an adult's sleep schedule. Sleep patterns in infants range from about 16 to 17 hours in the first week to 13 hours at age 2.

Respiratory Distress Syndrome

The last of the disorders to be discussed is **respiratory distress syndrome** (also called hyaline membrane disease). Although this problem is most common with prematures, it may strike full-term infants whose lungs are particularly immature.

RDS is caused by the lack of a substance called *surfactant,* which keeps open the air sacs in the lungs. When surfactant is inadequate, the lung can collapse. Since most babies do not produce sufficient surfactant until the 35th prenatal week, you can see why it is a serious problem for prematures. (Only 10 percent of a baby's lung tissue is developed at full-term birth.)

Full-term newborns whose mothers are diabetic seem especially vulnerable to RDS. Babies whose delivery has been particularly difficult also are more susceptible. The good news is that today 90 percent of these youngsters will survive and, given early detection and treatment, the outlook for them is excellent.

Nutrition

Developed countries have nearly eliminated malnutrition, although the familiar suspects of poverty, illness, and neglect can still cause considerable nutritional damage. In developed countries this issue focuses on concerns about the relative benefits of breast versus formula feeding. Newborn infants have a special need for protein, given the rapid tissue building occurring during these days. Their high metabolic rates also consume large amounts of their energy, thus they require substantial amounts of proteins, fats, carbohydrates, minerals, and vitamins—especially iron, zinc, and calcium (Moore, 1997).

Although breast versus formula has almost always caused controversy, it's interesting to note that breast-feeding in the United States declined noticeably from 1984 to 1989 (Lutz & Przytulski, 1997). Given the recent attention about the benefits of breast-feeding and the national goal of having 75 percent of mothers breastfeed, the trend has been reversed.

The composition of breast milk varies during the first weeks following birth. For the first 3 or 4 days, it's known as *colostrum,* a thin, yellowish fluid that is high in proteins. *Transitional milk* then appears until about the end of the second week. Finally, *mature milk* is available (Moore, 1997).

Guided Review

1. A _____ is a behavior in which a repeated stimulus elicits the same response.
2. The _____ is administered one minute after birth and measures, among other things, a newborn's muscle tone and skin color.
3. The _____ is a neonatal assessment technique that measures how an infant interacts with the environment.
4. Motor development occurs in a _____ to _____ direction.
5. The weight and height of _____ infants consistently remain below normal.

Answers

1. reflex 2. Apgar 3. Brazelton 4. head, foot 5. FTT

Infants quickly begin to attend to the objects in their environments, thus constructing their views about how the world "works."

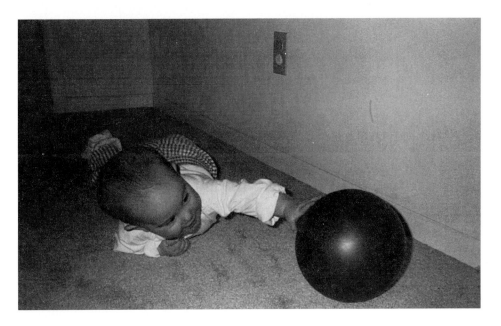

Field, T. (1990). *Infancy.* Cambridge, MA: Harvard University Press. A clear, simple, and carefully written account of infancy by a well-known commentator on these years.

Breast-feeding leads to two advantages that can't be duplicated by formula feeding. First is the protection against disease offered by a mother's milk. Breast-fed babies seem to have a lesser degree of illness than formula-fed babies, an important consideration in developing countries. Second, breast-fed babies are less at risk for allergic reactions than are formula-fed babies.

On the other hand, one of the advantages of formula feeding is that others, including the father, can feed the baby. Commercial formulas are good, containing more proteins than breast milk. Assuming that the formula is appropriate, nutritional problems should not arise. In the United States, infants are usually well-nourished either through breast or formula feeding. Other considerations, such as returning to work, may influence a woman's decision to either breast or formula feed (Lutz & Przytulski, 1997).

Perceptual Development

From what we've said so far, the current picture of an infant is that of an active, vibrant individual vigorously searching for stimuli. How do infants process these stimuli? Answering this question moves us into the perceptual world. We know now that babies not only receive stimuli, they interpret them. For example, Lewkowicz (1996) reported that when an investigator used both her voice and face as stimuli, 4, 6, and 8-month-old infants responded better to the combination of stimuli than to face or voice alone. Before attempting to chart perceptual development, let's explore the meaning of perception in a little more detail.

The Meaning of Perception

Infants acquire information about the world and constantly check the validity of that information. This process defines *perception:* getting and interpreting information from stimuli. Infants are particularly ingenious at obtaining information from the stimuli around them. They attend to objects according to the perceptual information the objects contain. As Bornstein (1995) noted, during infancy the capacity to take in information through the major sensory channels, to make sense of the environment, and to attribute meaning to information improve dramatically.

Seeking information leads to meaning. Objects roll, bounce, or squeak—in this way infants learn what objects are and what they do. During infancy, youngsters discover what they can do with objects, which furthers their perceptual development.

Remember: Infants are born ready to attend to changes in physical stimulation. Stimuli presented frequently causes a decrease in an infant's attention (**habituation**). If the stimuli are altered, the infant again attends, indicating awareness of the difference. For example, if you show an infant a picture (flower, birds, anything attractive), the child is first fascinated, then becomes bored; the child has habituated. If you now change the picture, you again capture the child's attention.

Infants, however, encounter a wide variety of objects, people, and events, all of which differ in many dimensions: color, size, shape. They must learn how to react to each, and how they react depends on many factors. For example, Clifton, Perris, and Bullinger (1991) found that when 6- and 7-month-old infants were in a dark setting and were presented with objects that made a sound, they reached accurately for the objects as long as they were within their reach. When the objects were out of reach, the infants were far less accurate. They thus perceive distance and direction and seem able to define their auditory space as long as an object is within reach of the body.

In a classic study, Brooks and Lewis (1976) studied how infants responded to four different types of strangers, a male and female child, a female adult, and a female midget. In this way, facial configurations and height were varied. The infants reacted to the children by continuous looking and some smiling. They reacted to the midget with considerable puzzlement but no positive response such as smiling or movement toward her. They reacted to the adult by sporadic looking, averting their eyes, frowning, and even crying. Thus the infants used size and facial configuration cues.

We may conclude, then, that perception depends on both learning and maturation. An infant's perceptual system undergoes considerable development following birth, resulting from greater familiarity with objects and events in the world as well as from growth.

Visual Perception

Infants are born able to see and quickly exhibit a preference for patterns. Do infants prefer looking at some objects more than others? In a pioneering series of experiments, Robert Fantz provided dramatic documentation of an infant's perceptual ability. Fantz (1961) stated that the best indicator of an infant's visual ability is eye activity. Infants who consistently gaze at some forms more than others show perceptual discrimination; that is, something in one form holds their attention.

A child's depth perception is tested on the visual cliff. The apparatus consists of a board laid across a sheet of heavy glass, with a patterned material directly beneath the glass on one side and several feet below it on the other.

Using a "looking chamber" in which an infant lies in a crib at the bottom of the chamber and looks at objects placed on the ceiling, Fantz could determine the amount of time that infants fixated on different objects. In one of his experiments, Fantz tested pattern perception by using six objects, all flat discs 6 inches in diameter: face, bull's-eye, newsprint, red disc, yellow disc, and white disc.

The face attracted the greatest attention (human faces are remarkably complex), followed by the newsprint, the bull's-eye, and then the three plain-colored discs (none of which received much attention). Infants, then, show definite preferences based on as much complexity as they can handle (Lewkowicz, 1996).

Visual Adaptation

Studying visual development spurs speculation about how growing visual skill helps infants to adjust to their environment. Gibson and Walk (1960), in their famous "visual cliff" experiment, reasoned that infants would use visual stimuli to discriminate both depth and distance.

The visual cliff is a board dividing a large sheet of heavy glass. A checkerboard pattern is attached flush to one half of the bottom of the glass, giving the impression of solidity. The investigators then placed a similar sheet on the floor under the other half, creating a sense of depth—the visual cliff.

Thirty-six infants from ages 6 to 14 months were tested. After the infant was placed on the center board, the mother called the child from the shallow side and then the cliff side. Twenty-seven of the youngsters moved onto the shallow side toward the mother. When called from the cliff side, only three infants ventured over the depth. The experiment suggests that infants discriminate depth when they begin crawling.

To conclude, we can state that by 2 to 4 months of age, infant perception is fairly sophisticated. Infants perceive figures as organized wholes; they react to the relationship among elements rather than single elements; they perceive color; and complex rather than simple patterns fascinate them. They scan the environment, pick up information, encode and process information. Why? Because they are well equipped to hear, to orient to, to perceive, and to distinguish sounds (Bornstein & Lamb, 1992).

Guided Review

6. The decrease in an infant's attention to stimuli presented frequently is called _____.

7. Investigators have discovered that using face plus _____ improves an infant's perceptual response.

8. A child's depth perception is tested on an apparatus called a _____ _____.

9. Neonates require about _____ hours of sleep per day.

10. Perception depends on _____ and _____.

Cognitive Development

How do infants develop an understanding of the world around them? Can infants really think? If they can, what is their thinking like? How do we explain the change in thinking from the newborn to the 2-year-old?

In their first year of life, infants seem to proceed through several stages. In the first month, they have no idea that objects are permanent—out of sight, out of mind. From 1 to 4 months, infants will continue to stare at the spot where an object disappeared and then turn their attention to something else. From 4 to 8 months, infants begin to show signs that an object still exists even if they can't see it; they'll look for a toy after they drop it; they love playing peek-a-boo. From 8 to 12 months, infants develop the notion of **object permanence** and will continue to hunt for a hidden object.

Recent studies indicate that object permanence is related to later cognitive development suggesting that roots of cognition lie in infancy. For example, Rose and his associates (1991) compared object permanence (among other cognitive indicators) in premature infants at 1 year with IQ measures at 5 years. They found a significant relationship between the two, suggesting developmental continuities in cognition.

To discover how infants develop such concepts as object permanence, we now turn to the work of the great Swiss scholar, Jean Piaget. You previously read about several of his important ideas in Chapter 2; here we'll examine his interpretation of infancy in some detail.

Piaget's Sensorimotor Period

Piaget (1967) stated that the period from birth to language acquisition is marked by extraordinary mental growth and influences the entire course of development. **Egocentrism** describes the initial world of children. Everything centers on them; they see the world only from their point of view. Very young children lack social orientation. They speak at and not to each other, and two children in conversation may be discussing utterly unrelated topics. (Likewise, egocentric adults know that other

Answers

6. habituation 7. voice 8. visual cliff 9. 14 10. learning, maturation

viewpoints exist, but they disregard them.) The egocentric child simply is unaware of any other viewpoint.

The remarkable changes of the **sensorimotor period** (about the first two years of life) occur within a sequence of six stages. Most of Piaget's conclusions about these stages were derived from observation of his own three children. (Jacqueline, Lucianne, and Laurent have become as famous in psychological literature as some of Freud's cases or John Watson's Albert.)

Stage 1. During the first stage, children do little more than exercise the reflexes with which they were born. For example, Piaget (1952) stated that the sucking reflex is hereditary and functions from birth. At first infants suck anything that touches their lips; they suck when nothing touches their lips; then they actively search for the nipple. What we see here is the steady development of the coordination of arm, eye, hand, and mouth. Through these activities, the baby is building a foundation for forming cognitive structures. (For a more extended discussion of the antecedents of these behaviors, see Smotherman & Robinson, 1996.)

Stage 2. Piaget referred to stage 2 (from about 1 to 4 months) as the stage of first habits. During stage 2, **primary circular reactions** appear, in which infants repeat some act involving their bodies. For example, they continue to suck when nothing is present. They continue to open and close their hands. Infants seem to have no external goal, no intent in these actions other than the pleasure of self-exploration. But they are learning something about that primary object in their world: their own bodies.

Stage 3. **Secondary circular reactions** emerge during the third stage, which extends from about 4 to 8 months. During this stage, infants direct their activities toward objects and events outside themselves. Secondary circular reactions thus produce results in the environment, and not, as with the primary circular reactions, on the child's own body.

For example, Piaget's son, Laurent, continued to shake and kick his crib to produce movement and sound. He also discovered that pulling a chain attached to some balls produced an interesting noise, and he kept doing it. In this way, babies learn about the world "out there," and feed this information into their developing cognitive structures.

Stage 4. From about 8 to 12 months of age, infants **coordinate secondary schemes** to form new kinds of behavior. Now more complete acts of intelligence are evident (Piaget & Inhelder, 1969).

The baby first decides on a goal (finding an object that is hidden behind a cushion). The infant attempts to move objects to reach the goal. In stage 4, part of the goal object must be visible behind the obstacle. Here we see the first signs of intentional behavior.

Stage 5. **Tertiary circular reactions** appear from 12 to 18 months of age. In the tertiary circular reaction, repetition occurs again, but it is repetition with variation. The infant is exploring the world's possibilities. Piaget thought that the infant deliberately attempts to provoke new results instead of merely reproducing activities. Tertiary circular reactions indicate an interest in novelty for its own sake.

How many times have you seen a baby standing in a crib and dropping everything on the floor? But listen to Piaget: Watch how the baby drops things, from different locations and different heights. Does it sound the same when it hits the floor as the rug? Is it as loud dropped from here or higher? Each repetition is actually a chance to learn. Thanks to Piaget, you will be a lot more patient when you see this behavior.

Stage 6. During stage 6, the sensorimotor period ends and children develop a basic kind of *internal representation*. A good example is the behavior of Piaget's daugh-

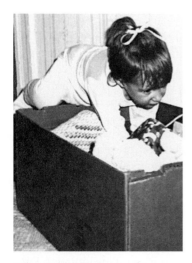

When infants begin to move things to get what they want, they are "coordinating secondary schemata." This is a clear signal of advancing cognitive development.

TABLE 5.4 OUTSTANDING CHARACTERISTICS OF THE SENSORIMOTOR PERIOD

The Six Subdivisions of This Period

Stage 1	During the first month the child exercises the native reflexes, for example, the sucking reflex. Here is the origin of mental development, for states of awareness accompany the reflex mechanisms.
Stage 2	Piaget referred to stage 2 (from 1 to 4 months) as the stage of primary circular reactions. Infants repeat some act involving the body, for example, finger sucking. (Primary means first, circular reaction means repeating the act.)
Stage 3	From 4 to 8 months, secondary circular reactions appear; that is, the children repeat acts involving objects outside themselves. For example, infants continue to shake or kick the crib.
Stage 4	From 8 to 12 months, the child "coordinates secondary schemes." Recall the meaning of schema—behavior plus mental structure. During stage 4, infants combine several related schemata to achieve some objective. For example, they will remove an obstacle that blocks some desired object.
Stage 5	From 12 to 18 months, tertiary circular reactions appear. Now children repeat acts, but not only for repetition's sake; now they search for novelty. For example, children of this age continually drop things. Piaget interpreted such behavior as expressing their uncertainty about what will happen to the object when they release it.
Stage 6	At about 18 months or 2 years, a primitive type of representation appears. For example, one of Piaget's daughters wished to open a door but had grass in her hands. She put the grass on the floor and then moved it back from the door's movement so that it would not blow away.

As infants acquire the ability to form representations of objects, they begin to move through their environments more skillfully.

ter, Jacqueline. At age 20 months, she approached a door that she wished to close, but she was carrying some grass in each hand. She put down the grass by the threshold, preparing to close the door. But then she stopped and looked at the grass and the door, realizing that if she closed the door the grass would blow away. She then moved the grass away from the door's movement and then closed it. She had obviously planned and thought carefully about the event before acting. Table 5.4 summarizes the accomplishments of the sensorimotor period.

Progress through the sensorimotor period leads to four major accomplishments:

- *Object permanence:* Children realize that permanent objects exist around them; something out of sight is not gone forever.

- *A sense of space:* Children realize environmental objects have a spatial relationship.

- *Causality:* Children realize a relationship exists between actions and their consequences.

- *Time sequences:* Children realize that one thing comes after another.

By the end of the sensorimotor period, children move from purely sensory and motor functioning (hence the name sensorimotor) to a more symbolic kind of activity.

Criticisms of Piaget

Although Piaget has left a monumental legacy, his ideas have not been unchallenged. Piaget was a believer in the stage theory of development; that is, development is seen as a sequence of distinct stages, each of which entails important changes in the way a child thinks, feels, and behaves. However, the acquisition of cognitive structures may be gradual rather than abrupt and is not a matter of all or nothing; for example, a child is not completely in the sensorimotor or preoperational stage. A child's level of cognitive development seems to depend more on the nature of the task than on a rigid classification system.

In one of the first important challenges to Piaget, Gelman & Baillargeon (1983), changed the nature of the task as follows:

- By reducing the number of objects children must manipulate

- By allowing children to practice (e.g., teaching children conservation tasks)

- By using materials familiar to children

These researchers found that children can accomplish specific tasks at earlier ages than Piaget believed. Such criticisms have led to a more searching examination of the times during which children acquire certain cognitive abilities. For example, Piaget believed that infants will retrieve an object that is hidden from them in stage 4, from 8 to 12 months. Before this age, if a blanket is thrown over a toy that the infant is looking at, the child stops reaching for it as if it doesn't exist.

To trace the ages at which object permanence appears, Baillargeon (1987) devised an experiment in which infants between 3½ and 4½ months old were seated at a table where a cardboard screen could be moved back and forth, either forward (toward the baby) until it was flat on the table or backward (away from the baby) until the back of the cardboard touched the table.

Baillargeon then placed a painted wooden block behind the cardboard screen so that the infant could see the block when the screen was in a forward, flat position. But when the screen was moved backward, it came to rest on the block, removing it from the infant's sight. Occasionally Baillargeon secretly removed the block so that the screen continued backward until it rested flat on the table. The 4½-month-old infants looked surprised at the change (they looked at the screen longer); even some of the 3½-month-olds seemed to notice the "impossible" event. These findings suggest that infants may develop the object permanence concept earlier than Piaget originally thought.

Infants and Memory

As infants progress through these first two years, behavior appears that can only be attributed to memory. The last half of the first year appears to be a time of rapid growth in memory ability (Schacter, 1996). Our discussion of Piaget's belief in the appearance of object permanence between 8 and 12 months is a good example of increasing memory ability. Analyzing the appearance of memory, Kail (1990, p. 1) states that between 4 and 7 months, a marvelous change occurs in the relationship between infants and their parents.

At 4 months, infants can distinguish between human and nonhuman objects in their environment (they smile and babble more to the human figures), but they are just as likely to smile at strangers as at parents. By 7 months, this has changed; infants will not smile at strangers and may appear threatened by them. (We'll discuss the psychosocial reasons for this change in Chapter 6. Here we'll concentrate on cognitive explanations.)

Testing Infant Memory

As you can well imagine, testing infant memory is difficult because infants can't tell us whether or what they remembered. Consequently, investigators have relied on experiments that measure the time that infants look at familiar and novel objects. Kail (1990) gives the example of presenting two groups of infants with a bull's-eye pattern and a set of stripes. One group saw the bull's-eye first and then the stripes; the other group had the procedure reversed: first the stripes and then the bull's-eye. If both groups looked longer at the second presentation (the stripes for the first group and the bull's-eye for the second), it shows that they preferred the novel stimuli, thus giving evidence of infant memory. That is, they remembered the first and habituated and were then more interested in the novel stimulus.

Newborns seem to recognize events they have heard or seen before (recall DeCasper's work that we mentioned in Chapter 4). By 2 to 3 months, infants will remember an event for several days, perhaps as long as a week. Memory continues to improve as infants "economize," that is, rather than remembering specific events, they begin to integrate their experiences (Shields & Rovee-Collier, 1992). This helps to explain how they find hidden objects (such as in the object permanence exper-

An Applied VIEW

What Do Infants Think About?

Examining cognitive development in infancy may lead you to say: Well, yes, infants are much more competent than I thought, but what do they think about? What do they feel? Answering these questions takes us from the observational and experimental world we have just explored into a psychodynamic view of infancy.

A Path of Sunshine: 7:05 A.M.

A space glows over there. A gentle magnet pulls to capture. The space is growing warmer and coming to life. Inside it, forces start to turn around one another in a slow dance. (Stern, 1990, p. 55.)

Stern, a sensitive interpreter of an infant's thoughts and feelings, has used these words to describe how a path of brilliant sunshine can attract an infant's attention. Infants react to attractive stimuli for all the reasons we have described in this chapter: intensity and complexity of the stimulation, visual ability, and the need for novelty. As we watch infants react to such stimuli, we may ask what subjective experiences accompany these behaviors.

We can't crawl inside an infant's mind, but speculating about what an infant's experiences may be like can shape our idea of what an infant is. We saw a good example of the power of these ideas in chapter 2. Freud's notion of infancy as a period seething with emotions is in stark contrast to Piaget's belief that the infant is like a little scientist busily constructing a model of its world. Both these theorists have made inferences about an infant's subjective experiences.

Is there a starting point for attempting to explain an infant's subjective experiences of its own social life? An infant's sense of self is probably the best guide for us to follow, because the qualitative changes we see in development testify to new forms of personality integration (Stern, 1990). Infants, as they undergo these changes, seem to portray a new "presence" or "social feel." For example, when an infant smiles into a parent's eyes and coos at about 3 months of age, it is more than a change of behavior. As observers, we recognize something unique and we react differently.

Stern (1990) believed that infants are predesigned to be aware of these self-organizing processes and experience four different senses of self:

- *The emergent self* appears in the time from birth to 2 months. If you observe infants of this age, they show joy, distress, anger, and surprise, clear signs of subjective experience.

- *The core self* emerges between 2 and 4 months. Infants use memory and a growing sense of physical competence to organize their experiences. They slowly realize that their actions have consequences.
- *The subjective self* develops between 7 and 15 months. Infants begin to realize that they can share their experiences with others; for example, the mother knows the infant wants the cookies, and the child knows the mother knows. How many times have you seen a child of this age find something and smilingly show it to the mother?
- *The verbal self* follows after 15 months. From this time on, language and symbolic play are tangible clues about what is occurring in the infant's subjective world.

We should also remember, however, that the subjective world of parents also influences their children's development. Parents tend to see their children in a way that relates to their own needs, values, desires, and experiences. For example, Brazelton and Cramer (1990) have identified three parental fantasies:

- *The infant as ghost,* in which the baby reminds the parents of someone (usually dead), which in turn unleashes a flood of emotional feelings and may affect a parent's relationships with the child; Selma Fraiberg (1980) has referred to this situation as the "ghost in the nursery." Other researchers, however, view intergenerational relationships as a powerful force (Wakschlag, Chase-Lansdale, & Brooks-Gunn, 1996). In other words, the mother-grandmother relationship exercises considerable influence on parenting style.
- *A parent's relationship with the infant reenacts a past mode of relationship.* Parents sometimes seek to recapture the relationships of their childhood through interactions with the infant. A mother who teased and fought with her brothers and sisters, or who might have kept a distance from them, adopts that same pattern with her children.
- *The infant as part of the parent.* Some parents attempt to project part of their selves on the infant: lazy, greedy, determined, stubborn.

The fantasy worlds of infants and parents affect children's development, and parents should be aware of such tendencies and avoid them where possible.

iments); they can now recall things and events (Kail, 1990). The growth of memory ability is a significant developmental accomplishment of the last half of the first year of life (Perris & Myers, 1990). We may conclude that memory during infancy is highly specific to the conditions surrounding the original encoding and that the last items forgotten are the first to be retrieved (Hayne & Rovee-Collier, 1995).

Infantile Amnesia

If memory seems to develop early in our lives, why do we have difficulty in remembering most of our experiences in infancy? You undoubtedly look with considerable skepticism at those individuals who claim to remember events from the first days of their lives. More common for all of us is a phenomenon called **infantile amnesia,** which refers to an inability to recall events from early in life. Is it that time has eroded our memory of these early experiences? Or is it that we simply did not encode these happenings? Or have we encoded these experiences but cannot access them?

Perhaps, as Newcombe and Fox (1994) speculate, as humans we have two types of memory: **implicit memory,** which affects our behavior without our being aware of it, and **explicit memory,** which are those events in our lives that we consciously remember. With our present knowledge, we're probably well advised to agree with Kail (1990) when he concludes that from early in life humans seem to be able to remember sights, sounds, and odors.

> Infancy culminates with the development of representational thinking and language. In the first year, for example, play with objects is predominantly characterized by sensorimotor manipulation and mouthing and fingering, whose goal seems to be the extraction of information about objects. In the second year, children's object play takes on an increasingly symbolic quality as they enact activities performed by self, others, and objects in simple pretense scenarios, for example by pretending to drink from empty teacups or to talk on toy telephones. (Bornstein, 1995)

Harris, J. R. & Liebert, R. (1992). *Infant and child.* Englewood Cliffs, NJ: Prentice-Hall. A thorough, well-documented account of the early years; particularly strong in its use of the transactional model.

Guided Review

11. Piaget's first stage of cognitive development is known as the _____ period.
12. _____ describes a phase of child development in which children perceive the world only from their point of view.
13. _____ _____ is when a child realizes that an object out of sight is not gone forever.
14. Children at the end of the sensorimotor period clearly demonstrate their ability to _____ things.
15. Children in stage _____ of the sensorimotor period are able to move things to get what they want.

Language Development

In our discussion, you probably noticed that in the latter stages of the sensorimotor period, language becomes increasingly important. Indeed, one of the most amazing accomplishments of human beings is their acquisition of language. Infants tune into the speech they hear and immediately begin to discriminate distinctive features. They also seem to be sensitive to the context of the language they hear; that is, they identify the emotional quality of speech.

Consequently, the forerunners of language appear immediately after birth in infant gazes and vocal exchanges with those around them (Akhtar, Carpenter, & Tomasello, 1996). With no formal learning and often exposed to dramatically faulty language models, children learn words, meanings, and how to combine them in a purposeful manner.

Answers

11. sensorimotor 12. egocentrism 13. object permanence 14. represent 15. 4

Context and Language

The Russian psychologist, Lev Vygotsky, whose ideas we discussed in Chapter 2, proposed a contextual view of language development that attracted considerable attention. Vygotsky (1978) believed that *speech* is one of the most powerful tools humans use to progress developmentally. Speech, especially inner speech, plays a critical role in Vygotsky's interpretation of cognitive development. In *Thought and Language* (1962), he clearly presented his views about the four stages of language development.

1. The first stage, which he called **preintellectual speech,** refers to such elementary processes as crying, cooing, babbling, and bodily movements that gradually develop into more sophisticated forms of speech and behavior. Although human beings have an inborn ability to develop language, we must then interact with the environment if language development is to fulfill its potential. Michael Cole (1996) employs a garden metaphor to help explain these issues: Think of a seed planted in damp earth in a jar and then placed in a shed for two weeks. The seed sprouts, a stem emerges, and then leaves appear. But for further development the plant must now interact with sunlight.

2. Vygotsky referred to the second stage of language development as "naive psychology," in which children explore the concrete objects in their world. At this stage, children begin to label the objects around them and acquire the syntax of their speech.

3. At about 3-years-of-age *egocentric speech* emerges, that form of speech in which children carry on lively conversations, whether anyone is present or listening to them.

4. Finally, speech turns inward **(inner speech)** and serves an important function in guiding and planning behavior.

For example, think of a 5-year-old girl asked to get a book from a library shelf. The book is just out of her reach, and as she tries to reach it, she mutters to herself, "Need a chair." After dragging a chair over, she climbs up and reaches for the book. "Is that the one?" "Just a little more." "OK." Note how speech accompanies her physical movements, guiding her behavior. In two or three years, the same girl, asked to do the same thing, will probably act the same way, with one major exception: she won't be talking aloud. Vygotsky believed she would be talking to herself, using inner speech to guide her behavior, and for difficult tasks she undoubtedly would use inner speech *to plan her behavior.*

In many cases, children who aren't permitted these vocalizations *can't accomplish the task!* In fact, the more complex the task, the greater the need for egocentric speech. Note how Vygotsky and Piaget disagreed about the function of egocentric speech: Piaget believed it simply vanishes; Vygosky believed it's an important transitional stage in the formation of inner speech.

Acquiring Their Language

How does this uniquely human achievement occur? Students of language, attempting to explain the richness and complexity of children's language, are convinced that this feat is possible because of two accomplishments. First, *children learn the rules of their language,* which they then apply in a wide variety of situations. Second, by the end of the second year, *children begin to fast map;* that is, they learn to apply a label to an object without anyone telling them. Even when children don't understand a word, they acquire information about it from the surrounding context (Hulit & Howard, 1997).

The process of acquiring language goes on at a furious pace until, at about the age of 5 for most children, they have acquired the fundamentals of their language. By the time children enter elementary school, they are sophisticated language users. After that it's a matter of expanding and refining language skills, a task that can often define success or failure. The speed of acquisition and the fact that it generally occurs, without overt instruction, for all children, regardless of great differences in a range of social and cultural factors, have led to the belief that there is some "innate" predisposition in the human infant to acquire language (Yule, 1996).

As an example of the world into which language development takes children, consider some of the intricacies of the English language that we, as adults, understand completely. Do you realize that you drive on a parkway and park on a driveway? Do you realize that you eat *ghoti* quite frequently? (*gh* as in tough, *o* as in women, *ti* as in nation—put them all together and you're eating fish.)

These examples (Pinker, 1994) illustrate what should be a stupendous task for children. But no matter how much difficulty children have with mathematics, for example, they move through their linguistic world with comparative ease. This is not to say, of course, that we all reach the heights of eloquent expression. Still, normal children will acquire the basics of their language with comparative ease.

Remember, however, children usually understand more than they articulate, which can be an important consideration in your assessment of their progress. For example, there seems to be a consistent difference between the rates of their comprehension (understanding) and their language production (speech). In their excellent series of studies, Menyuk and her colleagues (1995) found that 1-year-old children understand 50 words five months before they can produce them. As these authors stated (1995, p. 175):

> There is a great deal of variation among the children we observed in the rate at which they develop aspects of language. For the most part, these differences in the rate of development did not result in apparent problems in language development. Most of the differences in the rate of development occur in the production of language.

With this brief background, let's turn our attention to what we know about language development. All children learn their native language at about the same time and in a similar manner. During the infancy period, children at about 3 months use sounds in a similar manner to adults and at about 1 year they begin to use recognizable words. The specific sequence of language development during infancy appears in table 5.5.

Key Signs of Language Development

In the first year, babies continue to learn the sounds of their language (Sansavini, Bertoncini, & Giovanelli, 1997). During the first two months, babies seem to develop sounds that are associated with breathing, feeding, and crying. **Cooing** (sounds like vowels) appears during the second month. Between 5 and 7 months, babies play with the sounds they can make, and this output begins to take on the sounds of consonants and syllables, the beginning of **babbling.** Babbling probably appears initially because of biological maturation. At 7 and 8 months, sounds like syllables appear—da-da-da, ba-ba-ba (a phenomenon occurring in all languages)— a pattern that continues for the remainder of the first year (Pinker, 1994).

Late in the babbling period, children use consistent sound patterns to refer to objects and events. These are called **vocables** and suggest children's discovery that meaning is associated with sound. For example, a lingering "L" sound may mean that someone is at the door. The use of vocables is a possible link between babbling and the first intelligible words.

TABLE 5.5 LANGUAGE DEVELOPMENT DURING INFANCY

Language	Age
Crying	From birth
Cooing	2–5 months
Babbling	5–7 months
Single words	12 months
Two words	18 months
Phrases	2 years

First Words

Around their first birthday, babies produce single words, about half of which are for objects (food, clothing, toys). At 18 months children acquire words at the rate of a new word every two hours (a condition that lasts until about 3 years of age and is frequently referred to as the **language explosion**). Vocabulary constantly expands, but estimating the extent of a child's vocabulary is difficult because youngsters know more words than they articulate (Woodward, Markman, & Fitzsimmons, 1994). Estimates are that a 1-year-old child may use from two to six words, and a 2-year-old has a vocabulary ranging from 50 to 250 words. Children at this stage also begin to combine two words (Pinker, 1994).

Holophrases. If you have the opportunity, listen to a child's speech when single words begin to appear. You will notice a subtle change before the two-word stage. *Children begin to use one word to convey multiple meanings.* For example, youngsters say "ball" meaning "give me the ball," "throw the ball," or "watch the ball roll." They have now gone far beyond merely labeling this round object as a ball. Often called **holophrastic speech** (one word to communicate many meanings and ideas), it is difficult to analyze. These first words, or **holophrases,** are usually nouns, adjectives, or self-inventive words and often contain multiple meanings. As mentioned previously, "ball" may mean not only the ball itself but "throw the ball to me."

When the two-word stage appears (anytime from 18 to 24 months), children initially struggle to convey tense (past and present) and number (singular and plural). They also experience difficulty with grammatical correctness. Children usually employ word order ("me go") for meaning, only gradually mastering inflections (plurals, tenses, possessives) as they begin to form three-word sentences. They use nouns and verbs initially and their sentences demonstrate grammatical structure. (Although the nouns, verbs, and adjectives of children's sentences differ from those of adults, the same organizational principles are present.)

Children begin to use multiple words to refer to the things that they previously named with single words. Rather than learning rules of word combination to express new ideas, children learn to use new word forms. Later, combining words in phrases and sentences suggests that children are learning the structure of their language.

Telegraphic Speech. At about 18 to 24 months of age children's vocabularies begin to expand rapidly, and simple two-word sentences appear. Children primarily use nouns and verbs (not adverbs, conjunctions, or prepositions), and their sentences demonstrate grammatical structure. These initial multiple-word utterances (usually two or three words: "Timmy runs fast") are called **telegraphic speech.** Telegraphic speech contains considerably more meaning than superficially appears in the two or three words.

Word order and inflection (changing word form: e.g., "word"/"words") now become increasingly important. During the first stages of language acquisition, word order is paramount. At first, children combine words without concern for inflections, and it is word order that provides clues as to their level of syntactic (grammatical) development. Once two-word sentences are used, inflection soon appears, usually with three-word sentences. The appearance of inflections seems to follow a pattern: first the plural of nouns, then tense and person of verbs, and then possessives. (Table 5.6 summarizes several of the developmental highlights we have discussed in this Chapter.)

A youngster's effort to inject grammatical order into language is a good sign of normal language development. Several things, however, signal delay or difficulty in language acquisition. When children begin to babble beyond one year, problems may be present. For example, deaf children continue to babble past the age when other children begin to use words (Cole & Cole, 1996). Let's now look at several language accomplishments in more detail.

TABLE 5.6 DEVELOPMENTAL CHARACTERISTICS OF INFANCY

Age (months)	Height (in.)	Weight (lbs.)	Language Development	Motor Development	Cognitive (Piaget)
3	24	13–14	Cooing	Supports head in prone position	Primary circular reactions
6	26	17–18	Babbling—single syllable sounds	Sits erect when supported	Secondary circular reactions
9	26	20–22	Repetition of sounds signals emotions	Stands with support	Coordinate secondary schemata
12	29.5	22–24	Single words—mama, dada	Walks when held by hand	Same
18	32	25–26	3–50 words	Grasps objects accurately, walks steadily	Tertiary circular reaction
24	34	27–29	50–250 words, 2–3 word sentences	Walks and runs up and down stairs	Representation

Pinker, S. (1994). *The language instinct.* New York: Morrow. You would enjoy this fascinating, well-written account of the nature of language and how humans acquire their language.

As we complete this initial phase of examining infant development, remember that all phases of development come together in an integrated manner. Motor development is involved when a child moves excitedly toward its mother on her return. Language development is involved when infants intensify their relationships with their mothers by words that are now directed toward her. Cognitive development is probably less obvious but just as significant: Children are excited by their mothers' return because they remember their mothers. Consequently, a sound principle of development remains—all development is integrated.

Guided Review

16. _____ is sounds that approximate speech.
17. One word used to communicate many meanings is called _____ speech.
18. Vygotsky's work reflects a _____ view of language development.
19. A good sign of normal language development is a child's attempt to build _____ order into language.
20. For Vygotsky, _____ _____ plays a key role in cognitive development.

CONCLUSION

Our view of an infant today is of an individual of enormous potential, one whose activity and competence is much greater than originally suspected. It is as if a newborn enters the world with all its systems ready to function and eager for growth. What happens during these first two years has important implications for future development. Setbacks—both physical and psychological—will occur, but they need not cause permanent damage. From your reading in Chapter 1, you realize that human infants show remarkable resiliency.

How do infants first learn that they can trust those around them? The answer lies in the way their initial needs are satisfied. They have the ability to detect and react to parental signals. In Chapter 2 you read about Erikson's stages of development. In light of what you now know about infant potential, it is easier to accept Erikson's great contribution to our understanding of infants' development of trust.

In summary:

Physical and Motor Development

- Newborns display clear signs of their competence: movement, seeing, hearing, interacting.
- Infants' physical and motor abilities influence all aspects of development.
- Techniques to assess infant

Answers

competence and well-being are widely used today.

- Motor development follows a well-documented schedule.
- Infants can develop problems such as SIDS and FTT for a variety of reasons.

Perceptual Development

- Infants are born with the ability to detect changes in their environment.
- Infants are capable of acquiring and interpreting information from their immediate surroundings.

- Infants from birth show preferences for certain types of stimuli.

Cognitive Development

- Infants, even at this early age, are attempting to answer questions about their world, questions that will continue to occupy them in more complex and sophisticated forms throughout their lives.
- One of the first tasks that infants must master is an understanding of the objects around them.
- Piaget's theory of cognitive

development has shed considerable light on the ways that children grow mentally.

- A key element in understanding an infant's cognitive development is the role of memory.

Language Development

- Infants show rapid growth in their language development.
- Language acquisition follows a definite sequence.
- Language behaviors in infancy range from crying to the use of words and phrases.

KEY TERMS

Apgar	Failure to thrive (FTT)	Preintellectual speech
Apnea	Habituation	Primary circular reactions
Babbling	Holophrases	Reciprocal interactions
Brazelton Neonatal Behavioral Scale	Holophrastic speech	Reflex
Cooing	Implicit memory	Respiratory distress syndrome
Coordination of secondary schemes	Infantile amnesia	Secondary circular reactions
Crawling	Inner speech	Sensorimotor period
Creeping	Language explosion	Sudden infant death syndrome (SIDS)
Egocentric speech	Neonate	Telegraphic speech
Egocentrism	Neurological assessment	Tertiary circular reactions
Explicit memory	Object permanence	Vocables

WHAT DO YOU THINK?

1. The shift from considering an infant as nothing more than a passive sponge to seeing infants as amazingly competent carries with it certain responsibilities. We can't be overly optimistic about a baby's abilities. Why? What are some of the more common dangers of this viewpoint?
2. Testing infants has grown in popularity these past years. You should consider some cautions,

however. Remembering what you have read about infants in this Chapter, mention several facts you would be careful about.
3. You have been asked to babysit your sister's 14-month-old baby. When you arrive, the mother is upset because she has been repeatedly picking up things that the baby has thrown out of the crib. With your new knowledge, you calm her down by explaining

the baby's behavior. What do you tell her?
4. After reviewing the infancy work, what do you think about this period as "preparation for the future"? Select one phase of development (e.g., cognitive development) and show how a stimulating environment can help to lay the foundation for future cognitive growth.

CHAPTER REVIEW TEST

1. Which of the following is not a reflex?
   a. breathing
   b. sucking
   c. swallowing
   d. laughing

2. A _____ reflex is elicited by gently touching the infant's cheek.
   a. Moro
   b. rooting

   c. Babkin
   d. Babinski

3. _____ are brief periods when an infant stops breathing.
   a. Apnea
   b. Rooting
   c. Babbling
   d. Primary circular reactions

4. Depth perception in infants appears at

   a. birth.
   b. 7 to 10 days.
   c. 2 to 4 months.
   d. 4 to 5 months.

5. The Brazelton test assesses an infant's
   a. interaction with the environment.
   b. respiratory effort.
   c. reflex irritability.
   d. hearing.

6. Neurological assessment is not used for which of the following purposes?
   a. identification of a neurological problem
   b. treatment of a neurological problem
   c. monitoring a neurological problem
   d. prognosis about a neurological problem

7. The final area of the brain to develop is the
   a. sensory region.
   b. motor area.
   c. association area.
   d. auditory area.

8. _____ is a disorder caused by the lack of a substance called surfactant.
   a. SIDS
   b. RDS
   c. AIDS
   d. FTT

9. Infants see color at
   a. the neonatal period.
   b. 2 to 4 months.
   c. 6 to 7 months.
   d. 9 to 12 months.

10. The Brazelton test is a type of
    a. survival assessment.
    b. motor assessment.
    c. play assessment.
    d. behavioral assessment.

11. Infants from _____ show preferences for certain types of stimuli.

   a. birth
   b. 10 days
   c. two months
   d. six months

12. An infant's search for novelty during the sensorimotor period is seen in
    a. object permanence.
    b. secondary circular reactions.
    c. coordination of secondary schemes.
    d. tertiary circular reactions.

13. Infants initially show memory ability during
    a. the first and second weeks.
    b. the first three months.
    c. third to sixth month.
    d. sixth to 12th month.

14. In the development of language, children about 1 year of age begin to use recognizable
    a. vocables.
    b. holophrases.
    c. phrases.
    d. sentences.

15. According to Piaget, the acquisition of language in children depends on
    a. cognitive structures.
    b. biology.
    c. reinforcement.
    d. language acquisition devices.

16. By _____ months a child begins to run.
    a. 9
    b. 12
    c. 24
    d. 18

17. Which of the following is not a major accomplishment of the sensorimotor period?
    a. reversibility
    b. sense of space
    c. causality
    d. time sequence

18. _____ believes infants experience four different senses of self: emergent, core, subjective, and verbal.
    a. Erikson
    b. Skinner
    c. Piaget
    d. Stern

19. A 2-year-old child may have a vocabulary of as many as _____ words.
    a. 250
    b. 500
    c. 1,000
    d. 2,000

20. _____ believed the roots of language and thought were separate and only become linked through development.
    a. Chomsky
    b. Lenneberg
    c. Vygotsky
    d. Piaget

Answers

1. d 2. b 3. a 4. d 5. a 6. b 7. c 8. b 9. b 10. d 11. a 12. d 13. d 14. a 15. a 16. d 17. a 18. d 19. a 20. c

Psychosocial Development in Infancy

Janice watched with exasperation as her 1-year-old son, Joseph, sat crying. Her friend Laura had dropped in for a cup of coffee and had started to play with Joseph when he began to cry and pull away from her. Janice had noticed this happening often lately and was concerned that something was bothering him. She could tell that her friend, who had no children, was hurt; Janice wondered whether the problem was serious enough to call her doctor for advice. Joseph looked fine and seemed to show no symptoms of any illness, which made her hesitate.

Later that day, after her friend had left and Joseph was taking his nap, Janice thought about his behavior. If he wasn't sick, what was the problem? She was concerned that he might be so shy that he could have difficulty with relationships and in making friends. She was also bothered that she could be doing something wrong. Joseph was a first child; could she be keeping him too close to her and perhaps subconsciously resisting any contacts he might have with others?

Janice decided to take Joseph shopping the following day and visit the local bookstore. The next morning, Joseph was bright and cheerful and kept himself busy with a toy while Janice browsed through the books in the child-care section of the bookstore. At first she turned to those books that dealt with specific problems, but she didn't know what to look for, so she turned to more general discussions of child rearing. Still not satisfied, she was about ready to give up when she came across a book that described the milestones that occur during infancy.

Sure enough, there it was. "Beginning in the second half of the first year, infants start to show anxiety in the presence of strangers. This behavior is probably the first clue you will notice that tells you attachment is developing." Janice read the words again, relieved and delighted; Joseph was perfectly normal. Now, however, she was determined to learn more about attachment. ✪

Beginning at about six months of age, infants show signs of distress when approached by a stranger.

In showing his fear of strangers, Joseph was demonstrating perfectly normal behavior. His intense relationship with his mother is an example of what's called attachment. Typically attachment is between children and mothers, although it may be between children and someone else who is important to them, such as their father, grandmother, or aunt. Using these interactions with their mothers as a blueprint for future relationships, children like Joseph predict what to expect from others, which then shapes the path of their social development.

We have seen in the preceding chapters that children are not born as passive sponges; they immediately seek stimulation from their environment and *instantly interpret, and react to, how they are being treated,* a process called **reciprocal interactions.** Think of it this way: You react to me in a particular manner and I change. As a result of the changes that occurred in me, you change. Back-and-forth, on-and-on it goes, constantly changing the relationship. Consequently, we can now examine an infant's psychosocial development from a totally new and exciting perspective. Not only do infants attempt to make sense of their world as they develop cognitively, they also "tune into" the social and emotional atmosphere surrounding them and immediately begin to shape their relationships with others.

Think for a moment of what you have read about infants, especially their rapid brain and cognitive development. Infants take in information, and some of this information concerns how others, especially their mothers, treat them. Although they may not grasp the significance of what's going on around them, infants can understand the quality of their treatment. It is what Erikson has called the time of trust, which means that children acquire confidence in themselves as well as others. The degree of trust acquired does not depend as much on nutrition and displays of love as it does on the quality of the parent-child relationship. Parents can encourage a sense of trust by responding sensitively to their infant's needs. Physical contact and comfort are crucial for trust to develop.

Gradually, as children master motor control, they learn to trust their bodies, thus increasing their psychological sense of security. With the aid of their parents, and their own growing competence, children begin to think of the world as a safe and orderly place. An infant's relationships usually begin with its mother and then extend to father, siblings, friends, and so on. We know now that the entire range of a child's relationships contributes to social development.

To help us untangle this important network, in this chapter we'll first present several basic ideas about relationships (such as the active role that infants play in their own development). We'll then analyze the meaning of relationships: What are they and what do they consist of? Next, we'll examine the source of those first relationships and how they develop and influence later relationships. Finally, we'll explore the research on attachment that has attracted so much attention these past few years. Let's begin by looking at several basic ideas about relationships.

When you finish reading this chapter, you should be able to

• Describe how theory and research have contributed to our understanding of relationships.

• Assess the role of reciprocal interactions in any relationship.

• Distinguish the characteristics of a relationship.

- Identify the givens in a relationship.

- Trace the origins of relationships.

- Evaluate the significance of the parent-infant relationship.

- Analyze the impact of attachment on psychosocial development.

Relationships and Development

Infants immediately begin to take in information from their environment, and mothers are an important source of this information. From mothers, infants begin to develop a sense of how the world will treat them.

For most people, relationships with other people are the most important part of their lives.
Robert Hinde

Consider for a moment all that a single relationship incorporates: *Physical aspects* of development such as walking, running, and playing with a peer; *language aspects,* which enable youngsters to share one anothers' lives; *cognitive aspects,* which allow them to understand one another; *emotional aspects,* which permit them to make a commitment to another; and *social aspects,* which reflect both socialization and individuation. In other words, a relationship is a superb example of the influence of biopsychosocial interaction.

All of these features combine as youngsters interact with a remarkable variety of individuals, from those first crucial days with parents to later interactions with siblings, other family members, peers, teachers, and many others. Children continue to widen their circle of relationships as they grow. Our concern here, however, is with the origin of relationships in infancy, a concern that has grown out of the changing view of infancy we discussed. Let's briefly review several of the developmental concepts we discussed previously that have contributed to a greater understanding of how relationships develops.

Background of the Relationship Research

Several major reasons account for the current interest in relationships. First, developmental psychologists became dissatisfied with studying "the relationship" between mother and child. Greater precision was demanded: What do we know about the content of the interactions between mother and child? Can we study the quality of these interactions? Is it possible to determine the mother's commitment to the relationship? What does relationship mean?

A second important influence on relationship research has been the acceptance of a reciprocal interaction (or a **transactional model**) of development, which recognizes the child's active role in its development (Brazelton & Nugent, 1995; Brazelton & Cramer, 1990). As defined previously, reciprocal interactions means that I do something to the baby and the baby changes; as a result of the infant's change, I change; the process continues indefinitely. The unique temperamental distinctions that infants display at birth cause unique parental reactions. Visualizing how parents respond differently to a crying or cooing infant doesn't take much effort.

When parents change their behavior according to their child's behavior, they signal pleasure, rejection, or uncertainty about what their child is doing. Children act on their parents and change the parents; these changes are then reflected in how parents treat their children. The tone of the interactions between children and parents assumes a definite structure that will characterize the relationship for the coming years.

Remember: In any adult-child interactions, infants also exercise some control over the interactions. We, as adults, respond to infants partly because of the way that they have responded to us. An infant's staring, cooing, smiling, and kicking can all be employed to maintain the interactions. Thus these early interactions establish the nature of the relationship between parent and child, giving it a particular tone or style.

A third influence evident in studying relationships, the recognition that mothers react differently to different children, has introduced the concept of **sensitive responsiveness.** For example, we know that babies are temperamentally different

A Sociocultural View

Different Cultures, Different Interactions

In a thoughtful review of the literature analyzing minority infants (African-American, Hispanic-American, Asian-American, Native American, Alaskan native, and Pacific Islander), Garcia-Coll (1990) noted that during the first three years of life, infants develop those psychomotor, cognitive, and psychosocial skills that enable them to become accepted members of their cultural and social systems. Because of their families' backgrounds, minority infants are exposed to unique experiences that can influence their developmental outcomes in ways not yet understood.

Parents from a particular culture share a common system of beliefs, values, practices, and behaviors that differ from those of parents in other cultures. Parents from different cultural backgrounds differ in their views of infant competence, how to respond to crying, and what developmental skills are most significant (Garcia Coll, 1990). Consequently, infants are subject to different parental behaviors that are shaped by a particular culture.

Many interactions between parents and their infants are universal, such as baby talk, facial expressions, and play. Behaviors such as baby talk are so common that a mother's behavior may seem infantile. Many other maternal behaviors, however, are not that common. Eye contact and face-to-face talk are avoided in some cultures (Field,

1990). Specific examples include Chisholm's study (1983) of the use of cradle boards with Navajo infants. The arousal level and activity level of these infants seems to be lower than infants from other cultures, which affects mother-infant interactions. Mother-infant interactions are fewer and less intense. Navajo infants also have fewer contacts with strangers and are less fearful of them in the first year than Caucasian infants, but the pattern reverses in the second year.

But merely identifying specific differences in raising children in different cultures limits our perspective on development. As Garcia Coll and others (1996) have noted, to understand the development of minority children demands knowledge of how such variables as racism, prejudice, discrimination, and other sources of oppression influence developmental outcomes.

In addition, studies of children of color need to move from conceptualizing developmental outcome as either negative or positive to a more balanced conceptualization that reflects both the strengths and weaknesses in developmental processes and competencies of these children (Garcia Cole & others, 1996, p. 1895).

As babies begin to interact with their mothers, a pattern for future relationships is established. The more diverse the interactions that a baby engages in with its mother, the richer the relationship becomes.

at birth. An example of sensitive responsiveness would be that although most infants like to be held, some dislike physical contact. How will a mother react to an infant who stiffens and pulls away, especially if previous children liked being held? There's no escaping the importance of infant temperament in the development of attachment (Seifer, Schiller, & Sameroff, 1996). This research has contributed to a greater understanding of the role of relationships in development.

Infants instantly tune in to their environment. They give clues to their personalities so that a mother's and father's responses to their child's signals must be appropriate for *that* child. As Isabella (1993) has noted, maternal sensitivity is an all-important characteristic of reciprocal interactions that is consistently linked to attachment security.

The final influence came when investigators realized that, from birth, children are active processors of information. *Active processors of information* means that children don't only react to stimuli; they see and hear at birth and immediately begin the task of regulating their environment. They fight to control their breathing, and they struggle to balance digestion and elimination. But brief, calm periods appear after birth when infants take in information from the surrounding world. These fleeting but significant periods are the foundation for the appearance of key developmental milestones during the infancy period.

Infants are ready to respond to social stimulation. It is not only a matter of responding passively; infants in their own way initiate social contacts. Many of their actions (such as turning toward their mothers or gesturing in their direction) are forms of communication. Hinde (1993), too, noted that the interchange between infants and their environments is an active one. Those around infants try to attract

---

What's Your View?

Initial Encounters: Significant or Fleeting?

We cannot exaggerate the importance of the initial encounters that infants have with the adults around them. In a particularly significant study that was one of the first to focus on the lingering effects of these early interactions, Osofsky (1976, 1987) examined the link between neonatal characteristics and early mother-infant relations in 134 mothers and their 2- to 4-day-old infants.

Osofsky observed the infants at a scheduled feeding and in a 15-minute stimulation situation, during which the mothers presented tasks from the Brazelton Neonatal Assessment Scale to their children. The infants were next evaluated (between 2 and 4 days of age) using the full Brazelton scale.

A particularly significant finding showed that the overall pattern of interactions indicates consistent maternal and infant styles that appear soon after birth. Infants who were highly responsive during the Brazelton assessment were also highly responsive during the stimulation periods. Osofsky also found strong correlations between the mother's stimulation and the child's responsiveness: More sensitive mothers have more responsive infants.

These early findings have been consistently supported by recent research demonstrating that the mutual reciprocity between mothers and their children are critical in the socialization process (Maccoby, 1992). Efforts are currently underway to investigate and understand the specifics of the mother-child system of reciprocity (Kochanska, 1997).

When you consider the evidence supporting the importance of the mother-infant interactions, its significance for socialization is clear, given the contributions of both infant and mother to the style of the relationship. With the pattern of interactions formed almost from birth, a clearly defined relationship is set that will undoubtedly shape the course of social development.

Here's a project for your class. Either you or some of your classmates probably have relatives with infants. For those of you who do, observe the mother and child interacting. What's their reaction to this "mutual reciprocity"? What was the infant doing? How did the mother react to the baby's signals? Use these reports for class discussion and combine them with your reading of this chapter.

Do you still agree with the conclusion that the early mother-infant relationship shapes future relationships? Can you "fit" your interpretation of the importance of these early interactions with the reports of your classmates? What's your view?

---

their attention, but the babies actively select from these adult actions. In other words, infants begin to structure their own relationships according to their individual temperaments.

We can usually label relationships, using adjectives such as warm, cold, rejecting, and hostile. But we must be cautious. Any relationship may be marked by apparently contradictory interactions. A mother may have a warm relationship with her child as evidenced by hugging and kissing, but she may also scold when scolding is needed for the child's protection. *To understand the relationship, we must understand the interactions.*

Once developmental psychologists accepted these four views, investigations into attachment, first relationships, and peer relationships could be subjected to more precise and meaningful analysis. With this background, we now turn to an analysis of the role of relationships in development. First, however, just what do we mean by relationships?

The Meaning of Relationships

Think for a moment about your friends. What type of relationship do you have with them? with your parents? with a husband or wife? with a child? We can define a relationship as *a pattern of intermittent interactions between two people involving interchanges over an extended period of time* (Hinde, 1993). If you have a true relationship with someone, that relationship has continuity. That is, you can continue to maintain a relationship with a friend you have not seen for years.

An extended series of **interactions,** however, does not necessarily constitute a

Guided Review

1. Beginning at _____ children begin the task of regulating their environment.
2. Infants begin to structure their relationships according to their individual temperaments. This is also known as _____ processing of information.
3. A child's first relationship is usually with his or her _____.
4. An adult's appropriate response to an infant is called _____ _____.
5. A relationship is an excellent example of _____ interactions.

relationship. The cashier you frequently see at the supermarket, the receptionist at your dentist's office with whom you exchange pleasantries—none of these become partners in a relationship. If the interactions are nothing more than an exchange of money and a thank you, they cannot be classified as relationships.

Thinking about the type of interactions parents have with their child helps you to appreciate how the relationship has developed. For example, consider the kinds of things parents do with their children and the way they do them—all involving interactions. They play, they discipline, they explain; they provide correction and feedback; they answer questions. In other words, they're exercising their parental role in all of these interactions with their children. Analyzing these interactions helps you to realize that parents change as a result of their child's behavior and their children change in turn because of their parents' reactions. These *reciprocal interactions* demonstrate continuity over time and are a powerful force in the development of relationships (Freitag & others, 1996).

Although the history of the interactions defines a relationship, it is still more than the sum of these interactions. In a relationship, the interactions are integrated differently from the separate interactions (Hinde, 1993). It isn't just a matter of saying "Good morning. Isn't it a nice day?" to the cashier. A relationship also involves your perceptions, your mental picture, and your feelings for the other person. What one says or does is significant, but how the partner perceives and judges that behavior is even more important.

These ideas help us to understand the developing relationship between parents and infants. We think today that infants "tune into" their environment from birth. Thus they react to far more than their parents' behavior; the quality of the interactions instantly begins to establish the nature of the relationship (Hart & others, 1997).

But what are some of the major forces that influence a relationship? Physical appearance and temperament seem especially important.

Life is not simple, especially when it comes to the interactions between parents and their children.

The Givens in a Relationship

In the mother-infant relationship (or father-infant), both individuals bring to the relationship physical, biological, and psychosocial characteristics. We have previously discussed a person's genetic endowment, so here we'll concentrate on personal characteristics, such as personal appearance, temperament, and psychosocial characteristics such as role expectations.

Personal Appearance

Physical appearance has a powerful effect on a relationship. For good or ill, physical appearance affects how others react to us. The mere sight of a happy baby is

Answers

1. birth 2. active 3. mother 4. sensitive responsiveness 5. biopsychosocial

immensely appealing. Their facial expressions and the shape of their features are attractive to most people and help to ensure an infant's survival, given their immaturity and helplessness. Consequently, attractiveness is as important for infants as it is for adults (Langlois & others, 1995; Ritter & others, 1991).

On the other hand, the appearance of a sick baby generates concern. We almost instinctively react to their distress. However, we respond in a different manner to an unhappy, crying baby. Tired, frustrated parents may find it difficult to react positively, tending instead to be abrupt and stiff with their baby. From what we know of a baby tuning into its environment, we can understand how easily appearance can affect those first relationships.

Lest you think we're overly dramatizing the importance of personal appearance in determining how people react to others, consider the adult reflections of the great Russian novelist Leo Tolstoy, who considered himself physically ugly.

> I prayed to God for a miracle that would transform me into a handsome man, and I would have given all I had and all I might ever have in the future for a handsome face. . . . I am quite certain that nothing has such a telling impact on a man's cast of thought as his appearance, and not his appearance itself so much as his conviction that it is attractive or unattractive.

Powerful words that testify to the impact that the perception of attractiveness or unattractiveness has on a child's and adult's development.

The first mother-infant interactions quickly establish the style and tone of the relationship. If the infant's physical attractiveness alters the interactions, *sensitive responsiveness* becomes a matter of prime concern. Given the importance of reciprocal interactions, mothers can initiate a relationship in which an infant quickly realizes that something is wrong with the quality of the interactions.

Temperament

The second characteristic to explore is that of **temperament,** that is, an individual's unique behavioral style in interacting with the environment, which immediately begins to structure infants' relationships with those around them (DiPietro & others, 1996; Goldsmith & Campos, 1990). For example, Kagan (1997) has noted that 4-month-old infants who show a tendency to become upset at unfamiliar stimuli are more likely to become fearful and subdued during early childhood. Thus temperament is a critical personality trait, especially in the first days and weeks after birth.

Today's acceptance of the importance of temperament reflects the basic work of Chess and Thomas (1987), who were struck by the individuality of their own children in the days immediately following birth, differences that could not be attributed to the environment. As they noted, even mothers of identical twins can distinguish their infants by their differences in their reactions to faces, voices, and colors.

To test their hypothesis, Chess and Thomas designed a longitudinal study called the **New York Longitudinal Study.** In 1956 they began collecting data on 141 middle-class children. They observed the behavioral reactions of infants, determined the persistence of these behaviors, and attempted to discover how these behavioral traits interacted with specific elements in the infants' environments. From the resulting data they found nine characteristics that could be reliably scored as high, medium, or low, which they used to draw a behavioral profile of the children by 2 or 3 months of age. These nine characteristics clustered with sufficient frequency for the authors to identify three general types of temperament: **easy children, difficult children,** and **slow-to-warm-up children.** Table 6.1 summarizes their classification scheme.

The authors were able to classify 65 percent of the infants, leaving the other 35

TABLE 6.1 CATEGORIES OF TEMPERAMENT

Behaviors	Easy Children	Difficult Children	Slow-to-warm-up Children
Activity level	Varies	Low to moderate	Varies
Rhythmicity (regularity)	Very regular	Irregular	Varies
Approach or withdrawal	Positive approach	Withdrawal	Initial withdrawal
Adaptability	Very adaptable	Slowly adaptable	Adaptable
Sensory threshold (level of stimulation necessary to produce a response)	High or low	Tends to be low	High or low
Quality of mood	Positive	Negative	Slightly negative
Intensity of reactions	Low or mild	Intense	Moderate
Distractibility	Varies	Varies	Varies
Persistence and attention span	High or low	High or Low	High or low

percent with a mixture of traits that defied neat categorization. Knowing what kind of temperament their child has can help parents to adjust their own style of parenting to their child's temperament, which is a distinct advantage in forming positive parent-child relationships. The Thomas and Chess work suggests that infants immediately bring definite temperamental characteristics to the mother-infant relationship, characteristics that do much to shape those critical initial interactions.

The Origins of Temperament. Temperament appears to have a constitutional component that is observable, at least partially, during the first few days of life. Results of the *Colorado Adoption Project,* which compared matched adopted and non-adopted children, showed a clear genetic influence on temperament (Plomin & others, 1997; Plomin & others, 1993).

The ongoing *MacArthur Longitudinal Twin Study,* designed to study more than 330 same-sex twin pairs, has initially reported genetic influences on individual differences at 14 months of age; for example, behavioral inhibition and observed shyness showed a significant genetic influence (Emde & others, 1992).

As Kagan (1992, 1997) noted, given the individual differences in the biochemistry of the brain, it is little wonder that a child could be vulnerable to either sadness or anxiety. Thus, evidence continues to suggest a genetic role in temperament, with all that implies for the mother-infant relationship (Saudino & Eaton, 1991). What are some implications of these temperamental differences, and how do they influence parent-child relationships?

Goodness of Fit. When the interactions between parents and their children are compatible, a **goodness of fit** exists. As Chess and Thomas (1987) searched for some unifying theme to explain why a child's development was proceeding smoothly or not, they found that a goodness of fit existed when the demands and expectations of parents were compatible with their child's temperament. Goodness of fit signifies the match between the properties of the environment with its expectations and demands, and the child's capacities, characteristics, and style of behaving.

Poorness of fit exists when parental demands and expectations are excessive and not compatible with a child's temperament, abilities, and other characteristics. Poorness of fit produces stress and is often marked by developmental problems (Chess & Thomas, 1987). A simple way of phrasing this concept is to ask parents and their children how they get along together.

Parents need to be aware of the link between temperament and an infant's early behavior. For example, Vaughn and associates (1992) attempted to discover any association between security of attachment and an infant's temperament. They studied 555 children ranging in age from 5 months to 42 months and found a significant relationship between temperament and attachment at all ages. These researchers conclude that attachment and temperament are not isolated entities but influence each other.

Although goodness of fit established in infancy produces a good beginning for a child, no guarantee exists that this fit between parental demands and expectations and a child's temperament and capacities will last (Chess & Thomas, 1987). Children change and so do their parents' expectations, and as relationships become more complex (e.g., during adolescence) the goodness of fit may also change. For example, the parents of an infant with a low threshold for stimulation—a door closing or a light coming on may disturb her—may have adapted to her temperament. Later in school, however, the child may need extra time for homework or lose attention during a long lesson. Unless such environmental demands are made in light of the child's temperament, the goodness of fit could rapidly deteriorate.

Parental Roles: Expectations for a Relationship

Finally, parents bring basic preconceived ideas about the role they should play in their relationships with their children. Technically, role usually refers to behavior, or certain expectancies about behavior, associated with a particular position in society. Parents have certain expectations about how a mother should act, how a doctor should perform duties, or how a mechanic should work on a car. They have similar expectations about their role as a parent. *How they exercise that power and how their children react to their suggestions and encouragements, their demands and commands ultimately determine the success of the relationship.*

Both parents and children have expectations about a parent's role and a child's role, that is, how each should act. Parents' ideas about their child's behavior have come from many sources. For example, the interplay of how they were treated by their parents, their observation of those they consider good parents, and their reading about parenting, all are strong influences on what they see as their parental role. In an ideal world, their ideas, their expectations, and their sense of their role as a parent should mesh perfectly with their child's personality and abilities.

For example, let's pause for a moment and consider one source of their role expectations. Selma Fraiberg, a well-known child psychiatrist, has referred to the presence of **ghosts in the nursery,** which can have many consequences (1987). Do parents feel that their parents are looking over their shoulder, telling them how to bring up their child, ideas that they may well have rejected or even rebelled against? Does their child remind them of someone from their past, and they begin to react as they did to that other person? Do they tend to imitate a friend whom they admire? Or have they been impressed by the ideas of some "expert" they have read about or have seen on television?

The encouraging conclusion is that in spite of these findings, when parents are aware that ghosts from the past may influence them, they are able to overcome these relics and move on to positive relations with their children. Examining mother-grandmother relationships, Wakschlag, Chase-Lansdale, and Brooks-Gunn (1996) found that the quality of the existing mother-grandmother relationship is indeed related to parenting of the next generation. When the mother-grandmother relationship is open, flexible, and autonomous, the mothers demonstrated these qualities in their own parenting. Their findings also suggest that when the relationship between a mother and child is negative, *any intervention should include the grandmother.*

Having considered the nature and givens of relationships, we can now ask, what is the source of the interactions that lead to social relationship? How do an infant's first relationships develop?

Guided Review

6. Most parents have preconceived ideas about what their _____ as parents should be.
7. _____ and _____ are identified with the New York longitudinal study.
8. _____ is an individual's behavioral style in interacting with the environment.
9. Compatibility between parental and child behavior is known as _____ _____ _____.
10. When the behavior of parents and children are incompatible, this is called _____ _____.

First Relationships

In an intriguing statement about how early relationships develop, Brazelton and Cramer (1990) stated:

> For all parents-to-be, three babies come together at the moment of birth. The imaginary child of their dreams and fantasies and the invisible but real fetus, whose particular rhythms and personality have been making themselves increasingly evident for several months now, merge with the actual newborn baby who can be seen, heard, and finally held close. The attachment to a newborn is built on prior relationships with an imaginary child, and with the developing fetus which has been part of the parents' world for nine months. (p.3)

These interactions help infants to form their first relationships and influence how they relate to others. But how do these first relationships actually begin?

How Do Children Develop Relationships?

Infants typically react by general states of excitement and distress, which swiftly focus on the mother as infants recognize their mothers as sources of relief and satisfaction. Mothers rapidly discriminate their infants' cries: for hunger, attention, or fright. Thus infants learn to direct their attention to their mothers. Once the pattern is established, infants begin to evaluate the emerging interactions.

Three motives seem to be at work:

- *Bodily needs*—food, for example—lead to a series of interactions that soon become a need for social interaction.

- *Psychological needs* can cause infants to interrupt one of their most important functions, such as feeding. Children, from birth, seem to seek novelty; they require increasingly challenging stimulation. For infants, adults become the source of information as much as the source of bodily need satisfaction.

- *Adult response needs.* Adults, usually mothers, satisfy needs, provide stimulation, and initiate communication, thus establishing the basis for future social interactions.

Answers

6. role 7. Chess, Thomas 8. Temperament 9. goodness of fit 10. poorness of fit

The Developmental Sequence

These three influences at work during the infant's early days—bodily need satisfaction, a search for novelty, and adult responses to their overtures—form a basis for the appearance of social interactions similar to the following sequence.

- *During the first three weeks* of life, infants are not affected much by an adult's appearance. The only exception, as noted, is during feeding periods.

- *From about the beginning of the fourth week,* infants begin to direct actions at the adults. Emotional reactions also appear at this time, with obvious signs of pleasure at the sight and sound of adults, especially females.

- *During the second month,* more complex and sensitive reactions emerge, such as smiling and vocalizations directed at the mother, plus animated behavior during interactions.

- *By 3 months of age,* the infant has formed a need for social interactions. That need continues to grow and be nourished by adults until the end of the second or beginning of the third year, when a need for peer interactions develops (Hinde, 1987, 1992).

As these early interactions commence, several characteristics begin to identify the emergence of a successful relationship (Brazelton & Cramer, 1990). The first of these is **synchrony,** which refers to the ability of parents to adjust their behavior to that of an infant. Immediately after birth, infants are mostly occupied by their efforts to regulate such systems as breathing and heart rate, which demands most of their energy and attention. Once parents recognize these efforts—the baby's "language" (Brazelton & Cramer, 1990)—they can use their own behavior—talking softly, stroking—to help their infants adapt to environmental stimuli. This mutual regulation of behavior defines synchrony.

Another characteristic is **symmetry,** which means that an infant's capacity for attention and style of responding influence any interactions. In other words, how children interact with their parents reflects their temperaments. As Brazelton and Cramer (1990, p. 122) note, in a symmetric dialogue parents recognize an infant's thresholds, that is, what and how much stimuli an infant can tolerate.

Other characteristics include **entrainment,** a characteristic that identifies the rhythm that is established between a parent's and infant's behavior. For example, when the infant reaches toward the mother, the mother says something like, "Oh, yes, Timmy." The sequence involved in entrainment leads to playing games such as the mother making a face at the baby and the infant trying to respond similarly. Once infants realize that they have a share in controlling the interactions (about 6 months of age), they begin to develop a sense of **autonomy.** With these interactions, infants are beginning to form relationships and learn about themselves.

As the interactions between mother and child increase and become more complex, an attachment develops between the two. Figure 6.1 illustrates the sequence by which the first interactions, combined with developmental changes, gradually lead to specific relationships.

With the preceding ideas in mind, we turn now to the special topic of attachment.

Brazelton, T. B. & B. Cramer (1990). *The earliest relationship.* (Reading, MA: Addison-Wesley). You should enjoy reading this excellent, readable account of how relationships develop, presented from both a pediatric and psychoanalytic perspective.

Attachment

Because the roots of future relationships are formed during the first days of life, we may well ask: How significant is the mother-infant relationship in those first days and weeks after birth? We know that infants who develop a secure attachment to their mothers have the willingness and confidence to seek out future relationships.

Figure 6.1

The origin and development of relationships.

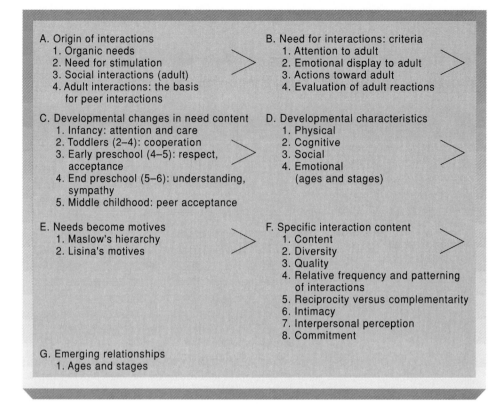

A. Origin of interactions
  1. Organic needs
  2. Need for stimulation
  3. Social interactions (adult)
  4. Adult interactions: the basis
     for peer interactions

B. Need for interactions: criteria
  1. Attention to adult
  2. Emotional display to adult
  3. Actions toward adult
  4. Evaluation of adult reactions

C. Developmental changes in need content
  1. Infancy: attention and care
  2. Toddlers (2–4): cooperation
  3. Early preschool (4–5): respect,
     acceptance
  4. End preschool (5–6): understanding,
     sympathy
  5. Middle childhood: peer acceptance

D. Developmental characteristics
  1. Physical
  2. Cognitive
  3. Social
  4. Emotional
     (ages and stages)

E. Needs become motives
  1. Maslow's hierarchy
  2. Lisina's motives

F. Specific interaction content
  1. Content
  2. Diversity
  3. Quality
  4. Relative frequency and patterning
     of interactions
  5. Reciprocity versus complementarity
  6. Intimacy
  7. Interpersonal perception
  8. Commitment

G. Emerging relationships
  1. Ages and stages

Both mother and child bring their own characteristics to the relationship (facial expressions, movements, vocalizations), and as they do, the interactions between the two become more complex and an attachment slowly develops between the two.

Guided Review

11. Infants' interactions with their mothers are motivated by three categories of needs: _____, _____, _____.

12. _____ is the ability of parents to adjust their behavior to that of an infant.

13. The need for peer interactions develops at the end of the _____ year.

14. Infants' capacity for attention and style of responding that influences their interactions is called _____.

15. The rhythm that develops between a parent's and infant's behavior is called _____.

One of the first researchers to recognize the significance of relationships in an infant's life was John Bowlby.

Bowlby's Work

The traditional notion of attachment was developed with great insight by John Bowlby (1969). Early in his professional career, Bowlby had been affected by the plight of children who had suffered negative family experiences (such as separation) early in life (Bretherton, 1992). Using concepts from psychology and ethology (ethology is the study of behavior in natural settings, Hinde, 1993.), Bowlby formulated his basic premise: A warm, intimate relationship between mother and infant is essential to mental health because a child's need for its mother's presence is

Answers 11. bodily, psychological, adult response 12. Synchrony 13. second 14. symmetry 15. entrainment

as great as its need for food. A mother's continued absence can generate a sense of loss and feelings of anger. (In his 1969 classic, *Attachment,* Bowlby states quite clearly that an infant's principal attachment figure can be someone other than the natural mother.)

Background of Attachment Theory

Bowlby and his colleagues, especially James Robertson, initiated a series of studies in which children aged 15 to 30 months who had good relationships with their mothers experienced separation from them. A predictable sequence of behaviors followed. *Protest,* the first phase, may begin immediately and persist for about one week. Loud crying, extreme restlessness, and rejection of all adult figures mark an infant's distress. *Despair,* the second phase, follows immediately. The infant's behavior suggests a growing hopelessness: monotonous crying, inactivity, and steady withdrawal. *Detachment,* the final phase, appears when an infant displays renewed interest in its surroundings, a remote, distant kind of interest. Bowlby describes the behavior of this final phase as apathetic, even if the mother reappears.

From observation of many similar cases, Bowlby defined attachment as follows:

> **Attachment behavior is any form of behavior that results in a person attaining or maintaining proximity to some other clearly identified individual who is conceived as better able to cope with the world. It is most obvious when the person is frightened, fatigued, or sick, and is assuaged by comforting and care-giving. At other times the behavior is less in evidence. (1982, p. 668)**

Bowlby also believed that while attachment is most obvious in infancy and early childhood, it can be observed throughout the life cycle. Table 6.3 presents a chronology of attachment behavior.

Bowlby, J. (1969). *Attachment.* New York: Basic Books. Here is Bowlby's classic statement about attachment. This book is very readable and is a reference with which you should be familiar.

TABLE 6.3 CHRONOLOGY OF ATTACHMENT DEVELOPMENT

Age	Characteristics	Behavior
4 months	Perceptual discrimination; visual tracking of mother	Smiles and vocalizes more with mother than anyone else; shows distress at separation
9 months	Separation anxiety; stranger anxiety	Cries when mother leaves; clings at appearance of strangers (mother is primary object)
2–3 years	Intensity and frequency of attachment behavior remains constant	Notices impending departure, indicating a better understanding of surrounding world
3–4 years	Growing confidence; tendency to feel secure in a strange place with subordinate attachment figures (relatives)	Begins to accept mother's temporary absence; plays *with* other children
4–10 years	Less intense attachment behavior, but still strong	May hold parent's hand while walking; anything unexpected causes child to turn to parent
Adolescence	Weakening attachment to parents; peers and other adults become important	Becomes attached to groups and group members
Adult	Attachment bond still discernible	In troubled times, adults turn to trusted friends; elderly direct attention toward younger generation

Source: From John Bowlby, "Attachment and Loss: Retrospect and Prospect," in *American Journal of Orthopsychiatry* 52:664–78. Reprinted with permission from the American Journal of Orthopsychiatry. Copyright © 1982 by the American Orthopsychiatric Association, Inc.

Attachment Research

Ainsworth (1973, 1979; Ainsworth & Bowlby, 1991), who accepted Bowlby's theoretical interpretation of attachment, devised the strange situation technique to study attachment experimentally. Ainsworth defined attachment as follows:

> The hallmark of attachment is behavior that promotes proximity to or contact with the specific figure or figures to whom the person is attached. Such proximity-and-contact-promoting behaviors are termed attachment behaviors. Included are signaling behavior (crying, smiling, vocalizing), orienting behavior such as looking, locomotions relative to another person (following, approaching), and active physical contact behavior (climbing up, embracing, clinging). (1973, p. 2)

A child's behaviors indicate attachment only when they are specifically directed at one or a few persons rather than to others. When infants first direct their attention to their mothers, it's their way of initiating and maintaining interaction with their mothers. Children also attempt to avoid separation from an attachment figure, particularly if faced with a frightening situation. Research also shows that children attach to insensitive, maltreating parents (Main, 1996).

Although the interactions between a mother and her child and a father and his child may appear quite different, a child will attach to both mother and father.

The Strange Situation Technique

To assess the quality of attachment by the *strange situation technique,* Ainsworth had a mother and infant taken to an observation room. The child was placed on the floor and allowed to play with toys. A stranger (female) then entered the room and began to talk to the mother. Observers watched to see how the infant reacted to the stranger and to what extent the child used the mother as a secure base. The mother then left the child alone in the room with the stranger; observers then noted how distressed the child became. The mother returned and the quality of the child's reaction to the mother's return was assessed. Next the infant was left completely alone, followed by the stranger's entrance, and then that of the mother. These behaviors have been used to classify children as follows:

- *Securely attached children,* who used their mothers as a base from which to explore. Separation intensified their attachment behavior; they exhibited considerable distress, ceased their explorations, and at reunion sought contact with their mothers.

- *Avoidantly attached children,* who rarely cried during separation and avoided their mothers at reunion. The mothers of these babies seemed to dislike or were indifferent to physical contact.

- *Ambivalently attached children,* who manifested anxiety before separation and who were intensely distressed by the separation. Yet on reunion they displayed ambivalent behavior toward their mothers; they sought contact but simultaneously seemed to resist it.

- *Disorganized/disoriented children,* who show a kind of confused behavior at reunion. For example, they may look at the mother and then look away, showing little emotion (Main, 1996).

Ainsworth also believed that attachment knows no geographic boundaries. Reporting on her studies of infant-mother attachment in Uganda, Ainsworth (1973) stated that of 28 infants she observed, 23 showed signs of attachment. She was impressed by the babies' initiative in attempting to establish attachment with their mothers and noted that the babies demonstrated this initiative even when no threat of separation or any condition that could cause anxiety existed. In tracing the developing pattern of attachment behavior, Ainsworth (1973) stated:

The baby did not first become attached and then show it by proximity-promoting behavior, but rather that these are the patterns of behavior through which attachment grows. (p. 35)

Ainsworth reported other studies conducted in Baltimore, Washington, and Scotland indicating that cultural influences may affect the ways in which different attachment behaviors develop. Nevertheless, although these studies used quite different subjects for their studies, all reported attachment behavior developing in a similar manner.

New Directions in Attachment Research

An added tool in attachment research has been the development of the **Adult Attachment Interview,** which assesses variations in the ability of parents to maintain a coherent, relevant discussion of the influences on their early attachments. Differences in responses to the questions of the AAI (that is, how truthful, clear, and orderly are the responses) predict the attachment categories of their infants (secure, insecure, etc.), *both before and after birth* (Main, 1996).

Continued research into the application of the AAI has focused on asking respondents to look back on their own childhood attachment. During a one hour interview, people are asked to support their memories by supplying evidence. For example, they are asked to furnish five adjectives describing their relationship to each parent. Later during the interview, they're asked to give memories of specific incidents supporting their earlier answers. Parental responses have been coded into categories that relate to the quality of their infants' attachment (see table 6.4).

Attachment researchers are also examining representational processes; that is, they're focusing on the relationship between early attachment and a child's drawings and stories in middle childhood. For example, when presented with instances of children who were separated from their mothers, secure 6-year-olds made up positive, constructive responses about the child in the story. But disorganized children gave frightened responses: "The mother is going to die," "The girl will kill herself."

Intergenerational Continuity

Several attachment topics have attracted considerable interest. The cognitive aspects of attachment have led to a closer scrutiny of how representations of a person's attachment history influence development. Studying 85 Icelandic children, Jacobsen, Edelstein, and Hofmann (1994) measured attachment representation at 7 years of age and then assessed cognitive functioning at 7, 9, 12, 15, and 17 years of age.

TABLE 6.4 THE ADULT ATTACHMENT INTERVIEW	
Adult Attachment Interview	**Strange Situation Response**
Secure–Autonomous–Coherent—values attachment, accepts any unpleasant, earlier experiences	*Secure*
Dismissing—Positive statements are unsupported or contradicted; they claim earlier unpleasant experiences have no effect	*Avoidant*
Preoccupied—Seems angry, confused, passive, or fearful; some responses irrelevant	*Resistant–Ambivalent*
Unfocused–Disorganized—Loses train of thought during discussion of loss or abuse; lapses in reasoning (speaks of dead people as alive)	*Disorganized/Disoriented*

They found that children with a secure attachment representation at age 7 did well on tests of concrete and formal operational thinking in childhood and adolescence. Those identified with an insecure-disorganized attachment representation at age 7 did poorly on cognitive tasks, especially deductive reasoning in childhood and adolescence.

In an attempt to discover if children's attachment representations had any effect on later school behavior and competence, Jacobsen and Hofmann (1997) studied 108 children in middle childhood and adolescence. These researchers used a story depicting a separation between a child and parent in which the parent is leaving on a plane, They then classified their subjects as secure or insecure. The children were then assessed by their teachers at 9, 12, and 15 years of age on competency and behavior. The secure children showed better results in attention-participation, self-esteem, and grade point average,

The intergenerational transmission of attachment patterns has also become a source of research interest. In other words, what are the internal models of attachment that influence how we treat our own children? Does deprivation in one generation lead to problems in the next? Evidence points to the reality of *intergenerational continuity,* that is, the connection between childhood experiences and adult parenting behavior.

A link has also been discovered between the way a mother recalls her childhood experiences and the present quality of the relationship with her child. Studying 100 pregnant women, Fonagy, Steele, and Steele (1991) wanted to assess how the attachment experiences of these women affected attachment with their children at 1 year of age. They found that 75 percent of the women who had been securely attached now had securely attached children. Of the remaining mothers, 23 percent had insecurely attached children. The researchers conclude that the internal representations of childhood attachment seem to carry to the next generation.

Exciting times for attachment research!

Fathers and Attachment

Historically, it has often been said that fathers are a biological necessity, but a social accident. Disagreeing with this view, Parke (1996) noted that today's fathers are pretty much the same as they were before—some are involved; some are even raising their children by themselves; some remain uninvolved. Although we have concentrated on the mother in our discussion of attachment, the father's role in the process has attracted growing interest. As fathers become more involved in child care (in the 1990s, about 90% of mothers will work full- or part-time), questions have arisen about an infant's attachment to both mother and father. Do infants react differently to each parent?

Commenting on the attachment between father and child, Bowlby (1988) noted that the patterns closely resembled those between mothers and their children. A finding that intrigued Bowlby was that there was no correlation between the attachment patterns for each parent; that is, an infant may have a secure attachment with the mother but not necessarily with the father or with the father but not necessarily the mother.

Other comparisons between the attachment of infants to mothers and fathers support Bowlby's conclusions. For example, a study of 15-month-old Dutch infants showed that the attachment behaviors directed toward mothers and fathers were linked (Goosens & Van Ijzendoorn, 1990). This, and other studies, suggest that although the mother usually remains the primary attachment figure, both mother and father have the potential to induce attachment (Fox, Kimmerly, & Schafer, 1991).

We can summarize these findings by stating that at 7 or 8 months of age, when attachment behavior (as defined by Bowlby and Ainsworth) normally appears, infants are attached to both mothers and fathers and prefer either parent to a stranger. The evidence indicates, then, that fathers can establish a close and meaningful relationship with their infants immediately from birth (Cox & others, 1992; Phares, 1992).

The interactions between a father and his child tend to be more physical than those between a mother and her child. The qualitatively different types of stimulation a child receives from each parent would seem to suggest implications for the staffing of day-care centers and preschool facilities.

Differences in Mother/Father Behavior

Research has also focused on demonstrating the differences between mothers' and fathers' behavior (nurturant versus playful), the similarity between parental behaviors (both exhibit considerable sensitivity), and the amount of involvement in the infant's care. For example, fathers tend to engage in more exciting activities such as bouncing, lifting, and tossing their infants into the air. Mothers are more verbal, tend to provide toys, and play more conventional games. In a relaxed setting, both parents seem to have equal attraction as attachment figures. When infants are hungry or sick, however, they turn more to their mothers.

Examining the antecedents of father-son attachment, Belsky (1996) studied 126 fathers and their sons in the strange situation. He found that fathers of secure infants were more extroverted and agreeable than fathers of insecure infants. They tended to have better marriages, and had a harmonious relationship between work and family. Temperament did not seem to distinguish between secure and insecure infants.

As you can tell from this brief summary, more research is needed to help us understand the dynamics of the interaction between fathers and their infants. A good conclusion would be this:

> When observed at home, infants react to naturally occurring separations from their fathers in the same way as to separations from their mothers. Nor were there any clear preferences for one parent over the other. (Parke, 1996, p. 122)

Guided Review

16. An early researcher into the significant relationships in an infant's life was _____.
17. Following separation from their mothers, Bowlby found a predictable sequence of behaviors: _____, _____, _____.
18. Attachment characterized by separation or stranger anxiety usually begins at the age of _____ months.
19. Studies showed that by _____ months of age, infants interact differently with their parents than with strangers.
20. _____ is known for the strange situation technique.

Early Emotional Development

As you read about the impact of attachment and early relationships on psychosocial development, you can understand how a child's emotional life is also affected. The study of emotions has had a checkered career in psychology. From the peaks of popularity, interest in emotions and their development plunged to the depths of neglect. Today we see once again a resurgence of enthusiasm for the study of emotional development.

First, however, what do we mean by *emotion?* Although philosophers and psychologists have trembled at the thought of defining emotion for almost as long as attempts have been made, the following definition hints at what underlies this emotional (!) term.

> Emotion is a feeling(s) and its distinctive thoughts, psychological and biological states, and range of propensities to act. (Goleman, 1995, p. 289)

Answers

16. Bowlby 17. protest, despair, detachment 18. 9 19. 8 20. Ainsworth

Goleman then goes on to ask the controversial question: Is it possible to classify the basic emotions? Answering his own question, he proposes several fundamental families of emotion, together with representative members of each family.

- *Anger:* fury, resentment, animosity

- *Sadness:* grief, sorrow, gloom, melancholy

- *Fear:* nervousness, apprehension, dread, fright

- *Enjoyment:* happiness, joy, bliss, delight

- *Love:* acceptance, trust, devotion, adoration

- *Surprise:* shock, astonishment, amazement, wonder

- *Shame:* guilt, embarassment, mortification, humiliation

You probably think Goleman's list is incomplete—what about blends such as jealousy? You could accurately point out that too much is missing from these categories. Yet efforts such as these undoubtedly will continue because of Paul Ekman's discovery that specific facial expressions for fear, anger, sadness, and enjoyment are recognized by people of all cultures around the world, thus suggesting their universality (Ekman & Davidson, 1994). Once Ekman stated that emotions evolved for their adaptive value in dealing with fundamental life tasks and identified four of these emotions, the stage was set and the task was identified: link these fundamental tasks with basic emotions. But our concern here is with emotional development.

You would enjoy reading Daniel Goleman's remarkably clear ananalysis of emotions, *Emotional intelligence* (1995). New York: Bantam.

Signs of Emotional Development

Recognizing that several issues surround emotional development will help you to understand this important part of children's lives (Dunn, 1994). You should first remember that changes occur in what elicits children's emotions at different ages. The amusement a 6-month-old child shows when tickled by her mother is far different from a 16-year-old's amusement at a funny story told by a friend. We may label both "amusement," but is the emotion the same? As children grow, the circumstances that elicit an emotion change radically; that is, the emotional experiences at different ages vary drastically.

Remember also that complex new emotions appear as children grow. For example, as early as 2 or 3 years of age children begin to display shame, guilt, and jealousy. These new emotions emerge from a child's increasing cognitive maturity and, as they do, they have a strong influence on self-esteem (Dunn, 1994). For example, embarassment or shame at giving a wrong answer in school may weaken a child's sense of competence.

As emotions appear, children must grapple with the issue of regulating them. Impulse control (see chapter 10) becomes an important learning experience early in life, strongly influenced by a child's temperament and how the environment (family, school, peers) reacts to emotional outbursts. We see here once again the importance of recognizing how biopsychosocial interactions affect behavior.

Emotional development seems to move from the general (positive versus negative emotions) to the specific—general positive states differentiate into such emotions as joy and interest; general negative states differentiate into fear, disgust, or anger. These primary emotions emerge during the first six months. Sometime after 18 months of age (recall Piaget's explanation of cognitive development), secondary emotions appear that are associated with a child's growing cognitive capacity for self-awareness. For emotions such as embarassment to appear, children must have developed a sense of self (Rothbart, 1994).

The Smile

One of the first signs of emotion is a baby's smile, which most parents immediately interpret as a sign of happiness. Two-month-old infants are often described as "smilers." Although smiles appear earlier, they lack the social significance of the smile

This 3-month-old infant is responding to its mother's face by smiling. In these interactions we see the roots of a child's psychosocial development.

that emerges at about 6 weeks. Babies smile instinctively at faces—real or drawn—and this probably reflects the human tendency to attend to patterns. Infants gradually learn that familiar faces usually mean pleasure, and smiling at known faces commences as early as the fifth month (Lewkowicz, 1996). Smiling seems to be a key element in securing positive reinforcement from those around the infant.

Smiling has a developmental history and, "for no reason" (that is, before infants discriminate among faces), appears soon after birth (Izard, 1994; Goleman, 1995). These smiles are usually designated as "false" smiles because they lack the emotional warmth of the true smile. By the baby's third week, the human female voice elicits a brief, real smile. By the sixth week the true social smile appears, especially in response to the human face. Babies smile at a conceptual age of 6 weeks, regardless of chronological age.

Why do infants smile? Several possible explanations are:

- Infants smile at human beings around them.

- Infants smile at any high-contrast stimuli, thus eliciting attention from those around them. The infant then links the human face with pleasure.

- Infants smile at discovering a relationship between their behavior and events in the external world.

These behaviors suggest that infants' emotions are much more organized than previously suggested. Recent research has examined the antecedents of emotional behavior. For example, tracing the roots of inhibition at 3 years of age, Park and others (1997) discovered that high negativity (fear, distress) in infancy, coupled with low positivity (laughter, smiling) predicted high inhibition in 3-year-olds—certainly no surprise.

But what was fascinating about this work was the role of parents. The investigators concluded that more demanding, less responsive parental care was associated with a *decrease* in later inhibition in children. In other words, those parents who are sympathetic and who accept their children's inhibition in the face of novelty, for example, actually encourage the development of inhibition. These findings, which support earlier work (see Arcus & others, 1992), remain controversial and need further research.

Also, studies have found that the antecedents of emotional understanding at age 3 are still in place at age 6 (Brown & Dunn, 1996). For example, participation in family discussions of the causes of people's behavior was related to later differences in how well children understood conflicting emotions.

Emotional Communication

Tronick (1989) questioned how some infants become sad and withdrawn, whereas others become happy, curious, and affectionate. To answer this question and to understand emotional development, Tronick turned to the nature of infant-caretaker emotional communication, in which both are active participants. (Again, note the importance of understanding that development is an integrated process—physical, cognitive, social, and emotional—and how important reciprocal interactions are to healthy growth.)

To begin his analysis, Tronick noted that infants, like all of us, have multiple goals: interacting with others, maintaining proximity to attachment figures, establishing homeostatic control, among others. To attain these goals, infants process information about themselves; in other words, there is an almost immediate cognitive input. Infants who attain their goals acquire a positive emotional state that encourages them to engage in additional interactions. Infants who determine that their goals are not being met experience negative emotions and begin to withdraw from any additional interactions. Obviously, infants can't reach these objectives on their own; they are too immature and limited in their abilities. They can, however, engage in reciprocal interactions that motivate others to help them.

Interactions between an infant and, usually, its mother display both

TABLE 6.5 A CHRONOLOGY OF EMOTIONS	
Age	**Emotions**
Birth	Ability to express emotions
1–3 months	Distress, rage, beginning of social smile
4–6 months	Sadness, disgust, beginning of attachment
7–9 months	Joy, anger, fear, separation and stranger anxiety

coordination and miscoordination. When miscoordination occurs—a mother misinterprets her child's behavior (for example, thinking that her child's cries are unnecessarily demanding when actually the child is tired or hungry)—the infant may turn away, frown, or whimper. Tronick labels these interactions as **interactive errors,** which can be corrected by **interactive repair,** thus returning the interactions to a positive state. Infants who consistently experience miscoordinated interactions gradually tend to distort their interactions with other people; they increasingly become more negative in their lifestyles. The nature of these interactions ultimately determines whether a child will be happy and cheerful or sad and depressed. Table 6.5 summarizes the time of appearance of several key emotions during the first year.

First Feelings

As you can tell from this brief excursion into emotional development, the resurgence of interest in emotional development has yet to be matched by hard experimental evidence. But given the changes in developmental research that we've described in these first chapters, it's only a matter of time before the path of emotional development becomes less obscure.

We have previously noted the current view of an infant as an active partner in development and have also described an infant's state with all of its meaning (Tronick, 1989). Today we are aware of the number of abilities an infant brings into the world. Using these insights, Greenspan and Greenspan (1985) and Greenspan (1995) have begun to probe the origins of emotions. They believe that the six emotional milestones they have identified can lead to parental practices that will help infants to establish more satisfying relationships with others.

- *Birth to 3 months.* The Greenspans believe that the major features of this period are self-regulation and interest in the world. For normal infants, each of these tasks supports the other.

- *2 to 7 months.* This is the infant's time of falling in love. Babies begin to focus on their mothers and are delighted by the mother's appearance, voice, and actions.

- *3 to 10 months.* During these months, an infant attempts to develop intentional communication. It is a time of reciprocal interactions as mothers and infants respond to each other's signals. When adults (usually the mother) respond to the baby's signals, the infant learns that its actions can cause a response.

- *9 to 18 months.* This is a time of dramatic observable achievements: standing, walking, talking. An organized sense of self begins to emerge. For example, when the mother returns, an infant of this age may walk to the mother, touch her, and perhaps say a word or two. The baby has put together several behaviors in an organized manner.

- *18 to 36 months.* Called the time of creating emotional ideas, this is a period of rapid mental growth. Children can form images of the mother in her absence.

They now link these cognitive capacities to the emotional world. They remember their mother's reading to them last night—why not tonight? They remember their father wrestling with them last night—why not tonight?

- *30 to 48 months.* The Greenspans believe that the emotional thinking of these months forms the basis for fantasy, reality, and self-esteem. In other words, children use their ideas to form a cause-and-effect understanding of their own emotions. Parents would be well-advised to follow Greenspan's advice.

> Each challenge, each new developmental milestone, is an opportunity not only for a child's growth, but for our own growth as well.—As we grow with our children through the daily trials, tribulations, joys, and pleasures of life, we can only make one simple demand of ourselves: to learn from our experiences. (Greenspan, 1995, p. 309)

Guided Review

21. _____ expressions for emotions are recognized by people of all cultures around the world.
22. One of the first signs of emotions is a baby's _____.
23. An infant's smile appears soon after _____.
24. The Greenspans have identified _____ emotional milestones in an infant's emotional development.
25. The Greenspans would describe the period of _____ to _____ _____ as a period of self-regulation and interest in the world.

CONCLUSION

The role of relationships in development has finally achieved a prominent place in our attempts to understand a child's growth. From the initial contacts with the mother to the ever-expanding network of siblings and peers at all ages, relationships exert a powerful and continuing influence on the direction of development.

We are slowly acquiring data about the function of relationships. For example, we have seen how important and persistent are the first interactions with parents. They set a tone for future relationships and set the direction for social and emotional development. Recent research has led to significant findings about the quality of relationships.

In summary:

Relationships and Development

- Acceptance of the transactional model of development and the idea of sensitive responsiveness has helped us to understand how children form relationships.
- Infants, as active partners in their development, help to shape their relationships.

The Meaning of Relationships

- Analyzing relationships by a system of categories such as Hinde's helps to make both theory and research more precise.
- Certain characteristics such as

appearance and temperament are intrinsic parts of any relationship.

- Appearance affects our initial impression of an individual.
- An infant's temperament immediately affects interactions with adults.
- The work of Chess and Thomas has helped us to understand the concept of goodness of fit—the match between an infant's and parents' temperaments.

First Relationships

- Developing relationships follow a sequence that incorporates all aspects of development: physical, cognitive, and psychosocial.

Answers

21. Facial 22. smile 23. birth 24. six 25. birth, 3 months

Attachment

- Bowlby and his colleagues, studying the separation of children from their parents, identified attachment as an important part of psychosocial development.
- Other explanations of attachment include the psychoanalytic, behavioral, and cognitive.
- Ainsworth's strange situation technique is designed to assess the security of an infant's attachment.
- Attachment is a cross-cultural phenomenon that knows no geographic boundary.
- Attachment develops early in life and offers clues to psychosocial development.
- The sensitivity of the infant-mother relationship in the moments following birth has led to considerable controversy.
- A mother's attachment to her infant seems to be influenced by the security of her attachment to her own mother.

Early Emotional Development

- Smiling is one of the first clues to emotional development.
- The Greenspans have identified several milestones of early emotional development.

KEY TERMS

Adult Attachment Interview
Attachment
Autonomy
Difficult children
Ghosts in the nursery
Easy children
Entrainment

Goodness of fit
Interactions
Interactive errors
Interactive repair
New York Longitudinal Study
Reciprocal interactions
Sensitive responsiveness

Slow-to-warm-up children
Strange situation technique
Symmetry
Synchrony
Temperament
Transactional model

WHAT DO YOU THINK?

1. Probably the basic issue for you to grasp is the extent of an infant's abilities: physical, social, and psychological. Do you think that infants are as we have described them in chapters 5 and 6, or do you think that we have over- or underestimated their competencies?

2. Depending on your answer to question 1, explain how you interpret an infant's participation in developing relationships. That is, given an infant's ability to smile, coo, and make physical responses, how much control do you believe infants exercise in their interactions with adults?

3. Think about the role of appearance and temperament in developing relationships. A well-known psychologist once said that some children are so difficult to love that parents may have to fake it. How do you react to this statement? Do you think an infant could detect such parental behavior?

4. Although Mary Ainsworth's research is the basis for our belief in the importance of attachment in social development, criticism has been directed at her studies because of the small number of subjects and the lack of consideration of the subjects' temperaments. Do you think these are valid criticisms? Do they raise questions in your mind about the universality of her conclusions?

CHAPTER REVIEW TEST

1. A reciprocal interactions model is also known as a (an) _____ model.
   a. transactional
   b. interaction
   c. main effects
   d. developmental model

2. Which of the following statements is not in agreement with an understanding of sensitive responsiveness?
   a. All children are temperamentally similar at birth.
   b. Children instantly tune into their environment.
   c. Children give clues to their personalities.
   d. Children, from birth, engage in reciprocal interactions.

3. A true relationship has
   a. reciprocity.
   b. continuity.
   c. spontaneity.
   d. longevity.

4. More sensitive mothers have infants who are more
   a. restless.
   b. nervous.
   c. detached.
   d. responsive.

5. The content of interactions would not include
   a. what the partners do together.
   b. how the partners see each other.
   c. distinguishing different relationships.
   d. labeling the relationship.

6. Langlois demonstrated that infants value _____ as much as adults
   a. hair color
   b. skin color
   c. gender
   d. attractiveness

7. Children's _____ contribute significantly to their interactions with their environments.
   a. ages
   b. gender
   c. temperaments
   d. culture

8. Chess and Thomas described a child with a low intensity of reactions and a somewhat negative attitude as
   a. slow to warm up.
   b. difficult.
   c. easy.
   d. depressed.

9. Which of the following influences is not at work during the first days of an infant's life?
   a. Bodily needs
   b. Psychological needs
   c. Cognitive needs
   d. Adult response needs

10. By the age of _____ the infant has formed a need for social interactions.
    a. 3 months
    b. 1 week
    c. 6 months
    d. 1 year

11. _____ is a characteristic that identifies the rhythm that is established between a parent's and infant's behavior.
    a. Synchrony
    b. Autonomy
    c. Entrainment
    d. Symmetry

12. According to Bowlby, _____ behavior is any form of behavior that results in a person attaining or maintaining proximity to some other clearly identified individual who is conceived as better able to cope with the world.
    a. detachment
    b. attachment
    c. protest
    d. emotional

13. Which statement is true?
    a. Only mothers have the potential to induce attachment.
    b. Fathers and mothers act quite differently with their infants.
    c. There is a sensitive period for parent-infant bonding.
    d. No sensitive period exists for parent-infant bonding.

14. The connection between childhood experiences and adult parenting behavior is described in
    a. intergenerational continuity.
    b. the New York Longitudinal Study.
    c. the origins of temperament.
    d. goodness of fit.

15. A smile is an early sign of a baby's
    a. cognitive development.
    b. emotions.
    c. physical needs.
    d. attachment.

16. By the _____ the true social smile appears.
    a. third day
    b. third week
    c. sixth week
    d. third month

17. Which is not a possible explanation of an infant's smile?
    a. Infants smile at human beings around them.
    b. Infants smile at high-contrast stimuli.
    c. Infants smile at discovering a relationship between their behavior and external events.
    d. Infants smile at the sound of rhythmic music.

18. Tronick refers to the miscoordination between a mother and her infant as
    a. misguidance.
    b. metacognitive misinterpretation.
    c. interactive error.
    d. symbolic miscoding.

19. According to the Greenspans, the age 3 to 10 months is characterized by
    a. standing, walking, and talking.
    b. an attempt to develop intentional communication.
    c. the infant falling in love.
    d. creating emotional ideas.

20. Early relationships
    a. can influence later relationships.
    b. are based on physical needs.
    c. are preprogrammed.
    d. are characterized by shyness.

Answers

1.a 2.a 3.b 4.d 5.b 6.d 7.c 8.a 9.c 10.a 11.c 12.b 13.d 14.a 15.b 16.c 17.d 18.c 19.b 20.a

PART IV

Early Childhood

One of the most obvious facts about grownups, to a child, is that they have forgotten what it's like to be a child.

Randall Jarrell

CHAPTER 7

Physical and Cognitive Development in Early Childhood

L iz, whom we met in chapter 5, felt she now had a good idea of what perpetual motion meant. Her two children, 3-year-old Maddi and 5-year-old Jackie, engaged in nonstop activities from the time they woke up in the morning until they went to bed—with great reluctance. (Be thankful for small favors, she thought; Maddi still took a long afternoon nap.) At least you could talk to Jackie, who was excited about entering kindergarten in September.

But Maddi—oh, that Maddi! She had discovered the thrill of saying "no" loudly and emphatically, was into everything, and sometimes pretended not to hear Liz's warnings. Liz was worried about what seemed to be a steady stream of threats she directed at Maddi. She was concerned that so many negative incidents could affect her relationship with Maddi.

These thoughts came to Liz as she opened a letter from the preschool where Maddi was registered for the fall. Also included was a form for her to fill out, and as she read the items, she became even more concerned.

The first item asked for a description of Maddi. Liz answered honestly that she was healthy, vigorous, active, and seemed to be progressing well. She was toilet trained, helped in dressing herself, and seemed quite independent. Liz thought Maddi was unusually curious, always poking into things, opening drawers, and looking into closets. Liz was often embarrassed by this behavior when she and Maddi visited other homes. On the other hand, Maddi was putting her words together nicely and played fairly well with other children.

In the next part of the form, Liz was asked several specific questions: How independent was Maddi? Was she left-handed or right-handed? Were there particular activities that Maddi really enjoyed, such as drawing? Did she like pretend play?

Liz answered the questions carefully: Maddi seemed quite independent; she didn't cling and could play by herself. She used her right hand for drawing and throwing. She loved to draw and Liz was able to understand what Maddi was trying to tell in her pictures. In her games and play, she often used objects for different purposes, such as a stick for a broom.

As Liz responded to the questions, she realized that Maddi seemed to be a fairly normal 3-year-old (whatever that might mean, Liz thought a little gloomily). Still, she was bothered by Maddi's incessant questioning and outbursts of negativism. Since she and Maddi were scheduled for an interview at the preschool the next week, Liz decided to mention her worries to the instructor who would be interviewing them. After all, preschool teachers worked constantly with children of this age.

The following week, while Liz talked with one of the instructors, Maddi played happily with a variety of toys. When the instructor commented that Maddi seemed quite well adjusted, Liz had the opportunity to mention how worried she was. The instructor listened and then began to laugh, saying that Maddi seemed to be perfectly normal for her age. She mentioned that Maddi was at that age when she wanted as much information as possible to feed her inquiring mind, which was steadily becoming involved in more symbolic activities, such as telling a story with her drawings and using one thing to represent another.

As Liz listened, she was delighted because these were just the things that Maddi was doing. She was acting as most youngsters of her age do. The instructor then went on to describe what Liz could expect for the next year or so. ✪

Early childhood youngsters find the world a fascinating place. Giving these children the freedom to explore and learn, coupled with sensible restrictions, encourages the development of mastery.

Many parents have an all too human reaction—disbelief—to the reality of dealing with a dynamo, which describes children of the age we're about to discuss. Physical activity, constant curiosity, and growing mental maturity all characterize children from 2 to 6 years of age. By age 2, typical children walk, talk, and eagerly explore their environment, gradually acquiring greater mastery over their bodies.

It's a time of rapid physical and cognitive change. The rounded bodies of infancy give way to the slimmer torsos of early childhood, muscles begin to firm, bones begin to harden, and continued brain development provides a foundation for a world of symbolic promise. When these changes combine with feelings of confidence—"No, no, I can do it"—parents and other adults working with children of this age face challenges that can try their patience.

Cognitively, it's the time of Piaget's *preoperational period,* which traces a child's mental odyssey during these years. Many of today's early childhood youngsters will also experience some form of preschool education. Finally, these are the years when children acquire their language so rapidly that we refer to the "language explosion."

Liz's concerns and what she was learning about these years is our task for the next two chapters. In this chapter we'll first trace the important physical changes of the period. We'll then analyze cognitive development and trace the growing symbolic ability of the early childhood youngster. Finally, during these years children experience the "language explosion" with all that it implies for development, so we'll conclude by discussing this critical phase.

When you finish reading this chapter, you should be able to

• Describe the outstanding physical and cognitive characteristics of the period.

• Analyze the importance of brain lateralization in a child's development.

• Identify the key phases in cognitive development during the preoperational period.

• Contrast Piaget's view of cognitive development with information-processing explanations.

• Designate the language milestones of the early childhood years.

• Indicate the speech irregularities that can occur in the early childhood period.

So our task for these next two chapters is clear: understanding the physical, cognitive, and psychosocial changes of these exciting years. Table 7.1 summarizes many characteristics of these youngsters.

Guided Review

1. The early childhood years coincide with Piaget's _____ period.
2. The period of early childhood extends from the age of _____ to the age of _____.
3. During this period a child can grow as much as _____ inches and gain _____ pounds.
4. These years are the time of the language _____.

Answers

1. preoperational 2. 6 3, 10-12, 18 4. explosion

TABLE 7.1 SOME DEVELOPMENTAL CHARACTERISTICS OF EARLY CHILDHOOD

Age (yrs)	Height (in.)	Weight (lbs.)	Language Development	Motor Development
2½	36	30	Identifies object by use; vocabulary of 450 words	Can walk on tiptoes; can jump with both feet off the floor
3	38	32	Answers questions; uses brief sentences; vocabulary of 900 words	Can stand on one foot; jumps from bottom of stairs; rides tricycle
3½	39	34	Begins to build sentences; vocabulary of 1200 words	Continues to improve 3-year-old skills; begins to play with others
4	41	36	Names and counts several objects; uses conjunctions; understands prepositions; vocabulary of 1500 words	Walks downstairs, one foot to step; skips on one foot; throws ball overhand
4½	42	38	Mean length of utterance 4.5 words; vocabulary of 1870 words	Hops on one foot; dramatic play
5	43	41	Begins to show language mastery; uses words apart from specific situation; vocabulary of 2100 words	Skips, alternating feet; walks straight line; stands for longer period on one foot
5½	45	45	Asks meaning of words; more complex sentences of 5 or 6 words; vocabulary of 2500 words	Draws recognizable person; continues to develop throwing skill
6	46	48	Good grasp of sentence meaning; continues to use complex sentences; vocabulary of 2600 words	Jumps easily; throws ball overhand very well; alternates standing on each foot

Physical and Motor Development

As you can see from table 7.1, growth in childhood proceeds at a less frantic pace than in infancy. Children during this period grow about another 12 inches and continue to gain weight at the rate of about 5 pounds a year. Body proportions are also changing, with the legs growing faster than the rest of the body. By about age 6, the legs make up almost 45 percent of body length. At the beginning of this period, children usually have all their baby teeth; and at the end of the period, children begin to lose them. Boys and girls show about the same rate of growth during these years.

Features of Physical Development

Look at figure 7.1, the human growth curve. (Note that 10 centimeters equal 4 inches.) This curve strikingly illustrates the regularity of physical growth. Most parts of the body (except the brain and the reproductive organs) follow this pattern (Tanner, 1989). With the exception of the two spurts at infancy and adolescence, growth is highly predictable for almost all boys and girls, given satisfactory conditions.

The Sequence of Early Childhood Growth

We know that different cells, tissues, and organs grow at different rates. (Some tissues never lose the ability to grow, such as hair, skin, and nails.) In humans, for example, body length at birth is about four times the length of the face at birth, so the head is relatively large. But the head grows more slowly than the trunk or limbs, so that they gradually become proportional.

Parents and children alike are quite conscious of the appearance and loss of

Figure 7.1

The human growth curve

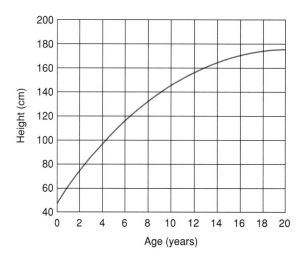

Children's rapidly developing motor skills are clearly seen in their drawings from uncontrolled scribbling to controlled "within the lines" attempts to their own creative expressions.

"baby" teeth and the arrival of the first permanent teeth. At about 2½ years all of the primary teeth have come through, which most children begin to lose between 5 and 6 years. At about this time, the first permanent teeth appear. Children continue to lose their primary teeth and gain new permanent teeth at about the same time. The timing can be different for some children, however, so that gaps between teeth may appear or new teeth arrive before the baby teeth have fallen out, causing a space problem that may require professional attention.

Continuing Brain Development

We traced the brain's rapid development during the prenatal period and the infancy years, and now we see a slowing process take hold (Fischbach, 1992). The brain's growth spurt effectively begins to decelerate during the early childhood years. For example, estimates are that about 75 percent of adult brain weight is present at 2½ years and 90 percent at 6 years, a figure that clearly indicates a slower growth pattern (Rose, 1990). In other words, while it took 2½ years to grow 75 percent, another 3½ years sees growth increasing only by 15%. Figure 7.2 illustrates this process.

Although the brain continues its development, the process resembles more a filling in of the structure that has grown to this point. Here we see another example of biopsychosocial forces interacting. For example, a child's experiences feed back into the developing nervous system and facilitates the multiplication and growth of cells. The new and exciting stimuli of the early childhood years also encourage the formation of new connections among the neurons that developed during infancy. (See chapter 5 for a review of early brain development.)

Figure 7.2

Slowing Growth of the Brain

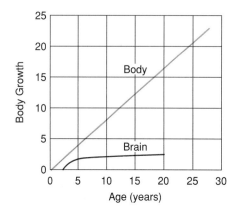

Figure 7.3

Lateralization of handedness

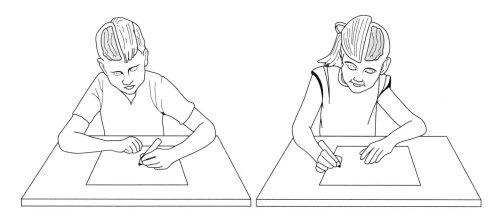

By the age of 2, the cortex has grown to a point where it more closely resembles the cortex of an adult brain. The cerebellum, which is that part of the brain controlling balance and fine motor skills, continues to grow fairly rapidly. The sensory area receives visual, auditory, and tactile stimuli that children must analyze and interpret, thus furthering their potential for cognitive development. Consequently, we can say that continued brain growth during the early childhood years parallels cognitive and language accomplishments, another example of continued impact of biopsychosocial forces (Lansdown & Walker, 1991).

Lateralization

During the early childhood years, as the brain continues to exercise its powerful control of behavior, children show a decided preference for using one hand or foot over the other. This preference, called **handedness,** starts to appear toward the end of infancy and becomes well established by the age of 5 or 6.

Which hand do you use for writing? If you were to kick a football, would you use the leg on the same side of your body as the hand you use for writing? Pick up a pencil or ruler and assume it is a telescope. Which eye do you use? Are you using the same side of the body that you used for writing and kicking? Your answers to these questions should give you some idea of the meaning of cerebral **lateralization.**

Language is a good example of lateralization. If you recall our earlier discussion in chapter 5, language entails the combining of discrete elements—letters, syllables, words. Since this fits the functioning of the left hemisphere, about 95 to 99 percent of right-handed people and about 70 percent of left-handed people are left lateralized for language. Yet we can't be absolutely sure that the right hemisphere is totally inactive in language usage. Blood-flow studies suggest that during language processing considerable blood flows to the right hemisphere (Temple, 1993). We also know that damage to the right hemisphere frequently causes perceptual and attentional disorders (Gershon & Rieder, 1992). Another possible role for the right hemisphere in language may involve humor (perceiving wit in stories and jokes).

Consequently, although the hemispheres seem to be almost identical, our discussion reveals important differences between the two. These differences are clues to your brain's organization. If you are right-handed, for example, your left cerebral hemisphere is lateralized for handedness and also for control of your speech—you are "left lateralized." Figure 7.3 illustrates lateralization.

Influences on Physical Development in Early Childhood

In an excellent overview of physical development, Tanner (1989) discusses how the interaction of heredity and environment produces the rate and kinds of physical growth. Among the chief contributing forces are the following:

The energy of the early childhood years is seen in the physical activities of the period: constant motion followed by periods of rest and nutrition.

- *Genetic elements*. Hereditary elements are of immense importance to the regulation of growth. The genetic growth plan is given at conception and functions throughout the entire growth period.

- *Nutrition*. Malnutrition delays growth and, if persistent, can cause lasting damage. Children in Stuttgart, Germany, were studied each year from 1911 to 1953. From 1920 to 1940 there was a uniform increase in average height and weight, but in the later years of each war (World Wars I and II) average height declined as food was curtailed. These children recovered, but it's difficult to draw definite conclusions from this and similar studies because of children's individual differences (Cole & Cole, 1996). Each of us has a differing ability to withstand deprivation of any kind.

- *Disease*. Short-term illnesses cause no permanent retardation of the growth rate, although they may cause some disturbance if the child's diet is consistently inadequate (an avoidance of empty calories). Major disease usually causes a slowing of growth, followed by a catch-up period if circumstances become more favorable.

- *Psychological disturbance*. Stress can slow development and occasionally lead to deprivation dwarfism. Small children under uncompromising strain (war conditions, abuse) seem to "turn off" their growth hormone and become almost dwarfed (Tanner, 1989).

- *Socioeconomic status*. Children from different social classes differ in average body size at all ages. Tanner gives the example of differences in height between British children of the professional class and those of laborers. Children of the professional class are from 1 inch taller at age 3 to 2 inches taller at adolescence. A consistent pattern appears in all such studies, indicating that children in more favorable circumstances are larger than those growing up under less favorable economic conditions. The difference seems to stem from nutrition, sleep, exercise, and recreation.

- *Secular trends*. During the past hundred years the tendency has been for children to become progressively larger at all ages. This is especially true in Europe and America.

This brief overview of physical development again illustrates the importance of the biopsychosocial model. For example, you may be tempted to think that physical growth is essentially biological, mainly determined by heredity. Note, however, the role played by nutrition and socioeconomic status. The interaction among biological, psychological, and social influences testifies to the power of the biopsychosocial model in explaining development.

TABLE 7.2 THE EMERGENCE OF MOTOR SKILLS		
Age	**Gross Skills**	**Fine Skills**
2	Runs, climbs stairs, jumps from object (both feet)	Throws ball, kicks ball, turns page, begins to scribble
3	Hops, climbs stairs with alternating feet, jumps from bottom step	Copies circle, opposes thumb to finger, scribbling continues to improve
4	Runs well, skillful jumping, begins to skip, pedals tricycle	Holds pencil, copies square, walks balance beam
5	Hops about 50 feet, balances on one foot, can catch large ball, good skipping	Colors within lines, forms letters, dresses and undresses self with help, eats more neatly
6	Carries bundles, begins to ride bicycle, jumps rope, chins self, can catch a tennis ball	Ties shoes, uses scissors, uses knife and fork, washes self with help

This child is using his right hand to dig, signaling that his left cerebral hemisphere is lateralized for handedness and control of speech.

Growing Motor Skills

When early childhood children reach the age of 6, no one—neither parents nor teachers—is surprised by what they can do physically. Think back to the infancy period and recall how often we referred to what children couldn't do. Stand, walk, run. We tend to take the accomplishments of the 6-year-old for granted, but a great deal of neuromuscular development had to occur before these motor skills became so effortless.

We are concerned here with two types of **motor skills:** *gross* (using the large muscles) and *fine* (using the small muscles of the hands and fingers). Thanks to perceptual and motor development, 3-and 4-year-old children can hold crayons, copy triangles, button their clothes, and unlace their shoes. Table 7.2 summarizes the development of motor skills.

The physical picture of the early childhood youngster is one of energy and growing motor skill. Adequate rest is critical and parents should establish a routine to avoid problems. For example, to reconcile a rambunctious child with the necessity of sleep, parents should minimize stimulation through a consistent, easily recognized program: washing, tooth brushing, storytelling, and gentle but firm pressure to sleep. Careful and thoughtful adult care should prevent undue difficulties.

The Special Case of Drawing

The early childhood years are a time when children show a great love for drawing. Not only are their drawings a sign of motor development, but they also indicate levels of cognitive development and can be emotionally revealing.

Children love to draw and their art work has long attracted the attention of scholars as far back as John Ruskin in 1857 with his book, *The Elements of Drawing*. In a finely tuned sequence, which no one has to teach them, children move from random scribbles to skillful creations. Some of their drawings are efforts to reproduce things that interest them; others tell a story; others are fanciful and combine real and imaginary elements (Schulman, 1991). When something is as natural and fascinating for children as drawing, we can only wonder why the vast majority of youngsters lose this desire and skill.

Children's drawings go through a sequence of stages: 2-year-olds grab markers and scribble enthusiastically (using dots and lines) and seem fascinated by their ability to produce lines as a result of their movements. Parents and preschool teachers should encourage this **random scribbling** as a necessary first step in children's creative growth, much as crawling preceded walking and cooing and babbling precede speech (Capacchione, 1989). During this phase of random scribbling, which continues until about age 3, children are free from any evaluation of their drawings; they're simply having fun.

Three-year-olds hold a crayon with their whole hand and then begin to use their wrists, which permits them to draw curves and loops. Called **controlled scribbling,** they become engrossed with geometric figures and are beginning to realize their lines can represent objects. (Rhoda Kellogg and her colleagues (1967) identified 20 basic scribbles.) Now their art matches their cognitive development and reflects their growing symbolic power. For example, they'll point to their creation and say, "That's a man." This phase lasts until about age 4.

Four- and 5-year-olds show greater control and attention to what they are doing, deliberately attempting to create representations of objects. For example, they'll use a circle to represent a head or the sun. Young children produce exciting creations, using a combination of symbols that vary widely from child to child (Wachowiak & Clements, 1997). Artistic expression seems to peak by the end of the early childhood period. During these years, children begin to paint and hold the brush with thumb and fingers. They hold the paper in place with the free hand. They give names to their drawings and begin to show representation (using one thing for another—see the cognitive section of the chapter). They work hard at their creations and take them seriously (Schulman, 1991).

Children's Love of Drawing—What Happens?

Well-known psychologist Howard Gardner (1980, 1982) has written sensitively about children's drawing and raised several important questions. Noting how drawings develop—from the scribbles of the 2-year-old to the 3-year-old's interest in design to the 4- and 5-year-old's drawing representations—Gardner commented on the liveliness and enthusiasm of their work. And then suddenly it stops! The end of the early childhood period sees the end of creative expression, except for a select few. Why?

Gardner (1982a) has argued that children limit their artistic efforts to copying forms or cease drawing altogether after the peak of creativity has been reached. This "reach for realism" may be a critical stage of development during which children reflect their cognitive level by following rules and obeying the dictates of convention. With growing cognitive ability, and a decrease in egocentrism, children may well compare their efforts with those of others and become discouraged—their work just isn't as good—and they lose interest. It is not until adolescence that a small number of children again manifest that creative spark. At this time inborn talent and a supportive environment help a child develop those skills needed to withstand immersion in rules and correct thinking.

Schulman (1991) takes a different view. Noting that art experts urge that children not receive formal training in art skills until the end of the middle childhood period, he argued that schools and parents encourage and develop their children's artistic skills at a young age. Children like to draw and paint, to express themselves through their artistry. They lose their interest, however, when they see no goal, when making another pattern no longer fascinates them. With no new objectives and challenges, children's enthusiasm vanishes, interest evaporates, and they turn their attention to other fields.

Whatever the explanation, most of us match Adams's (1986, p. 94) description of college-age students.

> A great deal of effort has been put into their formal education, but little into their visual ability. When they come to Stanford many are "visual illiterates." They often are not used to drawing, nor to using visual imagery as a thinking mode. Although their drawing is usually not good, it is usually good enough (especially with a few helpful hints) to use as a thinking aid. Nonetheless, they are usually extremely reluctant to draw because their drawings compare so badly with drawings made by professionals.

Children's drawings not only are good clues to their motor coordination but, as we'll see, provide insights into their cognitive and emotional lives, another example of how a biopsychosocial perspective helps us to understand development.

Guided Review

5. Optimum growth requires proper _____, _____, and _____ to stimulate growth hormones.
6. High-sugar and high-fat foods lead to the accumulation of _____ _____.
7. _____ scribbling continues until about 3 years of age.
8. A child using his/her left hand to draw, signals that the _____ cerebral hemisphere is lateralized for handedness.
9. Motor skills fall into two types _____ and _____.
10. Gardner has attributed the loss of a child's artistic creativity to the _____ _____ _____.

Cognitive Development

Physical developments during early childhood, while observable and exciting, are not the only significant changes occurring. Early childhood youngsters expand their mental horizons by their increasing use of ideas and by their rapid growth in language. This growing cognitive ability is a fact; explaining it is much more difficult. To help us understand what is happening and how it happens, we turn once more to Piaget.

Piaget's Preoperational Period

For Piaget, **preoperational** refers to a child who has begun to use symbols but is not yet capable of mentally manipulating them. Children who cannot take two things into consideration at the same time—take something apart and put it together again, who cannot return to the beginning of a thought sequence, that is, who cannot comprehend how to reverse the action of 2 + 2, who cannot believe that

These children, playing doctor and patients, are furthering all aspects of their development. They are discovering what objects in their environment are supposed to do, they are learning about the give and take of human relationships, and they are channeling their emotional energies into acceptable outlets.

Answers

5. nutrition, temperature, rest 6. empty calories 7. Random 8. right 9. gross, fine 10. "reach for realism"

water poured from a short, fat glass into a taller, thinner one retains the same volume—these children are at a level of thinking that precedes operational thought. Several examples of preoperational thinking are as follows:

Realism, which means that children slowly distinguish and accept a real world. They now have identified both an external and internal world.

Animism, which means that children consider a large number of objects as alive and conscious that adults consider inert. For example, a child who sees a necklace wound up and then released explains that it is moving because it "wants to unwind." Children overcome this cognitive limitation when they refuse to accept personality in things. Piaget believed that comparison with the thoughts of others slowly conquers animism as it does egocentrism. He identified four stages of animism:

- Almost everything is alive and conscious.

- Only those things that move are alive.

- Only those things that manifest spontaneous movements are alive.

- Consciousness is limited to the animal world.

Artificialism, which consists of attributing human creation to everything. For example, when asked how the moon began, some of Piaget's subjects replied, "because we began to be alive." As egocentrism decreases, youngsters become more objective and they steadily assimilate objective reality to their cognitive structures. They proceed from a purely human or divine explanation to an explanation that is half natural, half artificial: The moon comes from the clouds but the clouds come from people's houses. (The decline of artificialism parallels the growth of realism.)

Features of Preoperational Thought

For Piaget, the great accomplishment of the preoperational period is a growing ability to represent, which is how we record or express information. For example, the word "car" is a **representation** since it represents a certain idea. Pointing an index finger at a playmate and saying "Stick 'em up" is also an example of representation.

Other activities typical of preoperational children reflect their use of internal representation (Piaget & Inhelder, 1969) and include the following.

Deferred Imitation. Preoperational children can imitate some object or activity that they have previously witnessed; for example, they walk like an animal that they saw at the zoo earlier in the day. Piaget gave the example of a child who visited his home one day and while there had a temper tantrum. His daughter Jacqueline, about 18 months old, watched, absolutely fascinated. Later, after the child had gone, Jacqueline had her own tantrum. Piaget interpreted this to mean that Jacqueline had a mental image of the event.

Symbolic Play. Children enjoy pretending that they are asleep, or that they are someone or something else. Piaget argued eloquently for recognizing the importance of play in a youngster's life. Obliged to adapt themselves to social and physical worlds that they only slightly understand and appreciate, children must make intellectual adaptations that leave personality needs unmet. For their mental health, they must have some outlet, some technique that permits them to assimilate reality to self, and not vice versa. Children find this mechanism in play, using the tools characteristic of symbolic play. (We'll discuss the role of play in greater detail in chapter 8.)

Drawing. We have previously discussed drawing in a broad context but here Piaget concentrated on its cognitive elements. Children of this age project their mental representations into their drawings. Highly symbolic, their art work reflects the level of their thinking and what they are thinking. Encourage children to talk about their art.

Mental Images. Mental images appear late in this period because of their dependence on internalized imitation. Piaget's studies of the development of mental images between the ages of 4 and 5 showed that mental images fall into two categories. **Reproductive images** are images restricted to those sights previously perceived. **Anticipatory images** are images that include movements and transformations. At the preoperational level, children are limited to reproductive images.

A good illustration of the difference between the two types of images is Piaget's famous example of matching tokens. Piaget showed 5- and 6-year-old children a row of red tokens and asked them to put down the same number of blue tokens. At this age, children put one blue token opposite each red one. When Piaget changed the arrangement, however, and spread out the row of red tokens, the children were baffled because they thought there were more red tokens than blue. Thus, children of this age can reproduce but not anticipate, which reflects the nature of their cognitive structures and level of cognitive functioning.

Language. For preoperational children, language becomes a vehicle for thought. Children of this age need ample opportunities to talk with adults and with each other. (See the language section of this chapter.)

Limitations of Preoperational Thought

Although we see the steady development of thought during this period, preoperational thought still has limitations. As the word *preoperational* implies, this period comes before advanced symbolic operations develop. Piaget has stated consistently that knowledge is not just a mental image of an object or event.

To know an object is to act on it, to modify it, to transform it, and to join objects in a class. The action is also reversible. If two is added to two, the result is four; but if two is taken away from four, the original two returns. The preoperational child lacks the ability to perform such operations on concepts and objects.

Several reasons account for the restricted nature of preoperational thought. In the period of preoperational thought, children cannot assume the role of another person or recognize that other viewpoints exist, a state called **egocentrism.** This differs from sensorimotor egocentrism, which is primarily the inability to distinguish oneself from the world. For example, children may believe that the moon follows *them* around; everything focuses on them.

In Piaget's classic experiment, a child is shown a display of three mountains varying in height and color. The child stands on one side of the table, looking at the mountains; a doll is then placed at various spots around the mountains. The child is next shown several pictures of the mountains and asked to pick the one that shows what part of the mountains the doll saw. Egocentric children pick the photo that shows the mountains as they saw them.

Another striking feature of preoperational thought is the centering of attention on one aspect of an object and the neglecting of any other features—called **centration.** Consequently, reasoning is often distorted. Preoperational youngsters are unable to decenter, to notice features that would give balance to their reasoning. A good example of this is the process of **classification.** When youngsters from age 3 to age 12 are asked, "What things are alike?", their answers proceed through three stages. First, the youngest children group *figurally,* that is, by similarities, differences, and by forming a figure in space with the parts. Second, children of about age 5 or 6 group objects *nonfigurally.* They form the elements into groups with no particular spatial form. (For an interesting discussion of the development of children's analysis of spatial patterns, see Tada & Stiles, 1996.)

At this stage, the classification seems rational, but Piaget and Inhelder (1969) provide a fascinating example of the limitations of classification at this age. If in a group of 12 flowers, there are 6 roses, preoperational youngsters can differentiate between the other flowers and the roses. But when asked if there are more flowers or more roses, they are unable to reply because they cannot distinguish the

Figure 7.4

Lack of genuine classification

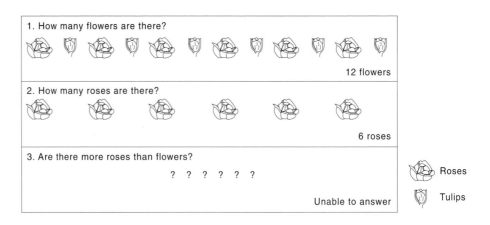

1. How many flowers are there?

12 flowers

2. How many roses are there?

6 roses

3. Are there more roses than flowers?

? ? ? ? ? ?

Unable to answer

Roses

Tulips

Figure 7.5

Piaget used the beaker task to determine whether children had conservation of liquid. In 1, two identical beakers (A and B) are presented to the child; then the experimenter pours the liquid from B into beaker C, which is taller and thinner than A and B. The child is asked if beakers B and C have the same amount of liquid. The preoperational child says no, responding that the taller, thinner beaker (C) has more.

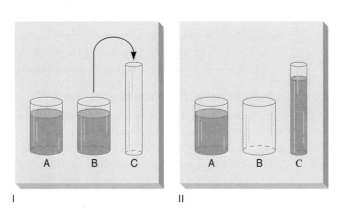

whole from the part (see figure 7.4). This understanding does not appear until the third phase of classification, at about the age of 8.

Another limitation of the period is the lack of **conservation.** Conservation means understanding that an object retains certain properties, no matter how its form changes. The most popular illustration is to show a 5-year-old two glasses, each half filled with water. The child agrees that each glass contains an equal amount. But if you then pour the water from one of the glasses into a taller, thinner glass, the youngster now says that the new glass contains more liquid (see figure 7.5).

Youngsters consider only the appearance of the liquid and ignore what happened. They also do not perceive the reversibility of the transformation. In their minds they do not pour the water back into the first glass.

Finally, preoperational thought lacks **reversibility.** A truly cognitive act is reversible if it can use stages of reasoning to solve a problem and then proceed in reverse, tracing its steps back to the original question or premise. The preoperational child's thought is **irreversible** and entangles the child in a series of contradictions in logic.

In the water-level problem, for example, the child believes that the taller, thinner glass contains more water. Youngsters cannot mentally reverse the task (imagine pouring the contents back into the original glass). At the conclusion of the preoperational period, children slowly decenter and learn reversibility as a way of mental life.

Challenges to Piaget

As we mentioned in our previous discussion of Piaget's sensorimotor period (see chapter 5), recent research has raised questions about Piaget's assumptions concerning the cognitive abilities of young children. For example, as we explained in the matching tokens problem, children of this age are likely to say that the spread-out row now has more tokens. Piaget believed that the children concentrated on the length of the row because they lacked a concept of number.

When Gelman and Baillargeon (1983) used similar problems with a smaller number of objects (up to four), however, children of this age successfully answered questions about the number of objects involved. Evidence continues to mount supporting the conclusion that Piaget underestimated the cognitive abilities of young children: They conserve, classify, and overcome egocentrism earlier than Piaget realized (Gardner, 1983).

Metacognition

As Flavell (1992, p. 999) noted, young children are quite competent—they are not as "pre this or pre that" as we used to think. He gives the example of 2-year-olds who know that a blindfolded person will not see what they themselves are looking at. Their understanding of numbers and their mental states are more advanced than previously realized. For example, we now think that children construct their own ideas of how their minds work, a theory of mind frequently referred to as **metacognition.**

Although interest in metacognition is relatively recent, its content has always been with us; for example, our thoughts about a decision we made or "how we are doing on a project" all entail metacognitive processes. Metacognitive skills seem to be involved in many mental activities: comprehension, evaluation, reading, writing, and problem solving among others. Flavell (1993) has analyzed metacognition by two domains: **metacognitive knowledge** and **metacognitive experiences.**

Metacognitive knowledge refers to a child's knowledge and beliefs about cognitive matters gained from experiences that are then stored in long-term memory (Flavell, 1993). Children acquire metacognitive knowledge about *people, tasks,* and *strategies.* For example, they may have come to believe that a particular person just does not like them; pupils may decide that a teacher has little confidence in their ability. Another example is seen in the recent interest in children's **theory of mind,** that is, their ability to understand how other people's ideas affect their behavior (Jenkins & Astington, 1996).

For example, children gradually learn that the nature of a task forces them to think about how they will attack it. If it's difficult, perhaps they will need more time, or perhaps they will take a different approach or seek adult help. As for strategies, children learn to make a distinction between cognitive strategies (achieving a goal) and metacognitive strategies (monitoring progress toward that goal). Over time, they will continue to learn about what strategies are best suited for success on a particular task.

Metacognitive experiences are either cognitive or affective experiences that relate to cognitive activities. For example, children, after studying, may feel a little uncertain or doubtful about one of the topics, or may be concerned that they didn't understand it. As Flavell (1993) noted, metacognitive experiences are most likely to occur when careful, conscious monitoring of cognitive efforts are required.

Flavell's statement (1993, p. 127) about cognition during the early childhood years seems particularly relevant here.

> The developmental psychologist's portrait of cognition during the period of early childhood used to be rather negative and unflattering. For example, preschool children's thinking was often characterized as "preoperational" or even "preconceptual." However, recent research has shown that an impressive number of fragile but nonetheless genuine competencies have been acquired by the end of this period. It seems we had underestimated the young child's abilities, just as we had underestimated the infant's.

Children and Their Humor

"Why did daddy tiptoe past the medicine cabinet?"

"Because he didn't want to wake the sleeping pills."

Jokes such as these have spurred Paul McGhee (1979, 1988; McGhee & Paniutsopoulous, 1990) to analyze children's humor and trace its developmental path. Noting that little is known about how children develop humor, McGhee turned to cognitive development as a possible explanation. Although humor also has psychodynamic and social features (Clay, 1997), McGhee believes that its cognitive properties offer the best basis for unraveling its secrets.

McGhee begins by noting that the basis of most children's humor is incongruity, which is the realization that the relationship between different things just isn't "right." Using this as a basis, he traces four stages of incongruous humor. He treats stages as does Piaget: The sequence of stages remains the same, but the ages at which children pass through them varies.

- *Stage 1: Incongruous Actions toward Objects.* Stage 1 usually occurs sometime during the second year, when children play with objects. They are able to form internal images of the object and thus start to "make believe." For example, one of Piaget's children picked up a leaf, put it to her ear, and talked to it as if it were a telephone, laughing all the time. One of the main characteristics of stage 1 humor is the child's physical activity directed at the object.
- *Stage 2: Incongruous Labeling of Objects and Events.* Stage 2 humor is more verbal, which seems to be its most important difference from

stage 1. McGhee (1979) notes that the absence of action toward objects is quite noticeable. Piaget's 22-month-old daughter put a shell on the table and said, "sitting." She then put another shell on top of the first, looked at them and said, "sitting on pot." She then began to laugh. Children in this stage delight in calling a dog a cat, a foot a hand, and then start laughing.

- *Stage 3: Conceptual Incongruity.* Around age 3, most children begin to play with ideas, which reflects their growing cognitive ability. For example, stage 3 children laugh when they see a drawing of a cat with two heads.
- *Stage 4: Multiple Meanings.* Once children begin to play with the ambiguity of words, their humor approaches the adult level.

"Hey, did you take a bath?"

"No. Why, is one missing?"

Children at stage 4 (usually around age 7) understand the different meaning of *take* in both instances. Stage 3 children could not understand the following joke:

"Order! Order! Order in the court."

"Ham and cheese on rye, your honor."

Stage 4 youngsters appreciate its ambiguity.

You can see how cognitive development is linked to humor: The effective use of humor with children can help stimulate new learning and creative thinking, instill an interest in literature, facilitate social development, and enhance emotional development and adjustment.

Guided Review

11. According to Piaget, _____ is the means that permits children to assimilate reality to self.
12. Attributing human activity or creation to things is known as _____.
13. To understand that an object retains properties no matter how its form changes is called _____.
14. Children's tendency to construct their own theories of mind is also called _____.

Answers

11. play 12. artificialism 13. conservation 14. metacognition

Early Childhood Education

Early education programs, often referred to as preschool and kindergarten programs, usually take one of two directions. They are either physically, socially, and emotionally oriented or more cognitively centered, which is not to say that programs are exclusively social or cognitive; typically elements of both occur in all programs (Bredekamp & Copple, 1997).

Given today's concern with educational achievement, many preschool programs rely on the ideas of individuals such as Piaget or Montessori.

Piaget and Montessori

In these programs, which are based on a developmental theory of behavior, children are encouraged to learn through interacting with their environments and to be active participants in constructing knowledge. Early childhood programs stress integrated subject matter; for example, mathematics is taught by having the children weigh different objects and measure amounts to cook. Peer relationships are stressed and the line between work and play fades. Teachers encourage, mediate, and try to extend children's thinking (Hauser-Cram & others, 1991).

Although Piaget himself never advocated using his developmental theory in this manner, you can see how his ideas could form the basis for early childhood programs. His emphasis on a child's progression through intellectual stages of development has clearly defined program implications (use of concrete materials, etc.). Since Piaget's is an *interactive* theory, children's energy and activities can be directed at interesting cognitive outcomes rather than having children passively accept facts.

In contrast, Montessori (1967) was a strong proponent of early childhood programs. She believed that developing children pass through different physical and mental growth phases that alternate with periods of transition, suggesting that children possess different types of minds at different periods. These periods differ so sharply that Montessori referred to them as a series of new births.

She described three major periods of development. The first stage, which is called the **absorbent mind** phase to indicate a child's tremendous ability to absorb experiences from its environment, extends from birth to age 6. The second stage, which is referred to as the **uniform growth** phase to identify these years as a time of considerable stability, extends from age 6 to age 12. Finally, the third stage extends from 12 to 18 years.

A youngster reaches this level by what Montessori calls the **prepared environment.** For children under age 6, the prepared environment includes sensorial materials, such as rods to teach lengths, cubes to teach size, and bells to teach musical pitch; materials for the acquisition of cultural geography, history, art, and arithmetic; and materials and techniques necessary for the development of a child's religious life. Montessori also devised concrete materials to encourage learning in 6- to 12-year-old children.

The stages we have just described lead to what is perhaps the best known of Montessori's ideas, that of **sensitive periods.** Montessori believed that there were times when a child was especially *sensitive* or ready for certain types of learning. One of the earliest and most vital of these periods is concerned with the attainment of their language, which, as we have seen, children acquire effortlessly, a good example of Montessori's sensitive periods.

Other preschool programs, such as Head Start, have also helped disadvantaged children.

Hauser-Cram, P., Pierson, D., Klein Walker, D., & Tivnan, T. (1991). *Early education in the public schools.* San Francisco: Jossey-Bass. An excellent review of early childhood programs designed according to developmentally appropriate principles.

Project Head Start

Originally conceived as part of President Lyndon Johnson's War on Poverty in the 1960s, **Project Head Start** was headed by Sargent Shriver, who had been as-

Head start was designed to offer developmental and educational services to preschool children from low-income families. With the increasing number of children living in poverty, such programs can provide much needed services.

tounded on examining the distribution of poverty in the United States. Data indicated that about one-half of the nation's 30 million poor were children and most of these were under age 12. His main objective thus became the preparation of poor children for entrance into kindergarten and the first grade. As Hauser-Cram and others. (1991) noted, Head Start was intended to provide educational and developmental services to preschool children from low-income families.

Improving children's health became a primary goal; children received pediatric and neurological assessments plus two nutritious meals a day (Zigler & Muenchow, 1992). Head Start programs had six components: preschool education, health screening and referral, mental health services, nutrition education and hot meals, social services for the child and family, and parental involvement (Zigler & Styfco, 1994). Since its beginning, Head Start has served more than 13 million children.

The IQ Controversy

Unfortunately, several of the early claims about the gains to be realized from Head Start programs revolved around changes in IQ; some proponents stated that as a result of participation in Head Start, a child's IQ would increase one IQ point a month. In the mid-1960s, critical evaluations of intelligence tests had not reached today's level of sophistication, but even then certain individuals such as Edward Zigler, a member of the Head Start Planning Committee, deplored reliance on increases in IQ scores as the means of evaluating Head Start.

His fears were quickly justified as follow-up studies of Head Start children showed a "fadeout effect." That is, although graduates of these preschool programs showed immediate gains in intelligence and achievement test scores, after several months in the public schools, the Head Start children seemed to lose these cognitive benefits (Zigler & Styfco, 1994, p. 128). Nevertheless, even if Head Start graduates do not maintain academic gains, they have improved their readiness for school and the advantages of Head Start extend to other parts of their lives.

Today, with the rapid increase in the number of working women and the stunning rise of children living in poverty, the need for early intervention programs to aid these children seems more compelling than ever. As Stipek & Ryan (1997)

Zigler, E. & Muenchow, S. (1992). *Head Start.* New York: Basic Books. A fascinating, well-written history of the early intervention movement and its role in attempting to prepare disadvantaged children for a successful school experience.

noted, disadvantaged children are every bit as eager to learn as their advantaged peers, but they have much further to go with regard to their intellectual skills and too often never catch up. In her summary of the need for greater support of preschool programs, Kassebaum (1994) pointed out that 21 percent of all American children live in poverty; 25 percent of all children live with a single parent; 25 percent of all babies are born to unmarried mothers; every night at least 100,000 children are homeless; the United States ranks 20th in the world with regard to infant mortality.

These statistics cry out for attention because the children they represent not only suffer educational disadvantages but they also face other developmental difficulties. For example, as we have seen, they are more frequently the premature babies; their families suffer devastating and widespread deprivation; the children themselves are more subject to physical illness and lowered cognitive performance. As more of these children enter the public schools, is it any wonder they are unable to meet the ordinary demands of the classroom (Hauser-Cram & others, 1991)? It is in meeting their needs that we see the value of programs such as Head Start and the hope of bringing these children successfully into the mainstream of school life and the wider community. If we are to succeed, we must identify the skills, both academic and social, that our students need.

Good Preschools

Several features distinguish good preschools: low teacher-child ratio, specially trained teachers, availability of resources, and recognition of children's individual differences. These programs are all child centered; that is, they are designed to emphasize individual children and to provide children with enriching, enjoyable experiences suitable for their years, which is especially desirable given the social needs of early childhood youngsters. Most studies of peer relationships during the early childhood period (2–6 years) have been conducted in day-care centers and nursery schools. Note the age progression in developing relationships: Social contacts occur more frequently among 5-year-olds than 3-year-olds. Aggressive interactions are quite common in the period, although aggression decreases in proportion to friendly interactions (especially true among middle-class boys).

Particularly interesting are the changes in quarreling during these years. As in their other social exchanges, older youngsters (4, 5, and 6 years) engage in fewer but longer quarrels with members of their own sex (Berk, 1997). Boys quarrel more frequently among themselves than girls, usually over objects, gradually changing from physical to verbal aggression toward the end of the period. Although solitary activity persists, older children of this period are more obviously bidding for the attention of their peers.

As you can tell from our discussion thus far, children of these years have marched firmly into a symbolic world, a major part of which is language.

Guided Review

15. Preschool programs are usually oriented to either _____ or _____/_____/_____ development.
16. Two individuals who have had great influence on the nature of preschool programs are _____ and _____.
17. A major goal of Project Head Start was improving children's _____.

Answers

15. cognitive, physical, social, emotional 16. Piaget, Montessori 17. health

The attention that adults (especially parents) give children encourages positive interactions and leads to satisfactory and fulfilling relationships. Adult attention will also further language development and enhance a child's self-concept.

Language Development

Youngsters soon acquire their native language, a task of such scope and intricacy that its secrets have eluded investigators for centuries. During the early childhood period, language figuratively "explodes." Remember: Children don't learn to speak by imitating adults, nor do most parents reward their children for good grammar (deCuevas, 1990). (Still, adults facilitate the process by their use of motherese or caretaker speech, that is, speaking to children in a high-pitched voice and using simple words.)

All children, however, learn their native language. At about the same age they manifest similar patterns of speech development, whether they live in a ghetto or in a wealthy suburb. Within a short span of time and with almost no direct instruction, children completely analyze their language. Although refinements are made between ages 5 and 10, most children have completed the greater part of the process of language acquisition by the age of 4 or 5. Recent findings have also shown that when children acquire the various parts of their language, they do so in the same order. For example, in English, children learn *in* and *on* before other prepositions, and they learn to use *ing* as a verb ending before other endings such as *ed* (Hulit & Howard, 1997).

Language acquisition is a tremendous accomplishment; if you remember how you may have tried to learn a foreign language as an adult, you'll recall how difficult it was to acquire vocabulary and to master rules of grammar and the subtleties of usage. Yet preschool children do just this with no formal training. By the time they are ready to enter kindergarten, most children have a vocabulary of about 8,000 words; use questions, negative statements, and dependent clauses; and have learned to use language in a variety of social situations. They are relatively sophisticated language users.

Language as Rule Learning

As children acquire the basics of their language, they are also learning the guidelines that make language such a powerful tool. For example, by the age of 4 or 5, children will also have discovered that rules exist for combining sounds into words, that individual words have specific meanings, and that there are rules for combining words into meaningful sentences and for participating in a dialogue. These rules help children to detect the meaning of a word with which they are unfamiliar. Called **fast mapping,** this technique enables children to use context for a word's meaning, thus helping them to continue rapid vocabulary development. (See also chapter 5.)

We can summarize these accomplishments as follows.

- The rules of **phonology** describe how to put sounds together to form words.

- The rules of **syntax** describe how to put words together to form sentences.

- The rules of **semantics** describe how to interpret the meaning of words.

- The rules of **pragmatics** describe how to take part in a conversation.

Simply by making noises with our mouths, we can reliably cause precise new combinations of ideas to arise in each other's minds.
Steven Pinker

As we trace the path of language development in the early childhood years, you should remember a basic distinction that children quite clearly demonstrate. At about 1 year (the infancy period), children show an ability for **receptive language** ("show me your nose"—they receive and understand these words). Now, in early childhood, they produce language themselves, **expressive language.** How do children acquire these language milestones?

Whole Language: Lasting Improvement or Passing Fad?

Building on a growing knowledge of language development, many educators, long dissatisfied with the teaching of reading and writing, have adopted a new strategy. Called **whole language,** this strategy refers to a technique by which all language processes (speaking, listening, reading and writing—including spelling and handwriting) are studied in a more natural context, as a whole and not as a series of isolated facts. For example, oral and written language are best acquired through actual use in meaningful situations (Levande, 1991). Instruction should be guided by the needs and interests of the learners and real literature should be used as much as possible (Giddings, 1992).

The proponents of whole language believe that it is consistent with Piaget's theory of human development because a child's use of language materials matches that child's level of cognitive development. Proponents also claim that it is consistent with Vygotsky's work because of the important role that context plays in a child's attempts to master reading and writing.

How the Whole Language Concept "Works"

Shifting from dependence on a basal language series to whole language requires teachers to rethink their assumptions about literature and language learning. For example, in the whole language strategy, many teachers will work with themes: friendship, loyalty, and honesty. First children will read a story that illustrates the theme. This is known as *experiencing the literature.* Next the teacher may read a related story or poem; pupils are *listening to the literature.*

Now the teacher may attempt to *expand* the concepts that the children experienced in their literature and simultaneously work on vocabulary using various techniques. Next children may read the selection cooperatively (taking turns with their partners or reading aloud about a particular character in the story). They can then discuss the characters in the story.

At this point, the children may *respond* to the literature by completing a story form (sentences with missing words, explaining the beginning and ending, telling how the story's problem was solved). The teacher may ask them to evaluate the characters' actions in the story or give their own opinions about the story. Some children may explore language; that is, if they need help with vocabulary or phonics, or with general reading strategies, they are guided to appropriate activities.

The children now shift from reading to writing. For example, they may write a paragraph explaining a particular part of the story. They use the words they have learned in their reading and apply them to their writing. They can be taught how to proofread and to revise in this phase.

With their reading and writing experiences completed, and if time permits, children may *extend their reading experiences.* That is, if the theme of their work was friendship, they may do independent research that could include examples of friendship in stories, friendship between leaders of nations, or friendship between people of different cultures.

The ideal time for the introduction of whole language is during the early childhood period. Children of this age are experiencing a rapid natural growth of language and enjoying the newfound power that language confers, which is the rationale for harnessing this exuberance and using it to further their learning.

Yet many critics of the whole language approach believe that children can miss many necessary fundamentals because of the lack of a structured curriculum. They focus particularly on a child's need for thorough phonics instruction. A controversial topic, the whole language issue needs additional research to provide clear answers to the many questions swirling around the concept at this time.

The Pattern of Language Development

As mentioned earlier, all children learn their native tongue, and at similar ages they manifest similar patterns of language development. The basic sequence of language development during early childhood is that at about 2½ years, most children produce complete sentences, begin to ask questions, and use negative statements. At about 4 years they have acquired the complicated structure of their native tongue, and in about two or three more years they speak and understand sentences that they have never previously used or heard.

As children grow, specifying the extent of their vocabularies is difficult. Do we mean spoken words only? Or do we include words that children may not use but clearly understand? Building a vocabulary is an amazing accomplishment. For example, the vocabulary of every language is categorized; that is, some words are nouns, some are verbs, still others are adjectives, prepositions, or conjunctions. If English had only 1,000 nouns and 1,000 verbs, we could form 1 million sentences (1,000 × 1,000). But nouns can be used as objects as well as subjects. Therefore the number of possible three-word sentences increases to one billion (1,000 × 1,000 × 1,000).

One billion sentences is the result of a starkly impoverished vocabulary. The number of sentences that could be generated from English, with its thousands of nouns and verbs, plus adjectives, adverbs, prepositions, and conjunctions, staggers the imagination. Estimates are that it would take trillions of years to say all possible English sentences of twenty words. In this context, the ability of children to acquire their language is an astounding achievement. Although most youngsters experience problems with some tasks during this period—difficulty with reading or mathematics—they acquire their language easily and in just a few years.

Language Irregularities

When speech emerges, certain irregularities appear in children's speech that are quite normal and to be expected. For example, **overextensions** mark children's beginning words. Assume that a child has learned the name of the house pet, *doggy.* Think what that label means: an animal with a head, tail, body, and four legs. Now consider what other animals "fit" this label: cats, horses, donkeys, and cows. Consequently, children may briefly apply *doggy* to all four-legged creatures; they quickly eliminate overextensions, however, as they learn about their world.

Overregularities are a similar fleeting phenomenon. As youngsters begin to use two- and three-word sentences, they struggle to convey more precise meanings by mastering the grammatical rules of their language. For example, many English verbs add ed to indicate past tense.

I want to play ball.
I wanted to play ball.

Other verbs change their form much more radically.

Did Daddy come home?
Daddy came home.

Most children, even after they have mastered the correct form of such verbs as *come, see,* and *run,* still add ed to the original form. That is, youngsters who know that the past tense of *come* is *came* will still say:

Daddy comed home.

Again, this phenomenon persists only briefly and is another example of the close link between language and thought. We know that from birth, children respond to patterns. They look longer at the human face than they will at diagrams because the human face is more complex. (Remember the Fantz study?) Once they have learned a pattern such as adding *ed* to signify past tense, they have considerable difficulty in changing the pattern.

An interesting development occurs as children's sentences grow longer: Their use of word order becomes closely linked to grammar rather than merely reflecting meaning. That is, their language has become more syntactic. Inflections such as "s" and "ed" are correctly added to words and, thanks to Roger Brown's groundbreaking work (1973), we now know quite a bit more about these grammatical morphemes (s, ed). He studied fourteen morphemes, including the three "s" inflections—plural (girls), possessive (girl's), and verb endings (runs).

Using them correctly requires considerable language sophistication. Children who correctly add *ed* to a word tell us in no uncertain terms that something happened in the past. Brown also discovered that *all* children acquire these fourteen morphemes in the same sequence. For example, although the three "s" look exactly alike—children learn the plural usage first, followed by the possessive, and finally the verb inflection.

During the early childhood years, children begin to display a growing mastery of meaning. As we mentioned, their vocabulary continues to increase quite dramatically, and they begin to combine words to refine their meaning. Yet they also display a sense of constraint in the way they use words; that is, they quickly learn to suggest the correct meaning for the correct word.

"That's right," suggesting correctness.
"That's right," suggesting direction.

As we saw with regard to fast mapping, children use many sources of information to acquire words, and probably follow the same strategies in pinpointing the meaning they intend to convey. How do we explain these and other remarkable language accomplishments? Flavell's words portray our current understanding (and lack) of language development.

> **Human children seem to be biologically equipped to acquire language of the human type; they encounter languages of rich and complex (and in part similar) grammatical structure in every human society; and they acquire such languages in an inexorable, age-and-stage-related fashion that does not appear—given our current, admittedly imperfect understanding— to be explicable on experiential bases but looks to be strongly maturational (Flavell, 1993, p. 318).**

The path of language development is similar for all children. For example, children will not speak before a certain time—this is a biological given and nothing will change it. A particular culture has little to do with language emergence, but it has everything to do with the shape that any language assumes. Bruner (1990) has argued that culture shapes cognitive development by imposing its symbolic systems, such as language, on the child's developing mind.

Summarizing, then, as children come to the end of the early childhood period, several language milestones have been achieved:

- Children become skillful in building words; adding suffixes such as *er, man,* and ist to form nouns (the person who performs experiments is an *experimenter*).

- They begin to be comfortable with passive sentences (the glass *was broken* by the wind).

- By the end of the early childhood period, children can pronounce almost all English speech sounds accurately.

- As we have noted, this is the time of the "language explosion" and vocabulary has grown rapidly.

- Children of this age are aware of grammatical correctness.

Moskowitz, B. (1979). The acquisition of language. *Scientific American* 239, 92–108. If you are like most readers encountering the basics of language development for the first time, you probably would like to do more reading about it. This article (still one of the best) is clear, thorough, and well written. You should find it easily in your library. You will find it helpful.

Bilingualism

Finally, we must recognize that many children in the United States do not speak or write English as their native language, and the number is growing. All evidence points to the conclusion that our country today is more diverse ethnically and linguistically than ever before. For example, while the country's population increased by 11.6 percent between the years 1970 and 1980, the Asian American community increased by 233 percent, Native Americans by 71 percent, Hispanics by 61 percent, and African Americans by 17.8 percent. Moreover, estimates are that at least 3.4 million pupils are limited in English language skills in a school system primarily designed for those who speak English (Lindholm, 1990).

Meet Genie—A Child You'll Never Forget

The tranquility of Temple City, California, was shattered in November 1970 by disquieting, almost unbelievable, news. Screeching headlines described the discovery of a young girl who had been "held prisoner" by her family for thirteen years. Her mother, almost completely blind and feeling the ravages of an abusive marriage, sought assistance for the blind in the local welfare office. With Genie, she mistakenly stumbled into a social services office where an alert eligibility worker became fascinated, not by the mother, but by the girl.

No wonder. The 13-year old girl weighed only 59 pounds and was 54 inches tall. She was even in worse condition than she looked. She wasn't toilet trained, she couldn't chew solid food, and she could barely swallow. She drooled continuously and had no compunction about spitting—no matter where she was. And these were only Genie's less obnoxious characteristics. Perhaps most important of all, she couldn't talk.

After her discovery, investigators began to trace the road that led Genie to her present state. The youngest child, Genie (not her real name), by then about 20 months old, received a rare physical examination by a pediatrician who stated that she seemed a little "slow," which the father interpreted as meaning that she was profoundly retarded. With the physician's label ringing in his ears, Genie's father, Clark, developed a weird and abusive style of child rearing for his youngest child.

He kept her in a small bedroom tied to an infant's potty seat. Trapped in this harness, Genie couldn't move anything but her hands and feet. She sat there, day after day, month after month, year after year. At night, she was placed in a sleeping bag designed by her father that kept her arms motionless much like a straitjacket. She was then placed in a crib with an overhead cover and wire mesh sides. She heard nothing—no human voices (only when her father swore at her), no radio, no language. When she made noise, her father beat her. She quickly learned to keep quiet rather than be beaten by a board her father kept in the room.

The room contained no other furniture, no pictures, one ceiling bulb. She was allowed to play with two dirty plastic raincoats, empty cottage cheese containers, and empty spools of thread. Her diet was baby foods, cereal, and an occasional soft-boiled egg. If she choked and spit out any food, he rubbed her face in it. Almost totally blind, Genie's mother was helpless; she was at the mercy of her husband. Finally, things became so bad that Clark relented, and called Genie's maternal grandparents, who took Genie and her mother with them, which eventually led to Genie's discovery. Her parents were arrested. Despondent about the emotional valleys in his life, Clark killed himself. Genie was hospitalized and became the object of intensive and prolonged study.

The startling case of Genie illustrates the durability of language but also demonstrates its vulnerability. After treatment in the Children's Hospital of Los Angeles, Genie was placed in a foster home where she acquired language, more from exposure than any formal training. Estimates are that she has acquired as much language in eight years as the normal child acquires in three. She continues to have articulation problems and difficulty with word order.

Although Genie made remarkable language progress, difficulties persist. For example, she does not appear to have mastered the rules of language (her grammar is unpredictable), she continues to use the stereotypic speech of the language-disabled child, and she seems to understand more language than she can produce. Thus the case of Genie suggests that while language is difficult to retard, sufficiently severe conditions can affect progress in language. Here we see the meaning of a sensitive period when applied to language development.

If you'd like to learn more about this tragic case, Rymer, R. (1993). *Genie: A scientific tragedy.* New York: Harper. This is one of the best summaries of Genie's years of hell.

To help make these figures more meaningful, consider this: The New York City school system, in the last several years, has enrolled more than 150,000 immigrant children. But suburban school systems are also experiencing the same increase. In one system of 5,300 students, the children speak 25 languages; in a larger Northeast system, the children speak 46 languages. How have the schools responded to these challenges?

Bilingual Education Programs

In a landmark decision in 1974 (*Lau v. Nichols*), the U. S. Supreme Court ruled that LEP students (*Limited English Proficiency*) in San Francisco were being discriminated against because they were not receiving the same education as their English-speaking classmates. The school district was ordered to provide means for LEP students to participate in all instructional programs. The manner of implementing the decision was left to the school district under the guidance of the lower courts. This decision provided the impetus for the implementation of bilingual education programs in the United States.

Two different techniques for aiding LEP pupils emerged from this decision. The *English as a second language program* (ESL) usually has students removed from class and given special English instruction. The intent is to have these pupils acquire enough English to allow them to learn in their regular classes that are taught in English.

With the *bilingual* technique, students are taught partly in English and partly in their native language. The objective here is to help pupils to learn English by subject matter instruction in their own language and in English. Thus they acquire subject matter knowledge simultaneously with English. Bilingual programs also allow students to retain their cultural identities while simultaneously progressing in their school subjects. In today's schools, bilingual education has become the program of choice.

Bilingual education programs can also be divided into two categories. First are those programs (sometimes called *transitional* programs) in which the rapid development of English is to occur so that students may switch as soon as possible to an all-English program. Second are those programs (sometimes referred to as *maintenance* programs) that permit LEP students to remain in them even after they have become proficient in English. The rationale for such programs is that students can use both languages to develop mature skills and to become fully bilingual.

The difference between these two programs lies in their objectives. Transitional programs are basically compensatory—use the students' native language only to compensate for their lack of English. Maintenance programs, however, are intended to bring students to the fullest use of both languages. As you can well imagine, transitional programs are the most widely used in the schools.

Research clearly shows that the native language does not interfere with second language development (Hakuta, 1986). Since the acquisition of language is a natural part of our cognitive system, both first and second language acquisition seem to be guided by similar principles (Hakuta & McLaughlin, 1996). Given the early childhood youngster's ability to acquire language, it is an ideal time to introduce a new language, both to help a child's adjustment and to prepare for school instruction.

Dialects. Some children speak with decided dialects. Think of a dialect as a variety of a language distinguished by vocabulary, grammar, and pronunciation that differs from a standard language. In the United States, for example, those from the Boston area are distinguished from those living in the South or the Midwest. You should remember that specific dialects such as Black English, although sounding different, are every bit as logical and rule-governed as standard English.

Pinker (1994) gives several examples of the systematic use of rules in Black English (BE) as Standard American English (SAE).

There's really a God. (SAE)
It's really a God. (BE)
Doesn't anybody know? (SAE)
Don't nobody know. (BE)
If you're bad (SAE)
If you bad (BE)

These linguistic facts raise interesting questions. What should teachers do with students who bring their dialect to the classroom? Here we have a clear illustration of what's meant by the distinction between cultural deficits and cultural differences. The children speaking Black English are using an undeniably logical system. Yet, at the same time, their speech may work against them in a nation that bestows achievement, occupational success, and status on those skillful in Standard American English.

Teaching Non-English-Speaking Students: Bilingual Education or ESL?

By the turn of the century, about 40 percent of public school students will be from ethnically diverse backgrounds, and these students may be at risk because of an English language deficit. Bilingual education, which offers these students course instruction in their native language while they study English separately is a major commitment because academic fluency takes about seven years. Many issues concerning bilingual education generate conflicting, often heated, opinions such as the following:

Issue Bilingual education is the way American public schools should educate non-English-speaking students.

Answer—Pro Students in bilingual education are not penalized because of a language deficit. They are able to stay current with their studies because they are taught in their native language, which helps to maintain students' self-esteem while they gain proficiency in English.

Answer—Con Bilingual education is not that helpful to these students. Students who eventually succeed in the marketplace are proficient in English. Bilingual education wastes valuable time reinforcing students' native languages instead of teaching them English.

Issue English as a Second Language (ESL) is a good alternative program to bilingual education.

Answer—Pro ESL is a desirable program because most of a student's course work is in English, with separate time allotted for specific English language instruction. Students are grouped according to grade level and the ESL teacher uses the student's classroom curriculum.

Answer—Con ESL does not give students support in their native language. In spite of English language training these students fall behind. Older students in particular may have difficulty with this technique.

Issue Since English is the official language of government and commerce in the United States, classroom instruction in public school classrooms should be in English.

Answer—Pro One of the goals of public school education is fluency in spoken and written English. If students are in an environment where only English is spoken, they will learn the language more quickly. These students may have initial difficulty but once they have acquired English proficiency, they typically catch up.

Answer—Con Non-English speaking students are often put in with students younger than themselves while gaining English proficiency. Or if they are put in with their peers, they suffer because they cannot keep up with the course work. Both of these conditions result in a loss of self-esteem for the students, which can then affect total academic performance and may cause the student(s) to drop out of school altogether.

A consensus seems to have gathered around techniques that in no way show disrespect to a student's language. For example, schools effective with culturally different populations are sufficiently flexible to accommodate a range of dialects that learners bring to school. Teachers are urged to allow dialects in social and recreational settings and encourage these students to use Standard English in school settings (Manning & Baruth, 1996).

Guided Review

18. Most children have completed the greater part of language acquisition by the age of _____.

19. _____ describes how to put sounds together to form words.

20. Calling all four-legged, furry animals doggy would be an example of _____.

21. The ability for receptive language demonstrated in the infancy period is advanced to include _____ language in early childhood.

22. The development of language can be hindered by _____ _____.

23. The two chief methods for instructing non-English-speaking students are _____ _____ and _____.

Answers

18. 5 19. Phonology 20. overextension 21. expressive 22. environmental conditions 23. bilingual education, ESL

CONCLUSION

Thus far in our discussion of the early childhood years, we have seen that although the rate of physical growth slows somewhat, it still continues at a steady pace. Physical and motor skills become more refined. Cognitive development during these years leads to a world of representation in which children are expected to acquire and manipulate symbols. Language gradually becomes a powerful tool in adapting to the environment.

In summary:

Physical and Motor Development

- Growth continues at a steady, less rapid rate during these years.
- Brain lateralization seems to be well established by the age of 5 or 6.
- Height is a good indicator of normal development when heredity and environment are considered in evaluating health.
- Increasing competence and mastery are seen in a child's acquisition of motor skills.

Cognitive Development

- These years are the time of Piaget's preoperational period and the continued appearance of symbolic abilities.
- Children's growing cognitive proficiency is seen in their use of humor.
- Many current early childhood programs have a cognitive orientation.

Early Childhood Education

- Many preschool programs are based on the ideas of Piaget and Montessori.
- Project Head Start was originally designed to offer educational and developmental services to disadvantaged children.
- Several positive social and emotional outcomes seem to be associated with Head Start programs.

Language Development

- Children acquire the basics of their language during these years with little, if any, instruction.
- All children seem to follow the same pattern in acquiring their language.
- Children whose native language is not English need a carefully designed program to support their native language and to help them acquire English as efficiently as possible.

KEY TERMS

Absorbent mind
Animism
Anticipatory images
Artificialism
Centration
Classification
Conservation
Controlled scribbling
Deferred imitation
Dialects
Drawing
Egocentrism
Expressive language
Fast mapping

Handedness
Irreversibility
Lateralization
Metacognition
Metacognitive experiences
Metacognitive knowledge
Motor skills
Overextensions
Overregulation
Phonology
Pragmatics
Prepared environment
Preoperational
Project Head Start

Random scribbling
Realism
Receptive language
Representation
Reproductive images
Reversability
Semantics
Sensitive periods
Symbolic play
Syntax
Theory of mind
Uniform growth
Whole language

WHAT DO YOU THINK?

1. As you can tell from the data presented in this chapter, early childhood youngsters continue their rapid growth, although at a less frantic rate than during infancy. Consider yourself a parent of a child of this age (boy or girl) for a moment. How much would you encourage them to participate in organized, directed physical activities (swimming, dancing, soccer, etc.)? Be sure to give specific reasons for your answer.

2. As you read Paul McGhee's account of the development of children's humor, could you explain his stages by comparing them with Piaget's work? Do you think this is a logical way to proceed? Why?

3. When you consider the tragic case of Genie compared to the enormous language growth of most children, what comes to your mind? Does it change your opinion about how language develops? In what way? What do you think this case implies for the existence of a sensitive period for language development?

CHAPTER REVIEW TEST

1. By the age of 2 a child should be able to
   a. jump from stairs.
   b. draw a recognizable person.
   c. stand on each foot alternately.
   d. throw a ball overhand.

2. The early childhood period coincides with Erikson's time of autonomy and
   a. sensitive responsiveness.
   b. attachment.
   c. initiative.
   d. goodness of fit.

3. A 5 year old may have as many as _____ words in his/her vocabulary.
   a. 5,000
   b. 2,100
   c. 500
   d. 900

4. During the early childhood period
   a. girls grow at a faster rate than boys.
   b. girls and boys grow at about the same rate.
   c. boys grow at a faster rate than girls.
   d. boys grow at a faster rate until age 4.

5. Children whose normal growth is interrupted are called
   a. disturbed.
   b. motorically lazy.
   c. developmentally delayed.
   d. slow learners.

6. Which of the following factors is not known to influence physical development?
   a. Genetic elements
   b. SES
   c. Disease
   d. Ethnicity

7. Which of the following would not be considered a motor skill?
   a. Running
   b. Skipping
   c. Tying shoes
   d. Singing

8. Controlled scribbling appears at about age
   a. 5
   b. 3
   c. 4
   d. 2

9. Which of the following behaviors is not associated with the preoperational period?
   a. Symbolic play
   b. Drawing
   c. Language
   d. Walks steadily

10. A child's belief that inanimate objects are real and conscious is known as
    a. artificialism.
    b. delusion.
    c. animism.
    d. centration.

11. By the time children are ready to enter kindergarten they have a vocabulary of about _____ words.
    a. 8,000
    b. 6,500
    c. 3,000
    d. 1,200

12. McGhee notes that the basis of most children's humor is
    a. irony.
    b. play on words.
    c. incongruity.
    d. sarcasm.

13. Effective use of humor is not credited with stimulating
    a. motor development.
    b. creative thinking.
    c. social development.
    d. emotional development.

14. Montessori's ideas concerning _____ periods are important in planning preschool programs.
    a. lengthy
    b. class
    c. sensitive
    d. time

15. Project Head Start was initiated in the
    a. 1960s.
    b. 1970s.
    c. 1980s.
    d. 1990s.

16. Studying language processes in a natural way refers to
    a. whole language.
    b. language acquisition.
    c. language rules.
    d. metalinguistic awareness.

17. The rules of _____ describe how to put words together to form sentences.
    a. phonology
    b. semantics
    c. syntax
    d. pragmatics

18. A child begins to build sentences by the age of _____ years.
    a. 2
    b. 3½
    c. 4
    d. 5

19. A 3-year-old stating, "Daddy camed home" is an example of
    a. overextension.
    b. mispronunciation.
    c. overregulation.
    d. delayed development.

20. By the end of the early childhood period children still cannot
    a. appreciate jokes and riddles based on ambiguities in syntax.
    b. pronounce almost all English speech sounds.
    c. increase their vocabulary greatly.
    d. gain awareness of grammatical correctness.

Answers

1.a 2.c 3.b 4.b 5.c 6.d 7.d 8.b 9.d 10.c 11.a 12.c 13.a 14.c 15.a 16.a 17.c 18.b 19.c 20.a

Chapter Outline

Barbara is a former nurse who now takes care of four neighborhood children, ranging in age from 9 months to 4 years. A neat, careful person who loves children (she has two of her own away at school), she is sensitive to their needs and aware of the developmental changes constantly occurring in her four children. Barbara is in great demand by neighborhood families because of these traits, but she refuses to take more than four children at a time.

It's eight o'clock in the morning and Gina, a 4-year-old dynamo, is at the door with her mother, Janice. Janice takes courses at the local college and leaves Gina with Barbara three days each week. Barbara smiles at the thought of Gina. Pretty, bright, and active, with springs in her legs, Gina usually leads the other children (and Barbara) on a merry chase. When you talk to her, Gina constantly bounces up and down.

Janice and Gina walk into the front room, which is spotless and filled with toys arranged attractively along the walls. It's apparent that this home is designed for children: bright, cheerful, and safe. Janice and Barbara talk about Gina for a few minutes; she had a cold the previous day and had a restless night, but Janice says she seems fine now. Upon seeing her 3-year-old friend, Amy, Gina darts over and begins to hug her.

Barbara and Janice watch as Gina asks Amy if she wants to see her new dance. (Gina takes a dance class and will be in a recital soon.) Without waiting for an answer, she goes through her dance and takes a deep bow. Amy laughs happily as Janice and Barbara applaud. Gina then takes Amy's hand and pulls her toward the backyard with its swings and sandbox.

It's so easy to tell how Gina feels by observing her play, Barbara thinks. Today she seems to be feeling better, has her energy back, and wants to play physically. At other times, Barbara has seen Gina working out a conflict with Janice by playing with dolls and assigning them mother-daughter roles. In her pretend play world, there were "mommy" dolls, "good" dolls, "bad" dolls, and "napping" dolls. As Barbara watches, she thinks to herself, as she does so often, what a wonderful time these years are. ✪

During the early childhood years, children blossom into quite distinctive personalities. Although personality differences are apparent at birth, they now flourish until even the most casual observer notices a child's "personality." Children of this age are entering a period in which they must learn to reconcile their individuality with the demands of the world around them. New abilities, new friends, new ideas come up against parental restrictions. Parents often find themselves searching for an ideal mix of firmness and love.

Children's personalities take on definite shadings. Their interactions with those around them begin to take shape, setting the stage for the kind of relationships they will form in the future. They now begin the process of widening their circle of relationships. Children from 2 to 6 will make new friends and, in our society today, almost inevitably have experience with preschool teachers. Some youngsters of this age are also faced with adjusting to a new sibling (or siblings), which can be a time of great frustration if not handled carefully.

This period is often described as one of socialization versus individuation. **Socialization** means the need to establish and maintain relations with others and to regulate behavior according to society's demands. **Individuation** refers to the fullest development of one's self, which we discussed in chapter 7. These two functions seem to pull in opposite directions. Society has certain regulations that its members must follow if chaos is to be avoided. Yet these rules must not be so rigid that the individual members who constitute the society cannot develop their potential to the fullest.

Children attempt to reconcile these tensions by mastering the following developmental tasks (Edwards, 1995):

- Learning to function more independently and becoming more involved in the family routine

- Recognizing and accepting who they are, that is, coming to grips with their self-concepts in a way that eases the very real struggle between socialization and individuation

- Developing strategies that lead to self-control and impulse control

- Beginning to understand and live by moral standards

- Acquiring a gender identity and a growing comprehension of gender roles

Television, one of the major socializing agents in a child's life, can have both prosocial and antisocial consequences. Consequently, parents should carefully monitor what their children watch.

• Knowing what it means to become a member of a society, with duties and responsibilities as well as rights

To help understand these issues, in this chapter we'll examine the modern family, tracing the stages through which it proceeds, the impact of parenting on children, the effect of divorce on development, and the growing importance of day care in our society. Throughout these years, a child's sense of personal identity is gradually emerging with its inherent temperamental characteristics tempered by the reactions of family members, teachers, and peers. Finally, we'll comment on the significance of play to children of this age.

When you finish reading this chapter, you should be able to

• Assess the impact of the family on a child's development.

• Evaluate the influence of parenting behavior on a child's development.

• Compare the various types of day-care centers.

• Describe the role of preschool education during the early childhood years.

• Determine the importance of self-esteem in a child's life.

• Appraise the function of play in a child's development.

Our initial task, though, is to examine that great socializing agent—the family.

The Family In Development

This section could have been written for any chapter in a lifespan book, but it is particularly pertinent here because the family is still recognized as *the* great socializing agent. Before we begin our analysis, it would be well to remember that any family is dynamic, not static. Families change, and as they do, they exercise different effects on a child's development—some significant, others not so (Scarr, 1992).

For example, children who remain in an intact family, or who experience the death of a parent, or who go through a parental divorce all undergo unique experiences that must affect development. We need not be so dramatic, however. All families sustain normal change in the course of the lives of their members.

The Changing Family

Defining *family* in our changing society is becoming increasingly difficult. As Garbarino (1992) noted, family takes many different forms, both across cultures and within societies. Traditionally, a man and woman marry and raise children. Today, however, we see many variations of this basic theme. Most of us are born into a family—the family of origin—and later in life usually start a family of our own—the family of procreation. You can see, then, that most people spend much of their lives in family units of one type or another.

The nature of that unit has changed dramatically. For example, in 1970, 70 percent of all households in the United States had married couples; in 1990, that figure had dropped to 56 percent. In 1970, 40 percent of married couples had children; in 1990, that figure had dropped to 26 percent. In 1970, 18 percent of families had three or more children; in 1990, that figure had dropped to 7 percent (U.S. Bureau of Census, 1991). About half of all children will spend some time in a single-parent household before they are 18.

Noting that these changes make defining a family a difficult task, Garbarino and Abramowitz (1992) used the following criteria: A family is any two people related by blood, marriage, or adoption. Whatever the particular type of family, *The National Commission on Children* (1991) has identified several characteristics of a strong family:

As social conditions change—working mothers, single-parent families—fathers have become more involved in child care. Children thus see their parents in roles different from the more stereotypical views of the past.

A Sociocultural View — What African American Children Consider Important

Although children attend to both the physical and social aspects of their environments, they seem to prefer one more than the other, and their preference depends on the guidelines of their culture (Banks, 1993; Banks & Banks, 1993). The urban environment and the social milieu in which most African Americans develop seem to predispose them toward the social elements of their environment, which then affects their school performance. Consequently, it's helpful to recognize the mechanisms by which students organize their lives.

Three categories seem to be significant.

- *The physical environment* that a family uses to shape a child's interactions with symbols and objects
- *The interpersonal relations* that provide feedback to students for their expectations and performances
- *The emotional and motivational climate* that influences a student's personality and behavior (Shade, 1987)

Within these categories, visual forms and family interaction patterns are particularly relevant. For example, research suggests that the visual forms within African-American homes are usually those of people (Martin Luther King, Jr., Jesse Jackson, John and Robert Kennedy). Middle-class white homes had more abstract paintings, pictures of flowers, and landscape scenes.

Interpersonal relationships within the family play a large role in the socialization of African-American children, with the ultimate goal of helping children to function independently within and without the family (Banks, 1993). Parents attempt to prepare their children for interactions with both peers and teachers and teach them how to act in social situations. Thus, parents are trying to provide a set of guidelines for behaving in novel situations that reflect the network of connections and kinship functions with which they are most comfortable (Manning and Baruth, 1996).

Such insights into the backgrounds of African-American children lead to a positive conclusion: These children face a brighter, more promising future for several reasons (Manning & Baruth, 1996).

- There is a growing recognition of the concept that "different is not deficient."
- As a result, African-American children are finally receiving more equitable educational opportunities.
- Their parents have better opportunities in employment, education, and housing, which will gradually lead to a more improved standard of living.
- Today's educators are better trained in diagnosis and remediation and more effectively employ the techniques of individualized education.

- Open and frequent communication among family members

- A feeling of belonging to a warm, supportive social unit

- Respect for individual members

- An ability to cope with stressful events

- Well-defined roles and responsibilities

Remember: Any analysis of family life contains two major themes. First is the nature of the family itself. In the late twentieth century, the identification of various forms of family living has sharply altered our view of the "family." Population projections and estimates of family styles present a fairly consistent pattern: Change will continue, but it will represent a modification of current styles. For example, the number of single mothers will increase, but as governmental support also increases, there will undoubtedly be more and better day-care services, increased after-school programs for the older children, and perhaps greater flexibility in the work schedules of working parents. The second major theme is the developmental consequences of these changes. Here we find much less certainty, since it is simply too soon to make definite statements.

As society changes, how families respond also changes. Children cannot escape the results, positive or negative, of these twists and turns of family living. We also know that one of the most important characteristics of any family is the way that parents treat their children. For example, Dekovic and Janssens (1992) found that popular and rejected children had different experiences. Parents of popular children used an authoritative/democratic style when interacting with their children, relying on verbal persuasion, positive reinforcement, and indirect methods of control. Parents of rejected children tended to be authoritarian/restrictive; that is, they were more critical and controlling.

The very idea of what constitutes parenting has drastically changed. Mothers, from economic necessity or personal preference, may work, which means that their children require some form of day care. Concerned with wanting children while pursuing a career, we have seen how the attachment research has raised additional questions: How much separation from its mother can a child tolerate? How far can the fibers of attachment be stretched before they break? We'll wrestle with these issues throughout the chapter, but if there's one thing we've learned about the relationships between parents and their children it's this: What's right means what works for parents and their children in their culture.

Children of different ages, with different problems, and from different cultures require different types of parenting. We're quite sure now that parents and children actually *construct* their relationships; no one model fits all children and parents. Parents do many things—select clothes, limit television time, impose rules—but they alone can't determine the nature of the relationship with their children. Parents and children are in it together, for better or worse.

Parenting Behavior

From our initial discussion concerning socialization, you probably realized that children's socialization emerges from the thousands of reciprocal interactions occurring among them and their family members over a period of many years. How this happens is a difficult knot to untie, but research and theory point to two major theories to explain what is meant by "effective parenting skills."

First is a *behavioral* explanation that assumes those parents who act in a noncontingent manner with their children can't correlate their behavior with what their child is doing. For example, a mother who remains disinterested and shows no positive behavior toward her child who is acting in a very prosocial way gives the child no clue that this is, indeed, the way to behave. How does this mother's child learn what's important or not, or how to react to the wider world? On the other hand, if the mother responds favorably to this behavior, then the world begins to look like a more predictable place. From the behavioral perspective, a parent's *contingent* behavior looms large, that is, the parents' response is appropriate for the child's behavior (Chamberlain & Patterson, 1995).

The second, and more prominent, theory attempts to link parental behavior with developmental outcomes. In a careful analysis of the relationship between parental behavior and children's competence, Baumrind (1967, 1971, 1986, 1991) discovered three kinds of parental behavior: authoritarian, authoritative, and permissive. Here is what she means by each of the types.

Authoritarian Parents

Authoritarian parents are demanding, and for them instant obedience is the most desirable child trait. When there is any conflict between these parents and their children (Why can't I go to the party?), no consideration is given to the child's view, no attempt is made to explain why the youngster can't go to the party, and often the child is punished for even asking.

Authoritative Parents

Authoritative parents respond to their children's needs and wishes. Believing in parental control, they attempt to explain the reasons for it to their children. Authoritative parents expect mature behavior and will enforce rules, but they encourage their children's independence and search for potential. They try to have their

TABLE 8.1 PATTERNS OF CHILD-REARING BEHAVIOR

	Authoritarian		Authoritative		Permissive	
	High	Low	High	Low	High	Low
Control	•		•			•
Clarity of communication		•	•		•	
Maturity demands	•		•			•
Nurturance		•	•		•	

TABLE 8.2 PARENTAL BEHAVIORS AND CHILDREN'S CHARACTERISTICS

	Parental Behaviors		
	Authoritarian	Authoritative	Permissive
Children's characteristics	Withdrawn	Self-assertive	Impulsive
	Lack of enthusiasm	Independent	Low self-reliance
	Shy (girls)	Friendly	Low self-control
	Hostile (boys)	Cooperative	Low maturity
	Low need achievement	High need achievement	Aggressive
	Low competence	High competence	Lack of responsibility

youngsters understand that both parents and children have rights. In the resolution of socialization versus individuation, authoritative parents try to maintain a happy balance between the two.

Permissive Parents

Baumrind believed that **permissive parents** take a tolerant, accepting view of their children's behavior, including both aggressive and sexual urges. They rarely use punishment or make demands of their children. Children make almost all of their own decisions. Distinguishing indulgence from indifference in these parents can be difficult.

Table 8.1 summarizes the relationship between Baumrind's categories of parenting behavior and levels of control, clarity of communication, maturity demands, and nurturance. As you can see, authoritative parents are high on control (they have definite standards for their children), high on clarity of communication (the children clearly understand what is expected of them), high in maturity demands (they want their children to behave in a way appropriate for their age), and high in nurturance (a warm, loving relationship exists between parents and children). Thus, according to Baumrind's work, authoritative parents are most desirable. Table 8.2 presents the relationship between Baumrind's classes of parenting behavior and children's characteristics.

Baumrind's findings have held firm over the years. As Holmbeck and others (1995) stated, authoritative parents have adolescents who achieve better and demonstrate more positive social adjustment than children whose parents adopted either authoritarian or permissive parenting styles. Yet these findings apply to white, middle-class families with both parents present. Children reared in single-parent families may experience quite different parenting behaviors. (See the section "Children of Divorce" that follows later.)

Parenting Styles

Examining the various types of families in a modern society, Chess and Thomas (1987) have identified the following six parenting styles. In so doing they have attempted to differentiate the behaviors a parent brings to child rearing from those that are a reaction to a child's behavior. **Secure parents** are confident of their techniques; if they make mistakes, they can change with no harm done. They assume they will cope successfully and look on parenting as an exciting challenge. This is not to state that all secure parents have the same parenting style, but the one defining theme is their security.

Insecure parents believe everything they do inevitably influences their child's destiny. The difficulties of parenting overwhelm them; when things turn out positively, they attribute it to luck. *Anything* to do with a child becomes a major issue. **Intimidated parents** lack the ability to be firm with their child. Whether from fear, guilt, or stress, their parenting style can only be described as one of appeasement. **Overinterpretive parents** feel they must explore in depth the complex psychological meanings behind their child's behavior. **Victimized parents** believe it just isn't fair if their child shows any sign of a problem after all *they* have done for the child; that is, it must be their child's fault. **Pathological parents** are those who actually suffer from a form of mental illness, which does not necessarily mean that their child will be subject to psychological disturbances. Remember: These different styles will *not* determine a child's psychological development. Rather it is the match between parenting behaviors and a child's temperament that is decisive, the *goodness of fit* that we discussed in chapter 6.

Finally, we must assess the question of how much children's temperaments affect the way they are treated; in other words, what the interaction is between a child's temperament and parenting behavior. In his elegant treatise on temperament, Kagan (1994), although arguing that temperament cannot be reduced to biology, noted that neither can physiology be removed from any analysis of temperament. That is, we cannot say that because a child is aggressive and uninhibited that parenting behaviors are solely at fault (Kagan, 1997). The biological input into temperament must also be considered. The critical question is: How do temperament and parenting behavior interact and *what* will be the resulting behavior? Recent research has indicated that different temperamental styles observed at 3 years of age continue to be present at 21 years of age (Newman, Caspi, Moffitt, & Silva, 1997). Baumrind has acknowledged the influence of temperament, but has also argued that parenting behavior must have a decided impact on a child's behavior.

No discussion of the family's influence on development would be complete without examining the role of siblings.

If you want to examine the research and discussion of parenting in more detail, you would find M. Bornstein (ed.), 1995, *Handbook of parenting* very helpful.

Siblings and Development

Growing up with **siblings** (brothers and sisters) is quite different from growing up without them. Brothers and sisters, because of their behavior toward one another, create a different family environment. As Dunn (1988) stated, the sibling relationship provides a context in which children demonstrate their varied abilities with frequency and intensity. During their early years, for example, siblings probably spend more time with each other than they do with their parents. An older sibling may spend considerable time taking care of younger brothers and sisters. These relationships last a lifetime, longer in most cases than those between husband and wife or parent and child (Dunn, 1988).

When you examine sibling relationships from this perspective, you can see how they affect development. In the early years, young brothers and sisters can provide security for babies who may feel frightened by strangers or anything different. (The attachment literature we discussed in chapter 5 shows that siblings definitely can attach to each other.) Older siblings are also models for younger children to imitate. They can become sounding boards for their younger brothers and sisters; that is,

Siblings play a major role in development. For those children with brothers and sisters, older siblings can act as models, help younger brothers and sisters in times of difficulty, and help smooth relations with adults.

the younger siblings can try out something before approaching a parent. Older siblings often ease the way for the younger by trying to explain to parents that what happened wasn't all that bad. In this way, bonds are formed that usually last a lifetime.

The Developing Sibling Bond

Attempts to analyze the influence of sibling relationships on development must reckon with age differences, friendships outside of the family, school experiences, sickness, accidents, gender differences, and socioeconomic status. Basic to all of these factors is the inborn temperamental disposition that each child brings to any relationship, which helps to explain the contradictions that seem to exist in the way that siblings relate to each other, sometimes affectionately and warmly, at other times hostilely.

Several cultural factors have contributed to the formation of a lifelong bond between siblings. For example, *longer lifespans* mean that brothers and sisters spend a longer period of their lives together than ever before, as long as 70 or 80 years! When parents have died, the siblings' own children have left, and spouses have died, siblings tend to tighten the bond and offer each other needed support. *Geographic mobility* means unavoidable separation. Friendships are lost; schools and teachers change; adjustments to new situations must be made. *Divorce and remarriage* typically bring unhappiness and hurt, and the need for support. During these troubled days, siblings may well be a trusted source of support and stability. For many children, the one anchor to be found is a brother or sister.

Sibling Relationships through the years. Here we may ask: Does the nature of the sibling relationship persist? In a study of sibling relationships from preschool through middle childhood to the beginning of adolescence, Dunn, Slomkowski, and Beardsall (1994) commented on the individual differences in sibling's relationships in middle childhood: Some are characterized by affection, others by hostility. Are these characteristics part of a pattern that began in early childhood? Considering our discussion thus far, you can see how it is possible to argue for continuity (yes, the nature of the sibling relationship is basically the same) since a child's personality and family dynamics usually remain stable. It is also possible to argue for discontinuity (no, the relationship changes over the years), since children's social relationships change over the years (e.g., they make new friends in and out of school) as do their perceptions of self.

Dunn and her associates (1994) found considerable continuity from early childhood to the beginning of adolescence in the positive and negative feelings of siblings toward each other. Many reasons contribute to the stability of these behaviors, especially the ongoing family dynamics. The siblings seemed to grow closer with adversity; that is, when one sibling had troubles with someone at school or became ill, other siblings offered support and sympathy. Gender differences also appeared: Adolescent girls were closer to their younger sisters than were adolescent boys with their younger sisters. Dunn and her associates (1994) attributed this finding to the tendency of adolescent boys to become more intensely involved with their male peer group.

How Siblings Help Each Other

As you might conclude from what we've said about siblings, conditions may exist that link siblings in a lifelong relationship. After all, why not? Think of the functions that siblings perform for one another, functions that contribute to the cementing of the bond. They have the freedom of accepting some of an older sibling's behaviors while rejecting others, which leads to differentiation, an important and necessary step in developing a healthy self-concept.

Siblings act as nonthreatening sounding boards for each other. New behaviors, new roles, and new ideas can be tested on siblings, and the reactions, whether positive or negative, lack the doomsday quality of many parental judgments. The emotional atmosphere is less charged. They exchange clothes as teenagers, borrow money before a paycheck, provide support in life's crises, in other words, they offer valuable services for each other.

Siblings also form subsystems that are the basis for the formation of powerful coalitions, often called the **sibling underworld.** Older siblings can warn their younger brothers and sisters about parental moods and prohibitions, thus averting problems. Older siblings frequently provide an educational service to parents by informing them of events outside the home that parents should be aware of.

We also know, however, that sibling relationships can be negative. *Rivalry,* whatever the cause, may characterize any bond. An older sibling can contribute to those feelings of inferiority that Erikson described as contributing to the crises of this period. Imagine the difficulty of a firstborn sibling forced to share parental attention, especially if the spacing between the children is close (less than two years). If the firstborns must also care for younger children, they can become increasingly frustrated.

The causes for rivalry are not one-sided (Ross, 1996). Younger children may only see the apparent privileges that are extended to the oldest: a sharing in parental power, authority, and more trivial matters such as a later bedtime or greater use of the television set (Kowal & Kramer, 1997). As Eisenberg (1992) noted, although the bond remains, siblings who help each other, share things, and frequently cooperate still have conflicts.

In fact, sibling discord is one of the problems that parents most frequently report. Researchers now realize that sibling conflict has multiple causes (Brody & others, 1992). For example, marital quality and conflict and the family's emotional quality seem to be related to sibling conflict. Studying 152 white children, Brody and his colleagues (1992) attempted to determine whether the way parents treated trouble between their children had any long-term consequences on sibling conflict. The researchers found that family harmony during discussions about sibling problems and the father's impartiality reduced sibling conflicts.

Next in our discussion of the role of family in development is a growing phenomenon in our society, one that affects an increasing number of children—homelessness.

Homeless Children

Traditional definitions of **homelessness** focused on the lack of a permanent place to live. Researchers now, however, tend to be more specific and concentrate on those who rely on shelters for their residence, or who live on the streets or in parks. The homeless today represent a different population from the days when they were seen as alcoholic men clustered together on skid rows. The so-called new homeless population is younger and much more mixed: more single women, more families, and more minorities. Families with young children may be the fastest-growing segment of today's homeless. On any given night, 100,000 children in this country will be homeless (Walsh, 1992). They are also characterized by few social contacts, poor health, and a high level of contact with the criminal justice system. Although the paths to homelessness are many, we cannot avoid discussing the role that poverty plays in this growing phenomenon.

The Children of Poverty

> Many children and adolescents in the United States today experience poverty at least occasionally, and for blacks poverty is more the rule than the exception. (Duncan, Brooks-Gunn, & Klebanov, 1994, p. 311)

In a penetrating essay, Weissbourd (1996) urged a more comprehensive view of poverty, suggesting that poverty hurts children in a range of subtle ways. Noting the tendency to equate poverty with disadvantaged, Weissbourd argued that most vulnerable children are *not* poor, and all the poor are *not* alike. For example, the

TABLE 8.3 NUMBER OF CHILDREN EXPERIENCING POVERTY

	Number	Percentage
Total Poor	36,425,000	13.8
Related Children	13,999,000	20.2
Total White Poor	24,423,000	11.2
Related Children	8,474,000	15.5
Total Black Poor	9,872,000	29.3
Related Children	4,644,000	41.5

African-American youth living in an urban ghetto experiences a quite different set of problems than a malnourished, chronically diseased white child in Appalachia.

Although about 8 percent of American children are poor for more than six years, close to 30 percent of our children experience poverty at some time in their lives.

> In the last three decades, huge numbers of skilled workers were laid off because of farm and factory closings, divorced middle-class mothers, and ousted professionals have suffered downward mobility, a sudden and severe loss of income, creating unfamiliar physical and emotional burdens for their children. (Weissbourd, 1996, p. 10)

The children of poverty experience more health problems, usually due to a lack of medical care. More of these children die in the neonatal and infancy periods. They also suffer more accidents than more fortunate children and are exposed to greater stress: occupational, financial, housing, neighborhood (Huston, McLoyd, & Garcia Coll, 1994). We know that parental stress can often translate into poor parenting practices (depression, irritability, abuse), which can lead to behavioral and emotional problems and academic difficulty for the children. Finally, as we know from the daily news, these children often witness and are the targets of violence, such as physical assault, rape, and shootings.

The conditions we have described put children at an immediate disadvantage: they are subject to school difficulties (perhaps culminating in their dropping out), low self-esteem, troublesome behavior, limited occupational opportunities, and encounters with the law. Erratic employment contributes to poverty, and the cycle commences again.

To give you some idea of the numbers involved, table 8.3 summarizes the number of individuals, including children, who fall below the current poverty level of $16,036 for a family of four.

It's an interesting table. You see immediately that children of all types are overrepresented in poverty, and, then, breaking the figures down by black and white, you note the large numbers of black children living in poverty.

Analyses of the children of poverty typically focus on income, education, occupation, and social status, yet other, potentially more powerful, psychological forces are also at work. For example, can children living in poverty avoid feelings of powerlessness? It doesn't take them long to perceive that they have little influence in their society, have access to fewer societal opportunities, and are more likely to have their lives directed by others (Reed-Victor & Stronge, 1997).

Classroom Performance

How do these facts translate into meaningful differences in the lives of these children? Classroom performance is a good example. Although our interpretation and use of intelligence tests has changed dramatically, these tests remain an indicator of achievement. Today children at a lower socioeconomic level score 10 to 15 IQ points below middle-class children; these differences are not only *present by the first grade,* they persist throughout the school years. Because the differences in these scores undoubtedly reflect social class distinctions, efforts have been made to discover any patterns that may exist. Profiles drawn from the data suggest that social class may cause an increase in scores, but the general pattern of intellectual ability was similar. That is, when profiles of lower-class children were drawn, they showed the children were like the middle-class children but they were lower on all abilities (Hetherington & Parke, 1993).

Consequently, socioeconomic status remains a reliable predictor of school achievement and suggests that students from the same social class will perform in a remarkably similar manner. For example, in a study of eighth graders, low SES white children are as likely as African American and Latino students to have poor grades. In this same study, low SES Asian American students did not achieve much better than other low SES students (Weiss, Farrar, & Petrie, 1989). These and similar results testify to the conclusion that socioeconomic status, more than any other variable, predicts educational outcome. Again, note the effect that biopsychosocial interactions have on development.

The Impact of Homelessness on Development

Saying that the well-being of homeless children is seriously threatened is no exaggeration. Defining the homeless as those in emergency shelter facilities with their families, Rafferty and Shinn (1991) state that these children are particularly vulnerable to health problems, hunger and poor nutrition, developmental delays, psychological problems, and educational underachievement. As we analyze these potential problems, it is well to remember that homelessness is a composite of several conditions and events: poverty; changes in residence, schools, and services; loss of possessions; disrupted social lives; and exposure to extreme hardship (Molnar & Rubin, 1991). Any one of these conditions, or any combination, may produce different effects on children.

- *Health problems.* Homeless children have much higher rates of acute and chronic health problems, which may have their roots in the prenatal period (Reed-Victor, 1997). For example, homeless women have significantly more low-birth-weight babies and experience greater levels of infant mortality. Their children are more susceptible to asthma, ear infections, diarrhea, and anemia. As you might expect, these children are also subject to immunization delays.

- *Hunger and poor nutrition.* Rafferty and Shinn (1991) summarized recent research on this topic when they described a homeless family's struggle to maintain an adequate and nutritionally balanced diet while living in a hotel: no refrigerator, no stove, poor food, and lack of food. Homeless children and their families often depend on emergency food assistance. But many times those facilities are themselves suffering from a lack of resources, such as a lack of playing areas, with the result that the children, and their families, go hungry (Bartlett, 1997).

- *Developmental delays.* Homeless children experience, to a significantly higher degree than typical children, coordination difficulties, language delays, cognitive delays, social inadequacies, and a lack of personal skills (e.g., do not know how to eat at a table). The instability of their lives, the disruptions in child care, an erratic pattern of schooling, and how parents adapt to these conditions also impede development (Molnar & Rubin, 1991).

- *Psychological problems.* Homeless children seem to suffer more than typical children from depression, anxiety, and behavioral problems. Again, remember the composites of homelessness discussed earlier that may contribute to these psychological problems. Data are simply lacking that enable us to identify the particular aspect of homelessness that causes a child's anxiety or depression.

We must also consider that parental depression affects children, and that children's problems may reflect the parents' feeling of helplessness.

- *Educational underachievement.* As we have seen, little research has been done on this issue other than to show that homeless children do poorly on reading and mathematics tests (Reed-Victor & Stronge, 1997). This finding should come as no surprise, given that these children have difficulty in finding and maintaining free public education for substantial periods. Missing educational opportunities is bad enough, but with the frequent moves their families make, these children also miss the remedial work they so urgently need. As Rafferty and Shinn (1991) noted, school is especially critical for homeless children because it can produce a sense of stability that is otherwise lacking.

In her interviews with homeless children, Walsh (1992) noted that children, because of their status and lack of power, cannot directly solve the problem of homelessness. Instead they concentrate on coping with the emotions that arise from becoming homeless, perhaps by restructuring the circumstances surrounding their homelessness. Younger children, for example, may unrealistically attribute their problems to some external event that is unrelated to them or their parents. Older children may try to explain away the cause, especially if it pertains to a parent. For example, rather than blame a parent's alcoholism or drug use, a youngster may say that the parent is sick or has problems.

Homelessness and poverty have robbed these children of a good part of their childhood. They have been forced to worry about the things that most children take for granted—food, safety, and a roof over their heads. Some become "little adults" in their efforts to help themselves and their families to survive. And yet, as their stories remind us, they are children. They cherish their toys, they play at the hint of any opportunity, they rush to get lost in the world of fantasy. They think in the magical and concrete ways of children, constructing their world with the logic of childhood. And they make clear in their stories that they would like to be treated as children—to be less burdened by worry and more able to depend on adults for the basics of survival. (Walsh, 1992, p. 178)

Guided Review

1. The early childhood years are frequently described as a period of socialization versus _____.
2. The sibling subsystem in a family is often called the _____ _____.
3. Parents who rely on verbal persuasion, positive reinforcement, and indirect methods of control are demonstrating _____ parenting behavior.
4. Today's new homeless are characterized by few _____ contacts, poor _____, and a high level of contact with the _____ _____ _____ .
5. Although homelessness has many causes, _____ remains a major contributing factor.

Children of Divorce

The United States has a larger number of single parents than any other developed country. About 25 percent of our children live with one parent. Who are these single parents? Although you probably answered that most of them are divorced (and

Answers

1. individuation 2. sibling underworld 3. authoritative 4. social, health, criminal justice system 5. poverty

you'd be right—about 65 percent of single parents are divorced), single parents represent a remarkably diverse group. They may be divorced, widowed, unmarried (about 2.5 million women have elected to have children outside of marriage), previously married, female, male (about 12 percent of all single parents are fathers, almost all of whom are divorced), adolescents or in their 30s, natural parents or adopting parents (Weinraub & Gringlas, 1995). Another distressing fact children must face is that the divorce rate following a remarriage is higher than that in first marriages. So children can experience the effects of divorce, usually several years in a single-parent home, and then the changed circumstances of a remarriage (Hetherington & Stanley-Hagan, 1995).

Nevertheless, the sheer overwhelming number of divorces demands consideration in our discussion of the early childhood years. Before examining these effects, let's look first at the divorce phenomenon.

Facts about Divorce

Nearly half of today's marriages will end in divorce and an estimated 50 percent of our children will live with a single parent before the age of 18. As mentioned earlier, any discussion of the effects of divorce (or any traumatic event) must begin with the child's level of cognitive development. Remember that early childhood youngsters are at Piaget's preoperational level, which means they are still quite egocentric. Their ability to engage in abstract thinking is still limited, and they lack that vital aspect of cognition—the ability to reverse their thinking. This colors their reaction to their parents' divorce; for example, they may think that *they* are responsible.

Children's Adjustment to Divorce

In about two or three years following the divorce, most children adjust to living in a single-parent home. This adjustment, however, can once again be shaken by what a parent's remarriage means: losing one parent in the divorce, adapting to life with the remaining parent, the addition of at least one family member in a remarriage.

The transition period in the first year following the divorce is stressful economically, socially, and emotionally. Conditions then seem to improve, and children in a stable, smoothly functioning home are better adjusted than children in a nuclear family riddled with conflict. Nevertheless, school achievement may suffer and impulsivity increases. In an interesting comment about the relationship between divorced mothers and their children, Hetherington and Parke (1993, p. 524) state:

> Divorced mothers may have given their children a hard time, but divorced mothers got rough treatment from their children, particularly their sons. In comparison with divorced fathers and parents in nuclear families, the divorced mother found that in the first year following divorce her children didn't obey, affiliate, or attend to her. They nagged and whined, made more dependency demands, and were more likely to ignore her. The aggression of boys with divorced mothers peaked at one year following divorce, then dropped significantly, but at six years after divorce was still higher than that of boys in nuclear families.

When Hetherington, a longtime student of the effects of divorce on children's lives, wrote these words, she undoubtedly had in mind the angry, tense times before separation and divorce and the difficult days following the divorce. Divorce affects children in complex ways we don't yet fully understand (Fagot, 1995). Not only is their physical way of life changed (perhaps a new home or reduced standard of living) but psychologically they are immersed in an emotionally charged home environment and in a world of deteriorating relationships, a condition that may affect the child's circle of competence in one or many ways.

Studies (Cherlin & others, 1991) suggest that more than the divorce itself may

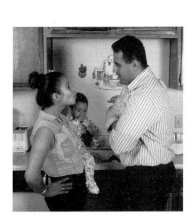

Children develop within a complex network of family relationships. What they are exposed to during these years can have long-lasting consequences.

be involved in a child's adjustment problems following parental divorce; that is, the conflict between parents may be the greatest culprit leading to a child's problems. Children from intact families in Great Britain and the United States were interviewed when the children were 7 years old and then again at 11 years of age. Children whose parents divorced between the two studies were then compared with children whose families remained intact. Children of divorced parents showed many more behavior problems than those children whose families remained intact. The investigators next went back and looked at the behavioral records of the children when they were 7 years old (when all the families were intact). They found that the children whose parents would later divorce were already exhibiting many behavior problems (tantrums, fighting, school problems), the kinds of behavior that accompany parental quarreling.

Children's Reaction to Divorce

Other conditions also affect children's reactions to their parents' divorce (Wallerstein & Blakeslee, 1989):

- The bitterness of conflict before the divorce

- The child's reaction to the loss of the parent who leaves

- Any change in the relationship between the child and the departed parent

- The effect the divorce has on the parent who retains custody of the children

- Any change in behavior toward the children on the part of the parent who retains custody

One potential source of problems for divorced mothers lies in the relationships they establish with their children right after the divorce. They may have given their children considerable freedom in those first months following the divorce and when they want to tighten the strings at adolescence, they are frequently faced with rebellion—daughters who become sullen and resentful, and sons who defy. The lesson here is that, as hard as it may be, mothers should try to maintain their role as authoritative parents immediately following the divorce. Mothers may at this time want to adopt a policy of what is called **coregulation;** that is, they talk things over with their children, plan what needs to be done, and then allow them to decide specifically how to do it, but with the mothers always shaping the general plan.

Searching for best-case scenarios, Ahrons (1994) found that in the 98 divorced families she studied, the most favorable results were found with those families where the fathers remained emotionally involved with their children, had more cooperative relationships with their ex-wives, and were current with child-support obligations.

And yet, questions remain. Commonly reported reactions of early childhood youngsters to divorce are shock, depression, and loyalty conflict (Buchanan, Maccoby, & Dornbusch, 1991). They fear that their parents no longer love them and are actually abandoning them. Another fascinating phenomenon reported by Hetherington and Blakeslee (1989) is what they termed **reconciliation fantasies.** Ten years after the divorce, and even if their parents had remarried, some children hoped their parents could get together again.

Divorced Fathers

As mentioned earlier, about 12 percent of all single parents are fathers, most of whom are divorced. The children in their families are usually older than those who remain with mothers and are more likely to be male. Fathers typically maintain their standard of living and have become the custodial parent because the mothers were judged to be incompetent or simply didn't want custody and the fathers accepted the idea of single parenthood. Single fathers have less control problems than mothers and do a better job of assigning household responsibilities. Like their maternal

For more information and reasoned discussion of the impact of divorce on children, we strongly recommend any of the writings of E. Mavis Hetherington.

counterparts, they report feelings of uncertainty and incompetence about their parenting skills in these new circumstances (Weinraub & Gringlas, 1995).

Day Care

Almost two-thirds of women with children under age 14, and more than one-half of mothers with children under age 1, are in the labor force. In fact, the single largest category of working mothers is those with children under age 3 (Zigler & Lang, 1991). Estimates are that by the year 2000, about 70 percent of mothers with children under 6 years will be employed (Clarke-Stewart & others, 1995). What happens to children while their mothers are at work? Obviously someone must be taking care of these youngsters, and it is precisely here that questions are raised about **au pairs, nannies,** and **day care.** How competent are the individuals who offer these services?

Au pairs, for example, are young women, often English, who want to spend time in America, typically 12 months because of the length of their work permits (U.S. Information Agency, 1996). They agree to provide child care services for up to 45 hours per week in no more than a 5½ day week (Peters, 1997). The United States Information Agency, which oversees the process recently stated that about 10,000 au pairs are working in the United States in any given year. Au pairs must be at least 18 and not more than 25, and possess a secondary school certificate. They are screened, determined to be of good character, and have a driver's license since America is such a car-oriented society. They receive anywhere from $100 to $130 per week plus room and board.

You can see how the au pair-family relationship demands compatibility given the live-in arrangements and the daily contact. When relationships are smooth, both sides are usually content with the circumstances. If problems arise, however, conditions can deteriorate quickly. (You may be interested in reading about the famous Louise Woodward case in Massachusetts in which the au pair was accused of murder in the death of a child in her care.)

Nannies present a different picture. Older, usually better educated, and higher paid (about $300 per week), they seem to provide a more stable environment. English nannies, for example, are often former nursery nurses with considerable experience. They typically receive careful developmental training such as a course that discusses age characteristics, nutrition, work with exceptional children, how to handle problems. etc. Many parents worry about the close relationship that develops between a child and nanny, many times feeling threatened by a growing attachment between the two. What's needed before care is actually begun is a frank discussion between the parents and nanny about duties, responsibilities, and limitations, particularly regarding the need for privacy for both parties.

Today, however, when we hear the term "caregiver," we tend to think of day care. What are the long-term developmental consequences of daycare placement? Is the day-care center healthy and stimulating? Is it safe?

(a) Day care has become an important phenomenon in our society as more and more mothers join the workforce. Research indicates that developmental outcomes are closely linked to the quality of day care. (b) Among the variety of day-care settings, home day-care centers are quite numerous. Often run by a family member or neighbor, they are smaller and more informal than large centers.

(a)

(b)

Types of Child Care

The following figures, based on data from the U.S. Bureau of Labor Statistics (1994), will give you an idea of the types of child-care arrangements and the number of children under 5 years of age in day care with employed mothers.

Care outside of home

Mother cares for child at work	6.2%
Kindergarten	1.0%
Nursery/preschool	11.6%
Group care centers	18.3%

Care in another home

By grandparent	10.0%
By other relative	5.5%
By nonrelative	16.6%

Care in child's home

By father	15.9%
By grandparent	6.5%
By other relative	3.3%
By nonrelative	5.0%

Note that the majority of these children are cared for in private homes. This may help to explain why we are uncertain about the influence of day care on development, since most research is done with children from day-care centers.

Facts about Day Care

Reliable facts about day care are hard to come by, chiefly because of the lack of any national policy that would provide hard data. About 35,000 to 40,000 "places" provide day-care services (i.e., principal income is from offering child care). "Places" is perhaps the best way to describe these facilities because of the wide variety of circumstances that exist: Zigler and Lang (1991) refer to them as a "patchwork of arrangements." For example, one mother may charge another mother several dollars to take care of her child. A relative may care for several family children. Churches, businesses, and charities may run large operations. Some may be sponsored by local or state government as an aid to the less affluent. Others are run on a pay-as-you-go basis. Almost everyone agrees that the best centers are staffed by teachers who specialize in day-care services (about 25 % of day-care personnel).

If we now sort out what is known about types of day-care centers, we can group them as follows (Clarke-Stewart, 1993; Clarke-Stewart & others, 1995). (Remember: Most states now have minimum standards for day-care operation.)

Care in the Child's Home. In this type of care, a relative is usually the caregiver, which is fairly common, but as Clarke-Stewart and others noted (1995), we probably know less about this care than any other. Although such an arrangement has several advantages (e.g., the child is familiar with the setting and the caregiver, the schedule can be flexible), several disadvantages also occur (e.g., the caregiver is usually untrained, the child misses peer activities).

Family Day Care. Here caregivers provide service in their homes, which may or may not be licensed and the number of children may range from 1 (family day-care home) to 12 (group day-care home). Family day-care homes are the most numerous and the least expensive. They are typically located near the child's home so transportation is no problem. A family atmosphere exists while simultaneously enabling a child to interact with a limited number of children of various ages. A major disadvantage is that in this type of day care the provider is the least accountable of providers. These settings typically are informal, unprofessional, and short-lived with little or no supervision (Clarke-Stewart, 1993, p. 45).

An Applied View — Desirable Qualities of Day-Care Centers

For those who want guidelines to identify important features in a day-care setting, here are several specific suggestions by the National Association for the Education of Young Children (1986).

1. Adult Caregivers
   - Adults should understand how infants and young children grow.
   - The number of adults available to meet the individual needs of the children should be adequate (see table 8.4).
   - Good records should be kept for each child.

2. The Program Itself
   - The setting should facilitate the growth and development of young children working and playing together.
   - Equipment and play materials should be adequate and readily available.
   - Instructors should be sufficiently skilled to aid youngsters in their language and social development.

3. Relations with Clients and Community
   - Parents should be actively involved with the center.
   - The community should be aware of activities at the center, and the center should be aware of community resources (recreational, learning centers).

4. The Ability to Meet the Demands of All Involved
   - The health of all members—children, staff, and parents—should be both protected and promoted.
   - Safety should be a primary concern.
   - Adequate space should be available to serve all activities (35 square feet of usable playroom floor space indoors per child and 75 square feet of play space outdoors per child).

Day-Care Centers. These centers are what people mean when they refer to "day care." They may be for profit (the number of these is increasing) or they may be nonprofit and they may provide for fewer than 15 or more than 300 children, whom they group by age. The average day-care center offers care for 60 children (Clarke-Stewart & others, 1995). Here is a summary of many of the day-care centers.

- *Private day-care centers* run for profit have no eligibility requirements and will accept almost anyone who can pay the fee. Typically staffed by two or three people (usually not professionally trained), these centers may operate in a converted store or shop. They probably are minimally equipped with toys and educational activities and usually offer no social or health services.

- *Commercial centers* are also private and run for profit. They may be part of a national or regional chain with uniform offerings and facilities. They usually are well equipped with good food and activities. The centers are a business, much as a McDonald's or Burger King. KinderCare, for example, runs about 900 centers.

- *Community church centers* are often, but not always, run for children of the poor. The quality of personal care (attention, affection) is usually good, but church centers often have minimal facilities and activities.

- *Company centers* are often offered as fringe benefits for employees. They are usually run in good facilities with a well-trained staff and a wide range of services.

- *Public service centers* are government sponsored, well run, and have high quality throughout. Unfortunately, few of these are available and they are designed to serve children of low-income families.

- *Research centers* are usually affiliated with a university and represent what the latest research says a day-care center should be. Most studies of day care have been conducted in these centers. But since the centers are of the highest

TABLE 8.4 SUGGESTED RATIO OF STAFF TO CHILDREN

	Age	Maximum Size	Staff-Child Ratio
For Centers	0–2	6	1:3
	2–3	12	1:4
	3–6	16	1:8
For Homes	0–2	10	1:5
	2–6	12	1:6

quality, the results of such studies do not give a true picture of day care throughout the country.

- *Other centers* include the family-run centers mentioned earlier and cooperative centers where parents rotate responsibility for child care under professional guidance. In another fairly popular form of care, a neighborhood mother, usually a former nurse or teacher, takes care of two or three children, thus avoiding state requirements concerning number of children, facilities, or insurance.

A National Concern

As you can see, the country is moving into a different era with regard to day care. Working mothers are now in the majority, and their numbers promise to increase. Given these events, regulation of day care has taken on new urgency. Legislative battles over standards for day-care centers have been constant, but the best the federal government has been able to do is to propose general standards, such as the suggested ratio of staff to children, which is illustrated in Table 8.4.

Despite the minimal salaries of day-care workers, costs are high because day care is labor intensive. Staff-child ratios usually average from 1:8 to 1:10, much too high considering children's needs and safety. But a new attitude is developing, one with political consequences. National surveys have consistently shown that more than one-half of the voters think a national policy regarding day care should be formulated.

Developmental Outcomes

Regardless of what you may have heard or read, no definite conclusions have been reached concerning the long-term developmental consequences of day care. One reason is that careful follow-up of children from day care is not yet available (Clarke-Stewart, 1993).

Attempting to summarize the research, Clarke-Stewart and others (1995) reached the following conclusions:

- *Physical development.* Children typically maintain their normal course of physical development during their time in day care. Disadvantaged children gain height and weight more rapidly and advance their motor skills in a day-care setting.

- *Cognitive development.* Children with experience in day care during the early childhood years manifest more advanced cognitive and language development than those who remain at home. These findings come from good quality centers (Broberg & others, 1997). But questions arise about the quality of other centers: What would be the results from centers of poorer quality? Do the individual differences in the children affect the results?

- *Social development.* Children in day care seem to be more assertive, independent, and self-confident. These children have also been found to be less pleasant, polite, and compliant with adults' requests.

As you read these conclusions you see how difficult it is to obtain reliable data. One example of a lack of good data relates to child abuse in day-care settings. Estimates are that the incidence rate of the sexual abuse of children under the age of 6 years in day care is 5.5 per 10,000 children compared to 8.9 per 10,000 children abused at home. The accuracy of these figures is indeed questionable and the topic cries out for extensive, objective research (Jackson & Nuttall, 1997). Another obstacle to definite conclusions has been the use of university-sponsored research centers to study children. These centers are usually lavishly equipped and overstaffed; they simply do not reflect the national norm. Consequently, the findings relating to the long-term developmental outcomes of day-care placement are shaky to say the least.

Guided Review

6. Nearly _____ of today's marriages will probably end in divorce.
7. A major factor in understanding children's reactions to divorce is level of _____ _____.
8. Reliable facts about day care are hard to come by because of the lack of _____ _____.
9. The developmental outcomes of day care are difficult to assess because most children are in _____ settings.
10. _____ day-care settings are the most numerous probably because they are the least _____.

The Self Emerges

Imagine for a moment you're looking in a mirror. What do you see? Don't laugh; you see *you*. But what exactly do you see? When you look in the mirror, you see yourself, of course. But there are two sides to this vision of yourself. The first is referred to as the "I" self, that part of you that is doing the actual looking. The second part of what you see is the "Me" self, that is, the "Me" is the person observed (Harter, 1993).

We have the great American psychologist, William James, to thank for this division of the self into two distinct parts. James believed that the "I" part of the self was the knower, that is, the "I" that thinks, makes judgments, recognizes it's separate from everything it sees, and controls the surrounding world. The "Me," on the other hand, is the object of all of the "I's" thinking, judging etc. Think of the "Me" as your self-image, which helps you to understand how the "I" develops feelings of self-esteem: As a result of the "I" evaluating the "Me's" activities, the self is judged good or bad, competent or incompetent, masterful or fumbling.

The Development of Self

Before tracing the path of self-development, we would like you to make the following distinctions.

• By self-concept, we mean that children know who they are and what makes them different from everyone else.

• By self-esteem, we mean that children possess feelings of confidence and satisfaction with one's self.

Answers

6. one-half 7. cognitive development 8. follow-up studies 9. private 10. Family, expensive

An Applied View

When I and Me Are We

Born in Taiwan, adopted by American Caucasian parents, product of an American upbringing, Julia Ming Gale often looks in the mirror and asks herself, "Who am I?" In her mind she sees a young woman with curly red hair, green eyes, and freckles, an image that causes her considerable sadness. Adopted by parents with two children of their own, the Gales had lived in Taiwan for three years, studied the Chinese language, had many Chinese friends, and kept a number of Chinese items in their American home—books, scrolls, and furniture.

But Ming's world was Caucasian and she couldn't recall a time when she didn't feel Caucasian, even though every time she looked in the mirror she faced an inescapable reality: the face looking back at her was Chinese. Periodic reminders of her Chinese heritage plagued her. Once doing the dishes, her younger brother came in with a friend. Telling his friend she was the maid and didn't speak any English, her brother was joking, but Ming still remembers the hurt. Bewildered, she began to fantasize that her birth mother was some famous Asian woman.

Nevertheless, her inner self didn't want to be any more Chinese than she had to be and she resisted any efforts her parents made to encourage the flourishing of her Chinese roots. She just wanted to be treated as another Caucasian. By the time she was 12, she learned she had been born in Taiwan, not in China, which only increased her sense of cultural rootlessness. She was bothered that she couldn't claim the culture she grew up in. She even tried to force herself to "go Chinese," but it didn't work. Wanting to be Caucasian, she couldn't bridge the gap between the two cultures.

When her parents realized what she was going through, they tried to help her reconcile her conflicts. Ming, at age 24, has slowly started to explore her Chinese background through language lessons, taking courses in Chinese history, and readings that show her interest in both China and adoption. The career she has chosen reflects her own background: helping Chinese adoptees discover their identities, to help them live with the duality that caused her so much pain.

In Ming's case two selves existed in conflict and she spent 24 years trying to reconcile the differences between them. A novelist couldn't dramatize a better example to illustrate how knowing who they are shapes children's development, giving them the poise and assurance to undertake challenges they may otherwise shun. Too often children feel a conflict between the self they want to be and what they actually see themselves as, two different versions of the same self—*When "I" and "Me" are "We."*

The infant shown here touching his nose and mouth against the mirror reveals the development of a sense of self, which most infants accomplish by about 18 months of age.

How do children construct a sense of **self,** this sense of who they are and what makes them different from everyone else? In a famous and ingenious study of self-development, the psychologists Michael Lewis and Jean Brooks-Gunn (1979) devised different strategies for uncovering how children discover they are distinct from their surroundings.

- Working with infants between 5 and 8 months old, the investigators placed them before a mirror. The children looked at themselves intently, smiled at their images, and even waved at the mirror, but gave no indication that they knew they were looking at themselves.

- Next, infants between 9 and 12 months reached out to the mirror to touch their bodies and turned toward other people or objects reflected in the mirror.

- The researchers then dabbed red rouge on the noses of infants between 15 and 18 months. When they saw themselves in the mirror, they pointed to their noses (on their own faces, not in the mirror) and tried to rub off the rouge.

- Finally, between 21 and 24 months, infants used their names and correctly applied personal pronouns. When placed with other same-sex infants in front of the mirror, they accurately identified themselves.

We're safe in saying, then, that children will usually have acquired a sense of self by 18 months of age and that after age 2 children clearly distinguished themselves from others (Pipp-Siegel & Foltz, 1997).

After infants take this initial step on the path to self-development and understanding, the next phase centers on the early childhood years. Children's growing—

even astonishing—ability to understand things provides them with ever-deepening insights into themselves. When asked to tell who she was, a 4-year-old replied as follows.

> I go to preschool. I like it. I play with my brother a lot. I have dark brown hair. I like to talk. (Oh yes!)

Here are the comments of a 6-year-old girl when asked to describe herself.

> I'm the youngest in my family. I'm happy most of the time. I like riding my bike. I eat a lot and I like different kinds of food. I have brown eyes. I have lots of freckles. I like almost everybody and I have lots of friends. Sometimes I get a little scared. When I'm a little older, I want to be a babysitter and I'll protect people. When I grow up I'm going to be a librarian.

Her reactions are fairly sophisticated for a 6-year-old. Note the more abstract ideas of happiness, friendship, and protecting others, concepts that usually appear at later ages. Most children of her age focus on the physical, such as hair color and color of eyes, or on tangible objects such as food, toys, even freckles. As children grow, their sense of self isn't limited to their reflections in a mirror; they have acquired language and are able to tell us what they think of themselves.

Note how children change from identifying themselves by physical characteristics (hair or eye color) to more social and emotional characteristics (feeling good or bad about themselves). In these later years, they usually begin to compare themselves to others. Among the many factors contributing to a sense of self are the following.

		SELF		
Physical	**Cognitive**	**Language**	**Psychosocial**	**Gender**
Health	Representation	Speech	Attachment	Identity
Coordination	Evaluation	Referents	Separation	Role
Appearance	Problem solving	Labeling	Relationships	Stereotypes

Another powerful input into a child's sense of self is that of gender.

The Role of Gender in Development

"Manhood" needs to be redefined in a way that allows women equality and men pride. Our culture desperately needs new ways to teach boys to be men. Via the media and advertising, we are teaching our sons all the wrong lessons. Boys need a model of manhood that is caring and bold, adventurous and gentle. They need ways to be men that don't involve violence, misogny, and the objectification of women.

Many young women are less whole and androgynous than they were at age ten. They are more appearance-conscious and sex-conscious. They are quieter, more fearful of holding strong opinions, more careful what they say and less honest. They're more likely to second-guess themselves and to be self-critical. They are bigger worriers and effective people pleasers. They are less likely to play sports, love math and science and plan on being president. They hide their intelligence. Many must fight for years to regain all the territory that they lost.

These words, taken from the remarkably popular book by Mary Pipher, *Reviving Ophelia* (1994), pose one of the major difficulties in our discussion of how children acquire their sense of gender in a way that they themselves and their society find acceptable. "Acceptable" means many things to many people, and although gender roles for boys and girls, men and women are slowly, even grudgingly, changing, sharp differences of opinion are still evident. For example, many parents want their children to follow traditional gender roles (sports for boys, dolls for girls), while other parents want to break down what they consider rigid gender role stereotypes. (See chapter 1 for definitions of gender identity, gender role, and gender stereotypes.)

Most parents today try to prevent negative gender images from occurring in their families, knowing that stereotypes begin to appear at an early age. Children construct categories from the world around them, attach certain characteristics to these categories, and then label the categories. Forming and labeling categories (boy–girl, dog–cat) is a critical and positive process because it helps children organize their world. Unfortunately, it may also be negative if the characteristics associated with a particular category are limiting. At this point you may well ask: How do boys become boys and girls become girls?

Children quickly learn what objects, activities, and friends are gender appropriate.

Males and females grow up in quite different learning environments with important psychological implications for development.
Jeanne Block

Acquiring Gender Identity: Heredity or Environment?

Before beginning our discussion of the role that gender plays in development you may find clues to the current status of women by examining the processes by which boys and girls acquire their sense of gender identity. The contributions of biology and the environment, however, interact in a complex, interactive manner, one that continues to cause controversy. Most psychologists today believe in a reciprocal interaction model of development to explain our behavior. That is, we respond to those around us and they change; their responses to us then change and we in turn change. The process is constant and you can see how the reactions to ideas of gender, particularly if they are stereotypical, can influence gender identity and also *behavior*. If girls are told that "girls don't make good scientists," then possibly their achievement in science classes will suffer. The first component of the heredity—environment interaction is biology.

Does Biology Count?

Whatever your ideas on gender identity, we start with an unavoidable premise: Parts of the sexual agenda are biologically programmed. John Money (1980), working in a Johns Hopkins clinic devoted to the study of congenital abnormalities of the sex organs, believed that sexual differentiation occurs through a series of four stages. First is *chromosomal sex*. The biological sexual program is initially carried by either the X or Y sex chromosome. Second is *gonadal sex*, in which the XX or XY combination pass on the sexual program to the undifferentiated gonads. Third is *hormonal sex*. Once the testes or ovaries are differentiated, they begin to produce chemical agents called sex hormones. Males produce more of the sex hormones called androgens than females, whereas females produce more estrogens (the female sex hormone).

Fourth is *genital sex*. A baby's sex is determined not only by chromosomes and hormones but also by its external sex organs. As you can well imagine, genital or morphological sex determines how society will treat the newly born baby. For example, recent research (Taylor, 1996) showed that 4- to 8-year-olds think that the biology of gender is most important in determining how boys and girls develop. It's not until the 9 to 10 year period that they come to recognize that the social context in which a person develops influences the kind of interests and activities a person pursues without affecting maleness or femaleness.

With these as the biological givens, we turn now to the role of socialization.

Does the Environment Count?

It doesn't take children long to discover what behavior "fits" boys and which "fits" girls (Fagot, Leinbach & O'Boyle, 1992). If you think about children's cognitive competencies and realize that they acquire their sex identity by 2 to 3 years of age, you can understand their rapid assignment of appropriate behavior to either male or female. (For an excellent and expanded discussion of this topic, see Unger & Crawford, 1996.)

In an attempt to explain these and similar findings, Martin, Wood, and Little (1990) found a developmental sequence to the appearance of gender stereotypes. In the first stage, children learn what kinds of things are associated with each sex (boys play with cars; girls play with dolls). From the ages 4 to 6 years, children move to the second stage where they begin to learn the more complex associations for their own sex (different kinds of activities associated with a toy). By the time of the third stage (roughly 6 to 8 years), children make the same types of associations for the opposite sex.

Becoming Boys and Girls

One of the first categories children form is sex related; there is a neat division between male and female. Children then move from the observable physical differences between the sexes and begin to acquire gender knowledge about the behavior expected of male and female. Depending on the source of this knowledge, gender role stereotyping has commenced and attitudes toward gender are being shaped. As Serbin and her colleagues (1993) noted, despite the societal changes we have seen in acceptable gender roles, gender role stereotypes have remained relatively stable. What do we know about this process?

Family

Evidence clearly suggests that parents treat boy and girl babies differently from birth. Adults tend to engage in rougher play with boys; give them stereotypical toys (cars and trucks), and speak differently to them. By the end of the second year, parents respond favorably to what they consider appropriate sexual behavior (i.e., stereotypical) and negatively to cross-sex play (boys engaging in typical girl's play and vice versa). For example, Fagot (1995) observed toddlers and their parents at home and discovered that both mothers and fathers differentially reinforced their children's behavior. That is, parents reinforced girls for playing with dolls and boys for playing with blocks, girls for helping their mothers around the house and boys for running and jumping.

Parents usually are unaware of the extent to which they engage in this type of reinforcement (Lips, 1993). In a famous study (Will, Self, & Data, 1976) 11 mothers were observed interacting with a 6-month-old infant. Five of the mothers played with the infant when it was dressed in blue pants and called "Adam." Six mothers later played with the same infant when it wore a pink dress and was called "Beth." The mothers offered a doll to "Beth" and a toy train to "Adam." They also smiled more at Beth and held her more closely. The baby was actually a boy. Interviewed later, all the mothers said that boys and girls were alike at this age and *should be treated identically.*

Siblings also influence gender development. Brothers and sisters differ markedly in personality, intelligence, and psychopathology in spite of shared genetic roots. Since about 80 percent of children have siblings and spend considerable time with each other, these relationships exercise a considerable influence. An older brother showing a younger brother how to hold a bat; a younger sister watching her older sister play with dolls; quarreling among siblings; each of these examples illustrates the impact that sibling relationships have on gender development (Furman, 1995).

Peers

Boys and girls have different expectations about their friends; girls quickly learn that relationships are a crucial part of their lives, while boys are urged to be independent and self-reliant (Lips, 1993). When children start to make friends and play, these activities foster and maintain sex-typed play. When they engage in "sex-inappropriate" play (boys with dolls, girls with a football) their peers immediately criticize them and tend to isolate them ("sissy; "tomboy"). Although we see increasing inroads into these stereotypes (girls in Little League and youth hockey, for example), the tendency to sexually compartmentalize behavior increases with age until most adolescents react to intense demands for conformity to stereotypical gender roles.

Here, again, we see the influence of imitation and reinforcement. During development, youngsters of the same sex tend to play together, a custom called **sex cleavage** and one that is encouraged by parents and teachers: boys guided to more large-group activities, girls forming more intense small groups (Fagot, 1995). If you think back on your own experiences, you can remember your friends at this age— either all male or female. In adolescence, despite dating and opposite sex attraction, both males and females want to live up to the most rigid interpretations of what their group thinks is ideally male or female. You can understand, then, how imitation, reinforcement, and cognitive development come together to intensify what a boy thinks is masculine and a girl thinks is feminine.

Media

Another influence on gender development, one that carries important messages about what is desirable for males and females and one that reaches into the home, is the media, especially television. Television has assumed such a powerful place in the socialization of children that it is safe to say that television is almost as significant as family and peers. What is particularly bothersome is the stereotypical behavior that it presents as both positive and desirable. As Lips (1993) has stated, television teaches gender stereotypes. The more television children watch, the more stereotypical is their behavior.

In spite of such shows as *Murphy Brown* and *Dr. Quinn,* the central characters of shows are much more likely to be male than female, the theme will be action-oriented for males, and the characters typically engage in stereotypical behavior (men are the executives and leaders, women are the housewives and secretaries). Much the same holds true for television commercials. There is little doubt that children notice the different ways television portrays males and females. When asked to rate the behavior of males and females, children aged 8 to 13 responded in a rigidly stereotypical manner: Males were brave, adventurous, intelligent, and make good decisions. Females, on the other hand, cried easily and needed to be protected (Lips, 1993).

These distinctions apply to other, much more subtle, features of television programming. For example, to understand a television program, children must know something about story form—how stories are constructed and presented. They use their knowledge of the world and general knowledge about situations and events in order to grasp television's content, which often reinforces what they are watching. They must also have knowledge of television's forms and conventions to help them understand what is happening on the screen. Music and visual techniques, plus camera angles, all convey information (Liebert & Sprafkin, 1988).

In other words, children learn more than the contents of a program from television. They learn the many cues that signal male or female. Loud music, rapid scene changes, multiple sound effects, and frequent cuts mean just one thing—a male-oriented show. Shows designed for females have soft background music, gentle cuts, and soothing sound effects. Children as young as 6 years can use these cues to identify shows that are intended for either males or females (Lips, 1993). Children understand television programs according to their level of development, and their level of development is affected by their television viewing, with all that implies for gender development.

For example, consider these words of Don Hewitt, a powerful network executive and producer of the popular *60 Minutes.*

> **We were learning how to serve it up, how to make it more dramatic, more exciting. We were dealing with something called the attention span; my job was to capture and hold the attention of the American public by putting on the best show, like putting a frame around a picture. (White, 1975)**

When the picture is gender, how it's framed shapes the meaning of that picture, and if the frame casts a shadow of gender stereotypes, the impact on developing minds is insidious, powerful, and long-lasting. Here we have a stunning acknowledgment of television's power. Imagine young minds sitting in front of such a dynamic and persuasive tool and being bombarded by gender stereotypes.

Let's now turn our attention to several theories that attempt to explain gender development.

Theories of Gender Development

Several theories of gender development have generated most of the research during the past 10 years: social learning theory, cognitive development, and gender schema theory. *Social learning theorists* believe that parents, as the distributors of reinforcement, reinforce appropriate gender-role behaviors. By their choice of toys, by urging "boy" or "girl" behavior, and by reinforcing this behavior, parents encourage their children to engage in gender-appropriate behavior. If the parents have a good relationship with their children, they become models for their children to imitate, encouraging them to acquire additional gender-related behavior. Thus children are reinforced or punished for different kinds of behavior. They also learn appropriate gender behavior from other male and female models (such as those in television shows) who display different kinds of behavior.

A second explanation, quite popular today, is *cognitive-developmental,* which derives from Kohlberg's speculations about gender development (1966). We know from Piaget's work that children engage in symbolic thinking by about 2 years of age. Using this ability, children acquire their gender identity and then, Kohlberg believes, they begin the process of acquiring sex-appropriate behavior. In other words, as a result of cognitive development—in a sense, constructing their own world—children begin to build the concepts of maleness and femaleness.

A newer, and different, cognitive-developmental explanation is called *gender schema* theory. A schema is a mental blueprint for organizing information, and children develop a schema for gender. Think back to our discussion of Piaget's schemes in chapter 2. Children form a mental blueprint of gender, which they use as a guide to interpret and store information about male and female. As Unger & Crawford noted (1996, p. 57):

> **According to this theory, learning of the gender schema begins very early, and the schema guides the individual in becoming gender typed. Gender typing occurs because the individual develops a generalized readiness to process information on the basis of the gender schema. Indeed, gender schema theory proposes that the self-concept itself gets assimilated into the gender schema.**

In other words, children use their cognitive abilities to form schema about gender and then shape any gender information coming from the environment to change and expand on the existing schema. The gender schema then becomes a powerful tool in connecting many ideas that otherwise seem unrelated (some *colors* are *feminine,* others *masculine*).

With this brief examination of the biological and environmental forces that contribute to gender and the theories that attempt to explain the process, let's next look at what happens when gender stereotypes are formed.

Children often find opposite-sex toys extremely attractive. Many parents encourage the use of such toys to help their children avoid the development of stereotypical gender-role attitudes.

Gender Stereotyping

As mentioned, gender stereotyping is the beliefs that we have about the characteristics and behavior associated with male and female. In other words, from an early age we form an idea of what a male and female should be, begin to accumulate characteristics about male and female, and assign a label to that category. This process certainly simplifies our ability to deal with our world: That rough, noisy person is a boy; that gentle, soft-spoken, obedient person is a girl. (As a result of such stereotyping, the "feminine" boy or "masculine" girl often has difficulties with their peers.)

Problems can arise, however, when the characteristics associated with a label create a negative image. "Oh, girls can't do math; girls can't do science; girls are always crying, girls can't be leaders." At this point we start to treat the individual according to the characteristics we associate with male or female. If you think about this for a moment, you can see some potential pitfalls, especially in the classroom. (For an excellent summary of the place of women in education, see Sadker & Sadker, 1994, pp. 15–41.)

Although sexual equality is widely accepted today—legally, professionally, and personally—gender stereotyping is still alive and well. But are males and females actually that different?

Gender Similarities and Differences

As knowledge about gender behavior increases, a growing consensus has emerged that the differences between the sexes are not as great as once thought. In a benchmark study of gender differences published in 1974, Maccoby and Jacklin concluded that males were superior in mathematical and visual-spatial skills, and females had better verbal skills. (Recent studies have continued to identify gender similarities and differences; for a summary of this research, see Berk, 1997.) We can summarize this research by stating that many more similarities exist than you probably expected, and that differences aren't necessarily caused by biological forces.

As an illustration of similarities, consider the recent work of Pinker (1994) who

TABLE 8.5 OBSERVED GENDER DIFFERENCES

Characteristic	Gender Difference
Physical differences	Although almost all girls mature more rapidly than boys, by adolescence, boys have surpassed girls in size and strength.
Verbal ability	Girls do better on verbal tasks beginning in the early years. Boys also exhibit more language problems than girls.
Spatial skill	Boys do well on spatial tasks, and continue to do so throughout schooling.
Mathematical ability	Little, if any, difference exists in the early years; boys continue to do well during the high school years.
Science	Gender differences seem to be increasing; females are falling more behind, whereas the performance of males is increasing.
Achievement motivation	Differences here seem to be linked to task and situation. Boys do better in stereotypical "masculine" tasks (math, science), girls on "feminine" tasks (art, music). In direct competition between males and females, beginning around adolescence, girls' need achievement seems to drop.
Aggression	Boys appear to be innately more aggressive than girls, a difference that appears early and is remarkably consistent.

noted that anthropologists frequently stress differences between peoples (the "strange behaviors" of others) and often understate the many similarities among all humans. For example, Pinker specifies such universal human characteristics as humor, insults, fear, anger, storytelling, laws, dreams, words for common objects, binary distinctions, measures, common facial expressions (happy, sad, angry, fearful), crying, displays of affection, and on and on. What we have here is a list of complex interactions between a universal human nature and the conditions of living in a human body on this planet (Pinker, 1994). Obviously, the point of this discussion is that humans are quite similar, regardless of male-female distinctions.

Nevertheless, differences do exist, as seen in table 8.5. By the way, we should point out that these differences are not fixed; that is, changes occur as more so-

Guided Review

11. Development is the integration of all aspects of growth: _____, _____, _____, and _____.
12. The "I" is the _____; the "Me" is the _____.
13. Children usually acquire a sense of self by _____ months of age.
14. When children develop a mental blueprint concerning gender, this is called _____ _____ _____.
15. Psychologists today are more alert to the proper use of the terms _____ and _____ to indicate the interacton of _____ and _____ to explain gender.

Answers

11. physical, cognitive, social, emotional 12. knower, known 13. 18 14. gender schema theory 15. sex, gender, biology, environment

phisticated research techniques produce new data. One example of this is the realization that differences in mathematical abilities are not as great as once thought.

An important part of the early childhood youngster's life is the role of play in physical, cognitive, social, and self-development.

The Importance of Play

Children shouting; children running; children chasing each other; children busy at games. All of these activities seem to fit what we mean by play. This seemingly simple, happy behavior is, nevertheless, difficult to define with any degree of precision. For example, is play really child's work, just a matter of "having fun"? Or is something else involved, something that contributes to a child's knowledge of the world? As Garvey (1990) stated, several descriptive characteristics of play are critical to its definition:

- Play must be enjoyable and valued by the player.

- Play has no extrinsic goals; that is, play is intrinsically motivated.

- Play is spontaneous and voluntary; no one is forcing a child to play; it is freely chosen by the child.

- Play demands that a child be actively engaged.

- Play has systematic relations to other behavior that is not play.

We'll see later that play is linked to other developmental considerations such as cognition, emotion, and the like. But for now, let's define **play** as *an activity that children engage in because they enjoy it for its own sake.*

Why do we play? Attempting to answer this question takes us into the realm of what interests us as human beings throughout our lifespan. As Bronson (1995, p. 1) noted:

> We are curious about the social and physical world and reach out to explore it. We manipulate and experiment to see what will happen and how things and people function. We try to master and control processes and produce desired effects by our own efforts. We also imitate what we perceive, and we play with these images in spontaneous variations on the captured themes.

Bronson goes on to point out that we play in a wide variety of situations; we play alone or with others, with objects, and with ideas. We play simply, but also with great skill and dexterity in complicated patterns. No matter how complex adult play becomes, one basic truth remains constant—the basic inclination that leads the child to play remains in the adult.

The Meaning of Play

Beginning with the notion that play has widespread consequences, we can say that play allows children to explore their environment on their own terms and to take in any meaningful experiences at their own rate and on their own level (e.g., running through a field and stopping to look at rocks or insects). Although students of play no longer believe that children engage in play as practice for tasks that will be useful to them as adults, you can see remnants of that belief in the notion that gaining experience in culturally valued roles remains a function of play (Uzgiris & Raeff, 1995).

Children also play for the sheer exuberance of it, which enables them to exer-

Play may be one of the most profound expressions of human nature and one of the greatest innate resources for learning and invention.
Martha Bronson

TABLE 8.6 TYPES OF PLAY

Play Type	Age	Definition	Examples
Functional Play	1–2 years	Simple, repetitive motor movements with or without objects	Running around, rolling a toy car back and forth
Constructive play	3—6 years	Creating or constructing something	Making a house out of toy blocks, drawing a picture, putting a puzzle together
Make-believe play	3–7 years	Acting out roles	Playing house, school, or doctor; acting as a television character
Games with rules	6–11 years	Understanding and following rules in games	Playing board games, cards, baseball, etc.

Source: After Berk, 1997

cise their bodies and improve motor skills. Such uninhibited behavior permits children to relieve tension and helps them to master anxiety (Watson, 1995). You probably remember the story of the child playing dentist after a visit to a dentist's office. Keep in mind, however, in our discussion, the interactive nature of play: Children can't play certain kinds of games until they reach a specific cognitive level, but they can't reach that level without environmental encouragement, some of which comes through their play.

The play interests that are encouraged and supported in childhood may influence the learning skills and conscious learning interests of the future. What children learn "is fun" becomes the foundation for intrinsic motivation now and later. Think back yourself: What kind of play did you really enjoy? Do you think it contributed to your success today? (Discuss this in class; it should provide some funny moments.) (Table 8.6 presents several types of play and the ages at which they occur.)

With this interactive model in mind, we can see that children play for various reasons, such as the following.

Cognitive Development

Play aids cognitive development; cognitive development aids play. Through play, children learn about the objects in their world, what these objects do (balls roll and bounce), what they are made of (toy cars have wheels), and how they work. To use Piaget's terms, children "operate" on these objects through play and also learn behavioral skills that will help them in the future.

Piaget is not the only theorist who has incorporated play into developmental theory. Once you accept the nature of play as pleasant and nonstressful, you see how other theorists such as Montessori incorporated play into their view of a motivated learning environment. Jerome Bruner, in his many influential writings on learning and development (especially his 1966 masterpiece, *Toward a Theory of Instruction*), argued forcefully that play provides the emotional security that leads to cognitive competence.

> Observations of young children and of the young of other species suggest that a good deal of their play must be understood as practice in coping with the environment. . . . The child's metalinguistic play is hard to interpret as anything other than pleasure in practicing and developing a new skill. Although competence may not "naturally" be directed toward school learning, it is certainly possible that the great access of energy that children experience when they "get into a subject they like" is made of the same stuff (Bruner, 1966, p. 118).

Social Development

Play helps social development during this period because the involvement of others demands a give-and-take that teaches early childhood youngsters the basics of forming relationships. Social skills demand the same building processes as cognitive skills. Why are some 5- and 6-year-olds more popular with their classmates than others? Watching closely, you can discover the reasons: decreasing egocentrism, recognition of the rights of others, and a willingness to share. These social skills do not simply appear; they are learned, and much of the learning comes through play.

Play provides an emotional release for youngsters (Fischer, Shaver, & Carnochan, 1990). There are not the right or wrong, life-and-death feelings that accompany interactions with adults. Children can be creative without worrying about failure. They can also work out emotional tensions through play.

Developmental Features of Play

Does play change over time? Are there age-related features of play that we can identify? Linking a specific kind of play to a specific age is difficult, but various kinds of play can be linked with the characteristics of a particular level (e.g., early childhood, middle childhood).

Until the age of 18 months to 2 years, children's play is essentially sensorimotor; that is, a great deal of repetition involving the body occurs (e.g., doing the same things with a toy). At age 2 a great divide is passed because children can engage their world symbolically: letting one thing represent another, adopting different types of roles, and indulging in fantasy and pretend activities. Children may pretend to drink from play cups, or feed a doll with a spoon, or use a clothespin as a doll. Pretend play is a major characteristic of the early childhood years.

 **An Applied View**

Children and Their Toys

From what we have said, you can see how important it is to provide appropriate play materials to match the needs and goals of children. As Bronson (1995) noted, the play materials we supply our children are loaded with multiple messages. They not only cause children to do certain things (because of the nature of the toy), they also convey clearly what parents think is acceptable. For example, some parents would never give a child a toy gun; others think guns are a normal part of growing up.

The appearance, structure, and complexity of play materials will certainly affect children's interests, depending on their age, skill, and cognitive maturity. For example, the condition of play materials teaches children whether or not to respect and take care of things. Broken or chipped toys are not only unappealing, they also teach children that carelessness and disregard are a way of life. Carelessness raises safety issues, which should be a primary concern in selecting play materials.

Play materials are typically grouped into four categories: social and fantasy; exploration and mastery; music, art, and movement; gross motor play. *Social and fantasy play materials* include items that encourage the use of

imagination and the mental representation of objects and events, as well as a deeper understanding of people and the rules we live by. Play materials in this category are often used in dramatic play, solitary fantasy play, and role play.

Exploration and mastery play materials increase children's knowledge about the physical world, encouraging them to devise ways to enrich their comprehension of "how things work." Materials that fit this category focus on explanation, experimentation, and mastery. Toys would include puzzles, pattern-making games, sand, water, and string. *Music, art, and movement play materials* aid in the development of artistic expression, and include arts, crafts, and instruments. Finally, *gross motor play materials* foster large muscle development and skills, and would include playground and gym equipment, push-and-pull toys, and sports equipment.

Remember: One basic principle should be at the heart of selecting play materials—their usefulness in supporting the growth and development of children. Table 8.7 illustrates the value of matching age, materials, and development, using games as an example.

Garvey, C. (1990). *Play.* Cambridge, MA: Harvard University Press. A brief, thorough examination of what we mean by play and how children play with objects, language, and rules, among others.

Play also becomes more social; interactions with other children become more important in play. With the beginning of the school years, play becomes even more social and rule dominated. Games with rules become important, which reflects children's ability to use abstract thinking in playing games. A strike in baseball, for example, is a ball thrown over the plate, one that a batter swings at and misses, or a "foul ball." School-age children, with their increased symbolic ability, understand these rules and apply them in their games. Table 8.8 summarizes the developmental changes in play.

TABLE 8.7 APPROPRIATE GAMES

Age	Appropriate Materials	Developmental Concerns
Older toddlers (2 years)	Simple games with few pieces; game pieces that are not too small (2–4 inches); simple matching games with few pairs (lotto-type); giant dominoes; magnetic fishing games	Enjoy games that they can do alone or with one other child and/or adult
Prechool and kindergarten children (3 through 5 years)	More complex matching games (more pieces), including lotto; dominoes (picture, color number); simple card games (Concentration); first board games (4–5 years); picture bingo (matching letter/number bingo at about age 5); games involving construction or balancing	Development of turn taking, concentration, attention to detail, and understanding of rule-based interaction supported by early games; can play games in which outcome is determined by chance, not strategy; may play with one or two peers but may have difficulty losing
Primary school children (6 through 8 years)	Simple guessing or deductive games, strategy games, trading games, card games, bingo, dominoes, marbles, checkers, Chinese checkers; word games, arithmetic games (simple adding games)	Increasing interest in games but hate to lose; can play competitive games by age 8; increasing capacity for cooperative interaction and use of strategy nurtured by games, but games should have relatively few rules and not require complicated strategies

Source: Bronson, M. (1995). *The right stuff for children birth to 8.* Washington, D.C.: National Association for the Education of Young People.

TABLE 8.8 DEVELOPMENTAL CHANGES IN PLAY

Type of Play	Description
Infant Play (first two years)	Reflects, as well as aids, physical and cognitive development; not dictated by the kind of object played with; in the second year uses toys and objects as they are used in daily life
Pretend Play (from the second year through middle childhood)	Behavior in the second year begins to mimic real-life activities; gradually becomes more social; begins to decline at about six years
Functional Play (peaks from two-to-three-years then shows steady decline through middle childhood)	Consists mainly of simple repetitive movements with or without objects
Constructive Play (common in preschool and kindergarten)	Using objects to create something
Games-with-rules (common in the seven-to-eleven-year age group)	More complex play involving the recognition, acceptance, and conformity to rules

Source: Based on data from Rubin, Fein, & Bandenberg, 1983

Guided Review

16. Any analysis of play must take into consideration that children play because they _____ it for its own sake.
17. Play is associated with four aspects of development: _____, _____, _____, and _____.
18. Early childhood youngsters seem to be especially involved in _____ play.
19. The _____ nature of play suggests play aids development, but also that development permits different aspects of play.
20. The play material we furnish children are laden with _____ _____.

CONCLUSION

At the beginning of the early childhood years, most children meet other youngsters. By the end of the period, almost all children enter formal schooling. Their symbolic ability enriches all of their activities, although limitations still exist. Given their boundless energy and enthusiasm, early childhood youngsters require consistent and reasonable discipline. Yet they should be permitted to do as many things for themselves as possible to help them gain mastery over themselves and their surroundings.

By the end of the early childhood period, children have learned much about their world and are prepared to enter the more complex, competitive, yet exciting world of middle childhood.

In summary:

The Family in Development

- The meaning of "family" in our society has changed radically.
- How parents treat their children has a decisive influence on developmental outcomes.
- Baumrind's types of parenting behavior help to clarify the role of parents in children's development.
- Research has demonstrated how divorce can affect children of different ages.
- Divorce plus remarriage produces a series of transitions to which children must adjust.
- Many children attend some form of day care, and the developmental outcomes of these experiences are still in question.

The Self Emerges

- The emergence of the self follows a clearly defined path.
- Self-esteem plays a crucial role in a child's development.
- Youngsters acquire their gender identity during the early childhood years.
- Children initially seem to acquire an understanding of gender before they manifest sex-typed behavior.

The Importance of Play

- Play affects all aspects of development: physical, cognitive, social, and emotional.
- The nature of a child's play changes over the years, gradually becoming more symbolic.

KEY TERMS

Authoritarian parents
Authoritative parents
Coregulation
Day care
Homelessness
Individuation
Insecure parents

Intimidated parents
Overinterpretive parents
Pathological parents
Permissive parents
Play
Reconciliation fantasies
Secure parents

Self
Sex cleavage
Sibling underworld
Siblings
Socialization
Victimized parents

Answers

16. enjoy 17. physical, cognitive, social, emotional 18. pretend 19. interactive 20. multiple messages

WHAT DO YOU THINK?

1. With today's accepted changes in the gender roles of males and females, do you think that a boy or girl growing up in these times could become confused about gender identity? Does your answer also apply to gender roles? Why?

2. Think back on your days as a child. Can you put your parents' behavior in any of Baumrind's categories? Do you think it affected your behavior? Explain your answer by linking your parents' behavior to some of your personal characteristics.

3. In this chapter you read about the "sleeper" effect of divorce (effects show up quite a bit later). Do you agree with these findings? Can you explain them by the child's age at the time of the divorce? (Consider all aspects of a child's development at that age.)

4. You probably have read about child abuse in some day-care centers. Do you think there should be stricter supervision? Why? By whom?

CHAPTER REVIEW TEST

1. The National Commission on Children has identified several characteristics of a strong family. Which of the following is *not* included?
   a. Open and frequent communication among members
   b. Respect for individual members
   c. An ability to cope with stressful events
   d. Extended generational membership

2. A child who is aggressive and demonstrates a lack of responsibility is associated with _____ parenting behavior.
   a. authoritative
   b. indifferent
   c. authoritarian
   d. doting

3. Conditions associated with homelessness can produce hardships on children. Which of the following conditions is not necessarily associated with homelessness.
   a. Health problems
   b. Hunger and poor nutrition
   c. Lower intelligence
   d. Developmental delays

4. About _____ percent of single parents are divorced.
   a. sixty-five
   b. eighty
   c. fifty
   d. twenty-five

5. Almost _____ percent of today's marriages will end in divorce.

   a. 25
   b. 50
   c. 10
   d. 75

6. Which one of the following is *not* a commonly reported reaction of early childhood youngsters to divorce?
   a. Lowered cognitive competence
   b. Shock
   c. Depression
   d. Loyalty conflict

7. Wallerstein discovered that even after 10 years following a divorce, children wished their parents would get together again. This phenomenon is called
   a. reconciliation fantasy.
   b. divorce-related depression.
   c. cognitive incompetence.
   d. separation anxiety.

8. Almost _____ of women with children under age 14 are in the labor force.
   a. ½
   b. ¾
   c. ⅔
   d. ⅓

9. Most children in day care are being cared for
   a. by a father at home.
   b. by a grandparent in another home.
   c. by a nonrelative in another home.
   d. in a nursery/preschool.

10. A long-term developmental consequence of day care is
    a. insecurity.

    b. adaptability.
    c. self-sufficiency.
    d. No definite conclusion is possible.

11. There are about _____ places providing day care services.
    a. 20,000–25,000
    b. 25,000–30,000
    c. 30,000–35,000
    d. 35,000–40,000

12. Probably the best type of day care is found in the _____ center, which may not provide an accurate picture of all centers.
    a. research
    b. company
    c. commercial
    d. family run

13. _____ is how children feel about themselves and how they value themselves.
    a. Self-identity
    b. Self-esteem
    c. Sense of belonging
    d. Sense of competence

14. The beliefs that we have about the characteristics and behavior we associate with male and female is called
    a. accommodation.
    b. gender practices.
    c. gender stereotypes.
    d. gender equality.

15. In cognitive development theory, children first acquire their
    a. gender identity.
    b. appropriate gender behavior.
    c. psychic stability.
    d. conditioned behavior.

16. Social learning theory depends on the concept of _____ to explain the acquisition of appropriate gender behavior.
    a. schema
    b. assimilation
    c. reinforcement
    d. adaptation

17. When children of the same sex tend to play together, it is referred to as
    a. sex differentiation.
    b. sex cleavage.
    c. sex bias.
    d. sex dichotomy.

18. Pretend play becomes more _____ with age.
    a. physical
    b. cognitive
    c. emotional
    d. social

19. Play materials are grouped into _____ categories.
    a. four
    b. six
    c. eight
    d. ten

20. The most typical type of play during the early childhood years is
    a. social.
    b. physical.
    c. adult sponsored.
    d. pretend.

1. d 2. b 3. c 4. a 5. b 6. a 7. a 8. c 9. c 10. d 11. d 12. a 13. b 14. c 15. a 16. c 17. b 18. b 19. a 20. d

PART V

Middle Childhood

*Always do right.
This will gratify
some people, and
astonish the rest.*

Mark Twain

CHAPTER 9

Physical and Cognitive Development in Middle Childhood

Cognitive theory has made us aware that children's language reveals much about their level of mental functioning.

I t was the week after school opened and 5-year-old Kenny Wilson and his 11-year-old sister Alice had just transferred to the Brackett School District. Mrs. Allan, the principal, took both pupils to their new classrooms and introduced them to their teachers.

"Good morning, Kenny. I'm delighted that you're going to be in this classroom," said Mrs. Groves, the first-grade teacher. "Some of the boys and girls in this room live near you. By the way, do you like your new house?"

Kenny, at first nervous, began to respond to Mrs. Groves' warm manner. "Oh, yes. I have my own bedroom. It has big windows."

Mrs. Groves laughed. "Can you see the moon from your window?" she asked.

"You bet. It follows me around the room," said Kenny.

At the same time, Alice was talking with Mr. Gallo, the sixth-grade teacher. "Welcome to the Brackett sixth grade, Alice. I think you'll enjoy being here," said Mr. Gallo. "Can you give me an idea of the kind of work you were doing?"

"Well, the social studies teacher was helping us with research skills," said Alice. "We were doing a project on Egypt and we had to pick one specific topic like housing. Then we outlined it and made a report to the class."

"That sounds as if you were doing good work, Alice. You'll like it here; we're doing a lot of the same things."

Both teachers were listening to and observing their pupils as they spoke, searching for clues that would help them work with these new pupils in their classrooms. And the clues were there, as you can tell from both conversations. Although each pupil spoke well, there are significant differences in both the thinking and speech of the two students. For example, Kenny's statement that the moon follows him around furnishes clues to his level of cognitive development, which we described in chapter 7 when we discussed cognitive development during the early childhood years.

Alice's skillful explanation of her use of research methods also revealed a level of cognitive development that one would expect of a typical sixth grader. Understanding the developmental achievements of children Alice's age—in middle childhood—will be our task in the next two chapters. ☮

In following the developmental path of children during these years, we find significant signposts in fiction. Can anyone describe the cognitive ability of a middle childhood youngster better than Mark Twain? Do you recall the memorable scene where Tom Sawyer was desperately trying to avoid whitewashing Aunt Polly's fence? One of his friends, Ben Rogers, passed by, imitating the "Big Missouri" riverboat. When Ben sympathized with him, Tom looked at him and said, "What do you call work?"

His friend asked, "Why ain't that work?" Tom neatly dodged the question and asked, "Does a boy get a chance to whitewash a fence every day?" By that time Ben was jumping up and down in his eagerness to paint. When that happened,

> **Tom gave up the brush with reluctance in face but alacrity in his heart. And while that late steamer Big Missouri worked and sweated in the sun, the retired artist sat on a barrel in the shade close by, dangled his legs, munched his apple, and planned the slaughter of more innocents. (Twain, 1980)**

What else can we do but acknowledge a sophisticated and subtle mind at work?

Do you remember Huck Finn meeting the Duke and the Dauphin? Not believing their stories about lost titles, Huck makes a decision:

> **It didn't take me long to make up my mind that these liars warn't no kings nor dukes at all, but just lowdown humbugs and frauds. But I never said nothing, never let on; kept it to myself; it's the best way; then you don't have no quarrels and don't get into no trouble. (Twain, 1979)**

As we'll see a little later, such thinking reflects a certain level of moral reasoning. Children of these years use their previous experiences with rewards and punishments and their growing cognitive ability to reach moral decisions.

This chapter, which analyzes the physical, cognitive, and moral milestones of middle childhood, will often take on the appearance of a mystery. Much is happening to 6- to 12-year-old youngsters that eludes initial detection. Cognitive complexities and subtle moral reasoning characterize these years between childhood and adolescence.

To help you discover clues to important developmental achievements, in this chapter we begin by tracing physical and motor development during the middle childhood years. We'll then turn again to Piaget and analyze his concrete operational period, that time of cognitive development when youngsters begin to engage in truly abstract thinking. Here we'll pause and examine the world of intelligence, which has caused so much controversy. But today's children are expected to do much more with their intelligence than just sit and listen and memorize: They're expected to develop thinking skills and to solve problems. We'll explore both of these worlds (cognitive and problem solving) and then trace the moral and language development of middle childhood youngsters.

As observers of this phase of lifespan development, we can't allow ourselves to be deceived by an apparent lull in development. Too much is going on. Deep-seated developmental currents are changing the very process by which children reason and make their moral decisions.

Think about what you read in this chapter; probe into what lies behind a child's behavior. It will help you to understand the developmental achievements that prepare a youngster to move from these last years of childhood to the different demands of adolescence.

When you finish reading this chapter, you should be able to

- Describe the physical development and growing motor skills of middle childhood youngsters.

- Indicate the cognitive accomplishments of the concrete operational period.

- Evaluate the importance of thinking skills in a child's life.

- Discriminate the skills involved in problem solving.

- Contrast theories of moral development.

- Assess language achievement in the middle childhood years.

- Identify the strategies children use as they begin to read.

Physical Development

In contrast to the rapid increase in height and weight during the first years of life, physical development proceeds at a slowed pace during middle childhood. Most children gain about 2 inches in height per year. The same pattern applies to weight gains. By 6 years of age, most children are about seven times their birth weight.

Nutrition

The physical picture of the middle childhood youngster is one of energy and growing motor skills. Parents often worry that their child isn't eating enough, but given the slower growth rate of the these years, less food is needed. Rather it's the quality of the food that's important; junk foods and excessive fats and sugars are to be avoided. Some parents in developed countries have children who are on vegetarian diets. In some cases, the children themselves dislike meat or avoid it because of their love of animals.

Vegetarian diets are in many ways desirable, but care must be taken that nutrients such as iron and zinc are obtained. Also, some fat is necessary because when the fat content of a diet falls below 20 percent, growth can be stunted. At the other extreme, obesity has many adverse consequences. These include an increasing susceptibility to physical problems, and a diminished sense of self that can cause psychological difficulties (Lutz & Przyltulski, 1997).

Obesity

With a slower growth rate children need fewer calories (Moore, 1997). Although their need for protein, vitamins, and minerals remain high, some children begin to accumulate empty calories from high-sugar and high-fat foods. Thus obesity, with its social, psychological, and medical consequences, looms on the horizon. (The best way to think of obesity is an excessive amount of fat on the body.) Recent research indicated that children who are overweight between the ages of 10 and 17 years will probably have a lifetime problem regardless of whether their parents were thin or fat (Whitaker & others, 1997). Even with slim parents, children who are overweight during the preteen and teen years have a 64 percent chance of becoming obese adults.

To help their children avoid obesity, parents should follow several safeguards (Lutz & Przyltulski, 1997).

- Carefully monitor their children's time spent watching television; the sarcastic label "couch potato" is, unfortunately, all too true given the tendency to munch while watching.

- Encourage appropriate physical activity as much as possible, *on a year-round basis.*

- Serve as much fruit and vegetables as possible.

- Watch fat intake because it is the most concentrated source of calories.

- Start as early as possible to make children aware of what they're eating.

- If a child is overweight, don't become obsessed with it; remember that obesity may well be a genetic problem.

Middle childhood youngsters show steady growth, usually good health, and an increasing sense of competence. Physical growth is relatively slow until the end of the period, when girls' development may spurt. Actually, American girls are reaching puberty earlier than previously realized according to recent research (Herman-Giddens & others, 1997). Nearly one-half of African-American girls and 15 percent of white girls begin to develop sexually by 8 years of age. In other words, girls in the second and third grades are facing issues of puberty (breast development, growth of pubic hair)

Variables such as genetic influence, health, and nutrition may also cause wide fluctuations in the growth of these children. Two youngsters may show considerable physical variation and yet both be perfectly normal. As Garcia Coll (1990) has reminded us, although most children achieve the major developmental milestones, the rate and content of development may well differ between cultures, subcultures, and ethnic groups.

Physical Changes in Middle Childhood

Changes in height and weight are not the only noticeable physical differences. Body proportion changes also. Head size comes more in line with body size. An adult's head size is estimated to be about one-seventh of total body size; the preschooler's is about one-fourth. This difference gradually decreases during the middle childhood years. Also, the loss of baby teeth and the emergence of permanent teeth change the shape of the lower jaw. By the end of the period, the middle childhood youngster's body is more in proportion and more like an adult's (Tanner, 1989).

Changes in arms, legs, and trunk size also occur. The trunk becomes thinner and longer, and the chest becomes broader and flatter. Arms and legs begin to stretch but as yet show little sign of muscle development. Hands and feet grow more slowly than arms and legs, which helps to explain some of the awkwardness that we see during these years. Children are tremendously active physically and gradually display a steady improvement in motor coordination (Tanner, 1989).

Healthy, active children of this age—both boys and girls—also demonstrate considerable motor skill. Lansdown and Walker (1991) summarized motor development during these years:

- Skill increases with maturity until, by the end of the period, some youngsters are highly skilled and much in demand for various sports.

- Boys are stronger than girls.

The middle childhood years are a time when children demonstrate considerable competence. Their continuing mastery of their bodies and their environment lead to emerging skills that are readily observable.

TABLE 9.1 PHYSICAL AND MOTOR DEVELOPMENT IN MIDDLE CHILDHOOD

Age (years)	Height (in.)		Weight (lb.)		Motor Development
	Girl	Boy	Girl	Boy	
7	48	49	52	53	Child has good balance; can hop and jump accurately
8	51	51	60	62	Boys and girls show equal grip strength; great interest in physical games
9	52	53	70	70	Psychomotor skills such as throwing, jumping, running show marked improvement
10	54	55	74	79	Boys become accurate in throwing and catching a small ball; running continues to improve
11	57	57	85	85	Boys can throw a ball about 95 feet; girls can run about 17.5 feet per second
12	60	59	95	95	Boys can run about 18.5 feet per second; dodge ball popular with girls

- Girls may be more graceful and accurate.
- Sex differences—especially strength—become more obvious toward the end of the period.
- Balance matures by the end of the period.
- Fine motor skills (writing and drawing) improve noticeably.

Table 9.1 summarizes the major physical/motor changes in middle childhood.

Guided Review

1. Girls as young as 8 years old today are faced with the issues of _____.
2. Motor development during these years shows an increasing degree of _____.
3. Changes in height, weight, and _____ _____ are major physical changes in middle childhood.

Cognitive Development

During the middle childhood years, children's cognitive abilities become remarkably complicated and sophisticated, reflecting in more observable form the complex mixture of heredity and environment. For example, in a series of studies, Rose and associates (1991) found that measures of object permanence made at 1 year of age were significantly related to cognitive performance at 5 years of age, suggesting that some of the roots of later cognition can be found in infancy.

Middle childhood youngsters now enter formal education, and their cognitive abilities should enable them to meet the more demanding tasks set by the school. We shall continue our practice of examining the cognitive abilities of children by beginning with Piaget and his explanation of these years—the **concrete operational period.**

Answers

1. puberty 2. coordination 3. body proportion

Piaget and Concrete Operations

During the period of concrete operations, children gradually employ logical thought processes with concrete materials, that is, with objects, people, or events that they can see and touch. They also concentrate on more than one aspect of a situation, an important accomplishment which is called **decentering.**

Several notable accomplishments mark the period of concrete operations:

- **Conservation** appears. If you think back to Piaget's famous water jar problem (see chapter 7), children in the concrete operational stage now mentally pour the water back. By reversing their thinking in this manner, they *conserve* the basic idea: the amount of water remains the same. Another of Piaget's classic experiments illustrates the process. To replicate this experiment, you'll need a 5-year-old child (in Piaget's preoperational stage), a 7-year-old child (in Piaget's concrete operational stage), six black tokens, and six orange tokens. Make a row of the black tokens. If you give the 5-year-old child the orange tokens with instructions to match them with the black tokens, the child can easily do it. When the tokens are in a one-to-one position, a 5-year-old can tell us that both rows have the same number.

But if we spread the six black tokens to make a longer row, the 5-year-old will tell us that the longer row has more tokens!

Even when Piaget put the tokens on tracks and let the child move and match them, the child still believed the longer row had more tokens.

Present the 7-year-old with the same problem. The child will think it is a trick—both rows obviously still have the same number.

- **Seriation** means that concrete operational children can arrange objects by increasing or decreasing size.

- **Classification** enables children to group objects with some similarities within a larger category. Brown wooden beads and white wooden beads are all beads.

Features of Concrete Operational Thinking

Children at the level of concrete operations can solve the water-level problem, but the problem or the situation must involve concrete objects, hence the name of the period. In the water-level problem, for example, children no longer concentrate solely on the height of the water in the glass; they also consider the width of the glass. But as Piaget noted, concrete operational children nevertheless demonstrate a true logic, since they now can reverse operations. Concrete operational children gradually master conservation—that is, they understand that something may remain the same even if surface features change.

Figure 9.1 illustrates the different types of conservation that appear at different ages. For example, if preoperational children are given sticks of different lengths, they cannot arrange them from smallest to largest. Or if presented with three sticks, A, B, and C, they can tell you that A is longer than B and C, and that B is longer than C. But if we now remove A, they can tell you that B is longer than C, but not

Middle childhood youngsters are at Piaget's stage of concrete operations. Now they demonstrate increasing mental competence, such as classifying.

Figure 9.1

Different kinds of conservation
appear at different ages.

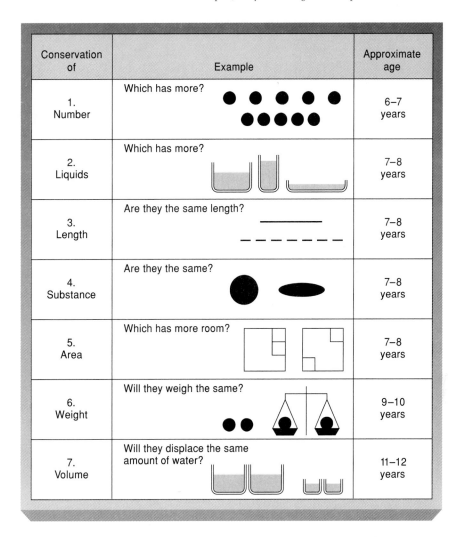

Conservation of	Example	Approximate age
1. Number	Which has more?	6–7 years
2. Liquids	Which has more?	7–8 years
3. Length	Are they the same length?	7–8 years
4. Substance	Are they the same?	7–8 years
5. Area	Which has more room?	7–8 years
6. Weight	Will they weigh the same?	9–10 years
7. Volume	Will they displace the same amount of water?	11–12 years

that A is longer than C. They must see A and C together. The child at the level of concrete operations has no difficulty with this problem.

But limitations remain. Piaget (1973) gave the example of three young girls with different colored hair. The question was: Who has the darkest hair of the three? Edith's hair is lighter than Suzanne's but darker than Lili's. Who has the darkest hair? Piaget believed that propositional reasoning is required to realize that it is Suzanne and not Lili. Youngsters do not achieve such reasoning until about 12 years of age.

Concrete operational children can also classify; that is, they can group different things that have something in common. For example, wooden objects may include both a table and a chair. In a classic experiment illustrating mastery of classification, Piaget showed a girl about 20 brown wooden beads and two or three white wooden beads. He then asked her to separate the brown from the white beads. Children at both the preoperational and concrete levels can do this. But then he asked her, "Are there more brown beads or wooden beads?" The preoperational child answered brown, whereas an older child answered correctly.

Another interesting feature of this period is the child's acquisition of the number concept, or **numeration.** This is not the same as the ability to count. If five red tokens are more spread out than five blue ones, preoperational children, although able to count, still think there are more red than blue tokens. Piaget then constructed an ingenious device that enabled a child to trace the blue to the red. The preoperational child can actually move the blue token to the corresponding red, but still thinks there are more red tokens! During the concrete operational period children understand oneness—that one boy, one girl, one apple, and one orange are all one of something (see figure 9.2).

Figure 9.2

Encouraging acquisition of number concept.

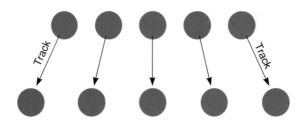

How do children's thought processes change so strikingly? Their growing physical abilities enable them to interact with increasingly complex objects, which, in turn, expands their mental lives. The game of *Battleship* is a good example. They must decide where to place their ships, determine which numbers and letters to use for their targets, and think about the sequence of moves. All of these activities contribute to sharpening such cognitive skills as reversing their thinking, classifying objects, and sequencing their moves, among others.

Piaget's Legacy

As we end our work on Piaget's analysis of cognitive development, what conclusions are possible? Two major contributions of Piaget come immediately to mind: Thanks to Piaget we have a deeper understanding of children's cognitive development. He also has made us more alert to the need for greater comprehension of how children think (the processes that they use) and not just what they think (the products of their thinking).

As we have seen, serious questions have emerged about Piaget's beliefs. By changing the nature of the task (e.g., reducing the number of objects children must manipulate), by allowing children to practice (e.g., teaching children conservation tasks), and by using materials familiar to children, researchers have found that children accomplish specific tasks at earlier ages than Piaget believed (Gelman & Baillargeon, 1983; Halford, 1989).

Although Piaget has left an enduring legacy, his ideas aren't the only explanation of cognitive development. Other psychologists, not entirely happy with Piaget's views, have devised new ways of explaining children's cognitive abilities.

New Ways of Looking at Intelligence

As we have seen, cognitive development is signaled by the acquisition of increasingly rich conceptual categories for thinking about and describing one's own thinking, that is, the metacognitive ability we mentioned in chapter 7 (Perkins & others, 1993). In our discussion of cognitive development from infancy through the middle childhood years, we have identified limitations in Piaget's theory. Addressing these shortcomings, several recent theories have been proposed to explain intelligence and cognitive development. Two of these seem particularly significant.

Sternberg's Triarchic Model of Intelligence

Robert Sternberg (1988, 1990, 1995, 1996) has designed a **triarchic model of intelligence,** containing three major categories.

1. *The components of intelligence.* Sternberg has identified three types of information-processing components: **metacomponents,** which help us to plan, monitor, and evaluate our problem-solving strategies; **performance components,** which help us to execute the instructions of the metacomponents; and **knowledge-acquisition components,** which help us to learn how to solve problems in the first place (Sternberg, 1988). These three components are highly interactive and generally act together.

   For example, consider writing a term paper. The metacomponents help you to decide on the topic, plan the paper, monitor the actual writing, and

Footprints in the History of Intelligence

The story of Alfred Binet and his search for the meaning and measurement of intelligence is one of the most famous in the history of psychology. In 1904, Binet was asked by the Parisian Minister of Public Instruction to formulate some means of identifying children most likely to fail in school. The problem was very difficult, because it meant finding some means of separating the normal from the truly retarded, of determining the lazy but bright who were simply poor achievers, and of eliminating the halo effect (assigning an unwarranted high rating to youngsters because they are neat and attractive).

Accepting this task meant that Binet had to begin with his own idea of intelligence, since it's impossible to fashion the means to measure something unless you know what that something is. Binet's view of intelligence contained three elements.

1. There is *direction* in our mental processes; they're directed toward the achievement of a particular goal and the discovery of adequate means of attaining the goal. In the preparation of a term paper, for example, you select a suitable topic and also the books and journals necessary to complete it.

2. We possess the ability to *adapt* by the use of tentative solutions; that is, we select and utilize some stimuli and test their relevance as we proceed toward our goal. Before writing the term paper, for example, you may make a field trip to the area you're researching, or to save time, you may decide to use relevant sources on the Internet or library resources.

3. We also possess the ability *to make judgments* and to criticize solutions. Frequently called *autocriticism,* this implies an objective evaluation of solutions. You may, for example, complete a paper, reread it, decide that one topic included is irrelevant, and eliminate it. This is autocriticism at work.

The items in Binet's early test reflected these beliefs. When an item seemed to differentiate between normal and subnormal, he retained it; if no discrimination appeared, he rejected it. Binet defined normality as the ability to do the things that others of the same age usually do. The fruits of his and his coworkers' endeavors was the publication in 1905 of the *Metrical Scale of Intelligence.*

Since their publication, Binet's mental age scales have pointed the way for intelligence testing. The success of the Binet scale led a leading American psychologist, Lewis Terman, to adapt it for American usage. Terman's revision, called the Stanford-Binet, first appeared in 1916 and was revised in 1937 and 1960. The fourth edition appeared in 1985 (Thorndike, Hagan, & Satler).

Another effort to measure intelligence appeared in the work of David Wechsler, who devised a series of tests intended to measure intelligence through the lifespan. Like Binet, Wechsler believed in a global theory of intelligence; that is, intelligent people, as measured on these tests, will be superior at anything they attempt. There are three forms of his test:

- *The Wechsler Adult Intelligence Scale—Revised (WAIS–111)* contains both verbal and performance items.

- *The Wechsler Intelligence Scale for Children–111 (WISC–111)* is designed for children 5 to 15 years old.

- *The Wechsler Preschool and Primary Scale of Intelligence—Revised (WPPSI–R)* is designed for children 4 to 6½ years old.

Considerable controversy has developed around these tests, mainly because those who have used them deviated from Binet's goal: to provide a means of identifying those students who needed help and *not* to classify people into rigid categories. Today we know that intelligence test scores change over the course of the lifespan for a variety of reasons. We also realize that these tests, which are highly verbal, are unfair to children from backgrounds different from middle-class white Americans. (For an extended discussion of these issues, see Travers & others, 1993.)

---

evaluate the final product. The performance components help you in the actual writing of the paper. You use the knowledge-acquisition components to do your research. Figure 9.3 illustrates how the components work together.

2. *Experience and intelligence.* Sternberg's second aspect of intelligence includes our experiences, which improve our ability to deal with novel tasks and to use pertinent information to solve problems.

3. *The context of intelligence.* The third aspect of intelligence in Sternberg's model refers to our ability to adapt to our culture. The major thrust of contextual intelligence is adaptation. Adaptation, for Sternberg (1996), has three meanings:

Figure 9.3

The relationship among the components of intelligence.

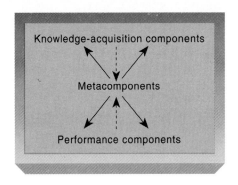

Knowledge-acquisition components

Metacomponents

Performance components

- *Adapting to existing environments,* so that you adjust to current circumstances
- *Shaping existing environments,* which implies changing the present environment to meet your needs
- *Selecting new environments*

Although Sternberg did not apply his theory directly to children, you can see how his work relates to the developing cognitive competence of the middle childhood youngster. To take one example, with their growing symbolic activity, children think about their thinking; that is, they are employing metacomponents. Sternberg (1988, 1995, 1996) has also compiled a list of reasons why we too often fail, which has important implications for children of this age.

Noting that all of us, children and adults, let self-imposed obstacles frustrate us, Sternberg stated that what is important is not the level of our intelligence but what we achieve with it. Sternberg has identified the most common obstacles:

- *Lack of motivation.* If children aren't motivated, it really doesn't matter how much talent they have. In a typical classroom situation, for example, the range of intelligence may be fairly narrow and differences in motivation spell success or failure.

- *Using the wrong abilities.* Although children acquire greater cognitive ability, they frequently don't use it or else fail to recognize exactly what is needed. For example, faced with a math test, they may fail to review solutions to word problems (knowledge-acquisition components) and instead depend on their previous experiences.

- *Inability to complete tasks.* Regardless of how skilled children may be in their use of Sternberg's components, if they are unable to sustain their efforts—for whatever reason—they are in danger of failure. The worry here is that this tendency may become a way of life, ensuring difficulty, frustration, and failure.

- *Fear of failure.* Some youngsters may develop a fear of failure early in life. This can prevent them from ever fulfilling their intellectual potential.

Gardner and Multiple Intelligences

Howard Gardner (1983, 1991, 1993, 1997) has forged a tight link between thinking and intelligence with his theory of **multiple intelligences.** An especially intriguing aspect of the insights it provides into those individuals who are capable of penetrating mathematical vision but who are baffled by the most obvious musical symbols. Gardner attempted to explain this apparent inconsistency by identifying eight equal intelligences.

1. *Linguistic intelligence.* The first of Gardner's intelligences is language—linguistic intelligence. For example, tracing the effects of damage to the language area of the brain, researchers have identified the core operations of any language (phonology, syntax, semantics, and pragmatics); and

Young, J. (1988). *Steve Jobs: The journey is the reward.* New York: Lynx. A penetrating account of the restless, inquiring mind of the middle childhood years that eventually led to the founding of Apple Computer.

language development in humans has been well documented and supported by empirical investigations. Gardner considered language a preeminent example of human intelligence.

As we shall soon see, during these years children change their use of language to a more flexible, figurative form. Gardner commented on this by noting that middle childhood youngsters love to expand on their accomplishments. They use appealing figures of speech: "I think I'll get lost," meaning that they're about ready to leave.

2. *Musical intelligence.* One has only to consider the talent and career of Yehudi Menuhin to realize that musical ability is special. At 3 years of age, Menuhin became fascinated by music, and by 10 he was performing on the international stage. The early appearance of musical ability suggests some kind of biological preparedness—a musical intelligence. The right hemisphere of the brain seems particularly important for music, and musical notation clearly indicates a basic symbol system. Although not considered intelligence in most theories, musical skill satisfies Gardner's criteria and so demands inclusion.

In regard to the middle childhood years, Gardner noted that most children (except for those who are musically talented) cease musical development after school begins. For the talented, up to the age of 8 or 9, talent alone suffices for continued progress. Around 9 years of age, serious skill building commences, with sustained practice until adolescence, when these children must decide how much of their lives they want to commit to music. In general, society accepts musical illiteracy.

3. *Logical-mathematical intelligence.* Unlike linguistic and musical intelligences, logical-mathematical intelligence, Gardner believed, evolves from our contact with the world of objects. In using objects, taking them apart, and putting them together again, children gain their fundamental knowledge about "how the world works." By this process, logical-mathematical intelligence quickly divorces itself from the world of concrete objects. Children begin to think abstractly.

Gardner then used Piaget's ideas to trace the evolution of thinking. The

Relationships with peers, abstract activities, and developing physical skills all occupy middle-childhood youngsters. The success that children achieve in these activities contributes significantly to an emerging sense of competence.

development of logical-mathematical thinking, as explored by Piaget, is used as an example of scientific thinking. You may want to review Piaget's ideas concerning the unfolding of intelligence to better understand Gardner's views.

4. *Spatial intelligence.* Brain research has clearly linked spatial ability to the right side of the brain. Here Gardner relied heavily on Piaget, noting that an important change in children's thinking occurs during these years, especially with the appearance of conservation and reversibility. Middle childhood youngsters can now visualize how objects seem to someone else. During these years, children can manipulate objects using their spatial intelligence, but this ability is still restricted to concrete situations and events. (For further discussion of spatial development in children, see Tada & Stiles, 1996.)

5. *Bodily-kinesthetic intelligence.* Gardner stated that our control of bodily motions and the ability to handle objects skillfully are defining features of an "intelligence"—bodily-kinesthetic intelligence. You may be puzzled by this statement, given that we normally divide the mind and reasoning from our physical nature. This divorce between mind and body is often accompanied by the belief that our bodily activities are somehow less special. But Gardner urged us to think of mental ability as a means of carrying out bodily actions. Thus thinking becomes a way of refining motor behavior, which raises the age-old question: Does increasing mental ability affect the performance of a bodily skill?

6 & 7. *Interpersonal and intrapersonal intelligence.* Gardner referred to interpersonal and intrapersonal intelligences as the personal intelligences. Interpersonal intelligence builds on an ability to recognize what is distinctive in others, while intrapersonal intelligence enables us to understand our own feelings. Autism is a good example of a deficit in this intelligence. Often competent in a certain skill, autistic children may be utterly incapable of ever referring to themselves.

8. Gardner recently identified the eighth of his intelligences as *naturalist intelligence,* by which he meant the human ability to discriminate among living things as well as a sensitivity to our natural world. He defined naturalist intelligence as:

the ability to recognize and classify plants, minerals, and animals, including rocks and grass and all variety of flora and fauna. The ability to

TABLE 9.2 GARDNER'S MULTIPLE INTELLIGENCES	
Type of Intelligence	**Meaning**
Linguistic	Communication, a preeminent example of human intelligence
Musical	Linked to brain location and a basic symbol system
Logical-mathematical	What we usually mean by "intelligence"
Spatial	Linked to brain location and symbol systems
Bodily-kinesthetic	Smooth development of bodily movements and adaptation
Interpersonal and intrapersonal	Linked to frontal lobe of brain; recognize what is distinctive in others
Naturalist	Ability to discriminate among living things.

recognize cultural artifacts like cars or sneakers may also depend on the naturalist intelligence (Gardner in Checkley, 1997, p. 9).

The middle childhood years are a time of greater social sensitivity, better social understanding, a keener awareness of others' motivations, and a sense of one's own competencies. For example, during the early phases of middle childhood, children seem to consolidate their understanding of *false beliefs*, which had commenced at about 4 years of age (Jenkins & Astington, 1996). False beliefs refers to children's ability to understand the reasoning of other people.

In a typical false belief task, children are shown a popular candy container that contains a pencil rather than candy. The child is then asked what another person would think was inside the container. Children younger than 4 years insist that others would think that pencils are inside (Ruffman & Keenan, 1996). Young children's ability to predict and explain the actions of others based on mistaken or false beliefs is the cornerstone of understanding other people and their behavior (Slomkowski & Dunn, 1996).

During these years, children begin to develop friendships and devote considerable time and energy to securing a definite place in a circle of friends. This effort can only increase their sensitivity to interpersonal relations. Greenspan and Benderly (1997) have commented on this emotional side of cognitive development by calling attention to research showing that the prefrontal area of the brain support-

Immigrant Children and Tests

Children's ability to take tests often powerfully influences the results of the test, especially intelligence tests. Tests can scare students or cause them anxiety. Test anxiety may come from parental pressure, their own concerns, or the testing atmosphere. At any rate, merely taking a test may affect a child's performance, which often is especially true for pupils with different cultural experiences. Language, reading, expectations, and behavior all may be different and influence their test performance (Stigler & others, 1990).

These children want to succeed, as reflected in interviews with many of them: Almost 50 percent were doing one to two hours of homework every night. (Twenty-five percent of the Southeastern Asian students reported more than three hours each night.) We have spoken throughout our work of the need for sensitive responsiveness. Here is an instance in which being sensitive to the needs of multicultural children will only aid their adjustment and achievement in school.

In an effort to ensure equity in testing, a new national system of authentic assessment has been proposed (Madaus, 1994). These tests supposedly engage students in real world tasks rather than multiple-choice tests (Darling-Hammond, 1994). For example, President Clinton's Goals 2000 rests on the assumption that the federal government can help state and local communities in their striving for educational reform by specifying goals, providing financial support to attain these goals, and establishing a voluntary assessment mechanism for account-

ability (Pullin, 1994). The intent is to ensure that all students will be competent in the core academic subjects, which will occur only if each disadvantaged group has an effective and complete opportunity to learn.

The goals are clear; the task itself is difficult. Since social and cultural groups differ in the extent to which they share the values that underlie testing and the values that testing promotes, any national testing system raises questions of equity (Madaus, 1994). The values of the test makers and the test takers aren't necessarily identical. For example, different cultural groups may have different intellectual traditions that tests, of whatever design, may not measure. As Madaus (1994) pointed out, who gains and who loses once again raises the issue of equity.

When children feel comfortable, they do better; this is particularly true for test taking. Multicultural children need information about why the test is being given, when it is being given, what material will be tested, and what kinds of items will be used. These are just a few topics to consider. In addition, language should not be a barrier to performance. For example, children need to understand the terms in the directions of the test—what analyze means; what compare means; what discuss means.

Helping multicultural students in this way means extra time and effort for teachers. But it is teaching, just as teaching English or history is teaching. As more and more multicultural students become users of classroom tests, they shouldn't do poorly because they don't understand the mechanics of the test.

Gardner, H. (1983). *Frames of mind.* New York: Basic Books. Gardner's book, which is available in paperback, is an excellent example of the new perspective on studying intelligence. Recognizing that we all seem to demonstrate different abilities, Gardner makes an appealing case for the existence of several intelligences.

ing emotional regulation, interactions, and sequencing shows increased activity during the second half of the first year. This is the same time that infants demonstrate the reciprocal interactions of attachment as well as the cognitive activities of making choices and searching for hidden objects. At the same time, they become more aware of themselves, furthering the development of their intrapersonal intelligences. If children of this age do not succeed in establishing harmonious relationships, they may develop feelings of inadequacy and isolation. This fuels a fear of failure that can produce diminished expectations.

Guided Review

4. Middle childhood corresponds with Piaget's _____ _____ period.
5. Concrete operations is characterized by the following cognitive accomplishments: _____, _____, and _____.
6. Sternberg's triarchic model of intelligence includes _____, _____, and _____ _____ components.
7. _____ is associated with the theory of multiple intelligences.
8. Gardner would describe an ability to recognize what is distinctive in others as an example of an _____ intelligence.

Thinking and Problem Solving

Advanced societies demand citizens who can do more with their intelligence than just survive. Rapid change requires the ability to cope. Yet 25 percent of the 14- to 18-year-old group are no longer in school. How many of these young people are adapting? Concern about these and similar statistics has prompted renewed interest in two topics that have been with us for years: critical thinking and problem solving.

Information Processing

As our society moves from an industrial base to one committed to an information technology, the skills that children need to adapt to these new directions likewise change. Unless parents and teachers equip themselves with the ability to teach innovative skills, children will be woefully unprepared to meet new demands (Ceci, 1996). Since a swift proliferation of knowledge characterizes an information technology, mastery of available content will not suffice once children leave home and school and attempt to become productive citizens. Rather, they need skills and strategies that will enable them to adapt to constant change. That is, critical thinkers are self-correcting; they discover their own weaknesses and act to remove obstacles and faults.

Using Intelligence

Once children have accumulated knowledge, they must plan what to do with the material, like a carpenter who has secured a desirable piece of wood and now has to decide how to shape it. Children need to shape their facts so that they squeeze as much value from them as possible. It's not enough just to obtain knowledge; children need to apply what they have learned, to integrate it with other facts, and then to stand back and ask themselves if they could do any better. Think of infor-

Answers

4. concrete operations 5. conservation, seriation, classification 6. metacomponents, performance, knowledge acquisition 7. Gardner 8. interpersonal

An Applied View
How Would You Answer These Questions?

1. Imagine that you were lucky enough to obtain two tickets to the great Broadway musical Phantom of the Opera for $100. As you walk down the street to the theater, you discover that you have lost the tickets. You can't remember the seat numbers. Would you go to the ticket window and buy another pair of tickets for $100?

2. Imagine that you are on the way to the theater to buy tickets for the Broadway play Phantom of the Opera. They will cost you $100. As you approach the ticket window, you discover that you have lost $100. Would you still pay $100 for the tickets?

These questions, originally posed by Tversky and Kahneman (1981) elicit some interesting answers. How did you answer them? Among their subjects, 46 percent answered yes to question 1, while 88 percent answered yes

to question 2. Note that many more people said they would buy new tickets if they had lost the money rather than the tickets. Yet the two situations are almost identical—in each instance you would have lost $100.

How can we explain the difference in the responses? Tversky and Kahneman believed that the way a problem is framed helps to explain our response. As they stated: The frame that a decision-maker adopts is controlled partly by the formulation of the problem and partly by the norms, habits, and personal characteristics of the decision-maker. (1981, p.453)

The point here is that our personal characteristics (such as motivation, persistence, and the like) and how questions and problems are structured influence our decisions. We can help children reach better decisions by teaching them the skills and strategies discussed in this chapter.

---

mation processing as encompassing such topics as attention, perception, thinking, memory, and problem solving. Parents and teachers attempting to help children improve their thinking shouldn't focus merely on questions or on facts. They should try to stretch children's thinking abilities by asking questions that require application, analysis, synthesis, and evaluation. They should also keep in mind the following:

- *Remember that ideas are only as valuable as the meaning they convey.* Be careful not to accept words alone as evidence that children have attained a concept. Continually question them to ensure that they understand and can use the idea(s). For example, you probably can define thinking strategies but can you describe them, explain the various types, and give examples of how you could use them?

- *Provide varied experiences for children.* For example, today's students can't avoid studying about DNA in science classes. Watching one of the many excellent PBS films illustrating the basic concepts about DNA provides vivid and memorable visualization. Ask them to show the location of DNA in a picture of a cell. In other words, offer opportunities for them to work with ideas under different conditions. Where possible they should see and feel and talk about them, using as many senses as possible. They should occasionally encounter examples of what is not DNA because negative examples are effective if mixed with many positive, clear instances.

- *Use different methods when helping children.* Teachers may want to sit with children individually or in small groups for a period and discuss a topic; they may want to ask them questions; they may want to show them a magazine article that relates to what they're studying. They may want to break the pattern completely. For example, if a child is studying the nineteenth century, they could say, "I'm not giving you any homework tonight. Take the night off and go see *Little Women*. We'll discuss it in class."

- *Encourage children to relate what they're studying now to their prior knowledge.* Discover if children know anything that can help them with their present work.

For example, if an assignment required them to discuss the relationship between the Northern states and England at the time of the Civil War, they should attempt to discover a pattern of interactions between the two countries: the Revolutionary War, the War of 1812, England's need for the cotton grown in the Southern states, which help to explain England's close ties to the South.

Encouraging the Use of Thinking Skills

Given the importance of developing and using thinking skills in our society today, parents and teachers should help children to develop the habit of analyzing, that is, to identify the parts in a problem or situation and to see how they relate to the whole. This is common in math and science classes, but children should apply these techniques in all aspects of their lives. Using these ideas as a basis, parents and teachers can take several steps to help children sharpen their thinking skills by using games and exercises.

- *Teach children not to be satisfied with the first thing they do.* For example, in doing a homework assignment, students should learn to evaluate the work according to certain criteria: Did I get all the information I could? Does it "fit" the topic? Is it what I was supposed to do?

- *Ask children to invent something they can use in their homes.* Give them simple examples, such as the need for a back-scratching instrument or a device that will pick up pins and needles from the floor. You can structure it in the form of a "back-to-the-future" game. But make them justify their invention: Is it necessary? What is the problem it will solve? Are materials available to build it? How much will it cost? You are forcing them to examine the basis of their judgments.

- *Teachers could have groups of students research the countries of origin of several of their classmates and create a "cultural corner,"* where one group at a time places their reports, magazines, pictures, literature about the country, and any other materials they may have collected. They could design holiday cards for the special holidays of that country and then specify class time for oral reports.

- *Children should be aware of current environmental concerns by discussing news accounts of dangerous incidents,* such as oil spills, toxic waste, and so on.

As children's decision-making abilities improve with age, they can be further aided by helping them to improve their thinking and problem-solving skills.

Try This Problem

Do you think you're a good problem solver? Before you answer, try to solve the following problem.

Two motorcyclists are 100 miles apart. At exactly the same moment, they begin to drive toward each other for a meeting. Just as they leave, a bird flies past the first cyclist in the direction of the second cyclist. When it reaches the second cyclist, it turns around and flies back to the first. The bird continues flying in this manner until the cyclists meet. The cyclists both traveled at the rate of 50 miles per hour while the bird maintained a constant speed of 75 miles per hour. How many miles will the bird have flown when the cyclists meet?

Many readers, after examining this problem, immediately begin to calculate distance, miles per hour, and constancy of speed. Actually this is not a mathematical problem; it is a word problem. Carefully look at it again. Both riders will travel for one hour before they meet; the bird flies at 75 miles per hour; therefore the bird will have flown 75 miles. No formulas, no calculations, just a close examination of what is given.

Have them write letters to the local papers expressing their concerns. In this way, you are encouraging them to work together to solve problems.

Parents and teachers are the primary motivators of a middle childhood youngster's cognitive potential to think critically. By appealing to a child's enthusiasms and abilities, adults encourage these youngsters to begin using "a thinking disposition."

Problem-Solving Strategies

Middle childhood youngsters then use their newly developed cognitive accomplishments, such as ability in critical thinking, to solve the problems they face in their daily lives. To give you an idea of what we're talking about, see how good you are at solving the problem in the accompanying box.

Obviously some people are better at problem solving than others due to intelligence, experience, or education. But it's possible to improve anyone's ability to solve problems, even children's. Some children and adults don't do well with problems because they're afraid of them. "I'm just not smart enough"; "I never could do these." Here is a good example. Group the following numbers in such a way that when you add them, the total is 1,000.

8 8 8 8 8 8 8 8

Teaching children the basics of problem solving will improve their abilities to recognize and solve problems, both in and out of the classroom.

Unintimidated elementary school children get the answer almost immediately. Some of you won't even bother trying; others will make a halfhearted effort; still others will attack it enthusiastically. What is important is how you think about a problem. This willingness to attack problems is known as *mindfulness,* which is a state of mind resulting from drawing novel distinctions, examining information from new perspectives, and being sensitive to context (Langer, 1993). Step back and decide what you have to do; then decide on the simplest way to get the answer.

In the eights problem, think of the only number of groups that would give you 0 in the units column when you add them—five. Try working with five groups and you will eventually discover that 888 + 88 + 8 + 8 + 8 gives you 1,000.

Many of the daily problems children face are vague and ill defined. If children lack problem-solving strategies, their task is next to impossible. This is one of the major reasons schools are under increasing pressure to teach problem-solving skills, either as a separate course or as a part of another course's content. Adults help children to become better problem solvers by teaching them a problem–solving method such as the DUPE technique.

The DUPE Model

Many models have been proposed to help people solve a wide variety of problems. Often these models employ acronyms to assist people in problem solving (e.g., SAC—Strategic Air Command; NATO—North Atlantic Treaty Organization; HOMES —The names of the Great Lakes: Huron, Ontario, Michigan, Erie, Superior). For our purposes we'll use an acronym that you'll remember easily and transfer to any problems (or teach to a child). The acronym is **DUPE** and its intent is to convey the message: *Don't let yourself be deceived.* The meaning of each letter is as follows:

D—*Determine* just exactly what is the nature of the problem. Too often meaningless elements in the problem deceive us; it is here that attention to detail is so important. How would you go about solving this problem?

There is a super psychic who can predict the score of any game before it is played. Explain how this is possible.

This problem, taken from Bransford and Stein (1993), poses a challenge to most of us because, as the authors noted, a reasonable explanation is difficult to generate. If you are having difficulty, it is probably because you have made a faulty assumption about the nature of the problem. You were not asked about the final score; the score of any game before it is played is 0 to 0. We deliberately presented a tricky problem to stress that you must attend to details.

U—*Understand* the nature of the problem. Realizing that a particular problem exists is not enough; you must also comprehend the essence of the problem if your plan for solution is to be accurate. For example, we frequently hear that a pupil's classroom difficulties are due to hyperactivity. Thus the problem is determined; but understanding the cause of the hyperactivity—physical, social, psychological—requires additional information. Here is an example of the need to understand the nature of a problem.

Tom either walks to work and rides his bicycle home or rides his bicycle to work and walks home. The round trip takes one hour. If he were to ride both ways, it would take 30 minutes. If Tom walked both ways, how long would a round trip take?

This problem illustrates a basic problem-solving strategy of dividing a problem's information into subgoals to help understand what's required. Think for a moment: What are the givens? How long would it take to ride one way? (15 minutes) How long is a round trip? (1 hour) How long does it take to walk one way? (45 minutes) How long is the round trip if Tom walked both ways? (45 + 45 = 90 minutes)

P—*Plan* your solution. Now that you know that a problem exists and you understand its nature, you must select strategies that are appropriate for the problem. It is here that memory plays such an important role. The accompanying box illustrates various memory strategies that aid memory.

E—*Evaluate* your plan, which usually entails two phases. First you should examine the plan itself in an attempt to determine its suitability. Then you must decide how successful your solution was.

All of these techniques, however, are useless unless children are motivated to use them.

Bransford, B. & Stein, B. (1993). *The IDEAL problem solver.* New York: Freeman. An excellent little book that explores the mysteries of problem solving in an engaging and practical way.

Children and Motivation

The renewed interest in critical thinking, problem solving, and motivation seems particularly pertinent to our study of middle childhood youngsters. With their developing cognitive sophistication, they are equal to the challenge posed by new

The Role of Memory

Most children have good memories that can be improved with adult help, which, in turn, helps them in solving problems. All memory strategies, however, are not equally effective. The appropriateness of the strategy depends on what you are asked to do. Try this memory problem.

The following list contains 25 words. Take 90 seconds to study these words. When time runs out, write as many of the words as you can without looking at the list.

paper	fruit	street	wheel
white	step	juice	time
spoke	shoe	car	note
ball	word	judge	run
banana	touch	hammer	table
dark	page	bush	official
walk			

How did you do? Or more importantly from our perspective, how did you do it? Were these among the strategies you used?

1. Rehearse each word until you have memorized it: car, car, car.

2. Rehearse several words: paper, white, spoke; paper, white, spoke.

3. Organize the words by category. Note that several words are related to cars; others could be grouped as fruit; still others could be categorized as relating to books.

4. Construct a story to relate as many of the words as possible.

5. Form images of words or groups of words.

You may have tried one or a combination of these strategies, but note that you were not told to memorize them in any particular manner. If you had received specific instructions, each of these strategies would not have been equally effective. For example, when we are asked to remember a particular telephone number, the tendency is to rehearse it for as long as we need to recall it. If you had been directed to memorize the words in the list in a certain order (e.g., the way that they were presented), grouping them by categories would not have been efficient. Thinking of a story to link them in the correct order would have been much more efficient.

ideas and welcome the opportunity to sharpen their mental skills, *provided they are motivated to do so.*

What Is Motivation?

When people ask about motivation, they want to know what causes a child to act in a particular way. To answer this question, we must first attempt to understand what motivation, a central construct in psychological research for the past 60 years, means (Weiner, 1990). No single best definition of motivation is recognized; thus to help us in our work, we'll think of motivation as consisting of three interrelated components: *goals, beliefs,* and *emotions* (Ford, 1992).

Thus we can say that *motivation arouses, sustains, directs, and integrates behavior.* When you are motivated, or when children are motivated, you usually discover what conditions caused the behavior. Something acted on you to produce a certain kind of behavior, which was maintained at a certain level of intensity, and which was directed at a definite goal. For example, a teenager may have been promised a ticket to a rock concert for passing an algebra course. Here a certain type of behavior was aroused and maintained long enough to achieve a specific goal, which raises the topic of intrinsic and extrinsic motivation.

Intrinsic and Extrinsic Motivation

Psychologists have long argued about the relative merits of intrinsic versus extrinsic motivation: Should children always be intrinsically motivated? Should adults avoid extrinsic motivation when working with children, since it may frustrate the development of intrinsic motivation? Or should we stress the role of the environment and learn as much as possible about the use of rewards to further learning?

Intrinsic motivation means that children themselves want to do something to achieve a specific objective. Obviously this is an ideal state that results in considerable learning. You can help children acquire intrinsic motivation by relating your knowledge of their abilities, needs, and interests to meaningful goals. For example, when a parent, teacher, or counselor recognizes that a child is interested in the medical field, knowing that child's ability enables them to channel that interest in an appropriate direction.

Although this is ideal, intrinsic motivation can be elusive. Consequently, adults use extrinsic motivation such as marks, prizes, and other tangible rewards to motivate children. When adults use these methods, they should always attempt to have children transfer these temporary external devices to intrinsic motives. How? By making sure that children succeed at some level and being there to reinforce their efforts.

Any society can ill afford to ignore the significance of motivated children if it desires harmony in the home, school, and community. Remember: Children are always motivated to do something, and if this energy is not focused on worthwhile goals, delinquency, violence, and maladjustment often, if not always, result.

As middle childhood youngsters think better, reason more maturely, and evaluate their actions, moral development becomes a matter of increasing importance.

Guided Review

9. A willingness to attack problems is called _____.
10. A memory strategy in which you go over material repeatedly is called _____.
11. The goal of the DUPE model is _____ _____ _____ _____ _____.
12. Good problem solvers share distinct characteristics such as a positive _____ and a concern for _____.
13. The letters in DUPE mean _____, _____, _____, and _____.

Moral Development

We want children to be good, truthful, kind, wise, just, courageous, and virtuous. We also want them to behave, *in all circumstances,* according to an internalized code of conduct that reflects these desirable characteristics. This is a formidable goal and you may well ask how do children reach this ideal state? As we attempt to answer this question, we would like you to keep three issues in mind as we study children's moral development.

1. *How do children think about moral development?* Here we'll present the theories and relevant research that shed light on this question. We'll then trace the powerful influence of gender and social class on children's thinking about moral issues.

2. *How do children feel about moral matters?* The role of emotions in morality deserve our attention because of the manner in which emotions interact with how children think and behave in moral situations. To make this more meaningful, think of yourself for a moment. For example, how do you "feel" when you know you hurt someone else by something you said, even if you didn't mean to. The answer is that you feel awful. So do children when they do the same thing.

Answers

9. mindfulness 10. rehearsal 11. don't let yourself be deceived 12. attitude, accuracy 13. determine, understand, plan, evaluate

3. *How do children behave in moral situations?* Do children's thoughts and emotions dictate how they act morally? An intriguing question, one that both fascinates and frustrates us, and one that will challenge our ingenuity to answer.

As we begin our analysis of children's moral progress, remember that moral behavior is a complex mixture of *cognition* (thinking about what to do), emotion (feelings about what to do or what was done), and *behavior* (what is actually done). A summary of children's moral development should help to put the theories and research in a more meaningful perspective.

The Path of Moral Development

Initially, young children (birth to about 2 or 3 years) begin to learn about right and wrong from their parents; these teachings immediately begin to interact with children's natural inclination to do good. So from an early age—as soon as possible— most parents try to combine direction with understanding. Continually forcing children to obey, as we know, loses its effectiveness as they grow older. During these early years, modeling is especially effective. Lacking cognitive sophistication, young children who have a good relationship with their parents usually are enormously impressed by what they see their parents doing.

The next phase (about 2 to 6 years) reflects children's growing cognitive maturity and their developing ability to decide what's right or wrong. They now begin to interact with a variety of authority figures—teachers, counselors, religious, coaches, directors—who make reasonable demands on them. These individuals assume great importance in children's lives and usually reinforce parental concerns about moral behavior. By their directions, explanations, expectations, and by pointing out the consequences of children's behavior for others (a process called *induction*), they provide welcome support to parents' efforts.

Parents and Moral Development

Recent research illustrates how influential parents are in their children's moral development. A team of psychologists at Pennsylvania State University probed the question of why children show marked differences in their sensitivity to moral issues, differences that have been widely documented (Dunn & others, 1995). The researchers concentrated on uncovering the possible reasons for these differences. Studying 6-year-old children, they made two important findings.

1. Children whose mothers treated them reasonably but firmly after transgressions seemed more sensitive to matters of right and wrong. These mothers also insisted that their children consider the harm or discomfort done to the *other* child.

2. Those children with older siblings who were friendly and supportive seemed more morally mature.

These findings testify to the significant input parents have into their children's moral development, which begins with the type of family relations they encourage. If parents urge (perhaps insist is a better word) their children to help and encourage each other, and if they deal with misbehavior with a judicious blend of firmness and understanding, they will have illuminated the moral pathway quite brightly for their children.

Parents who also encourage their children to express their opinions about moral issues and who themselves model a higher level of moral behavior help to advance their children's insights into matters of right and wrong (Walker & Taylor, 1991). In his biography of Erik Erikson (see chapter 1), the child psychiatrist, Robert Coles (1970, p. 176) commented on the process by which children develop a sense of right and wrong with the help of their parents.

We learn to trust because we learn about another person. Each of us learns to know a mother, to recognize her in a particular way—which is encouraged and sanctioned and given ritual form by a society and its traditions. Similarly, we learn about what is right and wrong, what is and is not ours, what we can and what we dare not initiate—all through the experience of approval and disapproval, through the meeting up with the applause or discouragement in more or less ritualized ways.

As children move into the next phase (about 7 to 11+ years), they interact more frequently and intensely with their siblings in their family lives, with their schoolmates in classroom experiences, and with their friends in games and other social activities. Here they again encounter the reality of rules, rules not established by parental edict. As a result they learn about making and following regulations as well as deriving insights into those children who don't. In this way, children are both participants (in games and activities where they must obey the rules) and authority figures (occasionally they will be among those who make the rules).

Let's now turn our attention to how children think about matters of right and wrong.

A cadet does not lie, cheat, or steal, or tolerate those who do. The West Point Honor Code

Piaget's Explanation

Youngsters realize that the opinions and feelings of others matter: What they do might hurt someone else. By the end of the middle childhood period, children clearly include intention in their thinking. For 6-year-olds, stealing is wrong because they might get punished; for the 11- or 12-year-old, stealing may be wrong because it takes away from someone else. During these years, children move from judging acts solely by the amount of punishment to judging acts based on intention and motivation.

Marbles and Morality

As might be expected, Piaget examined the moral development of children and attempted to explain it from his cognitive perspective (Piaget, 1932). Piaget formulated his ideas on moral development from observing children playing a game of marbles. Watching the children, talking to them, and applying his cognitive theory to their actions, he identified how children actually conform to rules.

While observing the children playing marbles Piaget also asked them their ideas about fairness and justice, what is a serious breach of rules, and how punishment should be administered. From this information, he devised a theory of moral development:

- Up to about 4 years, children are not concerned with morality. Rules are meaningless, so they are unaware of any rule violations.

- At about 4 years, they begin to believe that rules are fixed and unchangeable. Rules come from authority (e.g., parents, God) and are to be obeyed without question. This phase of moral development is often called *heteronomous morality* (or *moral realism*). Children of this age make judgments about right or wrong based on the consequences of behavior; for example, it is more serious to break five dishes than one. They also believe in *immanent justice;* that is, anyone who breaks a rule will be punished immediately—by someone, somewhere, somehow!

- From 7 to about 11 years of age, children begin to realize that individuals formulate social rules, which can be changed. This phase is referred to as *autonomous morality* (or the morality of reciprocity). At this age, children think punishment for any violation of rules should be linked to the intent of the violator. The person who broke five cups didn't mean to, so should not be punished any more than the person who broke one.

Piaget's ideas about moral development led to the advancement of a more complex theory devised by Lawrence Kohlberg.

Kohlberg's Theory

Among the more notable efforts to explain a child's moral development has been that of Lawrence Kohlberg (1975, 1981). Using Piaget's ideas about cognitive development as a basis, Kohlberg's moral stages emerge from a child's active thinking about moral issues and decisions. Kohlberg formulated a sophisticated scheme of moral development extending from about 4 years of age through adulthood.

To discover the structures of moral reasoning and the stages of moral development, Kohlberg (1975) employed a modified clinical technique called the **moral dilemma,** in which a conflict leads subjects to justify the morality of their choices. In one of the best known, a husband needs a miracle drug to save his dying wife. The druggist is selling the remedy at an outrageous price, which the woman's husband cannot afford. He collects about half the money and asks the druggist to sell the drug to him more cheaply or allow him to pay the rest later. The druggist refuses. What should the man do: steal the drug or permit his wife to die rather than break the law? By posing these conflicts, Kohlberg forces us to project our own views.

Kohlberg's theory traces moral development through six stages by successive transformations of cognitive structures (see table 9.3). Middle childhood youngsters are typically at Kohlberg's *preconventional level of morality.* Only as they approach ages 10 to 12 do they begin to edge into the *conventional level of morality,* where acts are right because that's the way it's supposed to be (determined by adult authority). The *postconventional level of morality* comes at age 13 and over.

According to Kohlberg, moral judgment requires us to weigh the claims of others against self-interest. Thus youngsters must overcome their egocentrism before they can legitimately make moral judgments. Also, anyone's level of moral development may not be the same as their moral behavior. To put it simply, people may

A major objective for those working with children should be to make them sensitive to their relationships with others, to recognize those times when a "helping hand" is needed.

TABLE 9.3 KOHLBERG'S STAGES OF MORAL DEVELOPMENT

Level I. Preconventional (about 4 to 10 years)

During these years children respond mainly to cultural control to avoid punishment and attain satisfaction. There are two stages:

Stage 1. Punishment and obedience. Children obey rules and orders to avoid punishment; there is no concern about moral rectitude.

Stage 2. Naive instrumental behaviorism. Children obey rules but only for pure self-interest; they are vaguely aware of fairness to others but obey rules only for their own satisfaction. Kohlberg introduces the notion of reciprocity here: "You scratch my back, I'll scratch yours."

Level II. Conventional (about 10 to 13 years)

During these years children desire approval, both from individuals and society. They not only conform, but actively support society's standards. There are two stages:

Stage 3. Children seek the approval of others, the "good boy-good girl" mentality. They begin to judge behavior by intention: "She meant to do well."

Stage 4. Law-and-order mentality. Children are concerned with authority and maintaining the social order. Correct behavior is "doing one's duty."

Level III. Postconventional (13 years and over)

If true morality (an internal moral code) is to develop, it appears during these years. The individual does not appeal to other people for moral decisions; these decisions are made by an "enlightened conscience." There are two stages:

Stage 5. An individual makes moral decisions legalistically or contractually; that is, the best values are those supported by law because they have been accepted by the whole society. If there is conflict between human need and the law, individuals should work to change the law.

Stage 6. An informed conscience defines what is right. People act, not from fear, approval, or law, but from their own internalized standards of right or wrong.

Source: Based on L. Kohlberg, "A Cognitive-Developmental Analysis of Children's Sex-Role Concepts and Attitudes" in *The Development of Sex Differences,* edited by E. Maccoby, Stanford University Press, Stanford, Calif., 1966.

Moral Development at Home and in the Classroom

Many schools are now using moral dilemmas as a teaching tool in their classrooms. These are thought-provoking dialogues that probe the moral bases for people's thinking. They're real or imaginary conflicts involving competing claims, for which there is no clear, morally correct solution. As you can imagine, both teachers and parents are interested in using them to further children's moral development. Here are several suggestions.

- *With younger children,* they might try something like this: Set the scenario with a newly arrived foreign student. Yasmin has just arrived from Lebanon, and she is being mocked by some classmates because of differences in language and customs. Ask children what they would do if their friends would no longer play with them if they were friendly with Yasmin. Would they risk their friendships by being nice to the new girl?

  Because most younger children have had little experience in resolving moral dilemmas, at first adults should act as a guide during the discussion and only later introduce more complex issues that require resolution at the stage above their present moral level.

- *Asking why* helps children to identify the dilemma and discover their level of moral reasoning. For example, after discussing Hong Kong's reunion with China with your older students, why not ask them what people should do if, while working on a Hong Kong newspaper, they were forbidden to write a story critical of the Chinese government. Their family's lifestyle and security could be at stake. Yet the writer feels strongly about freedom of the press. (Ask your students why theirs is a good solution.)

- *Complicating the situation* adds a new dimension to the problem. Pose this problem to older children: Imagine an official in the Cuban government with family in the United States. He is torn between trying to retain power in Cuba and moving to the United States and rejoining his family. Begin by discussing loyalty, then gradually introduce complications, such as civil conflict, family ties, regional or national commitment, and then ask, "What would you have done?"

Effective discussions of moral dilemmas also require an atmosphere, both at school and in the home, conducive to moral instruction, which can be encouraged by attention to the following four points.

1. *You must create an atmosphere of trust and fairness in which children are willing to reveal their feelings and ideas about the moral dilemma with which the group is wrestling.* Adults must work to bring children to the point where they will share their beliefs with others.

2. *Such an atmosphere results from respecting children and valuing their opinions.* Adults who are decent and fair in their relations with children and treat them with respect can do much to create a positive atmosphere for moral instruction.

3. *Adults must be sensitive to what children are experiencing.* They must be alert especially to those who find a discussion painful, for whatever reason. Make every effort to provide a forum—within the group or in private conversation—for them to express their feelings on their terms.

know what is right but do things they know are wrong. Not all students of moral development agree with Kohlberg. Strenuous objections have been made to Kohlberg's male interpretation of moral development, especially by Carol Gilligan.

Gilligan's "In a Different Voice"

The importance Kohlberg placed on justice triggered serious doubts by those who believe that he ignored gender differences. Carol Gilligan, in particular, questioned the validity of Kohlberg's theory for women (1982). She argued that the qualities Kohlberg associated with the mature adult (autonomous thinking, clear decision making, and responsible action) are qualities that have been traditionally associated with "masculinity" rather than "femininity."

Characteristics that supposedly define the "good woman" (gentleness, tact, concern for the feelings of others, display of feelings, caring) all contribute to a different concept of morality. As a result, the different images of self that boys and girls/men and women acquire lead to different interpretations of moral behavior:

Teaching Moral Values: In the School or in the Home?

Increasing crime and violence in this country is an issue of national attention. In particular, incidences of violence in American schools have never been higher. Many feel the time has come to formally teach moral values in our classrooms, but others disagree.

Issue: A formal in-school program of moral education should be mandatory in all schools.

Answer—Pro A growing consensus has emerged that violence, particularly among the young, is a national problem. As such, the schools, which contact all of our children, would be a logical place to introduce formal programs devoted to moral education. Such programs would guarantee all students access to these ideas and behaviors and would maintain uniformity of the content.

Answer—Con The school day is already too short. Something we are now teaching would have to be eliminated to include another subject. An informal treatment of these issues, designed to suit the problems of individual communities and integrated across the curriculum of the community's schools makes better sense.

Issue: Educators are best suited to develop and implement a program that instills values for children.

Answer—Pro Educators understand best how to develop and teach ideas. Since children spend the greatest part of the day in school, they should receive moral education within the educational system.

Answer—Con More and more schools are being asked to take up the responsibilities that have traditionally rested with the family, which is one reason that achievement scores have fallen. The schools can only do so much. Families and religious settings are the best contexts within which to impart moral values, not the public school.

Issue: Educators are well suited to develop the content of a moral education curriculum.

Answer—Pro Since teachers are assuming more and more responsibility for all aspects of their students' lives, they are the ideal choice to determine what their students need in a program of moral education. Schools can present a developmentally sensitive curriculum using aspects of ideas like respect, service, and integrity appropriately.

Answer—Con Whose values or morality will the school teach? We are an ever-increasing multicultural nation. Our many backgrounds mean we have many ways of looking at these issues. How do we decide whose view to choose?

Important and sensitive issues are involved here. Should issues that reach into the heart of families, but also impact on society-at-large be confined to home discussion? Yet, is it possible that classroom discussion, as general as it may be, could conflict with the values taught at home? Perhaps the safest conclusion at this moment is that there are no easy answers to these questions, and that time and continued research are needed.

---

women, concerned with caring and a strong interpersonal focus; men, raised with the belief that rights and justice are paramount.

Women's moral decisions are based on an *ethics of caring* rather than a *morality of justice,* which led Gilligan to argue forcefully for a different sequence for the moral development of girls and women. For example, initially, any moral decisions a girl has to make center on the self and her concerns are pragmatic: Will it work for me? Gradually, as her attachment to her parents continues, self-interest is redefined in light of "what one should do." A sense of responsibility for others appears (the traditional view of women as caretakers), and goodness is equated with self-sacrifice and concern for others.

Gilligan believes that women, with growing maturity, begin to include concern for self with their concern for others. In other words, is it possible to be responsible to one's self as well as to others? Women now realize that recognizing one's needs is not being selfish but rather being honest and fair; that is, the idea of doing good includes others but also one's self. Finally, women resolve the conflict between concern for self and concern for others because of their maturing ability to view their relationships from a broader perspective, which results in a guiding principle of nonviolence. Harmony and compassion govern all moral action involving self and others, which ultimately defines both femininity and adulthood.

For girls and women, issues of femininity or feminine identity do not depend on the achievement of separation from the mother or the progress of individuation. Since masculinity is defined through separation while femininity is defined through attachment, male gender identity is threatened by intimacy while female gender identity is threatened by separation. Thus males tend to have difficulty with relationships, while females tend to have problems with individuation. (Gilligan, 1982, p. 8).

To both their credit, neither Gilligan nor Kohlberg argued for the superiority of either a male or female sequence of moral development. Nevertheless, does the difference in emphasis on what constitutes the basis of moral development—caring or justice—carry the seeds of inevitable clashes of opinion when boys and girls/men and women look at moral issues? It shouldn't because the replies of boys and girls to moral dilemmas show both justice and caring themes. When Gilligan's and Kohlberg's theories are taken together, the moral person is seen as one whose moral choices reflect reasoned and deliberate judgments that ensure justice be accorded each person while maintaining a passionate concern for the well-being and care of each individual. Justice and care are then joined (Brabeck, 1983).

Continuing to refine her ideas about the sequence of moral development for women, Gilligan, Lyons, and Hanmer (1990) noted that adolescent girls face problems of connections: What is the relationship among self, relationships, and morality? Must women exclude themselves and be thought of as a "good woman," or exclude others and be considered selfish? The answer seems to reside in the nature of the connections that women make with others.

Whether boy or girl, middle childhood youngsters, through their rapid cognitive development, are aware of right and wrong. How do we know this? They write answers to questions; they talk to us. Thus, language development is another clue to their growing maturity.

Guided Review

14. According to Piaget, when children believe that anyone who breaks a rule will somehow be punished, this is called _____ _____.
15. The phase of moral development when children realize that individuals formulate social rules is known as _____ _____.
16. A _____ _____ was Kohlberg's clinical technique whereby a conflict leads subjects to justify the morality of their choices.
17. Middle childhood youngsters are, for the most part, at Kohlberg's _____ level of morality.
18. _____ has challenged Kohlberg's theory with regard to women.

Language Development

In middle childhood we find children immersed in a verbal world. By the age of 7, almost all children have learned a great deal about their language. They appear to be quite sophisticated in their knowledge yet considerable development is still to come. During the middle childhood years, children improve their use of language and expand their structural knowledge. By the end of the period, they are similar to adults in their language usage.

Answers

14. immanent justice 15. autonomous morality 16. moral dilemma 17. preconventional 18. Gilligan

Changes in Usage

Three changes in language usage occur during these years (Menyuk, 1982):

- *Children begin to use language for their own purposes,* to help them remember and plan their actions. They move from talking aloud when doing something, to inner speech. From about age 7 on, children use language to help them recall things. This applies not only to individual items (such as lists) but also to the relations between objects or actions (psychologists call this **encoding**).

- *Language during these years becomes less literal.* We saw the beginnings of this change in chapter 7, when we discussed children's humor. Now they use language figuratively. On going to bed, an 11-year-old may say, "Time to hit the sack." Children display this type of language by a process called **metalinguistic awareness,** which means a capacity to think about and talk about language. You can see how this is impossible until children acquire the cognitive abilities previously discussed.

- *Children are able to communicate with others more effectively.* They understand relationships; they can also express these relationships accurately, using appropriate language. In a sense, more effective communication is the product of the interaction of many developmental forces: physical growth as seen in the brain's development; cognitive development as seen in the ability to use symbols and to store them; and language development as seen in vocabulary development and usage. Language has now become an effective tool in adapting to the environment.

In regard to changes in structural knowledge, most middle childhood youngsters, especially by the end of the period, begin to use more complex words. Children begin to change word stems, which can produce syntactic changes as well.

I really like history.
I really like historical books.

They now understand the rules that allow them to form and use such changes. The same process applies to compound words. What does your instructor write on? Usually it's a blackboard. Middle childhood youngsters realize that a blackboard in this meaning is not a black piece of wood. The awareness of relations helps them to learn that the same relationship can be expressed in different ways.

Liz helped Janie.
Janie was helped by Liz.

As Menyuk (1982) states, much of children's language development during these years results from their awareness of language categories and the relationships among them.

During middle childhood the relationship of language development (in the sense of mastering a native tongue) to reading becomes crucial. Between the ages of 6 and 10, children must interpret written words wherever they turn: from signs on buses and streets as they go to school, to schooling that is massively verbal. When you consider a middle childhood youngster's competence, especially cognitive and linguistic, you conclude that they should be able to read effectively. The topics that engage reading researchers reflect the cognitive abilities of these children.

The Importance of Reading

In summarizing the reading research of the last decade, we can make several generalizations:

- *Reading is a constructive process,* which clearly implies that readers construct meaning from what they read (Mason & Au, 1990). The meaning that children

Every effort should be made to instill a love of reading in children, both for academic success and the lifelong pleasure reading affords.

glean from their reading also depends on their previous experiences, which may be rich or deficient. A related problem here is that even if children possess relevant knowledge about what they are reading, they may not use it.

- *Reading must be fluent,* which means that children must be able to decode quickly and accurately. We'll discuss this shortly.

- *Reading must be strategic,* which means that good readers, for example, adapt their reading techniques to the difficulty of the text and the purpose of their reading (Mason & Au, 1990).

- *Reading requires motivation,* which demands that reading materials be interesting and teaching be innovative and challenging.

- *Reading is a continuously developing skill,* which suggests that instruction and materials must match the changing abilities and skills of children.

With these guidelines, researchers are investigating topics such as the following.

Decoding, a controversial and elusive topic, refers to the technique by which we recognize words. Some reading theorists argue that children should focus on the whole word; others believe that individual letters must be taught—the phonics method. Research today indicates that early phonics instruction produces the most satisfactory results. Do middle childhood youngsters possess this ability? Absolutely.

Vocabulary, or word meaning, refers to teaching the meaning of a word, not how to pronounce it. Pause for a moment and consider the ramifications of this statement. Knowledge of vocabulary is highly correlated with intelligence, which is highly correlated with reading performance and school success. Is it any wonder, then, that the acquisition of vocabulary is high on any list of reading priorities?

Reading comprehension, which is the ultimate objective in any type of reading instruction, means that a reader not only recognizes words but also understands the concepts that words represent. Children of this age should have the capacity to understand the meaning of appropriate words.

You can see, then, that the goal of reading instruction during these years should be to enable children to control their own reading by directing attention where it is needed.

Keep in mind, also, that all of us, both children and adults, have a limited capacity for attention; that is, we attend to only a few things at once. If the tasks are simple and automatic, we attend to two or three. For children reading and studying there's an important lesson here: Focus on the significant and don't be distracted by the trivial. For example, when they're studying, there shouldn't be anything in their environment that's too novel or intense or incongruous that could easily distract them. Adults should urge children to develop the habit of searching for patterns. For example, after reading a story (or page or paragraph), children could be given a mixed series of statements and asked to arrange these statements in the order in which they appeared in the story. Garner (1992) has insisted that children automatically look for information in a systematic way; that is, they search for and develop strategies to guide their reading.

Strategies of Maturing Readers

In discussing the strategies that children of all ages use to obtain meaning from words, Booth (1994) stated that readers sample the text, confirming or rejecting possible meanings. They read along, pause to reflect on what they've read, perhaps skip words that they'll come back to, and reread to clarify meaning. As they do, they search for several types of cues in the text. The first type of cue that Booth (1994) identified are *pragmatic* cues, that is, those practical signals that help discover meaning. For example, a novel differs from a textbook, a shopping list differs from a statistical table.

Readers then relate the words themselves to what they signify, that is, to known facts and ideas. Using these *semantic* (meaning) cues, readers integrate this new information with what they already understand, which is remarkably similar to Piaget's discussion of assimilation and accommodation. *Syntactic* cues (knowledge of rules) enable readers to apply the rules of oral language that they have acquired to predict the meaning of words. Finally, readers use *phonological* cues (sound knowledge) to assess the relationship between the sounds of words and their written symbols.

Using these cues to assess reading capacity, Booth (1994) has identified several levels of reading ability. First are the emergent readers, who can identify letters and recognize some common words. They know what books "do" and they attempt to read by using semantic and syntactic cues. Next are developing readers, who are beginning to understand the relationship between sound and symbol. They pay close attention to the print in their efforts at decoding. Readers at this level use all four of the cueing systems previously mentioned. Finally, there are independent readers, who can read ably and without assistance using all of the cueing systems.

As children come to the end of the middle childhood years, they are in the independent reader category. They use their language more symbolically and understand abstract concepts such as time. (Again, note the agreement with Piaget's description of the concrete operational years.) Through these years, which are the elementary school years, children continue to expand the length of their oral sentences and continue to refine their understanding of the structure and function of language (Barchers, 1994).

You can understand why reading is so important to children of this age. As they move through the school curriculum, their work becomes increasingly verbal: They read about the history of their country, the story of science, the symbols of mathematics, or any subject you can mention. A youngster who has a reading problem is a youngster in trouble. Table 9.3 summarizes some of the language accomplishments of the middle childhood years.

TABLE 9.3 TYPICAL LANGUAGE ACCOMPLISHMENTS OF MIDDLE CHILDHOOD

Age (years)	Language Accomplishment
6	Has vocabulary of several thousand words; understands use and meaning of complex sentences; uses language as a tool; possesses some reading ability
7	Improving motor control helps writing skills; can usually print several sentences; begins to tell time; losing tendency to reverse letters (b,d)
8	Motor control continues to improve, aiding both printing and writing; understands that words may have more than one meaning (ball); uses total sentence to determine meaning
9	Describes objects in detail; little difficulty in telling time; writes well; uses sentence content to determine word meaning
10	Describes situations by cause and effect; can write fairly lengthy essays; likes mystery and science stories; acquires dictionary skills; possesses good sense of grammar

Guided Review

19. Middle childhood youngsters begin to use language for their own _____.
20. Readers construct meaning from what they read, which means that reading is a _____ _____.
21. When readers adapt their techniques to the difficulty of the text, this shows that reading is also a _____ _____.
22. The process by which we recognize words is called _____.
23. According to Booth,_____ cues help readers to discover meaning.

CONCLUSION

From our discussion so far, we know several things about middle childhood youngsters. But are they capable of meeting the problems they face? Yes and no. They can assimilate and accommodate the material they encounter but only at their level. For example, elementary school youngsters up to the age of 10 or 11 are still limited by the quality of their thinking. They are capable of representational thought but only with the concrete, the tangible. They find it difficult to comprehend fully any abstract subtleties in reading, social studies, or any subject.

According to Erikson, the middle childhood period should provide a sense of industry; otherwise, youngsters develop feelings of inferiority. With all

of the developmental accomplishments of the previous six or seven years, youngsters want to use their abilities, which means that they sometimes experience failure as well as success, especially in their school work. Physically active, cognitively capable, and socially receptive, much is expected of these children, especially in school.

In Summary:

Physical Development

- These are good years physically as middle childhood youngsters consolidate their height and weight gains.
- Middle childhood youngsters develop considerable coordination in their motor skills.

Cognitive Development

- Among the major cognitive achievements of this period are conservation, seriation, classification, and numeration.
- Children of this age show clear signs of increasing symbolic ability.
- Sternberg and Gardner have proposed new ways of explaining intelligence.

Thinking and Problem Solving

- Children today need critical thinking skills to adapt to sophisticated, technological societies.
- Good problem solvers have several observable characteristics.
- The DUPE model offers

Answers

19. purposes 20. constructive process 21. strategic process 22. decoding 23. pragmatic

suggestions for improving problem-solving skills.

Moral Development

- Piaget formulated a four-stage theory of moral development that is tightly linked to his explanation of cognitive development.
- Kohlberg proposed six levels of

moral development that follow a child's progress from about 4 years of age to adulthood.
- Gilligan has challenged the male-oriented basis of Kohlberg's work.

Language Development

- Children's language growth during these years shows increasing

representation and facility in conversing with others.
- During these years children develop several strategies to help them with their reading.

KEY TERMS

Classification
Concrete operational period
Conservation
Decentering
DUPE
Encoding

Extrinsic motivation
Intrinsic motivation
Knowledge-acquisition components
Metacomponents
Metalinguistic awareness
Moral dilemma

Multiple intelligences
Numeration
Performance components
Seriation
Triarchic model of intelligence

WHAT DO YOU THINK?

1. Imagine an 11-year-old boy—let's call him Tim—who lives in the suburbs of a large northeastern city. He shows signs of becoming a great baseball player (a pitcher). His father realizes that his son could eventually win a college scholarship and go on to become a professional if he continues to develop. He decides that Tim should not play pickup games with his friends, because he might hurt himself. He also decides that the family should move to the South so Tom can play ball all year. Neither his wife nor Tim's sister wants to move. As a family friend, you have been asked for advice. What would you suggest?

2. You are a fourth-grade teacher and you turn to Janice and say, "Janice, Barbara is taller than Janie, who is taller than Liz. Who's the tallest of all?" Janice just looks at you. You sigh and think, "Where's Piaget when I need him?" How

would you explain Janice's behavior?

3. Billy (9 years old) cuts through the parking lot of a supermarket on the way home from school. In the bike rack by the wall he sees a beautiful racing bike that he really wants. It seems to be unlocked and no one is around. With Kohlberg's work as a guide, what do you think is going through Billy's mind?

CHAPTER REVIEW TEST

1. Psychological characteristics of middle childhood include all but
   a. seriation.
   b. numeration.
   c. moral reasoning.
   d. random scribbling.

2. An average 11-year-old who stands 57 inches weighs about _____ pounds.
   a. 50
   b. 85
   c. 100
   d. 115

3. Which statement is not true?
   a. Girls and boys in the middle childhood years show equal grip strength.
   b. Girls are stronger than boys during middle childhood.
   c. Middle childhood boys and girls show equal interest in physical games.
   d. Balance matures by the end of middle childhood.

4. Which of the following is out of order? Conservation of
   a. number.
   b. volume.
   c. liquids.
   d. length.

5. The acquisition of the number concept is known as
   a. classification.
   b. seriation.

   c. numeration.
   d. conservation.

6. Sternberg's theory is based on components, experience, and
   a. context.
   b. gender.
   c. age.
   d. chromosomes.

7. According to Sternberg, obstacles to realizing the potential of our intelligence include all but
   a. lack of motivation.
   b. using wrong abilities.
   c. fear of failure.
   d. physical disability.

8. Howard Gardner's theory of multiple intelligences includes _____ equal intelligences.
   - a. 4
   - b. 5
   - c. 8
   - d. 10

9. In Sternberg's theory, learning how to solve problems is a function of
   - a. metacomponents.
   - b. genetic endowment.
   - c. environment.
   - d. knowledge-acquisition components.

10. When we plan, monitor, and evaluate our problem-solving strategies, we are using
    - a. knowledge-acquisition components.
    - b. performance components.
    - c. metacomponents.
    - d. general intelligence.

11. According to Sternberg, adapting to our culture is called the context of
    - a. intelligence.
    - b. organization.
    - c. assimilation.
    - d. accommodation.

12. Recognizing what is distinctive in others is an example of which of Gardner's intelligences?
    - a. linguistic
    - b. interpersonal, intrapersonal
    - c. logical-mathematical
    - d. bodily-kinesthetic

13. Which of Gardner's intelligences results from contact with the objects of the world?
    - a. Musical
    - b. Interpersonal, intrapersonal
    - c. Linguistic
    - d. Logical-mathematical

14. Which of Gardner's intelligences is linked to the right side of the brain?
    - a. Spatial
    - b. Interpersonal
    - c. Linguistic
    - d. Logical-mathematical

15. One problem with tests is that test takers and test makers may differ in their
    - a. relationships.
    - b. circumstances.
    - c. conditions.
    - d. values.

16. Our response to problems may be determined by how the problem is
    - a. framed.
    - b. referenced.
    - c. refined.
    - d. filtered.

17. Gilligan's developmental sequence is based on
    - a. social justice.
    - b. female superiority.
    - c. an ethic of care.
    - d. moral reasoning.

18. Piaget's ideas on moral development came from
    - a. structured interviews with children.
    - b. moral dilemmas.
    - c. an ethic of care.
    - d. observations of children playing marbles.

19. During the years 7 to 11, Piaget believed that children develop a form of morality he called
    - a. autonomous.
    - b. heteronomous.
    - c. individualized.
    - d. group-oriented.

20. Which statement is not accurate?
    - a. Knowledge of vocabulary is highly correlated with intelligence.
    - b. Intelligence is correlated with reading performance.
    - c. Reading performance is highly correlated with gender.
    - d. Intelligence is highly correlated with school success.

Answers

1. d 2. b 3. b 4. b 5. c 6. a 7. d 8. c 9. d 10. c 11. a 12. b 13. d 14. a 15. d 16. a 17. c 18. d 19. a 20. c

CHAPTER 10

*Psychosocial Development
in Middle Childhood*

Support and encouragement are needed during the middle childhood years if a realistic sense of self-esteem is to develop.

The two teen age boys were sitting on the top row of the spectator seats, talking quietly until the game began. (Let's call them Jack and Bill.) It was a beautiful spring afternoon and baseball was in the air as the two high school teams prepared to get the game underway. The two boys stopped talking for a moment and waved at one of the players, obviously a friend of theirs. As the umpire motioned the first batter of the visiting team into the batter's box to start the game, a tall, striking-looking man paused at the foot of the stands and scanned the seats. Seeing the two boys in the top row, he quickly climbed the steps to join them.

"Hi guys. What are you doing here? No classes today for you private school softies?"

Both boys laughed; they obviously were at ease with the older man and his brand of humor. Jack then replied, "No, we started exams today and got out at noon. We're about a week ahead of Phil (the older man's son). But don't forget, we started earlier in September."

"Sure, Sure, Sure. All I get from you two are excuses, excuses, excuses."

Bill turned to him and said, " Well, at least Phil has a longer season; I'd love to still be playing." (Both boys played varsity baseball on their school team.)

The man shrugged and said, "I dunno. If the season ended sooner, I wouldn't feel I had to come here and watch that kid of mine make a fool of himself. Game after game; sometimes I wonder what's wrong with him. But, you know, fathers are supposed to be here."

Both boys stared at the field and didn't say anything. They liked Phil's father. He was nice to them and always was glad to see them, but they couldn't understand his reaction to Phil. Nothing that he did seemed to please his father. And to make matters worse, his father had no hesitation in criticizing—sometime belittling—Phil in front of others, including Phil's friends.

Just as his father finished speaking, Phil entered the batter's box. Both Jack and Bill noticed how Phil glanced up at his father as he moved to the plate. "Here we go again," said his father, "I suppose it'll be another strikeout."

Jack and Bill were too respectful to say what they thought, but both of them, when they were talking later, mentioned how glad they were that their fathers either voiced their support or kept quiet when things went bad. Jack summed up their feelings nicely. "I don't know how Phil takes that, day after day. If that were my father, I wouldn't even go out for team. No one needs that kind of stuff." ✤

(The previous story, unfortunately true, was told to one of the authors.) Too often we tend to overlook the long-term consequences of the way parents, teachers, and adults in general sometimes treat children. The person who mentioned the above story to us went on to tell us Phil (the son in the story) today is timid, anxious, with not much drive, with little confidence in himself. Will he ever achieve to the extent he might have if his self-concept hadn't been so severely shaken during those early years?

We have encountered too many similar cases over the years not to recognize the importance of a child's self-esteem. Consequently, we want to study its role in healthy development, while simultaneously avoiding many of the pitfalls and exaggerated claims surrounding any discussion of this important topic. For example, if parents do something in one way or another will their children be geniuses, presidents, Mars-walking astronauts, or Hollywood movie stars? Well, maybe; but unfortunately it just doesn't work that way, as we'll see.

Among the prime influences on a child's developing sense of self is peer opinion, which at this age is becoming a powerful motivator of behavior. School, with its important network of social contacts and the emphasis placed on achievement, provides constant feedback that powerfully affects a child's feeling about self. The media, especially television with its stereotypical models, furnishes children with artificial, often self-destructive, goals of what the self should be. Finally, all children face occasional stress. Although some children find themselves under unrelenting pressure, how children cope with stress leaves an indelible mark on their feelings about themselves.

With the personal changes that middle childhood youngsters experience, their social contacts expand—perhaps the addition of brothers and sisters, new friends, new adult figures, and school with its challenges and achievements. All of these new contacts in their widening world become important influences on children's development because we know that the great socializing agents of childhood are family, peers, school, and the media.

When you finish reading this chapter, you should be able to

- Assess the critical role of self in healthy development.

- Analyze the role of peers in middle childhood development.

- Compare the different kinds of influence that schools exercise during the middle childhood years.

- Describe television's effect on the different aspects of development in middle childhood.

- Define the different kinds of stress that can affect children during this period.

- Distinguish the causes of violence in middle childhood youngsters.

The Changing Sense of Self

In chapter 8, we described the emerging sense of self and self-concept and traced their developmental path. Here we'll continue our narrative by demonstrating the tight link between realistic self-esteem and the attainment of competence. What do we mean by **self-esteem?** A good way to think of it is as a feeling of confidence and self-satisfaction with one's self.

Self-esteem seems to be composed of several elements that contribute to a child's sense of worth.

- *A sense of physical safety.* Children who feel physically secure aren't afraid of being harmed, which helps to develop feelings of confidence.

- *A sense of emotional security.* Children who aren't humiliated or subjected to sarcasm feel safe emotionally, which translates into a willingness to trust others.

- *A sense of identity.* Children who know "who they are" have achieved a degree of self-knowledge that enables them to take responsibility for their actions and relate well with others.

- *A sense of belonging.* Children who are accepted by others are comfortable in seeking out new relationships and begin to develop feelings of independence and interdependence.

- *A sense of competence.* Children who are confident in their ability to do certain things are willing to try to learn to do new things and persevere until they achieve mastery (Youngs, 1991).

Concern with competence appears at about 7 or 8 years of age and suggests that developmental changes occur in self-esteem. Interestingly, before beginning school children coming from a supportive home typically feel very good about themselves, very self-important. As they begin to measure themselves against their classmates, however, their confidence in their abilities becomes more realistic and by the second grade what they think about their self-esteem comes close to the opinions of those around them.

In other words, children's evaluations of their abilities match teacher ratings, test scores, and direct observations (Berk, 1997). A child's evaluation of self, self-esteem, and self-efficacy is tightly interwoven with their satisfaction with appearance, their need for support from someone they love and trust, and a belief in their competence.

Self-Esteem and Competence

Susan Harter, a developmental psychologist at the University of Denver, has been a long-time student of the self, self-development, self-concept, and self-esteem and her research has been a beacon of light in an otherwise murky field (Harter, 1993). Studying 8-to-13 year-old children, Harter and her colleagues identified five types of **competence** that seem to be central to a child's level of self-esteem: scholastic competence, athletic competence, likability by peers, physical appearance, and behavioral conduct. Trying to determine what produces a child's sense of self-esteem, Harter posed a basic question.

How do children's evaluation of their competency affect the level of their self-esteem?

Devising a questionnaire that tapped children's perception of their competence, the researchers used items such as the following.

Some kids have trouble figuring out the answers in school.
but
Other kids can almost always figure out the answers.

Children would then indicate which of the answers best described them, thus creating a profile of their feelings of competence. The results were fascinating.

Children don't feel they do equally as well in all five types of competence Harter identified. Most children show a "sawtooth" profile, indicating that they feel good about themselves in some activities but not so good in others. Not only that but some children who have noticeably different profiles have quite similar levels of self-esteem. Other children, with similar profiles, have vastly different levels of self-esteem. Here's an example of the children's profiles.

Child 1

	Scholastic Competence	Athletic Competence	Social Acceptance	Behavioral Conduct	Physical Appearance	Self-Esteem
High					•	•
Medium			•	•		
Low	•	•				

Child 2

	Scholastic Competence	Athletic Competence	Social Acceptance	Behavioral Conduct	Physical Appearance	Self-Esteem
High					•	
Medium			•	•		
Low	•	•				•

You can see in this example that each child has a similar profile but a much different level of self-esteem. Their self-esteem was affected only by the things they viewed as important (social acceptance, looks, etc.). The first child does not see school or athletics as important, therefore not doing well academically or athletically doesn't matter. The other child, however, probably does value sports and studies, and feels inadequate with an accompanying loss of self-esteem.

In the second phase of her study, Harter probed to discover how what others think about children affects their self-esteem. She used questions similar to the following:

Some kids have classmates that like the kind of person they are.
but
Other kids have classmates who do not like the kind of person they are.

The results were as you probably anticipated. Children who receive considerable support from the important people in their environment had a high regard for themselves. Those who obtain little, if any, support from their significant others showed the lowest self-esteem. Taken together, these findings provide penetrating insights into how children acquire their sense of self-esteem.

Ever the honest researcher, Harter proposed several troublesome questions about the information she and her colleagues uncovered. For example, in all of her studies there was a strong link between what children thought of their physical appearance and their level of self-esteem. In fact, what children think of their looks is the leading predictor of their self-esteem. As Harter asks, is self-esteem only skin deep?

Harter asked her subjects whether they felt that their appearance determined their self-esteem or did their sense of worth lead them to favorably evaluate their looks. She discovered that those who believed their looks determined their self-esteem felt worse about their appearance, had lower self-esteem, and were more subject to bouts of depression.

Summarizing, then, children and young adolescents for whom personal appearance and the opinion of others determined their sense of self had lower levels of self-esteem. Those who believed that their sense of self caused others to think highly of them and who felt that their sense of self-esteem led to feelings of competency had higher levels of self-esteem. The lesson is clear for those working with children: To help children enhance their self-esteem encourage them to examine their sense of worth carefully, but not to look through the glass darkly.

Parents and educators must walk a thin line between providing the necessary support and encouragement for children to face "the great battle of life" on the one hand and the equal necessity of keeping children's feet securely planted in reality on the other. We again want to emphasize the need to praise and recognize children's honest achievements.

But if an adult's reactions are an island of praise in a sea of neutral, even negative evaluations, eventually children will ignore them. Children shouldn't be subjected to a salvo of criticisms, but reactions to their efforts can't be transparently false. You can't fool children; they cut right through any sham, especially if something is meaningful to them. It's better to be honest. "You didn't do that well this time, but I know if you study (practice, rehearse, whatever the activity) hard, you'll do better next time." Honest evaluation, coupled with support and encouragement, go a long way toward deserved self-esteem.

To have high self-esteem is to feel confidently appropriate to life.
Nathaniel Branden

There is, however, a flip side to this positive look we've taken at the self. For their own good, and the good of those around them, children must develop self-control.

Children and Self-Control

On June 3, 1986, the state of Florida charged 9-year-old Jeffrey Bailey with murder. Making sure no one else was around, he had pushed a 3-year-old boy who couldn't swim into the pool. He pulled up a chair to watch the boy drown. Later, when the police had pieced together the circumstances of the murder, they arrested Jeffrey, who was described as calm, nonchalant, and enjoying the attention (Magid & McKelvey, 1987).

This story, as startling as it is true, is only one of many that appears with increasing frequency in our nation's newspapers and television news reports. Murder is the most dramatic example of a life gone wrong. The increasing rate of assaults, robberies, and arson raises a basic question: What happens to children to turn them into killers, thieves, and arsonists? Why didn't they ever develop those critical inner controls?

What is Self-Control?

Just exactly what is meant by **self-control?** As you know, self-control refers to many different types of behaviors: mastering fear, controlling eating, restricting drinking, keeping your temper in check, and refusing drugs. We'll focus on that element of self-control that saves children from unnecessary conflicts, unreasonable aggression, and senseless violence. A dictionary definition of self-control is a good starting point: restraint exercised over one's own impulses, emotions, or desires. In other words, children should possess the ability to control their actions in appropriate ways; they must develop a sense of inner control.

Let's examine several key reasons that help us to understand why some children become aggressive, even violent, adolescents and adults.

The Roots of Violent Behavior

Two well-known commentators on the social scene, James Wilson and Richard Herrnstein (1985) in their massive study of crime and human nature found clear evidence of a positive association between past and future antisocial behavior, which gives rise to the maxim that the best predictor of violence is past antisocial behavior.

The causes of violent and criminal behavior are multiple and complex. Nevertheless, most modern scientists believe that a tendency to commit crime is established early in life, *perhaps as soon as the preschool years,* and the behavior of these children provide ample clues to their possible future antisocial behavior. Aggression has been well established in preschoolers and recent research (Crick, Casas, & Mosher, 1997; Galen & Underwood, 1996) has indicated that these early signs of aggression are closely associated with social-psychological maladjustment.

A critical age for early signs of emerging delinquency is 7 to 12 years when children search for friends and want to become accepted members of a group. Some children, for whatever reason, tend to join groups that encourage antisocial acts (Tomada & Schneider, 1997). They may be drawn to a particular group because a friend is a member; it may be a sign of rebellion (my mother doesn't like those kids, but I think they're neat); it may just seem a daring thing to do.

Clues to Troublesome Behavior

If two boys are from the same family, with the same opportunities, why does one turn to a life of crime while the other leads a law-abiding life? Was there some subtle genetic transmission? Were the family relations similar for both boys? Were their friends radically different? Examining each case helps us to identify the causes of crime for that child. Family conditions may be the cause for one child but not an-

The Bully

Is there any reader who did not have nightmares sometime during school about that "monster" who loved to tease, humiliate, threaten, and fight? Even today most middle-school principals will list bullying among their major worries.

Who is the bully? Olweus (1982, 1993, 1995) identified **bullies** as those who have aggressive reaction patterns and have considerable physical strength. **Peer victimization,** on the other hand, describes those children who are anxious, insecure, cautious, and sensitive with low self-esteem. Many have been treated violently themselves, attended schools that treat violence ineffectively, or are members of a peer group that encourages aggression. As a result, these children avoid school if possible, and even at an early age begin to lead lonely lives (Kochenderfer & Ladd, 1996).

When we couple this kind of pupil with others who are almost "natural victims" (small, underweight, perhaps differently dressed, or having an obvious personal problem, such as anxiety), then conditions are ripe for bullying. These children seem ideal targets for bullies, who attack those most unlikely to retaliate (Schwartz, Dodge, & Coie, 1993).

Four causes seem significant in the development of a bully:

- *Indifference* (usually by the mother) is a form of silent violence
- Parents who are *permissive* with an aggressive child
- Parents who typically resort to *physical punishment*
- A *temperamentally aggressive* child

Be alert for this type of behavior. Often teachers and parents are the last to know because the victim is reluctant to talk about it. Among Olweus's suggestions for dealing with bullies are the following:

- Supervise recreation periods more closely
- Intervene immediately to stop bullying
- Talk to both bully and victim privately and insist that if such behavior does not stop both school and parents will become involved
- If the problem persists, therapy may be needed

other; that is, one child may experience the environment quite differently than another.

Does anything distinguish delinquents from nondelinquents? What are some characteristics of children who become delinquent? Here are some possible clues. (Once again note the influence of biopsychosocial elements.)

- There may be something *genetic* at work; for example, both members of identical twin pairs are more likely to be involved in delinquency than nonidentical twins. (For an excellent and thorough analysis of the interaction of genes and the environment in the development of antisocial behavior, see Rutter, 1997.)

- *Males* are more prone to criminal behavior than females, and younger males are more likely to commit crimes at a higher rate than older males; age is a major factor in understanding criminal behavior (Regoli & Hewitt, 1991).

- *Attitudinally,* most children prone to behavior problems are hostile, defiant, resentful, suspicious, and resistant to authority (Regoli & Hewitt, 1991).

- *Psychologically,* delinquents are more interested in the concrete than the abstract and are generally poor problem solvers (Elliott & others, 1996).

- *Socioculturally,* delinquents are frequently reared in homes that offer little understanding, affection, stability, or moral clarity. For example, some parents frequently, although unconsciously, reinforce aggressive behavior in an effort to defuse an explosive situation. A mother may tell a child to do something; the child refuses and becomes aggressive toward the mother. The mother may then "back off" and the child's aggressive behavior has been positively reinforced. (See the discussion of reinforcement in chapter 2.)

These findings testify almost unerringly to the conclusion that the causes of antisocial behavior are multiple, complex, and interactive and that these interactions begin at an early age. The roots of violence may stretch as far back as infancy. For example, children who do not form bonds with anyone (see chapter 4) constitute one of the largest deviant populations in the country (Wilson, 1993). These children cannot form relationships; they describe their reactions to others as making "no connections."

The words of convicted serial killer Ted Bundy hang like icicles in the chilling world of those deprived of friends and relationships (Magid & McKelvey, 1987).

> **I didn't know what makes things tick. I didn't know what made people want to be friends. I didn't know what made people attractive to one another. I didn't know what underlay social interactions.**

Magid, K. & C. McKelvey (1987). *High risk: Children without a conscience.* New York: Bantam. An excellent, readable account of the development of violent children.

As the screeching headlines of our newspapers tell us, children are becoming more and more involved in serious crime and violence. Consequently, identifying the causes of such behavior and formulating the means to prevent it become more urgent. The task is difficult, expensive, and lengthy but well worth while to prevent violence from becoming an accepted part of children's lives.

Children and Impulse Control

For children to be successful in any of their endeavors and enjoy pleasant relationships with others, they must exercise restraint in deciding what to do, how to do it, what to say, and how to say it. In other words, controlling their impulses becomes an increasingly important feature in their lives.

Psychologists have found the study of **impulsivity** alluring, similar to standing at a window and peering into the depths of a child's personality. And what they see is not only revealing but has serious long-term developmental implications. (You may also have seen impulsivity referred to as a child's lack of ability to delay gratification or, of course, self-control.) Children who are reflective as opposed to impulsive seem destined to achieve at higher levels, attain greater emotional maturity, and gain appreciable personal popularity (Mischel & Mischel, 1983; Yuochi & others, 1993).

Impulsivity and Development

What do we know about impulsivity and the developmental path it follows? Like the tributaries of a river joining to form the major body, the streams of research into impulsivity converge on delay of gratification studies. Picture this setting: Children are placed in a position in which they are presented with something they enjoy—candies, toys—and told if they don't eat the candy or play with the toy until the researcher returns, they can have two pieces of candy or an even bigger toy. The researcher then leaves the room and observers watch the children through one-way mirrors. The results were as you would expect: Some children ate the candy immediately or played with the toy; others resisted by trying to distract themselves.

The truly amazing part of this work, however, was the follow-up research. The same children who displayed impulsivity at 4 years of age were the more troubled adolescents; they had fewer friends; they experienced more psychological difficulties such as lower self-esteem; they were more irritable and aggressive, and less able to cope with frustration. Whereas the 4-year-olds who delayed their gratification could better handle frustration, were more focused and calm when challenged by any obstacle, and were more self-reliant and popular as adolescents. The behavior of the 4-year-olds on delay of gratification tests predicted success in both elementary and secondary schools, and even turned out to be a powerful predictor of how they would do on their SATs (Mischel & Mischel, 1983).

Transformations

Parents can help children to develop self-control when they're young by urging them to think of other things. As they grow a little older, perhaps by first grade, a phenomenon called **transformation** appears; that is, they learn to think about what they shouldn't do in different terms. If they're instructed not to eat marshmallows, for example, they may think of the marshmallows as white clouds. From this time on, children do well at devising their own strategies as they become more competent with their growing cognitive abilities. In fact, research indicates that children exercise greater self-control when using strategies they have devised rather than using those suggested by adults.

Middle childhood youngsters will bring to their interactions with those outside of the family the characteristics that they formed within the family circle. With this in mind, let's turn now to the impact of peers on development.

Guided Review

1. Children begin to acquire a realistic sense of self by the _____ grade.
2. Harter's work attempted to link level of self-esteem with various types of _____.
3. Level of self-esteem is affected powerfully by what children think of their _____ _____.
4. The best predictor of future antisocial behavior is _____ _____.
5. The resistance to temptation studies are an example of a child's ability to control _____.

The Influence of Peers

Do you sometimes wonder if we exaggerate the influence of peers? If you have any doubts, here is an example of the far-reaching power of peer relations, one that should answer this question. In the 1940s, Anna Freud (Sigmund Freud's daughter) and Sophie Dann worked with six German-Jewish orphans whose parents had died in the Nazi gas chambers. The six children were together in a concentration camp for several years, enduring horrible conditions, with few adult contacts.

When the war ended, the children were taken to England to recover. It soon became clear to observers that although the children showed some effects of their ordeal—thumb-sucking, fearfulness, restlessness—they were strongly attached to each other, to the point where they would comfort each other if disturbed and become upset if separated. With the loving care that the children received over the next years, coupled with their continued relationships with their peers, they gradu-

During middle childhood, peer relationships become increasingly important for social development. Children are attracted to those who share their interests, who play well with them, and who help them to learn about themselves.

Answers

1. second 2. competence 3. physical appearance 4. past behavior 5. impulses

ally showed normal patterns of development, a moving example of the strength and significance of peer relationships (Freud & Dann, 1951).

We typically use the word **peer** to refer to youngsters who are similar in age, usually within 12 months of each other. But equal in age does not mean equal in everything, for example, intelligence, physical ability, or social skills. Also, research shows that many of a child's interactions are with those who are more than 12 months older, although we know little about the nature of these relationships (Berk, 1997).

With these cautions, we turn now to the influence of peers during middle childhood. (Here you may want to return briefly to chapter 5 and the analysis of relationships. We'll assume that you understand the basics of a relationship at this point.) When we turn to same-sex and mixed-sex interactions, we can summarize the obvious findings quickly. Children of all ages associate more frequently with members of their own sex. Why? Adults encourage such relationships. Children of the same sex also share more mutual interests, and gender-role stereotypes operate powerfully to reinforce same-sex relationships.

Children's Friendships

Middle childhood youngsters, with the abilities that we have traced, can reach logical conclusions about their **friends.** Children of this age search for friends who are psychologically compatible with them. For example, does Jimmy share my interests? Does he want to do the same things I do? Children begin to realize, especially toward the end of the middle childhood period, that friends must adapt to each other's needs.

As Hartup (1996, p. 10) has noted:

> Supportive relationships between socially skilled individuals appear to be developmental advantages, whereas coercive and conflict-ridden relationships are developmental disadvantages, especially among anti-social children.

Loneliness

Children who feel rejected by their peers frequently are plagued by problems. For example, in studying 452 children aged 5 to 7, Cassidy and Asher (1992) found that children who believed that they had few friends were troubled by feelings of loneliness. Even the younger children in the study recognized that they had peer relationship problems and experienced unhappiness with their rejection. This study, with its focus on loneliness, testifies to the significance of peer relations to normal social development. Yet reactions to peer rejection may differ. As Boivin and Hymel (1997, p. 135) stated:

> Withdrawn, rejected children view themselves negatively on a variety of dimensions and report greater loneliness, whereas aggressive rejected children are less likely to acknowledge their social difficulties and report less loneliness.

In a similar study, Parker and Asher (1993) analyzed the relationship between group acceptance and friendship and concluded that a problem with group acceptance doesn't necessarily doom the possibility of satisfactory friendships. The authors discovered that not all highly accepted children had close friends and that friendships had a more powerful impact on children's feelings of loneliness than did peer group acceptance. For example, children without best friends were more lonely than children with best friends regardless of how well accepted they were. Parker and Asher (1993) concluded that feelings of loneliness arise from several sources—poor acceptance by peers, lacking a friend, or having a friendship that fails to meet relationship needs—that either singly or in combination can seriously undermine children's feelings of well-being.

These findings were confirmed by Morison and Masten's (1991) longitudinal study of peer reputation as a predictor of later adaptation. Believing that the ability to get along with peers is a critical developmental task of middle childhood, these authors studied 207 third to sixth graders, and seven years later restudied 88 percent of the group. They found that peer reputation assessed in middle childhood was a significant predictor of adolescent adjustment. Disruptive, aggressive, sensitive, and isolated behavior during the early childhood years was associated with antisocial, incompetent behavior in adolescence.

Peers in Middle Childhood

Think of the world these children are now encountering. Physical and cognitive abilities enable them to move steadily, although slowly, toward others such as neighborhood friends. Upon entering school, they increase their contacts and begin to realize that other children have ideas that may differ from their own. How children react to these different opinions may reflect their own home conditions (Kerns, Klepac, & Cole, 1996). Cassidy and her colleagues (1992) discovered that children whose parents are warm, responsive, and consistent disciplinarians have children who are more competent with peers than children whose parents are harsh and rejecting or overly permissive.

Peers and School Entrance

The first day of school is stressful for youngsters. For most children, however, this upset to their psychological equilibrium passes and they adapt quickly.

With school entrance children's lives change dramatically as they move toward Erikson's goal of industry for middle childhood. Their interactions with others contain revealing clues about the path of their future social development. During these years some children still find it difficult to tear themselves away from their mothers and have considerable difficulty in relating to their peers. Where is the problem here, with the mother or the child?

In one of the schools we visited, we noticed the mother of a fifth grade boy walking him to school every day while holding his hand. We discovered that the boy, while not a problem in school, was having difficulty with the other boys in his class and tended to drift off by himself or play with younger children. How to reach the mother, of course, was the issue because the boy was doing fairly well in school and was causing no difficulties. The matter was resolved by having the teacher gently point out the growing independence of boys of this age and by having the mother become a "room mother," where she could see the typical behavior of fifth grade boys.

During these years, children discover they must get along with peers, which forces them to think about their relationships, a major step in social development (Cassidy & others, 1996). For example, their growing abilities enable them to make definite judgments about the behavior of their peers. They become more astute at detecting meaning in facial expressions and in the way something is said. Since teachers have now become a force to be reckoned with, children no longer may ignore the wishes and ideas of those around them.

The Importance of Communication

Middle childhood children are better able to communicate with one another and to use reinforcements from their peers to shape their own behavior. Because of their cognitive, language, and perspective-taking skills, they cooperate better with one another than younger children, and aggression decreases somewhat. The desire to conform now becomes increasingly more important, especially at the end of the period when the adolescent horizon beckons (Newcomb, Bukowski, & Pattee, 1993).

Parents and teachers can help children with their peer relations by identifying behaviors that other children dislike: aggressive, whining, dominant. By talking to children (asking them how other children react to this kind of behavior, asking them what they think they should do to change their behavior), adults can help children to improve their relationships and maintain their self-esteem and group acceptance.

Cognitive development also helps middle childhood youngsters to accept differences. For Piaget, one of the major obstacles to more mature thinking is egocentrism, which affects a child's social perspective-taking ability. With the decline of egocentrism during middle childhood, children gradually see that other points of view exist. This in itself is an important developmental phenomenon, one that Robert Selman (1980) has carefully explored.

Social Perspective Taking

In his efforts to clarify emerging interpersonal relationships, Selman has developed a theory of **social perspective-taking** levels that springs from a social cognitive developmental framework. Selman (1980) stated that you can't separate children's views on how to relate to others from their personal theories about the traits of others. Thus, children construct their own version of what it means to be a self or other.

As a result of careful investigations of children's interactions with others, and guided by such theorists as Piaget, Flavell, Mead, and Kohlberg, Selman has identified several levels of social perspective taking and noted that in the middle childhood years a youngster gradually realizes that other people are different and have ideas of their own. By the end of middle childhood, a youngster's views of a relationship include self, someone else, and the kind of relationship between them, and also the desire to conform becomes important, especially at the end of the period.

Given the increase in friends during the school years, we should examine the role of schooling itself. How does it influence the development of middle childhood youngsters?

One's friends are that part of the human race with which one can be human.
George Santayana

Guided Review

6. Children who are within 12 months of age of each other are called _____.
7. Equal in age does not mean equal in _____.
8. Children who believed they had few friends were troubled by feelings of _____.
9. Selman's theory is referred to as _____ _____ _____.
10. Children in middle childhood gradually come to see that other points of view exist due to diminishing _____.

Schools and Middle Childhood

Much is expected of our schools and, in spite of dramatic headlines, much has been accomplished. In the 27th Annual Phi Delta Kappa/Gallup Poll of the public's attitudes toward the public schools, parents rated the schools in their communities much higher than they rated the nation's schools, which suggests that the closer parents are to their children's schools, the more satisfied they are (Rose, 1995). A well-known educational commentator, Albert Shanker (1995), stated that the number of students taking math and science courses has risen dramatically, as has the number of students enrolled in foreign language classes.

Scores on National Assessment of Educational Progress exams show an equally dramatic and encouraging rise. The positive signs just mentioned, however, can't be

Answers

6. peers 7. everything 8. loneliness 9. social perspective taking 10. egocentrism

Our schools should develop the reasoning faculties of our youth, enlarge their minds, cultivate their morals, and instill in them percepts of virtue and order.
Thomas Jefferson

allowed to mask the reality of what still needs to be accomplished. Problems remain, but progress continues. Unfortunately, defective schools do indeed exist, which is a tragedy given the influence schools have on children's development.

Are Schools Really That Important?

The question facing us, however, is: Do schools affect development during these years? Michael Rutter, an internationally respected researcher of children's issues, in a massive and meticulously conducted study of school effectiveness, found startling differences between schools in their impact on children (1983). His data led to several conclusions.

- Children are more likely to show good behavior and good scholastic achievement if they attend some schools rather than others.

- Differences between the schools are not due to the size or age of the buildings or the space available.

- Differences between the schools are due to a school's emphasis on academic success, teacher expectations of student success, time-on-task, skillful use of rewards and punishment, teachers who provide a comfortable and warm classroom environment, and teachers who insist on student responsibility for their behavior.

These criteria graphically demonstrate that *good instructional leadership* is critical, which means that principals, teachers, students, and parents agree on goals, methods, and content. Home-school cooperation supports good leadership, which in turn produces *an orderly environment* that fosters desirable discipline, academic success, and personal fulfillment. When teachers *sense the support of parents and administrators,* they intuitively respond in a manner that promotes student achievement and adjustment, encourages collegiality among teachers, and produces a warm, yet exciting atmosphere.

School is an important milestone for all aspects of development. Children must learn to respond appropriately to authority outside of the family and to get along with peers. It is an important part of psychosocial as well as cognitive development.

The Role of Teachers

Let's not forget the critical role of teachers. Reflecting on several outstanding teachers that he had in school, Ernest Boyer (1990), a well-known critic of American education, stated that several characteristics make teachers great.

- They employ language clearly and efficiently, an important observation because words swirl around classrooms in an almost unending current. If teachers present their ideas in colorful, exciting writing, and express themselves precisely in their oral language, students have superb models from which to learn. These teachers talk to their students, not at them.

- Well-informed teachers who are comfortable with the history and frontiers of their disciplines provide students not only with facts but also with a way of

---

Poverty, Culture, and Education

In his biting commentary on current conditions in America's schools, Kozol (1991) drew some vivid comparisons. In schools populated with children of the poor, students are crowded into small, squalid spaces, and in some cities overcrowding is so bad that some schools function in abandoned factories. Students eat their lunches in what was previously the building's boiler room. Reading classes are taught in what used to be a bathroom; science classes have no microscopes; one counselor serves 3,600 students in the elementary grades. In the high school of this district, a single physics section exists for 2,200 students; two classes are being taught simultaneously in one classroom.

As an example of these kinds of schools, listen to Kozol's words.

> The city was so poor there had been no garbage pickup for four years....On the edge of the city is a large chemical plant. There is also a very large toxic waste incinerator, as well as a huge sewage treatment plant. . . . The city has one of the highest rates of infant mortality in Illinois, the highest rate of fetal death, and also a very high rate of childhood asthma.
>
> The schools, not surprisingly, are impoverished. . . . The entire school system had been shut down after being flooded with sewage from the city's antique sewage system. "I did meet several wonderful teachers in the school, and I thought the principal of the school was excellent. The superintendent is also a very impressive person" (Kozol, 1991, p. 5).

A more affluent district in the same state presents a different picture. A greenhouse is available for students interested in horticulture; the physical sciences department offers 14 courses; there are 18 biology electives. The school's orchestra has traveled to the former Soviet Union. Beautifully carpeted hallways encourage students to sit and study; computers are everywhere. The ratio of counselors to students is 1 to 150. Parents of these students recently raised money to send the school choral group to Vi-

enna. Given these different conditions, is it any wonder that different educational outcomes are inevitable?

If, as frequently described, the school is a middle-class institution staffed mainly by white middle-class teachers, then students from different social classes immediately begin their schooling at a disadvantage (Hetherington & Parke, 1993). From everything we have said, you can understand that middle-class teachers can be expected to have different values and expectations than their economically deprived students.

These conditions can either be improved or made worse by the family's belief in education. As Garbarino and Benn noted (1992), parents may not be present in the classroom but they have a profound influence on the ways their children view school and learning. The extent to which the family supports the school's objectives directly affects their child's academic performance. Too often low parental expectations for their children reflect the parents' own educational experiences. If parents had encountered difficulties in school, they may exercise a negative impact on their children's attitudes, expectations, and performance. The reverse also holds true.

These conclusions are particularly significant for immigrant students.

> Individual children have individual histories and inner struggles as they wrestle with the changes in their lives. Their development began in another country; their lives were first attuned to a different culture (Igoa, 1995).

Frequently coming from crushing poverty, their backgrounds can be almost impossible for American teachers to understand. The economic hardships these immigrants previously lived with may continue here and they undoubtedly face a bleak economic future in the United States, especially when we realize minorities reach the poverty level at an ever-increasing rate. These facts point to an inescapable conclusion: Our schools must be as good as possible because they frequently are the only escape routes from poverty, crime, and violence.

thinking that serves them well in a complex world. For example, the science teacher who presents basic genetic facts and then goes on to show how this knowledge can lead to the future cure of serious diseases, breathes real life into what may seem to students as remote, abstract facts.

- Finally, as Boyer emphasized, effective teachers relate what they know to their learners so that students become aware of the beauty, the power, and the application of knowledge.

Given the physical, cognitive, and social changes that occur in children of these years, it's only reasonable to expect schools to play a decisive role. Let's first examine several of the academic issues that affect children in our schools.

Middle Childhood and Educational Change

As children pass through the elementary grades, they no longer satisfy society's needs by playing happily and behaving nicely. Now they face challenges to achieve and, like it or not, they face daily competition. They not only experience steady developmental changes, they also encounter constant subject matter change. It's almost as if knowledge that had been forced below a level of consciousness has burst through restraining barriers, and, as if to make up for lost time, has exploded before their eyes. Children, in the midst of all these discoveries, have a unique opportunity to acquire learning that will shape their future as never before. Interestingly, recent studies of children in Los Angeles, Tokyo, East and West Berlin, Moscow, and Prague have shown that children, across cultures, have similar developmental patterns in their beliefs about the importance of effort, ability, luck, teachers, and unknown causes as explanations of school success (Little & Lopez, 1997).

Reading

A topic that seems to have parents and educators in a constant state of crisis, the teaching of reading, has probably attracted more speculation, research, attacks, and apparent "breakthroughs" than any other school subject. No one questions its primacy in school, or, indeed, its critical function in a child's adjustment to a technological society. Alas, heat, more than light, surrounds the question: What is the best technique that will produce the best results for children

The Whole Language Controversy

What should you know about reading? In a widely read report, *Becoming a Nation of Readers,* reading was compared to the performance of a symphony orchestra. Like the performance of a symphony, reading is a holistic act. In other words, although reading can be analyzed into subskills such as discriminating letters and identifying words, performing the subskills one at a time does not constitute reading. Reading, like a superb orchestra, functions effortlessly and at a superior level only when the parts come together in a smooth, integrated performance. For the members of an orchestra, repeated practice assures a desirable performance, while good reading likewise comes from repetition over long periods of time.

As an example of how controversy attaches itself to the teaching of reading, consider the whole language technique, which we discussed in chapter 7. Furiously attacked by its opponents and passionately defended by its adherents, whole language has rekindled the fires of controversy that seem to be always smoldering beneath the surface of "reading methods." In whole language, meaning comes first. Children are not taught phonics in isolation; they learn to read by obtaining the meanings of words from context, with phonics introduced as needed. For example, if while reading a story, a child has difficulty with the word *dish,* the child stops and sounds it out. Children don't use basal readers; they read appropriate-level literature about themes that interest them; they then write about these ideas.

To help children with their reading parents should be good models. Children should see them reading and enjoying it, which will spur them on to learn as quickly as possible. Next, both parents and teachers should read to children; they love it, and it makes them even more eager to learn how to access these funny, exciting stories. Finally, parents should listen, attentively, to their children read and stop them occasionally at strategic points and ask them to explain what's happening.

Mathematics

American students have repeatedly scored poorly on international mathematics tests. A recent report of the *Third International Mathematics and Science Study* of 26 countries showed that although American children were doing well in science, they ranked 10th at the third grade level and 12th at the fourth grade level. Few gender differences were discovered. Singapore and South Korea are the top-ranked countries in mathematics at the third and fourth grade levels (Sullivan, 1997). These finding are consistently replicated in other studies (Geary & others, 1996).

As you can imagine, another wave of publicity about revising the mathematics curriculum followed the release of these tests results, which is nothing new. The "new math" of the 1960s was not an unqualified success chiefly because public school teachers and parents had little to say about its implementation. Parents, particularly, were upset because no one bothered to explain to them why it wasn't important, apparently, that Johnny didn't know that $9 \times 7 = 63$. A few years later, unhappiness with these new techniques produced the "back-to-basics" movement. Today's emphasis is less on skills for their own sake and more on thinking about and understanding the meaning of numbers by manipulating mathematical concepts.

Parental Involvement

The public's persistent problem with mathematics has been well documented and needs no additional comment here, except to say it's well founded. For example, some children experience problems with numbers in preschool and develop anxieties, even phobias, about mathematics that remain with them for a lifetime. Still other children are counting, adding, and "taking away" by 3 years of age. How do we explain these differences? Involved parents seem to make a major difference here—alertly seeing that a child is having trouble in math, taking the time to be with the child, and helping within the framework that the teacher has established. Children can stumble mathematically quite easily early in life, and if no one is there to pick up the mathematical pieces, the stumble can turn into a lifelong feeling of numerical inadequacy.

The National Council of Teachers of Mathematics (NCTM) (1989) has identified the basic goal of mathematics instruction as teaching math to all students in a way that produces an understanding of mathematical concepts, which also increases children's confidence in their ability to use math. In other words, learning math is doing math. What students learn depends on how they learn it. By asking their children to apply what they have learned in school to an everyday situation, parents emphasize the importance of mathematics, which seems to be a cross-cultural phenomenon (Guberman, 1996).

Science

Project 2061—a committee for constructing goals for science, mathematics, and technology education—identified what students need to achieve scientific literacy. In its first publication, *Science for All Americans* (Hoffman & Stage, 1993), readers were bluntly told that classroom science should be essential, enduring, and learnable; that is, science is an exciting and esteemed subject that all students should be able to master and use.

In the report just mentioned, the *Third International Mathematics and Science Study,* American children were well above the international average, third at both the third and fourth grade levels (Sullivan, 1997). *But, for science, boys significantly outperformed girls at the eighth grade level,* which reflects the major gender concerns discussed in chapter 8.

An Applied View

Translating Knowledge Into Practice

One of the best illustrations of how scientists think and how the great scientists shift their thinking from the highly technical to the practical, applies to the Nobel Prize winner, Richard Feynman (Gleick, 1992). Admittedly a genius, Feynman showed his abilities early in life. Fascinated by mathematics and an inveterate tinkerer, as a boy of 10 or 11 years he designed his own radios, invented a burglar alarm for his house, and invented a gadget for rocking his sister's cradle. He taught himself the tricks of mental arithmetic and speculated about the possibility of using atomic power for rockets. Even while deeply immersed in the atomic bomb project, Feynman, always intrigued by puzzles, taught himself how to pick locks, open safes, and infuriate his colleagues.

But it was the Challenger disaster and Feynman's ability to convert the highly technical to the readily understandable that demonstrated the utility of scientific thinking. If you recall, considerable speculation had centered on the O-rings that were designed to keep gases from escaping from the rocket. Feynman believed that at low temperatures (32 degrees) the O-rings would become brittle and permit gases to escape with disastrous consequences.

Appointed a member of the committee to uncover what had caused the tragedy, Feynman became disgusted by the bureaucratic thinking that was gripping the committee. To dramatize his ideas, on the morning of one of the hearings, he rose early, found a taxi, and cruised Washington, searching for a hardware store that would be open. He bought a C-clamp and a pair of pliers. When the hearing began, he asked for a glass of ice water and dropped a piece of O-ring into the glass. Onlookers immediately detected changes in the O-ring, changes that made failure of the critical seals inevitable. Feynman's simple experiment demonstrated scientific thinking at its best, the translation of theory into action.

You're probably saying to yourself that's fine for a Nobel prize winner, but in grade school? The answer is yes. Good science instructors will teach children to think in a similar manner: Don't be satisfied with the obvious. Do other, better solutions exist? What steps do I take for answers? Remember, it's not the subject matter that's important; it's the way of thinking. Disturbed by estimates that fewer than 10 percent of high school graduates have the skills necessary to perform satisfactorily in college-level science courses, science teachers today are using a more "hands-on" approach to their teaching. Instead of having students memorize lengthy formulas, they have them doing experiments starting in the early grades.

Guided Review

11. Parents' opinions about their children's schools differ from their opinions about the _____ schools.
12. A massive study showing that schools do indeed make a difference in children's development was conducted by _____ _____.
13. A recent controversial method of teaching reading is called the _____ _____ method.
14. Teaching mathematics today focuses on teaching students how to _____ math.
15. Teaching science today requires teachers to be at the _____ of their subject.

Effective science teachers, at all levels, guide their students through a logical progression of steps, from basic knowledge to solving scientific problems. Consequently, teachers must know not only the fundamentals of their subject but also be aware of the frontiers of discovery. Good teachers make science come alive before children's eyes. Not only will students experience the exhilaration of solving problems themselves, they also will learn to transfer these skills to problems they encounter outside the classroom. Their thinking becomes scientific; that is, they exercise care and precision when faced with a challenge.

You may argue that there's nothing new in this technique; good teachers have been doing it for years. There are differences, however. Where this approach has

The Extent of Television Watching

For an idea of the role that television plays in our society, try to answer these questions, which have been drawn from several national surveys:

1. What percentage of American homes have a TV set?
2. How long (on the average) is the set on per day?
3. By age 85, how many years of television has the average viewer seen?
4. How many hours of TV does the average viewer watch per week?
5. By age 18, a student has watched how many hours of TV?
6. By age 15, how many killings has a child seen on television?
7. Is there evidence that television influence a child's behavior?

If you had any doubts about the extent of television viewing, these figures should dispel them.

6. 13,000 killings 7. yes

1. 99 2. 7 hours 3. 9 years 4. 28 hours 5. 15,000 hours

been successful, teachers have acted as facilitators, not directors. Teachers are not forced to teach a specific amount of material; in a sense, teaching less can result in teaching more. That is, by teaching generalizable problem-solving strategies along with the concepts of basic subject matter, and by emphasizing that learners should know themselves, teachers can prepare students for a lifetime of learning. Also, these school systems have been totally committed to scientific discovery from the elementary grades through high school.

Television and Development

Do you have a television set in your home? Did you laugh at what appears to be a ridiculous question? You probably have at least one, more likely two or three. When you consider that American homes have at least one set and realize the colorful appeal of TV, you can better understand why television has become the school's great competition (Comstock, 1993).

Television has become one of the great means of socialization in a child's life. As such, and recognizing the relationship between program content and a child's age, adults should be particularly careful in what children watch.

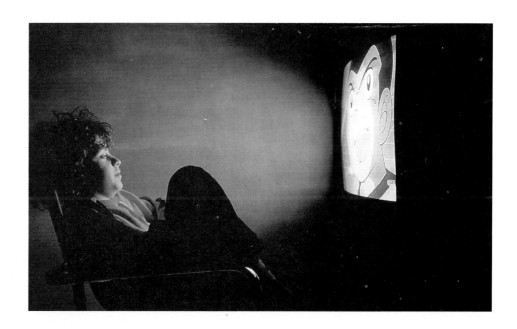

In the Surgeon General's report on television viewing, *Television and Behavior: Ten Years of Scientific Progress and Implications for the Eighties* (1982), one of the questions asked was, who watches television? The answer was simple: almost everyone. Elementary school children watch at least four hours each day. Today television viewing may be the most frequently shared activity among family members (St. Peters & others, 1991).

The pattern of children's viewing tells us quite a bit about the "how much" and "what" of the shows they watch. Babies are briefly attracted by the color and sound of the shows; 2- and 3-year-olds watch longer and with some understanding; elementary school children watch for long periods. The beginning of school attendance slows the time spent watching, but at about age 8 the rate increases dramatically; and teenagers spend less time watching television. What is particularly interesting is the match between children's ages and program content. For example, Comstock and Paik (1991) report that the popularity of *Sesame Street* declined between the ages of 3 to 5 (from 30 percent to 13 percent). *The Flintstones* rose in popularity in these same years, from 11 percent to 36 percent. Are there developmental effects from all this viewing?

Television and Cognitive Development

The moment we concede that children learn from watching television, certain questions arise:

- How active are children in the process?

- To what do they attend?

- How much do they understand?

- How much do they remember?

Answering these questions gives us insight into how TV watching and cognitive development are associated. For example, when you studied Piaget's work, especially his views on operations, you saw how he insisted that children were active participants in their cognitive development. They actively construct their cognitive world.

Cognitive theorists, reflecting Piaget's views, believe that children understand what they see according to their level of cognitive development. The cognitive structures that children form can be altered by what they see on television. Children attend to what they see; they learn from what they see; and they remember what they see. They can also apply these new ideas in new settings.

The same is true of their TV watching. They bring a unique set of cognitive structures to the TV set, structures that reflect their level of cognitive development. Remember what we said about middle childhood youngsters: attention span lengthens, memory improves, and comprehension increases. Children don't drop these abilities when they watch TV; they apply them to what they are seeing (Liebert, Sprafkin, & Davidson, 1988). Specifically, we know that:

- *Children remember what is said,* even when they are not looking at the screen. Auditory attention is also at work (voices, sound changes, laughing, and applause).

- *The amount of time spent looking at the set is directly related to age.* By age 4, children attend to TV about 55 percent of the time, even when there are many other distractions in the room (Comstock, 1993).

- *Specific features of programs attract children:* women, movement, and camera angles; they look away during stills and animal shots (Wright & others, 1994).

- *Children quickly learn to relate sound to sight:* chase music means a chase scene (Wright & others, 1994). (Note the ideal combination of auditory and visual effects that produces powerful attractions.)

- *Comprehension depends on age and experience* (Comstock & Paik, 1991). To understand television, children need three accomplishments. First, they must know something about story form—how stories are constructed and understood. Second, they must have world knowledge or general knowledge about situations and events in order to grasp television's content. Finally, they must have knowledge of television's forms and conventions to help them understand what is happening on the screen. Music, visual techniques, and camera angles all convey information.

Consideration of these three requirements helps to put children's viewing in perspective: They simply lack the maturity and experience to grasp fully much of what they are watching. For example, children have the perceptual skills to see and recognize a car moving away. But then the camera may cut to another scene (the sky, a police officer, or the corner of a house). The significance of the cut introduces another theme, embedded in the story, that completely eludes youngsters.

We can conclude, then, that much of what children see on television is not just content. They also learn TV's codes: sound effects, camera techniques, and program organization. Some researchers believe that changes in children's behavior following the viewing of televised violence come from their responding to fast action, loud music, and camera tricks (Clifford & others, 1995).

Children understand television programs according to their level of development, and their level of development is affected by their television viewing. For example, in a study of 261 subjects age 5 and 7, Wright and his colleagues (1994) found that the older children better understood that the fictional characters in the shows they watched differed from the way they acted in real life, a finding that supports Piaget's conclusions about the concrete operational period. Let's turn our attention now to different explanations of how children interpret what they see on television.

Liebert, R. & Sprafkin, J. (1988). *The early window,* 3d ed. New York: Pergamon. This paperback is one of the best single sources on the impact of television on our society today. Once you read this, you'll understand why TV is considered a major socializing force in a child's life.

Television's Impact: By Understanding or Modeling?

We have repeatedly noted how different theorists (especially the major theorists discussed in chapter 2) can interpret the same data differently. Television violence is a good example. Because we have discussed cognitive theory in detail, let's turn to the behaviorists.

Behaviorists, especially in the social learning theory of Bandura (1986, 1997), offer a different interpretation. Bandura believes that considerable evidence exists to show that learning can occur by observing others, even when the observer doesn't reproduce the model's responses. Referring to this as **observational learning,** Bandura states that the information we obtain from observing other things, events, and people influences the way we act.

In a series of experiments beginning in 1963 (Bandura, Ross, & Ross, 1963), Bandura conducted a now-famous experiment (discussed earlier in chapter 2). Preschool children observed a model displaying aggression toward an inflated doll under three conditions: In one situation the children saw a film of a human model being aggressive toward the doll. In the next, children witnessed filmed cartoon aggression. Finally, live models exhibited the identical aggressive behavior. The results: Later, all children exhibited more aggression than youngsters in a control group!

Television and Violence

In 1977 Ronny Zamora, a 15-year-old, shot and killed the 82-year-old woman who lived next door to him in Florida. Not guilty, pleaded his lawyer, Ellis Rubin, by reason of the boy's having watched too much television. From watching television Ronny had become dangerously inured to violence (Stossel, 1997, p. 87).

Sound familiar? The staggering amount of television violence has led many to conclude that programming violence is at the heart of our alarming crime rate. (In-

Figure 10.1

Incidents of Television Violence

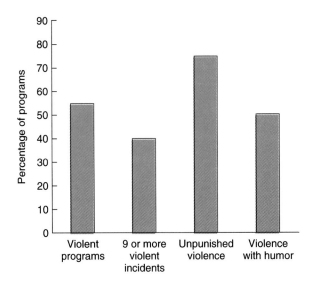

cidentally, Ronny's lawyer didn't sway the jury; Ronny was convicted of first-degree murder.)

Although research and theory point to television's role in **aggressive behavior,** almost total agreement exists that television is *a* cause, not *the* cause of aggressive behavior (Comstock & Paik, 1991). Nevertheless, after decades of research, we can safely conclude that televised violence may cause aggressive behavior in the children who observe it (Comstock & Paik, 1994). Are children exposed to much television violence? Figure 10.1 leaves little doubt as to the answer (adapted from Berk, 1997).

Remember that almost every American home has at least one television set, which children watch for many hours each day. Recall also that much of television's programming contains violence as a common feature. A survey by the *Center for Media and Public Affairs* of one day's programming (on April 7, 1994) tallied 2605 violent acts shown on TV that day (Stossel, 1997).

Consequently, we cannot ignore the possible long-term negative effects of violence on TV, particularly when you realize the power of observational learning (Crick, 1996). Most children watch television with few, if any, parental restrictions. (Our concern here is with middle childhood youngsters who tend to watch adult shows.) As Barry (1993, p. 42) noted:

> The discouraging point made in these studies is that, despite the massive research evidence of screen violence as a direct contributing factor to America's homicide rate, the screen violence level continues to rise.

Television and Prosocial Behavior

There is another side to television's role in development, however, and that is in its potential for the development of **prosocial behavior.** Nancy Eisenberg (1992), who has done so much to further our thinking about this important topic, has defined prosocial behavior as voluntary behavior intended to benefit others (such as helping, sharing, and comforting). Prosocial behavior, although it may have an ulterior motive (such as rewards or approval), may also include elements of altruistic behavior, that is, behavior motivated by sympathy for others (Eisenberg & others, 1996).

Many socialization techniques are designed to promote prosocial behavior (Grusec, 1996) and television, as one of the most powerful of these techniques, has the potential for encouraging this type of behavior. As Eisenberg (1992, p. 129) noted:

Clearly, television can be a negative influence on children; but can it also be a positive influence? If children model and learn from violent television shows and movies, they would be expected to learn positive behaviors and values from shows depicting helpfulness, generosity, cooperation, self-sacrifice, and the like. Recent studies suggest that the media can be used to foster development, although the effects of viewing prosocial television programming appear to be somewhat weaker than the effects of viewing violent programming.

Can the American public force television producers to decrease the level of violence in their programming, a level that slowly but steadily seems to be increasing? Or should we rely on the "V-chip," that ingenious little package that enables parents to program out shows that are too violent or sexual? Can we increase the number of shows dramatizing prosocial behavior? For many reasons, ranging from the appeal of violence to issues of free speech, these are difficult questions to answer. But all responsible adults can take one step with far-reaching consequences: Be alert to what children are watching, because television affects development.

Guided Review

16. When children watch television, they are usually _____ involved in the program.
17. Bandura's belief that learning can occur by watching others is called _____ _____.
18. Children's comprehension of a television program depends on _____ and _____.
19. In spite of all the studies, the level of _____ _____ continiues to rise.

Stress in Childhood

As youngsters of this age spend more of their time away from home, new contacts and new tasks can upset them. There is no escape; we all have faced similar circumstances. Were we scarred for life by these encounters? Probably not. Yet for some children, an inability to cope with **stress** has serious consequences, and today we are more alert to the signs of childhood stress.

But first, let's link what is known about childhood stress to development. We begin by admitting that no definition of stress exists that everyone agrees with. Let's use this definition: *Stress is anything that upsets our equilibrium—both psychological and physiological.*

Types of Stress

When each of us faces stress, we react differently. To begin with, not all of us would agree on what stress is. For example, some people are probably terrified of flying, whereas others see it as a pleasant, relaxing adventure. Table 10.1, based on Brenner's excellent and practical work (1984), summarizes specific childhood stressors.

Although many reasons help to explain these different responses, we can isolate several important individual differences.

Answers

16. actively 17. observational learning 18. age, experience 19. screen violence

TABLE 10.1 SPECIFIC CHILDHOOD STRESSORS	
Type	**Example**
Two-parent families	Changes associated with normal growth: new siblings, sibling disputes, moving, school, working parents
One-parent families	Multiple adults, lack of sex-role model, mother vs. father
Multiparent families	New relationships, living in two households
Death, adoption	Parental death, sibling death, possible institutional placement, relationships with different adults
Temporary separation	Hospitalization, health care, military service
Divorce	Troubled days before the divorce, separation, the divorce itself
Abuse	Parental, sibling, institutional; sexual, physical, emotional
Neglect	Physical (food, clothes), emotional (no response to children's needs for attention and affection)
Alcoholism	Secrecy, responsibility for alcoholic parent, suppress own feelings

Why Children React Differently To Stress

Stress, regardless of the source, produces a variety of reactions. Think of your own childhood when your parents were really angry with you. How did you react? Some children react in the same way to anything stressful, either with high anxiety, fear, avoidance, weakness, or even vomiting. Others rationalize that they'll do better next time and get on with their lives. Still others aren't bothered at all; they mentally shrug and say to themselves, "They'll (the parents) get over it." Although we could list many reasons for these varied responses, several important individual differences are at work.

Sex

Whether it's temporary separation, divorce, or hospitalization, boys are more vulnerable to stressful events in their lives. Boys are more likely to be exposed to the conversations and tensions surrounding separation, divorce, or illness, or any other stressor, whereas parents frequently try to shelter girls from as much unpleasantness as possible. Also parents may not be as sympathetic to the signs of a boy's distress as they are to a girl's.

> Boys tend to react more adversely to some types of psychosocial stress and adversity than do girls. The increased vulnerability of males does not apply to all situations, however. For example, it has not been found in relation to institutional rearing or head injury. This suggests that, although to some extent males may be generally psychologically more vulnerable than females, in parallel with their greater physiological vulnerability, it is most unlikely to constitute the whole explanation. (Rutter, 1996)

Once again, however, let's not forget the role of individual differences. Children with different temperaments act differently in similar situations. The history of these children with their parents is different, their interactions with their parents are different, and the events following the stressful situation (divorce, death, separation) are different. This is a good example of the problems researchers face as they attempt to penetrate the maze surrounding childhood stress and try to discover the psychological mechanisms at work.

Age

Children of different ages respond differently to distress. Below the age of 6 months, they simply don't have the cognitive capacity to recognize the various types of stress.

During the early childhood years (age 2 to 6), children don't really understand what's happening and tend to blame themselves for any problems. They don't have the cognitive ability to fully appreciate what's going on around them (it's my fault mommy and daddy are fighting), and also because of the intensity of their growing attachment (usually with their mothers).

Starting at about 6 years children begin to understand the circumstances surrounding them. For example, they realize their mother's hospitalization is only a temporary separation and not a sign of rejection or abandonment. Although middle childhood youngsters (about age 7 to 11) face more stressful situations than younger children, they have learned better ways to cope. They think more logically, they usually have mastered varied problem-solving strategies, they make their own decisions, and they plan ahead. All of these abilities help to combat stress, but don't completely eradicate all memories and effects of the stress they may have experienced.

As they move away from sole dependence on parents, peers begin to form a strong supportive network, especially toward the end of middle childhood. If children have good relationships with their parents, they'll recognize parents as authority figures, which gives them a sense of security, an effective buffer against stress. These emerging strengths, coupled with appropriate support, help children to adjust and move on with their lives.

At this point, why don't you re-read the basics of Piaget's preoperational period in chapter 7 to refresh your memory about children's thinking? If you recall, one of the limitations on children's thinking during the years from 2 to 6 was the struggle to eliminate the effects of their mental egocentrism, that tendency to center everything on themselves. For example, when parents decide to divorce, youngsters of this age may blame themselves. "Daddy's leaving because he thinks I wasn't nice to him the other day." "If I were nicer, Mommy and Daddy wouldn't fight."

So on the one hand, you see the stress caused by self-blame, and on the other, the tension aroused by not understanding the reasons for parents' battling. During infancy (birth to 2 years) it's usually not a problem, while older children (above 6 years) attempt to rationalize what's going on around them.

Temperament

Recall that children are all born with unique **temperaments,** differences that affect the way they interact with the environment. Consequently, their temperament influences the intensity of their reactions after a stressful event, such as parental separation. Kagan (1994, p. xix) has studied differences in temperament in children for many years and has attempted to identify the roots of the differences we're discussing.

> About one in five healthy Caucasian infants reacts to stimulation with vigorous motor activity and distress, and about two-thirds of these highly reactive four-month-olds become inhibited children. About two of every five infants inherit a bias that favors a relaxed, minimally distressed reaction to stimulation, and two-thirds of these become uninhibited in the second year.

In other words, there seem to be inborn temperamental differences that influence children through the later years, and probably for life. These are but a few of the many factors that help to explain different reactions to stress. But what can we say about their developmental effects?

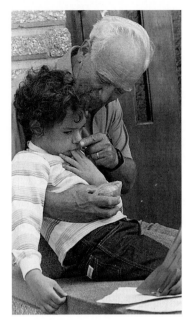

Children need emotional support from those in their environment. Even under the most difficult circumstances (divorce, death of a parent, hospitalization), the presence of a "significant other" can help a child to cope, to deal with stress in an appropriate manner for the child's developmental level.

Courage is the price life exacts for granting peace.
Amelia Earhart

Developmental Effects of Stress

If we attempt to link development and vulnerability to stress, we reach certain conclusions. For example, Maccoby (1988) notes that we can't be upset by events whose power to harm us we don't understand. We cannot be humiliated by failure to handle problems whose solutions are someone else's responsibility. Maccoby compares why some events are stressful and others are not and formulates several hypotheses. First, *age changes alone don't explain vulnerability.* Although the events that cause stress change with age, we all experience periods of stabilization and destabilization. In other words, we may be more vulnerable to change at certain times (e.g., we may react emotionally to bad news if we have been quite sick, a biopsychosocial reaction).

Second, *the environment can lessen vulnerability.* Youngsters can handle stress better if all other parts of their lives are stable. For example, entering school is stressful for almost all children. Home conditions that are warm and supportive help to ease what can be a difficult transition. But if parents have separated during these days, children can find school entrance quite painful. The environment—family, school, and friends—usually are pillars of support, but can also be major sources of stress for some children.

Next, *although middle childhood youngsters face more stressful situations than younger children, they have learned better ways to cope.* Their growing cognitive maturity enables them to reason more effectively. Finally, *with their growing cognitive ability,* children of this age begin to develop coping skills that help them to combat stress. Think of our discussion of this growing cognitive capacity: the ability to think abstractly, solve problems, reach decisions, and to plan ahead. All of these abilities help them to combat stress.

Let's focus now on one of the stressors we've mentioned—abuse—which, unfortunately, has become a major problem in modern society.

Abused Children

Most people consider the United States to be a nation of child lovers; thus, discussing **child abuse** always comes as a shock. Before we begin to discuss this topic, we should agree on what is meant by the term. Six major types of abuse are commonly identified: physical abuse, sexual abuse, emotional abuse, physical neglect, emotional neglect, and educational neglect (Jackson & Nuttall, 1997).

Child abuse has always been with us, but it has only been a matter of public awareness for the past quarter-century. Abuse still remains an elusive subject that defies precise definition because of its many forms. Physical and sexual abuses that leave evidence are easy to detect and describe (if they are reported), but other forms of abuse that emotionally wound youngsters are perhaps never detected. Professionals believe that abusive behavior involves direct harm (physical, sexual, deliberate malnutrition), intent to harm (which is difficult if not impossible to detect), and intent to harm even if injury does not result.

Another troublesome issue is that of incidence. Figures show tremendous variability. The actual data are only for reported cases and undoubtedly represent only the tip of the iceberg. The true extent of the problem may be staggering. For example:

- In 1995, more than 3 million cases of child abuse were reported, an increase of 100 percent since 1980.

- Estimates of national child abuse and neglect range from 35 percent to 53 percent of the child population.

- A 1995 state survey of child abuse indicated that 25 percent of reported abuse cases were due to physical abuse, 52 percent to neglect, 13 percent to sexual abuse, 5 percent to emotional abuse, and 17 percent other types.

- In 1995, over 1,000 children died from abuse or neglect. Ninety percent of these children were under age 5, and 50 percent were infants under age 1 (Hearings on the Child Abuse Prevention, Adoption, and Family Services Act, 1992).

The Nature of the Problem

Although child abuse is an age-old problem, not until recently did it become widely publicized. In the 1920s, Dr. John Caffey, studying bone fractures and other physical injuries, suggested that parents might have caused the injuries. The skepticism that greeted his conclusions prevented him from officially reporting his findings until the late 1940s. In 1961 C. Henry Kempe and his associates startled the annual meeting of the American Academy of Pediatrics by their dramatic description of the **battered child syndrome.**

Parental Characteristics

You may well ask: What kind of person could ever hurt a child? Although the parental characteristics leading to child abuse are not rigidly defined, several appear with surprising frequency. Here are some of the most frequently found characteristics (Rogosh & others, 1996):

- The parents themselves were abused as children.

- They are often loners.

- They refuse to recognize the seriousness of the child's conditions.

- They resist diagnostic studies.

- They believe in harsh punishment.

- They have unreasonable expectations for the child. (Children should never cry or drop things.)

- They lack control and are often immature and dependent.

- They feel personally incompetent.

A cycle of abuse becomes clear. The most consistent feature of the histories of abusive families is the repetition, from one generation to the next, of a pattern of abuse, neglect, and parental loss or deprivation. In each generation we find, in one form or another, a distortion of the relationship between parents and children that deprives children of the consistent love and care that would enable them to develop fully. Parents perceive the child as disappointing or unlovable, especially in times of stress and crisis. Finally, for most children, no lifeline exists; that is, no helpful sources can be accessed in times of crisis.

But what of the children themselves? Some observers believe that certain types of children are more prone to be abused than others. Remember: Children shape their parents as much as parents shape their children. If a child's actions or appearance irritate a parent predisposed to violence, then the results of the parent-child interaction may be preordained (which does not mean that the child is at fault).

Children as Victims

Children growing up in a hostile environment feel that to survive they must totally submit to their parents' wishes. They often exhibit continual staring and a passive acceptance of whatever happens. Only later, in a permissive setting does the pent-up fury explode, revealing the latent hostility. Abused children slowly develop complete distrust of others, which often translates into school problems.

When you consider the factors that may trigger abuse—parents, children themselves, poor family relations, socioeconomic conditions, lack of support—understanding the problem clearly requires considerable and careful research.

The Special Case of Sexual Abuse

Sexual abuse refers to any sexual activity between a child and an adult whether by consent or force. It includes fondling, penetration, oral-genital contact, intercourse, and the use of children in pornography. Estimates are that between 50,000 and 500,000 children are sexually abused each year (200,000 is the usual figure given, but these figures remain suspect because of the suspected enormous number of unreported cases). Most of the victims are female, but the number of male victims is on the rise (Burkhardt & Rotatori, 1995).

Abused children feel that they have lost control and are helpless when an adult sexually abuses them. All of their lives children have been taught to obey adults, so they feel forced to comply. This is particularly sensitive because most abusers are known to the family: a relative, friend, or some authority known to the children.

Effects of Sexual Abuse

What are the developmental effects of an adult's violation and betrayal of a child? Different ages seem to suffer different types of effects (Kendall-Tackett & others, 1993). For example, the highest rate of problems was found in the 7- to 13-year-old group. Forty percent of the abused children of this age showed serious disturbances; 17 percent of the 4- to 6-year-old group manifested some disturbance. About 50 percent of the 7- to 13-year-old group showed greatly elevated levels of anger and hostility compared with 15 percent of the 4- to 6-year-olds. Increase of anxiety, fear, and distress were common to all age groups.

Do adults who were sexually abused as children suffer long-term consequences? Among the possible effects are the following: depression (probably the most common finding), above normal levels of tension, aggression, a negative self-concept, and sexual problems, often becoming sexually promiscuous (Kendall-Tackett, 1993). Sexual abuse is a problem that every reader will find repugnant. Yet we can offer some positive conclusions. We are now better able to identify these children and provide help. Treatment techniques offer hope for the future. As the problem becomes more widely publicized, parents, teachers, and concerned adults are becoming more sensitive to the possibility of the occurrence of sexual abuse.

As we examine these children who have experienced severe stress, what can we learn from them that would benefit others? There are no guarantees of successful coping, for obvious reasons: the intensity of the stress, the immaturity of the children, and the amount of support they receive. Yet we also know that a small number of children seem oblivious to stress, at least for a time.

Resilient Children

The mother of three children was beset by mental problems. She refused to eat at home because she was sure someone was poisoning her. Her 12-year-old daughter developed the same fear. Her 10-year-old daughter would eat at home only if the father ate with her. Her 7-year-old son thought they were all crazy and always ate at home. The son went on to perform brilliantly in school and later in college and has now taken the first steps in what looks like a successful career. The older daughter is now diagnosed schizophrenic, whereas the younger girl seems to have adjusted after a troubled youth. How do we explain these different reactions?

First, understand what resilient means: These children have endured terrible circumstances and come through, not unscathed, but skilled at fending off feelings of inferiority, helplessness, and isolation. What we know about these children points to their ability to recover from either physiological or psychological trauma and return to a normal developmental path.

Identifying Resilient Children

Who are these resilient children who grow up in the most chaotic and adverse conditions, yet manage to thrive? Clues may be found in a remarkable long-term study conducted by Emmy Werner and Ruth Smith called *Overcoming the Odds* (1992). They studied all of the children (837) born on the island of Kauai in the year 1955. (Kauai is an island in the Hawaiian chain.) What's unusual about this study is that the authors studied 505 of these children from their prenatal days until they were 31–32 years of age. (The drop in numbers from the original 837 was due to some of the subjects dying, some moving to other islands or to mainland U.S.A.)

Of the 505 individuals followed over the 30+ year span, one in three was born with the odds stacked dramatically against them. They either experienced birth problems, grew up in poverty, or were members of dysfunctional families (desertion, divorce, alcoholism, mental illness). Two children out of three in this particularly vulnerable group encountered four or more risk factors before they were 2 years old and developed serious learning and/or behavior problems. *Nevertheless, one of three of these high-risk children developed into a competent, confident young adult by the age of 18.* What protective factors were at work in these children that let them overcome daunting adversity?

Characteristics of Resilient Children

Remember that the children we're focusing on here were battered by stressful events including desertion, divorce, discord, alcoholism, mental illness, neglect, and abuse. These conditions delivered a series of sledgehammer blows to their development, yet one of three of these children turned out to be a success in their personal and professional lives. They made good marriages, had happy families, and were good workers. What personal characteristics were at work here?

One way to answer this question is to search for the characteristics that mark the lives of resilient children.

- *They possess temperaments that elicit positive responses from those around them.* They are the easy children described in chapter 4: Eating and sleeping habits are quite regular; they show positive responses when people approached them; they adapt to changes in their environment. In spite of their suffering, they are friendly, likable children who possessed an inner quality that protects them from their hostile surroundings and enables them to reach out to an adult who could offer critical support.

- *Many of these children have a special interest or talent.* For example, some are excellent swimmers, dancers, and artists. Others have a special knack for working with animals. Still others show talent with numbers quite early. Whatever their interest, it served to absorb them and helped to shelter them from their environment. They use their talent to take advantage of the support systems available to them, whether in school, church programs, or community. These activities seem to provide the encouragement and stability often lacking in their home lives.

- *They are sufficiently intelligent to acquire good problem-solving skills,* which they then use to make the best of things around them; they attract the attention of helpful adults; they do well in school, where they are usually popular. Interestingly enough, their obvious competence elicits support from others, which produces a good sense of self. In turn, higher levels of self-esteem at age 18 produce individuals less inclined to have bouts of emotional disturbance at age 31–32. In other words, they use their abilities to adapt successfully to their circumstances.

- When children from troubled families (now the successful adults) recaptured the times when they were struggling and now linked them to their present happy circumstances, *they usually mention some person—grandparent, aunt, neighbor, teacher, religious figure, coach—who appeared on the scene in the nick of time.* The support, warmth, advice, and comfort offered by this friend-in-need and in-deed usually was crucial.

- *Children who are buffeted by events outside of the family, such as economic hardships, often find that one parent—frequently the mother—forms a tight bond with them.* Her behavior in accepting the hard times and doing everything she could to overcome crippling adversity sets a lasting example for her children. Here, as in everything else we've discussed, you can see the benefits and power of modeling.

Such characteristics—a genuinely warm, fairly easy-going personality, an absorbing interest, and the ability to seek out a sympathetic adult—help to distance them emotionally from a drugged, alcoholic, or abusive parent (sometimes a parent with all of these problems).

> The life stories of the resilient youngsters now grown into adulthood teach us that competence, confidence, and caring can flourish, even under adverse circumstances, if children encounter persons who provide them with the secure basis for the development of trust, autonomy, and initiative. From odds successfully overcome springs hope—a gift each of us can share with a child—at home, in the classroom, on the playground, or in the neighborhood. (Werner & Smith, 1992)

Table 10. 2 summarizes the characteristics of resilient children.

You will be both informed and encouraged by reading Werner, E. & Smith, R. (1992). *Overcoming the odds: High-risk children from birth to adulthood.* Ithaca, NY: Cornell University Press.

TABLE 10.2 CHARACTERISTICS OF RESILIENT CHILDREN

Age	Characteristics
At birth	Alert, attentive
1 year	Securely attached infant
2 years	Independent, slow to anger, tolerates frustration well
3–4 years	Cheerful, enthusiastic, works well with others
Childhood	Seems to be able to remove self from trouble, recovers rapidly from disturbance, confident, seems to have a good relationship with at least one adult
Adolescence	Assumes responsibilities, does well in school, may have part-time job, socially popular, is not impulsive

Guided Review

20. Anything that upsets our equilibrium, both psychological and physiological is known as _____.
21. The highest rate of problems resulting from sexual abuse was found in children aged _____ to _____.
22. _____, _____, and _____ are examples of external sources of stress.
23. Gender must be considered in responding to stress. _____ are more vulnerable to stress than _____.
24. Children who succeed under adverse conditions are called _____ children.

Answers

20. stress 21. 7, 13 22. Family, school, peers 23. Males, females 24. resilient

CONCLUSION

In this chapter, we followed middle childhood youngsters as they moved away from a sheltered home environment and into a world of new friends, new challenges, and new problems. Whether the task is adjusting to a new sibling, relating to peers and teachers, or coping with difficulties, youngsters of this age enter a different world.

But the timing of their entrance into this novel environment is intended to match their ability to adapt successfully, to master those skills that will prepare them for the next great developmental epoch, adolescence. From Tom Sawyer's subtlety to children learning to cope with stress, middle childhood youngsters require those skills that will enable them to deal with their widening social world.

Inevitably, though, they face times of turmoil, which, as we have seen, can come from internal or external sources. For some youngsters, these periods of stress are brief interludes; for others, there is no relief for years. Children cope uniquely using temperamental qualities and coping skills as best they can.

In summary:

The Changing Sense of Self

- The link between self-esteem and competence grows stronger during the middle childhood years.
- The development of self-control becomes a key element in a child's success, both cognitively and psychosocially.

The Influence of Peers

- During the middle childhood years, children begin to form close friendships.
- Children who have difficulty with their peers are often bothered by personal problems.
- Middle childhood youngsters learn to recognize the views of others.

Schools and Middle Childhood

- Children form and test social relations during these years.
- Children must learn to adjust to a wide variety of classmates, many of whom may be children of different cultures.
- School-age children are encountering considerable change in both curriculum and instructional methods.

Television and Development

- Television is the school's great competitor for children's time and attention.
- Some children spend more time watching television than they do in school-related activities.
- Controversy surrounds the issue of the effects of television violence.
- Television is also credited with the potential for encouraging prosocial behavior.

Stress in Childhood

- Children react differently to stress according to age, gender, and temperament.
- Some children, called resilient children, overcome the adverse effects of early stressors.
- Several theories have been proposed to explain how children become violent.
- Children acquire coping skills that enable them to adjust to stress in their lives.

KEY TERMS

Aggressive behavior
Battered child syndrome
Bullies
Child abuse
Competence
Friend
Impulsivity

Observational learning
Peer
Peer victimization
Prosocial behavior
Resilient children
Self-Control
Self-Esteem

Sexual abuse
Social perspective-taking
Stress
Temperament
Transformation

WHAT DO YOU THINK?

1. Recall Harter's studies investigating the association between self-esteem and physical appearance. Would you agree that the association was as strong as she found in her subjects? Could you make additional suggestions for helping children find other means of evaluating themselves?

2. It is generally accepted that friendships and groups become more important during the middle childhood years. With your knowledge of the developmental features of these years, do you think children of this age are ready for group membership?

3. For individuals to experience stress, they must understand the forces that are pressing on them. Do you think middle childhood youngsters are capable of such an interpretation of the events surrounding them?

4. Great concern exists today about the increasing rate of violence among children. Do you think the problem is as serious as the media indicate? From your knowledge of this topic, do you think the predictors of early criminal behavior are useful?

CHAPTER REVIEW TEST

1. Children who have similar levels of competence may have quite different levels of
   a. cognitive development.
   b. friendship.
   c. television viewing.
   d. self-esteem.

2. A peer is defined as one who is
   a. equal in intelligence.
   b. in the same grade.
   c. within 12 months of age.
   d. in a nearby house.

3. Which of the following differences between schools has little impact on children's development?
   a. Emphasis on academic success
   b. Teacher expectations
   c. Time-on-task
   d. Size of school

4. Impulse control at 4 years of age predicted
   a. the nature of interactions with siblings.
   b. future academic success.
   c. the health of the child.
   d. physical competence.

5. Friends provide certain resources for children that adults lack. Which of the following is *not* a resource provided by friends?
   a. Membership in the sibling underworld
   b. Opportunity for learning skills
   c. Chance to compare self with others
   d. Chance to belong to a group

6. Selman's theory of interpersonal relationships is known as
   a. observational learning.
   b. social perspective taking.
   c. linguistic interpretation.
   d. accommodation.

7. A critical factor in effective schools is
   a. condition of the school.
   b. recreational facilities.
   c. numbers of tenured teachers.
   d. good instructional leadership.

8. Which of the following is *not* a characteristic of good teaching?
   a. Gender of the instructor
   b. Efficient use of language
   c. Extensive knowledge of subject matter
   d. Good communication skills

9. The author of a scathing criticism of schools in low SES environments is
   a. Bruner.
   b. Skinner.
   c. Kozol.
   d. Deming.

10. Comprehension of the meaning of television programs depends on age and
    a. gender.
    b. exposure time.
    c. experience.
    d. parental guidance.

11. Which of the following is not a requirement for a child to be able to understand what they see on television?
    a. Must know something about story form
    b. Must have general knowledge about situations and events
    c. Must have knowledge about television forms and conventions
    d. Must be able to predict outcomes

12. Which of the following is not considered a severe stressor of childhood?
    a. Parental alcoholism
    b. School life
    c. Abuse
    d. Separation from parent

13. Child abusers often share parental characteristics. Which of the following is not such a characteristic?
    a. Perpetrator abused as a child
    b. Have unreasonable expectations for the child

c. Often immature and dependent
d. Low SES

14. There may be as many as _____ sexually abused children per year in the United States.
    a. 75,000
    b. 250,000
    c. 500,000
    d. 1,000,000

15. Which is not a long-term effect of sexual abuse?
    a. Permissive parenting
    b. Depression
    c. Negative self-concept
    d. Sexual problems

16. _____ notes that we cannot be upset by events whose power to harm us we do not understand.
    a. Maccoby
    b. Brenner
    c. Eisenberger
    d. Bruner

17. _____ _____ is a major factor in helping a child cope with stress.
    a. Denial pattern
    b. Parental support
    c. Imagined illness
    d. Voluntary withdrawal

18. Which of the following does not account for individual differences in the reaction to stress?
    a. Age
    b. Sex
    c. Temperament
    d. Athletic ability

19. Children react differently to stress according to all but
    a. age.
    b. gender.
    c. temperament.
    d. race.

20. Among the protective factors for resilient children is
    a. temperament.
    b. interactive error
    c. geographic mobility.
    d. assimilation.

Answers

*If men and women
are to understand
each other, to enter
into each other's
nature with
mutual sympathy,
and to become
capable of genuine
comradeship, the
foundation must
be laid in youth.*

Havelock Ellis

P eter and Lynn are wide awake at two in the morning, but they are not having a good time. They are having a teenager. Matty, their son, was due home two hours ago. He is sixteen, his curfew is midnight, and they have heard nothing from him. They are wide awake and angry, and most of all, they are worried.

But this is not going to be one of those nights that changes anyone's life. Nobody is going to die. Nothing of this night will be on the news. This is the ordinary night nobody writes about. Matty is going to come home in another half hour hoping his parents have long since gone to sleep, so he can assure them tomorrow that he was in "only a little past twelve." When his hopes are dashed by the sight of his wide-awake parents, he will have an excuse about somebody's car and somebody else's mother and a third person who borrowed the first person's jacket with his car keys and left the party early, and maybe it's just because it's now nearly three in the morning, but the story will sound to Peter and Lynn so freshly made up that all its pieces barely know how to fit together.

Lynn won't be thinking about it now, but only six years ago—not a long time to her—she had been struck by how independent Matty had become. This clingy kid who seemed to need her so much had become a little 10-year-old fellow full of purpose and plans, in business for himself, with a sign on his bedroom door—"Adults Keep Out." A part of her missed the little boy who didn't want to be left alone, but a bigger part of her was pleased for both of them by this development. But six years later, at two-thirty in the morning, it will not occur to her to say, "Matty, my son, I'm so impressed by the way you are able to take care of yourself, by how much you can do for yourself, by the way you just go wherever you want to and come home whenever you want to, by how little you seem to need your dad and me. You're really growing up, son. Your dad and I just wanted to stay up until two-thirty in the morning to tell you how proud we are!" No, what will occur to Lynn to say is something more like "This isn't a hotel here, buddy!" . . . Peter and Lynn want something more of Matty now than they wanted when he was 10. (Kegan, 1994, p. 15–16) ✪

Kegan believes we all want a lot from teens like Matty. We want him ". . . to be employable, a good citizen, a critical thinker, emotionally self-reflective, personally trustworthy, and possessed of common sense and meaningful ideals. This is a lot to want. It grows out of our concern for ourselves, our concern for others who live with Matty, and our concern for Matty himself. Will he be up to all these expectations?" (p. 19)

Kegan has suggested that in general, our expectations of our teenagers are too high (1994). There is considerable evidence today (Lerner, 1996) that the great majority of adolescents pass safely through this stage of life and become reasonably happy adults who make contributions to their families, friends, and communities. Nevertheless some researchers are finding that our youth are under greater stress than in previous decades, and that this is being reflected in an increase in a variety of high-risk behaviors (see the Applied View box below). In this and the next chapter, we will look closely at the most revealing studies and try to come to some conclusions about the nature of adolescence today. We begin by looking at some ways to better define our subject.

When you finish reading this chapter, you should be able to

- State some of the criteria in a definition of adolescence, such as ways we know it has started.

- State the attributes of and differences among the theoretical contributions of Anna Freud, Erik Erikson, and John Hill.

- Identify the important parts of the male and female reproductive systems and explain their functions.

- List the normal sequence of events in puberty for males and females.

- Describe the influence of timing on individual adolescents' emotional reactions to the physical changes of puberty.

- Identify the symptoms associated with anorexia nervosa and bulimia.

- Describe four factors that contribute to the development of eating disorders.

- Explain the cognitive development that takes place in early and late phases of the formal operations stage.

- Describe the major elements of egocentric thinking: the imaginary audience and the personal fable.

- Identify the differences between critical thinking and creative thinking and discuss the research that has investigated the processes of each.

- Establish the nature and prevalence of adolescent mental health issues.

- Discuss these issues from an applied, a sociocultural, and your own point of view.

How Should We Define Adolescence?

> "Who are you?" said the caterpillar. Alice replied, rather shyly, "I—I hardly know, Sir, just at present—at least I know who I was when I got up this morning, but I must have changed several times since then."
>
> Lewis Carroll, *Alice in Wonderland*, 1865

In writing his brilliant story, Carroll presaged in many ways current views of adolescence. For example, Graber and Brooks-Gunn (1996; see also Graber & other, 1996; Lerner, 1995; Lerner & others, 1996) stated that:

> Current approaches to studying adolescence frequently consider the precursors and outcomes of a variety of transitions, a constellation of events that define the transition period, or the timing and sequence of events that occur within a transitional period. For example, puberty and school events are frequently studied as key transitions signaling the entry into adolescence; finishing school or beginning one's full-time job are examined as transitional events that define the exit from adolescence or entry into adulthood.... The term **transition-linked turning points** is used to characterize this framework (pp. 768–69).

Lerner (1996) characterized the adolescent transition as being distinguished by four traits:

- Relative plasticity. There is always the potential for change, although past and contemporary contextual conditions may oppose severe limitations.

- Relationism. The basis for change lies in the multiple levels of the individual's relationships with others.

- Historical embeddedness. No level of organization functions as a result of its own isolated activity. All change is meaningful only in the context of the historical time in which it occurs.

• Diversity and individual difference. In the past, developmental psychology has emphasized the ways that all humans are alike (that is why we have behaviorist and stage theories). More and more, the emphasis is on the variety of ways individuals learn to cope with themselves and their environments.

In this chapter, some of the theories and research that we review conform to these newer views and some do not. Nowhere can the science of developmental psychology be seen to be more in transition than in its study of adolescence. Therefore, although we attempt to report the best of the newer work, we also retain an interest in the older, still classic contributions.

When Does Adolescence Start?

At what point did your adolescence begin? Many answers have been offered:

• When you began to menstruate, or when you had your first ejaculation

• When the level of adult hormones rose sharply in your bloodstream

• When you first thought about dating

• When your pubic hair began to grow

• When you became 11 years old (if a girl); when you became 12 years old (if a boy)

• When you developed an interest in the opposite sex

• When you (if a girl) developed breasts

• When you passed the initiation rites set up by society: for example, confirmation in the Catholic Church; bar mitzvah and bas mitzvah in the Jewish faith

• When you became unexpectedly moody

• When you became 13

• When you formed exclusive social cliques

• When you thought about being independent of your parents

• When you worried about the way your body looked

• When you entered seventh grade

• When you could determine the rightness of an action, independent of your own selfish needs

• When your friends' opinions influenced you more than your parents' opinions

• When you began to wonder who you really are

Although at least a grain of truth exists in each of these statements, they don't help us much in defining adolescence (Jarratt & others, 1997; Roche & Tucker, 1997). For example, although most would agree that menstruation is an important event in the lives of women, it really isn't a good criterion for determining the start of adolescence. The first menstruation (called *menarche*) can occur at any time from 8 to 16 years of age. We would not say that the menstruating 8-year-old is an adolescent, but we would certainly say the nonmenstruating 16-year-old is one.

Probably the most reliable indication of the onset of adolescence is a sharp increase in the production of the four hormones that most affect sexuality: progesterone and estrogen in females, testosterone and androgen in males. But determining this change would require taking blood samples on a regular basis, starting when youths are 9 years old. Not a very practical approach, is it?

Is interest in the opposite sex the best sign that a young person has reached puberty? What other indicators could you name?

G. S. Hall was the first American to publish research on the teen years, with his book *Adolescence* (1904).

Clearly, identifying the age or event at which adolescence begins is not a simple matter (Graber & Brooks-Gunn, 1996). We will need to look at it much more closely, from the standpoints of biology, psychology, sociology (biopsychosocial interactions). An American psychologist was the first to offer a specific theory to explain development in the teen years, one based almost entirely on biology.

G. Stanley Hall

G. Stanley Hall (1844–1924) is known as the father of adolescent psychology. Building on Charles Darwin's theory of evolution, Hall constructed a psychological theory of teenage development, published in two volumes and entitled *Adolescence* (1904). A major aspect of his theory was his speculation that this stage of life is characterized by "storm and stress," that most teens are by nature moody and untrustworthy. This stereotype has had many advocates ever since (Kegan, 1994).

Although Hall is to be admired for his efforts to bring objectivity to adolescent psychology through the use of empiricism, it has been suggested that he had several personal agendas. He was a strong preacher against what he viewed to be teenage immorality and was especially concerned that educators try to stamp out the "plague of masturbation," which he considered to be running rampant among male youth. Here is a little speech that he recommended high school teachers and clergy give to their youthful charges:

> If a boy in an unguarded moment tries to entice you to masturbatic experiments, he insults you. Strike him at once and beat him as long as you can stand, etc. Forgive him in your mind, but never speak to him again. If

---

An Average Day in the Life of Some North American Teens

Today (and every other day this year), some teens get into trouble:

- 8,441 teens become sexually active.
- 2,756 teens become pregnant.
- 1,340 babies are born to teen mothers.
- 2,754 babies are born out of wedlock.
- 638 babies are born to mothers receiving late or no prenatal care.
- 2,699 babies are born into poverty.
- 95 babies die before their first birthday.
- 2 children younger than 5 are murdered.
- 248 children are arrested for violent crimes.
- 176 children are arrested for drug abuse.
- 12,720 children are arrested for alcohol abuse or drunk driving.
- 135,000 children bring guns to school.
- 2,350 children are in adult jails.
- 167,500 students ages 16 to 24 drop out each school day.

On the other hand, today (and every other day this year), teenagers have engaged in many kinds of activities that enrich their own lives and those of the people around them. It is impossible to know exactly how many are in-

volved in each of these activities. (It is interesting that we know much more about teenagers' negative actions, isn't it?) Here are some examples:

- Have joined a service-oriented club (e.g., Scouts, 4-H, Future Farmers of America)
- Became members of Junior Achievement
- Competed in an athletic event
- Became a candy-striper (volunteer nurse's aide)
- Joined Students Against Drunk Driving
- Taught another teen in a peer tutor program
- Served food in a shelter for the homeless
- Volunteered at a day-care center or a nursing home for the elderly
- Answered phones on a drug abuse or suicide hotline
- Delivered newspapers, stocked supermarket shelves, or in some other way earned money at a part-time job

Obviously, we would wish that all adolescents were more interested in the ideals represented by these activities. Can you think of ways that you could help make this happen?

Adapted from Children's Defense Fund, 1996.

A book that also deals with the stereotype of lack of civility among adolescents is: William Goldman's *Lord of the flies*. New York: Coward-McGann. This tale of a group of teenage boys whose plane crashes on a Pacific island, killing the adults, is excellent reading. You watch the subgroups develop and proceed to the shocking ending.

he is the best fighter and beats you, take it as in a good cause. If a man scoundrel suggests indecent things, slug him with a stick or a stone or anything else at hand. Give him a scar that all may see; and if you are arrested, tell the judge all, and he will approve your act, even if it is not lawful. If a villain shows you a filthy book or picture, snatch it; and give it to the first policeman you meet, and help him to find the wretch. If a vile woman invites you, and perhaps tells a plausible story of her downfall, you cannot strike her; but think of a glittering, poisonous snake. She is a degenerate and probably diseased, and even a touch may poison you and your children. (1904, p. 136)

What's Your View?

Is a Bias Built into Adolescent Research?

Hall is hardly the only adolescent psychologist who can be accused of bias in his thinking. In a fascinating study, Enright and colleagues (1987) looked at 89 articles published during two economic depressions and two world wars to see if these events had an influence on research. The results were striking:

> In times of economic depression theories of adolescence emerge that portray teenagers as immature, psychologically unstable, and in need of prolonged participation in the educational system. During wartime, the psychological competence of youth is emphasized and the duration of education is recommended to be more retracted than in depression. (p. 541)

Is it likely that youth were viewed as immature during financial depressions in order to keep them from competing with adults for scarce jobs? Is their maturity seen as greater during wartime because they are needed to perform such adult tasks as soldiering and factory work? If so, is this societal bias conscious or unconscious? What do you think? Perhaps a search of the popular press for articles about teens, some written in war times and some when the economy was stagnant, would enlighten your thinking.

As you read the other theories in this chapter, see if you can spot what you believe to be biases in them. Do they emphasize some aspects of adolescent life at the expense of others? Is one more moralistic than the others?

Is adolescence typically a stage during which hormones run rampant, causing irrational and antisocial behavior? It is true that some misbehavior occurs (see the Applied box below), but there is also evidence that it is a time when many good deeds are done.

Why, then, has the "storm and stress" view of adolescence been so prevalent in the popular press? Could it be that there has been a bias in the research itself?

Guided Review

1. Graber and Brooks-Gunn hold that the precursors and outcomes of a variety of transitions are one kind of _____ _____ _____.
2. Lerner characterized the adolescent transition as being distinguished by four traits: relative plasticity, historical embeddedness, diversity and individual difference, and _____.
3. G. S. Hall, the father of adolescent psychology, saw child development paralleling the development of the human race, with adolescence being a time both of civilization and of storm and _____.

Answers

1. transition-linked turning point 2. relationism 3. stress

A Sociocultural View

Is Adolescence a Cultural Phenomenon?

In Western cultures, extended schooling keeps children out of full-time productive work so they do not start observing and participating in the adult economic world as they do in, for example, Guatemala. Schooling has become a substitute for adult roles. For instance, a college student spends years studying nursing (chemistry, psychology), but he is not a nurse (chemist, psychologist). Extended schooling, then, artificially stretches the period from childhood to adulthood. This delay or waiting period is unique in human history. Combined with the decreasing age of reaching menarche in middle-class Western girls, adolescence can be prolonged more than 10 years! Compare this to the Efe, hunters and gatherers in Zaire, who marry and assume adult roles soon after puberty. Is adolescence just a theoretical construct (see Chapter 2)? Is it peculiar to cultures with extended schooling? Has an extended adolescence altered our definition of maturity? What if our increasing need for high-level education were to extend adolescence into the middle or even late twenties? Would this change the meaning of adolescence? What do you think?

Theories of Adolescence

True, my theory is no longer accepted, but it was good enough to get us to the next one!
Donald Hebb

In this section, the theories of three famous adolescent theorists are reviewed. These theories were not chosen because they fully *explain* adolescence, but because they have done such a good job of spurring our thinking about the nature of this period. Thus it is with theories in general: they are respected not because they are true, but because they are generative.

Anna Freud's Psychological Theory

The daughter of Sigmund, Anna Freud (1895–1983) believed that his definition of adolescence was too sketchy. She suggested (1968) that her father had been too involved with his discovery that sexuality begins not at puberty but in early infancy. As a result, he overemphasized the importance of that earlier stage in the total developmental picture. Anna Freud spent the major part of her professional life trying to extend and modify psychoanalytic theory as applied to adolescence.

Anna Freud saw the major problem of adolescence as being the restoration of the delicate balance between the ego and the id, which is established during latency and disrupted by puberty. Latency, she felt, is the time when children adopt the moral values and principles of the people with whom they identify. Childhood fears are replaced with internalized feelings of guilt that are learned during this period. The id is controlled during latency by the strength of the superego. At puberty, however, the force of the id becomes much greater and the delicate balance is destroyed.

The problems brought about by this internal conflict cause the adolescent to regress to earlier stages of development. A renewed Oedipal conflict (see Chapter 2) brings about fears that are entirely unconscious and often produce intense anxiety. Therefore, the unconscious defenses of the ego tend to multiply rapidly, especially the typical ones of repression, denial, and compensation. The problem, of course, is that the use of these defense mechanisms causes new stresses within the individual and tends to further increase the level of anxiety.

Anna Freud described two additional adolescent defense mechanisms:

- Asceticism, in which, as a defense against the sexual, "sinful" drives of youth, the teenager frequently becomes extremely religious and devoted to God

- Intellectualization, in which the adolescent defends against emotionality of all kinds by becoming extremely intellectual and logical about life

Members of the Hitler Youth Corps were victims of "premature foreclosure," in which their identity was designed for them without their having any choice. They were taught exactly what to wear, how to act, what to think. Some actually turned their parents in to the secret police for what they believed to be violations of Hitler's creed.

Erikson wrote a fascinating book on Martin Luther: *Young man Luther.* New York: Norton. Erikson picked Luther as a subject because, in Erikson's view, he was a famous case of someone who struggled with his sense of identity. This book also closely examines the Protestant Reformation and so may appeal to you if you are interested in the beginnings of the Protestant religions.

Anna Freud may be seen as emphasizing the psychological aspect of the biopsychosocial model.

Erik Erikson's Psychosocial Theory

According to Erik Erikson (1902–1994), the main task of the adolescent is to achieve a **state of identity.** Erikson (1963, 1975), who originated the term **identity crisis,** used it in a special way. In addition to thinking of identity as the general picture one has of oneself, Erikson referred to it as a state toward which one strives. If you were in a state of identity, the various aspects of your self-images would be in agreement with each other; they would be identical.

Repudiation of choices is another essential aspect of a person's identity. Striving for identity means that we have to repudiate (give up) all the other possibilities, at least for the present. All of us know people who seem unable to do this. They cannot keep a job, they have no loyalty to their friends, they are unable to be faithful to a spouse. For them, "the grass is always greener on the other side of the fence." Thus they must keep all their options open and must not repudiate any choices, lest one of them should turn out to have been "the right one."

Erikson suggested that identity confusion is far more likely in a democratic society because so many choices are available. In a totalitarian society, youths are usually given an identity, which they are forced to accept. The Hitler Youth Corps of Nazi Germany in the 1930s is an example of a national effort backed by intense propaganda to get all the adolescents in the country to identify with the same set of values and attitudes. In democratic societies, where more emphasis is placed on individual decision making, choices abound; some children may feel threatened by this overabundance of options. Nevertheless, a variety of choices is essential to the formation of a well-integrated identity.

Erikson saw adolescence as a period of moratorium—a "time out" period during which the adolescent experiments with a variety of identities, without having to assume the responsibility for the consequences of any particular one. The moratorium period does not exist in preindustrial societies. Erikson stated that indecision is an essential part of the moratorium. Tolerance of it leads to a positive identity. Some youth, however, cannot stand the ambiguity of indecision. This leads to "premature foreclosure." The adolescent who makes choices too early usually comes to regret them. He or she is especially vulnerable to identity confusion in later life.

Although some youths tend to be overly idealistic, Erikson believed that idealism is essential for a strong identity. In young people's search for a person or an idea to be true to, they are building a commitment to an ideology that will help them unify their personal values. They need ideals to avoid the disintegration of personality that is the basis of most forms of mental illness.

Identity Status

Erikson's ideas on adolescence have generated considerable research on identity formation. The leader in this field is James Marcia, who has made a major contribution to our understanding through his research on **identity status.** He and his colleagues have published numerous studies on this topic (Marcia, 1980, 1983; Cote & Levine, 1988; Craig-Bray & others, 1988; Flum, 1994).

Marcia believes that two factors are essential in the attainment of a mature identity. First, the person must undergo several crises in choosing among life's alternatives, such as the crisis of deciding whether to hold or to give up one's religious beliefs. Second, the person must come to a commitment, an investment of self, in his or her choices. Since a person may or may not have gone through the crisis of choice and may or may not have made a commitment to choices, four combinations, or statuses, are possible for that person to be in:

Status 1. **Identity confusion:** No crisis has been experienced and no commitments have been made.

Status 2. **Identity foreclosure:** No crisis has been experienced, but commitments have been made, usually forced on the person by the parent.

Status 3. **Identity moratorium:** A number of crises have been experienced, but no commitments are yet made.

Status 4. **Identity achievement:** Numerous crises have been experienced and resolved, and relatively permanent commitments have been made.

Table 11.1 summarizes these definitions.

Erikson's eight stages (in addition to the six described in this book thus far, there are the stages of generativity and integrity) follow each other in a more or less unchangeable sequence. Research indicates that Marcia's identity statuses have a tendency toward an orderly progression, but not so clearly as Erikson's stages. Carol Gilligan (1982, Gilligan & others, 1990) and others have focused on possible gender differences in identity formation. They have concluded that women are less concerned than men with achieving an independent identity status. Women are more likely to define themselves by their relationships and responsibilities to others. Society gives women the predominant role in transmitting social values from one generation to the next. This role requires a stable identity, and therefore a stable identity appears to be more important to women than it is to men.

TABLE 11.1   SUMMARY OF MARCIA'S FOUR IDENTITY STATUSES

	Identity Status			
	Confusion	Foreclosure	Moratorium	Achievement
Crisis	Absent	Absent	Present	Present
Commitment	Absent	Present	Absent	Present
Period of adolescence in which status often occurs	Early	Middle	Middle	Late

A Sociocultural View

Ethnic Self-Concept

One African American male recalls, "Much of my junior and high school years were difficult because, on top of the typical problems of this time period, I had to combine the struggle of being Black and having my race always looked down upon, expected to fail, expected to cause trouble, and expected to be unproductive. During this time, I had to fight to maintain my confidence. I did not know who I was . . . I was confused." He went on to describe how he was kicked off the football team for a failing grade, but when his parents spoke to the teacher, it was discovered that he actually had a C+. "He had given me an F not because I earned it, but because he expected me to deserve it" (John B. Diamond in Schoem, 1991).

A Mexican American male stated, "As I moved to junior high, the issue of my ethnicity became a problem. I remember thinking that I would be a great deal more popular if only I had Bobby's face and body and brains. I

would look in the mirror and imagine what I would look like. The mythical Bobby was, of course, always white and popular with girls. This fantasy ate away at my self-esteem, and I found myself bitterly questioning why I had been born a brown-faced Mexican. . . . From this point on, all my energies were spent on the elusive quest for acceptance by my peers—and unconsciously, by myself" (Carlos Manjarrez in Schoem, 1991).

Do you think ethnic prejudice can make the development of self-concept and positive self-esteem difficult? Do you think the African American teen felt that he mattered to his teacher? What are the social expectations for him and how might they influence self-concept? What values of American society make the development of self-concept and positive self-esteem challenging for adolescents of color?

John Hill's Biopsychosocial Theory

The first biopsychosocial theory of adolescence was produced by John Hill (Adams & others, 1996; Hill, 1973; 1983; Hill & Holmbeck, 1986). Figure 11.1 illustrates his theory. The concentric rings are meant to portray the interrelatedness of the three factors. Biological factors are in the center because they are present at birth, as are some of the psychological factors. However, all the psychological and social factors begin playing a part immediately after birth. The major point is that each is imbedded in the other two. The meaning of each is inextricably connected to the other two. A fourth factor running through the others is time—not only the aging process from early to late adolescence, but also the events going on during this historical period.

The biological factors Hill considered important are considered later in this chapter, and the social factors are reviewed in chapter 12. However, some additional comment in Hill's conception of the psychological factors is required here.

By detachment, Hill did not mean emotional independence from parents, as did many other theorists of his time. According to their view (which was primarily psychoanalytic), because teens are shifting their sexual attachments from their parents to their peers, there is bound to be a lot of "storm and stress." It was seen as natural for parents and their adolescent children to fight with each other on a regular basis. Hill rejected this view on the basis of actual research of his own and others. He saw the shift as more a matter of moving from dependence to interdependence (see Chapter 12).

The nature of the shift, he felt, was more a matter of growing autonomy, which means ". . . independence in decision making and feelings of confidence in personal goals and standards of behavior" (1973, p. 37). There *is* a lessening of dependence, but the emphasis should be placed on increases in autonomy.

As to sexuality, once again Hill disagreed with the psychoanalytic view, which was that change in one's sense of a sexual self follows a gradual continuous pattern. He argued that puberty is brought on not only by physiological changes of a rather abrupt nature (menarche, nocturnal emotions, the growth spurt—see below). Rather the social changes involved in acquiring the new self-concept of adolescence force teens to view themselves in a whole new light sexually. Thus the change is discontinuous, not gradual.

The new adolescent ability to become intimate with another, Hill believed, is basically tied to sexuality. It begins with feelings of affection for a close friend (which are not overtly sexual but are more intimate than the feelings that characterized earlier relationships). For most people, intimacy and sexual attraction then move to focus on opposite-sex friends. The integration of intimacy and sex, Hill believed, is one of the basic tasks of adolescence.

Achievement motivation and behavior are related to the standard of excellence individuals set for themselves and the relative proficiency they see themselves as having. Achievement behavior is different from achievement motivation, because the former may be affected by other motives too (having a good time, for instance). This difference is a particularly good example of the role that social context may play. For example, a girl may be highly motivated to play the violin, but if her friends treat that activity with contempt, and if she cares more and more about their opinions as she passes into adolescence, then the violin is likely to be relegated to its case.

Finally, Hill paid Erikson the compliment of saying that his concept of identity ". . . appears to integrate much of what is known about adolescence" (1973, p. 64). Hill felt that the six psychological factors he highlighted (see Fig. 11.1) fit well with and added to the concept of psychological identity. He did caution, however, that more research would be needed to determine if the adolescent years are always the time in which identity issues are most likely to be addressed (Adams & others, 1996). His concern has been borne out: it is now clear that many young people, es-

Figure 11.1

John Hill's theory of adolescence.

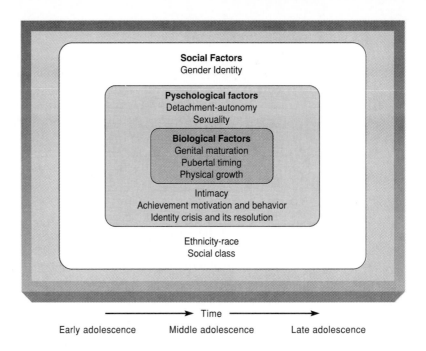

pecially college students, do not come to a clear identity crisis until they are in their early twenties, if then.

Although much progress in understanding the building blocks of adolescence has been made since Anna Freud, Erik Erikson, and John Hill theorized about it, it is abundantly clear that our progress would have been far less without the work of these three titans.

In summary, it may be said that the adolescent's personality is undergoing many changes, but these changes are probably no more traumatic than at any other stage of life. There is the danger of overreliance on defense mechanisms. Another danger is staying in the moratorium period too long. The major concern is to begin to form an adult identity, which means choosing certain values and repudiating others. It is considered necessary to work one's way from identity confusion through the moratorium to an achieved identity, while avoiding foreclosure. In the next two sections of this chapter, we will be dealing with the two foundations of adolescence: physical and cognitive development.

Guided Review

4. Anna Freud sees adolescence as a time to restore the delicate balance between the ego and the id, and sees _____ and intellectualization as two defense mechanisms unique to the period.
5. The phrase "identity crisis" is associated with the theorist _____ _____ and is his fifth stage of development.
6. Identity status is achieved through crises and commitment in four stages: identity confusion, identity foreclosure, identity _____, and identity achievement.
7. Marcia believes that to attain a mature identity, a person must undergo several crises in choosing from life alternatives and come to a _____ in his/her choices.
8. James Hill was the first to see that the causations of adolescent changes are always embedded in the intricate interactions among _____, _____, and _____ forces.

Answers

4. asceticism 5. Erik Erikson 6. moratorium 7. commitment 8. biological, psychological, social

Physical Development

Gretchen, my friend, got her period. I'm so jealous, God. I hate myself for being so jealous, but I am. I wish you'd help me just a little.

Judy Blume

Prior to the twentieth century, it appears that children moved directly from childhood into adulthood with no period of adolescence in between.

To better understand physical development in adolescence, we'll answer the following questions in this section: What parts of our body are involved? When does puberty start? What are the effects of timing?

> The girls are clearly beginning to look like young ladies, while the boys with whom they have thus far played on scarcely equal terms now seem hopelessly stranded in childhood. This year or more of manifest physical superiority of the girl, with its attendant development of womanly attitudes and interests, accounts in part for the tendency of many boys in the early teens to be averse to the society of girls. (King, 1914, p. 13)

Your Reproductive System

Today more is known about many aspects of **puberty,** such as how the organs of our reproductive system function together. Just as important, we are learning how to present this knowledge to adolescents effectively.

The Female Sexual System

The parts of the female sexual system are defined here and are illustrated in Figure 11.2.

- *Bartholin's glands.* A pair of glands located on either side of the vagina. These glands provide some of the fluid that acts as a lubricant during intercourse.

- *Cervix.* The opening to the uterus located at the inner end of the vagina.

- *Clitoris.* Comparable to the male penis. Both organs are similar in the first few months after conception, becoming differentiated only as sexual determination takes place. The clitoris is the source of maximum sexual stimulation and becomes erect through sexual excitement. It is above the vaginal opening, between the labia minora.

- *Fallopian tubes.* Conduct the ova (egg) from the ovary to the uterus. A fertilized egg that becomes lodged in the fallopian tubes, called a fallopian or ectopic pregnancy, cannot develop normally and if not surgically removed will cause the tube to rupture.

- *Fimbriae.* Hairlike structures located at the opening of the oviduct that help move the ovum down the fallopian tube to the uterus.

- *Hymen.* A flap of tissue that usually covers most of the vaginal canal in virgins.

Figure 11.2

The female reproductive system

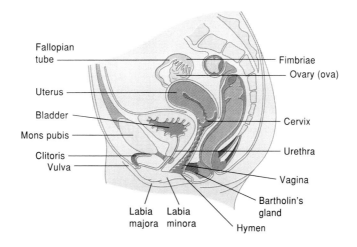

- *Labia majora.* The two larger outer lips of the vaginal opening.

- *Labia minora.* The two smaller inner lips of the vaginal opening.

- *Mons pubis or mons veneris.* The outer area just above the vagina, which becomes larger during adolescence and on which the first pubic hair appears.

- *Ova.* The female reproductive cells stored in the ovaries. These eggs are fertilized by the male sperm. Girls are born with more than a million follicles, each of which holds an ovum. At puberty, only 10,000 remain, but they are more than sufficient for a woman's reproductive life. Because usually only one egg ripens each month from the midteens to the late forties, a woman releases fewer than 500 ova during her lifetime.

- *Ovaries.* Glands that release one ovum each month. They also produce the hormones estrogen and progesterone, which play an important part in the menstrual cycle and pregnancy.

- *Pituitary gland.* The "master" gland located in the lower part of the brain. It controls sexual maturation and excitement and monthly menstruation.

- *Ureter.* A canal connecting the kidneys with the bladder.

- *Urethra.* A canal leading from the bladder to the external opening through which urine is excreted.

- *Uterus.* The hollow organ (also called the *womb*) in which the fertilized egg must implant itself for a viable pregnancy to occur. The egg attaches itself to the lining of the uterus from which the unborn baby draws nourishment as it matures during the nine months before birth.

- *Vulva.* The external genital organs of the female.

The Male Sexual System

The parts of the male sexual system are defined here and are illustrated in Figure 11.3.

- *Cowper's glands.* Located next to the prostate glands. Their job is to secrete a fluid that changes the chemical balance in the urethra from an acidic to an alkaline base. This fluid proceeds up through the urethra in the penis, where it is ejaculated during sexual excitement just before the sperm-laden semen. About a quarter of the time, sperm also may be found in this solution, sometimes called preseminal fluid. Therefore, even if the male withdraws his penis before he ejaculates, it is possible for him to deposit some sperm in the vagina, which may cause pregnancy.

Figure 11.3

The male reproductive system

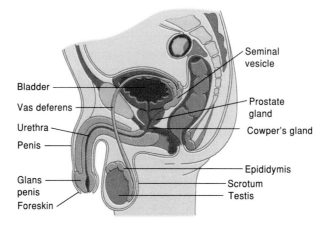

- *Epididymis.* A small organ attached to each testis. It is a storage place for newly produced sperm.

- *Foreskin.* A flap of loose skin that surrounds the glans penis at birth, often removed by a surgery called circumcision.

- *Glans penis.* The tip or head of the penis.

- *Pituitary gland.* The "master" gland controlling sexual characteristics. In the male it controls the production of sperm, the release of testosterone (and thus the appearance of secondary sexual characteristics such as the growth of hair and voice change), and sexual excitement and maturation.

- *Prostate gland.* Produces a milky alkaline substance known as semen. In the prostate the sperm are mixed with the semen to give them greater mobility.

- *Scrotum.* The sac of skin located just below the penis, in which the testes and epididymis are located.

- *Testes.* The two oval sex glands, suspended in the scrotum, that produce sperm. Sperm are the gene cells that fertilize the ova. They are equipped with a tail-like structure that enables them to move about by a swimming motion. After being ejaculated from the penis into the vagina, sperm attempt to swim through the cervix into the uterus and into the fallopian tubes, where fertilization takes place. If one penetrates an egg, conception occurs. Although the testes regularly produce millions of sperm, the odds against any particular sperm penetrating an egg are enormous. The testes also produce testosterone, the male hormone that affects other aspects of sexual development.

- *Ureter.* A canal connecting each of the kidneys with the bladder.

- *Urethra.* A canal that connects the bladder with the opening of the penis. It is also the path taken by the preseminal fluid and sperm during ejaculation.

- *Vas deferens.* A pair of tubes that lead from the epididymis up to the prostate. They carry the sperm when the male is sexually aroused and about to ejaculate.

When Does Puberty Start?

Is the beginning of adolescence marked by any one physiological event? The sequence of bodily changes in puberty is surprisingly constant. This holds true whether puberty starts early or late and regardless of the culture in which the child is reared. Table 11.2 lists the sequences of physiological change.

Which of these physical events in the life of the adolescent might we choose as the actual beginning of puberty? Change in **hormonal balance** is first, but its beginning is difficult to pinpoint. Skeletal growth, genital growth, pubic hair, breast development, voice change, growth spurt—all are inconvenient to measure. **Menarche** has been suggested as the major turning point for girls, but many women do not recall menarche as a particularly significant event. Sometimes the first ejaculation is suggested as the beginning of adolescent puberty for males, but this too is often a little-remembered (and possibly repressed) event.

Despite the fact that puberty is primarily thought of as a physical change in an adolescent, the psychological impact can be significant (Caspi & others, 1992; Lee, 1994; & Wierson & others, 1993). This is especially true with menstruation. Even in these "enlightened" times, too many girls experience menarche without being properly prepared. As a result, an event in a young girl's life that should be remembered as the exciting, positive beginning of the transition to adulthood is instead viewed as a negative, sometimes frightening, experience. Research suggests that better preparation for first menstruation results in more positive attitudes about it (Masters

TABLE 11.2	THE SEQUENCE OF PHYSIOLOGICAL CHANGE IN MALES AND FEMALES

Females	Males
• Change in hormonal balance • The beginning of rapid skeletal growth • The beginning of breast development • The appearance of straight, pigmented pubic hair • The appearance of kinky, pigmented pubic hair • Menarche (first menstruation) • Maximum growth spurt (when growth is at its fastest rate) • The appearance of hair on the forearms and underarms	• Change in hormonal balance • The beginning of skeletal growth • The enlargement of the genitals • The appearance of straight pigmented pubic hair • Early voice changes (voice "cracks") • First ejaculations (wet dreams, nocturnal emissions) • The appearance of kinky, pigmented pubic hair • Maximum growth spurt • The appearance of downy facial hair • The appearance of hair on the chest and underarms • Late voice change (the voice deepens) • Coarse, pigmented facial hair

Note: For more on these physiological changes, see Muuss (1996).

& others, 1995). The same is no doubt also the case for a male's first ejaculation. Accurate and accessible information about the changes our bodies undergo benefits adolescents for whom physical changes often lead to sexual activity (Bingham & Crockett, 1996).

Given our understanding of the physiology of adolescents and differences in individual psychology and culture, we would have to conclude that no single event but, rather, a complex set of events marks the onset of puberty, a process whose effects may be sudden or gradual. Thus biology alone cannot give us a definition of adolescence; we will need to include psychological and social factors to achieve that.

The Effects of Timing on Puberty

In a general sense, the onset of puberty affects all adolescents in the same way. However, the age at which these changes begin has some very specific effects on the adolescent's life. (The photograph in Figure 11.4, taken in 1914, illustrates how 14-year-old adolescents can differ greatly in their stage of physiological development—and did so even many years ago!)

In this section, eight adolescents (four females and four males) are compared to illustrate the differences that often occur among children even though they are all in the **normal range of development.** Each adolescent is 14 years old. The first female and male are early maturers, the second are average maturers, and the third are late maturers. They all fall within the typical range of all adolescents.

The Early-Maturing Female: Ann

At 5 feet, 5 inches and 130 pounds, Ann is considerably bigger than her age-mates. Her growth accelerated when she was 8 years old, and by the time she was 10½, her **maximum growth spurt** crested. She is still growing taller but at a slower rate. Her motor development (coordination and strength) had its greatest rate of increase two years ago. She is stronger than her age-mates, but her strength and coordination have reached their maximum.

She started menstruating three years ago, at age 11, and her breasts are already in the secondary (adult) stage. Her pubic and underarm hair are also at an adult

Figure 11.4

Comparison of male and female growth (King, 1914)

Culture and the Imaginary Audience

'Chin, chong, chin, chong, ah so! Yellow-face, can you see out of those eyes?!' Every day for nearly one year, I heard those words as I rode the bus to middle school. I was 11 years old in the seventh grade.

This experience was related by a young Korean girl. At that time she believed that she must have done something to deserve such anger. She experienced immense humiliation and pain. She wanted to be like the other children. "With the onset of puberty, my body began to change, and I did not want to change into something even more different from the other girls." Because she could not change her slanted eyes or her skin color, she decided she must learn to speak perfect English.

When she was 11, this young woman worked hard on her English to please an imaginary audience—all those peers whom she imagined were watching her every move. By the time she was 14, their opinion became much less important to her, and she began to feel pride in her ethnic identity.

Phinney (1993) has found that ethnic identity development has stages that parallel those of Marcia's ego statuses in adolescents: a combined foreclosure-diffusion stage in which teenagers had not explored their ethnic identity yet; ethnic identity search/moratorium; and ethnic identity achievement. This study found that the greater a teen's ethnic identity achievement, the higher was her or his self-esteem. In an interesting series of studies, Rotheram-Borus (1993) found that in an integrated school, biculturalism (identification with American culture and with the ethnic background of their parents) was common (44–45 percent). In a school with high cross-ethnic tension, however, most students (over 70 percent) were most strongly committed to the ethnic identity of their parents. Ethnicity, then, seems to become a more powerful conditioner of one's identity if one experiences strong ethnic tension in one's surroundings.

stage. She has clearly entered a period in which the **maturation** process is accelerated.

The Average-Maturing Female: Beth

Although Beth is also 14, she is different in almost every way from Ann. She represents the typical adolescent today in the sense of being average in her measurements and physical change. It is clear that from the standpoint of personality and behavior, no "average" adolescent exists.

Beth is 5 feet, 3 inches tall and weighs 120 pounds. She reached her maximum growth spurt two years ago and is also starting to slow down. She is presently at the peak of her motor development.

Her breasts are at the primary breast stage; she is beginning to need a bra, or thinks she does. She started menstruating two years ago. She has adult pubic hair, and her underarm hair is beginning to appear.

The Late-Maturing Female: Cathy

Cathy is at the lower end of the normal range of physical development for a 14-year-old girl. She is only 4 feet, 8 inches tall, weighs 100 pounds, and is just beginning her growth spurt. She is not too happy about this; she feels that the other girls have advantages in relationships with boys.

Cathy's breasts are at the bud stage; her nipples and encircling areolae are beginning to protrude, but she is otherwise flat-chested. She has just begun menstruation. Pubic hair growth has started, but as yet no hair has appeared under her arms.

The Early-Maturing Male: Al

Al finds that at 5 feet, 8 inches tall, he towers over his 14-year-old friends. He reached his maximum growth spurt approximately two years ago and weighs 150 pounds. He is now about two years before the peak of his motor development. His coordination and strength are rapidly increasing, but contrary to the popular myth he is not growing clumsier.

As adolescents reach their peak of motor development, they usually handle their bodies better, although adults expect them to have numerous accidents. It is true that when one's arms grow an inch longer in less than a year, one's hand-eye coordination suffers somewhat. However, the idea of the gangling, inept adolescent is more myth than fact.

Al's sexual development is also well ahead of that of his age-mates. He already has adult pubic hair, and hair has started to grow on his chest and underarms. He began having nocturnal emissions almost two years ago, and since then the size of his genitals has increased almost 100 percent.

The Average-Maturing Male: Bob

Interestingly, Bob is exactly the same height as his "average" female counterpart, Beth, at 5 feet, 3 inches tall. At 130 pounds, he outweighs her by 10 pounds. He is currently in the midst of his maximum growth spurt and is four years away from reaching the peak of his coordination and strength.

His sexual development began about a year ago with the start of nocturnal emissions, and he is just now starting to grow pubic hair. As yet he has no hair on his chest or under his arms. However, his genitals have reached 80 percent of their adult size.

The Late-Maturing Male: Chuck

Chuck is also similar in stature to his counterpart, Cathy. They are both 4 feet, 8 inches tall, although at 90 pounds, Chuck is 10 pounds lighter than Cathy. He is a year and a half away from his maximum growth spurt and must wait six years before his motor development will peak.

Chuck's sexual development is also lagging behind those of the other two boys. His genitals are 50 percent larger than they were two years ago, but as yet he has no pubic, chest, or underarm hair. He has not yet experienced nocturnal emissions, although these are about to begin.

The preceding descriptions illustrate the great variability in adolescent growth and in adolescent responses to growth. Keep in mind, however, that self-image and peer relationships are not entirely determined by physique. "Average-sized" adolescents do not always lead a charmed life, and many late and early maturers are quite comfortable with themselves. Adolescents who have clarified their values and set their own standards are not likely to be overly affected by pubertal changes or the peer approval or disapproval brought about by them (Alsaker, 1995).

An Applied View

Dealing with Early or Late Development

Petersen and others (1988) found an increased risk of sexual abuse for the early-maturing female. Significantly early or late development has been linked to depression and eating disorders in both boys and girls (Rierdan & others, 1988), so it is important for practitioners working with adolescents to be aware of negative reactions to their physical change (or lack of it). If you know a teen who is significantly early or late in body development, be on the lookout for psychological problems. If you find evidence

of such problems, make arrangements for the youth to have access to appropriate professional attention.

On the other hand, you should understand that "normal" covers a wide band of developmental time. We should help teens who "hate" their bodies because they are not perfectly average to be more accepting. Finally, if you do feel there is a problem, say nothing to the teen until you have an experienced person's advice on the best course of action.

The Secular Trend

 Three books that provide additional information are: (1) Judy Blume's *Are you there, God? It's me, Margaret.* New York: Bradbury. Although written for teens, this book has a wealth of insights into pubertal change, at least for females. Our women friends tell us that Blume really understands. (2) R. H. Curtis's *Mind and mood: Understanding and controlling your emotions.* New York: Scribner's. According to Curtis, knowing more about emotions and how they affect the body can help in understanding and controlling them. This book has chapters that describe the nervous system and endocrine system, addressing the physiological impact on emotions; a chapter on behavior modification; and a section with personality tests that you can take. (3) McCoy and Wibbelsman's *The teenage body book.* Los Angeles, CA: The Body Press. An excellent reference book for teenagers and those who work with them.

The average teenagers 100 years ago were physically similar in most ways to Cathy and Chuck, the late maturers described above. This fact is part of the phenomenon called the **secular trend.** The secular trend refers to the decreasing age of the onset of puberty, including a significant drop in the average age at which females in a particular country reach menarche. Earlier puberty affects other developmental factors such as sexual attraction (Alsaker, 1996; McClintock & Herdt, 1996). In Western countries, the average age of menarche has declined about three months per decade over the past hundred years. In the United States, 17 was the average age in the late eighteenth and early nineteenth centuries (Vaughan & Litt, 1990).

Today the average age of onset is 12.5 years. Most researchers feel that improved nutrition, sanitation, and health care are responsible for the trend, and that we are now at a period of leveling off (Brooks-Gunn & others, 1985). We think nutrition is involved because girls must typically achieve a certain proportion of body fat before they can menstruate (Frisch, 1988; Swarr & Richards, 1996). Studies of female athletes and dancers have shown that a lack of fat can delay menarche or can stop menstruation after it has begun (Brooks-Gunn, 1987). Childhood conflict also influences pubertal timing (Kim & others, 1997).

Will the secular trend continue in future years? No, the trend likely is a special case that pertains only to the period from the 1700s to today and is the result of improvements in nutrition, medicine, and health care in general.

Figure 11.5 details the age ranges considered normal for development. Adolescents who experience these changes earlier or later may have no medical problem, but consulting a doctor is probably a good idea. If a glandular imbalance exists, the doctor can usually remedy the problem with little difficulty.

In summary, we may say that the vast majority of human bodies proceed toward maturity in the same way, but that in the last few centuries the timing of the process in females has changed radically. Although timing is affected mainly by biology, psychological and social forces clearly influence it, too. An example of the biological consequences of psychological and social factors is the eating disorder (Swan & Richard, 1996).

Eating Disorders

Although still rather rare, eating disorders are so serious (about one-third of those who develop an eating disorder die) it is necessary to review what we know about them here. There are two main types, known as anorexia and bulimia nervosa.

Figure 11.5

Normal age ranges of puberty

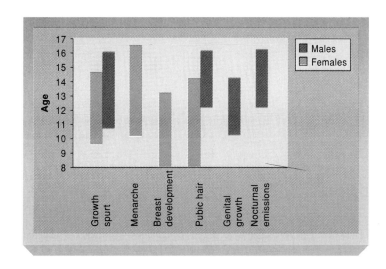

Christy Henrich, a gymnist who died of anorexia.

Anorexia Nervosa

Anorexia nervosa is a syndrome of self-starvation that mainly affects adolescent and young adult females, who account for 95 percent of the known cases. Professionals suspect that many males may also be victims (e.g., those who must maintain a low weight for sports), but their illness is covered up (Mintz & Betz, 1988). Anorexia is characterized by an "intense fear of becoming obese, disturbance of body image, significant weight loss, refusal to maintain a minimal normal body weight, and amenorrhea [suppressed menstruation]. The disturbance cannot be accounted for by a known physical disorder" (American Psychiatric Association, 1985).

Health professionals have seen an alarming rise in the incidence of this disorder among young women in the last 15 to 20 years (Anderson & others, 1992; Malowald, 1992). Whether anorexia nervosa has actually increased or whether it is now being more readily recognized has yet to be determined.

The specific criteria for anorexia nervosa are the following:

- Onset before age 25

- Weight loss of at least 25 percent of original body weight

- Distorted, implacable attitudes toward eating, food, or weight that override hunger, admonitions, reassurance, and threats, including
  —Denial of illness, with a failure to recognize nutritional needs
  —Apparent enjoyment in losing weight, with overt manifestations that food refusal is a pleasurable indulgence
  —A desired body image of extreme thinness, with evidence that it is rewarding to the person to achieve and maintain this state
  —Unusual hoarding and handling of food

- No known medical illness that could account for the anorexia and weight loss

- No other known psychiatric disorder, particularly primary affective disorders, schizophrenia, or obsessive, compulsive, or phobic (fearful) neuroses. (Even though it may appear phobic and obsessional, food refusal alone is not sufficient to qualify as an obsessive, compulsive, or phobic disorder.)

- At least two of the following manifestations: amenorrhea (loss of menses); lanugo (soft downy hair covering body); bradycardia (heart rate of less than 60); periods of overactivity; vomiting (may be self-induced).

Cauffman and Steinberg (1996) found that a higher incidence of anorexia is found among 12- to 13-year-old girls who have experienced menarche, and who are dating and are physically involved with their boyfriends.

Bulimia Nervosa

Bulimia nervosa is a disorder related to anorexia nervosa and sometimes combined with it. It is characterized by

> . . . episodic binge-eating accompanied by an awareness that the eating pattern is abnormal, fear of not being able to stop eating voluntarily, and depressed mood and self-deprecating thoughts following the eating binges. The bulimic episodes are not due to anorexia nervosa or any known physical disorder. (American Psychiatric Association, 1985)

Bulimia has been observed in women above or below weight, as well as in those who are normal. The specific criteria of bulimia are the following:

- Repeated episodes of binge-eating

- Awareness that one's eating pattern is abnormal

- Fear of not being able to stop eating

- Depressed mood and self-deprecation after binges

Anorectics and bulimics share emotional and behavioral traits, despite their clinical differences. The most characteristic symptoms specific to these disorders are the preoccupation with food and the persistent determination to be slim, rather than the behaviors that result from that choice (Cauffman & Steinberg, 1996; Moore, 1995).

The Athletic Body

At the age of 15, gymnast Christy Henrich narrowly missed making the United States Olympic team. Following the trials, a judge told Christy that she should lose a few pounds—at the time, Christy was 4 feet 10 inches and weighed 90 pounds! Comments such as these led to Christy having anorexia and bulimia. At one point Christy's weight was down to 47 pounds. In July 1994, as her parents and coach were helping her recover, Christy died of multiple organ failure at the age of 22. Her coach claims that gymnastics and its emphasis on slimness are not responsible for Christy's illness and death. He claims her intense drive to win contributed to her eating disorder. The gymnastic training system encourages young female athletes to keep their weight down, and many gymnasts live on diets of fruits, laxatives, and painkillers. In 1976 the average age of a U. S. gymnast was 18, with an average weight of 106 pounds. In 1992, the average age of a U. S. gymnast was 16, with an average weight of 83 pounds—a drop of 23 pounds! Cathy Rigby, a former gymnast who won a gold medal at the 1968 Olympics, fought a 12-year battle with anorexia and bulimia. Now recovering from her illness, Cathy states that gymnasts are trained to be slim through fear, guilt, and intimidation (Ryan, 1995).

A number of new approaches to treatment and therapy are currently being researched (Scott, 1988). Although success rates are not high, the situation in either disorder is usually so complex and potentially hazardous that only qualified personnel should attempt to treat victims.

Guided Review

9. Puberty is a relatively abrupt and qualitatively different set of physical changes in boys and girls that usually occurs at the beginning of the _____ years.
10. Although there is a rather wide normal range of development as relates to the onset of puberty, early- or late-maturing children can be affected socially and _____.
11. _____-maturing boys are often peer group leaders.
12. One hundred years ago the average-maturing girl was physically much like the late-maturing girl today. This phenomenon is called the _____ _____.
13. _____ _____ is a syndrome of self-starvation characterized, in part, by an intense fear of becoming obese, disturbance of body image, and significant weight loss.

Cognitive Development

I was about 12 when I discovered that you could create a whole new world just in your head! I don't know why I hadn't thought about it before, but the idea excited me terrifically. I started lying in bed on

Answers

Saturday mornings till 11 or 12 o'clock, making up "my secret world." I
went to fabulous places. I met friends who really liked me and treated me
great. And of course I fell in love with this guy like you wouldn't believe!
(Susan Klein, an eighth-grade student)

Adolescence is a complex process of growth and change (see, for example, Rushton & Ankney, 1996). Because biological and social changes are the focus of attention, changes in the young adolescent's ability to think often go unnoticed. Yet it is during early and middle adolescence that thinking ability reaches Piaget's fourth and last level—the level of abstract thought (see Chapter 2). To understand how abstract thought develops, we have to know more about cognition itself.

Variables in Cognitive Development: Piaget

Let us pause to review Jean Piaget's theory (described in Chapter 2). He argued that the ability to think develops in four stages:

- The *sensorimotor stage* (birth to 2 years), in which the child learns from its interactions with the world.

- The *preoperational stage* (2 to 7 years), in which behaviors such as picking up a can are gradually internalized so that they can be manipulated in the mind.

- The *concrete operational stage* (7 to 11 years), in which actions can be manipulated mentally, but only with things. For example, a child of 8 is able to anticipate what is going to happen if a can is thrown across the room without actually having to do so.

- The *formal operational stage* (11 years +), in which groups of concrete operations are combined to become formal operations. For example, the adolescent comes to understand democracy by combining concepts such as putting a ballot in a box and hearing that the Senate voted to give money for the homeless. This is the stage of abstract thought development.

We are like other animals, especially the primates, in many ways. They, too, can make plans, can cooperate in groups, and may well have simple language systems. But the ability to perform formal operations is what truly separates us (although we cannot say that all humans reach this stage, either). Piaget's conception of the formal operation is a remarkable contribution to psychology.

It was also Piaget who first noted the strong tendency of early adolescents toward democratic values because of this new thinking capacity. This is the age at which youths first become committed to the idea that participants in a group may change the rules of a game, but once agreed on, all must follow the new rules. This

Elementary school-age children compete at a chess tournament.

tendency, he believes, is universal; all teenagers throughout the world develop this value.

Having considered Piaget's ideas about adolescent cognition in some detail earlier in this book, let us turn now to a review of the findings of those researchers who have been diligently following him.

Culture and gender can also influence cognitive development. Piaget's theory seems to assume that the ideal person at the end point of cognitive development resembles a Swiss scientist. Most theorists focus on an ideal end point for development that, not too surprisingly, ascribes their own valued qualities to maturity.

Piaget (1973) acknowledged that his description of the end point might not apply to all cultures, since evidence had showed cultural variation. If one stresses the influence of context (sociocultural and individual) on development as Vygotsky (1978) and Barbara Rogoff (1990) do, then one sees multiple directions for development rather than only one ideal end point. For example, it may well be that for some agricultural societies, sophisticated development of the concrete operational stage would be far more useful than minimal formal operational thinking. That is, an understanding of the complicated workings of a machine may be concrete, but that does not make that type of thinking inferior to another person's ability to do formal operations. Thus believing that the formal operations stage is always superior would be intellectual snobbism.

A Sociocultural VIEW Personality Factors, Achievement, and Ethnicity

It is often assumed that economic disadvantages and poor academic achievement have led people of color in the United States to have low expectations for the future and negative self-concepts. A number of recent studies have examined the relationships among several personality factors and achievement as they are related within several ethnic groups. For example, Graham (1994) learned that although motivational factors are believed to be as important as intellectual competencies in understanding achievement in all people, this is especially so among African Americans. Graham's research reviewed 140 studies on motivation in African Americans covering strength of achievement motive, locus of control, causal attributions, levels of expectancy, and self-concept.

Graham concludes from this research that African Americans do not lack the motive to strive for success. Even in studies where African Americans appeared to be lower in achievement motive (and no studies after 1970 showed differences favoring whites over African Americans), African Americans reported educational and vocational aspirations equal to or higher than their white counterparts. They were just as likely as whites to aspire to go to college and/or enter high status professions. For all subjects, motive scores increased with higher social status. When socioeconomic class (SES) was controlled, differences between African Americans and whites diminished or reversed. In other words, high SES African American boys had higher achievement motive scores than did boys in a number of low SES white groups. Other studies found equally low motive scores for African Americans and whites in the lowest SES groups.

People with internal locus of control (those who see themselves as the main cause of what happens to them) are considered less susceptible to social influence, better information seekers, more achievement-oriented, and better psychologically adjusted. Graham's review found less internality among African Americans. However, studies examining the relationship between locus of control and other achievement-related variables did not support the argument that this lack of internality is a problem for African Americans. In fact, there appear to be positive consequences of this perception, such as increased social activism and militance.

African Americans and whites were equal in displaying an adaptive pattern by attributing success to one's ability and effort, and failure to one's lack of effort. Data also show African American subjects remained optimistic about the future even after achievement failure. Research on general self-concept in African Americans does not support the view that they have negative self views; they have consistently been shown to be equal to or higher than whites on a variety of self-concept measures.

Graham's overview of past research is generally supported by Taylor and associates (1994), who studied a sample of African Americans, by Lease and Robbins (1994), whose research was on Southeast Asian adolescent refugees, and by Yan and Gaier (1994), who studied Chinese, Japanese, Korean, and Southeast Asian college students.

Gender also plays a role in the definition of formal operations. Gilligan (1982) said that most theories of development define the end point of development as being male only, and that they overlook alternatives that more closely fit the mature female. She believed that if the definition of maturity changes, so does the entire account of development. Using men as the model of development, independence and separation are seen as the goals of development. But if women are used as the models, relationship with others or interdependence are the goals of development. This gender difference also leads to distinctions in the development of thinking about morality (Gilligan & others, 1990).

In a rare study that investigated all three aspects of the biopsychosocial approach, Casey and associates (1997) sought to explain the superiority of males on the Mathematics Scholastic Aptitude Test (SAT-M). Some scholars have argued that this perennial result is due to a male genetic advantage in doing math, whereas others have attributed it to female math anxiety, which they learn early in life. Casey and associates measured the relationships among sex and spatial skills (innate traits), math self-confidence and geometry knowledge (psychological variables) and math anxiety (a socially induced trait).

> All morality consists in a system of rules, and the essence of all morality is . . . in the respect which the individual acquires for these rules.
> Jean Piaget

(It should be noted that the sources of each of these variables are themselves biopsychosocial, at least to some degree.) Through a complex statistical technique known as path analysis, the researchers established that attitudinal variables accounted for only 36 percent of the variation in SAT-M scores, and spatial skills accounted for 64 percent. This finding does not mean that the greater math ability of boys is inevitable, however. Numerous approaches to the difference might be taken. For example, we could encourage girls to get more experience playing with toys and games and in sports that require a high degree of spatial skill.

Adolescent Egocentrism

Parents often feel frustrated at the seemingly irrational attitudes and behaviors of their adolescent children. One explanation is the reemergence of a pattern of thought that marked early childhood, egocentrism. **Adolescent egocentrism,** a term coined by Elkind (1978), refers to adolescents' tendency to exaggerate the importance, uniqueness, and severity of social and emotional experiences. Their love is greater than anything their parents have experienced. Their suffering is more painful and unjust than anyone else's. Their friendships are most sacred. Their clothes are the worst or the best. Developmentally speaking, adolescent egocentrism seems to peak around the age of 13 (Elkind & Bowen, 1979), followed by a gradual and sometimes painful decline.

Elkind sees two components to this egocentrism. First, teenagers tend to create an **imaginary audience** (Montgomery & others, 1996). They feel they are on cen-

Young teen-agers today are being forced to make decisions that earlier generations didn't have to make until they were older and more mature, and today's teen-agers are not getting much support and guidance.
David Elkind

ter stage, and the rest of the world is constantly scrutinizing their behavior and physical appearance. This accounts for some of the apparently irrational mood swings in adolescents. The mirror may produce an elated, confident teenager ready to make an appearance. Then one pimple on the nose can be cause for staying inside the house for days. In fact, school phobia can become acute during early adolescence because of concerns over appearance.

The second component of egocentrism is the **personal fable.** This refers to adolescents' tendency to think of themselves in heroic or mythical terms (Siegel & Shaughnessy, 1995). The result is that they exaggerate their own abilities and their invincibility. This type of mythic creation on the part of an adolescent can sometimes lead to increased risk-taking, such as drug use, dangerous driving, and disregard for the possible consequences of sexual behavior. Many teenagers simply can't imagine an unhappy ending to their own special story.

Critical Thinking

Although we discussed critical thinking at some length in Chapter 9, we should make a number of points about its role in adolescence. Guilford's (1975) distinction between convergent and divergent thinking is helpful here, because critical thinking is made up of these two abilities.

Convergent thinking is used when we solve a problem by following a series of steps that close in on the correct answer. For example, if we were to ask you to answer the question, "How much is 286 times 469?" you probably could not produce it immediately. However, if you used a pencil and paper or a calculator, you would almost certainly converge on the same answer as most others trying to solve the problem. Only one answer is correct. Critical thinking uses convergent thinking. As Moore and Parker (1986) state, it is "the correct evaluation of claims and arguments."

Divergent thinking, on the other hand, is just the opposite. This is the type of thinking used when the problem to be solved has many possible answers. For example, what are all the things that would be different if it were to rain up instead of down?

Other divergent questions are "What would happen if we had no thumbs?" and "What should we do to prevent ice buildup from snapping telephone lines?" Divergent thinking can be right or wrong, too, but considerably greater leeway exists for personal opinion than with convergent thinking. Not all divergent thinking is creative, but it is more likely to produce a creative concept. To be a good critical

---

What's Your View? Should Critical Thinking about Interpersonal Problems Be Taught in Our Schools?

Critical thinking is of tremendous importance to teens, as they learn to cope with the changes that life brings. One arena in which this skill is of great usefulness is in working out interpersonal problems. Here, too, we may easily see how an understanding of the concept of bidirectionality (see the section on contextualism in Chapter 1) also plays a role. The roots of interpersonal problems almost always involves bidirectional causes. Most teens are well aware of how the actions of others affect them, but sometimes fail to see how their own actions may bring about negative reactions. Here is

where following the five phases of critical thinking described above comes in. Practicing this procedure can greatly alleviate some of the hurt feelings and misunderstandings that inevitably occur.

Many educators agree that teaching critical thinking as it applies to school subjects is appropriate, but cannot agree that they should also apply these lessons to real-life teen problems. If you were a secondary teacher (or counselor or administrator), would you include adolescent interpersonal relations in your teaching of critical thinking? What's your view?

Video Games and Cognitive Development

The emergence of video games as a popular pastime among children and adolescents in the late 1970s created a firestorm of controversy. Parents and educators were warned that there may be detrimental consequences to prolonged exposure. Surgeon General C. Everett Koop cautioned that video games could contribute to the development of psychosis (Funk, 1993). Amidst all this controversy there is little empirical evidence to support the claims of the negative impact of video games (Subrahmanyam & Greenfield, 1994).

The 1990s offers an entirely different perception of this newest, information-age form of play. A Harvard study in 1993 found no significant ill effects from video games. Now that more than 34 percent of all households own a Nintendo game system, video games have a well-established role in American adolescent culture. Strong evidence indicates that just as various forms of play in all societies prepare children for the demands of adulthood, video games are an important cultural artifact to teach skills that relate to the mastery of computer technology. There has been speculation that video games may enhance eye-hand coordination, decision making, numerical concepts, and the ability to follow directions. Their extreme motivational qualities in a goal-directed activity make the games a subject of interest to a broad range of researchers (Subrahmanyam & Greenfield, 1994).

Video games are a type of symbolic play representing movement within actual space. The effect of video games on spatial skills has recently been studied (Subrahmanyam & Greenfield, 1994; and Okagaki & Greenfield, 1994). Action video games were shown to improve spatial relations skills more than an educational word game did. Although males of all ages have better spatial abilities (Greenfield, 1994), researchers found no difference in the rate of improvement in spatial skills between males and females playing six hours of the game Tetris after they had not played any video game during the previous year (Okagaki & Greenfield). This result was obtained in spite of higher pretest scores of spatial skill for the male subjects. In general, males have more experience in video game playing than do females (Greenfield). If spatial skills are acquired and not genetically determined, video games could be an excellent method to develop these skills and could contribute to gender balance in this domain of cognitive development (Subrahmanyam & Greenfield).

Another area of study has focused on divided attention and video games. Divided attention is necessary for many vocations such as air traffic controller, as well as for everyday tasks such as driving a car or playing certain sports. In a recent study involving both expert and novice video game players, strategies of divided attention were shown to improve in both categories of subjects (Greenfield & others, 1994).

It does appear that video games have been viewed too negatively; they do serve to socialize children to interact with artificial intelligence. A greater cause for concern may be that most video games contain violent themes. Boys tend to enjoy that type of aggressive competition, whereas girls do not. Because video games improve cognitive development and prepare individuals for skills related to computer technology, more games with active female characters and with nonviolent themes should be designed to ensure equal preparation for survival in this age of technology (Greenfield, 1994).

thinker, analyzing statements accurately is not enough. Often you will need to think divergently to understand the possibilities and the implications of those statements, too.

Because adolescents are entering the formal operations stage of intellectual development, they become vastly more capable of critical thinking than younger children. As they move through the teen years, they grow in their ability to make effective decisions. This involves five types of newly acquired abilities (Moore & others, 1985):

Phase 1. Recognizing and defining the problem (e.g., a 13-year-old boy notices that girls seem to avoid him, and when he stands near them, they move away)

Phase 2. Gathering information (he asks other boys if they get the same reaction, and several mention that he gets that reaction because he has body odor)

Phase 3. Forming tentative conclusions (he wonders if he should shower more than twice a week and change his clothes more often)

Phase 4. Testing tentative conclusions (he showers and changes clothes daily, and then strikes up conversations with several girls)

Phase 5. Evaluation and decision making (because he no longer experiences avoidance, he decides to continue his cleanliness program)

In the next section, we make a distinction between critical and creative thinking, but it is important that we not make too great a distinction. Paul (1987) describes this concern well:

> Just as it is misleading to talk of developing a student's capacity to think critically without facing the problem of cultivating the student's rational passions—the necessary driving force behind the rational use of all critical thinking skills—so too it is misleading to talk of developing a student's ability to think critically as something separate from the student's ability to think creatively. . . . The imagination and its creative powers are continually called forth. (p. 143)

Creative Thinking

> This is the story about a very curious cat named Kat. One day Kat was wandering in the woods where he came upon a big house made of fish. Without thinking, he ate much of that house. The next morning when he woke up he had grown considerably larger. Even as he walked down the street he was getting bigger. Finally he got bigger than any building ever made. He walked up to the Empire State Building in New York City and accidentally crushed it. The people had to think of a way to stop him, so they made this great iron box which made the cat curious. He finally got inside it, but it was too heavy to get him out of again. There he lived for the rest of his life. But he was still curious until his death, which was 6,820,000 years later. They buried him in the state of Rhode Island, and I mean the whole state. (Ralph Titus, a seventh-grade student)

The restless imagination, the daring exaggeration, the disdain for triteness that this story demonstrates—all are signs that its young author has great creative potential. With the right kind of encouragement, with the considerable knowledge we now have about how to foster creativity, this boy could develop his talents to his own and society's great benefit (Dacey, 1989a and c, 1998; Dacey & Lennon, 1998; Esquivel, 1995; Hennessey, 1995; Litterst & Eyo, 1993; Tavalin, 1995).

Creative thinking appears to have many elements—divergent thinking, fluency, flexibility, originality, remote associations. We will look more closely at these ele-

ments when we get to adult creativity later in this book, but one element that seems to be of special importance in adolescence is the use of metaphor.

The Use of Metaphor

A *metaphor* is a word or phrase that by comparison or analogy stands for another word or phrase. Common sense suggests a relationship between efficient metaphor use and creativity. Using a metaphor in speech involves calling attention to a similarity between two seemingly dissimilar things. This suggests a process similar to divergent thinking, and a growing body of research shows support for this relationship.

Kogan believed that the **use of metaphor** can explain the difference between ordinary divergent thinking and high-quality divergent thinking. A creative person must be able not only to think of many different things from many different categories but also to compare them in unique, qualitatively different ways. Although metaphors are typically first used by older children and adolescents, research has looked at the symbolic play of very young children and how it relates to creativity (see Kogan, 1983, for a good review). The early imaginative play of children is now being viewed as a precursor of later metaphor use and creativity.

Howard Gardner and his associates at Harvard University have studied the role of metaphor. Gardner's seminal *Art, Mind, and Brain: A Cognitive Approach to Creativity* (1982) offers many insights into the process (see also Csikszentmihalyi, 1994; Gardner, 1993a, 1993b). Gardner has based his research on the theories of three eminent theorists: Jean Piaget, Noam Chomsky, and Claude Levi-Strauss. He states that "These thinkers share a belief that the mind operates according to specifiable rules —often unconscious ones—and that these can be ferreted out and made explicit by the systematic examination of human language, action, and problem solving" (p. 4).

Gardner's main efforts have focused on the relationship between children's art and children's understanding of metaphor, both in normal and brain-damaged children. He describes talking to a group of youngsters at a seder (the meal many Jews eat to commemorate the flight of the Hebrews from Egypt). He told the children how, after a plague, Pharaoh's "heart was turned to stone." The children interpreted the metaphor variously, but only the older ones could understand the link between the physical universe (hard rocks) and psychological traits (stubborn lack of feeling). Younger children are more apt to apply magical interpretations (God or a witch did it). Gardner believes that the development of the understanding of metaphoric language is as sequential as the stages that Piaget and Erikson proposed and is closely related to the types of development treated in those theories.

Examining children's metaphors such as a bald man having a "barefoot head" and an elephant being seen as a "gas mask," Gardner and Winner (1982) found clear changes with age in the level of sophistication. Interestingly, two opposing features appear:

- When you ask children to explain figures of speech, they steadily get better at it as they get older. This ability definitely increases as the child attains the formal operations stage.

- However, very young children seem to be the best at making up their own metaphors. Furthermore, their own metaphors tend to be of two types (Gardner & Winner, 1982):

  The different patterns of making metaphors may reflect fundamentally different ways of processing information. Children who base their metaphors on visual resemblances may approach experience largely in terms of the physical qualities of objects. On the other hand, children who base their metaphors on action sequences may view the world in terms of the way events unfold over time. We believe that the difference may continue into adulthood, underlying diverse styles in the creation and appreciation of artistic form. (p. 164)

Child prodigies are distinguished by the passion with which they pursue their interests. Here we see the young Wolfgang Amadeus Mozart performing for a group of admiring adults. He was not merely precocious—able to perform at levels typical of older children; he was prodigious—able, at a young age, to write music that professional musicians still perform.

It is exciting to think that this discovery by Gardner and Winner may explain why some people become scientists and others writers. If this is so, it certainly is an important key to fostering such talent. Of course, this is not to say that they have the answers to such questions as why children develop one of the two forms of "metaphorizing" (or neither), but their work appears to be a giant step in the right direction.

These researchers believe that the spontaneous production of metaphors declines somewhat during the school years. This is probably because the child, having mastered a basic vocabulary, has less need to "stretch the resources of language to express new meanings" (Gardner & Winner, 1982, p.165). In addition, teachers and parents exert greater pressure on children to get the right answers, so they take fewer risks in their language. Gardner and Winner point to the *Shakespeare Parallel Text Series,* which offers a translation of the bard's plays into everyday English ("Stand and unfold yourself" becomes "Stand still and tell me who you are"), as a step in the wrong direction. "If, as we have shown, students of this age have the potential to deal with complex metaphors, there is no necessity to rewrite Shakespeare" (p. 167).

Creativity, Giftedness, and the IQ

As Feldman (1979; 1994a and 1994b) has pointed out, many studies of "giftedness" have been conducted, but only a few of exceptionally creative, highly productive youth have been undertaken. This is a serious omission because, as you will see later in this book, adolescence is a sensitive period in the growth of creative ability. Feldman believes that this unfortunate situation is mainly the fault of "the foremost figure in the study of the gifted," Lewis M. Terman. Terman (1925) was well known for his research on 1,000 California children whose IQs in the early 1920s were 135 or higher. Terman believed these children to be the "geniuses" of the future, a label he kept for them as he studied their development over the decades. His was a powerful investigation and has been followed by scholars and popular writers alike.

Precisely because of the notoriety of this research, Feldman argues, we have come to accept a numerical definition of genius (an IQ above 135), and a somewhat low one at that. Feldman notes that the *Encyclopedia Britannica* now differentiates two basic definitions of genius: the numerical one fostered by Terman; and the concept first described by Sir Francis Galton (1870, 1879): "creative ability of an exceptionally high order as demonstrated by actual achievement."

Feldman (1979) says that *genius,* as defined by IQ, really only refers to **precociousness**—doing what others are able to do, but at a younger age. **Prodigiousness** (as in child prodigy), on the other hand, refers to someone who is qualitatively higher in ability from the rest of us. This is different from simply being able to do things sooner. Further, prodigiousness calls for a rare matching of high talent and an environment that is ready and open to creativity. If such youthful prodigies as Mozart in music or Bobby Fischer in chess had been born 2,000 years earlier, they may well have grown up to be much more ordinary. In fact, if Einstein had been born 50 years earlier, he might have done nothing special—particularly because he did not even speak well until he was five!

So if prodigies are more than just quicker at learning, what is it that truly distinguishes them? On the basis of his intensive study of three prodigies, Feldman states that

> Perhaps the most striking quality in the children in our study as well as other cases is the passion with which excellence is pursued. Commitment and tenacity and joy in achievement are perhaps the best signs that a coincidence has occurred among child, field, and moment in evolutionary time. No event is more likely to predict that a truly remarkable, creative contribution will eventually occur. (1979, p. 351)

In summary, critical and creative thinking are similar in that they both employ convergent and divergent production. The main difference between them is that critical thinking aims at the correct assessment of existing ideas, whereas creativity is more aimed at the invention and discovery of new ideas. Although each requires a certain amount of intelligence, creativity also depends on such traits as metaphorical thinking and an independent personality.

Robert Sternberg (1990) said the intelligent person can recall, analyze, and use knowledge, whereas the creative person goes beyond existing knowledge and the wise person probes inside knowledge and understands the meaning of what is known (see Chapter 18). It should be noted that these conclusions appear to hold true not only for adolescence, but for all periods of the lifespan.

Mental Health Issues

A number of psychologists and psychoanalysts (most notably Freud) have suggested that having distressing, turbulent, unpredictable thoughts that in an adult would be considered pathological is normal in adolescence. This disruptive state is partly characteristic of the identity stages of confusion and moratorium. Identity confusion is sometimes typified by withdrawal from reality (Erikson, 1968). Occasional distortions in time perspective can occur. Mental disturbance also often makes intimacy with another person impossible. These characteristics are also seen in the moratorium stage, but they tend to be of much shorter duration.

How common and how serious are these problems? The picture is not clear. Summarizing decades of research, Kimmel and Weiner (1985) concluded that true psychopathology (mental illness) is relatively rare during adolescence. It is impossible to determine the frequency of mental illness, however, because of current disagreements over its definition. Weiner (1992) summarized numerous studies, which give us considerable reason to believe that "adolescent turmoil," though common, does not really constitute psychopathology.

Studies do indicate that when adolescents become seriously disturbed and do not receive appropriate treatment quickly, the chances of their "growing out" of their problems are dim (Eisen & others, 1992; James & Nims, 1996; Tolbert, 1996). Weiner warned that

> An indiscriminate application of "adolescent turmoil" and "he'll-grow-out-of-it" notions to symptomatic adolescents runs the grave risk of discouraging the attention that may be necessary to avert serious psychological disturbance. (p. 66)

There is evidence that living in an adoptive family is less of a factor in the emotional adjustment of adoptees than the mental health of biological parents. A recent study conducted by Ge and associates (1996b) found that the hostile and antisocial behaviors sometimes displayed by adopted children were in fact related to the psychiatric disorders of their biological parents. McGue and associates (1996) discovered that adolescents raised by adoptive parents are less well adjusted than children born to those same parents. Although adopted and birth children may be raised in the same environment, it appears that adopted children may face a more complicated transition into adolescence. McGue and associates concluded that "These findings provide further evidence of the minimal effect of common rearing on sibling psychological similarity, at least within the broadly constituted U. S. middle class" (p. 604).

Furthermore, the family environment may perpetuate adolescent depression and antisocial behavior. Pike and associates (1996) stated that responses to negativity questionnaires by parents and siblings showed signification relationship to unhealthy adolescent adjustment. Family factors were also examined by Henry and associates (1996), with regard to violent and nonviolent behaviors of adolescents. The authors concluded that whereas childhood temperament is associated with the adolescent's being convicted of primarily violent offenses, family characteristics were associated with both violent and nonviolent criminal behavior of adolescents.

Types of Mental Disorders

The question of what kinds of mental illness afflict adolescents has not received much attention, but interest is increasing (e. g., Compass & others, 1995; Reimer, 1996). Several studies (Culp & others, 1995; Hammond & Romney, 1995; Prosser & McArdle, 1996) have suggested that the prevalence of major depression and the incidence of suicide is increasing in adolescent populations, particularly among males. Petersen and associates (1993) found that for teens, who had *not* sought professional help, between 10 and 35 percent of the boys and between 15 and 40 percent of the girls reported that they had experienced the symptoms of depression.

Ethnic differences in depressed adolescents were examined by Greenberger and Chen (1996). They found that the ethnic variations among adolescents did not account for significant differences. However, whether the subjects were in the early or late stages of adolescent development produced more striking differences with regard to their perceived relationships with their parents. The perceived relationships accounted for more variance in depressed mood in early adolescents. Parental hostility toward teens when they were in the seventh, eighth, and ninth grades was observed by Ge and associates (1996a) as predictors of adjustment problems and depressive symptoms among these children when they were in the tenth grade. Although depression rates are about equal for boys and girls before they reach puberty, after it starts, girls are about twice as likely to feel seriously depressed as boys. A detailed description of the research on adolescent suicide rates and causes is presented in Chapter 19.

In conclusion, adolescence is not a time of turmoil and distress for most teens. Rates of mental disturbance among teens are very similar to rates of disturbance among adults. As you will recall, however, adolescents (and adults) are experiencing increasingly high levels of daily stress. Hechinger (1992) warns that teenagers are in greater danger than ever from the risks of alcohol and drugs, unwanted pregnancy, sexually transmitted disease, depression, and violence. It is not normal for adolescents to be experiencing high levels of psychological distress. When society exposes youth to serious risks, such as drugs and violence, psychological distress and mental disturbance are likely to increase (American Psychological Association, 1994).

A source on this subject is Gibson's *The butterfly ward.* New Orleans: Louisiana State University Press. This set of short stories tells what it is like to be between sanity and insanity. It is a sensitive look at the world of the mentally ill, both in and out of institutions.

Guided Review

14. In exploring cognitive development, we examine Piaget's four stages of cognitive development: sensorimotor, preoperational, _____ operational, and formal operational.
15. Formal operational means that a person can form _____ mental operations.
16. Elkind presents the concept of adolescent egocentrism, which includes an _____ _____ and the personal fable.
17. Thinking skills can be separated into convergent (coming together with a single correct answer) and _____ (exploring the many possible answers to a question).
18. David Feldman claims that some children are precocious (doing what others do, but at a younger age), while other children are _____ (having a qualitatively greater ability than the rest of us).
19. _____ _____ is sometimes typified by withdrawal from reality.

CONCLUSION

Defining adolescence is a complex task. Deciding when it begins and ends is even more complicated. We know that any definition must be biopsychosocial in order to be comprehensive. We know that, biologically, there is a marked increase in the flow of sex-related hormones, as well as a maximum growth spurt and the appearance of secondary sex characteristics. Psychologically, a new sense of self and the formation of the identity take shape, and cognitive changes such as formal operations, the personal fable and the imaginary audience occur. The social world of the teen undergoes many changes, including the inauguration of new privileges and new responsibilities. These changes constitute the bare bones of a definition, but even all the information in this and the following chapter only begin to tell the whole story.

We wish that all children could complete puberty with a normal, healthy body and body image. We wish they could negotiate adolescence so successfully that they become energetic, self-confident adults.

Unfortunately, we know that this is not always the case. Some youths suffer from a negative self-concept because, although they differ from the norm only slightly in their body development, they perceive this as "catastrophic." Others deviate significantly from the norm because of some physiological problem. Of particular concern for females is our society's obsession with thinness. Taken together, the various aspects of puberty can cause the adolescent quite a bit of chagrin.

The only solution is to get some perspective on these problems. The good news is that just when they need it, most adolescents develop improved mental abilities that enable them to get a more realistic view of themselves. Cognitive development is a complex matter, one about which we understood very little before this century. Our best evidence is that the intellect develops in stages. Contrary to earlier beliefs, thinking in childhood, adolescence, and adulthood are qualitatively different from each other. Furthermore, cognitive development has a number of other aspects: social cognition, information processing, egocentric thinking, critical thinking, creative thinking, and mental health.

In summary:

How Should We Define Adolescence?

- Most experts state that the majority of adolescents are happy and productive members of their families and communities.
- Hall's interpretation of adolescent development was greatly influenced by his observation that it is a period of storm and stress.
- It is likely that youth are viewed as immature during financial depressions in order to keep them from competing with adults for scarce jobs; their maturity is seen as greater during wartime because they are needed to perform such adult tasks as soldiering and factory work.

Theories of Adolescence

- Anna Freud believed that the delicate balance between the superego and the id, being disrupted by puberty, causes the adolescent to regress to earlier stages of development.
- According to Erik Erikson, human life progresses through eight "psychosocial" stages, each of which is marked by a crisis and its resolution. The fifth stage applies mainly to adolescence.
- Although the ages at which one goes through each Eriksonian stage vary, the sequence of stages is fixed. Stages may overlap, however.
- John Hill's biopsychosocial theory, with its emphasis on the six factors of dependence, autonomy, sexuality, intimacy, achievement, and identity, offers the most inclusive theory of adolescence.

Answers

14. concrete 15. abstract 16. imaginary audience 17. divergent 18. prodigious 19. Identity confusion

Physical Development

- Theories of adolescence in the early twentieth century were largely based on personal bias, because little empirical data existed.
- Those who work with adolescents need complete knowledge of the reproductive systems of both sexes.
- The order of physical changes in puberty is largely predictable, but the timing and duration of these changes are not.
- The normal range in pubertal development is very broad, and includes early, on-time, and late maturers.
- The adolescent's own perception of being normal has more influence on self-esteem than objective normality.
- Maturity of appearance affects whether adolescents are treated appropriately for their age.
- Early maturing is a positive experience for boys but may be negative for girls.
- Late maturing is often difficult for both boys and girls.
- Two of the most disruptive problems for adolescents are the eating disorders known as anorexia and bulimia nervosa.
- Adolescent girls develop eating disorders more than any other group.
- Developmental, cultural, individual, and familial factors are associated with the development of eating disorders.

Cognitive Development

- Piaget focused on the development of the cognitive structures of the intellect during childhood and adolescence.
- The infant and child pass through Piaget's first three stages: sensorimotor, preoperational, and concrete operational.
- Piaget's highest stage of cognitive development, that of formal operations, begins to develop in early adolescence.
- Adolescents focus much attention on themselves and tend to believe that everybody is looking at them. This phenomenon is called the imaginary audience.
- Many adolescents also hold beliefs about their own uniqueness and invulnerability. This is known as the personal fable.
- Critical thinking combines both convergent thinking, in which there is only one correct answer, and divergent thinking, in which there are many possible answers to a problem.
- Effective decision making, a formal operational process, is a part of critical thinking.
- Creative thinking includes divergent thinking, fluency, flexibility, originality, and remote associations.
- In adolescence, the understanding and use of metaphor appears to be an important aspect of creative thinking.
- Conventional schooling often has a dampening effect on students' willingness to risk doing creative, metaphorical thinking.
- Criticism of genius, as defined by IQ, holds that IQ indicates only precociousness but cannot account for prodigiousness.
- The idea that those who develop mental illness during adolescence will "grow out of it" is not supported by research. Depression can be an especially dangerous illness at this age.
- Adolescence is not a time of turmoil and distress for most teens. Rates of mental disturbance among teens are very similar to rates of disturbance among adults.

KEY TERMS

Adolescent egocentrism
Anorexia nervosa
Bulimia nervosa
Convergent thinking
Divergent thinking
Hormonal balance
Indentity crisis
Identity status

Imaginary audience
Maturation
Maximum growth spurt
Menarche
Normal range of development
Personal fable
Precociousness
Prodigiousness

Puberty
Repudiation
Secular trend
State of identity
Transition-linked turning points
Use of metaphor

WHAT DO YOU THINK?

1. Should children be taught about their body functions in school? Should this teaching include sexuality? If so, at what grade should it start?
2. How do sociocultural influences impact adolescent cognitive development? How do these influences differ for girls and boys?
3. Why do you suppose people develop eating disorders?
4. Why should adolescents be more prone than other age groups to having "imaginary audiences" and "personal fables"?
5. Do you believe you can "disinhibit" (free up) your creative abilities? How should you start? Why don't you?
6. What are some of the ways we can help adolescents to have better mental health?

CHAPTER REVIEW TEST

1. Which of the following is part of the male reproductive system?
   a. Fimbriae
   b. Vas deferens
   c. Cervix
   d. Ova

2. What controls sexual characteristics in both males and females?
   a. Pituitary gland
   b. Bartholin's glands
   c. Cowper's glands
   d. Epididymis

3. What marks the onset of puberty?
   a. Menarche for females; the first ejaculation for males
   b. The growth spurt for females and males
   c. The beginning of breast development for females; the enlargement of the genitals for males
   d. No single event marks the onset of puberty.

4. Adolescents who are dependent and childlike, who feel a growing dislike for their bodies, and who become more introverted and self-rejecting because of it are most likely to be
   a. early-maturing males.
   b. early-maturing females.
   c. average-maturing males.
   d. late-maturing females.

5. The identity status in which numerous crises have been experienced and resolved, and relatively permanent commitments have been made is called
   a. identity moratorium.
   b. identity achievement.
   c. foreclosed identity.
   d. confused identity.

6. The decreasing age of the onset of puberty is referred to as
   a. early physical maturation.

b. early psychological maturity.
   c. the evolutionary trend.
   d. the secular trend.

7. Specific criteria for anorexia nervosa include
   a. weight loss of at least 25 percent of original body weight.
   b. onset before age 25.
   c. distorted attitudes toward eating and weight.
   d. All of the answers are correct.

8. One of the traits by which Lerner characterized the adolescent transition is
   a. independence.
   b. eating disorders.
   c. relative plasticity.
   d. negative body image.

9. From the standpoint of adolescence, the most important of Erikson's eight stages is the _____ stage.
   a. identity
   b. autonomy
   c. intimacy
   d. industry

10. What occurs during Piaget's formal operational stage?
    a. Concrete operations combine to become formal operations
    b. Preoperations turn into formal operations
    c. Parts of the sensorimotor stage turn into formal operations
    d. The preoperational stage and the sensorimotor stage combine to become formal operations

11. One of the criticisms of Piaget's theory of cognitive development is that it
    a. is too broad.
    b. does not address abstract thought.

c. is too complex.
    d. does not account for culture and gender influences.

12. To think of oneself in heroic or mythical terms is known as
    a. egocentrism.
    b. imaginary audience.
    c. the personal fable.
    d. invincibility.

13. When teenagers believe they are being scrutinized for their behavior and physical appearance, they are
    a. egocentric.
    b. creating a personal fable.
    c. creating an imaginary audience.
    d. exaggerating their abilities and skills.

14. According to John Hill's biopsychosocial theory, which three factors are most involved?
    a. Biological, achievement, and social
    b. Biological, psychological, and sexual
    c. Intimacy, dependency and autonomy
    d. Biological, psychological, and social

15. To solve problems that have only one correct answer, we are using
    a. divergent thinking.
    b. convergent thinking.
    c. creative thinking.
    d. critical thinking.

16. New ideas are to creative thinking as existing ideas are to
    a. convergent thinking.
    b. critical thinking.
    c. divergent thinking.
    d. concrete operational thinking.

CHAPTER 12

Psychosocial Development in Adolescence

In the last chapter and in this one, evidence is presented of a serious increase in several types of high-risk behaviors (such as eating disorders, binge drinking, use of illegal substances, and unprotected sex) among a significant segment of today's adolescents. In a comparison of these youth with their parents, who became adults in the 1970s, William Pfaff (1997) offers a possible explanation for this phenomenon:

> The post-1960s generation felt itself liberated to set its own principles of life, rejecting hierarchies, patriarchies, tradition, established powers, repudiating the 'canons' set by famous dead white men, and moral codes established by repressed old men and women who knew nothing of life. People now were to be free, independent, 'self-actualizing' individuals.
>   What counted was each person's freedom to do whatever he or she wanted to do, within the professed limitation that it did not restrict anyone else's freedom to do whatever they wanted to do. All this, as we now know, did not work out in an entirely positive way. . . .
>   . . .A great many of the children of [today's] generation feel that they have been deserted by their parents. They have been given no standards. . . . This new generation is saying: You failed to transmit to us positive values in which you believed. We now must look for them elsewhere. (p. 15)

Is Pfaff's description of the situation today the explanation for the increase in high-risk activities? He is describing a relatively momentary trend in family life, one that seems likely to change as today's teens become parents (see the cartoon below). As you read the various sections of this chapter, ask yourself whether you believe Pfaff's explanation is sufficient, or whether you think there could be other forces, perhaps more biological or psychological, that also play a role in why adolescents are behaving as they are. ☻

*"This song is dedicated to our parents, and is in the form
of a plea for more adequate supervision."*
Drawing by Koren; © 1991 The New Yorker Magazine, Inc.

The topics in this chapter examine the evidence, pro and con, on Pfaff's position. Following a discussion of the changing life of the family, we look closely at peer relations and sexuality. We also cover four topics of psychosocial development that no one is happy about: sexually transmitted infections, teenage pregnancy, substance abuse, and criminal behavior.

When you finish reading this chapter, you should be able to

- Name the five main functions that have been lost by the family, as well as the role that remains.

- Describe the effects of divorce on adolescents.

- Define four types of parenting styles.

- List positive influences that the peer group can have on an adolescent's growth.

- Describe the developmental patterns of peer groups.

- List the functions of peer groups.

- Specify the various concerns that adults have about adolescents engaging in sexual intercourse.

- Discuss three theories of the origin of homosexuality and their implications for those who work with gay teens.

- Discuss reasons that teenagers engage in premarital sexual activity.

- Explain why some adolescents become runaways, prostitutes, or both.

- List the prevalence, symptoms, consequences, transmission, and treatment of sexually transmitted diseases found in adolescents.

- Discuss factors associated with causes and consequences of teenage parenthood.

- Describe the prevalence of drug use among different groups of adolescents and between different types of drugs, and state any major differences between groups.

- Describe the connection between school performance (including learning disabilities) and delinquent behavior.

- List and describe at least three reasons that youth join gangs.

Changing American Families and Their Roles in Adolescent Life

> It is, after all the simplest things we remember: A neighborhood softball game, walking in the woods at twilight with Dad, rocking on the porch swing with Grandma.
>
> Now, no one has time to organize a ballgame. Our woods have turned to malls. Grandma lives three states away. How will our children have the same kind of warm memories we do? (Barbara Meltz)

Of all the changes in American society in recent years, those affecting families have probably been the most extensive (also see Chapter 8). Let's begin with a look at the changing roles of families in modern society.

The Loss of Functions

In 1840 the American family fulfilled six major functions (Sebald, 1977). Table 12.1 lists those functions and suggests which elements of society now perform them.

TABLE 12.1 THE CHANGING ROLES OF FAMILIES

Former Family Roles	Societal Elements That Perform Them Now
Economic-productive	Factory, office and other business
Educational	Schools
Religious	Church or synagogue
Recreational	Commercial institutions
Medical	Doctor's office and hospital
Affectional	Still the family

Today professionals have taken over the first five functions—economic-productive, educational, religious, recreational, medical. It appears that the family has been left to provide but one single function—affection—for its members. In the nineteenth century, parents and children needed each other more than now, for the following three major reasons:

- *Vocational instruction.* For both males and females, the parent of the same sex taught them their adult jobs. Most men were farmers and most women, housewives. Parents knew all the secrets of work, secrets passed on from generation to generation. Today nearly 100 percent of men work at jobs different from their fathers, and an increasing percentage of women are not primarily housewives, as their mothers were.

- *Economic value.* Adolescents were a vital economic asset on the farm; without children, the farm couple had to hire others to help them. Work was a source of pride to the children. It was immediately and abundantly clear that they were important to the family. Today, instead of being an economic asset, most children are an economic burden on the family's resources.

- *Social stability.* When families almost never moved from their hometowns, parents were a crucial source of information about how to live in the town, knowing all the intricacies of small-town social relationships. One depended on one's parents to know what to do. Today, when the average American moves every five years, the adults are as much strangers in a new place as the children. In fact, with Dad, and now frequently Mom, driving out of the neighborhood to work, the children may well know the neighborhood better than their parents do.

A number of other factors also influence adolescent family life. For example, the social support of family was found to be positively related to self-reliance and good grades and negatively related to problem behavior in African American adolescents (Taylor, 1996). Greater parental religiosity can also have positive affects on adolescents' academic and socioemotional adjustment during this stage of their lives (Brody & others, 1996). Molina and Chassin (1996) found that parent alcoholism did not moderate the effects of puberty, but Mexican American and white children experienced more conflict with their parents than nonalcoholic parents and their children. Not surprisingly, Young and associates (1995) found that when parents routinely exhibit supportive behaviors, the later life satisfaction of the teenage children is high. The support of " . . . both mothers and fathers was equally important in predicting life satisfaction of adolescent offspring" (p. 813).

Fergusson and Lynsky (1996) examined the factors that affect resiliency in 940 New Zealand 16-year-olds who had experienced significant family adversity. The factors most associated with the absence of high-risk behaviors (i.e., resiliency) were higher than average IQ, low novelty seeking, and lower than average affiliation with delinquent peers. The findings emphasized the important role of positive peer models during this age period.

A humorous look at adolescence and the family in earlier times may be found in Carson McCullers's *Member of the Wedding.* New York: Bantam. Twelve-year-old Frankie yearns desperately to join her brother and his bride on their honeymoon. She learns a great deal about the transition from childhood to maturity from the devoted housekeeper.

How Well Do Parents Know What Their Teens Are Doing?

The Who's Who organization recently (1997) surveyed 3,370 teenagers 16– to 18-year-olds, all of whom have an "A" or a "B" average and are planning to attend college. Because these students are among the highest achievers in the United States one might assume that their parents would be reasonably well aware of their activities. As the chart below reveals, there are some serious discrepancies.

There are at least three important questions that are posed by these data: Why is there such a great distance between what the teens say they do and what their parents believe? Might these "good students" be underreporting their actual activities? As you will see in ot her chapters of this book, in some cases these students' rates of behavior are lower than for more ordinary students, and in some cases higher—why do you suppose this is so?

Do You Think that Your Child . . .	Parental Myth	Teen Reality
Has contemplated suicide?	9%	26%
Has cheated on a test?	37%	76%
Has had sex?	9%	19%
Has friends with drug problems?	12%	36%
Has driven a car while drunk?	3%	10%
Has worries about pregnancy?	22%	46%

Source: Who's Who Special Report, 1997.

The Effects of Divorce

A smoothly functioning family can provide support and nurturance to an adolescent during times of stress (Young & others, 1997). But when the family is itself in a state of disarray, such as during a divorce, not only is the support weakened, but the family often becomes a source of stress (Fergusson & Lynskey, 1996).

Divorce has become commonplace in American society. Even with slight decreases in the divorce rate in recent years, more than one million divorces still occur every year, which is roughly half the number of marriages performed during the same time (U. S. Bureau of Census, 1996). Divorce tends to occur most in families with a newborn, and second most in families with an adolescent present. Estimates suggest that divorce affects as much as one-third to one-half of the adolescent population.

What, then, are the effects of divorce on the development of the adolescent? Unfortunately, conclusions are often based as much on speculation as on research findings, due to problems in the research. Divorcing parents often refuse to let

themselves or their children participate in such studies, which makes random samples difficult to obtain.

Nevertheless, the divorcing family clearly contributes additional stress to a developing adolescent. One obvious effect is economic. The increased living expenses that result from the need to pay for two domiciles most often leads to a significant decrease in the standard of living for the children. Most adolescents, particularly young adolescents, are extremely status conscious, and status is often obtained with the things money can buy (clothes, stereos, cars, etc.). Young adolescents may well resent being unable to keep up with their peers in this regard. Older adolescents are better equipped to cope with this type of additional stress, both psychologically and financially, because they can enter the workforce themselves.

Another obvious effect of a divorce is the absence of one parent. Often custodial rights are given to one parent (usually the mother), and so the children are likely to lose an important source of support (usually that of the father). What support the noncustodial parent provides is sometimes jeopardized by the degree of acrimony between the divorced parents. One or both of the parents may attempt to "turn" the adolescent against the other parent. This sometimes results in disturbing, negative tales about a mother or father, forcing adolescents to cope with adult realities while they are still young.

Such distractions also can disrupt the disciplinary process during adolescence. Under any circumstances, administering consistent and effective discipline during this time often requires the wisdom of King Solomon. A difficult job for two parents becomes the primary responsibility of one. Preoccupied parents, perhaps feeling guilty over subjecting the child to a divorce, find it difficult to provide the consistent discipline that the child was used to previously. It should be noted however, that for adolescents in general, decreased contact with parents also produces these problems. Larson and associates (1996) noted that the daily interactions of adolescents with family decreased from 35 percent to 14 percent during the period from fifth to twelfth grade.

Because the father typically leaves a family during divorce, there are often more negative effects for males than for females (Hetherington & others, 1989). During the teenage years, the father often assumes primary responsibility for disciplining the male adolescents in the family. An abrupt change in disciplinary patterns can lead some adolescents to exhibit more antisocial and delinquent behavior. For example, divorce may force adolescents into growing up faster and disengaging from their families. Early disengagement from a family can actually be a good solution for teens, if they can devote themselves to school activities and rewarding relationships with friends or teachers (Hetherington & others, 1989). Further, Nelson & Vaillant (1993) found that "fatherless boys who have substitute male role-models were similar in personality to boys with fathers" (p. 435).

For girls, there can be greater problems if the father does not leave the family but has an unhealthy relationship with his wife. A study conducted by Jacobvitz and Bush (1996) examined the perception of family relationships in the minds of adolescent females. They found that the father-daughter alliance, which occurs when fathers turn to their daughters instead of their wives for intimacy and affection (as a consequence of emotionally unfulfilling marriage), contributed most to daughters' depression, anxiety, and decreased self-esteem.

Young adolescents often have difficulty accepting remarriage. Older adolescents, because of their greater maturity and self-confidence, seem to have an easier time accepting remarriage but are likely to confront or question aspects of the new family arrangements. In addition, their acute awareness of sexuality may foster resentment of the new marital closeness of their parents (Hetherington & others, 1989).

Despite the negative aspects we've outlined, you should keep in mind that not all aspects of a divorce have a negative impact on adolescents. Divorce is often a better alternative than keeping a stressful, unhappy family intact. In fact, the few studies that have compared adolescents from the two groups have shown that teenagers from divorced families do better in general than adolescents from intact but feuding families (Hetherington & others, 1989). Obviously the ability of the two parents to resolve their divorce as amicably as possible is an important factor in lessening the burden on the children. And although too many new or inappropriate responsibilities may inhibit ego formation, some added responsibilities may increase self-esteem and independence in the long run.

Hines (1997) summarizes the research findings:

> For the adolescent undergoing multiple developmental changes, divorce and its related transitions present additional challenges, promoting growth for some and constituting developmental vulnerabilities for others. A review of the literature on adolescent development, family relations and the impact of divorce on adolescents reveals that adolescents experience divorce differently from younger children and that a positive parent-adolescent relationship can ameliorate the negative effects of divorce. (p. 375)

Guided Review

1. Five functions that were provided by the family but are now provided elsewhere: educational, religious, recreational, medical and economic _____.
2. Within families that experience divorce, there are some interesting gender differences. Divorce generally has more adverse effects on _____ than on _____.
3. In a study on parenting styles in which at least one of the adolescents in a family was highly creative, parents were found to employ a style of parenting called _____.
4. Divorce tends to occur most often in families with a newborn and second most in families with an _____.
5. The three styles of parenting most often identified by researchers are authoritarian, permissive, and _____.

The Nurturing Parent

As we discussed in Chapter 8, most family researchers have agreed that three styles of parenting exist (Baumrind, 1986): the **authoritarian, permissive,** and **authoritative parenting** styles. In an extensive study of 56 families in which at least one of the adolescents was highly creative (Dacey, 1989c, 1998; Dacey & Packer, 1992; Dacey & Kenny, 1997; Dacey & Lennon, 1998), a picture of a fourth style clearly emerged. The parents in these families were found to be devotedly interested in their children's behavior, but they seldom make rules to govern it. Instead, by modeling and family discussions, they espouse a well-defined set of values and expect their children to make personal decisions based on these values.

After the children make decisions and take actions, the parents let the children know how they feel about what was done. Even when they disapprove, they rarely punish. Most of the teens in the study said that their parents' disappointment in them was motivation enough to change their behavior. All of the parents agreed that if their child were about to do something really wrong, they would stop her or him, but that this virtually never happens. This has been termed the **nurturing parenting** style (Dacey & Packer, 1992). Only some of the parents in the study are themselves creative, but all appear committed to this approach.

Answers

1. productive 2. boys, girls 3. nurturing 4. adolescent 5. authoritative

The success of nurturing parents is based on a well-established principle: People get better at what they practice. These parents provide their children with ample opportunities to practice decision-making skills, self-control, and, most vital of all, creative thinking. They serve as caring coaches as their children learn how to live. This research demonstrates the profoundly positive effects a healthy family can have on a person.

Peer Relations

Important debates have existed in the field of adolescent psychology concerning the value and influence of peer and parental relationships during adolescence. Recent research has helped to resolve some of these debates. The importance of parent and peer relationships and the ways in which peer relationships change during the adolescent years will be the focus of this section.

Developmental Patterns of Peer Groups

Peer groups are important in adolescent development. Although it is clear that friendships are vital throughout life, there seems to be something special about the role of the peer group during adolescence.

The role of peers as a source of activities, support, and influence increases greatly (Savin-Williams & Berndt, 1990). Perhaps it is for these reasons that adults and the media have been interested in and anxious about the role of the peer group. Brown (1990) described four specific ways in which the peer group changes from childhood to adolescence.

- As previously mentioned, adolescents spend much more time with peers than do younger children. As early as sixth grade, the early adolescent begins withdrawing from adults and increases time spent with peers. During high school, middle adolescents spend twice as much time with their peers as they spend with parents and other adults.

Although rigidly segregated into gender groups during middle childhood, boys and girls become much more willing to interact with each other as adolescence proceeds.

- Adolescent peer groups receive less adult supervision and control. Teenagers try to avoid close supervision by parents and teachers and are more independent and find places to meet where they are less closely watched. Even at home, teenagers seek privacy and places where they can talk to friends without being overheard by parents and siblings.

- Adolescents begin interacting more with peers of the opposite sex. Although boys and girls participate in different activities and friendship groups during middle childhood, the sexes mix increasingly during the adolescent years. Interaction with members of the opposite sex seems to increase at the same time as adolescents distance themselves from their parents.

- During adolescence, peer groups become more aware of the values and behaviors of the larger adolescent **subculture.** They also identify with certain **crowds,** which are groups with a reputation for certain values, attitudes, or activities. Common crowd labels among high school students include "jocks," "brains," "druggies," "populars," "nerds," "burnouts," and "delinquents." Interestingly, although the adolescent subculture changes over time, these crowds seem to exist in some form across all periods in which the adolescent subculture has been studied.

Brown (1997) made an important distinction between crowds and cliques, which are subgroups within crowds:

> Some might suppose that crowd labels are little more than vague, stereotypical categories, and because the constraints on selecting a crowd for oneself are substantial, the crowd niche would matter less to adolescents than their clique niche. Remember, however, that the clique affiliation indicates merely who an adolescent's close friends are; crowd affiliation indicates who an *adolescent* is—at least in the eyes of peers. It is a very personal evaluation of the adolescent by those whose opinions matter. Thus, it is not surprising that adolescents resist being labeled or pigeonholed as part of one crowd. (p. 184)

Brown (1990) also thought about why peer groups change in the preceding ways during adolescence and suggested several explanations. He maintained that the biopsychosocial changes of adolescence affect the development of a teenager's peer relationships. First, puberty seems to increase adolescents' interest in the opposite sex and contributes to withdrawal from adult activities and increased time with peers. Although adolescents are in the process of becoming less dependent on their parents they tend to increase their dependence on peers.

An adolescent's definition of a friend is quite different from a child's. Although both a 5-year-old and a 15-year-old might say a friend is "someone who is close to you," the same words would mean very different things to each. If questioned more carefully about what they mean by "close," the younger child might say it means "someone who lives near you, that you play with." The adolescent would have a much fuller set of requirements, which would not necessarily include living close by. By the teen years, the young person includes many psychological dimensions in her definition of a friend. These would include such things as values and interests in common, as well as the idea that a friend is someone to be trusted with very personal information (Selman & Schultz, 1990).

Functions of Peer Groups

In contrast with the popular view that peers are a negative influence during adolescence, peer influence serves important social and psychological functions. When adolescents do not have the chance to be part of a peer group, they miss out on important learning experiences. Kelly and Hansen (1990) described six important positive functions of the peer group. The group can help teens to:

- *Control aggressive impulses.* Through interaction with peers, children and adolescents learn how to resolve differences in ways other than direct aggression. Observing how peers deal with conflict can be helpful in learning assertive, rather than aggressive or "bullying," behavior.

- *Obtain emotional and social support and become more independent.* Friends and peer groups provide support for adolescents as they take on new responsibilities. The support adolescents get from their peers helps them to become less dependent on their family for support.

- *Improve social skills, develop reasoning abilities, and learn to express feelings in more mature ways.* Through conversation and debate with peers, adolescents learn to express ideas and feelings and expand their problem-solving abilities. Social interactions with peers give adolescents practice in expressing feelings of caring and love, as well as anger and negative feelings.

- *Develop attitudes toward sexuality and gender-role behavior.* Sexual attitudes and gender-role behaviors are shaped primarily through peer interactions (Hartup, 1983). Adolescents learn behaviors and attitudes that they associate with being young men and women.

- *Strengthen moral judgment and values.* Adults generally tell their children what is right and what is wrong. Within the peer group, adolescents are left to make decisions on their own. The adolescent has to evaluate the values of peers and decide what is right for him or her. This process of evaluation can help the adolescent to develop moral-reasoning abilities.

- *Improve self-esteem.* Being liked by a large number of peers helps adolescents feel good about themselves. Being called up on the telephone or being asked out on a date tells adolescents that they are liked by their peers, thereby enhancing feelings of positive self-esteem.

It is clear that the formation of intimate friendships is an important adolescent goal. One of the most important aspects of these friendships during adolescence is the growing trend for them to become sexual.

A Sociocultural VIEW

Racial Influences on Peer Groups

Steinberg (1990) examined whether parental or peer influence on academic values is stronger for adolescents of different races. Steinberg and his colleagues studied 15,000 high school students from nine different high schools in Wisconsin and California. They found that parental influence on academics was stronger only for the white students. For African American, Latino, and Asian American students, the peer group had a greater influence on school attitudes and behavior, including how much time students spent on their homework, whether they enjoyed school, and how they behaved in class. Fortunately for the Asian students, their peers generally valued academic achievement and positively influenced academic achievement. For African American and Latino adolescents, it was more difficult to find and join a peer group that rewarded academic success. Consequently, these youths often experienced conflict between the positive values of their parents for academic achievement and the negative values held by their peers and did less well in school.

Similarly, Fordham and Ogbu (1986) found that African American students felt that to be popular, they could not do well in school. When African American students of high ability attended school with only high-achieving students, they were no longer anxious about losing peer support and were more successful.

Further, the African American teen subculture does appear to promote a greater sense of loyalty and support among its members than does the white teen subculture. This provides a climate that helps nurture a positive identity and self-confidence.

Guided Review

6. Brown describes four ways in which the peer group changes from childhood to adolescence. These are (1) adolescents spend more time with peers; (2) adolescent peer groups receive less adult supervision; (3) adolescents begin interacting more with peers of the _____ _____; and (4) peer groups become aware of values of the larger adolescent subculture.

7. When describing what they like best about their "best friend," adolescents state that they like interpersonal qualities, _____, and physical qualities.

8. The influences of the peer group serve important social and_____ functions.

9. Whereas peers teach adolescents about social relationships outside the family, adults provide a source of guidance in forming _____ and setting goals.

Sexual Behavior

Few aspects of human behavior have changed more in this century than sexual behavior. Until the 1970s the popular belief about sex was, "They're talking more about it now, but they're not doing anything more about it!" This may have been true earlier in this century, but no longer.

Evidence shows that the forces that traditionally kept the majority of adolescents from engaging in sex are no longer powerful. Available data show that U. S. adolescents are becoming sexually active at increasingly earlier ages. Kann and associates (1993) found that for both sexes, 67 percent had experienced intercourse by the twelfth grade. Early sexual activity appears to have declined recently, however, probably due to a growing concern about AIDS and other sexually transmitted diseases. A study conducted by the National Survey of Family Growth (HHS News, 1997) indicates that in the current group of 15- to 19-year-olds, the percentage who have had sex is about 50 percent, down from a peak of 55 percent several years earlier. Results of studies vary, but the most likely percentage of college sophomores who are no longer virgins is about 75 percent for both males and females.

Stages of Sexuality

Many psychologists believe that human sexuality develops in three steps (Brooks-Gunn & Paikoff, 1993):

1. Love of one's self **(autosexuality)**

2. Love of members of one's own sex **(homosexuality)**

3. Love of members of the opposite sex **(heterosexuality)**

These stages appear to be natural, although some argue that it is as natural to stay in the second stage as to go on to the third.

In the autosexual stage, the child becomes aware of himself or herself as a source of sexual pleasure and consciously experiments with masturbation. The autosexual stage begins as early as 3 years of age and continues until the child is about 6 or 7, although in some children it lasts for a considerably longer period of time.

When the child enters kindergarten, the homosexual phase comes to the fore (please note that this does not necessarily refer to sexual touching, but rather to the direction of feelings of love). For most children from the age of 7 to about 13, best friends, the ones with whom he or she dares to be intimate, are people of the same

Answers

sex. Feelings become especially intense between ages 10 and 12, when young people enter puberty and feel a growing need to confide in others. They naturally are more trusting with members of their own sex, who share their experiences. Occasionally these close feelings result in overt sexual behavior (one study found this to be true more than one-third of the time). In most cases, however, it appears that such behavior results from curiosity rather than latent homosexuality of the adult variety.

The great majority of teenagers move into the third stage, heterosexuality, at about 13 or 14 years, with girls preceding boys by about a year. We discuss these three phases in the following sections.

Autosexual Behavior

Masturbation is probably universal to human sexual experience (Leitenberg & others, 1996; Meston & others, 1996; Weiderman & others, 1996). Although most people still consider it an embarrassing topic, it has always been a recognized aspect of sexuality, legitimate or not. Kinsey, in his 1948 study of male sexuality, found that 97 percent of all males masturbated, and the majority report they have erotic fantasies (Koch, 1993). As for women, approximately two-thirds have masturbated to orgasm by the time they reach 16 (Gagnon & Simon, 1969). Most 4- to 5-year-olds masturbate, are chastised for it, and stop, then start again at an average age of 14. If masturbation is so popular, why has it been considered such a problem?

For one reason, many believe that the Bible forbids masturbation. Dranoff (1974) pointed out that the Latin word *masturbari* means "to pollute oneself." For generations, people have taken as a prohibition the passage in Genesis 38:8 in which Onan is slain by the Lord because "he spilled his seed upon the ground." Dranoff argues that Onan was not slain by the Lord for masturbating, but because he refused to follow God's directive to mate with his brother's wife. Instead, he practiced coitus interruptus (withdrawal from the vagina before ejaculation).

Although most psychiatrists feel that no intrinsic harm exists in masturbation and believe it to be a normal, healthy way for adolescents to discharge their sexual drive, some teens (mainly boys) feel such a sense of shame, guilt, and fear that they develop the "excessive masturbation" syndrome. In this case, masturbation is practiced even though the child feels very bad about it. These feelings are reinforced by solitude and fantasy, which leads to depression and a debilitating sense of self-condemnation. Some teens are now being treated for an addiction to making 900 phone line sex calls.

In summary, most psychiatrists argue that masturbation in childhood is not only normal but helpful in forming a positive sexual attitude. It cannot be obsessive at 4, so it should be ignored at that age. However, it can be obsessive at 14, and if the parents suspect this to be the case, they should consult a psychologist.

Homosexual Behavior

A number of suggestions have been put forth about why people become homosexuals (Bailey & Pillard, 1991; McNeill, 1995; O'Conor, 1995; Taylor, 1995; White, 1994). The three most often cited explanations are the psychoanalytic theory of homosexuality, the learning theory of homosexuality, and the genetic theory of homosexuality.

The Psychoanalytic Theory of Homosexuality

Freud's **psychoanalytic theory of homosexuality** suggested that if the child's first sexual feelings about the parent of the opposite sex are strongly punished, the child may identify with the same-sex parent and develop a permanent homosexual orientation. Because researchers have noted many cases in which the father's suppression of the homosexual's Oedipal feelings was not particularly strong, this theory is not held in much regard today.

Clearly, some of the stereotypes about homosexuals are untrue and unfair. What generalizations, if any, do you believe can fairly be made about all homosexuals?

The Learning Theory of Homosexuality

The **learning theory of homosexuality** offers another explanation: Animals that are low on the mammalian scale follow innate sexual practices. Among the higher animals, humans included, learning is more important than inherited factors. According to this theory, most people learn to be heterosexual, but for a variety of little-understood reasons, some people learn to be homosexual.

The Biopsychosocial Theory of Homosexuality

No direct proof exists that people become homosexual because of genetic reasons. However, a number of studies (D'Augelli & Patterson; Diamonti & McAnulty, 1995; Hu, 1995; LeVay, 1993; LeVay & Homer, 1994; Patterson, 1995) have offered some evidence of genetic predisposition (an inborn tendency). Some theories argue that the fetus's brain reacts to sex hormones during the second through sixth month of gestation in a way that may create such a predisposition. In other words, those who favor a **biopsychosocial theory of homosexuality** suggest that if the biological predisposition is present and certain psychological and social factors (as yet unknown) are in place, then the contention of many homosexuals that their sexual orientation was not a matter of choice would be confirmed. The research of psychologist Daryl Bem (1996) has found support for a biopsychosocial approach. He found that genetic inheritance influences temperament, which then interacts with a long chain of psychological factors that influence whether the person will be homosexual or heterosexual. Because our current culture strongly favors heterosexuality, most people turn out that way. In another cultural setting, things might be different, he believes.

The Onset of Homosexuality

For a long time, psychologists believed that homosexuality does not manifest itself until adulthood. Recent studies of male homosexuals reviewed in the *Journal of the American Medical Association* (Remafedi, 1988), however, indicate that this belief was the result of interviews with teens, most of whom were ashamed or otherwise unwilling to tell about their feelings on the subject. The current studies, using better methods, are in remarkable agreement that at least one-third of all males have had "a homosexual experience that resulted in an orgasm" at least once during their adolescent years. About 10 percent "are exclusively homosexual for at least three years between the ages of 16 and 55" (p. 222).

Most adult homosexuals remember feeling that they were "different" at about 13 years old, the age when most boys are beginning to notice girls. One study followed boys who were seen by medical personnel because of gender-atypical behavior (dressing in girls' clothes, playing with dolls, etc.) between the ages of 3 and 6. The majority developed a homosexual identity during adolescence or adulthood.

Remafedi (1988) summed up the situation:

Professionals may deny the existence of gay or lesbian teenagers for a number of reasons, some benign and others more malignant. It is both reasonable and judicious to avoid applying potentially stigmatizing labels to children and adolescents. It is also understandable . . . to adopt a 'wait and see' approach to a teenager's homosexuality, while providing appropriate preventative and acute health care. However, the reluctance of some professionals to acknowledge the existence and the needs of homosexual adolescents is primarily related to the emotionalism surrounding the issue. (p. 224)

Two other studies reinforce Remafedi's position: those by Harry (1986) and Sullivan and Schneider (1987).

Whatever one believes about homosexuality being a natural stage of sexual development, the great majority of people in the United States today do engage in heterosexual behavior sooner or later—and the evidence indicates that they begin much sooner than they used to.

What's Your View? Is Homosexuality A Matter Of Choice?

On the one hand, we have the behavioral, psychoanalytic, and biopsychosocial theorists giving their explanations of how homosexuality is learned. On the other hand, we have many homosexuals who believe that their sexual orientation became clear so early in life that it could only have been caused genetically. Proponents of each of these positions agree that being homosexual is not a matter of choice for the homosexual. Thus it is argued that they should be accepted the same as heterosexuals, or at the very least be given sympathy, because their role in today's society is not an easy one.

Others believe that homosexuality is a matter of free choice and that those who choose it are behaving in an immoral way. Homosexuals don't have to be that way; they want to. What's your view? Do you think interviewing some gays and lesbians on this question would deepen your understanding?

Heterosexual Behavior

At the beginning of this section, we presented some statistics on teen sexuality that may have surprised you. To get a clearer picture of this situation, you will need to look at the data that a number of other studies have provided on heterosexual teen behavior (for an excellent summary, see Petersen & others, 1995).

First Coitus

Although sexuality develops throughout life, most people view first intercourse as the key moment in sexual development. When this moment occurs is influenced by numerous factors (diMauro, 1995; Lerner & Semi, 1997). For example, the more the adolescent engages in risk behaviors such as drug and alcohol abuse and delinquency, the earlier first coitus is likely to take place (Costa & others, 1995; Savin-Williams, 1995; Small & Luster, 1994; Zabin & others, 1993). Emotional distress encourages earlier sex (Borus & others, 1995), especially when caused by divorce and peer conflicts (Feldman, 1995; Feldman, Fisher, Ranson & Dimicelli, 1995; Feldman, Rosenthal, Brown & Canning, 1995; Whitbeck & others, 1994).

Early first coitus is highly associated with a number of adverse outcomes. The National Center for Health Statistics found that 22 percent of girls who had sex before they turned 15 described their first encounter as "not voluntary," and over one-third stated that their partner was a male over 18, which constitutes statutory rape in most states (HHS News, 1997). Rosenthal (1996) studied 171 girls, average age 14.5. She found that 42 percent of them were sexually experienced, having had first intercourse at an average age of 13.1 years. Of these girls, half had had an adverse outcome—a sexually transmitted infection, a pregnancy, or an abnormal Pap smear.

When do most Americans first experience intercourse? The statistics vary, but all research confirms that this experience occurs at a younger age than it did for previous generations (Alva & Jones, 1994; Annie Casey Foundation, 1995: Carnegie Corporation, 1995; Rosenthal, 1996). Table 12.2 makes this evident.

TABLE 12.2 PERCENTAGE OF HIGH SCHOOL STUDENTS WHO HAVE HAD SEXUAL INTERCOURSE			
	Ever Had Sexual Intercourse	Have Had 4 or More Sex Partners	Currently Sexually Active*
Sex			
Female	50.8	13.8	75.3
Male	57.4	23.4	64.1
Grade			
9	39.0	12.5	57.5
10	48.2	15.1	68.9
11	62.4	22.1	69.4
12	66.7	25.1	75.9
Race or Ethnicity			
White	50.0	14.7	67.9
Black	81.5	43.1	72.9
Hispanic	53.1	16.8	69.6

*Of those who had ever had sexual intercourse, the percentage who had had intercourse during the 3 months preceding the survey.

Source: L. Kann, W. Warren, J. L. Collins, J. Ross, B. Collins, and L. J. Kolbe, "Results from the National School-Based 1991 Youth Risk Behavior Survey and Progress Toward Achieving Related Health Objectives for the Nation" in *Public Health Reports, vol. 108,* supp. 1, 1993, pages 47–55.

The Many Nonsexual Motives for Teenage Sex

In recent years researchers have begun to pay more attention to the notion that teens engage in sex for many reasons other than the satisfaction of their prodigious sexual drives. In one of the most enlightening articles on this subject, two therapists who work with adolescents (Hajcak & Garwood, 1989) concluded that for many adolescents, orgasm becomes a "quick fix" for a wide variety of other problems. Among these alternative motives for sex are the desire to do the following:

- *Confirm masculinity/femininity.* For some teens, having sex with one or more partners (sometimes called "scoring") is taken as evidence that their sexual identity is intact. This is particularly relevant to those (especially males) who consciously or unconsciously have their doubts about it.

- *Get affection.* Usually some aspects of sexual behavior include physical indications of affection, such as hugging, cuddling, and kissing. To the youth who gets too little of these, sex is not too high a price to pay to get them.

- *Rebel against parents or other societal authority figures.* There are few more effective ways to "get even" with parents than to have them find out that you are having sex at a young age, especially if it leads to pregnancy.

An Applied VIEW

How to Talk to Teens about Sex (or Anything Else, for That Matter)

Adolescents are more likely to talk to adults who know how to listen—about sex, alcohol, and other important issues. But certain kinds of responses, such as giving too much advice or pretending to have all the answers, have been shown to block the lines of communication.

Effective listening is more than just "not talking." It takes concentration and practice. Below are six communication skills that are useful to anyone who wants to reach adolescents. By the way, these skills can also enhance communication with other adults.

Rephrase the person's comments to show you understand. This is sometimes called **reflective listening.** Reflective listening serves four purposes:

- It assures the person you hear what she or he is saying.
- It persuades the person that you correctly understand what is being said (it is sometimes a good idea to ask if your rephrasing is correct).
- It allows you a chance to reword the person's statements in ways that are less self-destructive. For example, if a person says "My mother is a stinking drunk!" you can say "You feel your mother drinks too much." This is better, because the daughter of someone who drinks too much usually can have a better self-image than the daughter of a "stinking drunk."
- It allows the person to "rehear" and reconsider what was said.

Watch the person's face and body language. Often a person will assure you that he or she does not feel sad, but a quivering chin or too-bright eyes will tell you otherwise. A person may deny feeling frightened, but if you put your fingers on her or his wrist, as a caring gesture, you may find that the person has a pounding heart. When words and body language say two different things, always believe the body language.

Give nonverbal support. This may include a smile, a hug, a wink, a pat on the shoulder, nodding your head, making eye contact, or holding the person's hand (or wrist).

Use the right tone of voice for what you are saying. Remember that your voice tone communicates as clearly as your words. Make sure your tone does not come across as sarcastic or all-knowing.

Use encouraging phrases to show your interest and to keep the conversation going. Helpful little phrases, spoken appropriately during pauses in the conversation, can communicate how much you care:

"Oh, really?"

"Tell me more about that."

"Then what happened?"

"That must have made you feel bad."

Remember, if you are judgmental or critical, the person may decide that you just don't understand. You cannot be a good influence on someone who won't talk to you.

- *Obtain greater self-esteem.* Many adolescents feel that if someone is willing to have sex with them, then they are held in high regard. Needless to say, this is often an erroneous conclusion.

- *Get revenge on or to degrade someone.* Sex can be used to hurt the feelings of someone else, such as a former boyfriend. In more extreme cases, such as "date rape," sex can be used to show the person's disdain for the partner.

- *Vent anger.* Because sex provides a release of emotions, it is sometimes used to deal with feelings of anger. Some teens regularly use masturbation for this purpose.

- *Alleviate boredom.* Another frequent motive for masturbation is boredom.

- *Ensure fidelity of girlfriend or boyfriend.* Some teens engage in sex not because they feel like it, but because they fear their partner will leave them if they don't comply.

Using sex for these reasons often has an insidious result. As Hajcak and Garwood (1989) described it:

Adolescents have unlimited opportunities to learn to misuse sex, alone or as a couple. This happens because of the powerful physical and emotional arousal that occurs during sexual activity. Adolescents are very likely to ignore or forget anything that transpired just prior to the sex act. Negative emotions or thoughts subside as attention becomes absorbed in sex. . . . The end result is that adolescents condition themselves to become aroused any time they experience emotional discomfort or ambiguity . . . sexual needs are only partially satisfied [and] the nonsexual need (for example, affection or to vent anger) is also only partially satisfied, and will remain high. . . . The two needs become paired or fused through conditioning. . . . Indulging in sex inhibits their emotional and sexual development by confusing emotional and sexual needs and, unfortunately, many of these teens will never learn to separate the two. (pp. 756–58)

This is not to say that adolescents don't experience genuine sexual arousal. They definitely do, but this does not by itself justify sexual activity. These therapists argue that teens need to be taught to understand their motives and to find appropriate outlets for them. In fact, this has led some experts to recommend sex education that teaches alternatives to premarital sex. Abstinence is one alternative, of course, but there is an increasing trend toward advising "outercourse" (e.g., Haignere & others, 1996; Kegan, 1994). This refers to sexual activity other than that which involves insertion of a penis into a vagina or anus. Those who advocate outercourse as a more reasonable recommendation than abstinence or "safe sex" point to adolescent cognitive skills as their main rationale. As Kegan stated:

The 'abstinence' norm's main failing is that it denies how irresistible sexual experience is. . . . The "safe sex" norm's biggest failing is that it unwarrantedly assumes an order of consciousness capable of such responsibility, far-sightedness, and future-mindedness. Given how infrequently even college-age youth make use of the condoms and dental dams passed out during freshman orientation week, is it not wildly unrealistic to believe that sexually active 12-, 13-, 14-, 15-, 16-, and 17-year-olds are going to have the presence of mind to involve these devices regularly in their sexual activity when these devices are completely unnecessary to, and unenhancing of, the only real goals and interests they have in mind at the moment? (p. 60)

Actually, contraceptive use is becoming more common among teens than many experts had realized (Leeming & others, 1995), as the data in Table 12.3, compiled by the Alan Guttmacher Institute, make clear. Although the percentages of contraceptive users indicate an increased acceptance of this protection, there are still large numbers who use no protection at all. Also, over two-thirds use contraceptives that provide no protection against infections. Finally, it should be remembered, too, that contraceptives are no protection against the emotional turmoil that can result from immature sexual encounters.

Sex educators, educational administrators, religious leaders, adolescent psychologists, and political officials (as well as parents, of course) are in the midst of a great debate over the best course to take in terms of sex education for teens. It is a thorny question, and one that does not appear destined for resolution any time soon.

Sexual Abuse

When adolescents are abused, typically it is by someone they know and trust. It is often just a continuation of abuse that started during childhood. The most common type of serious sexual abuse is incest between father and daughter. This type of relationship may last for several years. The daughter is often manipulated into believing it is all her fault and that if she says anything to anyone, she will be seen as a bad person, one who may even be arrested and jailed. The outcome is usually another adolescent statistic: a runaway or even a prostitute (Friedman & others, 1996; Gary & others, 1996; Green, 1995; Jezl & others, 1996; Karp & others, 1996).

TABLE 12.3 AVOIDING PREGNANCY

Most sexually experienced women and their partners use a contraceptive, primarily the pill or condoms.

By Age

More than seven out of 10 sexually active girls aged 15 to 17 use contraceptives, a figure that rises to nearly nine out of 10 young women 20 to 24.

Age	Pill	Condom	Other*	Total (%)
15–17	38	29	5	72
18–19	52	24	8	84
20–24	60	13	15	88

By Race and Ethnicity

Young Hispanic women aged 15 to 19 trail blacks and whites in use of contraceptives.

Race	Pill	Condom	Other*	Total (%)
Hispanic	37	26	2	65
Black	58	17	2	77
White	45	28	8	81

By Income

Seven out of 10 low-income young women aged 15 to 19 use contraceptives, as do eight of 10 higher-income women.

Income level	Pill	Condom	Other*	Total (%)
Low**	41	27	3	71
High	47	27	9	83

*Other methods include the diaphragm, sponge, spermicide, and IUD.

**Low income* means from 100–199 percent of the poverty level. For example, a family of four that earned $14,000 to $28,000 in 1992 would be considered low income.

Source: Leeming et al, *Issues in Adolescent Sexuality.* Needham Heights, MA. Allyn & Bacon, 1996.

Most sexual offenses are discussed with a friend or with no one. Very few are reported to parents, police, social workers, or other authorities. It has also been found that the effects of abuse may influence a youth's future relationships. Directly following the experience, children may engage in such "acting out" behaviors as truancy, running away, sexual promiscuity, and damage to school performance and family relationships (Gary & others, 1996).

Adolescents are not only the victims of sexual abuse; they also are perpetrators of it (Ryan & Lane, 1997). Juveniles are responsible for about one-third of all reported abuses (Finfelhor, 1996). This share of responsibility for abusive acts has remained steady for several decades (Snyder & others, 1996).

Several researchers (Mateen & others, 1996; Tingus & others, 1996) have called for improved education to sensitize people to prevent incest, as well as improved reporting systems, legal definitions, and treatment of victims. These may help us better understand and intervene, so that victims can receive professional attention earlier that may reduce the long-term effects of abuse.

Sexuality in the lives of late adolescents and young adults in the last decade of this century is very different from in earlier decades (although perhaps not so different from several centuries ago). What is the relationship between this fact and the problem covered in the next section about sexually transmitted infection? That is a complex question.

Guided Review

10. Some psychologists describe three stages of human sexuality. These include autosexuality, _____, and heterosexuality.

11. Currently the three theories that attempt to explain homosexuality include psychoanalytic theory, _____ theory, and the biopsychosocial theory of homosexuality.

12. It is estimated that by the end of adolescence, more than 80 percent of the boys and _____ percent of the girls will have been sexually active.

13. Many nonsexual motives contribute to teenage sex, such as getting even, confirming one's _____ or _____, and rebelling against authority figures.

14. Considering some of the reasons for adolescent sexual activity, it is not surprising that nearly 70 percent of twelfth graders report having had _____ _____.

Sexually Transmitted Infections

In this section, we cover research on AIDS and other infections that are sexually contagious.

AIDS

Not long ago, when people thought about **sexually transmitted infections (STIs),** gonorrhea came to mind. In the 1970s, it was herpes. Today, **AIDS (Acquired Immune Deficiency Syndrome)** causes the most concern (Brown & others, 1996; Johnson & others, 1996; Steers & others, 1996; Whalen & others, 1996).

AIDS was first diagnosed at Bellevue-New York University Medical Center in 1979 and has quickly approached epidemic proportions. What is known about AIDS is that a virus attacks certain cells of the body's immune system, leaving the person vulnerable to any number of fatal afflictions such as cancer and pneumonia. In addition, the disease can directly infect the brain and spinal cord, causing acute meningitis.

The virus that leads to AIDS—**human immunodeficiency virus (HIV)**—is transmitted through the transfer of substantial amounts of intimate bodily fluids such as blood and semen. The virus is most likely to be transferred through sexual contact, the sharing of hypodermic needles, and, much less likely, through blood transfusions (a test for AIDS is now available at blood banks and hospitals). In addition, the virus can be transmitted from an infected mother to an infant during

First diagnosed in 1979, AIDS has quickly approached epidemic proportions.

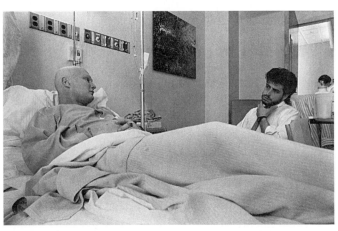

TABLE 12.4 AIDS STATISTICAL TRENDS		
HIV-positive Patients (in thousands)		
	In 1981	In 1992
Age 13–29	23	194
% Male	93	86
% Female	7	14
% White	60	49
% Black	26	35
% Latino	14	15
Other	1	1
AIDS Deaths by Age		
Age	1981	1992
0–4	96	192
5–12	10	36
13–29	1329	3809
30–39	3013	10265
40–49	1396	5855
50–59	590	1760
60+	248	758

Source: *Statistical Abstract of the United States,* U. S. Department of Commerce, Washington, D. C., 1994.

pregnancy or birth. Table 12.4 shows the concentrations of AIDS in each of these groups, as well as the percentages of cases by race/ethnicity. In the most recent report available (C.D.C.P., 1997), powerful new drugs were credited with bringing about a 6 percent decline in AIDS cases in the United States, the first decline since the epidemic began in the 1980s.

In the initial stages of the spread of the disease in this country, HIV has most often been found in certain segments of the population such as male homosexuals and intravenous drug users and, to a much lesser degree, among hemophiliacs. But that could easily change over time. In some Central African countries, where AIDS is thought to have originated, HIV is found equally among men and women throughout the population. After a slow start, large-scale education efforts by grassroots organizations, as well as by state and federal government agencies, have begun to get these messages out, but the problems remain extremely serious (Cooksey & others, 1996; Ford & Norris, 1995).

First, as mentioned, the virus has been identified with a few select groups. If you're not gay or a drug user, you might think you don't have to consider preventive measures. However, a person exposed to HIV may not show any symptoms for as many as 15 years. Further, this same person can expose other people to the virus during this incubation phase. Some people have reacted to this by becoming more particular about their sexual partners. Monogamous relationships were on the rise again during the 1980s, after the "liberated" days of the sexual revolution of the 1960s and 1970s. And as condom use increases, the educational message seems to be getting through. But many still ignore the dangers, and the consequences may be years away.

This may be particularly true among adolescents. Adolescents currently constitute only about 1 percent of all diagnosed cases of AIDS in the United States (Cooksey & others, 1996). But given the long incubation period and the research findings that suggest that adolescents are not very well informed about AIDS, many researchers think this may be an underestimation. Adolescents are also more prone than the general public to misconceptions and prejudices generated by the frightening new disease.

For example, some adolescents have the misconception that AIDS can be transmitted through casual contact such as kissing or hugging someone with AIDS, or sharing their utensils or bathroom facilities. Such misconceptions unnecessarily increase fear and anxiety in everyone. AIDS prevention efforts aimed at adolescents often have as their main goal the dispelling of such myths (Greene & others, 1996; Sigelman & others, 1996).

 *An Applied View*

How Adolescent Hypocrisy Can Affect Condom Use

The incidence of HIV infection among adolescents has been steadily rising. At the same time condoms, the only effective preventative measure against HIV for those engaged in sex, are used by only 17 percent of teens every time they have sex (Azar, 1994a). Why the discrepancy?

University of California researcher Eliot Aronson believes this occurs because of two widespread hypocrisies:

- Obsession with sex versus the puritanical view of sex
- Condom use promotes early sexual practices versus condoms provide safety

Denial, Aronson believes, is the mechanism that makes otherwise savvy students accept these obviously hypocritical positions. Neither threatening adolescents with dire results nor trying to "eroticize" condoms was found to have any lasting effects (cited in Azar, 1994b). Therefore Aronson tried a different approach: He got groups of college students to make videotapes promoting safe sex and then used these tapes to teach high school students. Compared with a control group of college students who simply made videotapes, the "teachers" reduced unsafe sex practices significantly. Apparently actually talking to others made it harder for them to use denial, and thus they were more likely to change their own behavior.

Other Sexually Transmitted Infections

Often lost in the public focus on the burgeoning AIDS problem is a truly epidemic increase in the prevalence of other STIs. Because of its fatal nature, AIDS gets most of the press and the major funding. But STIs such as gonorrhea, syphilis, chlamydia, and herpes are running rampant compared with AIDS, particularly among adolescents. The effects of such venereal diseases range from the mildly annoying to the life-threatening. More than 50 diseases and syndromes other than AIDS account for over 13 million cases and 7,000 deaths annually (National Institute of Allergy and Infectious Diseases, 1987).

Some of the more common STIs (other than AIDS) include the following:

- *Chlamydial infection.* **Chlamydia** is now the most common STI, with about 5 to 7 million new cases each year (Subcommittee on Health and the Environment, 1987). In one state, black and Hispanic female teens have rates of chlamydia infection more than 10 times higher than rates reported in white female teens (Massachusetts Department of Public Health, 1991). Often chlamydia has no symptoms. It is diagnosed only when complications develop. It is particularly harmful for women and is a major cause of female infertility, accounting for 20 to 40 percent of all cases (Hersch, 1991b). Untreated, chlamydia can lead to pelvic inflammatory disease (see the information to follow). As with all of these diseases, it can be transmitted to another person whether symptoms are present or not. The news about this infection, however, is excellent. A single-dose antibiotic treatment has been found to be very effective (Martin & others, 1992).

- *Gonorrhea*. The well-known venereal disease **gonorrhea** infects between 1.5 and 2 million persons per year. One quarter of the cases reported are adolescents (Klassen & others, 1989). Gonorrhea is caused by bacteria and can be treated with antibiotics. When penicillin was introduced in the 1940s, the incidence of gonorrhea declined dramatically. Today, however, the number is rising and has reached the highest level in 40 years (Hersch, 1991a). The most common symptoms are painful urination and a discharge from the penis or the vagina.

- *Pelvic inflammatory disease*. **Pelvic inflammatory disease (PID)** frequently causes prolonged problems, including infertility. It is usually caused by untreated chlamydia or gonorrhea. These infections spread to the fallopian tubes, resulting in PID. The scarring the infection causes often prevents successful impregnation. More than 1 million new cases per year occur in the United States (Washington & others, 1986). Women who are most likely to get it are those who use an intrauterine device for birth control, have multiple sex partners, are teenagers, or have had PID before. PID is so widespread that it causes $2.6 billion in medical costs per year!

- *Genital herpes*. **Genital herpes** is an incurable disease, with about 500,000 new cases every year. Spread by a virus during skin-to-skin contact, the major symptom of genital herpes is an outbreak of genital sores, which can occur as often as once a month. Estimates suggest about 30 million people in this country suffer from this infection. Unlike chlamydia, problems associated with herpes are mainly emotional and social rather than medical (Hersch, 1991b). People with herpes often experience embarrassment and low self-esteem about their bodies.

- *Syphilis*. Like gonorrhea, **syphilis** is no longer the killer it was before penicillin. However, this sexually transmitted disease still accounts for 70,000 new cases per year. In the state of Massachusetts, 76 percent of these cases were teens of color (Massachusetts Department of Public Health, 1991). Caused by bacteria, the first sign of syphilis is a chancre ("shan-ker"), a painless open sore that usually shows up on the tip of the penis and around or in the vagina. This disease must be treated with antibiotics or it can be fatal.

- *Hepatitis B*. About 200,000 new cases of **hepatitis B** occurred in the United States in 1990, and 300,000 were predicted to occur in 1991 (Hersch, 1991a). This viral disease is transmitted through sexual contact and also through the sharing of infected needles. Although a preventive vaccine is available, those who are most at risk for hepatitis B (intravenous drug users, homosexual men, and inner-city heterosexuals) usually do not have the vaccine readily available to them.

Figure 12.1 depicts the relative percentage of new cases of each type of STI in the United States each year.

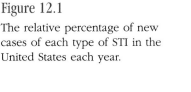

Figure 12.1

The relative percentage of new cases of each type of STI in the United States each year.

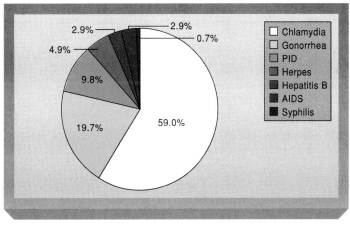

Three books that should be of interest to you are: (1) Jean Auel's *Clan of the Cave Bear.* New York: Bantam. Auel's wonderful imagination and excellent knowledge of anthropology make this book on the beginnings of the human family a winner. In fast-paced fiction, she describes the relationships, sexual and otherwise, of early humans who, she speculates, were unaware that sex causes pregnancy! (2) Mary Calderone and John Ramsey's *Talking to Your Child About Sex.* New York: Ballantine. This book offers a creative interpretation of human sexuality in a family setting. (3) Erich Fromm's *The Art of Loving.* New York: Harper & Row. Although most of us think of love as a very personal topic, it would be hard to think of anything that has been the subject of more novels, articles, poems, plays, and psychological treatises. Most of these are not particularly helpful, and many are downright corny. Fromm's book is a distinct exception.

Studies have shown that the age group at greatest risk for STIs are individuals between 10 and 19 years old (National Institute of Allergy and Infectious Disease, 1987; Steers & others, 1996). This age group is particularly difficult to educate in any area concerning sexuality. The obstacles to education include individuals who refuse to take the information seriously, and parents who won't let the information be taught.

The AIDS crisis and the STI epidemic have several features in common. On the negative side, misconceptions contribute to both problems. Many young people believe that only promiscuous people get STIs, and that only homosexuals get AIDS. Having multiple sexual partners does increase the risk of contracting STIs, but most people do not view their sexual behavior, no matter how active, as being promiscuous. Recent research also suggests machismo gets in the way of proper condom use, an effective prevention technique for all STIs. A "real man" doesn't use condoms. And, finally, when people do contract a disease, strong social stigmas make accurate reporting difficult.

On the positive side, the preventive and educational measures are basically the same for AIDS and other STIs: Dispel the myths, increase general awareness and acknowledgment of the problem, and encourage more discriminating sexual practices. Perhaps some of the educational efforts made on behalf of AIDS prevention and treatment will have a helpful effect on the current STI epidemic. Historically the health focus on STIs has been on treatment, typically with antibiotics, but recently the Public Health Service has shifted its focus to prevention for all STIs. So perhaps comprehensive efforts of this kind that emphasize all STIs will prove fruitful.

In summary, it seems safe to say that major changes in adolescent sexual practices have occurred in recent decades. Many of them must be viewed with considerable alarm, especially when you consider the tragic increases in STIs and pregnancy.

Guided Review

15. The nature of our concern about sexually transmitted infections has changed since the spread of AIDS, or _____ _____ _____ syndrome.
16. HIV attacks the body's _____ _____, thus leaving the person vulnerable to a number of fatal afflictions.
17. Other sexually transmitted infections include chlamydia, _____, pelvic inflammatory disease, syphilis, genital herpes, and hepatitis B.
18. Studies show that the age group at greatest risk for sexually transmitted infections is _____.

The Teenage Parent

"You're pregnant," the doctor said, "and you have some decisions to make. I suggest you don't wait too long to decide what you'll do. It's already been seven weeks, and time is running out!"

"Look, it just can't be true!" I replied. I was trying to convince myself that the clinic doctor was lying. It wasn't supposed to be like this! I was tired of the bitter quarrel I had been having with the doctor. I resented him with every passion. How could I let myself be seen like this?

Answers

15. acquired immune deficiency 16. immune system 17. gonorrhea 18. adolescence

Except for the youngest adolescents, birthrates for adolescents have been dropping in recent years. However, the extent to which young adolescents have been becoming pregnant is certainly a cause for great concern because physically, emotionally, and economically, they are at the greatest risk.

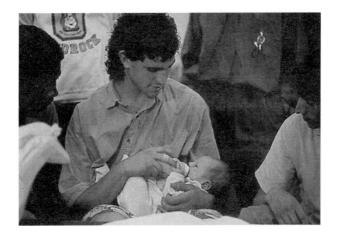

I had been fearing this answer. I suppose I knew the truth all along, but I really didn't want to face it. I didn't want an abortion, that much I was sure of. Besides, where would I get the money?

For ages now, I had been thinking my period would come any day. Now the truth was in the open! I walked out of the office and headed aimlessly down the street. I looked around and saw only ugliness. I thought about God and how even He had deserted me. It all hurt so much.

"How could this have happened to me?" I thought. "Good girls don't get pregnant!" All of the things my mother had told me were lies. According to her, only the "fast girls got pregnant." The ones who stayed out late and hung around with boys. I wasn't part of that category!

I looked down at my stuffed belly and thought about my family. Would they be understanding? After all, they had plans for my future. They would be destroyed by the news.

"I'm not a tramp," I said to myself. "Then again, I'm only 16 and who would believe that Arthur and I really are in love?"

The feelings of this unmarried girl are all too typical. Each year, about one million teenage girls in the United States become pregnant (diMauro, 1995), and by 18 years, 25 percent of American females have been pregnant. About half have babies (Children's Defense Fund, 1995).

Trends in Behavior

As Figure 12.2 makes clear, out-of-wedlock child bearing is on the increase in all age groups for both white and African American teenage females. As would be expected, the rate is highest for those under 15. In most states, 10 to 20 percent of all females have been pregnant at least once by the time they reach their 19th birthday. Clearly this is unfortunate, but the rate for 15- to 17-year-olds, which is about one-third as high, might even be described as catastrophic. The largest increases in teen pregnancy rates have occurred in those under the age of 15 and overall, more unmarried teens become parents than ever (Furstenberg, 1990). Furthermore, two-thirds of births to teenage girls resulted from unintended pregnancies (compared to the 31 percent unintended pregnancies for women of all ages) (HHS News, 1997). Table 12.5 lists the percentage of adolescent fathers by age. To further complicate matters, the younger the father at the time of the child's birth, the less likely he is to be married.

Two variables that have a negative effect on teen pregnancy are work and alcohol use. In a study of 384 pregnant girls (mean age = 15.9 years), those who worked 16 or more hours per week were 4.6 times more likely to deliver a below-average weight infant than those who did not. There was no difference in preterm delivery, however (Zwillich, 1995a). In her study of 378 pregnant girls up to 17 years old, Weimann found that 108 denied using alcohol and 48 had stopped within the last 30 days. As many as 54 percent had used alcohol while pregnant (Zwillich, 1995b).

Figure 12.2

Trends in out-of-wedlock child bearing among U. S. females under age 20 by race, 1969–87

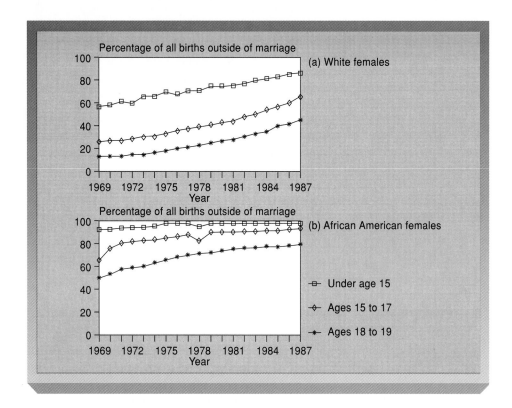

TABLE 12.5 ADOLESCENT FATHERS WHO REPORTED HAVING FATHERED A CHILD BEFORE THE AGE OF 20, BY FATHER'S AGE AT CHILD'S BIRTH AND MARITAL STATUS AT CONCEPTION

Father's Age at Child's Birth	Males Who Reported Having Fathered a Child Before Age 20		Single at Conception		Married at Conception	
	N = 555		N = 446		N = 109	
Age 11 to 16	66	(10.1%)	66	(12.7%)	0	(0.0%)
Age 17	85	(15.8)	76	(18.3)	9	(5.8)
Age 18	181	(30.6)	158	(32.8)	23	(22.1)
Age 19	223	(43.5)	146	(36.2)	77	(72.0)
Age 11 to 19	555	(100.0)	446	(100.0)	109	(100.0)

Source: *Adolescent Health (vol. 1–3)*, Office of Technology Assessment, Washington, D. C., 1991.

Illegal Behavior

Although they are not necessarily developmental in nature, we include brief sections on substance abuse and criminal behavior in this chapter because they often play a role in other aspects of development during adolescence. For the most part, that role clearly is negative.

The Role of Ethnicity in Teen Pregnancy

Many studies have reported that teens of color are at great risk of having unwanted pregnancies. To understand this finding, however, it is important to sort out ethnic values from socioeconomic factors. Poor teens, whether African American, Asian American, Native American, white, or Latino, are three to four times as likely to become unwed parents than economically advantaged teens (Children's Defense Fund, 1989).

The higher rates of teenage parenthood among economically disadvantaged youth are understandable. Teens who are behind in school, who lack basic skills, and who see few opportunities for their future are more likely to become parents as teenagers. For adolescents lacking educational and job opportunities, parenting may be one of the few available ways of achieving adult status. Unfortunately, becoming pregnant as teenagers often makes their lives and the lives of their young children more difficult.

To solve the problem of teenage parenthood, we have to solve problems of education and job opportunities for all teenagers, regardless of ethnicity. We must also consider ways to help teenage mothers provide their babies with the needed emotional, intellectual, and physical care, while also enabling the mothers to continue their education. These factors, as you will recall from our discussion of the consequences of teenage pregnancy, often make a difference in the futures of the mothers and their children. Support from family members can be important.

Talking to Teens about Pregnancy

Nurses, teachers, and counselors frequently have opportunities to help teens to clarify their attitudes toward pregnancy, whether they are currently involved with a pregnancy or not. For a number of reasons, these conversations seldom take place, however.

Sometimes those who work with teens feel that discussing pregnancy with them means pushing their own values on them. Others feel that this subject is very delicate and should not be discussed outside the church or home. Others refrain from discussing it because they feel like they just don't know enough (readers of this book, of course, will not have to be concerned about this problem!). It does seem reasonable to make sure that teens have the objective facts about pregnancy and its repercussions for baby, mother, and father. Does this make sense to you?

It should be noted that some of the suggestions for talking to teens about sex in the box on page 323 are useful here, too.

Guided Review

19. The largest increase in the pregnancy rate is occurring among those under the age of _____.
20. Early coitus has been found to be highly associated with three adverse conditions: _____, _____, and _____ _____ _____.
21. Contrary to the stereotype, most teenagers who become pregnant had been in a relationship for at least _____ _____.

Answers

Two excellent books on this topic are : (1) Cohen and Cohen's *A Six-Pack and a Fake I.D.: Teens Look at the Drinking Question.* New York: M. Evans. According to the authors of this book, the decision to drink or not to drink is personal rather than moral. They recognize the tragedy that alcohol can bring into people's lives, but they still "do not see moderate drinking as a problem; indeed, it is often a positive pleasure." They do, however, feel that before coming to conclusions about the use of alcohol, you should have reliable and believable information to help you make the best and most informed decision. (2) Harris's *Drugged Athletes: The Crisis in American Sports.* New York: Four Winds Press. Athletes take drugs to increase speed, strength, and accuracy; to mask pain; to relax muscles; to relieve stress; to improve performance; and to gain pleasure. Harris provides an overview and discusses specific problems of drugs in sports at all levels.

Substance Abuse

It is difficult to say precisely how widespread substance abuse is. Studies differ from year to year, from region to region, and disappointingly, from one another (even when year and region are the same). Nevertheless there have been some sound studies. For example, Johnston and associates (1996) found a slight decrease in all categories of drug use (see Table 12.6). Gfroerer and associates (1997) learned that high school dropouts had the highest rate of illicit drug and cigarette use, and college students had the highest rate of alcohol use.

TABLE 12.6 PERCENTAGE OF HIGH SCHOOL SENIORS WHO USED PARTICULAR DRUGS IN THE LAST 30 DAYS

	Class of 1978	Class of 1986	Class of 1996
Approximate Number of Students	17,800	15,200	14,300
Marijuana/Hashish	37.1	23.4	21.9
Inhalants	3.2*	3.2	2.5
Hallucinogens	5.3*	3.5	3.5
Cocaine	3.9	6.2	2.0
Heroin	0.3	0.2	.5
Stimulants	8.7	5.5	4.1
Sedatives	4.2	2.2	2.1
Tranquilizers	3.4	2.1	2.0
Alcohol	72.1	65.3	50.8
Cigarettes	36.7	29.6	34.0

*Class of 1979

Source: Johnston, L.D., O'Malley, P.M., & Bachman, J.G. (1996). *The rise in drug use in teens continues in 1996.* Ann Arbor, MI: Institute of Social Research, Table 4.

Contrary to the stereotype, several studies have found that adolescents of color are often less susceptible to substance abuse than European-American youth, in part because of religious influence (Alva & Jones, 1994; Barnes & others, 1994; Flannery & others, 1996; Jessor & others, 1995; Schulenberg & others, 1996). This appears not to be true of Native American teens, however (Gfellner, 1994; Mitchell, 1996).

In her study of the relationship between alcohol use and risky sexual behavior, Graves (1995) found that having multiple sexual partners was more likely among adolescent males who consumed five or more drinks per sitting. She also learned that condom use was less likely among this group. Adolescent males studied by Schulenberg and associates (1996) exhibited other risk factors such as drinking "to get drunk," which was related to lack of self-efficacy and was predictive of binge drinking later in life.

Criminal Behavior

Although much could be said about juvenile delinquency, it is so changeable and varying by region, gender, and social class that we will not be able to go into it all here. Instead, we will limit this discussion to one aspect of adolescent criminal behavior, gang behavior, which has been moving in a most disturbing direction lately.

Gangs often offer youths the fulfillment of basic needs (Burke & Hagedorn, 1995; Dishion & others, 1995; Graham & others, 1994; Popenoe, 1996; Sanyika, 1996; Scheidlinger, 1994; Vigil, 1996). Some of their functions clearly coincide with those of the larger society (Sheley & others, 1995). Gangs typically provide protection, recognition of the desire to feel wanted, and rites of passage that mark

achievement, status, and acceptance, such as the initiation rite of a potential gang member. Thus we may say that the gang is a kind of subculture, a "subculture of violence" (Hammond & Yung, 1993, p.145).

According to a study commissioned by the New York City Youth Board (1989), urban gangs possess the following characteristics:

- Their behavior is normal for urban youths; they have a high degree of cohesion and organization; roles are clearly defined.

- They possess a consistent set of norms and expectations, understood by all members.

- They have clearly defined leaders.

- They have a coherent organization for gang warfare.

The gang provides many adolescents with a structured life they never had at home. What makes the gang particularly cohesive is its function as a family substitute for adolescents whose strong dependency needs are displaced onto the peer group. The gang becomes a family to its members (Dishion & others, 1995).

The formation of juvenile gangs typically follows a sudden increase in this country of new ethnic groups due to immigration. The children of new immigrants have a difficult time breaking through cultural barriers such as a new language and racism. Perceiving their prospects of succeeding in the new society as bleak, some of these children form gangs, which provide the structure and security discussed, but also serve as an outlet to attack the society that seemingly will not accept them. In times past, these gangs were composed of Jewish, Irish, and Italian Americans. Today's gangs are frequently formed by Latinos, Asian Americans, and African Americans (Burke, 1990). The gang becomes a vehicle for tearing its members away from the main social structures and authorities, in particular the family and school.

But today's gangs have some disturbing differences from those of years past (Sheley & others, 1996). They are much more heavily armed and seemingly much more willing to use their weapons. Movies like *West Side Story* (1961) depict gang members carrying knives, chains, and pipes. Today's urban gangs are often armed with AK-47 assault rifles and UZI submachine guns, grenades, and even cluster bombs.

To what can we attribute the growth of gang membership? Numerous studies have pointed to the absence of an effective father's presence, or at least the presence of an effective male role model (Burke & Hagedorn, 1995; Palmer & Tiller, 1995; Popenoe, 1996; Sanyika, 1996; Scheidler, 1994; Vigil, 1996). For many, the violence of gang life is a means of proving masculine capability, which the absence

As early as the early 1960s, Leonard Bernstein's *West Side Story* signaled society's concern that glib sociological excuses would only worsen the handling of behavior disorders. Public opinion and public institutions are turning back to a punishment model.
John Meeks

of a father figure has unconsciously put in doubt. Fortunately, professionals are improving in their ability to assess violence risk (Borum, 1996; Grisso & Tomkins, 1996). In addition, a number of new programs, such as those that feature collaborative work situations, are having some success in combating this problem (Tate & others, 1995; Wolford & others, 1996).

A Sociocultural View

Portrait of a Gang Girl

Tamika was just the gang leader's girlfriend. Then he went to jail, and now the gang depends on her to hold things together (LeBlanc, 1994).

She feels that being in the gang gives her a sense of family; it provides her with companions on the streets that she used to walk alone when she would run away from the father who sexually abused her. Gang life gives her more than a way to hang out with the boys; it also affords her the comfort, protection, and public code of behavior she desires.

Few after school programs exist for mid-teen girls like Tamika. She prefers handball and softball to cheerleading, and would enjoy exercising her mathematical skills, except that people wouldn't "get down with that." The Brooklyn Navy Yard gang she belongs to is a loosely formed group of Puerto Rican teens who hang out, drink beer, and occasionally get into trouble. Tamika's grandmother's house, where she lives, is an hour's train ride from the Navy Yard, but she makes that journey every day because for her, the confusion there is more predictable and less personal than it is at home.

Although Tamika's gang isn't particularly violent, the members do commit small crimes such as mugging to get money. The gangs depersonalize the victims of their crimes, and prefer mugging to begging overwhelmed parents for money, because mugging only lasts a few minutes. Many of the members come from homes where parents are rarely sober, and these teens feel shame, guilt, and obligation for their family. The goal of the gang is not theft, but rather to promote pride in its cultural heritage.

Tamika's boyfriend, Manny, is currently in prison, which allows her freedom she wouldn't otherwise enjoy with him around. Ordinarily, when Manny goes out with friends, Tamika would be in "lock down," which means that she couldn't leave his mother's apartment. She wouldn't drink beer or smoke without him; she would be more quiet, and go to school regularly. In Manny's absence, Tamika has become close with another male member of the gang, Cee-lo, who provides her with sharp objects, such as paper clips and broken pens, which she uses to cut herself. The feeling of cutting helps her escape, she explains.

Aside from the scars on her body, Tamika also has a tattoo of the name Ruby inside a heart. Ruby, Tamika's grandmother, is the person Tamika loves more than anyone in the world. Tamika is proud of the way her grandmother cares for her: how she gets upset when Tamika is late and doesn't call; how worried she gets if Tamika doesn't come home. One of Tamika's dreams is to get rich and send her grandmother to a beautiful place where she doesn't have to work.

While Tamika waits for Manny's release from prison, she continues to search for the feeling of belonging that is diminishing in her gang. Although she considers joining other gangs, it is important to her that girls are appreciated as much as the boys. She doesn't want to join any organization that doesn't understand the most basic strengths girls have to offer: heart and knowledge.

Guided Review

22. In general, the study by Johnston and associates found a slight _____ in abuse of substances in recent years.
23. Some of the functions of a gang include protection, recognition of desire to feel wanted, rites of passage that mark _____, status, and acceptance.
24. Gangs can be cohesive because of their function as a _____ _____ for adolescents with strong dependency needs.
25. Gangs can become a vehicle for tearing their members away from the main _____ _____ of society.

Answers

22. decrease 23. achievement 24. family substitute 25. social structures

CONCLUSION

For each of the aspects of social interaction reviewed in this chapter—family interactions, peer relations, sexual behavior, sexually transmitted infections, teenage parenthood, criminal behavior—all adolescents must deal with one consistent trend: fast-paced change. Some of this change derives from ground swells in today's society, and some results from the nature of adolescence itself. Here again we see the biopsychosocial model demonstrated.

There are many changes ongoing in the American family. Many functions formerly fulfilled by the family are now the province of other agencies. The stress of divorce has a variety of outcomes, many of which we are learning to understand and deal with. The nurturing parenting style appears to promote many desirable traits.

Interactions among teenage peers change with each generation. Gang behavior is a growing threat to healthy development. Yet perhaps nothing has had a more resounding impact on adolescent life than the recent changes in our attitudes toward sexuality. The four areas of greatest change have been in homosexuality, sexually transmitted infections (including AIDS), the earlier and more widespread participation in sex by teenage females, and the increase in pregnancy and child bearing among younger teenagers.

Some observers have suggested that the biggest problem facing adolescents today, and one intertwined with those just listed, is the difficulty in knowing when childhood and youth have ended and adulthood has begun. When the societal lines between these stages of development are blurred, youth cannot be blamed for not knowing how to behave. We will look into this phenomenon more fully in the next chapter.

As to a comprehensive definition of adolescence (the goal of this section of the book), we have seen that only by including biological, psychological (both cognitive and affective), and social factors can we begin to define this complex stage of life. We have reviewed numerous such factors: the sequence of physiological changes that occur in virtually every teen's body as well as the timing of those changes; the remarkable advances made in cognitive abilities; the social and emotional alterations that occur in relations with family, peers, and

the larger society. Together these provide markers for the onset of the adolescent period. You should be aware, however, that a really adequate biopsychosocial definition cannot be presented in two chapters of a book, or even in one whole book. We learn more about this complex subject every day, and so our definition must be considered still in process.

In summary:

Changing American Families and Their Roles in Adolescent Life

- American families have lost five of their six main functions; the only remaining one is providing affection for family members.
- A number of effects of divorce pertain only to adolescents.
- There are four recognized parenting styles: authoritarian, permissive, authoritative, and nurturing.

Peer Relations

- Peer groups provide adolescents with a source of social activities and support, and an easy entry into opposite-sex friendships.
- The biological, psychological, cognitive, and social changes of adolescence affect the development of a teenager's peer relationships.
- Peer groups serve to control aggressive impulses, encourage independence, improve social skills, develop reasoning abilities, and form attitudes toward sexuality and sexual behavior. They may also strengthen moral judgment and values and improve self-esteem.
- Peer groups also aid in the development of self-concept and allow an adolescent to try out a new identity.

Sexual Behavior

- Many teenagers are becoming sexually active at increasingly younger ages.
- Sexuality develops in three stages, from love of self to love of members of the same gender to love of members of the opposite gender.
- Masturbation is believed to be a harmless and universal form of human sexual expression.
- Homosexual behavior has been surrounded by many myths throughout history.

- Several theories suggest different origins of homosexual orientation: psychoanalytic, learning, and biopsychosocial.
- Many researchers now believe that homosexual orientation may already be set by adolescence.
- Many teens still obtain a great deal of information and misinformation about sex from their peers.
- Youths from stable family environments are less likely to engage in premarital sexual relations.
- Effective listening skills are essential for parents who wish to maintain good communication with their adolescents.
- Teenagers misuse sex for many nonsexual reasons, including a search for affection, rebellion against parents, venting anger, and alleviating boredom.
- Many adolescent runaways and prostitutes are the products of sexual abuse, often by someone they know, a family member, or parent.

Sexually Transmitted Infections

- Today a high prevalence of sexually transmitted infections (STIs) is found in sexually active adolescents.
- AIDS (acquired immune deficiency syndrome) causes the most concern, because it is currently incurable and fatal. As yet, it is not very common in adolescents, but because it usually lies dormant for 10 to 15 years, it is a cause for great concern.
- Other STIs that affect adolescents are increasing in epidemic proportions, including chlamydia, gonorrhea, genital herpes, syphilis, and hepatitis B.
- In spite of increased availability and information about contraceptive methods, many teenagers continue to engage in unprotected sex.

The Teenage Parent

- Teenage pregnancy and parenthood are on the rise among younger teens. With rare exceptions, this situation causes a lot of heartache for the teenage parents, their parents, and their child.
- Teenage mothers who receive emotional support from their families, who continue in school, and who have no additional children while they are still teenagers are

likely to have better-adjusted children and avoid the cycle of poverty.

• When teens possess strong self-esteem, feelings of hope concerning the future, and job and academic skills for entry into the job market, they are less likely to become teenage parents.

Illegal Behavior

• Drug and alcohol abuse is still prevalent among teens. Tobacco use is on the rise again as is use of marijuana, cocaine, and LSD.
• Gangs typically have a high degree of cohesion and organization, a consistent set of norms, clearly

defined leaders, and coherent organization for warfare.
• Gangs have become much more violent in the past decade, probably in part as a response to increased drug trafficking.

KEY TERMS

AIDS (acquired immune deficiency syndrome)
Authoritarian parenting
Authoritative parenting
Autosexuality
Biopsychosocial theory of homosexuality
Chlamydia

Crowds
Genital herpes
Gonorrhea
Hepatitis B
Heterosexuality
Homosexuality
Human immunodeficiency virus (HIV)
Learning theory of homosexuality

Nuturing parenting
Pelvic inflammatory disease (PID)
Permissive parenting
Psychoanalytic theory of homosexuality
Reflective listening
Sexually transmitted infections (STIs)
Subculture
Syphilis

WHAT DO YOU THINK?

1. Do you think that your adolescent peer group followed the developmental patterns described in this chapter?
2. What are some of the most important effects that your teenage peer group had on your life?
3. Do you agree with the theorists who claim that there are three stages in the development of love and sexuality and that this development is natural?

4. In what ways do you believe family life in the United States will be different in 50 years from the ways it exists today?
5. If you were the mayor of a medium-size city, what actions would you take to try to reduce the incidence of sexually transmitted infections?
6. A number of large, urban high schools are creating day-care facilities for the babies and

children of high school students. Do you think public schools should be providing these services? What services, if any, should junior and senior high schools provide to teenage parents?
7. In what cases should juvenile offenders be tried as adults? Should they always be treated as adults? Should they be treated differently because of their age? What things need to be considered?

CHAPTER REVIEW TEST

1. **Brown (1991) states that the peer group can change in four ways during adolescence: adolescents spend more time with peers; they receive less adult supervision; they interact more with peers of the opposite sex; and they**
   a. interact with peers in a work setting.
   b. become sexually active.
   c. begin to identify with certain crowds.
   d. interact more with peers in school and service activities.

2. **Most family researchers have agreed that the three styles of parenting are**

   a. authoritarian, permissive, and devoted.
   b. permissive, aggressive, and impassive.
   c. authoritarian, authoritative, and permissive.
   d. aggressive, impassive, and devoted.

3. **What reason is cited in the text for why there may be a decline in early sexual activity?**
   a. Concern about AIDS and other STIs
   b. Prevailing conservative attitudes
   c. More people devoting time to making money

   d. The increasing influence of religion

4. **The first stage of sexuality**
   a. is heterosexuality.
   b. is homosexuality.
   c. is autosexuality.
   d. depends on the individual.

5. **Parents who practice a nurturing parenting style are**
   a. interested in their child's behavior but seldom prescribe rules, relying instead on modeling and family discussions to instill a well-defined set of values.
   b. controlling but loving in

guiding their children through development.

c. nurturing but providing little structure in the family.

d. nurturing yet strictly controlling of the way in which the family functions.

6. The genetic theory on homosexuality claims that
a. people learn to be homosexual.
b. as children homosexuals identified with the same-sex parent.
c. persons born with a predisposition toward homosexuality can be influenced by the environment to either select or avoid homosexuality.
d. many homosexuals are in denial about their genetically predisposed orientation.

7. Although he has a girlfriend, Steve wants to prove to his friends that he can "score" with a number of different girls in school. Steve's nonsexual motive for sex is to
a. get affection.
b. confirm his masculinity.
c. ensure fidelity of his girlfriend.
d. obtain greater self-esteem.

8. A female adolescent who "acts out" by running away, engaging in sexual promiscuity, or damaging her school performance may be a victim of
a. drug abuse.
b. peer pressure.
c. extreme loneliness.
d. sexual abuse.

9. The CDC estimates how many people in the United States are currently infected with the initial virus of AIDS?
a. 50,000
b. 100,000
c. 500,000 to 600,000
d. 1 to 1.5 million

10. Intravenous drug users, homosexual men, and inner-city heterosexuals are groups most at risk for contracting
a. syphilis.
b. genital herpes.
c. hepatitis B.
d. gonorrhea.

11. The highest rates of teen pregnancy occur for those
a. under age 15.
b. 15 to 16 years of age.
c. 16 to 18 years of age.
d. 18 to 19 years of age.

12. Sara is an African American teenager who grew up in a poor, single-parent home, and has low occupational aspirations. Sara fits the profile of a
a. drug abuser.
b. gang member.
c. pregnant teenager.
d. domestic abuse victim.

13. Held (1981) conducted a study of teenage girls in the third trimester of pregnancy. It was found that social support among the ethnic groups differed in that _____ keeping their baby had the highest self-esteem.
a. Mexican Americans

b. whites
c. African Americans
d. None of the answers are correct.

14. Important racial differences can be found in recent research on teenage pregnancy. It seems that studies of low-income nonwhite girls focus on societal factors, whereas studies of white, middle-class girls tend to focus on
a. social causes.
b. psychological causes.
c. cognitive ability causes.
d. moral reasoning ability causes.

15. John joins a gang because it serves as a pseudo-family for him. Most likely John has strong _____ needs that are being displaced onto the peer group.
a. dependency
b. friendship
c. financial
d. All of the answers are correct.

16. Recent research indicates that gangs have which of the following characteristics?
a. They possess a consistent set of norms and expectations that are understood by all gang members
b. Members have lower expectations of success than do nonmembers
c. Members are as likely to have divorced parents as are nonmembers
d. Members are more likely to score high on IQ tests than are nonmembers

Answers

1.c 2.c 3.a 4.c 5.a 6.c 7.b 8.d 9.d 10.c 11.a 12.c 13.c 14.b 15.d 16.a

PART VII

Early Adulthood

You grow up the day you have the first real laugh—at yourself.

Ethel Barrymore

CHAPTER 13

Physical and Cognitive Development in Early Adulthood

Yudia cannot believe how rapidly her feelings keep changing. One moment she is curious and excited, the next, nervous and afraid. Tonight begins her igubi, the rite that celebrates her induction into adulthood. Yudia has longed for this day most of her 11 years, but now she wonders if she really wants the responsibilities of a grown-up.

Though it seems much longer, only a week has passed since the excruciating beginning of her initiation. The memory of it is already dimming: the bright fire, her women relatives pinning her down on the table, her grandmother placing a thin sharp stone against her vulva, the searing pain.

The women had held and consoled her, empathizing fully with her feelings. Each had been through the same agony. For them, too, it occurred shortly after their first menstruation. They had explained to her that this was just the beginning of the suffering she must learn to endure as an adult woman. All during the past week, they had been teaching her—about the pain her husband would sometimes cause her, about the difficulties of pregnancy and childbirth, about the many hardships she must bear stoically. For she is Kaguru, and all Kaguru women accept their lot in life without complaint.

It has been a hard week, but tonight the pleasure of the igubi will help her forget her wound. There will be singing, dancing, and strong beer to drink. The ceremony, with its movingly symbolic songs, will go on for two days and nights. Only the women of this Tanzanian village will participate, intoning the time-honored phrases that will remind Yudia all her life of her adult duties.

In a large hut less than a mile from the village, Yudia's male cousin Mateya and seven other 13-year-old Kaguru boys huddle close, even though the temperature in the closely thatched enclosure is a stifling 110 degrees. Rivulets of sweat flow from their bodies and flies dot their arms, backs, and legs. They no longer pay attention to the flies, nor the vivid slashes of white, brown, and black clay adorning all their faces. Their thoughts are dominated by a single fear: Will they cry out when the elder's sharpened stone begins to separate the tender foreskin from their penises? Each dreams of impressing his father, who will be watching, by smiling throughout the horrible ordeal.

Three months of instruction and testing have brought the young men to this point. They have learned many things together: how to spear their own food, how to tend their tiny gardens, how to inseminate their future wives, and most important, how to rely on themselves when in danger.

The last three months have been exhausting. The boys have been through many trials. In some, they had to prove they could work together; in others, their skill in self-preservation was tested. For most of them, being out of contact with their mothers was the hardest part. They have not seen any of the female members of their families since they started their training. Unlike Yudia's initiation, which is designed to draw her closer to the adult women of the tribe, Mateya's initiation is designed to remove him forever from the influence of the females and to align him with the adult men.

Now it is evening. Mateya is the third to be led out to the circle of firelight. Wide-eyed, he witnesses an eerie scene. His male relatives are dancing in a circle around him, chanting the unchanging songs. The grim-faced elder holds the carved ceremonial knife. Asked if he wishes to go on, the boy nods yes. Abruptly the ritual begins: The hands of the men hold him tight; the cold knife tip touches his penis; a shockingly sharp pain sears his loins; he is surprised to hear a piercing scream; then, filled with shame, he realizes it comes from him.

Thus far, Yudia's and Mateya's initiations have been different. Mateya's has been longer and harder than Yudia's. She is being brought even closer to the women who have raised them both, but Mateya must now align himself with the men.

The initiations are similar, though, in that both youths have experienced severe physical pain. In both cases, the operations were meant to sensitize them to the vastly greater role sex will now play in their lives. Furthermore, their mutilations made them recognizable to all as adults of the Kaguru tribe.

At this "coming out" ceremony, males and females also receive new names, usually those of close ancestors. This illustrates the continuity of the society. The beliefs of the tribe are preserved in the continuous flow from infant to child to adult to elder to deceased and to newborn baby again. When all is done, Yudia and Mateya can have no doubt that they have passed from childhood to adulthood. ✪

We open this chapter with a discussion of the passage from adolescence to adulthood. Then we investigate the physical and cognitive development of the young adult.

When you finish reading this chapter, you should be able to

- Discuss the purpose of initiation rites and the effects on adolescents of there being no formal rite of passage into adulthood in our culture.

- Describe the components of some initiation rites in preindustrial societies.

- List activities in our own society that may be parallel to these rites.

- Specify some activities that could serve some of the purposes of an initiation rite.

- Discuss how early adulthood signifies the peak in physical development.

- Define what is meant by "organ reserve."

- Suggest ways in which lifestyle choices, such as food, tobacco, and alcohol use and marriage, affect health.

- List Perry's nine stages of intellectual/ethical development.

- Contrast women's and men's "ways of knowing."

- Appraise Holland's and Super's theories of career selection.

- List the pros and cons of a dual-career family.

Initiation into Adulthood

The horrors of the college fraternity initiation have been softened by legal restrictions and by more humane attitudes. Nevertheless, most of us have heard of cases of maimings and even deaths of young men who have been put through **hazing,** the initiation rite that proceeds full acceptance into fraternity membership. People at all socioeconomic levels and of most cultures hold such trials (Lesesne & others, 1995). They are organized by sports teams and criminal gangs and are not limited to males, either. Cults, for example, whether secular or religious, attract males and females for many reasons, and appear to be on the rise. Curtis and Curtis (1993) examined factors related to the appeal and recruitment of cults. They found that low self-esteem, poor family relations, physical and substance abuse, and stress are factors that may help convince a person to become initiated into the cult. The findings of Collins and Weatherburn (1995) further support the increase of unemployed adolescents into criminal behavior as some form of initiation. They reported that those who become unemployed are more likely to commit crimes and to continue to do so for longer periods.

Why do some people, and the groups they wish to be associated with, seem to enjoy holding initiation rites so much? And why are so many adolescents, many of them otherwise highly intelligent and reasonable, willing and eager to endure such pain? Is it simply because they want to join the group, to feel that they belong? There seems to be more to it than that. Throughout the world, adolescents readily engage in such activities because they seem to want to be tested, to prove to themselves that they have achieved the adult virtues of courage, independence, and self-control. And the adults seem to agree that adolescents should prove they have attained these traits before being admitted to the "club of maturity."

The Transition to Adulthood in the United States

How are youths inducted into adulthood in the United States? Are Western initiation rites adequate? These are questions we will now address. In the industrial past of the United States, it used to be fairly clear when one became an adult. In their late teens, boys and girls usually got married and assumed an adult role. Males were accepted as partners in the family farm or business; females became housewives. This has changed in many ways. In his article on the nature of Christian initiation, Isaacs (1994) argued that

> Of all the significant aspects of [Christian] life, possibly the most taken for granted is initiation into the community of faith. Unlike ordination, marriage, or many other Christian rites which are optional, it is assumed that every Christian will have taken part in the rites of initiation. Yet the full meaning of Christian initiation is so often lacking in the understanding of those upon which it is practiced that it actually has little impact on the lives it is supposed to have changed. (p. 163)

This is not to say that Americans have no activities that signal the passage to maturity. We have a number of types of activities, which usually happen at various stages and ages of adolescence. Here is a list of the types and some examples of each:

Religious

Bar mitzvah or bas mitzvah
Confirmation
Participating in a ceremony, such as reading from the Bible

Sexual

Menarche (first menstruation)
Nocturnal emissions (male "wet dreams")
Losing one's virginity

The tuxedo and party dress might be considered costumes in one of America's initiation rites.

The Cultural Role of the Bridal Shower

Although numerous differences occur in the ways our different religious and ethnic cultures unite men and women in marriage, one aspect of the wedding festivities that is common among most American ethnic groups is the bridal shower. Cheal (1989) has suggested that this is because all these groups use the shower, in which brides-to-be receive tokens of their new status such as kitchen utensils and household furnishings, to reenact the dependence of women on men. They also emphasize the interdependence of women on each other. In this view, bridal showers are a rite of passage designed to subjugate women to male dominance. What do you think?

Social

"Sweet Sixteen" or debutante parties
Going to the senior prom
Joining a gang, fraternity, or sorority
Beginning to shave
Being chosen as a member of a sports team
Moving away from one's family and relatives
Joining the armed forces
Receiving a bridal shower
Getting married
Becoming a parent
Voting for the first time

Educational

Getting a driver's license
Graduating from high school
Going away to college

Economic

Getting a checking or credit card account
Buying a first car
Getting a first job

This list offers a good example of the biopsychosocial approach. Some of the occurrences are mainly biological (menarche), some psychological (going away to college), and some social (getting married). Which activities help in the passage from adolescence to adulthood? How might we improve this passage? In this and the next chapter, we will look at the developmental trends and needs of young adults, which will help us to better answer these important questions.

Implications of the Lack of an Initiation Ceremony

For most adolescents in our society today, the teen years are a kind of "time out," a moratorium for trying out different ways of being. More and more, we are having doubts that this moratorium is turning out to be effective. In fact, it appears that crime is one of the ways that some youth are initiating themselves into adulthood. Males especially seem to need to do something dangerous and difficult. Males raised without fathers or father substitutes are especially vulnerable to the attractions of criminality (Dacey & Kenny, 1997). This may be because they experience poorer peer adjustment and male self-image than those with fathers at home (Beaty, 1995). There is little evidence to support the idea that involvement of nonresident fathers has positive benefits for children (King, 1994). Further, the academic achievement of adolescents in general tends to be lower if they do not have ade-

The Components of Maturity

Think of the woman and the man who are the most mature persons you know—people with whom you are personally familiar, or people who are famous. Then ask yourself, "Why do I think these people are so much more mature than others?" In the spaces to the right, for both the male and the female, create a list of the characteristics that seem to distinguish them in their maturity.

How much do the lists differ? Is male maturity significantly different from female maturity? Which of the two people is older? Which of the two do you admire more? Which of the two are you more likely to want to imitate? Were you able to think of many candidates for this title of "most mature adult," or was it difficult to think of anyone? Are either or both of the people you picked professionals? Are either or both of these persons popular with their own peer group? What is the significance of your answers to you?

Female	*Male*
1.	1.
2.	2.
3.	3.
4.	4.
5.	5.
6.	6.
7.	7.
8.	8.
9	9.
10.	10.

It has been suggested that sports play the same role in life as the arduous tasks performed by youths in centuries past: learning coordination, cooperation, and the other skills necessary in adult work. Can you think of ways that sports might serve as initiation rites?

quate interactions with their fathers (Cooksey & Fondell, 1996). When they are leaving adolescence, many of them seem to feel they must prove their adulthood by first proving their manhood in risk-taking behavior.

For most adolescents, the transition into adulthood raises questions about what a person hopes to become as opposed to what a person is afraid she or he may become (Oyserman & Markus, 1990). Unfortunately, when these possible selves are not in balance, people often become involved in delinquent behavior. However, Collins and Weatherburn (1995) pointed out that unemployment may or may not affect one's decision to engage in such behavior. However, the result of being unemployed may affect one's image of one's self, which may influence an adolescent's decision to engage in delinquent behaviors.

In the 1960s and early 1970s, American youths sought to establish their identities by imitating the very rituals of the preindustrial tribes described earlier in this chapter. Known as "hippies" and "flower children," they attempted to return to a simpler life. Many of them returned to the wilderness, living on farms and communes away from the large cities in which they were brought up. Many totally rejected the cultural values of their parents. The most famous symbol of their counterculture was the Woodstock musical marathon in 1969. With its loud, throbbing music, nudity, and widespread use of drugs, the event was similar to many primitive tribal rites. Yet these self-designed initiation rites also seem to be unsuccessful as passages to maturity. Most of the communes and other organizations of the youth movement of the 1960s have since failed. Most American youths have decided "you can't go back again."

Organized sport is another attempt to include initiation rites in American life. The emphasis on athletic ability has much in common with the arduous tasks given to preindustrial youth. In particular, we can see a parallel in the efforts by fathers to get their sons to excel in Little League Baseball and Pop Warner Football. Fathers (and often mothers) are seen exhorting the players to try harder, to fight bravely, and when hurt, to "act like a man" and not cry.

Thus, in delinquency, the counterculture, and sports, we see evidence that members of several age groups today yearn for the establishment of some sort of initiation rite. Adolescents and adults alike seem to realize that something more is needed to provide assistance in this difficult transitional period. But what?

You might enjoy a book by Maya Angelou on this subject: *I know why the caged bird sings.* New York: Random House, (1970). Ms. Angelou recounts her childhood in rural Arkansas. Her strength and resilience model the building of a strong personal and cultural identity.

Traditional initiation rites are inappropriate for American youth. In preindustrial societies, individual status was ascribed by the tribe to which the person belonged. Social scientists call this an *ascribed identity.* The successes or failures of each tribe determined the prestige of its members. Family background and individual effort usually made little difference. In earlier times in the United States, the family was the prime source of status. Few children of the poor became merchants, doctors, or lawyers. Today, personal effort and early commitment to a career path play a far greater role in the individual's economic and social success. This is called an *achieved identity* (see Chapter 11). For this reason (and others), preindustrial customs are not compatible with Western youth today.

Guided Review

1. Rites of passage use _____ to capture elements of adult life that have been denied the youth and are now accessible to them as they are initiated into adulthood.
2. In the United States today, initiation activities occur in religious, _____, social, educational, and _____ settings.
3. The "time out" period, when adolescents explore possibilities and continue their education, is called the adolescent _____.
4. Organized sports, countercultural involvement, and _____ _____ are evidence that adolescents yearn for the establishment of some form of initiation rite.

The rate at which a person can mature is directly proportional to the embarrassment he can tolerate.

Physical Development

Adult psychologist Malcolm Knowles (1984) has stated:

> As I see it, there are four definitions of "adult." First, the biological definition: we become adult biologically when we reach the age at which we can reproduce. . . . Second, the legal definition: we become adult legally when we reach the age at which the law says we can vote, get a driver's license, marry without consent. . . . Third, the social definition: we become adult socially when we start performing adult roles. . . . Finally, the psychological definition: we become adult psychologically when we arrive at a self-concept of being responsible for our own lives, of being self-directing. From the viewpoint of learning, it is the psychological definition that is most crucial. But it seems to me that the process of gaining a self-concept of self-directedness starts early in life, . . . and grows cumulatively as we become biologically mature, start performing adult-like roles, . . . and take increasing responsibility for making our own decisions. So we become adult by degree as we move through childhood and adolescence, and the rate of increase by degree is probably accelerated if we live in homes, study in schools, and participate in youth organizations that foster our taking increasing responsibilities. But most of us probably do not have full-fledged self-concepts of self-directedness until we leave school or college, get a full-time job, marry, and start a family. (p. 6)

Let us begin our exploration of young adulthood with a consideration of Knowles' first criterion, physical development. We address three main questions about physical development in this section: When is peak development reached? What is organ reserve? and What are the effects of lifestyle?

Answers

1. rituals 2. sexual, economic 3. moratorium 4. delinquent activities

The Peak Is Reached

Early adulthood is the life period during which physical changes slow down. Table 13.1 provides some basic examples of physical development in early adulthood.

TABLE 13.1   SUMMARY OF PHYSICAL DEVELOPMENT IN EARLY ADULTHOOD
Height
Female: maximum height reached at age 18. Male: maximum height reached at age 20.
Weight (age 20–30)
Female: 14-pound weight gain and increase in body fat. Male: 15-pound weight gain.
Muscle Structure and Internal Organs

From 19–26: Internal organs attain greatest physical potential. The young adult is in prime condition as far as speed and strength are concerned.
After 26:   Body slowing process begins.
          Spinal disks settle, causing decrease in height.
          Fatty tissue increases, causing increase in weight.
          Muscle strength decreases.
          Reaction times level off and stabilize.
          Cardiac output declines.

Sensory function changes
The process of losing eye lens flexibility begins as early as age 10 and continues until age 30. This loss results in difficulty focusing on close objects. During early adulthood, women can detect higher-pitched sounds than men.
Nervous system
The brain continues to increase in weight and reaches its maximum potential by the adult years.

Source: Bureau of the Census, 1996.

In sports, young adults are in their prime condition as far as speed and strength are concerned. A healthy individual can continue to partake in less strenuous sports for years. As the aging process continues, however, the individual will realize a loss of the energy and strength felt in adolescence.

Early adulthood is also the time when the efficiency of most body functions begins to decline. For example, cardiac output and vital capacity start to decrease. As Table 13.2 clearly shows, these declines are quite steady right through old age. It is important to remember that this chart gives the average changes; considerable differences will occur from individual to individual.

Organ Reserve

Although Table 13.2 makes it look all downhill from what is probably your present age, the actual experience of most people is not that bad. This is because of a human capacity called organ reserve. **Organ reserve** refers to that part of the total ca-

TABLE 13.2 APPROXIMATE DECLINES IN VARIOUS HUMAN FUNCTIONAL CAPACITIES WITH AGE

	Percent of Function Remaining		
	30 Years	60 Years	80 Years
Nerve conduction speed	100	96	88
Basal metabolic rate	100	96	84
Standard cell water	100	94	81
Cardiac index	100	82	70
Glomerular filtration rate	100	96	61
Vital capacity	100	80	58
Renal plasma flow	100	89	51
Maximal breathing cap.	100	80	42

From Alexander P. Spence, *Biology of Human Aging*, ©1989, p. 8. Adapted by permission of Prentice-Hall, Inc., Englewood Cliffs, NJ.

pacity of our body's organs that we do not normally need to use. Our body is designed to do much more than it is usually called upon to do. Much of our capacity is held on reserve. As we get older, these reserves grow smaller. The peak performance that each of our organs (and muscles, bone, etc.) is capable of declines. A 50-year-old man can fish all day with his 25-year-old son and can usually take a long walk with him without becoming exhausted, but he has no chance at all of winning a footrace against him.

This is why people are aware of little decline during the early adult years and often do not experience a sharp decline in most of their everyday activities even into middle age. Our organ reserves are diminishing, but we are unaware of it because we call on them so seldom.

Of course, some individuals regularly try to use the total capacity of their organ reserves. Professional athletes are an example. Here again we see the biopsychosocial model in action. Biology sets the limits, but psychological factors (e.g., personal pride) and social factors (e.g., the cheering crowd) determine whether the person "gives it her all."

The Effect of Lifestyle on Health

Young adults are healthier than older adults in just about every way. All of the body's systems reach peak functioning at this age. Less illness occurs, too. For example, young adults have fewer hospitalizations and visits to the doctor's office than older adults, and those that do occur are caused mainly by injuries. Even catching a cold happens more rarely at this stage than at any other stage of life (U. S. Bureau of the Census, 1992).

There is good news about one of the most threatening diseases among young adults, AIDS. In 1996, there was an overall drop of 23 percent in deaths from AIDS (CDC, 1997). Decreases were greatest among homosexual men who also inject drugs. They were least among heterosexual men and women who inject drugs. The latter two groups have not yet been the targets of AIDS information as have homosexual men.

Good health is clearly related to factors such as genetics, age, and the medical treatment locally available. But these factors are generally beyond the control of the individual. Increasingly, people are beginning to realize that their style of life plays an enormous role in their own health.

The impact of lifestyle on health is dramatically illustrated by the observations in the book *The Healing Brain* (Ornstein & Sobel, 1987). These researchers determined that the miraculous technological gains in medicine over the last 100 years have not had as great an impact on health as one might think. It is true that at birth, we can expect many more years of life than people could in the last century. However, a person who has reached the age of 45 today has a life expectancy of only a couple years more than the person who had reached the age of 45 a hundred years ago, in spite of all the money and effort now spent on medicine after that age.

As a counterexample, Ornstein and Sobel offer the people of Nevada and Utah, two states and populations that are similar in geography, education, income, and availability of medical treatment. Yet Nevada's death rate is 40 percent higher than Utah's. Utah is largely composed of Mormons who live a relatively quiet and stable lifestyle, including very low incidences of smoking and drinking. In Nevada, people drink and smoke much more heavily, and it shows. The rates of cirrhosis of the liver and lung cancer are 100 to 600 percent higher in Nevada than in Utah. A man who reaches the age of 45 in Utah can expect to live 11 years more than the man who reaches age 45 in Nevada. The point is that simple, cost-free choices under the control of the individual are much more effective at improving health than all the expensive, time-consuming medical advances of the last century. Perhaps our priorities are misplaced.

Based on this information, we could conclude that a simple difference in style of life can have more of an effect on health than medical advances. Let's look at the influence on health of some specific lifestyle choices.

Choices of Foods

Nutrition plays an important role throughout human development, from neonates to the elderly. By the time we reach middle adulthood, however, increasing evidence demonstrates the influence of nutrition on two major health concerns, heart disease and cancer. Medical science has recently established a link between heart disease and a substance in the blood, **cholesterol.** Cholesterol has been found to leave deposits along the walls of blood vessels, blocking the flow of blood to the heart and resulting in a heart attack. The main culprit in high levels of cholesterol has been found to be diets high in fat. Typically Americans consume 40 percent of their total calories as fat. The American Heart Association (1984) recommends changes in diet, such as eating fish and poultry instead of red meat, yogurt and cottage cheese instead of cheese, margarine instead of butter, fewer eggs, and drinking skim milk instead of whole milk, as ways of lowering cholesterol in the body. Exercise is also very helpful.

A similar link has been found between diet and certain types of cancer, such as cancer of the breast, stomach, intestines, and the esophagus. The American Cancer Society has also come out with a set of recommendations for an improved, healthy diet. They too recommend lowering fat intake to no more than 30 percent of the daily caloric total and following a diet that is high in fiber, a substance that helps the digestive process. High-fiber foods include leafy vegetables such as cauliflower, broccoli, and brussels sprouts, as well as whole-grain cereals and breads. The proliferation of new products that feature lower levels of fat and higher levels of fiber indicates that the American public is taking this new knowledge to heart (no pun intended).

Anyone who is 10 percent over the normal weight for their height and build is considered overweight. Anyone who is 20 percent over the normal weight is considered obese. Obesity has been a very serious health concern and is rapidly getting worse. The percentage of our population that is obese has gone from one-fourth to one-third over the past 10 years! The problem is especially crucial for African American women (National Institute for Health Statistics, 1994).

What are the main causes of obesity? According to obesity expert F. X. Pi-Sunyer (1994), lack of exercise and snacking are the culprits. As he put it, "We drive everywhere. Nobody wants to walk anywhere. And we use a lot of other labor-saving devices. For example, if people cut lawns, they're sitting on the lawn mowers. They don't push them around" (p. 238).

An Applied View

Dealing with Adult Children of Alcoholics (ACoA)

According to Woititz (1990), clear agreement exists on three aspects of alcoholism: Alcoholism runs in families; children of alcoholics run a higher risk of developing alcoholism than other children; children of alcoholics tend to marry alcoholics. She also found that adult children of alcoholics usually manifest 13 characteristics. They

- are often not clear on what normal behavior is
- have difficulty following a project through from beginning to end
- lie when it would be just as easy to tell the truth
- judge themselves without mercy
- have difficulty having fun
- take themselves very seriously
- have difficulty with intimate relationships
- overreact to changes over which they have no control
- constantly seek approval and affirmation
- usually feel that they are different from other people
- are overly responsible or irresponsible
- are extremely loyal, even in the face of evidence that the loyalty is undeserved
- are impulsive (They tend to lock themselves into

a course of action without giving serious consideration to alternative behaviors or possible consequences.)

Woititz suggested that although these traits can make life difficult, it is important that the adult children of an alcoholic recognize that they are likely to possess most of them. "They could decide to work on changing aspects of themselves that cause them difficulty, or they could choose not to do so. In either event they have greater self-knowledge, which leads to greater self-understanding, which helps in the development of a sense of self. It is a win-win situation" (p. 98). She urged that: "Being the adult child of an alcoholic is not a disease. It is a fact of your history. Because of the nature of this illness and the family response to it, certain things occur that influence your feelings, attitudes, and behaviors in ways that cause you pain and concern. The object of ACoA recovery is to overcome those aspects of your history that cause you difficulty today and learn a better way. The process of recovery for adult children is very disruptive. It means changing the way you have perceived yourself and your world up until now." (p. 101)

The impact on health is significant and widespread. Obesity increases the risk of such diseases as heart disease, diabetes, arthritis, and cancer. In addition, our society places great importance on physical appearance. Overweight persons are likely to suffer from low self-esteem or even depression because of the way they are treated by others.

At the other extreme, some disagreement exists over what is considered to be too thin. Some researchers suggest that it is better to be a little overweight than it is to be underweight. Recent research on animals indicates that a restricted diet that leaves the animal lean and thin might be healthiest (Campbell & Gaddy, 1987; Masoro, 1984). A severely restricted diet leads to some of the complications associated with eating disorders such as anorexia nervosa (see Chapter 13). Once again, moderation is the safest course to follow.

Use of Alcohol

The consumption of alcohol is another great health concern to our society. Alcohol abuse is estimated to cost our economy more than $100 billion annually (Holden, 1987). This figure includes medical treatment for cirrhosis of the liver, osteoporosis, ulcers, heart disease, nervous system damage, and certain types of cancer such as breast cancer; the insurance and medical costs incurred by automobile accidents resulting from drinking and driving; the drug treatment necessary to help people control their addiction; and the enormous cost of labor that is lost when heavy drinkers are unable to come in to work.

Creeden (1990) examined reports of fraternity drinking and alcohol-related behavioral problems on college campuses. The influence of peers, accessibility of alcohol, and pressure to be accepted by the group affect behavior and consumption in fraternities. The socialization process within the fraternity system places high em-

What's Your ? *VIEW.*   Can Drinking Alcohol Have Positive Effects?

In most articles you may have read about alcohol consumption, it has been associated with a variety of negative biological and psychological effects. Earlier research seemed to indicate that alcohol had no redeeming qualities. More recently, studies have indicated that alcohol may have some beneficial effects, such as a decreased risk of heart attack. According to Criqui (1990), "The consistency of results across studies and the biological plausibility of alcohol's beneficial impact through high-density lipoprotein cholesterol and blood pressure suggest a potential benefit of several drinks per week" (p. 857).

Light social drinking may also encourage cross-cultural interactions. For example, vanWilkinson (1989) attempted to investigate the possible lifestyle influences on alcohol use among south Texas Mexican-Americans. He surveyed 247 respondents who were classified into six subgroups: working class, urban middle class, farmworkers, farmer/ranchers, migrants, and upper-class Mexican-Americans. All subgroups drank at home and at parties. "Almost all pachangas (parties) are held at someone's home and transcend any social class structure. Important for the rich as well as the poor, these events tend to make equals of those who might be unequals."

Do you think the consumption of alcohol can have positive physiological and social effects? What advice would you get if you called your local Board of Health? The Alcoholics Anonymous Central Service Office? The Ask-A-Nurse Hotline?

phasis on drinking. Johnson & others (1995) found that alcohol use is commonly associated with smoking and hostile behaviors, which may lead to increased risk of heart disease and high cholesterol. White males consume more than women or African Americans.

Most people consume alcohol to attain the relaxed, uninhibited feeling that alcohol tends to produce. The fact is, alcohol dulls the senses. Specifically, it decreases reaction times in the brain and nervous system. Continued drinking may affect the sex life of males, by making it difficult for them to attain and keep an erection.

Even though problems associated with alcoholism (e.g., with family, the law, and one's health) have been highlighted in the popular press, college presidents continue to rank alcohol abuse as the number one problem on campuses (Wechsler, 1996). Binge drinking (defined as five or more drinks in a row for men, and four or more drinks in a row for women, one or more times during a two-week period) has become widespread. The practice is not only harmful for those who drink, but also for those in their immediate environment. For example, bingeing is associated with injuries from fights and automobile accidents. This is supported by Honan (1997), who noted that the number of drug arrests on major college campuses increased almost 18 percent in 1995, according to an annual survey of campus crime. Although the survey emphasized a rise in drug arrests, college health specialists cited alcohol abuse as a far greater problem. For example, almost all sexual assaults at one major Westcoast university were alcohol related. Some college officials attribute the rise in arrests to stricter enforcement of the laws, rather than an actual increase in substance abuse. However, the rise in the number of arrests is worth noting, because arrests for other crimes, such as murders, robberies, and burglaries, decreased.

Ironically, some research has indicated that a daily, moderate intake of alcohol may be beneficial (although not for those over the age of 50—see Chapter 15). Such small amounts of alcohol seem to produce a protein in the blood that helps lower cholesterol. Unfortunately, the addictive qualities of alcohol make it impossible for many people to drink in only moderate amounts. This is why treatment programs such as the very successful Alcoholics Anonymous ask their clients to abstain totally from alcohol rather than try to control their drinking.

Use of Tobacco

The use of tobacco has been falling rapidly, at about 1 percent per year since 1987. About 28 percent of American men are smokers, as compared with 23 percent of American women ("Cigarette Smoking among Adults," 1992).

As with immoderate use of alcohol, tobacco use is also linked to a variety of health problems. The most common way to use tobacco is to smoke cigarettes. Most people are now aware that heavy cigarette smoking greatly increases the risk of lung cancer. The notoriety of the trials in which cigarette companies are being successfully sued is facilitating this awareness. They are perhaps less aware of the links between smoking and cancer of the kidney and stomach, along with the links to other diseases such as heart disease and emphysema (Engstrom, 1986).

The main culprit in tobacco is nicotine. Nicotine is a stimulating drug that the Surgeon General of the United States has concluded is as addictive as heroin or cocaine. Individuals can be affected by nicotine in ways other than by smoking cigarettes. Recent attention has focused on the dramatic increase in the use of smokeless chewing tobacco, primarily in young men. This type of tobacco use leads to a higher risk of cancer of the larynx, mouth, esophagus, and stomach. Awareness of this type of health risk is quickly spreading, as people see news photos of teenage boys who have had to have entire portions of their face removed due to cancer. Smokers are 14 times more likely to die from cancer of the lungs, and twice as likely to die of a heart attack as nonsmokers. Other diseases linked to smoking are bronchitis, emphysema, and increased blood pressure.

The Department of Health and Human Services (1996) has outlined the personality types of smokers versus nonsmokers. Adult smokers tend to be risk-takers, impulsive, defiant, and extroverted. Blue-collar workers tend to be the heaviest smokers among men. For females, white-collar workers are the heaviest smokers, and homemakers tend to smoke more than women who work.

Peer pressure from friends is the major reason that young adults smoke. As in adulthood, young people who smoke tend to be extroverted and more disobedient toward authority than nonsmokers. Some young adults see smoking as a way of appearing older and more mature. Young adults who go on to college smoke less than those who do not continue their education. Among young women, smokers are less athletic, more social, study less, get lower grades, and generally dislike school more than nonsmoking females.

You may also involuntarily be exposed to the dangers of tobacco use. A growing body of research is documenting the deleterious effects of passive smoking. Passive smoking is the breathing in of the smoke around you that others produce. For example, a nonsmoker who is married to a heavy smoker has a 30 percent greater risk of lung cancer than someone who is married to a nonsmoker (National Institute for Health Statistics, 1995). (The role of smoke in the environment is also covered in Chapter 4.) Evidence also indicates that children can be affected when their mothers smoke. This mounting evidence has led to a flurry of legislation prohibiting smoking in certain public areas such as elevators, airplanes, and restaurants and the designation of smoking areas in workplaces.

The message does seem to be reaching the public. Overall, fewer people smoke now than at any time in the past 25 years (with the exception of teenage females). Numerous stop-smoking programs spring up all the time. These programs run the gamut from classic behavioral techniques to hypnosis. But perhaps the most telling evidence that smoking is on the decline in the United States is the reaction of the giant tobacco companies. In recent years these companies have increasingly targeted foreign markets (a growing ethical controversy, because these markets are typically Third World countries) while diversifying their domestic market with different and healthier products.

Physical Fitness

One of the most popular trends of recent years has been the so-called fitness craze. Health benefits are the obvious reason for this enthusiasm for exercise. Regular, strenuous exercise can increase heart and lung capacity, lower blood pressure, decrease cholesterol in the blood and keep weight at normal levels ("Coronary Disease Attributable to Sedentary Lifestyle," 1990).

During a physical workout, oxygen travels more deeply into the lungs, and the heart pumps harder to carry more blood into the muscles. Healthy lungs and heart are vital for a long life. Persons who do not exercise and have inactive jobs are at twice the risk for a heart attack compared with persons who do exercise. Individuals who exercise report other health benefits, including better concentration at work and better sleep patterns (VanderZanden, 1989).

One study (Ossip-Klein & others, 1989) assigned a number of clinically depressed women to one of three groups: a group that did regular running, a group that lifted weights regularly, or a control group that did nothing special. The women in both exercise groups showed increased self-concept over the women in the control group. The two types of exercise worked equally well.

Many corporations are now providing the time and facilities for employees to build regular exercise into their workday. The reasoning is that work time lost in this way is more than made up for by more productive employees, who end up losing less time due to illness. In one new trend, some health insurance programs are offering free access to exercise facilities, again looking at the long-term gain of having healthier members.

Marital Status

Another lifestyle factor that appears to affect health is marital status. Despite comedians' jokes, married people seem to be healthier than single, divorced, or widowed people (Horwitz & others, 1995). They tend to have less frequent and shorter stays in hospitals. They tend to have fewer chronic conditions and fewer disabilities. Never-married and widowed people are the next healthiest. Divorced and separated people show the most health-related problems. A number of possible explanations could account for this, but clearly one must consider the emotional and economic support that an intact family can provide.

Based on the preceding information, we could conclude that a healthy lifestyle consists of a diet with reasonable caloric intake that is low in fat and high in fiber, moderate or no consumption of alcohol, no tobacco use, plenty of regular, strenuous exercise, and a supportive spouse. In fact, this accurately describes the Mormon lifestyle in Utah, which allows the average resident of Utah to live years longer

---

Guided Review

5. Early adulthood is the time when the efficiency of most body functions begins to
_____.

6. Although physical ability has peaked, bodily responses in adulthood are supplemented by _____ _____; that is, the part of the total capacity of our body's organs that we do not normally need to use.

7. Our lifestyle affects our health, mainly through our choices of foods, use of alcohol, use of tobacco, _____ _____, and marital status.

8. Cholesterol, a substance in the blood related to heart attack, can be controlled by
_____.

9. Alcohol not only affects the person who drinks it. _____ children of alcoholics often have problems, including difficulty finishing projects, having fun, and constantly seeking the _____ of others.

10. Regular exercise that brings _____ deep into the lungs and enables the heart to take more blood to the muscles contributes to overall health.

11. Research indicates that married people tend to be _____ than single people.

Answers

5. decline 6. organ reserve 7. physical fitness 8. diet 9. Adult, approval 10. oxygen 11. healthier

than the average resident of Nevada. This, of course, is no reason to go out and change your religious preference, but it is reason to examine your current lifestyle and consider some prudent changes.

As you can see, health is also an aspect of life in which all three factors of the biopsychosocial model are clearly evident. For example, Verbrugge (1989) found important gender differences in health. Whereas women tend to have higher rates of acute illnesses and more nonfatal chronic conditions, men have higher rates of fatal conditions. Now let us turn to another complex area, sexuality.

As with physical development, there has not been a great deal of research on the cognitive development of young adults. Possibly this is because cognitive functioning appears to peak during this period, and so there is less concern over change.

Cognitive Development

There are important characteristics that distinguish young adult learners from older learners (Darkenwald & Novak, 1997; Edwards & Usher, 1997; Saul, 1997). For instance, Nunn (1994) found that younger college students (ages 17 to 30) tend to be less positive in their self-concepts and less internally oriented than older students (ages 31 to 65). Younger students prefer less formal learning methods, more physical movement in learning, and dislike variety in learning styles. Young adult learners are less goal and achievement oriented than older students. They are more anxious and impulsive and perceive themselves as less abstract in their thinking than the older students. In addition to learning factors, a major emphasis of research has been on the relationship between intellectual and ethical growth.

Intellectual/Ethical Development

Perry (1968a, 1968b, 1981) studied the intellectual/ethical development of several hundred Harvard college students, a group of males ages 17 to 22. These students responded to several checklists on their educational views and were interviewed extensively on the basis of their responses. The results of these studies led Perry to suggest a sequence of intellectual and ethical development that typically occurs during the transition from late adolescence to early adulthood. This sequence consists of nine positions, which indicate progress from belief in the absolute authority of experts to the recognition that one must make commitments and be responsible for one's own beliefs.

Perry's nine stages are divided among three broader categories, as follows:

I. **Dualism** ("Things are either absolutely right or absolutely wrong.")
   - Position 1: The world is viewed in such polar terms as right versus wrong, we versus they, and good versus bad. If an answer is right, it is absolutely right. We get right answers by going to authorities who have absolute knowledge.
   - Position 2: The person recognizes that uncertainty exists, but ascribes it to poorly qualified authorities. Sometimes individuals can learn the truth for themselves.
   - Position 3: Diversity and uncertainty are now acceptable but considered temporary because the authorities do not know what the answers are yet. The person becomes puzzled as to what the standards should be in these cases.

II. **Relativism** ("Anything can be right or wrong depending on the situation; all views are equally right.")
   - Position 4a: The person realizes that uncertainty and diversity of opinion are often extensive and recognizes that this is a legitimate status. Now

he or she believes that "anyone has a right to an opinion." It is now possible for two authorities to disagree with each other without either of them being wrong.

- Position 4b: Sometimes the authorities (such as college professors) are not talking about right answers. Rather, they want students to think for themselves, supporting their opinions with data.

- Position 5: The person recognizes that all knowledge and values (including even those of an authority) exist in some specific context. It is therefore relative to the context. The person also recognizes that simple right and wrong are relatively rare, and even they exist in a specific context.

- Position 6: The person apprehends that because we live in a relativistic world, we must make some sort of personal commitment to an idea or concept, as opposed to looking for an authority to follow.

III. **Commitment** ("Because of available evidence and my understanding of my own values, I have come to new beliefs.")

- Position 7: The person begins to choose the commitments that she or he will make in specific areas.

- Position 8: Having begun to make commitments, the person experiences the implications of those commitments and explores the various issues of responsibility involved.

- Position 9: The person's identity is affirmed through the various commitments made. There is a recognition of the necessity for balancing commitments and the understanding that one can have responsibilities that are expressed through a daily lifestyle. Perry (1981) described this position:

This is how life will be. I will be whole-hearted while tentative, fight for my values yet respect others, believe my deepest values right yet be ready to learn. I see that I shall be retracing this whole journey over and over—but, I hope, more wisely. (p. 276)

Some students move through these stages in a smooth and regular fashion; others, however, are delayed or deflected in one of three ways:

- **Temporizing.** Some people remain in one position for a year or more, exploring its implications but hesitating to make any further progress.

- **Escape.** Some people use opportunities for detachment, especially those offered in positions 4 and 5, to refuse responsibility for making any commitments. Because everyone's opinion is "equally right," the person believes that no commitments need be made and, thus, escapes from the dilemma.

- **Retreat.** Sometimes, confused by the confrontation and uncertainties of the middle positions, people retreat to earlier positions.

Perry's theory has been criticized because all of the subjects of his research were all males. However, his work spurred considerable research on females, which we now overview.

"Women's Ways of Knowing"

In a continuing collaborative study, Belenky and associates (1986, 1997) set out to answer the questions, "Do female ways of knowing develop differently from those of males? If so, how do they come to learn and value what they know?" The study was rooted in Perry's work and the work of Carol Gilligan, whose ground-breaking research on the morality of care and responsibility versus the morality of rights and justice was covered in Chapter 9.

Belenky and her associates conducted a series of lengthy and intense interviews with 135 women of diverse socioeconomic backgrounds. The researchers found five general categories of ways in which women know and view the world. Though some of the women interviewed clearly demonstrated a progression from one perspective to the next, the researchers contend that they are unable to discern a progression of clear-cut stages, as did Perry and Gilligan. The five perspectives are silence, received knowledge, subjective knowledge, procedural knowledge, and constructed knowledge.

1. **Silence.** Females in the silence category describe themselves as "deaf and dumb." These women feel passive and dependent. Like players in an authority's game, they feel expected to know rules that don't exist. These women's thinking is characterized by concepts of right and wrong, similar to the men in Perry's first category of dualism. Questions about their growing up revealed family lives filled with violence, abuse, and chaos. The researchers noted that "gaining a voice and developing an awareness of their own minds are the tasks that these women must accomplish if they are to cease being either a perpetrator or victim of family violence" (Belenky & others, 1986, p. 38).

2. **Received knowledge.** Women in the received knowledge category see words as central to the knowing process. They learn by listening and assume truths come from authorities. These women are intolerant of ambiguities and paradoxes, always coming back to the notion that there are absolute truths. Received knowers seem similar to the men that Perry described as being in the first stage of dualism, but with a difference. The men Perry interviewed felt a great affiliation with the knowing authority. The women of this perspective were awed by the authorities but far less affiliated with them. In contrast to the men of Perry's study, women of received knowledge channel their energies and increased sense of self into the care of others.

3. **Subjective knowledge.** The researchers noted that women in the subjective knowledge category often had experienced two phenomena that pushed them toward this perspective: some crisis of male authority that sparked a distrust of outside sources of knowledge, and some experience that confirmed a trust in themselves. Subjectivists value their "gut" or firsthand experience as their best source of knowledge and see themselves as "conduits through which truth emerges" (p. 69). The researchers note that subjectivists are similar to males in Perry's second category of relativism in that they embrace the notion of multiple truths.

4. **Procedural knowledge.** The women in the procedural knowledge category have a distrust of both knowledge from authority and their own inner authority or "gut." The perspective of procedural knowledge is characterized by an interest in form over content (how you say something rather than what you say). Women in this category also have a heightened sense of control. This category is similar to Perry's position 4b, where students learn analytic methods that authorities sanction. But analytic thinking emerges differently in women because they are less likely to affiliate with authorities.

    The researchers describe women as having two kinds of procedural knowledge: separate knowing and connected knowing. These terms are reminiscent of Gilligan's work. Separate knowers are analytical and try to

What's Your VIEW? How Does Age Affect High School Graduation Rates?

In the following table, you can see that a larger percentage of young adults aged 25 to 29 have a high school diploma and have four or more years of college than do all adults 25 and older. Why do you suppose this is true? Another interesting fact found in this table is that although educational level in general has risen steadily since 1940, there has been a slight decrease in high school graduation among the 25- to 29-year-olds in recent years. To what do you attribute this surprising finding?

Level of School Completed

	% Ages 25 to 29		% Ages 25 and over	
Year	H. S. or more*	4 or more years years of college	H. S. or more*	4 or more years of college
1940	38.1	5.9	24.5	4.6
1950	52.8	7.7	34.3	6.2
1960	60.7	11.0	41.1	7.7
1970	75.4	16.4	55.2	11.0
1980	85.4	22.5	68.6	17.0
1986	86.1	22.4	74.7	19.4
1987	86.0	22.0	75.6	19.9
1988	85.9	22.7	76.2	20.3
1989	85.5	23.4	76.9	21.1

*Includes recipients of high school equivalency certificates

Source: National Center for Education Statistics. *American Education at a Glance.* Office of Educational Research and Improvement, Washington, D. C., 1992, page 8.

I think the one lesson I have learned is that there is no substitute for paying attention.
Diane Sawyer

separate the self, to reveal the truth. Connected knowers learn through empathy with others.

5. **Constructed knowledge.** Those in the constructed knowledge category have integrated the subjective and procedural ways of knowing (types 3 and 4). Women of this perspective note that "all knowledge is constructed and the knower is an intimate part of the known" (p. 137). They feel responsible for examining and questioning systems of constructing knowledge. Their thinking is characterized by a high tolerance of ambiguity and internal contradiction. Indeed, the women whose ways of knowing are of this perspective often balance many commitments and relationships, as well as ideas.

The work of Perry and Belenky and her associates (as well as that of Piaget, Kohlberg, and Gilligan, discussed earlier in this book) has greatly advanced our knowledge of intellectual and ethical development in the late adolescent and early adult years. It has also produced much controversy. Many questions remain to be answered. For example, does socioeconomic level make any difference? What about cultural background? We hope that the research in this area will provide further insights into how we can help youth progress through this period successfully. We could say the same for the next aspect of development we will review, love in young adulthood.

Guided Review

12. William Perry examined the intellectual and ethical changes in Harvard males and found them to move through three broad categories of change. These categories include _____ (things are absolutely right or wrong), relativism (all views are equal), and _____ (holding to beliefs based on the best available evidence and values).

13. Perry describes nine stages within these three categories. Some students move through the stages smoothly, others are delayed by _____, escape, and _____.

14. Mary Belenky and her colleagues, building on Perry's work and the work of Carol Gilligan, examined the _____ and _____ development of women.

15. Belenky and others found five general categories of ways in which women view the world. The five perspectives include silence, _____ _____, subjective knowledge, procedural knowledge, and _____ _____.

Patterns of Work

> Waste of time is thus the deadliest of sins. Loss of time through sociability, idle talk, luxury, or more sleep than is necessary for health (six hours) is worthy of absolute moral condemnation. Thus inactive contemplation is also valueless, or even reprehensible if it is at the expense of one's daily work.
>
> —Max Weber, *The Protestant Ethic and the Spirit of Capitalism*

Weber, a philosopher and economist, was a leading spokesperson on the role of labor at the turn of the century. How differently we view that role today! Table 13.2 displays a brief summary of the history of work in Western society and indicates

TABLE 13.2   THE PRIMARY ROLES OF WORK

Years	Approximate Primary Role of Work
Early history	Search for food.
8000 B.C.E.	Cultivation of cereal grains, domestication of animals.
5000 B.C.E.	Greater division of labor, surplus production of goods, trade.
500 B.C.E.	Work seen as degrading and brutalizing by upper classes; done as much as possible by slaves.
500	Serfdom (lord of manor system replaces slavery).
1350	Black Death makes workers scarce. Move to towns; guilds of craftspersons formed. Cottage industry, capitalism start.
1750	Inventions cause "industrial revolution," demise of small business. Factory system takes advantage of cheap labor.
1900	Unions, government regulations, electricity and automation, new management policies greatly improve life of workers.
1950	Computers, technology create world of highly skilled, white-collar workers.
1970	Age of information processing.

Answers

12. dualism, commitment 13. temporizing, retreat 14. ethical, intellectual 15. received knowledge, constructed knowledge

how much our attitudes toward work have changed. Changes in the world of work have been coming more rapidly in recent years than ever before. Working in the United States today is complicated. The rest of this section is devoted to explicating the major trends, their causes, and likely results.

Getting a Job

How many jobs have you held so far in your life? Do you remember how you got them? What do the people who hire workers consider when they are hiring? Do blue-collar jobs have significantly different criteria than white-collar jobs?

To find out, you might interview the managers of a bank and a supermarket and ask what they look for in a new employee. Are there differences in behavioral, attitudinal, cognitive, or appearance criteria? Why or why not?

Employment Patterns

Most of the total population 16 years old and older who choose to work are working (U. S. National Center for Health Statistics, 1992). The figure is decidedly lower for the African American population—around 89 percent, compared with 93 percent for whites. Not surprisingly, the highest percentage of unemployment is found among persons 16 to 19 years old. For African Americans in that age group, the percentage is a disconcerting 40 percent, as compared with 15 percent for whites.

Another important aspect of employment patterns has to do with the effects of education. The lower the level of education, the more likely a person is to be unemployed. Unfortunately, this is even more true for African Americans than for whites and Latinos. For example, of those with less than four years of high school, 19.9 percent of whites and 15.8 percent of Latinos are unemployed, compared with 35.9 percent of African Americans.

How People Choose Their Careers

Two theories are described here, those of John Holland and of Donald Super. These two theories have achieved the most acceptance in this field.

Holland's Personality Theory

On the basis of research still considered to be highly reliable, Holland (1973) developed an interesting theory on how people choose their careers. He suggested

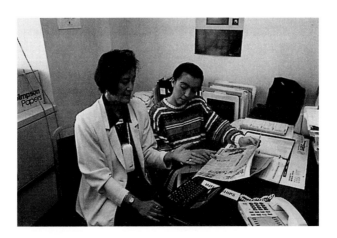

that in our culture, all people can be categorized as one of six personality types: realistic, investigative, artistic, social, enterprising, or conventional. An individual's personality pattern is estimated by figuring out how much a person's attributes resemble each type.

For example, a person might resemble an artistic type most. This type exhibits "a preference for ambiguous, free, unsystematized activities that entail the manipulation of physical, verbal, or human materials to create art forms or products, and an aversion to explicit, systematic, and ordered activities" (p. 120). This kind of person learns to be competent in artistic endeavors such as language, art, music, drama, and writing.

Our hypothetical person may next most resemble the social type. Such an individual is likely to be cooperative, friendly, generous, helpful, idealistic, insightful, responsible, tactful, and understanding. This person is then rated on the remaining four types in descending order. The six-category composite is the person's personality pattern.

The theory also holds that people live in six kinds of environments. These have the same names as the personality types. According to Holland (1973),

> each environment is dominated by a given type of personality, and each environment is typified by physical settings posing special problems and stresses. For example, realistic environments are "dominated" by realistic types of people—that is, the largest percentage of the population in the realistic environment resembles the realistic type. A conventional environment is dominated by conventional types. (p. 22)

People tend to search out environments in which they feel comfortable and competent. Artistic types seek out artistic environments, enterprising types seek out enterprising environments, and so forth. You can take a test—the Strong Vocational Interest Blank—to see which personality type is most like you.

Super's Developmental Theory

Donald Super has been one of the most influential figures in advancing theories of career choice and development during recent years. Super (1983, 1990) developed a life stage theory of career development to explain how career identity develops over time and to determine a person's readiness to make a career choice. Super described five career stages, which he originally associated with different developmental periods. In more recent revisions of his theory (Super, 1990), Super suggested that we recycle through each of these stages several times during our lives.

The exploration stage is associated primarily with early adulthood. Through school, leisure, and part-time work activities, the adolescent or young adult is exposed to a wider variety of experiences. Through these experiences, individuals further define their self-concept and have the opportunity to test out abilities and interests. Early in this stage, initial work-related choices are made by assessing interests, abilities, needs, and values. By the end of this stage, a beginning full-time job is often selected. Super believes that most adolescents are not ready to make definite career choices because they have not yet had the chance to adequately explore available opportunities.

The Phenomenon of the Dual-Career Family

The old family pattern of the husband who goes off to work to provide for his family and the wife who stays home and manages that family is almost extinct. Economic realities and the women's movement have led to the development of a new family dynamic—the **dual-career family.** The goals of the American Dream, achievement and self-sufficiency, have not changed. What has changed, as Hertz

Careers, like rackets, don't always take off on schedule. The key is to keep working on the engines.

(1991) noted, is that now both spouses want to realize this dream. Both want the upward progression in rank, responsibility, status, and pay that ultimately result in independence—a life of one's own.

First, women are still considered responsible for the maintenance of the family. Therefore, women are often considered unreliable by employers for the more important, higher-paying jobs. Women in general have better access to low-paying jobs with little opportunity for advancement. Women often choose jobs that fit in well with the needs of their family. Women tend to work shorter hours and change the nature of their work more often than men do. As Serakan (1989) found, women experience increased self-esteem and feelings of self-worth and self-regard when working, critical variables that moderate the relationship among work factors and job satisfaction. Women who spend more time at work, though, experience less job satisfaction because of guilt over not being home than those who work less.

A study by Guelzow and associates (1991) confirmed that multiple roles in dual-career families are not necessarily related to stress but did find that longer working hours were associated with higher role strain for women; and larger family size and inflexible work schedules were associated with stress for men. Flexibility of work for men was related with role sharing in the household. Hertz (1989) found that when a wife's career became as demanding as her husband's, there was no time for a wife to be a wife; hence, the role of wife was the first to change. Sharing housework became inevitable; as one man put it, "If both of us were relying on the other to fix meals, we'd both starve."

Hertz also found that men have had to adjust psychologically to the increased role of their wives as providers for the family. Men have historically derived much of their self-image and personal satisfaction from their work and their ability to "provide" for their family. Women now contribute much more of the family income than in previous times, and in a small but increasing number of cases, women are the primary breadwinners.

Working-class men have adapted better to this change, perhaps because the financial reality gives them little choice. The more dependent a family is on the contributions of a wife's income, the more accepting the husband is of the new role of his spouse (Rosen, 1987). All classes of men and women, however, try to continue to portray the husband as the primary provider and the wife as providing secondary support. According to a recent study by Rosin (1990), "Research indicates, however, that many husbands believe that membership in a dual-career marriage leads to marital satisfaction because of a sense of companionship and partnership with their wives, an increased vitality in the relationship, and a greater feeling of independence" (p. 182).

Although women are entering the workforce in increasing numbers, in general men are not participating more in the family work. Whereas some research suggests, for example, that husbands of employed women perform more hours of housework than husbands of unemployed women, the differences are fairly small (Greenstein, 1996). Most wives do about two to three times as much family work as the husbands. Women tend to do all the everyday work, including most of the child care, washing of clothes, cooking, and general cleaning. They tend to work alone, during the week and on the weekends, and during all parts of the day. Greenstein has found that the beliefs men and women have about gender and marital roles play the biggest role in the division of domestic labor. Spouses that take a more egalitarian view of their respective roles share the housework more than those spouses who hold a more traditional view.

Men tend to do the less frequent, irregular work, such as household repairs, taking out the trash, mowing the lawn, and so on. They tend to do family work in the company of others, on the weekend, or perhaps during the evening. In the evening, this work may involve child care while the wife does the after-dinner chores. The tasks that men are most willing to share are the very tasks that women find most enjoyable: cooking and child care. During the inevitable argument over who does what around the house, the husband may point out that he helped out in these areas, not recognizing that he left the more onerous jobs for his wife.

We mentioned that men seem to derive their self-image and identity from their work and that this is increasingly threatened by the entrance of women into the workplace. One obvious way men could derive more satisfaction is by taking on a greater role in the care of their children. This change, however, does not appear to be occurring at the same pace as women entering the workforce. It is estimated that mothers are actively involved with their children three to five times as much as fathers (Lamb, 1987). Mothers do all the routine chores such as feeding, bathing, and dressing. Fathers primarily play with their children. Fathers tend to spend their time with the children when the mothers are around, whereas mothers spend much more time alone with the children.

Today it is more difficult for some to define themselves according to their jobs (Seppa, 1997). As the number of two-income households continues to grow, women are taking many of the new high-growth jobs, which affects men's traditional image as chief provider in the family. Although many people welcome more equal division of responsibility in marriages, the effects of such positive changes have psychological ramifications for men, who now may find they have lost their role as dominant breadwinner as they become a more active parent.

This conflict may not be a serious problem for future generations of workers, as children are socialized very differently today. In Seppa's view (1997), boys raised by working mothers are likely to have new views of adult gender roles, and a new definition of masculinity will arise. Women's contributions to family income will provide positive benefits to the family, and men will need to define themselves in a way that differs from the old idea that they must compete to be successful. Compared to the rapid changes for women brought on by the feminist movement, this new definition of men is likely to emerge at a slower pace, but will, nevertheless, be the cause of role adjustments for many.

> It seems that men in a dual career marriage, no longer cushioned by the traditional wife, need to learn to balance competing demands of work and family. Where these men do not have role models, their changing roles may increase stress or change men's relationship to work, the cornerstone of male identity and self-esteem. (Rosin, 1990, p. 175)

Guided Review

16. The nature of work has changed, moving from a primary focus on food gathering (early human history) to a factory system (1750–1950) to an emphasis on _____ _____ (1970).
17. Level of education affects employment status, with less education related to higher unemployment rates. African Americans suffer more from less education than do whites or _____.
18. Holland's theory on how people select careers is based on a categorization of six _____ _____.
19. According to Holland, people choose careers that will place them in environments in which they feel _____ and _____
20. In a dual-career family, men can get more satisfaction in their marriage by taking on an increased responsibility for _____ _____, as well as household duties.

Answers

16. information processing 17. Latinos 18. personality types 19. comfortable, competent 20. child care

Some male participation occurs regardless of whether the mother is employed. However, as economic necessity forces women to spend more time at a paid job, they are demanding that men help out more equitably. Recent research suggests that men who are forced to participate more in child care may form better relationships with their children. At the same time, this results in significantly more marital distress (Crouter & others, 1987). One of the challenges of the family in the 1990s will be to get husbands to take on voluntarily more of the responsibility of child care (not to mention equitable household management).

The results may lead to increased communication and interaction between husband and wife, enhancing the marriage, as well as an increase in job satisfaction for the working wife and mother who is able to devote more time to work without feeling stress over family obligations. (Serakan, 1989, p. 115)

CONCLUSION

We began this chapter by comparing how youths are inducted into adulthood in preindustrial tribes and in the modern United States. We concluded that our situation is much more complex than that of the tribes and that the absence of clear initiation rites still causes problems for us.

Young adulthood is a period during which many changes are taking place. The peak of physical development is reached, and the decline of certain abilities begins. These declines are almost never apparent, however, because of organ reserve. Our style of life has a powerful effect on this development, including our diet, use of alcohol, drugs and nicotine, and marital status.

The major change occurring in the area of cognitive development involves the relationship between intellectual and ethical growth. Research also suggests that there are five "women's ways of knowing."

The nation's workers experience a very different environment than their predecessors of 50 years ago, as we leave the industrial age and enter the age of "information processing." Many problems still must be solved—especially the treatment of persons of color and women.

In summary:

Initiation To Adulthood

- Initiation rites in other cultures offer a formal ceremony marking the transition from child to adult.

- Some researchers have suggested parallels to the initiation process in the crimes juveniles are often required to commit in order to become a member of a gang, and in the sequence of experiences that so often lead to drug addiction.
- The purpose of initiation rites in preindustrial societies is to cushion the emotional disruption arising from the transition from one life status to another.
- Entry into adulthood is far more complex for adolescents today, largely due to the increase of sophisticated technologies and the need for many more years of formal education.
- Organized sports, the adolescent counterculture, and delinquency all provide some sort of trials that must be passed for acceptance into adulthood.
- Five types of activities signal the passage to maturity in America today: religious, sexual, social, educational, and economic.

Physical Development

- Early adulthood is the period during which physical changes slow down or stop.
- The human body is designed to do much more than it is usually called upon to do. Much of its total capacity is held in "organ reserve."
- Lifestyle, food choices, alcohol and tobacco use, physical fitness, and

marital status all play an enormous role in the health of a young adult.

Cognitive Development

- Perry suggested three categories of intellectual and ethical development that typify transition from late adolescence to early adulthood: dualism, relativism, and commitment. By avoiding the three obstacles that might impede their progress (temporizing, escape, or retreat), young adults should be able to achieve commitments that are the hallmark of the mature person.
- Belenky and associates suggest women know and view the world through five perspectives: silence, received knowledge, subjective knowledge, procedural knowledge, and constructed knowledge.

Patterns of Work

- Most of the total population 16 years old and older who choose to work are working.
- Holland suggested that, in our culture, all people can be categorized in one of six vocational interest types as to career choice: realistic, investigative, artistic, social, enterprising, or conventional.
- Economic realities and the feminist movement have given rise to dual-career families in which both husband and wife work outside of the home.

KEY TERMS

Cholesterol
Commitment (Perry's term)
Constructed knowledge
Dualism
Dual-career family

Escape
Hazing
Organ reserve
Procedural knowledge
Received knowledge

Relativism
Retreat
Silence
Subjective knowledge
Temporizing

WHAT DO YOU THINK?

1. Do you remember any experiences from your own youth that were particularly helpful in your transition to adulthood?
2. Societal changes have led to a change in the nature of initiation rites for adolescents. Are adolescents better off today as a result, or should we try to return to the family and societal structures of the past?

3. The media offers countless advertisements to help a person look younger, feel better, be better. Why are these ads so effective? What do they say about Western society?
4. Most college students are making the transition from Perry's category of dualism to relativism and, finally, to commitment. What types of behaviors might you observe

from a college student at each of these levels of intellectual development?
5. Many of the problems in the American family today have been attributed to the phenomenon of the dual-career couple. Is there any truth to this perception? In what ways do two working parents alter (positively and negatively) the family's operation as a unit?

CHAPTER REVIEW TEST

1. A bar mitzvah or bas mitzvah is an example of a(n) _____ rite of passage.
   a. religious
   b. sexual
   c. social
   d. educational

2. For most adolescents, the transition to adulthood raises questions about
   a. relationships with a loving mother.
   b. lifestyle decisions they made while still a child.
   c. how they feel about their fathers.
   d. who they hope to become.

3. Because we seldom call on its total capacity, people often are not aware of the decline of their _____ _____ during early adulthood.
   a. aerobic capacity
   b. blood pressure
   c. heart rate
   d. organ reserve

4. Research indicates that heart disease and cancer are linked to
   a. nutrition.
   b. other related diseases.

   c. exercise.
   d. None of the above.

5. Lack of exercise, snacking, and use of labor-saving devices are the main causes of
   a. leukemia.
   b. cancer.
   c. obesity.
   d. high blood pressure.

6. A survey among college students on alcohol use showed that alcohol consumption was directly related to
   a. low grade-point average.
   b. poor relations with peers.
   c. memory loss.
   d. length of time needed to earn a college degree.

7. What is the major reason that young adults smoke?
   a. Stress
   b. Economic reasons
   c. Peer pressure
   d. Get a fix

8. According to the Department of Health and Human Services, what are some common characteristics of adult smokers?

   a. They are defiant and extroverted
   b. They are impulsive, risk-taking, and extroverted
   c. They are risk-takers and obedient to others
   d. They are introverted, defiant, and stubborn

9. Which marital status group shows the most health-related problems?
   a. Single
   b. Married
   c. Divorced and separated
   d. Widowed

10. The theory on career choice that suggests that in our culture, all people can be categorized into six personality types was developed by whom?
    a. Super
    b. Holland
    c. Erikson
    d. Miller

11. Donald Super has been one of the most influential figures in developing a life stage theory of _____ _____ to explain how career identity develops over time.
    a. vocational training

b. career development
c. educational openness
d. human development

12. Perry's stages of dualism, relativism, and commitment refer to a person's
    a. relationship development.
    b. intellectual and ethical development.
    c. ability to make moral decisions.
    d. interpersonal relationships.

13. In a study of women's perspectives on knowledge (Belenky & other), received knowledge refers to

a. the view that words are central to the knowing process.
b. an experience that resulted in a distrust of outside sources of knowledge.
c. a distrust of knowledge from authority.
d. learned passivity and dependency in relationships.

14. Belenky's category of procedural knowledge is most similar to which of Perry's stages?
    a. Dualism
    b. Commitment
    c. Affirmation
    d. Relativism

15. The ability to recognize that certainty is impossible but _____ to or toward a certain position is necessary, even without certainty, describes Perry's third stage.
    a. aspiring
    b. commitment
    c. ambivalence
    d. disgust

16. At home, men tend to do the
    a. more frequent, regular work.
    b. less frequent, irregular work.
    c. work of their choice.
    d. dishes.

Answers

1.a 2.d 3.d 4.a 5.c 6.a 7.c 8.b 9.c 10.b 11.a 12.b 13.a 14.d 15.b 16.b

CHAPTER 14

Psychosocial Development in Early Adulthood

When things go wrong in society, we immediately inquire into the condition of family life. When we see society torn apart by crime, we cry, 'If only we could return to the good old days when family was sacred.' But were the good old days so good? Was the family ever free of violence? Many people who come to therapy these days were raised in the so-called golden age of the family, and they tell stories of abuse, neglect, and terrifying moralistic demands and pressure. Looked at coldly, the family of any era is both good and bad, offering both support and threat. This is why adults are so ambivalent about visiting their families and spending time with them: they want the emotional rewards of the sense of connection. But they also want the distance from painful memories and difficult relationships.

Today professionals are preoccupied by the 'dysfunctional family.' But to some extent all families are dysfunctional. No family is perfect, and most have serious problems. (Moore, 1992, pp. 15–16) ✻

You may disagree with Moore's assessment of the American family, but most researchers agree that the rapid changes this institution has been experiencing may well be cause for concern, if only because the family is the foundation from which so many other social and emotional elements of our lives spring. No aspects of young adult lives are more vital than those dealt with in this chapter: marriage and the family, work and leisure, and personal development.

When you finish reading this chapter, you should be able to

- Discuss changes regarding American marriages and young families that are ongoing today.

- Define the different types of marriage relationships.

- Discuss Levinson's theory of adult development as it relates specifically to men.

- Compare Levinson's theory with Erikson's young adult stage of intimacy and solidarity versus isolation.

- Define what is meant by individuation and discuss how it applies differently to women and men.

- Distinguish between sexual identity and gender role.

- Define three aspects of gender role, as well as the concept of androgyny.

- Demonstrate awareness of gender-role stereotypes and how they influence adolescent behavior.

- Discuss Gagnon and Simon's notion of "sexual scripts."

- Explain Wilson's sociobiological view of the objective of sex.

- Describe young adults' premarital and marital sexual practices.

- Identify Sternberg's seven forms of love.

- Define Fromm's notion of "validation" as it relates to love.

Marriage and the Family

When two people are under the influence of the most violent, most divisive and most transient of passions, they are required to swear that they will remain in that excited, abnormal, and exhausting condition continuously until death do them part.

—George Bernard Shaw

Changing American Marriages and Families

The modern American family is quite different from those of the last century. Those families were larger and much more likely to live near each other in the same city or town. What are the advantages and disadvantages of this tendency?

Finding critics of marriage is not difficult (e.g., Kathrin Perutz's book, *Marriage Is Hell*). Not many Americans are paying attention, though. Almost 95 percent of Americans get married at some point in their lives (U. S. National Center for Health Statistics, 1995). To better understand the present situation, let us take a look at the trends in marriage and family relations.

Today 25 percent of all people who get married for the first time are likely to marry someone who has been married before. In 20 percent of all marriages, both partners were married previously. Trends in the rates of first marriage, divorce, and remarriage since the early twentieth century reflect patterns of change in economic and social conditions in the United States. These changes can be clearly seen in Table 14.1. One of the most interesting trends has been the change in the average age at first marriage. At the turn of the century, the average age for females was almost 22 years, and for males almost 26 years. With the exception of the late Depression and war years, the trend has been toward earlier and earlier marriages.

This trend led demographers to make erroneous predictions. For example, Duvall (1971) predicted that marriages in 1990 would come even earlier, at about age 20 for both males and females. Several other investigators (e.g., Neugarten & Moore, 1968) said the same thing in the late 1960s. But these miscalculations only demonstrate the difficulty of predicting the behavior of human beings.

The average age at first marriage in the United States has gradually increased since the record lows during the mid-1950s (Table 14.1). Small increases in the age at first marriage occurred from 1955 to 1975. However, sharper increases have occurred in the last two decades. This U-shaped curve (from a high age in the 1890s to a relatively low age in the 1950s back to a high age today) is an excellent example of contextualism (see Chapter 1). One example of the effect of the current context for marriage is the rising number of women who have entered the workforce during this period.

An interesting change has been the nearly triple rise in the proportion of young adults who have not married during the past two decades. Eighty percent of men aged 20 to 24 years had never married in 1991, up from 55 percent in 1970. In this same time period, the rate went from 19 percent to 47 percent for men 25 to 29

TABLE 14.1 MEDIAN AGE AT FIRST MARRIAGE, BY SEX: 1890 TO 1990					
Year	**Men**	**Women**	**Year**	**Men**	**Women**
1990	26.3	24.1	1950	22.8	20.3
1985	25.5	23.3	1940	24.3	21.5
1980	24.7	22.0	1930	24.3	21.3
1975	23.5	21.1	1920	24.6	21.2
1970	23.2	20.8	1910	25.1	21.6
1965	22.8	20.6	1900	25.9	21.9
1960	22.8	20.3	1890	26.1	22.0
1955	22.6	20.2			

Source: From A. F. Saluter, "Marital Status and Living Arrangements: March 1991" in *Current Population Reports,* P-20 (No. 461), U. S. Bureau of the Census, Washington, D. C., 1991.

years old, and from 9 percent to 27 percent for men aged 30 to 34. As expected, because men marry later, men have higher proportions of the never-married in all age groups. For African Americans, however, the proportions are very similar for both genders (Saluter, 1991). An explanation may be that African American females may view African American males as poor marriage prospects because of their lack of employment opportunities (Chapman, 1988).

Another aspect of young adult relationships is cohabitation, which involves sharing a residence and personal assets, and sometimes having a child, without being married. Brown and Booth (1996) compared the relationships of married couples to those of couples who are cohabitors. Although cohabitors generally reported poorer relationship quality than the married couples, they also reported more frequent interaction with their partners than did married couples. In general, however, the relationships do not differ significantly.

More Americans are marrying outside of their racial groups, according to the major 1990 U. S. Census data (Reyes, 1997). Table 14.2 provides a comparison of interracial marriages in the 1950 and 1990 for African Americans and whites.

TABLE 14.2 A COMPARISON OF INTERRACIAL MARRIAGES IN 1950 AND 1990 FOR AFRICAN AMERICAN AND WHITE WOMEN AND MEN		
Racial Group	**1950**	**1990**
African American Women	1%	4%
White Women	>1%	3%
African American Men	>2%	8%
White Men	1%	4%

White men who had served in the military were three times as likely to marry outside their racial group as men who had never served. White women in the military were seven times as likely to marry outside their racial group as men who had never served.

The rate of divorce and, as a result, the rate of remarriage are higher. In their study of the responses of thousands of women, Norton and Moorman (1987) discovered several trends: "Currently many young adult women (particularly African Americans) will never marry, remarriage after divorce is becoming less frequent, and data indicate that divorce is leveling [at almost 50 percent]" (p. 3). Interracial marriage represents only one-half of 1 percent of all marriages. However, this number indicates a rapid increase over earlier periods.

The Bureau of the Census (1996) suggested that the recent trend in increased divorced rates is probably caused, at least in part, by four factors:

• Liberalization of divorce laws

• Growing societal acceptance of divorce and of remaining single

• The reduction in the cost of divorces, largely through no-fault divorce laws

• The broadening educational and work experience of women that has contributed to increased economic and social independence, a possible factor in marital dissolution

Other factors that affect divorce rates are ethnicity, the wife's workforce participation, husband's employment status, and residence status. A recent study conducted by Brunstein, Dangelmayer, and Schultheiss (1996) has shown that when one partner provides social support related to the personal goals of the other partner, the result is higher satisfaction with the relationship. Personal goals may include objectives both within and outside of the spouses' relationship, such as career projects or major life transitions.

Is the Increase in the Number of Working Mothers Seriously Harming the American Family?

No doubt you have recently heard at least one politician wringing his or her hands over what serious shape the American family is in. In Chapter 12, we reported on many of the changes affecting the relationship between parents and children in today's families—for example, the loss of such family functions as job training, and economic dependence. Some even worry that the family itself is on the way out. They prophesize that professionals will have ever-increasing roles in raising our children, as more and more American women seek careers.

Are other countries as concerned about this as we are? There are countries in which the family has always been of tremendous importance—Asian countries such as Japan and China, and Western countries such as Italy and Spain, for example. Is this becoming a big problem for them? What about Russia, where 50 percent of children 1 to 3 years old, and 90 percent of children 4 to 5 years old, are in day care? Do you think they have solved the problem of how to raise children when both parents work full time? What's your view?

Three marvelously well-written books that deal with this subject area are: (1) John Fowles's *The magus* (revised edition). Boston: Little, Brown. This is surely one of the best psychological mystery stories ever written. (2) Mary Gordon's *Final payments*. New York: Random House. The heroine of this marvelously revealing novel struggles with numerous obstacles, from within and without, to gain her independence as a responsible adult. (3) John Updike's *Rabbit, run*. New York: Knopf. This is the first of four books that chronicles the development of an ordinary man whose nickname is "Rabbit." We follow his efforts to leave behind his exciting life as a sports star and become a responsible family man. It is not an easy trip.

Although adults are certainly concerned about every aspect of their family lives, the crucial part of family life for most of them is how they manage their relationship with their spouse. Their major concern is: "What kind of marriage will I have, and how can I make it a happy marriage?" Simpson and associates (1996) have found that the level of attachment between spouses contributes to marital satisfaction. Couples who are most securely attached look to each other as a base of comfort and security when faced with stress or when they are upset. Those couples who are less secure or more ambivalent experience more anxiety and try to solve most problems by themselves.

Researchers have also asked the question, "When a marriage produces a sense of well-being, is that due to the state of marriage itself, or because mentally healthy people are more likely to marry than those with problems?" Horvitz and associates (1996) completed a study of 450 males and females age 12, 15 and 18 years old in a longitudinal study that took place from 1982 to 1994. They concluded that:

> . . . with controls for premarital rates of mental health, young adults who get married and stay married experience higher levels of well-being than those who remain single. In addition, although men—but not women—who become married report less depression, women—but not men—who become married report less problems with alcohol. . . . When both male-prevalent and female-prevalent outcome measures are used, both men and women benefit from marriage. (p. 895)

Although there are confounding effects of cohorts and age with length of marriage, VanLear and Zietlow (1991) found that high marriage satisfaction was associated with less deference in couples who had been married a short time and with more deference and less equality for long-term couples.

More than 40 percent of marriages are remarriages (Wilson & Clarke, 1992). And many of these remarriages involve children: One in five married couples with children had a stepchild in 1985. Stepparenting may involve considerable strain because of feeling excluded from the family or trapped in the role. High expectations, especially for a stepmother who sees herself as a nurturer and caretaker, may contrast sharply with her feelings about her stepchildren (Whisett & Land, 1992). A third of the stepfathers in one study (Marsiglio, 1992) felt that to some degree they are more like a friend than a parent to their stepchildren; 52 percent disagreed somewhat that it is harder to love a stepchild than your own child. Researchers are continuing their investigation of the special characteristics of stepfamilies.

A Sociocultural View

Ethnic Differences in Expectations about Marriage

A national survey of 2,000, unmarried, noncohabitating 19- to 35-year-olds from the National Survey of Families and Households was used to explore marital aspirations and perceived costs and benefits of marriage among African Americans, Hispanics, and whites (South, 1993). A larger percentage of Hispanic men was found to be more desiring of marriage than African American or white men, although Hispanic women are less desiring of marriage than white women. South suggests that this may be due, in part, to the importance of family to Hispanic men as an indication of personal achievement and adult responsibility. There is an emphasis on male dominance and superiority, a paternal authoritarianism that fosters dependence and submission among wives. On the other hand, Hispanic women did not differ from non-Hispanics in the anticipated impact of marriage on their economic and emotional well-being.

Both African American men and women were less desiring of marriage than their white and Hispanic counterparts. It is suggested that the limited educational and economic opportunities available to African American men may contribute to the perception of a wife and child as an economic burden. It also appeared from these findings that lower marriage rates among African Americans may be more a function of African American men's (than of African American women's) reluctance to marry. African American men anticipate less improvement from marriage in their sex lives and personal relationships.

Types of Marriage

Attitudes toward marriage, and therefore types of marriage, vary greatly throughout the world. Despite many variations in the ways humans begin their married lives, there are basically four kinds of marriage throughout the world: monogamy, polygamy, polyandry, and group marriage.

Monogamy is the standard marriage form in the United States and most other nations, in which there is one husband and one wife. In **polygamy,** there is one husband but two or more wives. In earlier times in this country, this form of marriage was practiced by the Mormons of Utah. There are still some places in the world where it exists, but the number is dwindling. **Polyandry** is a type of marriage in which there is one wife but two or more husbands. The rarest type of marriage, it is practiced only in situations where there are very few females. **Group marriage** includes two or more of both husbands and wives, who all exercise common privileges and responsibilities. In the late 1960s this form of marriage received considerable attention, but it accounts for a minuscule percentage of the world's population and has lost considerable popularity in recent years.

Homosexual marriages, although not officially sanctioned in many parts of the world, are beginning to be accepted in some religions. Such marriages, according to Wyers (1987),

can provide individuals with an intimate, mature relationship. At the same time, though, this type of relationship presents a number of unique challenges to the couple. Aside from prejudice and lack of understanding from society at large, in the United States many social service networks and agencies are unprepared to offer services to gay and lesbian men and women. (p. 148)

Guided Review

1. The sharpest increases in the average age at first marriage have occurred in the last two decades. One reason for this trend may be that higher numbers of women have entered the _____ during this time.
2. Couples married for a longer time _____ their spouses more, but couples married for a shorter time saw their partner as more equal.
3. A stepmother who sees herself as _____ may feel conflicted in her feelings about her stepchildren.
4. Four factors are attributed to a recent trend in increased divorce rates. These factors include liberalization of divorce laws, growing _____ _____ of divorce, reduction in cost of divorces, and the broadening educational and work experience of women.
5. Basically, four types of marriage exist in the world: monogamy, polygamy, _____, and group marriage.

Personal Development

In this section, we discuss the theories of Daniel Levinson and Erik Erikson. Each of these theories is somewhat dated, but each offers insights into the development of the adult personality that are still of great value. We also consider gender differences in individuation.

The Adult Life Cycle: Levinson

Yale psychologist Daniel Levinson, who died in 1994, was one of the most respected researchers in adult developmental psychology. Working with his colleagues at Yale, he derived a theory of adult development based on intensive interviews with 40 men and 40 women. Rather than depend on questionnaire data from a large number of individuals, Levinson decided that intensive interviewing and psychological testing with a small number of representative cases would more likely provide him with the information for a theory of adult development. Because of the number of hours necessary in this study (almost 20 hours were spent on interviews with each subject), Levinson decided to limit the number of cases so that he could get more detailed information.

Key to Levinson's (1978, 1986, 1990a) theory of adult development is the notion of **life course.** *Life* refers to all aspects of living—everything that has significance in a life. *Course* refers to the flow or unfolding of an individual's life. Life course, therefore, looks at the complexity of life as it evolves over time.

Equally important to Levinson's theory is the notion of **life cycle.** Building on the findings of his research, Levinson proposed that there is "an underlying order in the human life course; although each individual life is unique, everyone goes through the same basic sequence" (1986, p. 4). The life cycle is a general pattern

Answers

1. workforce (or job market) 2. respected 3. nurturing 4. social acceptance 5. polyandry

An Applied View

Responsibility for Self

One of the clearest indexes of maturity is the ability to be responsible for your own life and behavior. This exercise asks a number of questions involving responsibility for your own behavior.

1. Name two major purchases you have made in the past year by yourself without a strong influence by anyone else.

   _____

   _____

2. Wherever it is that you live, do your parents support you, or do you pay for your own housing?

   _____

3. Are you completely in charge of what time you come home at night, or do you have to answer to someone else?

   _____

4. Are you the sole person who decides what clothing you wear?

   _____

5. To what extent have your parents influenced your career, that is, whether you have chosen to go to college or work, the acceptability of your grades or pay, and so on?

   _____

6. Are you able to make independent decisions about your sex life? Do you let your parents know what you have decided?

   _____

You might compare your answers with those of some of your friends to get a relative idea of how responsible you are for your life.

of adult development, whereas the life course is the unique embodiment of the life cycle by an individual. As Nurmi (1992) noted in his study of Finnish people, the individual life course is shaped by the goals and concerns people experience at a given age. Young adults frequently mention future education and family-related goals, and have concerns related to themselves and their friends. Middle-aged people have goals related to their children's lives and property, and are concerned about their occupations. Elderly people have goals that revolve around their health, retirement, leisure activities, and the world, and experience health-related fears.

Through his studies, Levinson further defined parts of the life cycle. He defined the life cycle as a sequence of eras. Each era is **biopsychosocial** in character: It is composed of the interaction of the individual, complete with his or her own biological and psychological makeup, with the social environment. Each era is important in itself and in its contribution to the whole of the life cycle. A new era begins as the previous era approaches its end. That in-between time is characterized as a **transition.**

The intricacies of Levinson's theory of adult life course and life cycle are further elaborated by his concept of the adult **life structure.** Life structure is the underlying pattern or design of a person's life at a given time. Levinson noted that "a theory of life structure is a way of conceptualizing answers to a different question: 'What is my life like now?'" (1986, p. 6). The primary components of a life structure are the relationships that an individual has with significant others. It is through relationships that we "live out" various aspects of ourselves. Levinson regarded relationships as actively and mutually shaped. Life structure may have many components, but generally only one or two components are central in the structure at a given time. The central component(s) is the one that most strongly influences the life structure of the individual.

The evolutionary sequence of the life structure includes an alternating series of **structure-building** and **structure-changing** transitions. During the structure-building periods, individuals face the task of building a stable structure around choices they have made. They seek to enhance the life within that structure. This period of relative stability usually lasts five to seven years. During that time, the stability of the life structure affords individuals the freedom to question their choices and to consider modifying their life.

This process of reappraising the existing life structure and exploring new life structures characterizes the structure-changing period. This period usually lasts around five years. Its end is marked by the making of critical life choices around which the individual will build a new life structure. Levinson noted that the individual decides at this point, "This I will settle for" (1986, p. 7).

In considering the periods of stability and change in the adult life cycle, Levinson noted, "We remain novices in every era until we have had a chance to try out an entry life structure and then to question and modify it in the mid-era transition" (1986, p. 7). Individuals enter into new stages of adult development as they become focused on certain developmental tasks. You will understand these tasks better when we describe each stage in the following pages.

Levinson gave equal weight to periods of stability and transition. This captures the evolution of the focus of an individual and the flowing quality of adult development. Unlike most theories of child development, in which development takes the form of positive growth, Levinson's study of adult development recognized a coexistence of growth and decline.

Seasons of a Man's Life: Levinson

Levinson made two separate studies, one of men (1978) and one of women (1990b) (both to be further described in Chapter 16). In his first study, which was solely of men, 40 male subjects ranging in age from 35 to 45 were selected, representing four categories (10 each): blue-collar workers paid on an hourly basis, middle-level executives, academic biologists, and novelists.

The hourly workers and the executives were employees of an industrial firearms manufacturer or an electronics plant (about half from each). The biologists were employed at two highly rated universities located between Boston and New York. Of the writers, some were highly gifted novelists whose work had already been accepted by critics; others were less well known but were regarded as promising and worthy of serious consideration. Of course, this sample cannot be considered to represent the average male in the United States, but the diversity of the people selected in social class origins, racial, ethnic, and religious backgrounds, education, and marital status does make it typical of a great deal of American society today.

The study concentrates on the choices made by each man during his life and how he has dealt with the consequences of his choices, especially as they affect the main components of living: occupation, marriage, and family. After studying these components, Levinson suggested that there are four main seasons of life: (1) childhood and adolescence—birth to 22 years; (2) early adulthood—17 to 45 years; (3) middle adulthood—40 to 65 years; and (4) older adulthood—60 years and older.

Obviously, considerable overlap occurs between each of his stages. Between these major stages are substages that help to bring about the transitions necessary for development. Figure 14.1 gives a description of various stages and substages. Levinson himself concentrated on the early and middle adult periods, leaving further consideration of the childhood and late adult periods to others.

He believed that "even the most disparate lives are governed by the same underlying order—a sequence of eras and developmental periods" (1978, p. 64). The purpose of these developmental transitions is to cause greater individuation. **Individuation** refers to our becoming more individual; we develop a separate and special personality, derived less and less from our parents and teachers and more from our own behavior.

Although Levinson hypothesized more than 10 substages in the course of life, he chooses to concentrate on three phases in male development. These are the novice phase, the settling-down phase, and the mid-life transition (the latter two are discussed in Chapter 16).

Figure 14.1

Model of Levinson's theory. Levinson's initial phase of human development extends from ages 17 to 33 and includes the early adult transition, entering the adult world, and the age-30 transition.

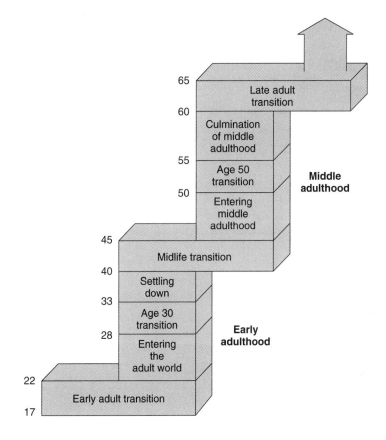

The Novice Phase

The **novice phase** of human development extends from age 17 to 33 and includes the early adult transition, entering the adult world, and the age-30 transition (see Figure 14.1). In this phase of life, four major tasks are to be accomplished. The individual in the novice phase should form

- *The dream.* "Most men construct a vision, an imagined possibility that generates vitality" (p. 91).

- *Mentor relationships.* Each man should find someone who is older, more experienced, and willing to make suggestions at each of the choice points in his early adult life.

- *An occupational decision.* A man should begin to build on his strengths and to choose a vocation that values those strengths.

- *Love relationships.* Each man should make decisions on a marriage partner, the number of children, and the type of relationship that he wants to have with wife and children.

The Mentor

In Greek mythology, Mentor was the guardian of Telemachus, the son of Odysseus. The concept of **mentoring** has received considerable attention in recent years (Bly, 1990; Field, 1994; Glasgow, 1996; Hamilton & Darling, 1996; Luna & Cullen, 1995; Nolinske, 1995, Perkins & others, 1994; Reid, 1994; Sorcinelli, 1994; Tentoni, 1995; Wunsch, 1994). Of particular interest are Robert Bly's notions on the subject (which, by the way, he calls "male mothering").

Bly suggested that two events have wreaked havoc with the modern American male's sense of himself. The first, which began in the first half of the nineteenth century, was the Industrial Revolution. As a result of this, fathers were forced to leave home, where they traditionally worked by the side of their sons, and seek

A solid relationship with an older mentor is crucial to the career success of a young adult, according to Levinson. Why is it, do you think, that older males are more likely to take a mentoring attitude toward their younger colleagues than are older females toward their younger colleagues?

A Sociocultural View

The Gender-Role Training of Western Men

Judith Jordan (cited in Bergman, 1991) stated:

I used to think that what we have here is just Western culture—competitive, individualistic, self-sufficient. But the cross-cultural data suggests that this country is off the scale—that we are so far into the individualistic, competitive ethic, and that, in fact, we continue to socialize males to be soldiers—whether on the battlefield or in industry—and you don't socialize soldiers to be empathic, listening, caring people. I think, ultimately, the individualistic ethic is starting to fail in terms of ecological and economic success in the world, and it will push the system to move into some new paradigms, and I feel some hope about that.

The well-being of young American men has been found to be influenced by closeness to child and wife, adjustment to the husband role, and the number of close friends (Julian & others, 1992). If Jordan is right that men are socialized to be soldiers and dread close relationships, this would indicate that the emotional health of American men is endangered by their gender-role training. If they are not taught to be caretakers of relational processes in the way women are, then they will have difficulty being emotionally close to their wives and children, and thus their personal well-being will suffer. What's your opinion? What new paradigms for men might Ms. Jordan be referring to?

An insightful book on this topic is Robert Bly's *Iron John.* Reading, MA: Addison-Wesley. A teacher of both poetry and philosophy, Bly combines the two in this fascinating tale of a journey into the self. Among other insights, he explores the modern young man's grief over his inability to become close to his father.

Yearn to understand first and to be understood second.

employment in factories. The second, which began in the 1960s with "no-fault" divorce, led to the proliferation of single-parent families, about 90 percent of which are headed by females.

With each of these events, much of the teaching and appreciation that boys used to get from their ever-present fathers was lost. Mothers have tried to make up for this loss, but because of deep-seated gender differences, only another male can induct a boy into adulthood successfully (see Chapter 13). Bly believed that only those young men who achieve a mentor relationship with some other older man are likely to attain a mature personality. This man may be an uncle, one of the father's friends, or some older man at work. Without such a person, the young man will not be brave enough to confront himself, and he will sink into a defensive, self-deluding lifestyle. Bly also suggested that because the typical conflicts that exist between sons and fathers are absent in the mentor relationship, the mentor actually can be more helpful to the young man.

Levinson found that after each man selects a dream, mentor relationship, occupation, and love relationship, at around age 30 (plus or minus two years) he comes to reexamine his feelings about the four major tasks. Important decisions are made at this time, such as an alteration of the dream, a change in mentor, a change in occupation, and sometimes a change in marital status. For some, this transitional period proves to be very smooth. In most cases, however, it challenges the very foundations of life itself. Although he often keeps it to himself, the typical male at this stage undergoes a seriously disturbing period of self-doubt. Fortunately, most emerge from these doubts with a clearer understanding of their strengths and weaknesses, and a clearer view of what they wish to make of themselves.

Thus, for Levinson, the transition from late adolescence to early adulthood (and also for the years to come) tends to proceed in stages as orderly as those we have seen in the earlier stages of life. More variation occurs as we grow older, because we are controlled less and less by our genetic inheritance and more and more by the environment in which we find ourselves, and by our own individual decisions. This growing independence from our genes and our early experiences is reflected clearly in these two theories. Even if we have had a hard childhood, with alcoholic parents and traumatic accidents, we should be developing the ability to be in charge of our lives. As we grow older, we have the opportunity, and indeed the responsibility, to reinvent ourselves. Of course, how we reinvent ourselves depends on our culture. Some have suggested that Levinson's theory is culturally limited to the United States. What do you think? The next personality theorist we will cover, Erikson, would certainly have agreed.

Intimacy versus Isolation: Erikson

We last talked about Erikson's theory in Chapter 11, where we discussed his fifth stage (adolescence), identity and repudiation versus identity confusion. Now we will consider his sixth stage, intimacy and solidarity versus isolation. This stage applies to what he defined as young adulthood, ages 18 to 25.

In his definition of intimacy, Erikson stated that it should include

1. Mutuality of orgasm
2. with a loved partner
3. of the other sex
4. with whom one is able and willing to share a mutual trust
5. and with whom one is able and willing to regulate the cycles of
   a. work
   b. procreation
   c. recreation
6. so as to secure to the offspring, too, all the stages of a satisfactory development (1963, p. 266).

Erikson pointed out, however, that sexual intercourse should not be assumed to be the most important aspect of intimacy between individuals. He was speaking here of far more than sexual intimacy. He was talking about the ability to relate one's deepest hopes and fears to another person and to accept another's need for intimacy in turn.

Those who have achieved the stage of **intimacy** are able to commit themselves to concrete affiliations and partnerships with others and have developed the "ethical strength to abide by such commitments, even though they may call for significant sacrifices and compromises" (1963, p. 262). This leads to **solidarity** between partners.

Erikson was fond of quoting Freud's response when asked what he thought a normal person should be able to do well: "Lieben und arbeiten"—"to love and to work." To Freud, then, sharing responsibility for mutual achievements and the loving feelings that result from them are the essence of adulthood. Erikson fully agreed with this. Thus when Freud uses the term *genitality* to describe this same period, he does not merely mean sexual intercourse; he is referring rather to the ability to share one's deeply held values, needs, and secrets with another through the generosity that is so important in intimacy.

It must be admitted, nevertheless, that Freud was far more concerned with the physical aspects of sex than Erikson, who deserves major credit for moving the school of psychoanalysis away from its fascination with genitalia and toward a greater concern for adult intimacy in general.

The counterpart of intimacy is **distantiation**. This is the readiness all of us have to distance ourselves from others when we feel threatened by their behavior. Distantiation is the cause of most prejudices and discrimination. Propaganda efforts mounted by countries at war are examples of attempts to increase distantiation. It is what leads to **isolation.**

Most young adults vacillate between their desires for intimacy and their need for distantiation. They need social distance because they are not sure of their identities. They are always vulnerable to criticism, and because they can't be sure whether the criticisms are true or not, they protect themselves by a "lone wolf" stance.

The 1960s were a time when many grassroots action groups, such as Students for a Democratic Society, came into being. They were anxious to promote "justice, peace, equality, and personal freedom."

Although intimacy may be difficult for some males today, Erikson believed that it used to be even more difficult for females. "All this is a little more complicated with women, because women, at least in yesterday's cultures, had to keep their identities incomplete until they knew their man" (1978, p. 49). Now that less emphasis occurs in the female gender role on getting married and pleasing one's husband, and more emphasis is on being true to one's own identity, Erikson believed that both sexes have a better chance of achieving real intimacy.

A growing number of theorists, however, many of them feminist psychologists, argue that females still have a harder time "reinventing" themselves, because of the way our society educates them. In the next section, we present their position.

Guided Review

6. Daniel Levinson's theory looks at adult development by examining life _____ (the unique development of the individual) and the life _____ (the general pattern of adult development).
7. Life structure is the underlying pattern or design of a person's life at a given time. It is _____ in character, with a primary component being the _____ that an individual has with significant others.
8. Erik Erikson's sixth stage of psychosocial development, intimacy versus isolation, focuses on building a _____ as opposed to Levinson's more career-oriented approach.

Sexual Identity and Gender Roles

The problem lay buried, unspoken, for many years in the minds of American women. It was a strange stirring, a sense of dissatisfaction, a yearning that women suffered in the middle of the twentieth century in

Answers

6. course, cycle 7. biopsychosocial, relationships 8. relationship

the United States. Each suburban wife struggled with it alone, as she made the beds, shopped for groceries, matched slipcover material, ate peanut butter sandwiches with her children, chauffeured Cub Scouts and Brownies, lay beside her husband at night—she was afraid to ask even of herself the silent question—"Is this all?" (Betty Friedan, 1963, p.1)

This paragraph, which opened Betty Friedan's famous book, *The Feminine Mystique* (1963), marked the beginning of a major reexamination of the female gender role. Today we are still undergoing a searching societal inquiry into the appropriate gender roles of both sexes. But are we any nearer to the answers we seek?

Consider this statement that the famed Greek philosopher Aristotle made more than 2,000 years ago: "Woman may be said to be an inferior man." Most of us would disagree with his viewpoint publicly. On the other hand, its underlying attitude is still widespread. People today are far less willing to admit to a belief in female inferiority, but many still act as though it were so. However, the influence of the women's movement, as well as of science and other forms of social change, is profoundly affecting the way we view sexual identity and gender role.

First, we should make a distinction between the two. Sexual identity results from those physical characteristics that are part of our biological inheritance. They are the genetic traits that make us males or females. Genitals and facial hair are examples of sex-linked physical characteristics. Gender role, on the other hand, results largely from the specific traits in fashion at any one time and in any one culture. For example, women appear to be able to express their emotions through crying more easily than men, although no known physical cause accounts for this difference. The results of recent studies have shown that people have different ideas about how their sexual identities formed (Eliason, 1995). Although some subjects claimed not to have thought about the formation of their sexual identities, others stated that society was responsible for their heterosexuality or that gender determined their sexual identities. Other themes were issues of choice versus innate feelings toward sexuality, having no alternative to heterosexuality, and the influence of religion in determining sexual identity.

People may accept or reject their sexual identity, their gender role, or both. For example, Jan Morris (1974), a British author, spent most of her life as the successful author James Morris. Although born a male, she deeply resented the fact that she had a male sexual identity and hated having to perform the male gender role. She always felt that inside she was really a woman. The cause of these feelings may have been psychological—something that happened in her childhood, perhaps. Or the cause may have been genetic—possibly something to do with hormone balance. Such rejection is rare, and no one knows for sure why it happens. Morris decided to have a transsexual operation that changed her from male to female. The

The beginning of the "feminist revolution" in the 1960s opened an era of changing views toward gender roles. Do you believe that society's views of gender roles are significantly different today from what they were ten years ago?

Some people are so unhappy with their sexual identity that they have it changed surgically. Renee Richards (a) before the surgery, and (b) the female tennis star, used to be a man by the name of Richard Raskind.

(a)   (b)

change caused many problems in her life, but she says she is infinitely happier to have her body match her feelings about her gender role.

Aspects of Gender Role

Some people are perfectly happy with their sexual identity but don't like their gender role. Gender role itself has three aspects:

- **Gender-role orientation.** Individuals differ in how confident they feel about their sex identity. Males often have a weaker gender-role orientation than females. (This will be discussed later in the chapter.)

- **Gender-role preference.** Some individuals feel unhappy about their gender role, as did Jan Morris, and wish either society or their sex could be changed, so that their gender role would be different. The feminist movement of the last few decades has had a major impact on many of the world's societies in this regard.

- **Gender-role adaptation.** Adaptation is defined by whether other people judge individual behavior as masculine or feminine. If a person is seen as acting "appropriately" according to her or his gender, then adaptation has occurred. People who dislike their gender role or doubt that they fit it well (e.g., the teenage boy who fights a lot because he secretly doubts he is masculine enough) may be said to be poorly adapted.

The traditional view holds that sexual identity is the result of interaction between sex chromosome differences at conception and early treatment by the people in the child's environment (Miller & Dyk, 1993). Once culture has had the opportunity to influence the child's sexual identity, it is unlikely to change, even when biological changes occur. Even in such extreme cases of **chromosome failure** as gynecomastia (breast growth in the male) and hirsutism (abnormal female body hair), sexual identity is not affected. In almost all cases, adolescents desperately want medical treatment so they can keep their sexual identities.

Although sexual identity becomes fixed rather early in life, gender roles usually undergo changes as the individual matures. The relationships between the roles of the two sexes also change and have altered considerably in the past few decades.

An excellent reference book on this topic is Judy Blume's *Letters to Judy: What your kids wish they could tell you* (1987). New York: G.P. Putnam's Sons. Blume offers letters from young adults who confide their concerns over the stresses of friendships, families, abuse, illness, suicide, drugs, sexuality, and other problems. In return, the author shares similar moments from her own life, both as a child and as a parent. She does not hesitate to reveal her own embarrassing situations to help us feel less alone. A special "Resources" section lists books for additional reading and addresses of special-interest organizations.

The Young Adolescent's Rigid View of Gender

The term *gender* is used all the time. But what does it mean? Gender refers to our conceptions of what it means to be male or to be female. Ronald Slaby (1990) explored gender as a social category system. By that he meant a mental filing system; that is, we use the categories of male and female to organize the information we receive. Slaby argued that gender categories are loaded with meaning. For example, when we hear of a person named Mary, before even meeting her, we hold certain preconceptions of what she will be like. She will (probably) always be female (and there are few traits that remain so stable). If you're female, then a person named Mary shares with you the things you think that all females experience. If you're male, then there are things that you think only males experience that you feel certain a person named Mary does not experience. In this manner, gender acts as a powerful organizing system. As Sandra Bem (1975) described it, once we have our sexual identity, we begin to view the world through gender "filters." All new stimuli are processed through these filters according to gender roles.

Most adolescents wrestle with what it means for them to be male or female. In doing so, they develop their gen-

der categories. Studies of adolescents' ideal men and women reflect very stereotyped notions of the sexes. According to Slaby, this is due to the inflexibility of their developing gender categories. When children and adolescents are just forming their concepts of gender, they are more likely to use **gender-role stereotypes** of male and female in a rigid manner. That clarity helps adolescents solidify their understanding of gender. When they become confident and comfortable in their ability to figure out maleness or femaleness, then they become able to use the gender categories more accurately. Then they are able to understand that even though Mary might fit their category of female in most ways, in some ways she may not.

Another problem is that adolescents often use gender stereotypes that are inaccurate or exaggerated. In a study by Allen (1995), young men and women were asked to rate how well they and others fit certain gender stereotypes. The findings showed that the way the people in the study viewed themselves was much less stereotypical than the way they viewed others. Hence, an important goal of adolescent education is to help them not to overestimate or underestimate differences between genders.

Erik Erikson's Studies

Erik Erikson's ideas (see Chapters 2 and 11) about the biological determinants of male and female gender roles came from his studies of early adolescents (1963). He tossed wooden blocks of various shapes and sizes on a table and asked each child to make something with them. Girls, he found, tend to make low structures like the rooms of a house. Having finished these structures, the girls then use other blocks as furniture, which they move around in the spaces of the rooms. Boys, on the other hand, tend to build towers, which, after completion, they usually destroy.

Erikson likened the roomlike structures of the girls to their possession of a womb, and the towerlike structures of the boys to their possession of a penis. He felt that these differences account for greater aggressive behavior in males. Penis and tower alike are seen as thrusting symbols of power. He attributed these behaviors to inherited tendencies of the two sexes. As you would expect, many researchers and most feminists disagree with his interpretation, arguing that his findings are more likely the result of learning that occurred in the childhoods of his subjects.

For more on this subject, read *Adulthood* (1978). New York: Norton. Edited by Erikson, this collection of essays explains what it means to become an adult and is written by experts from a wide variety of fields.

Androgyny

One gender-role researcher, Sandra Bem (1975), argued that typical American roles are actually unhealthy. She said that highly masculine males tend to have better psychological adjustment than other males during adolescence, but as adults they tend to become highly anxious and neurotic and often experience low self-acceptance. Highly feminine females suffer in similar ways.

Bem believed we would all be much better off if we were to become more

Figure 14.2

Relationships among the three gender roles

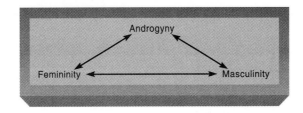

Our gender-role stereotypes define what actions are and are not appropriate for each sex. What would most people say if they saw this young woman chopping wood? What would people have said a hundred years ago?

androgynous. The word is made up of the Greek words for male, *andro,* and for female, *gyne.* It refers to those persons who are more likely to behave in a way appropriate to a situation, regardless of their sex.

For example, when someone forces his way into a line at the movies, the traditional female role calls for a woman to look disapproving but to say nothing. The androgynous female would tell the offender in no uncertain terms to go to the end of the line. When a baby left unattended starts to cry, the traditional male response is to try to find some woman to take care of its needs. The androgynous male would pick up the infant and attempt to comfort it.

Androgyny is not merely the midpoint between two poles of masculinity and femininity. Rather, it is a more functional level of gender-role identification than either of the more traditional roles. Figure 14.2 illustrates this relationship. Not surprisingly, Bursik (1995) found that people with higher levels of ego development are more likely to be androgynous.

Another criticism has been leveled by Harris (1994), who examined an instrument developed by Bem, the Bem Sex Role Inventory (BSRI), which is used to evaluate one's definitions of masculinity and femininity. He conducted an interesting study to determine if the BSRI is valid for people with different cultural backgrounds. Results showed that the BSRI was valid in terms of general American cultural definitions, but that it was less reliable among Hispanic American and African American subjects. Harris suggested that researchers develop culture-specific sex role inventories to take into account the various backgrounds of cultural groups in America.

Before we look at the relationship between gender roles and sexuality, we need to examine one other factor. This is the difference between female and male identity.

Male versus Female Identity

Identity precedes intimacy for men. . . . For women, intimacy goes with identity, as the female comes to know herself as she is known, through her relationships with others. (Gilligan, 1982, p.12)

The androgynous man is not afraid to be seen being kind to an infant.

Sigmund Freud would have concurred with this statement by Gilligan, but for reasons with which many modern women would disagree. According to feminist Betty Friedan, Freud believed "that women need to accept their own nature, and find fulfillment the only way they can, through 'sexual passivity, male domination, and nurturing maternal love'" (Friedan, 1963, p. 43).

The view of the feminists is that because females are trained to believe in the necessity of their maintaining relationships within the family, and because this role often involves self-sacrifice, women find it harder to individuate—that is, to develop a healthy adult personality of their own. They argue that for the young adult male, identity formation "involves separating himself from dependency on his family and taking his place in the adult world as an autonomous, independent being, competent, with a clear sense of career and confidence in his ability to succeed" (Wolfson, 1989, p. 11).

For the young adult female, career and self-assurance are not so emphasized. Winning the attention and then the commitment of a man are more important as-

For most young adults, society's gender roles determine their careers and the type of relationships they have.

pects of her identity, and intimacy is the major goal. This is seen as unhealthy. As Wolfson (1989) put it, "It is difficult to have a sense of yourself that is internally consistent and congruent if your identity is dependent on the identity of someone else. 'I am who you are' is very different from 'I am who I am'" (p. 12).

This new point of view arose in the 1960s, primarily with the publication of Betty Friedan's book, *The Feminine Mystique* (1963). The affluent 1950s had "created a generation of teenagers who could forgo work to stay in school. Inhabiting a gilded limbo between childhood and adult responsibility, these kids had money, leisure, and unprecedented opportunity to test taboos" (Matusow, 1984, p. 306). At this time many youths, particularly those of the newly affluent middle class, "wanted to live out the commitments to justice, peace, equality and personal freedom which their parents professed" (Gitlin, 1987, p. 12) but, the young people felt, failed to live up to. Groups such as the Students for a Democratic Society sprang up. Programs such as Rennie Davis's Economic Research and Action Project, whose goal was to "change life for the grassroots poor," developed (Matusow, 1984, p. 315). This movement worked for justice and equality not only for the poor and racial minorities but also for women.

The movement fostered a new commitment to women's issues and to studies of women themselves. For example, as a result of her research on the female perspective (see Chapter 9), Harvard psychologist Carol Gilligan (1982, 1990) has come to believe that

> for girls and women, issues of femininity or feminine identity do not depend on the achievement of separation from the mother or on the progress of individuation. Since masculinity is defined through separation while femininity is defined through attachment, male gender identity is threatened by intimacy while female gender is threatened by separation. (1982, p. 9)

Research has also pointed to two other concerns about women's identity formation. One has been the tendency of society to "objectify" women, which means seeing them as a particular type of creature or object rather than as individuals. Psychoanalyst Erich Fromm (1955) suggested that "To be considered an object can lead to a deep inner sense that there must be something wrong and bad about oneself" (p. 323).

The second concern involves the ability to admit vulnerability. "Men are taught to avoid, at all costs, showing any signs of vulnerability, weakness, or helplessness, while women are taught to cultivate these qualities" (Wolfson, 1989, p. 44). Obviously more work is needed to resolve this question of the role of gender in the development of the adult personality. Erikson (1963) himself appears to have endorsed this point of view, by stating that

> there will be many difficulties in a new joint adjustment of the sexes to changing conditions, but they do not justify prejudices which keep half of mankind from participating in planning and decision-making, especially at a time when the other half [men], by its competitive escalation and acceleration of technological progress, has brought us and our children to the gigantic brink on which we live, with all our affluence. (p. 293)

As to the development of male identity, Bergman (1991) has argued that the new feminine concepts have more to offer than the older theories, which hold that:

> Identity comes *before* intimacy. Men are taught to fight for power-over and for possession of women, and then, *despite* that as a context, to relate to them. Given the power of transference, Freud implies that true, intimate relationship is difficult, if not impossible; we are always shouting across

an unbridgeable gap . . . Erikson and the neo-Freudians are on the same train. . . .

> While it is easy for men to envision self, and even self and other, it seems less easy to envision the *relationship* between self and other, with a life of its own, in movement, as a process, arising from and reflecting all participants, its realness defined by the qualities inherent in mutual empathic connection. (Italics are Bergman's emphasis.). (pp. 2–3)

This last sentence of Bergman's is a mouthful, but think about it and you will come to understand this new view of identity—a concept of identity that holds that men and women are really more like each other, especially in our need to interrelate, than we have realized. It may be that males and females have seemed so different only because we have been taught to think so—the self-fulfilling prophecy.

In each of the theories described in this section on personality, the role of psychological and social forces is evident. Do you believe that biology also plays a part? For example, might hormones make a difference? Remember, virtually all human traits are the result of biopsychosocial causes. Although we could not find recent research on any biological aspect of personality development, based on trends in other areas of research on adult development, we would not be surprised to discover reports of such investigations soon.

Guided Review

9. With regard to gender roles, many people are not willing to admit a belief in female _____ but act as if it were so.
10. Sexual identity refers to our physical characteristics, whereas gender roles refer largely to the specific social _____ in fashion at a given time in a culture.
11. The three parts of gender identity are: gender-role _____, gender-role preference, and gender-role adaptation.
12. Erik Erikson believes that gender differences are _____ determined, based on his experiments with girls and boys as they played with building blocks.
13. According to Bem, _____ is characterized by more functional levels of role identification than by either male or female roles.

Sexuality

Sexuality plays a significant role in most of our lives. Most people who disregard or repress their sexuality suffer for it. Of course, the sex drive, unlike other instinctual drives such as hunger and thirst, can be thwarted without causing death. Some people are able to practice complete chastity without apparent harm to their personalities. The great majority of us, however, become highly irritable when our sexual needs are not met in some way. There is also reason to believe that our personalities do not develop in healthy directions if we are unable to meet sexual needs in adulthood. Why is sexuality so important to us? Although the answer may seem obvious, in fact a number of sexual motivations exist.

For Freud, human sexuality is the underlying basis for all behavior (see Chapter 2). He held that *genitality* (the ability to have a successful adult sex life) is the highest stage of development. He believed that those people who do not have adequate adult sex lives fail to do so because they have become fixated at some earlier and less mature level. Today psychologists view sexuality rather differently.

Answers

9. inferiority 10. characteristics 11. orientation 12. biologically 13. androgyny

Psychologist John Gagnon argues that humans learn to behave sexually according to scripts established by the culture in which they live. For most people, this learning takes place during adolescence and young adulthood.

Sexual Scripts: Gagnon and Simon

Psychologists John Gagnon and William Simon (1987) viewed sexual behavior as "scripted" behavior. They believed that children begin to learn scripts for sexual attitudes and behavior from the other people in their society. They view sexuality, therefore, as a cultural phenomenon rather than a spontaneously emerging behavior. They believed that

in any given society, [children] acquire and assemble meanings, skills, and values from the people around them. Their critical choices are often made by going along and drifting. (1987, p. 2)

Learning sexual scripts occurs in a rather haphazard fashion throughout childhood, but this changes abruptly as children enter adolescence. Here much more specific scripts are learned: in classrooms, from parents, from the media, and most specifically, from slightly older adolescents. This process continues throughout early adulthood, through a process of listening to and imitating older adults whom the individual admires. For these researchers, then, the roles sexuality plays in a society come about largely through transmission of the culture by idealized adults.

The Sociobiological View: Wilson

Whatever we see as our reasons for seeking sex, this complicated behavior has obviously evolved through a number of complex stages over which we have had no control. What genetic purposes has the evolution served? In a renowned publication, Harvard sociobiologist E. O. Wilson (1978) had a number of unorthodox suggestions:

• Sex is not designed for reproduction. Sociobiologists argue that the primary motivation of all human behavior is the reproduction of the genes of each person. Wilson, however, believed that if reproduction were the primary goal of the human species, many other techniques would have been far more effective:

Bacteria simply divide in two (in many species, every twenty minutes), fungi shed immense numbers of spores, and hybrids bud offspring directly from their trunks. Each fragment of a shattered sponge grows into an entire new organism. If multiplication were the only purpose of reproductive behavior, our mammalian ancestors could have evolved without sex. Every human being might be asexual and sprout new offspring from the surface cells of a neutered womb. (p. 121)

• Sex is not designed for giving and receiving pleasure. Wilson pointed out that many animal species perform intercourse quite mechanically with virtually no foreplay. Furthermore, lower forms achieve sex without benefit even of a nervous system. Thus, he suggests that pleasure is only one of the means of getting complex creatures to "make the heavy investment of time and energy required for courtship, sexual intercourse and parenting" (p. 122).

• Sex is not designed for efficiency. The very complexity of human genital systems makes them subject to a variety of disorders and diseases, such as ectopic pregnancy and venereal disease. The genetic balance brought about by sex is easily disturbed, and if the human being has one sex chromosome too many or too few, abnormalities in behavior and in physiology often result.

• Sex is not designed to benefit the individual's drives. If an individual's drive is to reproduce himself or herself, sex is actually an impairment. When sexual reproduction is employed, the organism must accept partnership with an individual whose genes are different. Only with asexual reproduction is multiplication of self totally possible.

What's Your VIEW?

Is Sexuality Mainly the Result of Genetic Influences?

As you might imagine, the whole theory of sociobiology (which is also covered in other sections of this book) is not without its critics. Obviously, genes do affect our behavior, but not nearly as much as they do in the other species of the animal kingdom. Many experts say that sociobiology has made a valuable contribution to the theory of human sexuality but that it overemphasizes the role of genes.

We find that many of our students reject sociobiology completely. "Wilson treats people as though we are no better than animals," they say. It might prove interesting to interview some of your friends about this idea. Also, what position do faculty members and students in the biology department of a local college or university take on this controversy? What do you think?

- Sex does create diversity. Wilson concluded that the only possible reason that evolution brought about the human sexual system is to create a greater diversity of individuals. The purpose of this diversity is to increase the chances of the survival of the species. As conditions have changed throughout history (e.g., during an ice age), some individuals have had a greater chance to survive than others. If only one type of human being with only one set of genes had existed, and that inheritance had not been suited to the changing environment, the species would have become extinct.

Wilson pointed out that when two different individuals mate, there is the possibility of offspring like individual A, offspring like individual B, and offspring with the characteristics of both. As these individuals mate with others, the possible variations increase exponentially. Diversity, brought about through sex, leads to adaptability of the species, and therefore its greater survival rate.

Why are there not hundreds of sexes instead of just two? Wilson argued that two sexes are enough to create tremendous diversity while keeping the system as simple as possible. Diversity may not only be responsible for variation in the offspring but may contribute to the wide range of values people place on sexuality.

Weinrich (1987) extended the sociobiological theory to explained homosexuality. He suggested that homosexual behavior is the result of a "reproductively altruistic trait." That is, homosexuals give up their right to reproduce their genes. The theory, Weinrich qualified, is applicable only in societies like ours that do not strictly require marriage and reproductivity.

Practices of Young Adults

Premarital Attitudes and Behavior

A number of findings of the Janus Report (Janus & Janus, 1993) are relevant to the premarital behavior and attitudes of young adults. Here are some of the most important findings:

- More than 80 percent of respondents were seriously concerned about sexually transmitted diseases, but most respondents reported increased rather than decreased sex activity in the past three years.

- Although many singles are exercising more caution, more men than women reported they had become more cautious about sex in the past three years.

- Nineteen percent of the single men and 23 percent of the single women surveyed reported using no contraception.

- The majority of singles do not find their lifestyle gratifying, but only one in three would prefer being married.

- Thirty-eight percent of single men and 45 percent of single women would like to become parents even if they do not marry.

- Middle-income women had had less premarital sexual experience than either low- or high-income women.

- For both men and women, premarital sex experience has increased: from 48 percent to 55 percent for men, and from 37 percent to 47 percent for women.

- Abortion has become more acceptable in the intervening years between phase 1 (1985) and phase 2 (1992)—from 36 percent to 30 percent agreement that abortion is murder, and from 29 percent to 53 percent disagreement.

Although these findings are probably reliable, some criticisms of their collection of data on actual practices have been made (Laumann & others, 1994). These researchers have published what they argue are more reliable findings, because of the data techniques they have used. Their result as to sexual practices in general and oral sexual practices in general may be found in Table 14.3. The findings that pertain to middle-aged adults will be discussed in Chapter 16. Perhaps the most surprising data in this table is the mean frequency of sex per month. For young adults, sexual acts (intercourse plus oral and anal intercourse) ranges from 7.2 to 6.7 for ages 18 to 34. There appears to be a general consensus that having sex slightly less than twice a week is the norm. There is very little difference between males and females on these ranges. Of course, it must be noted that because we do not have standard deviation data for these means, we do not know if there is a lot of variation around them. Men are somewhat more active in terms of oral sex (or say they are—perhaps the women were a little more reluctant to state their activity in this realm). Cohabiting singles do have a higher average frequency than those who are not cohabiting. Can you think of an explanation of this? What other conclusions can you draw from this table?

We have considerable evidence that sexual experience has increased among college students. Roche and Ramsbey (1993) examined college students' attitudes toward premarital sex. They found that there has been a change in students' behavior in the direction of conservatism since hearing about AIDS. For example, there is an increase in the use of birth and disease prevention materials (HHS, News, 1997).

Many studies of the premarital experiences of college students have been conducted, but few studies of persons who have not gone to college have been undertaken. We know from the classic studies that the noncollege educated are almost always more conservative (i.e., less experienced) than those who go to college (Kinsey & others, 1948, 1953; Masters & Johnson, 1966, 1970) but that they are subject to the same kinds of societal influence. Therefore we can expect that although noncollege populations have a lower experience rate, theirs, too, is considerably higher than it used to be. One factor related to dating and mating among college students is prestige (Whitbeck & Hoyt, 1991). Amount of money spent on dates, frequency of dating, alcohol use when dating, and sexual permissiveness are all factors that influence students' sexual experiences.

A study of university students by Wilson and Medora (1990) sought to examine attitudes of males and females towards premarital sex and other sexual behaviors. Differences were found between males' and females' attitudes toward premarital sex when the couple is casually acquainted, and toward extramarital sex, oral sex, and anal sex. Males were significantly more approving of premarital sex than were females. However, no significant differences were found among males and females with regard to masturbation, homosexuality, sexual fantasizing, and premarital sex when the couple is in love or when the couple is engaged.

TABLE 14.3 SELECTED SEXUAL PRACTICES

	Mean Frequency of Sexual Intercourse per Month		Sexual Practices							
			Occurrence of Active Oral Sex (%)				Occurrence of Receptive Oral Sex (%)			
			Men		Women		Men		Women	
Master Status Variable	Men	Women	Life	Last Event	Life	Last Event	Life	Last Event	Life	Last Event
Total population	6.5	6.3	76.6	26.8	67.7	18.8	78.7	27.5	73.1	19.9
Age:										
18–24	7.2	7.4	72.4	27.7	69.1	19.1	74.2	28.9	74.7	24.2
25–29	7.6	7.5	84.8	32.0	76.2	23.8	84.8	33.7	79.8	24.3
30–34	6.7	6.8	78.9	29.6	76.6	19.1	78.9	32.2	83.1	22.3
35–39	6.6	6.1	82.3	30.4	71.3	21.0	87.5	29.8	73.7	23.3
40–44	5.9	5.5	84.0	31.2	72.7	16.9	85.7	28.9	76.8	12.6
45–49	6.2	5.5	73.4	21.2	65.2	21.6	77.4	22.1	72.7	18.3
50–54	5.5	4.6	60.0	16.1	48.5	11.7	66.0	13.8	59.4	12.6
55–59	4.4	3.5	58.4	9.9	38.9	5.5	58.0	14.1	44.3	6.9
Marital status:										
Nev. marr., not coh.	5.6	5.3	66.7	28.9	59.4	21.0	70.3	32.8	67.7	26.8
Nev. marr., coh.	8.6	8.8	85.7	30.2	72.2	21.5	89.3	34.0	76.4	22.7
Married	6.9	6.5	79.9	25.2	70.7	16.9	80.4	23.0	73.9	16.9
Div./sep./wid., not coh.	5.4	5.1	81.5	30.1	64.1	25.4	88.1	34.5	73.1	24.2
Div./sep./wid., coh.	8.0	7.6	80.0	29.7	79.6	16.3	80.0	37.8	85.2	20.4
Education:										
Less than HS	6.5	6.3	59.2	16.4	41.1	10.1	60.7	16.4	49.6	13.2
HS grad. or eq.	6.9	6.3	75.3	30.1	59.6	16.4	76.6	25.3	67.1	18.5
Some coll./voc.	6.6	6.3	80.0	31.3	78.2	20.7	84.0	31.0	81.6	22.2
Finished coll.	6.0	6.4	83.7	23.7	78.9	22.9	84.6	31.1	83.1	20.7
Master's/adv.deg.	6.1	5.1	80.5	20.6	79.0	28.8	81.4	30.4	81.9	27.0
Religion:										
None	6.7	6.3	78.9	33.8	77.9	29.2	83.2	35.2	83.3	30.6
Type I Prot.	6.2	5.8	81.9	26.9	74.5	19.6	82.8	23.5	77.4	18.7
Type II Prot.	6.8	6.7	67.1	22.4	55.6	12.9	70.2	24.3	64.8	16.1
Catholic	6.6	6.2	82.4	27.2	73.6	21.5	82.1	29.2	76.6	21.8
Jewish	NA	NA	NA	NA	NA	NA	NA	NA	NA	NA
Other	5.6	NA	65.8	NA	65.7	NA	73.7	NA	65.7	NA
Race/ethnicity:										
White	6.6	6.3	81.4	28.3	75.3	21.0	81.4	28.7	78.9	21.2
Black	6.4	6.2	50.5	16.9	34.4	9.3	66.3	18.2	48.9	13.1
Hispanic	7.7	7.8	70.7	23.5	59.7	18.7	73.2	25.5	63.7	22.0
Asian	5.9	NA	63.6	NA	NA	NA	72.7	NA	NA	NA
Total N	1,200	1,437	1,321	1,109	1,661	1,380	1,038	1,109	1,660	1,384

Source: Laumann and associates, 1994.

Pregnant, Poor, and Alone in the Inner City

Hera is a 22-year-old African American woman who lives in Los Angeles. She describes a situation that is tragically not so unusual for poor women who live in large urban areas (Otteson, 1993).

I went to visit my boyfriend to tell him I was pregnant. When I arrived he was painting his room, so I decided to put it off until later that evening. When I got home, I felt empty, my heart began to beat very fast and my mind traveled beyond unhappiness for some reason. So I decided to call my boyfriend for comfort. I recognized his voice on the answering machine but I just hung up the phone. Then I went to his home where I found the lights on but no one was there. I sat in my car waiting for his return. A half hour went by and he didn't come. So I went home.

The next day I received a phone call. It was his sister and she said, "Bernard was killed the same day you came to visit him. Two gang members tried to take his car at the hamburger stand and they shot him in the back." I did not believe it to be true. I hung up the phone, reached for his picture, held it tight to my heart and began to cry. I thought someone would call and say it was a joke. I waited an hour and no one called so I called his mother to ask her if it was true and she said it was.

In four years of being with Bernard, every quiet moment we shared together he always asked, "When can we have a baby?" Now I was angry and hurt. How could they kill an innocent person over a car? And not only did they take one life but they scarred our lives forever. My child would never have the opportunity to know its father. But I knew I had to stay strong for my baby's sake. I knew that in spirit he would always be with us. The gang members were arrested and thrown into

jail. I thought of going to see them. I wanted to let them know the pain they had caused by taking that one life.

I did go to the trial of one of the gang members, to support Bernard's mother. I stared at this man who killed my baby's father. The anger was there but my thoughts were only, why? I listened closely as they repeatedly told the story. The gang member always looked around to see who was in the room. No one came to support him except his younger sister who testified of his abusive childhood. I felt sorry for her because she really loved her brother, but he let her down when he chose gangs over her. The lawyer gave her no sympathy and tortured her with questions. When she cried, the gang member showed some feelings for her and I realized this guy still had some deep feelings inside of him. This changed my heart from anger to crying out for God to help him.

After all the arguments, the jury decided he was guilty of murder. His sentence was the gas chamber. The gang member was shocked and his lawyer comforted him. As he looked over his shoulder, I looked him in the eyes.

The gang member's face is in my mind everyday. The incident travels with me daily, especially when my daughter asks, "Mommy, where is my daddy?" As I try to find the right words to tell her, my mind relives it all. My daughter is only three years old and will still ask questions until she's grown to understand what really happened.

I've been given strength through this tragedy. Learning about God has given me a more positive outlook on the situation. I have forgiven the gang member and I hope he can realize that now God is the one from whom he should ask forgiveness.

Pack Dating

A growing trend in dating, known as "pack dating," has been occurring at colleges across the country (Gabriel, 1997). Instead of pairing off, undergraduates go out to dinner, movies, and parties in groups. Although these packs may bolster students' confidence and sense of identity, it may keep them from forming deeper, more committed relationships. One possible reason for this behavior is that students of families in which parents have divorced may fear that there is no such thing as a successful romantic relationship. Pack dating resolves this dilemma by allowing one to have sexual relations while avoiding intimacy and deep involvement.

Some experts suggest that pack dating may be an attempt, in part, to deal with the risk of disease. Although HIV infection rates appear to be relatively low on campuses, rates of other STIs, such as venereal warts and chlamydia, are soaring. Because HIV can remain dormant for up to 15 years before becoming AIDS, we really don't know its incidence. Choosing a sex partner from a small circle of friends allows a person to know the histories and habits of the potential partners, which could possibly reduce risk of contracting an STI.

Another explanation for pack dating is that students simply don't have time for relationships. Many students hold at least one job while carrying a full course load, and others are focused on earning grades that will help get them into graduate school.

Marital Intercourse

Intercourse between a husband and wife is the only type of sexual activity totally approved by American society. Much is expected of it, and when it is unsatisfactory, it usually generates other problems in the marriage (McCary, 1978). Sexual closeness also tends to lessen significantly with the birth of each child, except in cases where the couple has taken specific steps to maintain the quality of their sexual relationship. Two studies (Whitehead & Mathews, 1986) learned that when young couples who are having sexual difficulties regularly attend therapy sessions, they are usually able to resolve their problems. Interestingly, those couples who received placebos (sugar pills) or small doses of testosterone did better than those who did not. This indicates how important the mind is in the area of sexuality.

A number of findings of the Janus Report (Janus & Janus, 1993) are relevant to the marital behavior and attitudes of young adults. Among the most important findings are:

- Women who lived with their spouses before marriage are more likely to be divorced than women who didn't; men, less likely. Couples still married had lived together, on the average, for a shorter period of time before marriage than those who are now divorced.

- Among the divorced, men cite sexual problems as the primary reason for the divorce three times more frequently than women. Women cite extramarital affairs twice as frequently as men. But both cite emotional problems as the most frequent cause of divorce.

- Among the divorced respondents, 39 percent of the men and 27 percent of the women reported using no contraception.

In the next section we turn to an examination of the deepest aspect of human relationship, love.

Guided Review

14. According to Freud, sexuality was the underlying basis for all behavior. He taught that if people did not have a healthy adult sex life, it was because they had _____ at an earlier stage.

15. Gagnon and Simon see sexual behavior as "scripted." Children learn sexual _____ and _____ much as they would learn a script for a play.

16. Gagnon and Simon argue that the roles sexuality plays in a society come about largely through transmission of the _____ by idealized adults.

17. Wilson suggests an unorthodox rationale for seeking sex. He claims that _____ leads to adaptability of the species and, therefore, its greater survival rate.

18. Research on marital intercourse indicates that sexual closeness between many couples tends to _____ significantly with the birth of each child.

Answers

14. fixated 15. attitudes, behaviors 16. culture 17. diversity 18. lessen

The Nature of Love

The words written about love over the course of human history are uncountable. In this book, we will limit ourselves to describing the developmental aspects of this emotion: the seven forms of love that psychologist Robert Sternberg has suggested, and psychoanalyst Erich Fromm's definition of the essence of love.

The Seven Forms of Love: Sternberg

Sternberg (Beall & Sternberg, 1995; Sternberg, 1986, 1993, 1995) argued that love is made up of three different components:

- **Passion.** A strong desire for another person, and the expectation that sex with them will prove physiologically rewarding.

- **Intimacy.** The ability to share one's deepest and most secret feelings and thoughts with another.

- **Commitment.** The strongly held conviction that one will stay with another, regardless of the cost.

Each of these components may or may not be involved in a relationship. The extent to which each is involved defines the type of love that is present in the relationship. Sternberg believed that the various combinations actually found in human relations produce seven forms of love (see Table 14.4).

TABLE 14.4 STERNBERG'S SEVEN FORMS OF LOVE	
Liking	Intimacy, but no passion or commitment
Infatuation	Passion, but no intimacy or commitment
Empty love	Commitment, but no passion or intimacy
Romantic love	Intimacy and passion, but no commitment
Fatuous love	Commitment and passion, but no intimacy
Companionate love	Commitment and intimacy, but no passion
Consummate love	Commitment, intimacy, and passion

From R.J. Sternberg, "The Triangular Theory of Love" in *Psychological Review* 93:119–35. Copyright © 1986 by the American Psychological Association. Reprinted with permission.

For more and more engaged couples, premarital counseling is becoming a part of their plan to marry.

This is not to say that the more of each, the better. A healthy marriage will usually include all three, but the balance among them is likely to change over the life of the marriage. For example, early in the marriage, passion is likely to be high relative to intimacy. The physical aspects of the partnership are new, and therefore exciting, although probably not enough time has passed for intimacy to develop fully. This is a dangerous time in the marriage, because when intimacy is moderate, the couple may misunderstand each other in many situations or may make unpleasant discoveries about each other. Such problems are often much more painful than they are later, when deeper intimacy and commitment have developed.

Passion, Sternberg states, is like an addiction. In the beginning, the smallest gesture can produce intense excitement. As the relationship grows older, however, larger and larger "doses" are needed to evoke the same feelings. Inevitably, passion loses some of its power. Of course, wide differences exist among couples. Some never feel much passion, whereas others maintain at least moderately passionate feelings into old age. Some appear to have strong commitments from the earliest stage of their association (love at first sight?), whereas others waver for many years.

Sternberg's theory has numerous implications for couples, and for marriage therapists as well. For example, more and more couples are engaging in premarital

For an expanded view of this subject, read Robert Sternberg's The triangular theory of love. *Psychological Review* 93: 129-35, and Love as a story. *Journal of Social and Personal Relationships* 12 (4): 541-46. These articles, too, offer a penetrating view of this most elusive topic.

counseling. In this, they analyze with their counselor the three factors of love, and how each person feels about them. This often helps them to avoid later problems and to get their relationship off to a good start. For some, it provides information that makes them realize that although their passion is high, their intimacy and commitment may not be, and they wait until these develop or decide not to get married at all. In their analysis of responses to the "Love Attitudes Scale," Butler and associates (1995) found that factor structure by age to be quite similar. That is, the attitudes of young adults were seen to have much in common with those of middle adulthood. It is hoped that findings such as Sternberg's and Bulter and associates will improve counseling efforts, which will in turn help to bring about a decrease in our nation's high divorce rate.

Validation: Fromm

In his highly enlightening book on this subject, *The Art of Loving* (1968), Erich Fromm gave us a highly respected understanding of the meaning of love. First, he argued, we must recognize that we are prisoners in our own bodies. Although we assume that we perceive the world around us in much the same way as others, we cannot really be sure. We are the only one who truly knows what our own perceptions are, and we cannot be certain they are the same as other people's. In fact, most of us are aware of times when we have misperceived something: We heard a phrase differently from everyone else; had a hallucination when under the influence of a fever, alcohol, or a drug; and so on.

Thus we must constantly check on the reality our senses give us. We do this thousands, maybe millions, of times every day. Let us give you an example. We assume you are sitting or lying down while you are reading this book. Did you make a conscious check of the surface you are sitting or lying on when you got on it? Probably not. Nevertheless your brain did. You know that if it had been cold, sharp, or wet, you would have noticed. That it is none of these things is something your unconscious mind ascertained without your having to give it a thought.

With some insane people, this is the major problem. Their "reality checker" isn't working right. They cannot tell fact from imagination. They dwell in "castles in the air," out of contact with the real world. We need the feedback from all our senses, doing repeated checks at lightning speeds, to keep in contact with reality.

Fromm's point is this: As important as these "reality checks" on our physical environment are, how much more important are the checks on our innermost state—our deepest and most important feelings and thoughts! To check on the reality of these, we must get the honest reactions of someone we can trust. Such a person tells us, "No, you're not crazy. At least I feel the same way, too!" Even more important, these individuals prove their insight and honesty by sharing with us their own secret thoughts and feelings. In Fromm's words, others give us **validation.**

Validation is essential to our sanity. We are social animals, and we need to know that others approve of us (or, for that matter, when they don't). When someone regularly makes you feel validated, you come to love them. This is the essence of what Erikson has called intimacy. Intimacy fulfills what Maslow calls the need for self-esteem.

We can do no great things—only small things with great love. Mother Theresa

There is, however, great risk in receiving validation. The person who gives it to you is able to do so only because you have let him or her in on your deepest secrets. This gives the person great power, for good or for ill. Because that individual knows you and your insecurities so well, she or he has the capability to hurt you horrendously. This is why many divorces are so acrimonious. No one knows how to get you better than a spouse with whom you have shared so many intimacies. This is why it is said that "There is no such thing as an amicable divorce."

Nevertheless, we truly need love and the validation that leads to it. As studies of mental illness make clear, those who try to live without love risk their mental health.

How's Your Individuation Index?

A number of theorists have stressed that maturity involves becoming more and more of an individual as one goes through life's stages; that is, one becomes less dependent on the opinions of one's parents, other relatives, teachers, and friends. The person is better able to determine her or his own personality, using these other influences only as guides. Thus one index of maturity level is the extent to which one is "individuating." Fill in the blanks below to get an idea of your own individuation.

1. Can you think of any occasion within the last month when your friends asked you to do something with them and you refused?

_____

_____

_____

2. Can you think of three important decisions you have made within the past year that were definitely not influenced by your parents?

_____

_____

_____

3. Can you name at least two things about yourself that you used to hate but that you now feel are not all that bad?

_____

_____

4. Can you name at least two people who used to have a big influence on your life but who are no longer able to influence you very much?

_____

_____

5. Can you name two things that you now like to do by yourself that you previously didn't like to do?

_____

_____

6. Can you name two beliefs or values you hold with which your friends would disagree?

_____

_____

7. Can you name three things you do of which your parents would disapprove? Three things of which they would approve?

_____

_____

_____

8. Do you think you organize your time differently from most of your friends? Name three ways in which you do things differently from them.

_____

_____

_____

9. Are you an "individual"? Suggest five ways in which you are different from everybody else.

_____

_____

_____

_____

_____

The answers to these questions do not prove or disprove that you are fully mature. They should help you gain some insight into yourself. Do you like your answers?

Guided Review

19. Robert Sternberg examined the nature of love, claiming that love is made up of three different components: passion, _____, and commitment.
20. A healthy marriage, according to Sternberg, will involve _____ among all three of his components.
21. Erich Fromm's concept of _____ is closely related to what Erikson calls intimacy.
22. Erik Erikson's theory considers _____ _____ to be less important than other forms of intimacy in his sixth stage—intimacy versus isolation.

Answers

19. intimacy 20. balance 21. validation 22. sexual intercourse

CONCLUSION

By now you can see that the study of human development is mainly the study of change. Few chapters in this book, however, have described a more changing scene than this one.

Americans are getting married later for a variety of reasons. They are staying married for shorter periods, having fewer children, and are more reluctant to remarry if they become divorced or widowed. As we discussed previously, the functions of the family itself have changed tremendously in this century, and some have even predicted the family's demise.

Perhaps the liveliest area in developmental study in recent years has been the field of personality research. More and more we are realizing that, just as in childhood and adolescence, adulthood has predictable stages. Distinct life cycles apparently exist, the goals of which are individuation and maturity. And differences between male and female development are becoming apparent.

Next we looked at definitions of sexual identities and gender roles, and at specific aspects of each. We examined Erikson's studies and looked into the concept of androgyny. We considered Ronald Slaby's ideas about the young adolescent's rigid view of gender.

There are several quite different explanations of why sexuality develops as it does and a number of important changes in the current sexual practices of young adults. Love, too, may be var-iously explained, for example with the theories of Sternberg and Fromm.

In summary:

Marriage and the Family

- Almost 95 percent of Americans get married at some point in their lives.
- Basically four kinds of marriage exist throughout the world: monogamy (one husband, one wife), polygamy (two or more wives), polyandry (two or more husbands), and group marriage (two or more of both husbands and wives). Homosexual marriages are also beginning to win acceptance.

Personal Development

- Levinson suggested that adults develop according to a general pattern known as the life cycle. Each individual's own personal embodiment of the life cycle is known as his or her life course.
- Levinson also described stages of development unique to men.
- According to Erikson's theory, early adulthood is defined in terms of intimacy and solidarity versus isolation.

Sexual Identity and Gender Roles

- Sexual identity results from those physical characteristics and behaviors that are part of our biological inheritance.
- Gender role, on the other hand, results partly from genetic makeup and partly from the specific traits in fashion at any one time and in any one culture.
- Views of acceptable gender-role behaviors have changed considerably during the past 20 years. Androgyny is now considered an acceptable alternative to masculine and feminine gender roles.

Sexuality

- Freud believed that human sexuality is the underlying basis for all behavior.
- Gagnon and Simon see sexual behavior as culturally derived, "scripted" behavior.
- Wilson concludes that the only possible reason that evolution brought about the human sexual system was to create a greater diversity of individuals in a species.
- Sexual experience has increased among college students.
- Intercourse between a husband and wife is the only type of sexual activity totally approved by American society.

The Nature of Love

- Sternberg argues that love is made up of three different components: passion, intimacy, and commitment.
- Fromm states that people need to have their deepest and most important thoughts and feelings "validated" by others who are significant to them.

KEY TERMS

Androgyny
Biopsychosocial
Chromosome failure
Distantiation
Gender-role stereotypes
Group marriage
Homosexual marriage
Individuation

Intimacy
Isolation
Life course
Life cycle
Life structure
Mentoring
Monogamy
Novice phase

Polyandry
Polygamy
Solidarity
Structure building
Structure changing
Transition
Validation

WHAT DO YOU THINK?

1. Which of the four types of marriage described in this chapter do your parents have? Your grandparents?

2. Which of the types of marriages described in this chapter are likely to exist 100 years from now?

3. Levinson believed that forming a mentor relationship is an essential part of the novice phase. Have you formed such a relationship? What are its characteristics?

4. To be intimate, you must know your own identity. But to achieve an identity, you need the feedback you get from being intimate with at least one other person. How can this catch-22 be resolved?

5. Do you agree with Wilson's sociobiological theory of sexuality? Why or why not?

6. How can you tell if you are truly in love?

CHAPTER REVIEW TEST

1. The average age at first marriage in the United States has
   a. increased for males and decreased for females.
   b. increased for females and decreased for males.
   c. increased for both males and females.
   d. decreased for both males and females.

2. A group marriage can be defined as
   a. when there is one husband and two or more wives.
   b. when there is one wife and two or more husbands.
   c. when one husband marries two or more sisters.
   d. when there are two or more of both husbands and wives, who all exercise common privileges and responsibilities.

3. The lower the level of education, the more likely a person is to be unemployed. Which cultural group is affected the most?
   a. Caucasians
   b. African Americans
   c. Latinos
   d. Japanese

4. According to Freud, human sexuality is the underlying basis for
   a. aggression.
   b. pleasure.
   c. human behavior.
   d. the fear of death.

5. Young adolescents learning sexual scripts are learning
   a. the need for intimacy.
   b. the need for belonging.
   c. the desire for submission.
   d. sexual attitudes and behavior in society.

6. In Sternberg's conceptualization of love, when a person is able to share his or her deepest feelings and thoughts with another, they are experiencing
   a. passion.
   b. commitment.
   c. intimacy.
   d. true love.

7. Androgyny refers to
   a. persons who are more likely to behave in a way appropriate to a situation, regardless of their sex.
   b. women who have higher than average male elements in their personalities.
   c. men who have higher than average female elements in their personalities.
   d. the midpoint between the two poles of masculinity and femininity.

8. If someone forced his way into a line at a football game, an androgynous female
   a. would accept the fact that he probably had good reason to cut in line.
   b. would be angry, but not let her feelings show.
   c. would look disapproving.
   d. would tell the offender to go to the end of the line.

9. According to Levinson, the purpose of the developmental periods in our lives is to cause greater individuation, which refers to
   a. our developing separate and special personalities, derived less and less from our parents and teachers and more from our own behavior.
   b. the realization that one does not need to be in a relationship to attain happiness.
   c. the recognition of our distinct interests.
   d. the inability for peers to have great influence on major life decisions.

10. Erikson used the term distantiation to describe
    a. the distance we keep between ourselves and others during personal conversation.
    b. our ability to distance ourselves from our families of origin.
    c. the time we need to progress between one developmental stage to the next.
    d. the readiness all of us have to distance ourselves from others when we feel threatened by their behavior.

11. Who finds fault with Erikson because of his belief that women are judged through their relationships with others?
    a. Levinson
    b. Gilligan
    c. Friedan
    d. Bem

12. Researcher Carol Gilligan states that because femininity is defined through attachment, female gender is most threatened by
    a. divorce.
    b. personal loss.
    c. separation.
    d. dispassionate males.

13. Over the last two decades, one reason for the increase in the age of people at first marriage may be higher numbers of women
    a. entering the workforce.
    b. traveling alone.
    c. afraid of divorce.
    d. having children.

14. The term biopsychosocial refers to the interactions of biology, psychology, and _____ in relation to the individual.
    a. sociology
    b. theology
    c. environment
    d. heredity

15. The role of a _____, according to some theorists, is to provide an individual with guidance during life transitions, assistance with decision making, and a clearer view of what

the individual wishes to make of himself or herself.

a. teacher
b. mentor
c. partner
d. sibling

16. The person who used the term validation to describe our need, as humans, to feel loved and accepted is

a. Fromm.
b. Levinson.
c. Bem.
d. Erikson.

Answers

1. c 2. d 3. b 4. c 5. d 6. c 7. a 8. d 9. a 10. d 11. d 12. c 13. a 14. c 15. b 16. a

PART VIII

Middle Adulthood

In the valleys you looked for the mountains. In the mountains you've searched for the rivers. There is nowhere to go. You are where you belong. You can live the life you dreamed.

Judy Collins

CHAPTER 15

Physical and Cognitive Development in Middle Adulthood

The idea that there is a "middle" phase in adult life is a rather modern idea. Most non-Western and preindustrial cultures recognize only a mature stage of adulthood, from about 25 to about 60 years old, followed by a stage of old age decline. Many Western scientists (including the authors of this book) now recognize four stages of adult life: young adulthood (approximate age range from 19 to 34); middle adulthood (approximate age range from 35 to 64); young elderly (approximate age range from 65 to 79), and old elderly (80+).

One non-Western country that does recognize middle adulthood is Japan. The Japanese word for middle age, *sonen,* refers to the "prime of life," the period between early adulthood and senility. Another quite positive word often used for the middle adult years in Japan is *hataraki-zakari,* meaning the "full bloom of one's working ability."

Not all Japanese words for middle adulthood are quite so joyful. The word *kanroku* means "weightiness" or "fullness," both as in bearing a heavy load of authority, and in being overweight.

Why do you suppose industrialized cultures like North America and Japan have several words for middle adulthood, and other cultures have no words at all? ✪

When you finish reading this chapter, you should be able to

- Identify health concerns of particular importance to middle-aged adults.

- Discuss how muscular and sensory abilities change in middle adulthood.

- Explain the role of hormone treatments in dealing with the climacteric and other aspects of aging.

- Contrast the various positions presented regarding the nature of intelligence as people pass through middle age.

- Describe creative individuals and suggest ways in which creativity develops in middle adulthood.

- Decide whether you believe that learning ability declines as people age.

- Highlight particular employment concerns among middle-aged adults.

- Describe the five major problem areas for working women.

- Discuss what is meant by a "midcareer crisis," as well as ways of dealing with it.

Physical Development

"You're not getting older, you're getting better!"

You may hear middle-aged people saying this to each other. They hope that the changes they are experiencing are minor and not too negative, but let's face it, physical systems do decline with age. As you will see, biological forces greatly in-

Figure 15.1

The decline of basal metabolism rate through the life cycle. BMR varies with age and sex. Rates are usually higher for males and decline proportionally with age for both sexes.

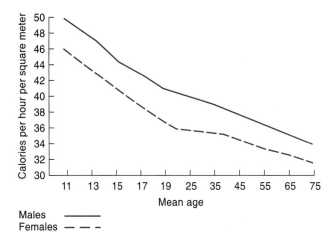

Males ———
Females — — —

fluence physical development, but be on the lookout for ways that psychological and social forces are at work as well. Now let us take a closer look at some of these functions.

Health

In general, concerns about health rise in the middle years. For example, a person's image of what they will be like in the future becomes increasingly health-related in mid-life. These thoughts are more often negative than positive, expressing fears about future health (Hooker & Kaus, 1994). This is not to say that middle-aged people are sickly. Their worries probably result more because they experience a greater number of serious illnesses and deaths of their loved ones than do younger people, and from the fact that the changes in their bodies are more abrupt than in the bodies of young adults.

As one moves into middle adulthood, weight gain becomes a matter of concern. For example, about one-half of the United States adult population weighs over the upper limit of the "normal" weight range. For some, this is the result of genetic inheritance—about 40 percent of the people with one obese parent become obese, as compared with only 10 percent of those whose parents are not obese (U. S. National Center for Health Statistics, 1986). Others become overweight simply because they do not compensate for their lowering **basal metabolism rate (BMR).**

BMR is the minimum amount of energy an individual tends to use when in a resting state. As you can see from Figure 15.1, this rate varies with age and gender. Males have a slightly higher rate than females. The rate drops most quickly during adolescence, and then more slowly during adulthood. This is caused by a drop in the ratio of lean body mass to fat, which "results in a lower BMR, since the metabolic needs of fat tissue are less than those of lean. Even for those who exercise regularly, fewer calories need to be consumed" (Kart & others, 1988, p. 171).

Thus if you continue to eat at the same rate throughout your life, you will definitely gain weight. If you add to this a decreased rate of exercise, the weight gain (sometimes called "middle-age spread," referring to wider hips, thicker thighs, a "spare tire" around the waist, and a "beer belly") will be even greater. If you expect this to happen, it probably will (another **self-fulfilling prophecy**).

Many people think that weight gain in middle age is natural, but in fact a number of studies (e. g., Clifford & others, 1991; Troumbley & others, 1990) clearly demonstrated that increased levels of health problems and risk of death do result from being overweight. A study conducted by Garvey and Schaffer (1994) found depression to be associated with weight gain in middle adulthood. Increased appetite and weight gain were two observed symptoms associated with depression in the subjects they examined.

On the other hand, the warnings against "crash diets" should be heeded,

Many men in their thirties find it hard to accept that their muscular ability is slowly declining. Unfortunately, this sometimes causes them to overexert themselves, leading to such dire results as serious injury and heart attack.

especially by middle-aged people. Probably the most popular diet these days includes the use of dietary supplements, and the most popular ingredient in them is an amino acid known as L-tryptophan. This acid has been linked to a blood disorder in which white blood cells increase to abnormally high numbers (American Association of Retired Persons, 1990a). This can result in swelling of extremities, severe pain in muscles and joints, fever, and skin rash. To date there have been almost 300 cases in 37 states, and one known death.

Cardiovascular Health

Cardiovascular reaction to stressful challenges is normal (Manuck, 1994). Jennings and associates (1997) investigated the causes when reactions are abnormal. They presented 902 men of ages from 46 to 64 with four tasks designed to measure their reactivity. They examined the subjects for cardiovascular disease such as hypertension (abnormally high blood pressure) and recorded their use of medications. They concluded that age and disease contributed about equally as causes of reactivity, with medications being a smaller independent influence.

Effects of Alcohol

📖 An interesting book on this topic is Janet Woititz' *Adult children of alcoholics*. Lexington, MA: Health Communications, Inc. Woititz describes the characteristics of the adult children of alcoholics but insists that these are not character defects. This book provides readers with basic tools that will enable them to achieve greater self-knowledge and understanding.

Anyone over the age of 50 should "go on the wagon" and stay there, according to Teri Manolio of the National Heart, Lung and Blood Institute (cited in AARP, 1990b, p. 7). Even one or two drinks each day can be dangerous, because they can cause enlargement of the left ventricle of the heart. Such enlargement causes the heart to work harder and often can cause irregular heartbeats. If a person's heart is already enlarged, the danger is even greater. These data come from the Framingham (Massachusetts) Heart Study, which has also furnished the following findings:

- The older the person and the larger the number of drinks per day, the greater the risk.

- The risk is smaller for women.

- Men who are obese or have high blood pressure are at the greatest risk.

Muscular Ability

Muscle growth is complete in the average person by age 17, but improvements in speed, strength, and skill can occur throughout the early adult years. In fact, most people reach their peak around age 25—females somewhat earlier than that and males somewhat later. Variations in peak muscular ability depend very much on the type of activity. Consider, for example, the 20-year-old female Olympic gymnast who is thought of as an "old lady" because peak ability in this area tends to come at around age 16.

Between the ages of 30 and 60, loss of strength is gradual—about 10 percent on the average (Spence, 1989):

- Most loss occurs in the back and legs.

- Muscle tone and flexibility decrease.

- Injuries take longer to heal.

- Muscle is gradually replaced by fat.

A 175-pound man has 70 pounds of muscle at age 30 but typically loses 10 pounds of that muscle to fat by the time he reaches old age (Schulz & Ewen, 1988). However, the current popularity of aerobic activities may be reversing this trend. Aerobic activity such as swimming and brisk walking appears to help maintain general health because it demands that the heart pump a great deal of blood to the large muscles of the legs.

In the middle period of adulthood (35 to 64) there is a common but unnecessary decline in muscular ability. Unfortunately, the majority of people in this stage of life do not get much exercise. Both males and females may undergo a marked change in lifestyle. Growing success in one's chosen field often leads to greater leisure and indulgence in the so-called finer things of life.

Sensory Abilities

The five physical senses—vision, hearing, smell, taste, and touch—are responsible for gathering information about the world around us. Although the stereotyped image of an older person losing hearing or vision is sometimes made fun of, the gradual loss of function of one of the senses is a serious concern for all of us. We often take everyday experiences such as reading a good book, watching television, driving a car to the grocery store, tasting or even smelling a good meal, or just holding a child in our arms for granted. Yet all these experiences depend on one or more of the five senses. What changes in sensory ability can we expect as we pass through middle adulthood? The following trends are only general and vary widely from one individual to another.

Vision

Because of changes in the eye that occur when we reach our forties, glasses are often necessary.

Vision is the sense that we most depend on for information about what's going on around us. The eye begins to change physically at about age 40. The lens becomes less elastic and more yellow. The cornea begins to lose its luster. By age 50 the cornea is increasing in curvature and thickness. At 50, the iris begins to respond less well to light (Schulz & Ewen, 1988).

What do these physical changes mean for our vision? In general, our eyes don't adapt to sudden intense light or darkness as effectively as they once did. The ability to focus on nearby objects decreases, leading to a diagnosis of farsightedness and possibly a prescription for bifocals. The ability to detect certain colors can also be hampered by age-related changes in the eye. As the lens yellows, shades of blue and green become more difficult to discern. The ability to detect moving objects may also decrease as we grow older (Warabi & others, 1984). For most people, these changes in visual ability pose a problem only when lighting is reduced, such as in night driving.

Eye disease is a more serious matter. Increasing age often brings a heightened risk for such diseases. **Glaucoma** results from a buildup of pressure inside the eye due to excessive fluid. The resulting damage can destroy one's vision. Glaucoma is increasingly common after the age of 40 and is the leading cause of blindness by age 70. Routine eye examinations, however, now usually include a glaucoma test and blindness is often prevented.

Less well known but more dangerous is **senile macular degeneration.** This disease of the retina is also a cause of blindness. It begins as blurred vision and a dark spot in the center of the field of vision. Advances in laser surgery have shown promise in treating diseases of the retina such as this.

Hearing

Hearing also seems to be susceptible to decline at about age 40. This is when we begin to lose the ability to detect certain tones. As you progress from middle to old age, certain frequencies, the higher ones in particular, may need to be much louder for you to hear them (Schulz & Ewen, 1988). Our ability to understand human speech also appears to decrease as we grow older. The most likely result is an inability to hear certain consonants. Cognitive capacity may play a role in the fact that the ability to listen to speech in a crowded environment (e.g., a party) declines faster than the ability to listen to someone alone with no background noise.

Our visual system is a more reliable sense than our auditory system. In fact, in contrast to the success that medical science has made in fighting blindness, deafness in the United States appears to be increasing. In 1940 you could expect to find deafness in 200 out of every 10,000 people in this country. Forty years later, you could expect to find it in 300 (Hunt & Lindley, 1989). Bear in mind, however, that these effects are partly a result of choice. Cross-cultural studies have shown that our relatively loud, high-tech culture contributes to our society's general loss of hearing.

One curious aspect of the age-related decline in hearing is that, of the five senses, hearing is easily the most stigmatized loss. People who wouldn't think twice about getting prescription eyeglasses will refuse to get a hearing aid or even admit they are suffering a hearing loss.

Smell

Although not used as often as vision or hearing, the **olfactory sense** does a little more than just tell us when dinner is about ready. First, the olfactory sense works closely with our taste buds to produce what we think of as the "taste" of a given food. In fact, it is difficult in studies to separate which sense—taste or smell—is actually contributing to the decline in performance on a certain task. Besides bringing us pleasurable smells, this sense warns us against spoiled foods, smoke or fire, and leaking gas (Stevens & Cain, 1987).

Various studies suggest that our sense of smell decreases as we grow older (Stevens & Cain, 1987). The decline seems to begin slowly around age 50 and increases rapidly after age 70.

Taste

As we mentioned, our sense of taste is closely tied to our sense of smell, which makes studying age-related effects on taste very difficult. Recent studies have suggested that older adults may experience a decline in the ability to detect weak tastes but retain their ability to discriminate among those foods that have a strong taste, such as a spicy chicken curry (Spence, 1989). The decline in the ability to taste (and smell) may account in part for the decrease in weight that many elderly persons experience.

In general, we can say that although our senses do decline somewhat throughout middle age, we are finding more and more ways to compensate for the losses, so they cause only slight changes in lifestyle. Another physical concern in our middle years is the climacteric.

The Climacteric

The word **climacteric** refers to a relatively abrupt change in the body, brought about by changes in hormonal balances. In women, this change is called **menopause.** It normally occurs over a four-year period at some time during a woman's forties or early fifties (Masters & Johnson, 1966). The climacteric also refers to the **male change of life,** whereas the menopause refers only to the cessation of menstruation, most often between the ages of 48 and 52. The term **climacterium** refers to the loss of reproductive ability. This occurs at menopause for women, but men tend to be quite old when they are no longer able to produce fertile sperm. In aging men there is a decline or loss of both libido (the part of sexuality involving conscious experience) and potency (the physical capacity to react to sexual stimuli), although there is a lesser decline in libido (Davidson, 1989). Whereas in females the body ceases to produce certain hormones, the sex hormone that controls normal sex behavior in males, testosterone, has been shown to remain fairly stable over age groups (Rowland & others, 1993). These findings suggest that while men may experience a decrease in physiological function, other factors are important to the overall satisfaction of one's sex life.

The main physical change in menopause is that the ovaries cease to produce the hormones estrogen and progesterone, although the adrenal glands continue to produce some estrogen. Does this decline in hormonal output always cause significant changes in female behavior? The question is difficult to answer. At the onset of menopause, symptoms are often affected by women's attitudes toward sexuality, lifestyle, function within the family, and hormone levels (Huerta & others, 1995). These factors interact as they impact a woman's life in different ways throughout the climacteric. Some researchers feel that negative feelings are related to a lack of social support at this time in a woman's life (Montero & others, 1993).

Undoubtedly a lack of understanding of menopause, coupled with normal fears of growing old, accounts for at least some of the negative feelings about menopause. It should be noted that many women have positive feelings. For example, they no longer have to be concerned about becoming pregnant.

Matthews and associates (1990) found no negative mental health consequences from menopause for the majority of middle-aged women sampled. In a study of Israeli women, those from traditional backgrounds (Moslem Arab villagers) and modern backgrounds (Central European immigrants) were found not to regret the loss of fertility brought on by menopause (Datan, 1995). Also on the positive side, Sheehy (1992) found that menopause is a time of "coalescence," a time of integration, balance, liberation, confidence, and action. A menopausal woman no longer worries about pregnancy; many feel relief when their children leave the nest.

The menopausal woman moves from the old age of youth to the youth of old age or, in other terms, she moves into a second adulthood. Many women in their fifties may find themselves in the prime of their lives (Fodor & Franks, 1990). They have good health, autonomy, security in their major relationship, freedom, higher income, status, and confidence. Brown (1982) found that many postmenopausal women in a variety of cultures experience greater powers, freedoms, and higher-level responsibilities when their children become adults; but as one study cautions, it may be that only women of higher status feel this increase in power (Todd & others, 1990).

For those women who experience serious problems with menopause, **estrogen replacement therapy** (ERT) can offer considerable relief. When estrogen was first instituted, ERT was found to increase the risk of cancer. Today, however, it is given in quite low levels and is combined with progesterone, which greatly reduces the risk (Col & others, 1997). The choice of whether or not to take hormone replacement therapy is a difficult one for postmenopausal women and must be undertaken on a case-by-case basis. In many women, hormone replacement can increase life expectancy by lowering the risk of developing coronary heart disease or hip fracture. However, hormone replacement therapy is linked with increases in breast cancer. Menopausal women are advised to consult with their gynecologists so they can weigh their risk factors for coronary heart disease, hip fracture, and breast cancer before deciding whether to undergo hormone replacement therapy.

Estrogen, which eliminates the symptoms of menopause, also stems the deterioration of the cardiovascular, urinary, genital, and nervous systems; slows the aging of the bones and skin; and cuts the death rate from heart disease for women in half. Recent Veterans Administration research, using human growth hormone, initially found that 60 men aged 60 to 80 may have regained the vitality of men 15 to 20 years younger. A study by the National Institute on Aging has begun testing two other hormones, DHEA and testosterone, suspected of retarding age-related symptoms such as loss of strength and vitality and the diminishing size of internal organs in frail, elderly men. Perhaps in the future, doctors may routinely prescribe hormone therapy for both men and women to slow the aging process (Rudman, 1992).

At one time, it was thought that the male hormone balance parallels that of the female. According to a well-designed study conducted by the National Institute on Aging (1979), however, the level of testosterone declines only very gradually with age. Dr. Mitchell Hermann, who conducted the study on men from age 25 to 89, said that his findings contradict earlier results because most of those previous studies were of men in hospitals and in nursing homes who were afflicted with obesity, alcoholism, or chronic illness. All of his subjects were healthy, vigorous men.

Hermann suggested the decrease in sexual potency that men experience in later years is probably not the result of hormone changes, but rather slowing down in the central nervous system, together with a self-fulfilling prophecy (men expect to become impotent, so they do). There have been numerous speculations in the popular press about the nature of "male menopause," as it referred to in Jed Diamond's book by that name (reviewed in White, 1997), but scientifically speaking the effects of hormonal changes on the appearance and emotional state of men are unclear at the present.

It seems likely that as we better understand precisely how hormone balances change and how the different changes interact with each other, the impairments that have been attributed to these changes will decrease.

Although middle-aged people are generally healthier than the elderly, chronic health problems are especially prevalent for poor African American middle-aged women. African Americans also sustain 39 percent more work-related injuries and diseases than whites and thus are more likely to drop out of the labor force before retirement (Jackson & Gibson, 1985). These socioeconomic and racial differences are a good place to see how the biopsychosocial model operates. What role would you say each of these three major forces play in causing these differences?

Health also plays a role in the cognition of middle-aged adults. In the next section, we examine this important developmental capacity.

> 📖 Two works that include sections on middle-aged physical development are: (1) The Boston Women's Book Collaborative. (1984). *Our bodies, growing older.* Boston: Author. An excellent update of the popular *Our bodies, our selves,* this book is for middle-aged and elderly women. (2) L. Nilsson and J. Lindberg. (1974). *Behold man: A photographic journey of discovery inside the body.* New York: Delacorte. A book of photographs, many of them pictures enlarged thousands of times. This is a magnificent description of the human body.

Guided Review

1. Adulthood has recently been thought of as having four stages: young adulthood (19 to 34 years of age), _____ _____ (35 to 64 years of age), _____ _____ (65 to 79 years of age), and old elderly (80+ years of age).
2. Basal metabolic rate is the _____ amount of energy an individual uses when in a resting state.
3. Our basic metabolism rate decreases with age, meaning that if we eat the same amount all our lives we will _____ weight.
4. According to recent research people over the age of 50 should be concerned about the effects of alcohol as its use can result in enlargement of the _____, causing it to work harder.
5. All five senses decline during middle adulthood, but _____ loss has the greatest social stigma attached to it.
6. "Climacteric" is the term used for the abrupt change that occurs in the body due to changes in _____ balances.
7. The term "menopause" refers to the _____ change of life, which includes the cessation of menstruation.
8. A number of women experience positive consequences from menopause, including a time of coalescence, of integration, and _____.
9. _____ _____ therapy can be used to offer relief to women who are experiencing problems with regard to menopause.

Answers

1. middle adulthood, young elderly 2. minimum 3. gain 4. heart 5. hearing 6. hormonal 7. female 8. liberation 9. Estrogen replacement

Cognitive Development

I am all I ever was and much more, but an enemy has bound me and
twisted me, so now I can plan and think as I never could, but no longer
achieve all I plan and think.

—William Butler Yeats

Of course, the "enemy" Yeats refers to is age. Was he right in believing he could
think as well as ever or was he just kidding himself? The question of declining intelligence across adulthood has long concerned humans.

Theories about Intelligence

Indeed, no aspect of adult functioning has received more research than intelligence.
Despite this considerable research, investigators still do not agree on whether we
lose intellectual ability as we grow old. In fact, three basic positions exist: yes, it
does decline; no, it does not decline; and yes, it does in some ways, but no, it
doesn't in others. Let's look at the evidence for these positions.

Wechsler's Answer: Yes

Undoubtedly the strongest proponent of the hypothesis that intelligence declines
with age is psychologist David Wechsler, whose seminal work in the 1940s and
1950s provoked much discussion. He stated that

> Beginning with the investigation by Galton in 1883 . . . nearly all studies
> dealing with the age factor in adult performance have shown that most
> human abilities . . . decline progressively, after reaching a peak somewhere
> between ages 18 and 25. (1958, p. 135)

The most widely used test of adult intelligence was designed by Wechsler himself
(1955).

Terman's Answer: No

Lewis Terman began his study of
the development of intelligence
in the 1920s.

Lewis Terman's work began even earlier than Wechsler's. His classic research (1925)
is an excellent longitudinal study that found an increase in intelligence with age.
That study was started in 1924 and used the Stanford-Binet Intelligence Test for children. The subjects were tested 10 years later, in 1941, and then retested in 1956 with
the Wechsler Adult Intelligence Scale (WAIS), which is highly correlated with the
Stanford-Binet. At the end of the second 15-year interval, when the subjects were
in their twenties, there was an average increase of scores (Bradway & others, 1958).

The subjects were retested in 1969 by Kangas and Bradway (1971). The average subject was then 40 years old. Their scores were found to have increased to an
average of nearly 130! Another study supporting the no-decline hypothesis is reported by Owens (1953). In 1919 a group of 363 students entering Ohio State College had their intelligence tested. Thirty years later Owens retested 127 of them, and
all but one of the subjects showed an increase over the 30 years. In 1966, when the
individuals were approximately 61 years old, 97 of the subjects were retested and
none of the scores had changed significantly.

Canestrari (1963) found that adults in middle age do more poorly on speed tests
than do younger subjects. However, when they were given more time, for example, to memorize digits, they did as well as the younger subjects.

Horn's Answer: Yes and No

J. L. Horn believed that intelligence does decline in some ways, but in other ways
it does not. The picture is probably more complicated than either of the first two
positions reveals. Evidence indicates that

- One type of intelligence declines, whereas another does not.

- Some individuals decline, whereas others do not.

- Although decline does eventually occur, it happens only late in life.

Horn has described two dimensions of intelligence: fluid and crystallized. The two can be distinguished as follows: **fluid intelligence** depends on the proper functioning of the nervous system. It is measured by tasks that show age-related declines (speeded tasks, tests of reaction time). **Crystallized intelligence** demonstrates the cumulative effect of culture and learning of task performance and is measured by tests of verbal ability and cultural knowledge (Labouvie-Vief & Lawrence, 1985).

Horn (1975, 1978) hypothesized that whereas crystallized intelligence does not decline and may even increase, fluid intelligence probably does deteriorate, at least to some extent (see Figure 15.2). Horn and his colleagues (1981) found that this decline in fluid intelligence averages three to seven IQ points per decade for the three decades spanning the period from 30 to 60 years of age.

Some older research has suggested that some kinds of achievement may rely more on one type of intelligence than on the other (Lehman, 1964). For example, in fields such as mathematics, music, chemistry, and poetry, the best work is usually produced at a relatively young age and therefore may rely most on fluid intelligence. Other major achievements, such as in history, astronomy, philosophy, writing, and psychology, usually occur later in life, which may indicate greater reliance on crystallized intelligence (more on this later).

A number of cross-sectional studies have attempted to validate Horn's theory. A good example is the work of Alan Kaufman and associates (1989). They studied groups of subjects ages 20 to 74 who were given the revised version of the WAIS-R. These researchers wanted to see whether the level of education subjects had completed would have any effect on their performance on the WAIS-R, and the relationship those performance scores would have to the age of each subject group. Results of the study appear to support Horn's theory of fluid and crystallized intelligence. Test scores showed a decline in verbal IQ, performance and full-scale IQ. However, when education was accounted for statistically, the decline in subjects' scores for verbal IQ disappeared, yet remained for performance and full-scale IQs. A subsequent study showed that ethnic differences occur in tests of crystallized abilities, regardless of educational attainment (Kaufman & associates, 1992). As was pointed out in Chapter 2, however, cross-sectional designs like this may be flawed. The problem is that people of different ages, having grown up at different periods,

Figure 15.2

Horn's three types of intelligence

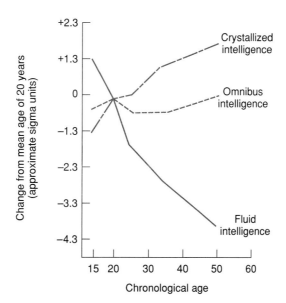

have necessarily had different life experiences. Therefore, the results may be more due to this cohort effect than to aging.

A longitudinal study avoids this weakness because it looks at the same group of people over an interval of time. Schaie and Hertzog (1983) conducted a longitudinal study on cognitive abilities and found evidence that they decline as one ages. The evidence for a decline after the age of 60 was strong. They also found evidence that this process starts after the age of 50, although it is probably not observable in everyday life. Making the situation even more complex, Hertzog's latest research suggested that a decline in speed of performance makes declines in intelligence look worse than they are. "It may be the case that a substantial proportion of the age changes actually observed by Schaie in his longitudinal studies is not loss of thinking capacity per se but, rather, slowing in rate of intelligent thought" (Hertzog, 1989, p. 650). Perhaps you simply need more time to think and respond when you get older.

You should recall from Chapter 1, however, that longitudinal studies may suffer from the problem that studies done at different points in time may be distorted by historical effects. Only a sequential design can resolve this difficulty and as of this time, no such study has been carried out.

The lifelong efforts of K. Warner Schaie (summarized in Schaie, 1994) are noteworthy; he has made powerful attempts to understand the adult life course of intellectual abilities. The Seattle Longitudinal Study examined, but was not limited to, the presence or absence of age-related changes and difference in individuals. Consequently, this study has provided data on the importance of age-related changes, variables that may explain such changes, and the basis for future interventions. By adopting the sequential format of studying a cross-sectional sample every seven years since 1956, Schaie has eliminated many limitations that accompany a strictly cross-sectional study or a longitudinal study.

New Views of Intelligence

Part of the debate is a matter of definition. What, exactly, is intelligence? How is it measured? It is certainly composed of several different cognitive abilities, such as memory, language, reasoning, and the ability to manipulate numbers. Each of these mental processes can, in turn, be divided into various subprocesses.

Different definitions of intelligence lead to different measures of it. Each measure emphasizes different mental abilities. For example, if you define intelligence as rank in class or school achievement, then cognitive abilities such as verbal comprehension and general information may be much more important than rote memory and perceptual tasks (for a review, see Horn & Donaldson, 1980). In fact, most of the commonly used IQ tests measure only a few of the cognitive abilities that could be measured. Under these circumstances, the question of whether intelligence declines with age becomes unanswerable. Clearly, more specific questions must be asked.

Increasingly, general intelligence is being abandoned as a scientific concept and subject of study. More and more, researchers are proposing several quite distinct cognitive abilities. Horn has now added supporting abilities to the concepts of fluid and crystallized intelligence. These include short-term memory, long-term memory, visual processing, and auditory processing. Howard Gardner (1983) contended that there are seven different cognitive abilities. His list includes linguistic, musical, logical-mathematical, spatial, bodily-kinesthetic, self-understanding, and social understanding abilities. Other researchers have generated other lists (e.g., Sternberg, 1990).

Baltes and his associates (1993) suggested a resolution to the question of how intelligence develops with age. They have proposed a **dual-process model** of intelligence. This model considers the interaction of the potential and the biological limits of the aging mind. Gains and losses are recognized as part of intellectual development. There is likely to be a decline in the mechanics of intelligence, such as

📖 If you want to learn more on this subject, read Gardner's *Frames of mind: The theory of multiple intelligences* (New York: Basic Books). It offers a comprehensive view of the numerous faces of intelligence.

classification skills and logical reasoning. These mechanics are largely dependent on genetics, and are comparable to fluid intelligence. Clearly, variables such as memory play an important role in this. Pragmatics of intelligence remain stable or increase with age, and include social wisdom, which is defined as good judgment about important but uncertain matters of life. Culture is the major influence on pragmatic intelligence.

This model seems to offer the most reasonable position. There are just too many famous people whose thinking obviously got better as they got older. To name a few: George Burns, Coco Chanel, Benjamin Franklin, Albert Einstein, Mahatma Gandhi, Helen Hayes, Michelangelo, Grandma Moses, Georgia O'Keefe, Pope John XXIII, Eleanor Roosevelt, Bertrand Russell, George Bernard Shaw, Sophocles, Frank Lloyd Wright, and so on and so on. It is no coincidence that these people also maintained their creative abilities well into old age. As we have said, a key factor in the ability to continue to be productive well into the later years is memory. Thus, an important question is what is memory?

Certainly intelligence cannot be separated from memory. Your mind can process information like lightning, but if you cannot recall the proper information, processing abilities are useless. Does memory decline with age? The stereotype is of the doddering old person who can't quite seem to remember the names of his grandchildren. But the research does not always confirm the existence of a decline.

Memory

The study of memory has caused considerable excitement in the scientific community in the last few years, as great strides have been made in solving the mystery of how it works (e. g., Bito & others, 1996; Frankland & others, 1997; Greenberg & Frank, 1994; Kamino & others, 1997; Kaestner & others, 1996; Kiebler & others, 1996; McGaugh & Guzowski, 1997; Moore & others, 1995). Although all the microbiological studies thus far have involved animals, experiments with human subjects are planned.

Sea Slugs, Fruit Flies, Mice, and CREBs

On the basis of the research on the animals studied thus far (sea slugs, fruit flies, and mice), it is clear that the memory process is controlled by the flow of a variety of proteins. This flow is governed by a master protein known as CREB. There are four distinct steps in the process (see Figure 15.3):

Figure 15.3

Diagram explaining the memory process at the neuronal level

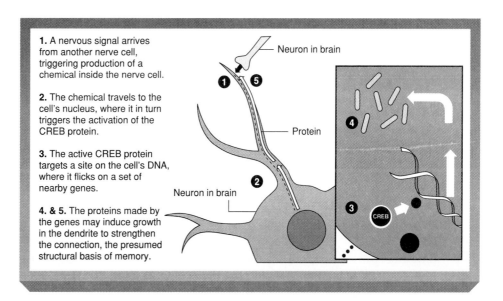

1. A nervous signal arrives from another nerve cell, triggering production of a chemical inside the nerve cell.

2. The chemical travels to the cell's nucleus, where it in turn triggers the activation of the CREB protein.

3. The active CREB protein targets a site on the cell's DNA, where it flicks on a set of nearby genes.

4. & 5. The proteins made by the genes may induce growth in the dendrite to strengthen the connection, the presumed structural basis of memory.

- An electrochemical signal sent from another neuron moves up the dendrite of the receiving neuron, which triggers a reaction in it.

- If the signal is of a certain type, it also triggers a reaction in the neuronal nucleus that activates CREB proteins.

- A site on the cell's DNA is targeted, which then "turns on" a set of nearby genes.

- Proteins produced by these genes travel back down the dendrite to the synaptic junction and strengthen the connection to the emitting axon by producing more neurotransmitter receiving points. This makes the next transmission from the sending neuron more likely to pass across the junction. In essence, this is the definition of memory.

Thus CREBs are the central factor in what will and what will not be remembered (Hawkins & Kandel, 1996). To be more specific, there are CREB activator proteins and CREB inhibitor proteins (DelVecchio & others, 1995; Tully & Yin, 1996). It has been found that animals given a dose of the inhibitor protein have impaired memory and those given the activator protein have much sharper memory storage ability. For example, fruit flies typically need 10 training sessions to associate an odor with an electric shock. Those that were inhibited could form no lasting memories at all. Those given the activator protein dose learned the association in one trial! Neurobiologist Timothy Tully stated that:

> **"This implies these flies have photographic memory. They are just like students who could read a book once, see it in their mind, and tell that the answer is in paragraph 3 on page 274"** (cited in Wickelgren, 1996, p. 3).

Both aspects of CREB proteins are essential to all thought. We need to remember the essential items, while not memorizing trivia, such as the habitual use of the word "like." It has also been found that short learning periods with rest or recreation in between facilitates long-term memory, presumably so that CREB activator proteins can be rejuvenated (Tully & Yin, 1996).

How humans operate the CREB process is not yet known, but it appears likely that highly intelligent persons are better at it than others. Where this inquiry will lead is an interesting question. Will we someday ingest synthetic CREB activator when involved in a complex learning task, or a CREB inhibitor when we wish to withdraw from the stimulation of our busy environment?

Memory in Middle Adulthood

Not surprisingly, a number of studies have found deterioration in some types of memory function as people age. For example, prospective memory is the memory "required to carry out planned actions at the appropriate time, such as meeting a friend for lunch or taking a medication. Prospective memory involves retrieval of an intention to act that has been stored in long-term memory" (Hertzog & others, 1997, p. 314). This type of memory may decline with age. Hertzog and associates (1997) found that middle adults have more difficulty than younger adults with prospective memory, particularly when it involves monitoring of time.

On the other hand, some researchers have produced differential results. For instance, Whiting and Smith (1997) found that middle adults have more difficulty than younger adults in memory tasks requiring more cognitive effort, such as recall. More automatic processes, such as recognition, do not decline as much with age. Also, middle adults have more difficulty than younger adults in spatial learning, according to Gold and associates (1997). In a study of how adults learn a route from one location to another, middle adults had greater difficulty in remembering the route than younger adults, but were as good at recognition of landmarks along the route.

A Sociocultural View

Cultural Bias and Cognitive Decline

A chief result of Schaie's studies (1994) has been the identification of variables that reduce the risk of cognitive decline. These are:

- The absence of cardiovascular and other chronic diseases.
- Living in favorable environmental circumstances, such as those who are above average in wealth tend to enjoy.
- Substantial involvement in activities found in stimulating environments such as travel and extensive reading.
- Having a flexible personality style.
- Being married to a spouse who has a high cognitive functioning level.
- Engaging in activities that require quick perception and thinking (such as verbal jousting with friends).
- Being satisfied with one's life accomplishments through mid-life.

No doubt all of these variables are biopsychosocial in origin. We can probably do little about the biological fac-

tors involved. Now that these variables have been identified, however, there may be many actions we as a society could take to affect the psychological and environmental elements. Can you think of any?

Furthermore, some of these variables are particularly related to economic level, culture, and lifestyle. Two of the most important are rating one's self as being satisfied with one's life accomplishments and reporting a flexible personality style at mid-life. These in turn tend to be related to having a high socioeconomic level, a complex and intellectually stimulating environment, being married to a spouse with high cognitive status, maintaining high levels of perceptual processing speed, and the absence of chronic diseases, especially cardiovascular disease. In summary, the richer you are and the higher your social class, the less your cognitive abilities decline.

These findings are strong evidence for a class bias in cognitive decline. What reasons can you give to explain the results?

The "grande dame" of modern dance, Martha Graham's contributions to choreography make her one of the most creative adults in the twentieth century.

The Development of Creativity

As the world changes more and more rapidly, the role of creativity becomes more crucial. In this section, we explore the development of creative ability in the adult years. But first, here is a description of creative individuals.

Traits of the Highly Creative Adult

A number of studies (reviewed in Dacey, 1989a and 1989c; Dacey & Kenny, 1997; Dacey & Packer, 1992) have compared highly creative and average adults in a number of important traits. In general, highly creative adults

- like to do their own planning, make their own decisions, and need the least training and experience in self-guidance.

- do not like to work with others and prefer their own judgment of their work to the judgment of others. They therefore seldom ask others for opinions.

- take a hopeful outlook when presented with complex, difficult tasks.

- have the most ideas when a chance to express individual opinion is presented. These ideas frequently invoke the ridicule of others.

- are most likely to stand their ground in the face of criticism.

- are the most resourceful when unusual circumstances arise.

- can tolerate uncertainty and ambiguity better than others.

- are not necessarily the "smartest" or "best" in competitions.

The "artistic" type of person, according to Holland, has a preference for ambiguous, free, unsystematized activities.

In their compositions, creative adults typically

- show an imaginative use of many different words.

- are more flexible; for example, in a narrative they use more situations, characters, and settings. Rather than taking one clearly defined train of thought and pursuing it to its logical conclusion, creative adults tend to switch the main focus quickly and easily and often go off on tangents.

- tend to elaborate on the topic assigned, taking a much broader connotation of it to begin with, and then proceeding to embellish even that.

- are more original. (This is the most important characteristic. The others need not be evidenced, but this one must be.) Their ideas are qualitatively different from the average person's. Employers frequently react to the creative person's work in this way: "I know what most of my people will do in a particular situation, but I never know what to expect from this one!"

Now let us turn to the research on the development of creativity.

Psychobistorical Studies of Creative Achievement

Lehman (1953) examined biographical accounts of the work of several thousand individuals born since 1774. He studied the ages at which these persons made their creative contributions. He compared the contributions of deceased persons with those still living. On the basis of his study, he concluded that

> on the whole it seems clear that both past and present generation scientists have produced more than their proportionate share of high-quality research not later than at ages 30 to 39, and it is useless to bemoan this fact or to deny it. (p. 26)

Figure 15.4 portrays Lehman's general results.

In his report of his own research on this subject, Dennis (1966) criticized Lehman's work, stating that it included many individuals who died before they reached old age. Dennis points out that this biased the study statistically, because we cannot know what proportion of creative contributions these deceased people would have made had they lived longer.

Dennis studied the biographies of 738 creative persons, all of whom lived to age 79 or beyond, and whose contributions were considered valuable enough to have been reported in biographical histories. He did this because he believed "that no valid statements can be made concerning age and productivity except from longitudinal data involving no dropouts due to death" (1966, p. 8).

He looked at the percentage of works done by these persons in each of the decades between the ages of 20 and 80. When creative productivity is evaluated in

Figure 15.4

Graph of Lehman's findings

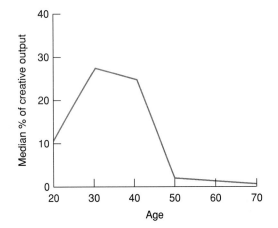

What's Your
VIEW?   **Do Most People Become More Creative as They Grow Older?**

Think of five people over 35 whom you know and most admire. Write their names here:

_____   _____

_____   _____

_____

Now, ask yourself, how many of these people are among the most creative people you know? If most are, do you think there is something about growing old that contributes to creativity? If your answer is no, what do you think does contribute? Would you say that, on the average, most people get more creative as they grow older?

this way, the results are quite different. Dennis found that scholars and scientists (with the exception of mathematicians and chemists) usually have little creative output in their twenties. For most of them, the peak period is between their forties and sixties, and most produce almost as much in their seventies as they did in their earlier years. The peak period for artists tended to be their forties, but they were almost as productive in their sixties and seventies as they were in their twenties. Figure 15.5 depicts these relationships.

Dennis offered an interesting hypothesis to explain the difference in creative productivity between the three groups. The output curve of the arts rises earlier and declines earlier and more severely because productivity in the arts is primarily a matter of individual creativity. Scholars and scientists require a greater period of training and a greater accumulation of data than do others. The use of accumulated data and the possibility of receiving assistance from others causes the scholars and scientists to make more contributions in later years than people in art, music, and literature. Most of the productive persons in Dennis's study were males. It would be interesting to investigate the patterns of productivity among a comparable all-female group.

Studies by Simonton (1975, 1976, 1977a, 1977b) have attempted to resolve the differences between the Lehman and Dennis research. In general, Simonton found evidence that quantity declines with age, which favors Lehman, but that quality does not, which favors Dennis. Unfortunately, because of differences in design and criteria (e.g., differing data sources, differing criteria for inclusion in the studies), it cannot be said that this issue is fully resolved at this time (Simonton, 1993).

We started this section on cognitive development by looking at the measurement of changes in intelligence over the adult years. Then we reviewed what we

📖 A highly respected source on the topic of creativity is *The Journal of Creative Behavior.* Pick up any volume of this fascinating journal at your library and browse through it. A wide variety of interesting topics are covered, and more often than not the articles are written creatively.

Figure 15.5

Graph of Dennis's findings

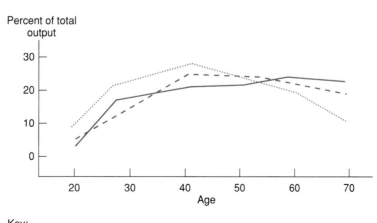

Obstacles and Aids to Creativity

We may agree that creativity is a valuable trait and should be fostered, but how? A number of theorists offered excellent suggestions (see, for example, Sternberg and Davidson, 1995), but educator Ralph Hallman's suggestions (1967) on the obstacles and aids to creativity are still classic. According to him, creativity has several persistent obstacles:

- *Pressures to conform.* The pressure on the individual to follow standardized routines and inflexible rules is probably the major inhibitor. Authoritarian parents, teachers, and managers who demand order are responsible for destroying a great deal of creative talent.
- *Ridicule of unusual ideas.* This destroys one's feelings of worth and makes one defensive and compulsive.
- *An excessive quest for success and the rewards it brings.* An overconcern with material success is often the result of trying to meet the standards and demands of others to obtain the rewards they have to give. In the long run, this distorts one's view of reality and robs one of the strength of character to be creative (Amabile & others, 1986).
- *Intolerance of a playful attitude.* Innovation calls for playing around with ideas, a willingness to fantasize and make believe, and a healthy disrespect for accepted concepts. Creative persons often are seen as childlike and silly and their activity wasteful, but these are only appearances. As Hallman remarks, "Creativity is profound fun."

In addition to recommending that we avoid these obstacles, Hallman urges that we promote the following aids in ourselves and others:

- *Engage in self-initiated learning.* Most people who are in charge of others (managers, teachers, parents) find it hard to encourage others to initiate and direct their own learning. After all, this is certainly not the way most people were taught. They fear that if their subordinates are given greater freedom to explore reality on their own, they will learn wrong things or will not learn the right things in the proper sequence. We must put less emphasis on learning "the right facts," and more on learning how to learn. Even if we do temporarily mislearn a few things, in the long run the practice in experimentation and imagination will be greatly to our benefit.
- *Become deeply knowledgeable about your subject.* Only when people make themselves fully familiar with a particular situation can they detach themselves enough to get an original view of it.
- *Defer judgment.* It is important to make wild guesses, to juggle improbable relationships, to take intellectual risks, to take a chance on appearing ridiculous. Refrain from making judgments too early.
- *Be flexible.* Shift your point of view; to dream up new ideas for things, imagine as many possible solutions to a particular problem as possible.
- *Be self-evaluative.* When a person comes up with a creative idea, he or she is always a minority of one. History is replete with examples of ideas that were rejected for years before people began to realize their worth. Therefore, the creative person must be one who knows his or her own mind and is relatively independent of the judgment of others. To become a good judge of their own thinking, people must practice making many judgments.
- *Ask yourself lots of open-ended questions.* One extensive study showed that 90 percent of the time the average teacher asks questions to which there can be only one right answer, which the teacher already knows. Questions that pique curiosity and allow many possible right answers were asked only 10 percent of the time. Realize that you were probably taught that way, and take steps to rectify the tendency.
- *Learn to cope with frustration and failure.* Thomas Edison tried more than 2,000 combinations of metal before he found just the right kind for the electric element in his first lightbulb.

know about creative development. Now we will consider a third aspect, one that attempts to pull together a variety of intellectual factors.

Learning Ability

Is there a serious drop from early to late adulthood in the ability to learn? Despite some classic studies (e.g., Eisdorfer & Wilkie, 1973; Hulicka, 1967; Knowles, 1989; Taub, 1975), considerable disagreement over this matter still exists.

An Applied View

The Lifelong Learning Resource System

As work environments undergo more and faster changes, there is a growing emphasis on learning how to learn, rather than on mastering a specific skill that may become obsolete. Secondary education or even a college education may no longer suffice for an entire career. Workers require "regular booster shots of education and training" (Abeshouse, 1987, p. 23). We need a system for "lifelong learning." Corporations and policymakers are grappling with the issues of retraining technologically displaced workers, especially older workers (Wallace, 1989).

Knowles (1984) made a marked distinction between teaching aimed at children and youths **(pedagogy)** and the teaching of adults **(androgogy).** Adults differ from younger persons in the following ways:

- *The need to know.* Adults need to know why they need to learn something before undertaking it.
- *The learners' self-concept.* Adults have a self-concept of being responsible for their own decisions, for their own lives.

- *The role of the learners' experience.* Adults come into an educational activity with both a greater volume and a different quality of experience than youths.
- *Readiness to learn.* Adults become ready to learn those things they need to know and be able to do in order to cope effectively with their real-life situations.
- *Orientation to learning.* In contrast to children's and youths' subject-centered orientation to learning (at least in school), adults are life-centered (or task-centered or problem-centered) in their orientation to learning.
- *Motivation.* Although adults are responsive to some external motivators (better jobs, promotions, higher salaries, and the like), the most potent motivators are internal pressures (the desire for increased job satisfaction, self-esteem, quality of life, and the like).

Does the apparent drop in learning ability from early to late adulthood occur strictly because of ability, or because of factors such as motivation and dexterity?

For example, many studies have shown a marked decline in paired associate learning (the ability to remember associations between two lists of words) (Kimmel, 1974). Obviously, memorizing pairs of words is itself of no great importance, but much essential learning is based on this skill. In most of these studies, however, the measure of how well the associations have been learned is speed of response. Do older persons perform poorly because they are slower to learn, or only because they take longer to show what they have learned? As Botwinick (1977) reported:

> The research strategy has been to vary both the amount of time the stimulus is available for study and the amount of time that is available for response. A general finding is that elderly people need more time for responding than typically is provided; they are at a disadvantage when this time is not available. When sufficient time for response is available, the performance of elderly people is only slightly inferior, or not inferior at all, to that of young people. (p. 278)

Another factor in learning ability that has been studied is motivation to learn (Botwinick, 1977). It has been suggested that persons in middle and late adulthood are less motivated to learn than younger people. Further, it appears that often they are aroused and anxious when placed in a laboratory situation for testing their learning ability. To the extent that this is true, their ability to learn is underestimated.

It has also been found in laboratory experiences that older adults are more likely than younger adults to make the "omission error." That is, when they suspect they may be wrong, they are more likely to refrain from responding at all, and therefore are scored as having not learned the task. But when asked what they think the answer is, they are often right.

Also, the meaningfulness of the task affects motivation. It is clear that the motivation for middle-aged and elderly adults is different from that of younger adults, and many experiments have not taken this into consideration in studying learning ability.

Decline in cognitive ability due to aging can often be offset through motivation and new learning experiences. This is shown by the growing number of adults who return to formal education in middle adulthood.

Why are more and more adults going back to school? In the past, children could be educated to deal with a society and workplace that would remain essentially unchanged for their entire lives. Today the rate of change and innovation is too rapid. Fifty-year-old men and women who were born before the computer was being invented, and certainly didn't learn about computers in school as children, are now routinely asked to use them at work. It is now commonplace for people to return to school in order to advance or even maintain their present career. Also, sometimes an adult returns to school in order to learn a new skill or hobby that will be enjoyable during retirement.

Women in particular are going back to school in large numbers. Middle-aged women of today were not encouraged to pursue higher education when they were young. Some women are trying to catch up to be competitive with their male counterparts. Other women may return to school, not to study accounting or computer science, but to study literature or history, just to broaden their knowledge and for their own personal enjoyment. Many need occupational training to support themselves and their families after a divorce.

The education system is having to adapt to this change. Most adults cannot afford to quit their current jobs to go back to school. More schools are now offering evening and part-time programs. Many schools offer courses that can be taken at home, in some cases taking advantage of technology such as TV or computers.

Not all new learning by middle-aged adults takes place in a formal school setting. Employees in many different types of work settings are asked to keep abreast of new innovations. Other social experiences, such as practicing a religion, going to a library, watching television, and serving as a volunteer, involve new learning. Learning is now more than ever a lifelong task.

The beautiful thing about learning is nobody can take it away from you.

Guided Review

10. Despite extensive research on intelligence during adulthood, investigators do not agree on the state of intellectual ability. For instance, Terman's longitudinal study showed an increase in IQ scores with age among his gifted population. Horn's studies, however, show decline in _____ intelligence, with an increase in _____ intelligence.

11. According to Horn, fluid intelligence depends on the proper functioning of the nervous system. Crystallized intelligence indicates the cumulative effects of _____ and _____ of task performance.

12. Memory is closely related to intelligence. Short-term memory (SAR—the ability to hold things in your mind while processing them) _____ with age, whereas long-term memory (TSR—tertiary storage and retrieval dimension) appears to _____ with age.

13. Highly creative people like to do their own planning, are the most _____ when unusual circumstances arise, and can tolerate uncertainty and _____ better than others.

14. Today more adults are going back to school because the rate of change and _____ in our society is so rapid.

Answers

10. fluid, crystallized 11. culture, learning 12. decreases, increase 13. resourceful, ambiguity 14. innovation

Patterns of Work

As the "baby boom" generation enters middle age, many changes are beginning to occur in the workplace. Fewer and fewer new young workers will be available to enter the workforce. Employers will find themselves with a larger number of older workers. This shrinking labor pool is leading many employers to pay more attention than ever to the welfare of their employees. Some of the new issues of the 1990s are child care, elderly care, home-based work, nontraditional work schedules, and the spiraling cost of health-care benefits.

O'Connor and Wolfe (1991) have identified several factors that enable adults to experience personal growth during the mid-life transition that results in positive emotional outlook and enthusiasm for career. Examples of these factors are understanding and changing organization of one's career, ego development, and commitment to learning. Other studies have found that some changes in adults' life structure are best accounted for by a process of shifting one's internal models (Wolfe & others, 1990). An example of this notion is moving from the existing structure of an adult's self and world to a commitment to new choices that help form a new structure.

Employers are also attempting more creative approaches to development and training. In the past, employers have tended to spend the majority of their training and development resources on younger employees. Perhaps this is just a matter of employers being unaware of the problems and concerns of their older employees. Or perhaps money and time invested in younger employees were considered better spent than that on older employees.

But in recent years, a trend has emerged among employers to recognize some of the concerns of middle-aged employees. Among them are the following:

- Awareness of advancing age and awareness of death

- Awareness of body changes related to aging

- Knowing how many career goals have been or will be attained

- Search for new life goals

- Marked change in family relationships

- Change in work relationships

- Sense of skills and abilities becoming outdated

- Feeling of decreased job mobility and increased concern for job security

Businesses have responded to these issues with continuing education, seminars, workshops, degree programs, and other forms of retraining. Employers are beginning to have an increasing appreciation for the contribution of older workers. There is growing recognition that each individual has different career choices, patterns, and promotional opportunities (Sterns & Miklos, 1995). As the labor pool shrinks, the welfare of the older, established workforce becomes more valuable. Another concern is the midcareer crisis.

Special Problems of the Working Woman

It is probably not news to you that the problems facing women in the workplace are different from those of men. But what actual difference does being a woman make? A review of this literature reveals the following four major problem areas.

Sexual Harassment on the Job

Sexual harassment can take many forms (Gelfand & others, 1995), such as verbal sexual suggestions or jokes; leering; "accidentally" brushing against your body; a "friendly" pat, squeeze, or pinch, or arm around you; catching you alone for a quick

On the average, the wife in a family does two to three times as much of the family's work as the husband.

kiss; explicit propositions backed by the threat of losing your job; and forced sexual relations.

Although harassment of professional women has received considerable media attention in recent years (e.g., Justice Thomas's nomination hearings), blue-collar women have even more difficulty with this problem. Many women who work in the trades report that their marriages are strained by their jobs; not only do their husbands not like their nontraditional occupation, but they are unwilling to support them against the sex discrimination and harassment they suffer (Dinnerstein, 1992; Grossman & Chester, 1990).

Most blue-collar women have been verbally harassed (88%), and many have been pinched, fondled, and otherwise physically assaulted (28%). They have little support from their supervisors; in fact, 20 percent of the perpetrators are the supervisors. These women also suffer discrimination: Their competence is questioned, the job requirements are stiffer, they are denied advancement, and necessary job information is withheld. They have little support for their complaints (Schroedel, 1990).

Fiske and Glick (1995) theorized that male sexual harassment in the workplace results from a combination of factors: ambivalent motives on the part of men and male gender stereotyping of women and jobs. Ambivalence refers to both hostile and mild motives, and the complex interaction of these motives with gender stereotyping promotes different types of sexual harassment. Some women do not consider their personal experiences with sexual harassment as a form of sex discrimination (Murrell & others, 1995). However, both sexual harassment and sexual discrimination result in negative work attitudes for women.

Equal Pay and Promotion Criteria

The Equal Pay Act was passed in 1963 and states that men and women in substantially similar jobs in the same company should get the same pay. Under this act, the complainant may remain anonymous while the complaint is being investigated.

In spite of these legal protections, women make less money on the average than men and are less often promoted to management-level jobs. Why? Male prejudice is one reason, no doubt, but there are probably others. Among the several explanations that have been offered (but for which little current research evidence exists) are: Women may be absent more from work due to illness of children and are much more likely to take parenthood leave; many women seem to have greater anxiety about using computers than males; and women take less math in school.

Career and/or Family

The research reported on the dual-career family in Chapter 14 applies here as well.

Travel Safety

Working women are exposed to a considerable number of hazards to which the average housewife and mother is not subjected. Crimes against women are no longer limited to the inner city but now occur in suburban and even rural areas with a high frequency.

These four problems are gradually being recognized in the workplace, and there is hope that they will be alleviated.

The Midcareer Crisis

Considerable attention is now being given to the crisis many people undergo in the middle of their careers. For some it is a problem of increasing anxiety, which is troublesome but no serious problem. For others a **midcareer crisis** is a reality, and it is truly threatening.

A number of changes in the middle years are not caused by work: the awareness of advancing age, the death of parents and other relatives, striking changes in family relationships, and a decrease in physical ability. Other changes are entirely work related.

Coming to Terms with Attainable Career Goals

By the time a person reaches the age of 40 in a professional or managerial career, it is pretty clear whether she or he will make it to the top of the field. If individuals haven't reached their goals by this time, most adjust their level of aspirations and, in some cases, start over in a new career. Many, however, are unable to recognize that they have unrealistic aspirations and thus suffer from considerable stress.

Even people whose career patterns are stable, such as Catholic priests, often have a midcareer letdown. Nor is this crisis restricted to white-collar workers. Many blue-collar workers, realizing that they have gone about as far as they are going to go on their jobs, suffer from depression.

This is also the time when family expenses, such as college education for teenage children, become great. If family income does not rise, this obviously creates a conflict, especially if the husband is the sole provider for the family. If the wife goes back to work, other types of stress often occur. Forthofer and associates (1996) found that marital problems are associated with work loss, specifically financial loss. Based on the average earnings of participants in this study, work loss related to marital problems came to approximately $6.8 billion per year. The authors suggest that family interventions be targeted at the prevention of marital problems to provide both psychosocial and economic benefits to society.

The Change in Work Relationships

Relationships with fellow employees obviously change when one has come to the top of one's career. Some middle-aged adults take a mentoring attitude toward younger employees, but others feel resentful toward the young because they still have a chance to progress. When people reach their forties and fifties, they often try to establish new relationships with fellow workers, and this contributes to the sense of conflict.

A Growing Sense of Outdatedness

In many cases, an individual has to work so hard just to stay in a job that it is impossible to keep up-to-date. Sometimes a younger person, fresh from an extensive education, will join the firm and will know more about modern techniques than the middle-aged person does. These circumstances usually cause feelings of anxiety and resentment in the older employee because he or she is afraid of being considered incompetent.

Inability to Change Jobs

Age discrimination in employment starts as early as age 35 in some industries and becomes pronounced by age 45. A federal law against age discrimination in employment was passed in 1968 to ease the burden on the older worker, but to date the law has been poorly enforced on both the federal and state levels. Many employers get around the law simply by telling older applicants that they are "overqualified" for the available position.

The Generativity Crisis

Erikson suggested that people in the middle years ought to be in the generativity stage. This is a time when they should be producing something of lasting value, making a gift to future generations. In fact, this is definitely a concern for middle-aged workers. The realization that the time left to make such a contribution is limited can come with shocking force. Braverman and Paris (1993) found that at midlife, using work as a defense against dealing with emotional conflicts tends to break down, and problems of childhood can re-emerge as mid-life crises.

The generativity crisis is similar to the identity crisis of late adolescence in many ways. Both often produce psychosomatic symptoms such as indigestion and extreme tiredness. Middle-aged persons often get chest pains at this time. These symptoms are rarely caused by organic diseases in people younger than 50 and usually are due to a depressed state associated with career problems.

The resolution of this crisis, and of other types of crises that occur during early and middle adulthood, depends on how the person's personality has developed during this period. In the following section, we continue our examination of this topic, which began in Chapter 14.

Some Suggestions for Dealing with the Midcareer Crisis

Levinson and others found that a fair number of workers experience a stressful midlife transition. One major way of dealing with it is for the middle-aged worker to help younger employees make significant contributions. Furthermore, companies are taking a greater responsibility for fostering continuing education of their employees. More equitable patterns of responsibilities in the home are also develop-

---

Guided Review

15. A number of concerns face middle-aged employees. These concerns include knowing how many career goals have been or will be reached, changes in family relationships, change in work relationships, feelings of decreased job _____ and concern for job _____.

16. Some middle-aged workers may experience a _____ crisis upon the realization that there may be limited time remaining for them to make contributions for future generations.

17. Some of the problems facing women in the workplace are _____ _____, equal pay, and travel safety.

18. Some women in the workplace experience _____, resulting in a questioning of competence, tougher job requirements, and blocks to career advancement.

Answers

15. mobility, security 16. mid-life 17. sexual harassment 18. discrimination

ing among dual-career middle-aged couples, although there are many exceptions (Coltrane & Ishii-Kuntz, 1992; Dancer & Gilbert, 1993).

We should continue the type of job transfer programs for middle-aged people that we now have for newer employees. Although sometimes the changes can be threatening, the move to a new type of job and the requisite new learning experiences can bring back a zest for work.

Perhaps the federal government should consider starting midcareer clinics. Such clinics could help workers reexamine their goals, consider job changes, and provide information and guidance. Another solution might be the establishment of "portable pension plans" that would move with workers from one company to another so they would not lose all they have built up when they change jobs.

Can you imagine any other remedies?

CONCLUSION

What is true of personality and social development appears to be true, though probably to a lesser extent, of physical and mental development: What you expect is what you get. If you expect

- your weight to go up,
- your muscles to grow flabby and weak,
- your senses to dull,
- your climacteric to be disruptive,
- your intelligence to drop,
- your creativity to plummet, and
- your sexual interest and ability to decline, they probably will.

This is called the self-fulfilling prophecy. People who take a positive outlook, who enthusiastically try to maintain their bodies and minds, have a much better chance at success. They are also better able to deal with the stresses that life naturally imposes on us all. This is not to say that we can completely overcome the effects of aging. It means that through our attitudes, we can learn to deal with them more effectively.

This phenomenon is also seen in the world of work. There are, of course, major changes that occur to most workers as they age, but the disruption of these alterations will usually be more severe if the person is sure they are go-

ing to be. Many workplaces are establishing programs to help their employees deal with these stresses. Of particular concern are the special problems that afflict female but not male workers. In summary:

Physical Development

- Health concerns in middle adulthood include increasing weight and lower metabolism.
- In the middle period of adulthood there is a common but often unnecessary decline in muscular ability, due in part to a decrease in exercise.
- Sensory abilities—vision, hearing, smell, and taste—begin to show slight declines in middle adulthood.
- The climacterium, the loss of reproductive ability, occurs at menopause for women but at much older ages for most men.

Cognitive Development

- Horn suggests that although fluid intelligence deteriorates with age, crystallized intelligence does not.
- Baltes has proposed a dual-process model of intelligence, which suggests a decline in the mechanics

of intelligence (classification skills, logical reasoning), yet an increase in the pragmatics of intelligence (social wisdom).

- Creativity, important in a rapidly changing world, manifests itself at different peak periods throughout adulthood.
- Learning in middle adulthood can be enhanced through motivation, new learning experiences, and changes in education systems.

Patterns of Work

- In recent years, a trend has emerged among employers to recognize some of the concerns of middle-aged employees.
- Four major problem areas are related to working women: sexual harassment on the job, equal pay and promotion criteria, career and/or family, and travel safety.
- Considerable attention is now being given to the crisis many people undergo in the middle of their careers.
- One major way of dealing with the mid-life crisis is for the middle-aged worker to help younger employees make significant contributions.

KEY TERMS

Androgogy
Basal metabolism rate (BMR)
Climacteric
Climacterium
Crystallized intelligence
Dual-process model

Estrogen replacement therapy (ERT)
Fluid intelligence
Glaucoma
Male change of life
Menopause
Midcareer crisis

Olfactory sense
Pedagogy
Self-fulfilling prophecy
Senile macular degeneration

WHAT DO YOU THINK?

1. When you look at the physical shape your parents and grandparents are in, and their attitudes toward the subject, do you see evidence of the self-fulfilling prophecy?

2. If you are a female and have not yet gone through menopause, what do you anticipate your feelings will be about it?

3. If you are a male, can you imagine what women facing menopause must be feeling?

4. What are some ways that our society might foster the creative abilities of its adult citizens?

5. What are some ways that our society might foster the learning of its adult citizens?

6. What remedies can you think of for the midcareer crisis?

CHAPTER REVIEW TEST

1. **Basal metabolism rate refers to**
   a. the minimum amount of energy an individual tends to use after exercising.
   b. the minimum amount of energy an individual tends to use when in a resting state.
   c. the maximum amount of energy an individual tends to use after exercising.
   d. the maximum amount of energy an individual tends to use when in a resting state.

2. **For persons over age 50, even one or two drinks each day can be dangerous, because they can cause**
   a. permanent liver damage.
   b. irreversible kidney damage.
   c. clogged arteries.
   d. enlargement of the left ventricle of the heart.

3. **During middle adulthood, how does one's vision change?**
   a. the lens becomes more elastic
   b. the cornea decreases in curvature and thickness
   c. the iris responds less well to light
   d. the ability to focus on nearby objects increases

4. **Due to physical changes in middle adulthood, our vision can be affected in what ways?**
   a. eyes do not adapt to sudden intense light or darkness as effectively
   b. detection of certain colors can be more difficult
   c. there is a heightened risk of eye diseases
   d. all of the answers are correct

5. **During middle adulthood, how does hearing ability change?**
   a. Higher frequencies need to be louder to be heard.
   b. Lower frequencies need to be louder to be heard.
   c. The ability to hear human speech remains constant.
   d. The ability to listen to speech in a crowded environment declines, while the ability to listen to someone alone without background noise increases.

6. **Estrogen replacement therapy has offered relief for women who experience serious problems with**
   a. mid-life crises.
   b. menopause.
   c. weight loss.
   d. fertility.

7. **What type of intelligence deteriorates with age, to some extent?**
   a. Learned
   b. Natural
   c. Crystallized
   d. Fluid

8. **What is an example of crystallized intelligence?**
   a. Arithmetical reasoning
   b. Letter grouping
   c. Recalling paired associates
   d. Dominoes

9. **People who like to do their own planning, make their own decisions, are flexible, and are able to stand their ground in the face of criticism demonstrate traits of a**
   a. highly creative person.
   b. career-oriented person.
   c. person with strong cognitive abilities.
   d. person who has successfully individuated him/herself from significant others.

10. **An aid to creativity is**
    a. self-initiated learning.
    b. deferring judgment and being flexible.
    c. self-evaluation.
    d. All of the answers are correct.

11. **While being tested on paired associate learning tasks the group most at a disadvantage if the amount of time available for response is not sufficient is the**
    a. group in early adulthood.
    b. group in middle adulthood.
    c. group in late adulthood.
    d. All groups would be at a disadvantage.

12. **Groups of middle-aged and elderly subjects are tested on their ability to remember associations between two lists of words. How are they most likely to respond when they suspect they may be wrong?**
    a. Take an educated guess
    b. Refrain from responding
    c. Confer with other group members
    d. State that they do not know the answer

13. **Research indicates that adults need to know why they need to learn something before undertaking it, that they have a self-concept of being responsible for their own decisions, and that they are life-centered in their orientation to learning. These findings highlight the difference between children and adults in**
    a. cognitive abilities.
    b. level of individuation.
    c. self-fulfillment.
    d. the learning process.

14. A factor in learning ability during middle adulthood is motivation to learn. It is important for researchers to keep in mind that _____ affects an adult's level of motivation.
    a. level of education
    b. meaningfulness of the task
    c. interest
    d. external distractions

15. Consequences of discrimination against women in the workplace include
    a. stiffer job requirements.
    b. inability to advance in their career.
    c. questioning of a woman's competence.
    d. All of the answers are correct.

16. When an accountant 20 years younger than Dan joined his marketing firm, Dan felt resentful and anxious because he feared he would be considered incompetent. Dan has a growing sense of
    a. job distress.
    b. outdatedness.
    c. the "gold watch" syndrome.
    d. job reluctance.

Answers

1.b 2.d 3.c 4.d 5.a 6.b 7.d 8.a 9.a 10.d 11.c 12.b 13.d 14.b 15.d 16.b

Recently, a middle-aged woman friend shared some reflections with me:
I remember walking to school one day in the second grade, chatting with my girlfriend's mother as she escorted us. I told her that I had noticed how much more quickly the day seemed to pass than it used to. Seven seemed a very advanced age to me then, so I was sure this phenomenon was related to being finally grown-up. Later that year we moved into a new house in a new community. Moving day was very exciting. The real grown-ups were very busy, so the most entertaining thing I had to do was to sit around and think about my life. Moving seemed to have wrapped up the first part of my life into a discrete little package. And it came to me that there I was, almost 8 years old, and I didn't have a feeling for all that time. I promised myself, as I sat in our old, soft maroon chair, holding some of my accumulated possessions dislocated by their recent journey, that five years later to the day I would sit again in the same spot, in the same position, holding the same objects. Then, I figured, with all the awareness born of old age, I would really know what five years would feel like. And five years later I did just that.

I am still trying to comprehend or capture a sense of time passing. Now only the units have changed. Every once in a while I hold very still and try to catch 20 years. Twenty years feel like those five did long ago. Twenty from now, if I'm lucky, I'll be staring my death in the face. It's all so odd. Somewhere inside I was all grown-up when I was 7. That "me" hasn't really aged or changed much, and it's still watching as the world wrinkles on the outside. Days are minutes, months are weeks, and years are months. I'll probably be menopausal in the morning!

Quoted by Lila Kalinich ✹

When you finish reading this chapter, you should be able to

- Define stress and identify common sources of stress.

- Describe the relationship between stress, physical illness, and mental health.

- List the three stages of Selye's general adaptation syndrome.

- Explain the relationship between risk and resiliency.

- Explain what is meant by "emotional divorce" and the "empty nest syndrome."

- List some components of a happy marriage.

- Discover how relationships with parents and siblings change in middle adulthood.

- Discuss the positive and negative effects of divorce on middle-aged adults and their families.

- Determine your position on whether personality development is continuous or changing.

- List Levinson's three major developmental tasks for middle-aged men, along with the four polarities men must confront.

The Chinese . . . are reported to
have a way of writing the word
"crisis" by two characters, one of
which signifies danger, and the
other opportunity.
Louis Wirth

- Describe the differences between Levinson's research with men and his more recent research with women.

- Define the NEO model of personality.

Dealing with the Stresses of Adulthood

We have included this section in the middle adult part of our book because the stresses of adulthood are different in one important way: More and more, adults are expected to deal with stress entirely on their own. True, we adults can and should expect help from others, but an increasing number of crises call for independent decisions and actions. For example, many more families today exist in a state of on-going, unending crisis. These families often have only one parent, who is unable to work and therefore is below the poverty level, and who has one or more handicapped or highly disruptive children (Smith, 1990).

As should be clear by now, stress has many sources, regardless of your age. Mainly, stress is due to change. It is the nature of human development to produce inexorable change in every aspect of our existence. This situation is difficult enough when we are young, but at least then we have the support of parents, teachers, and other adults, as well as a more resilient body. More stress does seem to occur as we get older. As we move from early to late adulthood, we must rely more and more on knowledge and insight to avoid having a stressful life.

The General Adaptation Syndrome

In 1936 Hans Selye (the father of stress research) was studying a little-known ovarian hormone, which led to the discovery of the **general adaptation syndrome** (Selye, 1956, 1975). In one of the experiments, hormones from cattle ovaries were injected into rats to see what changes would occur. Selye was surprised to find that the rats had a broad range of reactions:

- The cortex became enlarged and hyperactive.

- A number of glands shrank.

- Deep bleeding ulcers occurred in both the stomach and upper intestines.

Further experiments showed that these reactions occurred in response to all toxic substances, regardless of their source. Later experiments also showed them occurring, although to a lesser degree, in response to a wide range of noxious stimuli, such as infections, hemorrhage, and nervous irritation.

Selye called the entire syndrome an **alarm reaction.** He referred to it as a generalized "call to arms" of the body's defensive forces. Seeking to gain a fuller understanding of the syndrome, he wondered how the reaction would be affected if stress were present for a longer period of time. He found that a rather amazing thing happens. If the organism survives the initial alarm, it enters a **stage of resistance.** In this second stage, an almost complete reversal of the alarm reaction occurs. Swelling and shrinkages are reversed; the adrenal cortex, which lost its secretions during the alarm stage, becomes unusually rich in these secretions; and a number of other shock-resisting forces are marshalled. During this stage, the organism appears to gain strength and to have adapted successfully to the stressor.

However, if the stressor continues, a gradual depletion of the organism's adaptational energy occurs (Selye, 1982). Eventually this leads to a **stage of exhaustion.** Now the physiological responses revert to their condition during the stage of alarm. The ability to handle the stress decreases, the level of resistance is lost, and the organism dies. Figure 16.1 portrays these three stages. Table 16.1 lists the physical and psychological manifestations of the three stages.

As you grow older, your ability to remain in the resistance stage decreases. Activity over the years gradually wears out your "machine," and the chances of sus-

Figure 16.1

The general adaptation syndrome

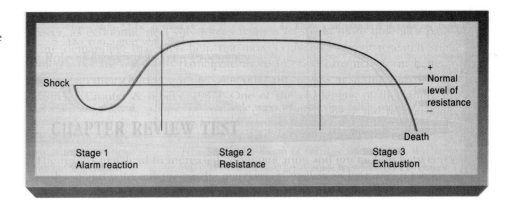

taining life are reduced. As we will discuss in Chapter 17, no one dies of old age. Rather, they succumb to some stressor because their ability to resist it has become weakened through aging.

Selye compared his general adaptation stages with the three major stages of life. Childhood, he said, is characteristic of the alarm stage: Children respond excessively to any kind of stimulus and have not yet learned the basic ways to resist shock. In early adulthood, a great deal of learning has occurred, and the organism knows better how to handle the difficulties of life. In middle and old age, however, adaptability is gradually lost, and eventually the adaptation syndrome is exhausted, leading ultimately to death.

Selye suggested that all resistance to stress inevitably causes irreversible chemical scars that build up in the system. These scars are signs of aging. Thus, he said, the old adage that you shouldn't "burn the candle at both ends" is supported by the body's biology and chemistry. Selye's work with the general adaptation syndrome has also helped us to discover the relationship between disease and stress.

TABLE 16.1   SELYE'S STRESS ADAPTATION SYNDROME

Stage	Function	Physical Manifestations	Psychological Manifestations
Stage I: Alarm reaction	Mobilization of the body defensive forces.	Marked loss of body weight. Increase in hormone levels. Enlargement of the adrenal cortex and lymph glands.	Person is alerted to stress. Level of anxiety increases. Task-oriented and defense-oriented behavior. Symptoms of maladjustment, such as anxiety and inefficient behavior may appear.
Stage II: Stage of resistance	Optimal adaptation to stress	Weight returns to normal. Lymph glands return to normal size. Reduction in size of adrenal cortex. Constant hormonal levels.	Intensified use of coping mechanisms. Person tends to use habitual defenses rather than problem-solving behavior. Psychosomatic symptoms may appear.
Stage III: Stage of exhaustion	Body resources are depleted and organism loses ability to resist stress.	Weight loss. Enlargement and depletion of adrenal glands. Enlargement of lymph glands and dysfunction of lymphatic system. Increase in hormone levels and subsequent hormonal depletion. If excessive stress continues, person may die.	Personality disorganization and a tendency toward exaggerated and inappropriate use of defense mechanisms. Increased disorganization of thoughts and perceptions. Person may lose contact with reality, and delusions and hallucinations may appear. Further exposure to stress may result in complete psychological disintegration (involving violence or stupor).

Source: Adapted from *Adult Health Nursing* by Carol Ren Kneisl and SueAnn Wooster Ames. Addison-Wesley, Menlo Park, Calif., 1986.

Dave Mack, an urban worker in Chicago, observes that a variety of differences exist among Asian people living in America, and these differences can cause intense stress (cited in Borgman, 1986). Referring to someone as an "Asian" may be misleading. The Chinese are proud of their vast history and the cultures it has spawned. Koreans also possess a rich, though separate, history. Filipinos, Burmese, and Vietnamese, though possibly educated in Chinese schools, nevertheless associate with some Asians while dissociating with others. For instance, among Southeast Asian people, a great deal of animosity exists between Cambodians and the Hmong.

These attitudes of cultural pride provoke endless problems, especially in our large cities. Mack tells of a group of Vietnamese waiting for a bus in the rain after a basketball game. They got on the bus when it arrived, just as some Chinese people appeared at the bus stop. Since another bus was not immediately available to transport everyone, the Vietnamese bus driver ordered his riders off of the bus and into the rain so that the Chinese people could get onto the bus first.

Assimilation into urban American culture, itself a smorgasbord of ethnicities all within a few square miles, often proves immensely stressful for all involved. The tension also involves how far one should go in regard to becoming "American." Is there such a thing as an "ethnic American"? Should people who immigrate into America be expected to set aside cultural conflicts for the sake of their new home? Given the stress that is bound to result from such an acclimation, is it worth the cost? Is it harder if you are middle aged or older than it would be for younger people?

Risk and Resilience

Individuals who deal well with stress and who have few psychological, behavioral, or learning problems as a result of it are said to have **resilience** (see Chapter 10). In recent years, researchers have become interested in studying the characteristics of resilient individuals. The stressors that individuals experience are called **risk factors.** Risk factors include poverty, chronic illness, parental mental illness and drug abuse, exposure to violence through war or some of the tragedies in the inner cities, and the family experiences of divorce and teenage motherhood. Researchers have been interested in identifying **protective factors** (characteristics of resilient individuals that protect them from stress). Three kinds of protective factors have been found so far: family environments, support networks, and personality characteristics (Hauser & Bowlds, 1990).

Prevention

Psychologists have been enthusiastic about identifying risk and protective factors in the hope that this knowledge will contribute to the prevention of psychological difficulties. Successful prevention programs reduce the occurrence of maladjustment and clinical dysfunction by reducing risk factors (when possible) and enhancing protective factors and effective coping strategies. Primary prevention programs try to eliminate problems before they begin. Secondary prevention programs intervene during the early stages of a problem to reduce its severity or the length of time it will last.

Prevention programs vary in whether they are directed toward all children and adolescents in a particular school or city, or whether only students identified to be at particular risk are invited. Among adolescents, prevention programs are most often delivered in the schools or in a community agency. School-based programs have been effective in building social skills and reducing at-risk behaviors. Effective programs have been developed for reducing the onset, use, and abuse of cigarettes, marijuana, and alcohol, reducing teen pregnancy, curbing dropout rates, improving academic performance, and reducing delinquent behavior (Kazdin, 1993). Accord-

A relevant source on dealing with stress is: Benson, H. & Proctor, W. (1985). *Beyond the relaxation response.* New York: Berkeley. A stress reduction program that has helped millions of people live healthier lives. It includes Benson's concept of the "faith factor."

Another good book on this subject is Csikszentmihalyi, M. (1990). *Flow.* New York: Harper & Row. "This book summarizes, for a general audience, decades of research on the positive aspects of human experience." A fine example of optimal reaction to stress.

ing to research by the Carnegie Council on Adolescent Development (1995), families, schools, and community organizations must work together to reduce risks, enhance protective factors, and promote healthy adolescent development.

Unfortunately, prevention programs are still limited and are not able to prevent the occurrence of mental disturbance. Psychotherapy, psychiatric hospitalization, and medications are needed to improve dysfunction for those individuals already suffering from mental disturbance.

Guided Review

1. Hans Selye outlined three stages of a general adaptation syndrome. These include: alarm reaction; a stage of _____, and a stage of exhaustion.
2. Each of Selye's stages can be understood in terms of its _____, physical manifestations, and _____ manifestations.
3. The stressors that people feel are called risk factors, whereas the characteristics that increase resilience are called _____ factors.
4. _____ prevention programs try to eliminate problems before they begin.

Marriage and Family Relations

In this section, we consider four important aspects of middle-aged life today: relationships in marriage, relationships with aging parents, relationships with brothers and sisters, and divorce. Although not all would agree, we define this part of life as going from 35 to 64 years of age.

Marriage at Middle Age

Middle age is often a time when husbands and wives reappraise their marriage. The **midlife transition** (a period during which people seriously reevaluate their lives up to that time) often causes a person to simultaneously examine current relationships and consider changes for the future. Often, whatever tension that exists in a marriage is suppressed while the children still live at home. As they leave to go off to college or to start families of their own, these tensions are openly expressed.

Sometimes couples learn to "withstand" each other rather than live with each other. The only activities and interests they share are ones that revolved around the children. When the children leave, they are forced to recognize how far apart they have drifted. In effect, they engage in **emotional divorce.** Often, the experience of divorce can be thought of as a cluster of small divorces (Steefel, 1992).

But most couples whose marriages have lasted this long have built the type of relationship that can withstand reappraisal, and they continue for the rest of their lives. U.S. Census data (1996) suggest that the highest rates for separation and divorce occur about five years after the beginning of the marriage. The period after the children leave home is like a second honeymoon for many. After the initial period of negative emotions that follow this disruption of the family, often called the **empty nest syndrome,** married couples can evaluate the job they have done with their children. They can pat themselves on the back for a job well done and then relax now that a major life goal has been accomplished. They then realize that they have more freedom and privacy and fewer worries. They usually have more money to spend on themselves. And this period after the children leave home is now much

The period in a marriage after which there is no longer a need to care for children is often a time for pursuing dreams that were previously impractical.

Answers

longer than it used to be. Husbands and wives now can look forward to spending 20 or 30 years together as a couple rather than as a large family.

An Applied View

Marriage Therapy in Middle Adulthood

Iwanir and Ayal (1991) suggest that the midlife phase in the marital relationship is a complicated transition period, one that challenges the flexibility and coping skills of every couple. If a couple finds their marriage to be in trouble (the authors call this "Separation/Divorce Initiation"— S/DI), they recommend a three-step process to help. The steps include: (1) assessment of the relationship's stamina and the function of the S/DI; (2) treating symptoms and reactions to the traumatic event in an 'emergency intervention' mode; (3) steps and techniques to help the couple overcome the traumatic effects of the S/DI and to rebuild their relationship on a more appropriate basis. (p. 609)

Three wonderful descriptions of middle-aged marriage are: (1) Breslin's Table money. *New York: Ticknor & Fields. An empathetic tale of matrimony, alcoholism, and the struggle to attain maturity, focusing on a poor middle-aged Irish American couple. (2) Guest's* Ordinary people. *New York: Ballantine. The evocative story of the relationships among a middle-aged couple, their teenage son, and his psychiatrist. (3) Hansberry's* A raisin in the sun. *This moving drama portrays the inner lives of an African-American family.*

The Happy Marriage

What does research have to say about the components of a happy, or at least a lasting, marriage? Gottman and Krokoff (1989) conducted a longitudinal study looking at the types of interactions between husband and wife and the effect on marital satisfaction. Earlier research suggested that there was always more negative interaction in unhappy marriages than in happy marriages. An exception to this appears to be the marriages of Chinese people. Shek (1995 a & b) found that although Chinese men feel happier in their marriages the longer they last, the opposite was true for the women in this large study of 1,500 subjects.

Gottman and Krokoff decided to look at the effect of different types of negative interactions rather than one global category. They found that certain types of conflict may in fact be positive factors in a happy, lasting marriage. They also found that certain types of conflict, particularly defensiveness, stubbornness, and withdrawal on the part of the husband, indicated that a marriage was in trouble.

Gottman and Krokoff assigned to the wife the role of manager of marital disagreements and suggested that she get her husband to "confront areas of disagreement and to openly vent disagreement and anger" (p. 50). Most husbands tend to try to avoid relational confrontations (Moyers & Bly, 1990). Therefore, overcoming this reluctance can have extremely beneficial long-term effects on the marriage.

The Unmarried Individual

About 1 in 20 people in middle age have never been married (U. S. Census, 1996). In general, a person who has never married by middle age will not get married. Such people tend either to have very low or very high education levels. At the low extreme, of those who have less than five years of school, one person in seven has never married. The factors that kept these people from completing school, such as mental illness or other handicaps, are probably the same ones that make them less likely to get married. At the other extreme, 13 percent of middle-aged women with 17 or more years of education have never been married.

A number of possible explanations could account for this. These women may choose higher education and a career over marriage. They may believe marriage will hold them back. A cultural factor may be at work, because some men feel threatened by women with more education than they have. Perhaps women who delay marriage to pursue an education end up having a smaller pool of available men to choose from, because men die, on the average, at an earlier age. Finally, the number of persons who live together without marrying is rapidly increasing (see Figure 16.2).

Figure 16.2

The number of unmarried couples in the U. S. is climbing rapidly.

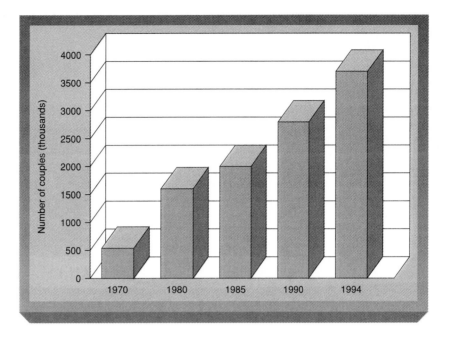

Relationships with Aging Parents

Middle age is also a time when most people develop improved relationships with their parents. Middle-aged children, most of them parents themselves, gain a new perspective on parenthood and so reevaluate the actions taken by their own parent. Also, grandchildren can strengthen bonds that may have weakened when people left their parents' home during early adulthood.

In many cases, however, the relationship begins to reverse itself: As elderly parents grow older, they sometimes become as dependent on their middle-aged children as those children once were on them. Most people fail to anticipate the costs and emotional strains that the aging of their parents can precipitate. This can lead ultimately to new sources of tension and rancor in the relationship. Often, early family experiences may have a positive or negative affect on the later relationship between adult children and their aging parents (Whitbeck & others, 1994). For example, young children who have close relationships with their parents, and whose parents provided consistent, frequent care, will have more positive later relationships.

The most frequently cited problem of middle-adult women is not menopause

Relationships and roles among the generations are always changing.

Sibling Relationships in Industrial and Nonindustrial Societies

In industrial societies, close relationships among siblings tend to be optional, based on the siblings' desires to be friendly toward one another or not. In nonindustrial societies, sibling relationships are based on the constraints that cultural norms impose. Such norms demand that siblings should behave in certain ways toward each other. These differences, in large part, are due to differences in economic structure.

Nonindustrial societies tend to be agrarian, village-centered, and relatively poor. Because resources are limited in such societies, sibling cooperation is necessary to accomplish tasks, to maintain family functioning, and to attain economic goals. In these societies, a greater number of siblings exists and they are expected to fulfill certain responsibilities. Siblings share caretaking and act as educational and socializing agents for each other's children. Parents usually have this role in industrial societies. In these societies, sibling relationships are secondary to spouse-spouse and parent-child relationships.

In nonindustrial societies, sister-brother and brother-brother relationships are closest, whereas sister-sister relationships are closest in industrial societies. Control mechanisms exist in nonindustrial societies to deal with tension and conflicts, such as an emphasis on the authority of older children over younger siblings.

or aging, but caring for their aging parents and parents-in-law (James, 1990). This is not so surprising when we realize that it is virtually always the daughter(s) in the family who is responsible for the care of the elderly parents (Kendig & others, 1992). Green (1991) found that the daughter who is the primary caretaker relies on siblings, especially her sisters if she has them, for emotional support. These sisters typically feel guilty about not doing enough. On the average, brothers provide less help and feel less guilty about it. Recent findings have maintained the idea that social support is of foremost importance to daughters who are the primary caregivers for aging parents (Pohl & others, 1994). By social support the authors mean emotional, financial, or other support offered by friends and family. Daughters may feel more positive about caregiving when they have secure income, health, marital status, and educational level. It seems that the demands on women to fulfill the role of family nurturer are deeply rooted and powerful. Of course, as more women enter the workplace, and as more of them become assertive about equitable family responsibilities, this pattern may well change, with males assuming more of the burden.

Caserta & others (1996) examined caring for elderly parents or in-laws, and have proposed a multidimensional view of this burden. The authors determined several aspects of the caregiving task, such as the emotional strain, the time constraints involved (e.g., amount of time elderly relatives depend on one's care), and physical health of the caregiver. The well-being of the caregiver, therefore, is important to the person receiving the care. Because the burden of caregiving is not easily measured, each of the various dimensions should be considered as having a possible effect on the relationship.

We will deal here with two other features of family life in middle adulthood: relationships with siblings and the problems of divorce.

Relationships with Siblings

Developmental psychology has, for some time now, recognized the importance of sibling relationships for a child's cognitive and social growth. But do these special relationships stop contributing to a person's development after adolescence? Does the relationship slowly decline in importance as one ages? Are the characteristics of the relationship the same in middle adulthood as they were in childhood? Psychological research has recently begun to focus on some of these questions.

Sibling relationships have the potential to be the most enduring that a person can have. You don't usually meet your spouse until young adulthood or at least adolescence. Your parents usually pass away before you do. You usually pass away before your children do. But most siblings are born within a few years of each other, and such a relationship can last 60, 80, or even 100 years!

One would hope that a growing maturity would lessen rivalry. Certainly adult siblings are faced with more serious and important tasks than are childhood siblings. For example, most middle-aged siblings must make mutual decisions concerning the care of their elderly parents and eventually deal with the aftermath of their death.

Another consideration is the effect of changing family patterns on sibling relationships. Couples now are having fewer or even no children. Children will therefore be less available to parents for companionship and psychological support. On the other hand, parents and their siblings will be living longer, more active lives. The obvious conclusion is that sibling relationships will become more and more important in the future.

Friendships

Middle age is a time when friendships become fewer and more precious. Actually, the findings of Carstensen (1992) suggest that individuals begin narrowing their range of social partners long before middle age. The most dramatic decline occurs between the ages of 18 and 30. In early adulthood, interaction frequency with acquaintances and close friends begins to decline while at the same time it increases with spouses and siblings. It would seem that at about age 30, individuals choose a select few relationships with which to derive support, self-definition, and a sense of stability. Emotional closeness, however, increases throughout adulthood in relationships with relatives and close friends. These relationships with a select few, then, become increasingly close and satisfying during the middle adult years. Further, the idea that face-to-face contact is necessary for closeness cannot be supported. In fact, many parents report feeling closest to their adult children when they see them the least.

The Middle-Aged Divorced Person

Because divorce rates have been increasing for those over 40, mid-life divorce will become an important focus in the future (Uhlenberg & others, 1990). The divorce rates are higher for second or subsequent marriages, for African Americans, and for those who are less educated and who have lower earning ability. Mid-life is a time when a divorce is less likely to occur—most divorces take place during the first five years of marriage and the number tapers off rapidly after that (see Figure 16.3). Nevertheless, the proportion of divorced persons in mid-life is relatively high, because many who divorced earlier have never remarried. Men and women over 40 experience significantly more turmoil and unhappiness than younger people at the same stage of divorce (Chiriboga, 1989). The reasons are clear: length of time of marriage, complex economic and property linkages, a web of social relationships, and a generally higher standard of living.

In respect to the last point, it should be noted that women, especially at mid-life, are often hard hit economically by divorce. The National Longitudinal Survey found they experience significant declines in income, increased rates of poverty, and dramatic lifestyle changes upon separation, divorce, or widowhood; they do not recover unless they remarry (Hoffman & Duncan, 1988). Furthermore, because most women who divorce at mid-life are already working, they have little room to maneuver for more income after divorce. This is especially true for African American women, because the only notable increase in workforce participation after divorce is for white women (Morgan, 1991).

More and more children are living in homes without fathers. More than half of

Figure 16.3

This chart of divorces in the United States shows that most divorces occur within the first five years of marriage, with the peak at three years. Interestingly, the same pattern is found in most other societies, ranging from contemporary Sweden to the hunting and gathering groups of southwest Africa.

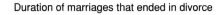

Duration of marriages that ended in divorce

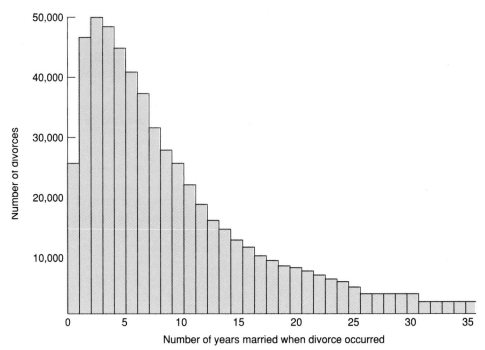

single-parent mothers are not receiving full child support, and half of those are not receiving any. Whereas 68 percent of white women were awarded child support, only 35 percent of African American women and 41 percent of Latina women received such awards (Crohan & others, 1989). Until recently, child support was awarded mainly because of the mother's limited income. Now, most states use a specific formula that relates child support to both parents' incomes. This requires both parents to provide adequate financial support regardless of with which parent the child actually lives (Cancian & Meyer, 1996).

A discomforting finding of White (1992) is that children of divorce, even after they have left home and their parents enter middle age, receive significantly less support (child care, advice, transportation, loans, and so forth) than do children whose parents have remained married. Remarriage does not seem to increase or decrease this support deficit.

In general, new divorce laws were considered to have a liberating effect on women. Until the liberalization of divorce laws and attitudes, women usually had no choice but to endure a difficult and sometimes even abusive marriage. Cultural norms allowed men much more moral latitude, the so-called double standard. Women basically just had to put up with it.

Before liberalization, it was necessary to establish "reasonable grounds" for divorce, such as adultery or physical abuse. Women who were granted divorces were almost always awarded larger alimony settlements than they receive today, to make up for the loss of income. This was necessary because women lagged far behind men in their earning potential, and often women stayed at home to raise the children and run the household while the husband advanced a career. A woman could not survive a divorce if it left her and her family destitute.

In 1970 the divorce laws were liberalized in California, a change soon followed across the country. This was the introduction of a **no-fault divorce.** A major facet of the new laws was supposed to be their gender neutrality. Men and women are treated equally under the divorce law, and this includes the division of property and alimony. But perhaps these laws were premature. Men and women did not in 1970, and still do not today, live in an economically equitable system. Men still possess a competitive advantage in earning potential, and the culture still holds women responsible for raising the children and running the household. When a divorce judge divides up the property equally, grants little or no alimony, and provides inadequate child support, it is the woman and children who suffer.

This is particularly true of the middle-aged homemaker. The courts seldom give much recognition to the years spent running the household while the husband invested time in advancing a career. Such a woman cannot reasonably be expected to compete with others who have been gaining experience in the marketplace while she stayed at home.

Another effect is that no-fault divorce laws mandate an even division of property. This often means that the family house must be sold. Before these laws, the house was almost always given to the woman and her children. Besides being an economic burden, the loss of the house has psychological consequences for the development of the children. The dislocation often requires that the children leave their school, neighborhood, and friends. And this usually comes just after the divorce, a period of tremendous stress for any child.

Some indications show that reform is on the way. In California the rules for division of property and spousal support are being revised. More things are now being considered family assets, to be divided equally, such as the major wage earner's salary, pension, medical insurance, and future earning power. In addition, some states have now become aggressive at pursuing husbands who are delinquent on child support payments. Their names are being published and a part of their wages is being withheld and given to the ex-wife. Massachusetts is even considering paying spouses the money lost through delinquent payments and reimbursing itself through taxes and garnishments of the other spouse.

Divorce will probably never be the "civilized" process that the early proponents of no-fault divorce laws hoped it would become. At best, we can expect the suffering of spouses to become more equal, and the suffering of the children to be reduced.

Marriage and family life are closely related to two other factors that play an important role in middle age: sex and love.

Guided Review

5. During middle age, marriage is sometimes affected by emotional _____ (which means drifting apart while still married).
6. After the initial period of negative emotions that follow after the children leave home, called the "_____ _____ syndrome," couples can evaluate the job they have done in raising their family.
7. Certain types of conflict in a marriage can be positive and are particularly beneficial if the _____ is willing to confront areas of disagreement.
8. It is unlikely that a middle-aged person who has never married will marry. Such people tend to have either very high or very low levels of _____.
9. One of the most challenging problems facing middle-adult women is that their parents or parents-in-law are now _____ on them.
10. New divorce laws were considered to have a _____ effect on women. These laws, however, have had the result of impoverishing many women.

Sex and Love in Middle Adulthood

At mid-life, minor physiological changes occur in both male and female sexual systems. For the male, there may be lower levels of testosterone, fewer viable sperm, a decrease in sex steroids affecting muscle tone and the cardiovascular system,

Answers

5. divorce 6. empty nest 7. husband 8. education 9. dependent 10. liberating

slight changes in the testes and prostate gland, and a change in the viscosity and volume of ejaculate (Hunter & Sundel, 1989). There is usually a need to spend more time and to give more direct stimulation to the penis to attain erection. None of these changes is sufficient to alter significantly the man's interest and pleasure in a sexual and sensual life.

For the female, the reduction in estrogen occurring during and after menopause may cause changes, such as less vaginal lubrication and possible vaginal irritation at penetration, that can eventually affect the ease and comfort of sexual intercourse. Sexual arousal may be somewhat slower after the fifth decade, but orgasmic response is not impaired. As with the males, females may need more time and appropriate stimulation for vaginal lubrication and orgasmic responsivity. Some studies have found a reduction of female interest and desire, whereas others have found a decrease in frequency of intercourse (Cutler & others, 1987). Bretschneider and McCoy (1988) argued that low estrogen levels are associated with decreased sexual interest in women. Hysterectomies can catapult a woman into premature menopause and can cause her to experience postoperative sexual problems that may require estrogen replacement therapy (Leiblum, 1990).

A study of lesbian women at menopause (Cole & Rothblum, 1990) found very few sexual problems. The 10 percent who did list one or more symptoms qualified their responses to say there were differences, not problems. Masters and associates (1986) found that lesbians make smooth transitions into the middle years, usually in lasting relationships.

As you can see, by the time people reach middle adulthood, sexual preferences are clearly a very individual matter. Some couples engage in sexuality a lot right into their old age, and some have a fine marriage without making love very much at all.

A report on frequency of sexual activity among the adults of all ages, the Janus Report, gives a picture that weakens the stereotype that as we grow older, we become more inactive sexually. As Table 16.2 illustrates, there is a small increase in sexual activity in the middle years, as compared with early adulthood. For men, middle age is a time when opportunity, if not desire, is at a peak. For women, age makes little difference across the adult lifespan. These findings are supported by Deacon and associates (1995), who found that the physical and pathological changes associated with advancing age do not necessarily reduce the opportunity to enjoy sex.

Many couples find that when they reach middle age, their relationship becomes more romantic.

TABLE 16.2 FREQUENCY OF SEXUAL INTERCOURSE BY AGE

| | Ages (Years) | | | | | | | | | |
| | 18 to 26 | | 27 to 38 | | 39 to 50 | | 51 to 64 | | 65+ | |
	M	F	M	F	M	F	M	F	M	F
N =	254	268	353	380	282	295	227	230	212	221
a. Daily	15%	13%	16%	8%	15%	10%	12%	4%	14%	1%
b. A few times weekly	38	33	44	41	39	29	51	28	39	40
c. Weekly	19	22	23	27	29	29	18	33	16	33
d. Monthly	15	15	8	12	9	11	11	8	20	4
e. Rarely	13	17	9	12	8	21	8	27	11	22
Active = lines a + b	53%	46%	60%	49%	54%	39%	63%	32%	53%	41%
At Least Weekly = lines a through c	72%	68%	83%	76%	83%	68%	81%	65%	69%	74%

From S. Janus and C. Janus, *The Janus Report on Sexual Behavior.* Copyright ©1993 Wiley & Sons, New York. Reprinted by permission of John Wiley & Sons, Inc.

An award-winning novel that examines, among other aspects of middle age, several views of sexuality, is Tom Wolfe's *The bonfire of the vanities*. New York: Farrar, Straus & Giroux. With his customary verve, Wolfe looks inside the heads of five men and two women, all New Yorkers in early middle age, and shows us how they think.

Generally speaking, attitudes toward love remain constant into middle age. However, Butler and associates (1995) learned that older adults differ in their conceptions of love from younger adults in several important ways: "Specifically, greater age was related to lower agreement with items thought to reflect passive, dependent love (Mania) and all-giving, selfless love (Agape), and these tendencies were more pronounced in females than in males. Furthermore, the age-related decrease in agreement with Mania items was more pronounced among those who were currently in love" (p. 292).

The experts pretty well agree on the nature of physical alterations that occur through the middle years of adulthood. Much less agreement exists, however, on the course of cognitive development in these years.

Guided Review

11. Bretschneider and McCoy claimed that low _____ levels are associated with decreased sexual interest for women.
12. The Janus Report indicates that the stereotype that people become less _____ sexually as they age is not supported by the Januses' research.
13. The Janus Report found that middle age is the _____ sexual time for men with little change with age. For women, age makes little difference across the adult _____.

Personality Development: Continuous or Changing?

In earlier chapters, we have examined the controversy over whether personality is stable or changing. This debate is concerned with middle adulthood, too.

Continuity versus Change

Most of us have heard someone say, "Oh, he's been like that ever since he was a baby!" Such a comment doesn't sound like a philosophical statement, but think about what it implies. It implies that individuals can remain basically the same throughout their lifespan. This is the fundamental question that the issue of change versus continuity of development addresses. Do human beings really change very much over the course of their lives, or do we all stay pretty much the same? It is the focus of great debate by child-development and lifespan psychologists alike because of its implications.

If we assume that people remain the same regardless of what happens to them as their life continues, then the period of early childhood takes on great meaning. Several of the developmental theorists we have discussed (e.g., Freud and Piaget—see Chapter 2) have focused much of their attention on the early years of childhood in the belief that what happens to a person during childhood determines much of what will happen to him or her in the future.

Conversely, others (e.g., Erikson and other adult development theorists—see Chapter 2) believe that because people are constantly changing and developing, all life experiences must be considered important. In that case, early childhood becomes a somewhat less significant period in the whole of development, and adolescence and adulthood come more into focus. It also implies that getting children "off on the right foot" is not enough to ensure positive development. These are just some of the implications of the debate about personality continuity versus change.

Answers

In the study of adulthood, the issue of continuity versus change gets even more complex. In general, two distinct theoretical positions influence the study of adult personality. Some theorists feel that adults remain basically the same—that the adult personality is stable. This is continuity in adult development. Other theorists view the adult as constantly in a process of change and evolution. That is what the position of change refers to.

The study of continuity versus change in adulthood is complicated by the many ways that the issue is studied. Some researchers look at pieces of the personality (personality traits) as measured by detailed questionnaires. They argue that the answers to such questionnaires assess adult personality. These researchers are known as **trait theorists.**

Others note that such questionnaires measure only parts of the personality. They argue that adult personality is much more complicated than any list of personality traits. What is interesting to them is how those traits fit with the whole of the person. Beyond that, they are also interested in how an adult's personality interacts with the world around him or her. They believe that research based on personality traits is too narrow in focus and that we must also look at the stages of change each person goes through. These researchers are known as **stage theorists.** The old saying, "you can't see the forest for the trees," sums up their position—the parts prevent you from seeing the whole.

The differences in how to go about measuring adult personality complicate the study of continuity and change in adulthood. Researchers use extremely different methods of measuring adult personality and then relate their findings to support either the position of continuity or change. In general, trait theorists have found that the adult personality remains the same: Their work supports continuity (Costa & McCrae, 1995). These researchers summed up their findings in the title of an article: "Still Stable after All These Years." They recently proposed that personality traits are organized hierarchically, with narrow traits combining to define broad factors (Costa & McCrae, 1995 a & b). For example, it is common that a person who is kind, unselfish, and empathizes with others is a very compassionate person. Researchers looking at the whole of the adult personality through extensive interviews found support for the notion of change in adulthood (Levinson, 1990a, 1990b).

The study of continuity versus change in adult psychology has important implications, just as it does in childhood psychology. The findings of personality studies add to our knowledge of what "normal" adult development means. Yet as we have seen, the studies vary in their definitions of what adult personality is and how it should be measured. Not surprisingly, studies also differ in what they tell us about normal adult development. Theorists have different answers to the question: "If nothing very unusual happens (like a catastrophe), how will the adult personality develop?"

Trait theorists like McCrae and Costa might say, "If nothing unusual happens, then the adult personality will stay relatively the same. Normal adult personality development is really the maintenance of personality." Levinson, Vaillant, and Erikson, looking at the whole of the adult, would respond differently (see also Chapter 14). They might say, "The adult personality naturally and normally develops through change. Normal adult personality development is a continual process of growth and change."

Who is right? We suggest you read our summary of the studies that each camp provides, and try to make up your own mind. We begin with Daniel Levinson's theory, as it applies to middle age.

Seasons of a Man's Life: Levinson

This section continues a discussion of Levinson's theory that was begun in Chapter 14. Figure 16.4 reproduces that part of his theory that applies to middle adulthood.

Figure 16.4

Levinson's theory—middle age

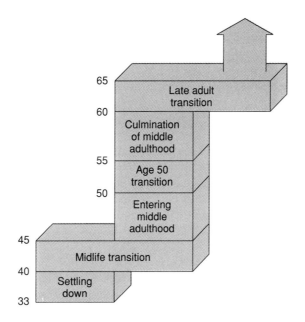

Settling Down

The settling-down phase usually extends from age 33 to 40. At this time, most men have pretty well decided what occupation they choose to pursue. During this period, most men attempt to achieve two tasks: (1) establish a niche in society, and (2) advance up the ladder of the occupational group. During this phase, the male attempts to overcome his dependency on his mentor and slowly is able to "become his own man." This is a step in the direction of greater individuation, in that the man thinks less and less as others want him to, and more and more as his own views dictate. He is now ready to go into the third phase of his adulthood, the mid-life transition.

The Mid-Life Transition

The mid-life transition, which usually lasts for five years, generally extends from age 40 to 45. It involves three major developmental tasks:

- The review, reappraisal, and termination of the early adult period

- Decisions as to how the period of middle adulthood should be conducted

- Dealing with the polarities that are the source of deep division in the man's life at this stage. These polarities, which represent the continual struggle toward greater individuation, are (1) young/old, (2) destruction/creation, (3) masculinity/femininity, and (4) attachment/separation

The so-called mid-life crisis—do you think most middle-aged men go through one?

Young/Old. Young/old is the major polarity to be dealt with during the mid-life transition. Levinson referred to Freud's disciple, Carl Jung (1966), who suggested that the experience of thousands of generations of human beings has gradually produced deep-seated ideas that each of us must learn to deal with. The major one is that although we begin to grow old even at birth, we are also interested in maintaining our youth, if only to avoid the ultimate consequence of our mortality: death.

In tribal symbolism, the word *young* represents fertility, growth, energy, potential, birth, and spring. *Old*, on the other hand, encompasses termination, death, completion, ending, fruition, and winter. Until the age of 40, the man has been able to maintain his youthful self-image. Through producing and raising children, and in some cases through a creative product such as a book, invention, or painting, he has been able to see himself as part of a new and youthful recycling of life. Subconsciously, at least, he has been able to maintain the myth of immortality.

At about the time of his 40th birthday, he is confronted with evidence of his own declining powers. He is no longer able to run, play tennis, or shoot basketballs as effectively as he could in his twenties. He sometimes forgets things, and his eyesight may not be as good. Even more damaging to his hope for immortality is the illness of his friends. Heart attacks, strokes, and other serious illnesses are more frequent among people of his age. In many cases, his parents suffer serious illnesses, or even die. These events lead to one inevitable realization: He is going to die, and perhaps in the not-too-distant future. Even the 32 years left him (on the average) do not seem like much, because over half of life is now already past.

A sense of wanting to leave a legacy now emerges. Most individuals want to feel that their life has made some difference, and they want to leave something behind them that can be remembered. Therefore, it is typical at this time that the individual becomes more creative and often works harder than he has in the past to make a contribution considered worthwhile by those who follow him.

Destruction/Creation. The male going through a mid-life transition realizes not only the potential of the world to destroy but also his own capacity to be destructive. He recognizes the evil within himself and his own power to hurt, damage, and injure himself and others. He knows, if he is honest with himself, that he has not only hurt others inadvertently but sometimes with clear purpose. He sees himself as both victim and villain in the "continuing tale of man's inhumanity to man" (Levinson, 1978, p. 224).

The more honest he is with himself, the more he realizes how tremendous is his capacity to destroy. This honesty has a bonus, however: In recognizing his power to be destructive, he begins to realize how truly powerful he can be in creating new and useful forms of life. As with the young/old polarity, he now attempts to strike a new balance between his destructive and creative sides.

Masculinity/Femininity. Levinson again borrowed from Jung, using his concept that all persons have a masculine and feminine side and that they emphasize one over the other because of the demands of society. This emphasis often costs us greatly. A rich adulthood can be achieved only by compensating for that part of us that was denied during our childhood. In most males, the feminine side has typically been undernourished and now must come to the fore if they are to be all they are capable of being.

According to Levinson, in early adulthood, femininity has a number of undesirable connotations for the male. To the young man, masculinity connotes bodily prowess and toughness, achievement and ambition, power, and intellectuality. Also to the young man, the feminine role represents physical ineptness, incompetence and lack of ambition, personal weakness, and emotionality. Now is the time when the polarity between these self-concepts must be seen and reconciled.

The male who is to achieve greater individuation now recognizes that these dichotomies are false and that he does indeed have a feminine side that must also be nourished. The mature male is able to allow himself to indulge in what he before has disparaged as feminine aspects of his personality. Such a male feels secure enough in his masculinity to enjoy his ability to feel, to nurture, to be dependent. Levinson suggests such men are now freer to assume more independent relationships with their mothers, to develop more intimate love relationships with peer women, and to become mentors to younger men and women alike.

Attachment/Separation. By the attachment/separation process, Levinson meant that each of us needs to be attached to our fellow members of society but also to be separate from them. As the human being develops, a fascinating vacillation occurs between each of these needs. In childhood, a clear-cut attachment to mother and later to family exists. Children need support because of their incompetence in dealing with the complexity of the world around them. Nevertheless, children do begin the separation process by forming attachments to their peers.

You might enjoy reading the third in Updike's series about an ordinary American male: Rabbit is rich. New York: Knopf. In this volume, Rabbit reaches middle age.

During adolescence, this need switches toward an emphasis on separateness from family, as the individual proceeds through the identity moratorium. During this time, most adolescents need to separate themselves not only from their parents but also from the entire society around them in order to try out new ways of being. This need vacillates back toward attachment during early adulthood. The ultimate goal, of course, is interdependence (see Chapter 6).

Throughout their twenties and thirties, most men are involved in entering the world of work and in family and have a strong attachment to others who can help them be successful in these goals. Now, in the midlife transition, a new separateness, perhaps a second adolescence, takes place. The man, especially the successful man, begins to look inside and to gain greater awareness of his sensual and aesthetic feelings. He becomes more in touch with himself by being temporarily less in touch with the others around him.

Because the men interviewed so extensively by Levinson and his colleagues were between the ages of 35 and 45, their study of adult development ends at the mid-life transition. Levinson recognized, however, that a great deal is still to be learned about development after this stage. He ends his book by encouraging those who are attempting to develop theory and research on the periods following this stage of life.

Seasons of a Woman's Life: Levinson

More recently, Levinson (1990b) turned his attention to female progress toward maturity. For his research, he selected three groups of women between the ages of 35 and 45. One-third are homemakers whose lives have followed the traditional family-centered pattern, one-third are teachers at the college level, and one-third are businesswomen. He saw these women as representing a continuum from the domestic orientation to the public orientation, with the college teachers being somewhere in between. Each of the 45 women has been interviewed eight to ten times by the research staff (half of whom are female) for a total of 15 to 20 hours.

Of greatest importance is the finding that females go through a sequence of stages very similar to the stages experienced by the males who were studied. Each gender may be seen as going through an alternating series of structure-building and

For women, an important transition appears to occur at about 30 years of age. The transition involves a period of self-evaluation that usually leads to greater satisfaction with life.

A Sociocultural View — Does Having a "Mid-Life Crisis" Depend on Your Ethnic Background?

Over the years, a number of researchers have noticed that people of color are less likely to report having had a "mid-life crisis" than are whites. A number of hypotheses have been proposed as to why this might be so (can you guess what they might be?). In her extensive review of the literature, however, Gallagher (1994) refuted this conclusion. She believed that encountering a mid-life crisis depends mainly on one's socioeconomic status, and the higher that is, the more likely is the individual to feel that she or he has been through such an experience. Because persons of color are more likely to be in the lower socioeconomic level, they are less likely to report the experience:

Mid-life crises are an affliction of the relatively affluent: rosy illusions are easier to maintain when a person is already somewhat shielded from reality. Just as childhood is often constricted among the poor, who early in life face adult realities and burdens, so middle age may be eclipsed by a premature old age brought on by poverty and poor health. Among working-class people, for whom strength and stamina may mean earning power, middle age may begin at thirty-five rather than the forty-five often cited by respondents drawn from the sedentary middle class. (1994, p. 74)

In Gallagher's view, then, just as "the moratorium of youth" we considered in Chapter 11 is mainly experienced by middle- and upper-class adolescents, the so-called midlife crisis is primarily a problem for those who have the time and money to afford it. Can you think of any other life crises that may pertain only to one socioeconomic group? How about one ethnic group?

structure-changing stages. Levinson found, for example, that men in their late thirties want to "become their own man." He also found that at just this time, women desire to "become their own woman"; that is, they want greater affirmation both from the people in their world and from themselves.

Although male and female growth toward maturity may be in similar stages, Levinson and his associates also believed that major differences exist between the genders within these similar stages. Sociohistorical differences are important. For women, the central themes are gender splitting, the traditional marriage enterprise, and the emerging gender revolution.

Gender Splitting

All societies support the idea that a clear difference should exist between what is considered appropriate for males and for females: **Gender splitting** appears to be universal. Women's lives have traditionally been devoted to the domestic sphere; men's to the public sphere. Human societies have seen a need for females to stay at home to protect the small number of offspring (compared with other species) while the male goes about being the "provisioner" (getting the resources the family needs outside of the home).

The Traditional Marriage Enterprise

In the final analysis, everyone gets married because they believe they can have a better life by doing so. Some exceptions may occur, but they are probably rare. At any rate, the main goal of the **traditional marriage enterprise** is to form and maintain a family. Gender splitting is seen as contributing to this goal.

Being supportive of the husband's "public" role—that is, getting resources for the family—is seen by the woman as a significant part of her role. When she goes to work, this goal is not largely different. Levinson reported that it is still a source of conflict when a female does get to be the boss. Women pay a heavy price for the security this role affords. Many find it dangerous to develop a strong sense of self.

The Gender Revolution

But the meanings of gender are changing and becoming more similar. This is because young and middle-aged adults have so much more work to do. The increase in life expectancy has created a large group, the elderly, who consume more than they produce. This, together with the decrease in birthrate, has brought many more women out of the home and into the workplace. Two other factors have also been at work in creating the **gender revolution:** the divorce rate, which has reached 50 percent, and the increase in the educational levels of women.

In his study of women, Levinson found support for the existence of the same stages and a similar midlife crisis as for men (Levinson, 1986). A major study of women's development (Reinke & others, 1985) used a methodology similar to Levinson's and found important transitions in the lives of women, but not exclusively clustered around the midlife period (ages 40 to 45). Instead, women described important transitions in their lives at ages 30, 40, and 60.

We are, in Levinson's opinion, at a cultural crossroads. The old division of female homemakers and male providers is breaking down, but no clear new direction has yet appeared. Researchers will be watching this dramatic change closely.

Levinson operated from the viewpoint of psychology. The next theory is that of a psychiatrist, most of whom are trained in the Freudian tradition. As we shall see, that makes for a rather different view of adult personality development.

Adaptations to Life: Vaillant

The subtitle of George Vaillant's book *Adaptation to Life* (1977) is *"How the Best and the Brightest Came of Age."* Vaillant's claim that the subjects of his study were among the smartest young men of their time seems to be justified. He investigated mountains of data collected on a carefully selected group of students from Harvard University's classes of 1939 through 1944. The investigation included 260 white males.

The young men were selected because of the superiority of their bodies, minds, and personalities. A major consideration was that each subject be highly success oriented. Although their intelligence was not greatly higher than that of other students at Harvard, almost two-thirds of them graduated with honors (as compared with one-fourth of their classmates), and three-fourths went on to graduate school.

Almost all had solid, muscular builds and were in excellent health. Their average height was 70 inches, and their average weight was 160 pounds. Interestingly, 98 percent were right-handed. If the current theory is correct (Dacey, 1989a), persons dominated by the left side of the brain (which is indicated by right-handedness) tend to be somewhat more intelligent but somewhat less imaginative. Left-handed people are thought to be more creative. It would be interesting to know how creatively productive this group of men has been, but because he was interested only in their mental health, Vaillant has not addressed this question.

Almost 20 hours of physical, mental, and psychological tests were administered to the men. Their brain waves were recorded, and anthropologists measured each man to determine his body type, although these last two measurements had little bearing on the results of the study. Finally, the family history of each of the subjects was carefully recorded. Using this voluminous data, Vaillant set out to describe the personal development of these special people.

As in the theories of Sigmund Freud and Erik Erikson, defense mechanisms are important in Vaillant's explanation of the mental health of these subjects. He believed that everyone uses defense mechanisms regularly. Thus defense mechanisms can range all the way from serious psychopathology to perfectly reasonable "adaptations to life." As he put it:

> These intrapsychic styles of adaptation have been given individual names by psychiatrists (projection, repression, and sublimation are some well-known examples). . . . In this book, the so-called mechanisms of

psychoanalytic theory will often be referred to as coping or adaptive mechanisms. This is to underscore the fact that defenses are healthy more often than they are psychopathological. (1977, p. 7)

On the basis of his data, Vaillant concluded that adaptive mechanisms, as he called them, are as important to the quality of life as any other factor. Nevertheless, he did not challenge Freud's definition; that is, these mechanisms are subconscious defenses of the ego (see Chapter 2). Vaillant made a number of generalizations about these mechanisms on the basis of his observations. He believed that they

- are not inherited;

- do not run in families;

- are not related to mental illness in the family;

- cannot be taught;

- are discrete from one another; and

- are dynamic and reversible.

Vaillant believed that four other generalizations also emerge from the data:

- Life is shaped more by good relationships than by traumatic occurrences during childhood.

- The constantly changing nature of human life may qualify a behavior as mentally ill at one time and adaptive at another.

- To understand the healthiness or psychopathology of the individual, it is necessary to understand what part these adaptive mechanisms play in the healing process. Furthermore, most people have a natural tendency to progress to higher-level mechanisms as they grow toward maturity.

- Because human development continues into adulthood, it is necessary to have a longitudinal study such as this to understand that development.

Generativity versus Stagnation: Erikson

Let us turn now to a theory that is considered a classic. In this final section, we will put forth Erikson's explanation of personality development in middle adulthood: generativity versus stagnation.

Generativity means the ability to be useful to ourselves and to society. As in the industry stage, the goal here is to be productive and creative. However, productivity in the industry stage is a means of obtaining recognition and material reward. In the generativity stage, which takes place during middle adulthood, one's productivity is aimed at being helpful to others. The act of being productive is itself rewarding, regardless of recognition or reward. Erikson added that generativity is

that middle period of the life cycle when existence permits you and demands you to consider death as peripheral and to balance its certainty with the only happiness that is lasting: to increase, by whatever is yours to give, the good will and the higher order in your sector of the world. (1978, p. 124)

Although Erikson certainly approved of the procreation of children as an important part of generativity for many people, he did not believe that everyone needs to become a parent in order to be generative. For example, some people, who from misfortune or because of special and genuine gifts in other directions, cannot apply this drive to offspring of their own and instead apply it to other forms of altruistic concern and creativity (Erikson, 1968).

Generativity, Erikson's term for the major goal of the middle years of adulthood, includes coming to understand those who are different from you and desiring to make a lasting contribution to their welfare.

At this stage of adulthood some people become bored, self-indulgent, and unable to contribute to society's welfare; they fall prey to **stagnation.** Such adults act as though they were their own only child. People who have given birth to children may fail to be generative in their parenthood and come to resent the neediness of their offspring.

In terms of promoting generativity, Wacks (1994) has suggested that each individual has an "inner elder-child," which combines both shame and fear of aging with a childlike appreciation of life and wisdom. Although he refers to an "elder-child," Wacks found that this phenomenon occurs in the middle years of adulthood. By nurturing this inner elder-child, the individual can gain maturity by learning from life experiences, including those that are painful or fearsome. This can help in integrating the young self with the older self at mid-life, that in turn tends to foster more generative attitudes.

Although generativity may provide great satisfaction to those who reach it, theorists have suggested that the picture is not as clear as it might appear (McAdams & others, 1993). In a cross-sectional study that looked at generativity across age groups, McAdams and associates examined four different features of generativity: generative concern, commitments, action, and narration. They found some evidence for Erikson's hypothesis that generativity is relatively low in young adulthood, peaks at mid-life, and declines in the older years. These researchers reported that several studies have suggested differences between men and women. Most men appear to become fixed in the industry stage, doing work merely to obtain the social symbols of success. Most women, these studies suggested, become fixed in the identity stage, confused and conflicted about their proper role in life, which prevents them from achieving intimacy and reaching the stage of generativity. Is Erikson's more optimistic view correct or not? Only more sophisticated investigation of the question will resolve it.

Becoming generative is not easy. It depends on the successful resolution of the six preceding Eriksonian crises we have described in this book. People who are able to achieve generativity have a chance to reach the highest level of personhood in Erikson's hierarchy: integrity. We will examine that stage in Chapter 18.

As you can see, all of the theories described thus far hold that as we age we go through many important changes. Let us turn now to the other side of the coin: the position that the adult personality is made up of traits that remain continuously stable, in most cases, throughout adulthood.

Continuous Traits Theory

In their extensive study of men at mid-life, McCrae and Costa (1984; see also Costa & McCrae, 1995a & b) found no evidence of personality change over the adult years, nor any evidence for the existence of mid-life crisis. The research measured the stability of several different personality traits over a period of six years (a longitudinal study) and also looked at those same personality traits in a cross-age population (a cross-sectional analysis).

At the first testing, McCrae and Costa administered several personality inventories to men ranging in age from 17 to 97. When they combined the data they gathered from the inventories, they defined three major personality traits that they feel govern the adult personality: neuroticism, extroversion, and openness to experience. Each of those three traits is supported by six subtraits or "facets" (see Figure 16.5). The three major traits together are termed the **NEO model of personality.** The researchers found relative stability of those traits throughout male adulthood.

Neuroticism is described as an index of instability or a predisposition for some kind of breakdown under stress. Behaviors associated with this trait include the following:

• A tendency to have more physical and psychiatric problems (without medical problems)

Figure 16.5

Schematic representation of the three-dimensional, 18-facet NEO (neuroticism, extroversion, openness) model of McCrae and Costa.

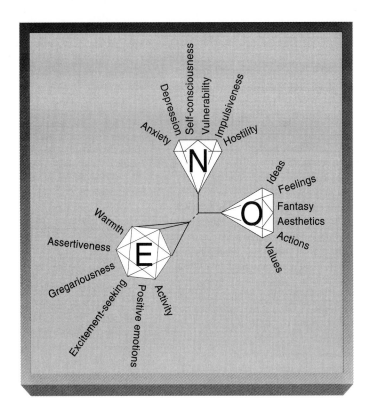

- Greater tendencies to smoke and drink

- More general unhappiness and dissatisfaction with life

Extroversion, the tendency to be outgoing and social, is the second global trait found by McCrae and Costa. Extroversion seems to spill over into almost all aspects of the personality, because it implies an overriding interest in people and social connections.

Openness to experience, the third general trait, is exactly that: an openness to new ideas, fantasies, actions, feelings, and values. Overall, a lack of rigidity in regard to the unfamiliar characterizes openness to experience.

The researchers noted that although habits, life events, opinions, and relationships may change over the lifespan, the basic personality of an individual does not (McCrae & Costa, 1984). They felt that people who experience a midlife crisis probably have the personality makeup that biases them toward that behavior. The Costa and McCrae research, however, lacks consideration of the reciprocal nature of influence of a person with his or her environment. Even so, the rigor of McCrae and Costa's work warrants careful consideration from those interested in personality development across the lifespan.

One study that examined the interaction of the individual and the environment was conducted by Caspi and others (1989). Two kinds of person-environment interaction that contribute to continuities in behavior patterns were discussed—cumulative continuity and interactional continuity. **Cumulative continuity** exists when a person's interactional style places the individual in environments that reinforce that style, thereby sustaining the behavior pattern across the lifespan. An example would be older teens joining a cult or a gang in order to insure that their parents will be replaced by some other authority figure who tells them how to behave. **Interactional continuity** exists when a person's style evokes reciprocal responses from others in ongoing social interaction, thereby sustaining the behavior pattern across the lifespan when a similar interactive event occurs. The findings support the concept that the individual's primary social-developmental task is the negotiation of transitions to new roles and relationships across the lifespan.

What's Your VIEW?

Traits versus Stages

As you can see, a clear conflict exists between the trait researchers and the positions of the three stage theorists. It appears that they cannot both be correct, although the truth may lie somewhere in between. We have devoted much more space to the stage theories. In part this is because they have received so much attention in the popular press, as well as by scholars. It is also because we are biased toward them. (It is certainly obvious throughout this book that we have a great deal of admiration for the ideas of Erikson.)

Whatever the case may be, the important thing is that, through discussion, further reading, and observation, you try to come to your own opinion. What do you think?

Guided Review

14. Two theoretical positions influence the study of personality: Trait theorists believe that adults remain basically the same, and _____ theorists believe that the adult is constantly changing and evolving.

15. In his discussion on mid-life transition, Daniel Levinson identifies four polarities that are a source of division in the life of a middle-adult man. These polarities are young/old, destruction/creation, masculinity/femininity, and _____.

16. From his studies on women, Levinson stated that the stages of women's development are similar to the stages for men, but he found three women's themes: _____ _____, the traditional marriage enterprise, and the emerging gender revolution.

17. As a result of his study on a group of Harvard men, Vaillant suggests that life is shaped by good relationships and that the changing nature of life means that a behavior might be considered indicative of a mental illness at one time and _____ at other times.

18. Erikson saw generativity (the ability to be useful to ourselves and society) versus _____ as the challenge for middle adulthood.

19. According to McCrae and Costa, _____, extroversion, and openness to experience are the three traits they found to be stable in middle-age adult males.

CONCLUSION

Dealing with change is as serious a challenge in mid-life as at any other time. Learning new ways to get along with one's spouse, parents, siblings, and children is necessary at this time of life. Considerable debate occurs over whether personality changes much during this period. Some think it goes through a series of predictable changes; others view it as continuous with earlier life. Workers often experience a "mid-life crisis" at this time, and women workers have an additional set of burdens to handle. Yet with any luck, we make it safely through middle age and move on to late adulthood.

In summary:

Dealing with the Stresses of Adulthood

• Many life events, including major events and daily hassles, contribute to stress in our lives.
• Selye's concept of the general adaptation syndrome includes the stages of alarm reaction, resistance, and exhaustion.

• It is not unusual for disease to result from stress.
• People who are exposed to many risk factors but develop few behavioral or psychological problems are called resilient.

Marriage and Family Relations

• Middle age offers a time for marriage reappraisal, which proves positive for most couples.
• Middle age is also a time when most people develop improved

relationships with their parents, though in some cases the relationship begins to reverse itself when those parents become dependent on their middle-aged children.

- Sibling relationships have the potential to be the most enduring that a person can have, with the relationship between sisters being strongest. It is usually one of these sisters who cares for the elderly parents.
- Reducing the number of one's friends begins in early adulthood. A deepening of the friendships that remain begins in middle age and goes on throughout the rest of life.
- Liberalization of divorce laws has improved the position of women following divorce; however, Weitzman argues that serious inequity still exists.

Sex and Love in Middle Adulthood

- Frequency of sexual intercourse as well as marital satisfaction appear to increase over the middle years.
- Some minor changes in sexual physiology occur for both sexes, but usually these need not hamper sexual satisfaction.

Personality Development: Continuous or Changing?

- Research by trait theorists such as Kagan, and McCrae and Costa generally supports the notion that human beings remain fairly stable throughout life.
- By contrast, theorists such as Erikson, Levinson, and Vaillant argue that human beings are best described as constantly changing and developing throughout life.
- Levinson suggested that most men go through a mid-life transition in

which they must deal with the polarities between young and old, masculinity and femininity, destruction and creation, and attachment and separation.
- Levinson also suggested that females go through a similar experience to that of males, with some notably different influences.
- Vaillant, in his study of the "smartest" young men of their time, concluded that adaptive mechanisms are very important to quality of life.
- Erikson's theory placed middle adulthood within the stage labeled "generativity versus stagnation." Generativity means the ability to be useful to ourselves and to society without concern for material reward.
- McCrae and Costa defined three major personality traits that they feel govern the adult personality: neuroticism, extroversion, and openness to experience.

KEY TERMS

Alarm reaction
Cumulative continuity
Emotional divorce
Empty nest syndrome
Gender revolution
Gender splitting
General adaptation syndrome

Generativity
Interactional continuity
Mid-life transition
NEO model of personality
No-fault divorce
Protective factors
Resilience

Risk factors
Stage of exhaustion
Stage of resistance
Stage theorists
Stagnation
Traditional marriage enterprise
Trait theorists

WHAT DO YOU THINK?

1. In what ways does Selye's concept for the general adaptation syndrome play a part in your life? In those of your friends?
2. What is the best way for middle-aged people to take

care of their ailing, elderly parents?
3. What changes would you make in our divorce laws?
4. Why is the mid-life transition so stressful for some men and not for others?

5. What are the main differences between male and female personality development?
6. Who's right, the stage theorists or the trait theorists?

CHAPTER REVIEW TEST

1. If a person is alerted to stress, the level of anxiety increases, and task-oriented and defense-oriented behavior takes place, the person is experiencing the psychological manifestations of
   a. alarm reaction.

   b an anxiety attack.
   c defense mechanisms.
   d denial.

2. According to Selye, your ability to remain in the resistance stage decreases when you are

   a experiencing optimum drive.
   b experiencing an alarm reaction.
   c an adolescent.
   d growing older.

3. Under continual stress, the gradual depletion of an organism's

adaptational energy eventually leads to

a   stage of resistance.
b   stage of exhaustion.
c   collapse of the nervous system.
d   increased energy.

4. Francis and Joan have drifted apart over the years but remain married to each other because of their children. Their relationship illustrates the

a. functional marriage.
b. practical marriage.
c. functional divorce.
d. emotional divorce.

5. According to Gottman and Krokoff's longitudinal research on marital interactions, those who tend most to avoid relational confrontations are

a. divorcing couples.
b. couples married for more than 25 years.
c. husbands.
d. wives.

6. What is the most frequently cited problem of middle-aged adult women?

a. Aging
b. Menopause
c. Caring for their children
d. Caring for their aging parents

7. Research suggests that the best indicator of a sibling relationship is

a. proximity.
b. frequency of contact.
c. mutual caring for elderly parents.
d. feelings of closeness.

8 Because the no-fault divorce laws do not account for an inequitable economic system, who suffers most financially by divorce?

a. The middle-aged homemaker
b. The career oriented woman
c. The middle-aged father
d. The adult children

9. The notion that adult personality changes over time is supported by

a. stage theorists.
b. transition theorists.
c. trait theorists.
d. lifespan theorists.

10. Trait theory is to _____ as stage theory is to _____.

a. lifespan development; stair step transition
b. continuity in adult development; change in adult development
c. change in adult development; continuity in adult development
d. stair step transition; lifespan development

11. The _____ that occur during Levinson's mid-life transition represent the continual struggle toward greater individuation.

a. attachments
b. separations
c. level of intimacy
d. polarities

12. The idea that a clear difference exists between what is appropriate for males and for females is referred to as

a. gender splitting.
b. the gender revolution.
c. role strain.
d. the traditional marriage.

13. In Vaillant's research on adaptations to life, he concluded that adaptive mechanisms are an important factor to

a. a person's reactive mechanisms.
b. a person's defense mechanisms.
c. the quality of a person's life.
d. a person's coping mechanisms.

14. According to Erikson, during the generativity stage one's productivity is aimed at

a. career advancement.
b. material rewards.
c. being helpful to others.
d. recognition.

15. McCrae and Costa defined three major personality types as neuroticism, extroversion, and

a. introversion.
b. openness to experience.
c. outdatedness.
d. None of the above.

16 The two kinds of person-environment interaction that contribute to continuities in behavior patterns are _____ continuity and _____ continuity.

a   introverted, extraverted
b   open, closed
c   cumulative, interactional
d   introverted, open

Answers

PART IX

As a white candle
In a holy place,
So is the beauty
Of an aged face.

Joseph Campbell

And just as young people are all different, and middle-aged people are all different, so too are old people. We don't all have to be exactly alike. . . . There are all kinds of old people coping with a common condition, just as kids in puberty when their voices start cracking. . . .

Every one of them is different. We old folks get arthritis, rheumatism, our teeth fall out, our feet hurt, our hair gets thin, we creak and groan. These are the physical changes, but all of us are different. And I personally feel that you follow pretty much the pattern of your younger years. I think that some people are born young and some people are born old and tired and gray and dull. . . . You're either a nasty little boy turned old man or a mean little old witch turned old or an outgoing, free-loving person turned old.

As for myself, I feel very excited about life and about people and color and books, and there is an excitement to everything that I guess some people never feel. . . . I have a lot of friends who are thirty-year-old clods. They were born that way and they'll die that way. . . . But me, I'm happy, I'm alive, and I want to live with as much enjoyment and dignity and decency as I can, and do it gracefully and my way if possible, as long as possible.

Author M.F.K. Fisher, who died recently at 82

A special session of the British House of Lords was being held to honor Winston Churchill on his ninetieth birthday. As he descended the stairs of the amphitheater, one member turned to another and said, "They say he's really getting senile." Churchill stopped, and leaning toward them, said in a stage whisper loud enough for many to hear, "They also say he's deaf!" ❂

Even when he was very old and ill, Winston Churchill's fabled sense of humor never left him. In addition, it was only in his later years that he found time to sharpen his artistic skills, which brought him world renown in that realm. He was an excellent example of how fruitful the last third of life can be.

Although positive, these vignettes remind us of the stereotypes of old age as being a rather negative stage of life. Multiple-choice and true-false tests given to college students have shown that this and other stereotypes continue to exist (Harris & others, 1996). How much truth is there to them? Must growing old mean decline? Must the teeth and hair fall out, the eyes grow dim, the skin wrinkle and sag? Must intelligence, memory, and creativity falter? Must old age be awful?

Or is there actually only a relatively slight decline in capacity, a decline greatly exaggerated by our values and presumptions? Many elderly people seem to be having the time of their lives! Could it be that the negative aspects of aging are largely the result of a self-fulfilling prophecy (people expect to deteriorate, so they stop trying to be fit, and then they do deteriorate)? Could most of us in our later years be as capable as those famous few who seem to have overcome age and remained vigorous into their nineties and beyond? In Chapter 17, we will investigate these questions.

When you finish reading this chapter, you should be able to

- Compare the major physiological theories of aging.

- Determine the contribution of genetics and the environment to aging.

- Explain changes that occur in late adulthood related to reaction time and sensory abilities.

- Describe the ways in which the skeletal system, skin, teeth, and hair alter in appearance as people age.

- Evaluate the nature of the relationship of hormone balance to physical ability.

- Define Alzheimer's disease and identify several theories about its cause.

- List Gerson and associates' findings regarding the relationship between mental and physical health.

- Explain other factors in the relationship between cognition and aging.

- Appraise the theory known as terminal drop.

- Discuss Dacey's theory of creativity and list critical periods of life during which creative ability can be cultivated most effectively.

The questions that introduced this chapter concern most of the 23 million men and women over 65 who constitute 12 percent of our population today. In 1900 the over-65 population was 3 million, only 3 percent of the total. By the year 2040 it will have reached 20 percent (see Figure 17.1). Such questions should also concern those of us who hope to join their ranks some day. In the next section we look at the answers to these questions, as revealed by considerable new research.

Must We Age and Die?

"Nothing is inevitable except death and taxes," the old saying goes. But is death inevitable? True, no one so far has attained immortality; the oldest known person in the United States, as certified by the Social Security Administration, is 114 years old. And, of course, the vast majority of the people who have ever lived are dead.

But not all organisms die. Some trees alive today are known to be more than 2,500 years old; they have aged but show no sign of dying. Bacteria apparently are able to live indefinitely, as long as they have the requirements for their existence. The fact is, we are not sure why we age, and until we are, we cannot be certain that aging and death are absolutely inevitable. Nor can we overlook those who appear to age well, which is often referred to as "successful" or "robust" aging (Garfein & Herzog, 1995). Robustly aging individuals report greater social contact and better health and vision than those who age less successfully. Furthermore, cover stories in the popular press (e.g., Darrack, 1992) have trumpeted as yet unpublished

A Sociocultural View

Percentage of Elderly in Japan Soon to Be Much Higher than Here

As can be seen in Figure 17.2, the percentage of the Japanese population over the age of 65 was about the same as the United States in 1990 (about 12 percent). By the year 2020, however, when the percentage of U. S. elderly will have risen by 3 percent, Japan's will have increased by 13 percent. That means that 25 percent of all Japanese will be elderly.

Two factors account for most of the increase in Japan (Kakuchi, 1997). The country is known for its excellent health care and nutrition. The Japanese also have a greatly decreased birthrate. For example, the percentage of those 14 or younger has dropped from 35 in 1955 to about 15 percent today. Can you imagine what the impact of this huge change will be on Japanese social conditions?

Figure 17.1

Age distribution of United States population, selected years

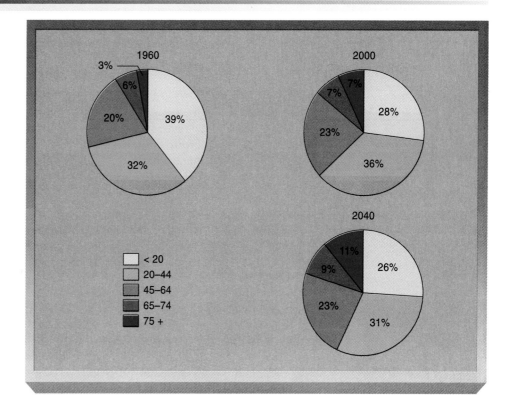

Figure 17.2

A comparison of the percentage of elderly persons in the U. S. and Japan from 1990 to 2020. More than a fourth of the Japanese population is projected to be older than 65 by 2020.

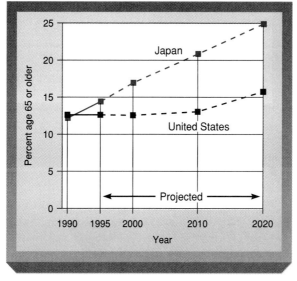

Source: Japan Information Network

This olive tree found in Greece is more than 2,500 years old. Do you think it's possible that it might live forever?

It is never too late to be what you might have been.
George Eliot

research that offers hope that aging can be slowed, stopped, or even reversed! Let's look now at the three types of explanations of aging that have been documented (Spence, 1989): physiological, genetic, and environmental aspects of aging.

Physiological Theories of Aging

It is apparent that organisms inherit a tendency to live for a certain length of time. An animal's durability depends on the species it belongs to. The average human lifespan of approximately 70 years is the longest of any mammal. Elephants, horses, hippopotamuses, and asses are known to live as long as 50 years, but most mammals die much sooner.

Some doctors are fond of stating that "no one ever died of old age." This is true. People die of some physiological failure that is more likely to occur the older one gets. One likely explanation of aging, then, is that the various life-support systems gradually weaken. Illness and death come about as a cumulative result of these various weaknesses. Seven different physiological factors have been suggested as accounting for this process.

Wear and Tear Theory

The **wear and tear theory** seems the most obvious explanation for aging, but there is actually little evidence for it. To date, no research has clearly linked early deterioration of organs with either hard work or increased stress alone.

A complex interaction, however, may be involved. It is known that lower rates of metabolism are linked to longer life and that certain conditions, such as absence of rich foods, cause a lower metabolism. Therefore, the lack of the "good life" may prolong life. On the other hand, it is also known that poor people who seldom get to eat rich foods tend to die at an earlier age than middle-class or wealthy people. Therefore, the evidence on this theory is at best conflicting.

Aging by Program

According to the **aging by program** theory, we age because it is programmed into us. It is hard to understand what evolutionary processes govern longevity (if any). For example, the vast majority of animals die at or before the end of their reproductive period, but human females live 20 to 30 years beyond the end of their reproductive cycles. This may be related to the capacities of the human brain. Mead (1972) argued that this extra period beyond the reproductive years has had the evolutionary value of helping to keep the children and grandchildren alive. For example, in times when food is scarce, older people may remember where it was obtained during the last period of scarcity. On the other hand, it may be that we humans have outwitted the evolutionary process and, due to our medical achievements and improvements in lifestyle, are able to live on past our reproductive usefulness.

Another enduring hypothesis, originally proposed by Birren (1960), is known as the "counterpart" theory. According to this concept, factors in human existence that are useful in the earlier years become counterproductive in later years. An example is the nonreplaceability of most cells in the nervous system. The fact that brain cells are not constantly changing enhances memory and learning abilities in the earlier years, but it also allows the nervous system to weaken because dead cells are not replaced.

Spence (1989) suggested that the hypothalamus may well be an "aging chronometer" (p. 17), a "timer" that keeps track of the age of cells and determines how long they should keep reproducing. Although research on aging by program is in its infancy, some findings indicate that older cells may act differently from younger cells. Although cells in the nervous system and muscles do not reproduce themselves, all the other cells in the body do reproduce, at least to some extent.

But these cells are able to reproduce only a limited number of times, and they are more likely to reproduce imperfectly as they get older. There is also reason to believe that reproduced older cells do not pass on information accurately through the DNA. This weakens the ability of older cells to continue high-level functioning.

Homeostatic Imbalance

It may be a failure in the systems that regulate the proper interaction of the organs, rather than wear of the organs themselves, that causes aging and ultimately death. These homeostatic (feedback) systems are responsible, for example, for the regulation of the sugar and adrenaline levels in the blood. Apparently there is not a great deal of difference in the systems of the young and the old when they are in a quiet state. It is when stress is put on the systems (death of a spouse, loss of a job, a frightening experience) that we see the effects of the elderly **homeostatic imbalance.** The older body simply isn't as effective, qualitatively or quantitatively, in reacting to these stresses. Figure 17.3 shows graphically the relationship between problems with the homeostatic systems and the competence of the organism to react effectively to dangers in the environment.

Figure 17.3

Homeostasis and health. Progressive stages of homeostasis from adjustment (health) to failure (death). In the healthy adult, homeostatic processes ensure adequate adjustment in response to stress, and even for a period beyond this stage compensatory processes are capable of maintaining overall function without serious disability. When stress is exerted beyond compensatory capacities of the organism, disability ensues in rapidly increasing increments to severe illness, permanent disability, and death. When this model is viewed in terms of homeostatic responses to stress imposed on the aged and to aging itself, a period when the body can be regarded as at the "limit of compensatory processes," it is evident that even minor stresses are not tolerable, and the individual moves rapidly into stages of breakdown and failure.

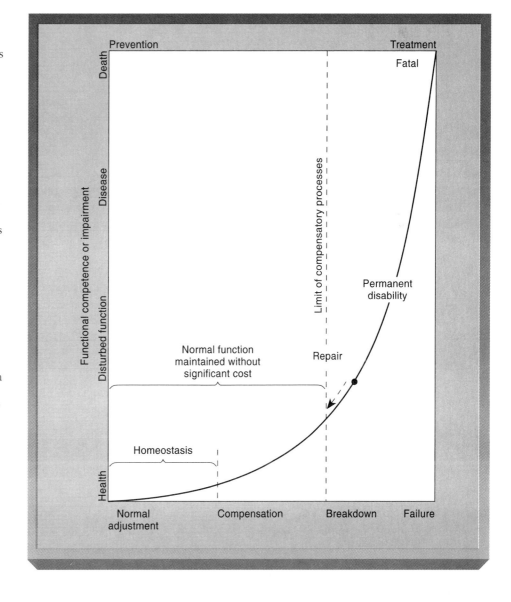

Cross-Linkage Theory

The proteins that make up a large part of cells are composed of peptides. When cross-links are formed between peptides (a natural process of the body), the proteins are altered, often for the worse. For example, **collagen** is the major connective tissue in the body; it provides, for instance, the elasticity in our skin and blood vessels. When its proteins are altered, skin and vessels are adversely affected. This is known as the **cross-linkage theory.**

Accumulation of Metabolic Waste

Although the connection has not been clearly established as yet, it may be that waste products resulting from metabolism build up in various parts of the body and contribute to the decrease in competence of those parts. Examples of this effect of the **accumulation of metabolic waste** are cataracts on the eye, cholesterol in the arteries, and brittleness of bones.

Autoimmunity

With increasing age, there is increasing **autoimmunity,** the process by which the immune system in the body rejects the body's own tissue. Examples of this are rheumatoid arthritis, diabetes, vascular diseases, and hypertension. It may be that, with age, the body's tissues become more and more self-rejecting.

This may be the result of the production of new **antigens,** the substances in the blood that fight to kill foreign bodies. These new antigens may come about for one of two reasons:

- Mutations cause the formation of altered RNA or DNA.

- Some cells may be "hidden" in the body during the early part of life. When these cells appear later, the body does not recognize them as its own, and forms new antigens to kill them. This in turn may cause organ malfunction.

Patients with a confirmed diagnosis of such ailments are usually instructed to begin drug therapy and change their lifestyles according to prescribed instructions (Clyman and Pompei, 1996 a & b). If patients continue to suffer from disabling pain, surgery is an alternative solution. However, elderly people who are bedridden, wheelchair-bound, or have heart disease are not often candidates for surgery. Fortunately, doctors are considering alternate treatments that may be effective.

Accumulation of Errors

As cells die, they must synthesize new proteins to make new cells. As this is done, occasionally an error occurs. Over time, these errors mount up. This **accumulation of errors** may finally grow serious enough to cause organ failure.

Genetic Theories of Aging

Gene theory also suggests that aging is programmed but says that the program exists in certain harmful genes. As Spence (1989) explained it,

> Perhaps there are genes which direct many cellular activities during the early years of life that become altered in later years, thus altering their function. In their altered state, the genes may be responsible for the functional decline and structural changes associated with aging. (p. 19)

Whatever the reason, little doubt exists that genes affect how long we live. Kallman and Jarvik's (1959) research into identical twins still offers strong evidence of this. They found that monozygotic twins (those born from the same egg) have more similar lengths of life than do dizygotic twins (those born from two eggs). This effect is illustrated in Figures 17.4 and 17.5.

Figure 17.4

One-egg twins at the ages of 12, 17, 67, and 91 years (note the long separation of these twins between the ages of 18 and 66).

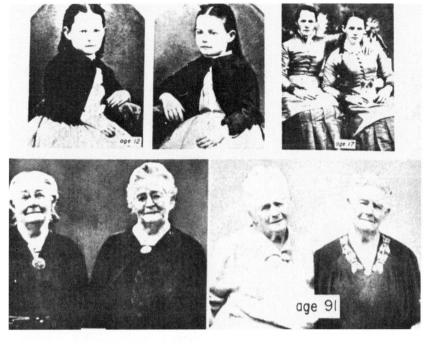

Figure 17.5

One-egg twins at the ages of 5, 20, 55, and 86 years

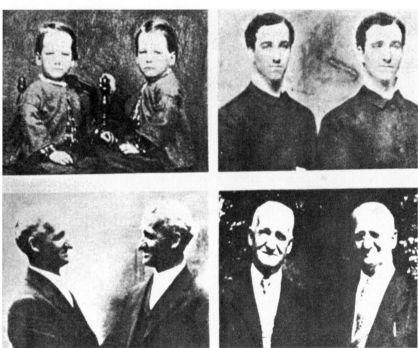

Effects of the Natural Environment on Aging

Our genes and the physiology of our organs greatly affect the length of our lives. This may be seen in the extreme accuracy with which insurance companies are able to predict the average number of deaths at a particular age. A mathematical formula to predict the number of deaths within a population was produced as early as 1825 by Gomertz. The formula is still quite accurate except for the early years of life.

Today many fewer deaths occur in early childhood, because vaccines have eliminated much of the danger of diseases at this age. This shows that the natural environment is also an important factor in the mortality rate. Many of today's elderly would have died in childhood had they been born in the early part of the nineteenth century.

Considering mortality rates for specific cultures rather than world population shows the effects of the environment more specifically. Starvation in Africa and earthquakes in Guatemala obviously had a tragic effect on the mortality rates of those two countries. A number of authors have reported on the effects of radiation (Spence, 1989). Some evidence indicates that the nuclear testing in the Pacific in the 1950s is affecting the aging process of some of the residents there. Little or no evidence exists, however, to suggest that the radiation we are all exposed to every day is having any impact on aging. It remains to be seen if events such as the nuclear accident at Three Mile Island will have adverse effects.

A Sociocultural View

The Role of Relatives in the Health of Persons of Color

A number of studies have indicated that although African American and Latino elderly are more susceptible than whites to health problems, if their relatives are involved in their lifestyle choices, this difference is greatly lessened. For example, persons of color are more susceptible to diabetes and hypertension, in part because they often have inadequate diets (too much sugar and fat, not enough fresh vegetables, etc.). Relatives can make sure that appropriate foods are purchased and properly prepared. They can also provide informal health care and intervene with health services to ensure that help is provided to the elderly when needed.

Other Modifiers of Ability

In addition to genetic, physiological, and natural environmental factors that indirectly affect the individual's rate of aging, other factors can modify a person's level of ability more directly. Many of these modifiers interact with one another in complex ways. Some of the major modifiers are training, practice, motivation, nutrition, organic malfunction, illness, injury, stress level, educational level, occupation, personality type, and socioeconomic status.

For example, although it appears that social networks (the number and extent of friendships a person has) do not directly affect the survival of elderly people, they are related to their quality of life. Within nursing homes, those who tend to be aggressive and verbally agitated have poor social networks and generally lack intimacy with their fellow patients. It is less clear whether the behavior causes the poor quality of network, or vice versa (Cohen-Mansfield & Marx, 1992). Socioeconomic factors such as amount of income and quality of housing do promote superior networks, however (Shahtahmasebi & others, 1992).

Figure 17.6 summarizes the relationships between the hypothesized factors that affect aging of physical and mental systems. These include two genetic, five physiological, and five environmental factors, as well as twelve other modifiers of human abilities. You could find no clearer example of the biopsychosocial model at work!

More recent research (Krause & Wray, 1991) indicates, however, that when these relatives are not knowledgeable about appropriate health procedures such as dietary concerns, they can do more harm than good. What is needed is a concerted effort to teach relatives and others on whom the elderly depend for health assistance the information they need to do the job well.

Figure 17.6

Influences on adult mental and physical systems

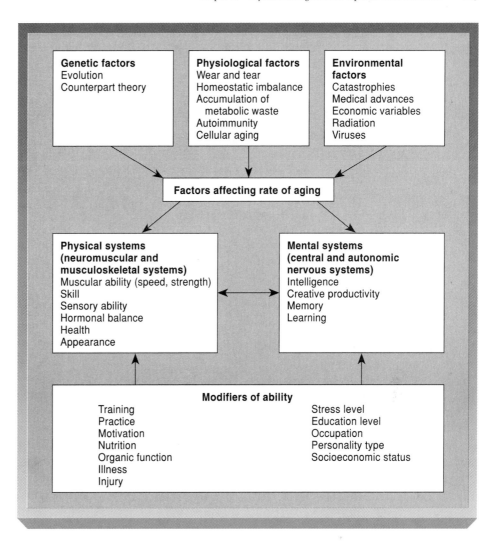

Genetic factors
Evolution
Counterpart theory

Physiological factors
Wear and tear
Homeostatic imbalance
Accumulation of
   metabolic waste
Autoimmunity
Cellular aging

Environmental factors
Catastrophies
Medical advances
Economic variables
Radiation
Viruses

Factors affecting rate of aging

**Physical systems
(neuromuscular and
musculoskeletal systems)**
Muscular ability (speed, strength)
Skill
Sensory ability
Hormonal balance
Health
Appearance

**Mental systems
(central and autonomic
nervous systems)**
Intelligence
Creative productivity
Memory
Learning

Modifiers of ability
Training   Stress level
Practice   Education level
Motivation   Occupation
Nutrition   Personality type
Organic function   Socioeconomic status
Illness
Injury

Guided Review

1. Theorists have proposed three generic explanations for aging and death: physiological aspects, _____ aspects, and environmental aspects.
2. Within the physiological aspects, one of the explanations is called the _____ and _____ theory, meaning that hard work and stress gradually destroy body parts.
3. The other physiological aspects are: aging by program, homeostatic imbalance, _____ theory, accumulation of metabolic waste, autoimmunity, and accumulation of errors.
4. The impact of the environment on aging and death helps us understand that our genes and the _____ of our organs affects the length of our lives.
5. According to Spence, a follower of the aging by program theory, the _____ may serve as a timer that keeps track of the age of cells and determines how long our cells should keep reproducing.

Answers

1. genetic 2. wear, tear 3. cross-linkage 4. physiology 5. hypothalamus

Before reading the next section, you might try your hand at the true–false test on the topic of aging in the following box.

An Applied View

The Facts on Aging Quiz

Mark the items T for true or F for false.

1. A person's height tends to decline in old age.

2. More older persons (over 65) have chronic illnesses that limit their activity than younger persons.

3. Older persons have more acute (short-term) illnesses than persons under 65.

4. Older persons have more injuries in the home than persons under 65.

5. Older workers have less absenteeism than younger workers.

6. The life expectancy of African Americans at age 65 is about the same as whites.

7. The life expectancy of men at age 65 is about the same as women's.

8. Medicare pays over half of the medical expenses for the aged.

9. Social Security benefits automatically increase with inflation.

10. Supplemental Security Income guarantees a minimum income for needy aged.

11. The aged do not get their proportionate share (about 11%) of the nation's income.

12. The aged have higher rates of criminal victimization than persons under 65.

13. The aged are more fearful of crime than are persons under 65.

14. The aged are the most law abiding of all adult groups, according to official statistics.

15. There are two widows for each widower among the aged.

16. More of the aged vote than any other age group.

17. There are proportionately more older persons in public office than in the total population.

18. The proportion of African Americans among the aged is growing.

19. Participation in voluntary organizations (churches and clubs) tends to decline among the healthy aged.

20. The majority of the aged live alone.

21. About 3 percent less of the aged have incomes below the official poverty level than the rest of the population.

22. The rate of poverty among aged African Americans is about three times as high as among aged whites.

23. Older persons who reduce their activity tend to be happier than those who remain active.

24. When the last child leaves home, the majority of parents have serious problems adjusting to their "empty nest."

25. The proportion widowed is decreasing among the aged.

The key to the correct answers is simple: Alternating pairs of items are true or false (i.e., 1 and 2 are true, 3 and 4 are false, 5 and 6 are true, etc.; and 25 is true).

Seniors usually find that their coordination declines with the years, and so they often quit playing sports. Now there is a strong movement to reverse this trend.

Physical Development

In this section, we consider development from the standpoints of reaction time, sensory abilities, other body systems, health, and appearance.

Reaction Time

It is obvious that physical skills decline as people grow older. This appears to be especially true of manual dexterity. Although older people are able to perform short, coordinated manual tasks, a long series of tasks such as playing a stringed instrument becomes increasingly difficult for them. Famed Spanish guitarist Andrés Segovia and pianist Vladimir Horowitz are notable exceptions.

Is this because the human nervous system is deteriorating through aging? To answer this question, psychologists have completed numerous studies of "reaction time," the time between the onset of a stimulus and the actual muscle activity that indicates a reaction to it. Studying reaction time is a scientific way of separating the effects of the central nervous system from the ability of the rest of the body to perform manual tasks.

We can conclude that variables other than sheer neural or motor activities account for most change in physical skills over time. One example of an alternative factor is ageism. It has been shown that young people process and respond to the speech of older people in stereotypical ways such as "baby talk" or pandering (Giles & others, 1992). This type of prejudice is known as **ageism.** Several studies (e.g., Dellman-Jenkins & others, 1986; Harris & Fiedler, 1988) found that ageism is as serious a problem today as it was several decades ago.

Because they are often treated in a condescending way, elderly persons sometimes behave in a less competent manner than they are capable of. Ageism is a prejudice that can seriously affect the elderly, lowering the quality of their lives. Furthermore, it robs our society of the diverse contributions that might otherwise be made by elderly persons, if their feelings of self-esteem and competence were not undermined by this prejudice.

What are some things you could do to fight this unfair attitude? For example, how might you help change the stereotype that senility is normal in the elderly?

Other factors that influence the reaction time of the elderly are motivation, depression, anxiety, response strategies, and response style. Older adults can improve their ability in any of these areas if they desire.

Sensory Abilities

Sensory functioning may be among the important determinants of individual differences in cognitive performance. Lindenberger and Baltes (1994) see old age as often being a time of "sensory deprivation"—reduced opportunities for stimulating exchanges with the environment. Lack of sensory stimulation is one of many factors that emerges during later phases of life, and helps regulate the process of aging. Such late-life factors of development are powerful influences, and may account for developmental changes in old age. We look at some of those changes in the following paragraphs.

Vision

A number of problems may affect the eye as the adult ages, such as cataract, macular degeneration, open-angle glaucoma, and diabetic retinopathy (Klein, 1991).

The lenses may become less transparent, thicker, and less elastic. This tends to result in farsightedness. The illumination required to perceive a stimulus also increases with age. Retina changes almost never occur before the age of 60, but Elias and associates (1977) argued that conditions that affect the retina, such as glaucoma, are often not detected, so problems may occur without causing noticeable changes in the eye.

Cataracts are the result of cloudy formations on the lens of the eye. They form very gradually and inhibit the passage of light through the eye. Cataracts are most common after the age of 60. If they become large enough, they can be removed, usually by laser surgery. Psychosocial adjustment to decline in vision, however, does not go unnoticed in late adulthood (Davis & others, 1995). Psychosocial factors such as depression, satisfaction with life, social support, self-esteem, stress, and motivation are all related to age-related decline in visual capabilities.

At any rate, with recent improvements in ophthalmology and optical surgery, the declining ability of the human eye need not greatly affect vision in older age (with the single exception of poor night vision, which hampers driving). Recent studies indicate that such improvements may reduce the level of depression associated with poor vision caused by aging (Fagerstrom, 1994).

Does society have the responsibility to provide transportation for people when it takes away their licenses? If not, does government have any responsibility to help such people? What's your view? To widen your understanding, you might interview

We are always the same age inside.
Gertrude Stein

several young adults who will bear the brunt of the cost for elderly transportation, and some older adults who will be isolated without it.

What's Your VIEW?

What Should Happen When the Elderly Lose Their License?

By 2020, up to one out of every five Americans will be 65 or older, and the vast majority will possess a driver's license. This is of concern because statistics show that accidents caused by drivers over the age of 75 equal or surpass those of teenagers, who have been considered the most dangerous group of drivers. A number of states are moving to monitor older drivers more aggressively. However, in those cases where a license is denied or revoked, the drivers may find themselves stranded without crucial transportation (Harvard Health Letter, 1991).

Hearing

Decline in hearing ability may be a more serious problem than decline in vision. However, we seem to be much less willing to wear hearing aids than we are to wear glasses, perhaps because we rely on vision more.

Most people hear fairly well until late adulthood, but men seem to lose some of their acuity for higher pitches during their middle years (Marshall, 1981). This difference may occur mostly in men who are exposed to greater amounts of noise in their occupations and in traveling to and from their jobs.

Smell

Some atrophy of olfactory fibers in the nose occurs with age. When artificial amplifiers are added, however, the ability of the older people to recognize foods by smell is greatly improved.

Taste

Studying the effects of aging on the sense of taste is difficult because taste itself is so dependent on smell. About 95 percent of taste derives from olfactory nerves. It is clear, however, that there is decline in tasting ability among the elderly (Cowart & others, 1994). Whereas young adults have an average of 250 taste buds, elderly adults have an average of no more than 100.

Touch

The tactile sense also declines somewhat after the age of 65 (Turner & Helms, 1989), but the evidence for this comes strictly from the reports of the elderly. Until scientific studies are performed, this finding must be accepted with caution.

Other Body Systems

Included in the category of body systems are the skeletal system, skin, teeth, hair, and locomotion (ability to move about).

Skeletal System

Although the skeleton is fully formed by age 24, changes in stature can occur because of the shrinking of the discs between spinal vertebrae (Mazess, 1982). As mentioned earlier, collagen changes. Frequently this causes bone tissue to shrink (Twomey & others, 1983). Thus the bones become more brittle. Because the entire skeletal system becomes tighter and stiffer, the aged frequently have a small loss of

A number of factors can cause the body to become shorter and stiffer with age.

height. Diseases of the bone system such as arthritis are probably the result of changes in the collagen in the bones with age.

Diseases such as osteoporosis can be very crippling. In this regard there is good news. Studies at Tufts University indicate strong evidence that if people over 50 (men as well as women) increase their daily intake of calcium to 1,200 milligrams and their vitamin D intake to about 500 international units, they can substantially decrease their risk of osteoporosis (Howe, 1997).

Skin

Collagen is also a major factor in changes in the skin. Because continuous stretching of collagen causes it to lengthen, the skin begins to lose its elasticity with age. Other changes are a greater dryness and the appearance of spots due to changes in pigmentation (Walther & Harber, 1984). The skin becomes coarser and darker, and wrinkles begin to appear. Darkness forms under the eyes, more because of a growing paleness of the skin in the rest of the face than because of any change in the under-eye pigmentation. Years of exposure to the sun also contribute to these effects.

Another important cause of the change in skin texture has to do with the typical weight loss among the elderly. They have a tendency to lose fat cells, which decreases the pressure against the skin itself. This tends to cause sagging, folds, and wrinkles in the skin. Older persons not only need less nourishment, but they also lose the social motivation of eating at meetings and parties that younger persons have (Carnevali & Patrick, 1986). As the elderly eat less, their skin becomes less tight and wrinkles appear.

Teeth

The loss of teeth is certainly one physical aspect that makes a person look older (Pizer, 1983). Even when corrective measures are taken, the surgery involved and the adjustment to dentures have a major impact on the person's self-image. In most cases, the loss of teeth is more the result of gum disease than decay of the teeth themselves. Education, the use of fluorides, the use of new brushing techniques, and daily flossing likely will make this aspect of aging far less of a problem in the future.

Hair

Probably the most significant signature of old age is change of the hair. Thinness, baldness, grayness, stiffness, and a growing amount of facial hair in women are all indications of growing old. Hormonal changes are undoubtedly the main culprit here. Improvements in hair coloring techniques and hair implants may make it possible to avoid having "old-looking" hair (for those to whom this is important).

Locomotion

It is generally assumed that the decrease in locomotion by older adults is due to aging. However, a recent study suggests that although older people do indeed walk more slowly, the pattern of coordination between their limbs remains essentially the same as for younger adults. Thus if people maintain good health and an active lifestyle, there is reason to believe that this locomotive decline can be kept to a minimum (Williams & Bird, 1992).

Health

It is well known that health declines when one reaches the older years. This decline, however, usually does not occur until quite late in life (Kart & others, 1988). Table 17.1 shows rates of death per 100,000 people. (A number of interesting comparisons can be found in this table—can you spot them?)

Illness is not a major cause of death until one reaches the thirties, and only then among African American females. This is probably because they receive fewer pre-

TABLE 17.1 DEATH RATES BY AGE, SEX, AND ETHNICITY [NUMBER OF DEATHS PER 100,000 POPULATION IN SPECIFIED GROUP.]

Sex, Year, and Race	All ages	Under 1 yr. old	1–4 yr. old	5–14 yr. old	15–24 yr. old	25–34 yr. old	35–44 yr. old	45–54 yr. old	55–64 yr. old	65–74 yr. old	75–84 yr. old	85 yr. old and older
Male												
1960	1,105	3,059	120	56	152	188	373	992	2,310	4,914	10,178	21,186
1989	922	1,077	47	32	152	203	302	628	1,570	3,415	7,950	17,695
Female												
1960	809	2,321	98	37	61	107	229	527	1,196	2,872	7,633	19,008
1989	817	891	41	21	54	76	142	338	888	1,997	5,083	14,070

Source: From *Vital Statistics of the United States,* U. S. National Center for Health Statistics, 1992.

ventive health services, and because medical treatment is frequently delayed until the later stages of disease. Not until adults reach the age of 40 does ill health, as opposed to accidents, homicide, and suicide, become the major cause of death. Arteriosclerotic heart disease is the major killer after the age of 40 in all age, sex, and race groups.

Another major cause is "cerebrovascular accidents" such as strokes. Due to a new treatment, victims who receive a clot-busting drug treatment known as tissue plasminogen activator (TPA) in time have a much better chance of surviving and recovering from the effects of a stroke. Symptoms that indicate need for a quick administration of the therapy (call 911) include paralysis of part of the body, drooping of facial muscles, and/or impairment of speech or motor abilities.

Alcoholism

For adults aged 60 or older, both continuation of problem drinking and late-onset problem drinking are known to occur. Welte and Mirand (1993) studied heavy drinking among elderly Americans in order to examine its relationship to the stress they encountered in their lives. Such stressors include "death or illness of family members and friends, caretaking of infirm spouses, decline of their own physical and mental abilities, loss of relationships with friends and associates, and retirement" (p. 67). Unfortunately, alcohol abuse is often difficult to recognize in elderly adults, who may exhibit conditions related to aging in general. For those taking medications, alcohol may cause them to suffer from negative reactions or may interfere in the aging process.

Prostate Cancer

Until recently, one of the leading causes of death among men, prostate cancer, was seen as unrelated to lifestyle (Harvard Men's Health Watch, 1997). New research has discovered links between a number of behaviors and the disease. These dangerous behaviors are:

• Eating excessive dietary fat (red meat is the leading culprit).

• Drinking too much alcohol (those who had more than 22 drinks a week had a 40 percent greater risk than light drinkers, and for those who had 57 or more, the risk was 90 percent higher).

• Smoking (even light smoking is risky).

• Too little exercise (those who burned 4,000 calories per week cut their risk in half).

Alzheimer's Disease

Alzheimer's disease is one of the two most common forms of dementia that affect the elderly, and is probably the single greatest source of affliction and debilitation (National Institute on Aging, 1993). The German neurologist Alois Alzheimer discovered the disease in 1906, but it did not gain attention until the 1970s. Researchers have announced that they have found a gene that is implicated in the cause. This does not, however, mean they have found a cure for it. Alzheimer's is difficult to diagnose and even more difficult to treat. Relatively few of its symptoms, which can include the deterioration of one's ability to learn, reason, remember, control behavior, or perform basic tasks of daily life, respond to any type of treatment, and then only in the earliest stages. Alzheimer's disease usually follows a 6- to 20-year course (Eastman, 1997).

Alzheimer's differs from what is called multi-infarct dementia in several ways. Those who exhibit signs of multi-infarct dementia are likely to remain stable for long periods of time or show signs of improvement, then suddenly develop new symptoms. The symptoms associated with Alzheimer's begin slowly and become steadily worse.

The normal brain consists of billions of nerve cells (neurons), which convey messages to one another chemically by way of branchlike structures called dendrites and axons. Neuron groups generate specific chemical transmitters that travel between cells at the synapses. Although Alzheimer's victims look normal externally, their brains are undergoing severe changes. Brain autopsies unmask severe damage, abnormalities, and even death of neurons. Once neurons die, they can never be replaced. Current research on Alzheimer's, however, is developing medications that might actually preserve the health of nerve cells before they die. Researchers hope one day to be able to identify very early, presymptomatic cases of the disease and treat the individual with these medications in order to prevent the appearance of symptoms of the disease (Eastman, 1997). Often as little as 10 percent of the normal amount of acetylcholine exists, and the degree of its loss corresponds closely to the severity of the disease (Gelman, 1989).

Several theories have been put forth to explain the causes of Alzheimer's. Some theorists believe that a virus causes the disease, whereas others think that environmental factors are involved. A popular theory is that an overabundance of metal accumulation in the neurons, mainly aluminum, causes it. Some dispute this theory, because although we all ingest aluminum, our bodies reject it by refusing to digest it. There is also some indication that Alzheimer's burns hole in the cells, thus impairing their function. Administering large doses of vitamin E may help prevent the disease, and may slow its progress. All of these possibilities are currently being studied scientifically.

It now appears that Alzheimer's may be transmitted genetically, because we know that a sibling of an Alzheimer's patient has a 50 percent chance of contracting the disorder. Almost all persons with Down syndrome, a genetic disorder, will develop Alzheimer's disease if they live long enough. It may be that a defective gene makes a person likely to get it if environmental conditions are present.

It is also known that Alzheimer's does not discriminate on the basis of ethnicity (Exploring the Environment, 1996). Women are somewhat more likely to contract the disease, but to date it is not known why, and some research has shown that being female is not a risk factor.

The president of the Alzheimer's Association reports that the cost of caring for an Alzheimer's patient in the home is $18,000 to $20,000 per year, whereas nursing home care may reach anywhere from $40,000 to $70,000 per year (Alzheimer's Association, 1996). The financial burden is usually placed on the patient's family, because neither Medicare nor most private health care insurance covers the cost of the long-term care these patients need. As a result, seven out of ten Alzheimer's patients live at home and nearly 75 percent of homecare is provided by family and friends (Alzheimer's Association, 1996). Another alternative to chronic care is the adult-care

Facts about Alzheimer's

- Approximately 10 percent of the 65-and-over population may have Alzheimer's. Forty-seven percent over 85 already have the disease.
- The National Institute of Health allocated $5.1 million for Alzheimer's research in 1978, and $123.4 million for research in 1989. Though the dollar amount allocated for research has increased each year, more money is needed.
- Heredity is the cause in 10 to 30 percent of all Alzheimer's cases.
- There are always at least two victims of Alzheimer's: the afflicted person and the primary caregiver. The stress of caring for Alzheimer's patients makes the primary caregiver much more vulnerable to infectious disease, as well as vulnerable to all the problems that go with dealing with high levels of stress.
- Although caring for the Alzheimer's patient may often seem to be a thankless task, evidence indicates that sensitive listening and attempts to enter the patient's reality may help prevent antisocial behavior and anxiety-related outbursts (Bohling, 1991).
- Family members and friends can help Alzheimer's patients maintain their daily routines, physical activities, and social contacts. Keeping these patients informed about what is going on in their daily lives may prevent brain activity from failing at a more rapid pace (National Institute on Aging, 1993). Some people find it helpful to use a big calendar, notes about daily plans and safety measures, and instructions about how to use household items.
- Proper nutrition is important for those victims of Alzheimer's. A balanced diet greatly helps to maintain health, because no special diets or supplements have been able to prevent or reverse dementia (National Institute on Aging, 1993).

Two books that offer many suggestions on how to care for Alzheimer's patients at home are: (1) Carly Hellen's *Alzheimer's disease: Activity-focused care,* Butterworth-Heinemann, Woburn, MA. (2) The Alzheimer's Association's *Activity programming for persons with dementia,* Chicago, IL.

facility. These programs provide help with daily tasks such as feeding, washing, toileting, and exercising.

At this time the outlook is bleak for patients and families suffering with Alzheimer's. This disease is becoming linked more frequently to the debate over physician-assisted suicide, as victims of Alzheimer's wish to avoid the inevitable pain and suffering that lies ahead (Glass, 1993). If you desire further information on what is known about the disease, write to the Alzheimer's Association, 70 East Lake Street, Suite 600, Chicago, Illinois, 60601.

The Gastric System

For years doctors have assumed that digestive problems of the elderly have been the result of a decline in the secretion of gastric acids. Reasoning that the elderly seem to get ulcers as readily as younger people, Hurwitz and associates (1997) tested a group of 250 elderly and found only a small percent to be low secreters. This is good news for older adults because it means they do not have to worry about absorption rates of the medications they need to take, among other concerns.

The Relationship between Physical and Mental Health

In their study of the general health of 1,139 elderly persons living in an urban community, Gerson and associates (1987) made a number of interesting findings:

- A strong relationship exists between physical and mental health.
- Married men have better health than unmarried men (married women are not healthier than unmarried women). This may be because their wives take care of them, or because they feel responsible to their families to maintain their health.
- Social resources are strongly associated with mental health for women, but less so for men. Probably women are more likely than men to use their social

Gateball and the Japanese Elderly

Gateball, developed in post–World War II Japan, is a team sport combining elements of golf and croquet. It employs strategies that exercise both mind and body. Although the object is to score the most points, a great deal of emphasis is placed on the individual's contributions to the team as opposed to individual achievement.

In addition to these benefits, gateball also provides a social outlet, building relationships around a common interest. Gateball has become immensely popular among "silver agers," as older people are called by the Japanese. In a modern, crowded, industrial country like Japan, with early retirement and the highest life expectancy in the world, gateball provides a way for seniors to continue their lifelong pattern of group participation in something worthwhile.

Observations of gateball players in action found people who share information, laughter, and a relaxed sense of belonging. When a player who hadn't been there for some time reappeared, he or she was warmly welcomed back. Exchange of food occurs routinely on the break, and people often encourage others to take some home with them.

In America, this kind of community spirit among seniors is evidenced in some sports (such as golf and bowling), but the stereotype of the elderly person in the rocking chair remains pervasive. Sports provide a means by which older people can remain healthy as well as connected to other people. It is another important lesson we might glean from Japanese culture.

resources to help them maintain their mental health. Many men hate to admit to their friends that they are having a mental disturbance, because it is not considered "manly."

• Economic resources are clearly related to mental health. As previously pointed out, this is especially true for African American women.

A stereotype exists that the older people get, the less health-conscious they become. The picture is usually more complex than this. For example, compared with those in their sixties and eighties, centenarians (those over 100) ate breakfast more regularly, avoided diets, ate more vegetables, and relied on their doctor more than on the news media for nutrition information (Johnson & others, 1991). They also were found to be more dominant and imaginative (Martin & others, 1992). On the other hand, they did not tend to avoid fats or comply with nutritional guidelines designed to reduce the risk of chronic disease (Johnson & others, 1991). Here again we see the complex interaction of biopsychosocial factors as they affect health and the aging process.

Recent findings further refute the stereotype that elderly people are less health conscious (Anderson, 1996). In fact, elderly patients tend to worry about well-being more than younger patients, but what they worry about is not necessarily of concern. For example, elderly people may worry about getting enough fiber in their diet and disregard the very real danger of falling.

Health and Retirement

Muller and Boaz (1988) stated: "Many studies of the retirement decision have found that poor health increases the probability of retirement. Yet doubts have been expressed whether self-reported deterioration of health is a genuine cause of retirement, rather than a socially acceptable excuse" (p. 52). These researchers studied the actual health status of retirees and found support for the idea that the majority of those who say they are retiring for health reasons are telling the truth.

Health unquestionably affects the physical abilities of adults across the age range. Yet it is also clear that social circumstances are the main factor in health in the older years. Thus, the healthiness of adults appears to be more a result of the cultural conditions in which they find themselves than of their age.

Appearance

All of the physical factors treated earlier have an effect on the person's self-concept, but none has a stronger impact than physical appearance. Appearance is of great importance in the United States. A youthful appearance matters a great deal, and to women more than to men. Because women are affected by the "double standard" of aging, they are more likely to use diet, exercise, clothing, and cosmetics to maintain their youthful appearance. Nevertheless, significant changes in physical appearance occur with age that cannot be avoided.

Guided Review

6. Physical abilities such as reaction time are not only affected by the aging process but also by motivations, depression, anxiety, _____ _____, response style, and ageism.
7. All five senses decline with age but hearing ability may be a more serious problem than _____, because people are less likely to wear a hearing aid than they are _____.
8. Because of continuous stretching of _____, the skin begins to lengthen and lose its elasticity with age.
9. Alzheimer's disease, a serious mental loss in some elderly persons, is caused by the inability of the _____ to produce acetylcholine.
10. Research indicates that Alzheimer's disease may be transmitted _____, because we know that a _____ of an Alzheimer's patient has a 50 percent chance of contracting the disorder.
11. When it comes to appearance in aging, there is a _____ _____ for men and for women.

Sales of products that promote youth and beauty are booming.

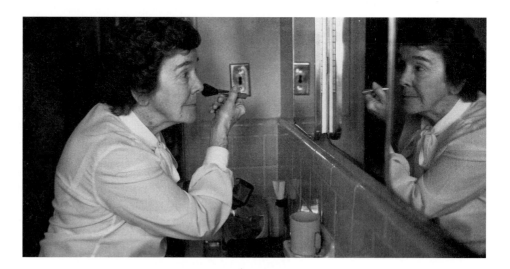

As you can see from the data presented in this chapter, a certain amount of physical decline happens in later life, but it does not occur until most people are quite advanced in age. And with the new medical technologies and marked trend toward adopting more healthy living styles, you can expect to see a much more capable elderly population. Will this happy news also be true for cognitive development?

Answers

6. response strategies 7. vision, glasses 8. collagen 9. brain 10. genetically, sibling 11. double standard

A Comparison of Physical Abilities

One of the best ways of comprehending adult development is to do a miniseries of experiments of your own. In this activity, you can compare the physical development of friends and relatives with just a few simple pieces of equipment. Pick at least three people in at least two age groups. The results might surprise you.

You may find that you need to alter the instructions of the following experiments to make it more convenient for you to do the study. This is perfectly all right, as long as you make sure that each test is the same for every person who takes it. The greater the variety of the adults you enlist in the study, in factors such as age, sex, and religion, the more interesting your results will be.

A. *Muscular strength.* Several of the following tests require a heavy table. Simply have each subject grasp a leg of the table with one hand and raise the leg off the ground 3 inches. Subjects who can hold it up 3 inches for 30 seconds have succeeded in step 1. Now have them try to hold it up another 3 inches, and if they succeed they get credit for step 2 (each step must be done for 30 seconds). In step 3 they must hold it at a height of 1 foot, in step 4 they must hold it at a height of 1 1/2 feet, and in step 5 at a height of 2 feet. Record one point for each step successfully completed.

B. *Vision.* The subject should be seated at the table with chin resting on forearms and forearms resting on the table. Set a magazine at a distance of 2 feet and ask the subject to read two lines. Next 3 feet, then 4 feet, then 5 feet, and finally at 6 feet. One point is given for each step.

C. *Hearing.* The subject is seated with his or her back to the table. You will need some instrument that makes the same level of noise for the same period of time. For example, a portable radio might be turned on a brief moment and turned back off, each time at the same volume. A clicker might be used. Whatever you use, make the standard noise at 2 feet behind the subject and have him or her raise a hand when the sound is heard. Then make the sound at 4 feet, 6 feet, 10 feet, and 20 feet. You may need to vary these distances, depending on the volume of the instrument you are using. Be sure to vary the intervals between the noises that you make, so that you can be sure the subject is

really hearing the noise when you make it. Give points for each appropriate response.

D. *Smell,* E. *Taste,* and F. *Touch.* For these three tests, you will need five cups of equal size. The cups should hold milk, cola, soft ice cream, yogurt, and applesauce. Each food should be chilled to approximately the same temperature. Blindfold subjects and ask them to tell you what the five substances are.

G. *Reaction Time—I.* For this test you will need three squares, three circles, three triangles; one of each is 1 inch high, 2 inches high, and 3 inches high. Make them of cardboard, plastic, or wood. Arrange the nine figures in random order in front of the subject. Tell the subject that when you call out the name of one of the figures (e.g., a large square), he or she is to put a finger on it as quickly as possible. Call out the name of one of the figures, and time the response. Repeat this test five times, calling out a different figure each time, and compute the total time required for the five trials.

H. *Reaction Time—II.* Again arrange the nine pieces randomly in front of the subject. You will call out either the shape ("circle") or a size ("middle-size"). The subject puts the three circles or the three middle-size pieces in a pile as quickly as possible. Repeat this experiment five times, using a different designator each time, and compute the total time the task requires.

I. *Health—I.* Ask subjects to carefully count the number of times they have been in the hospital. Give them one point if they have been hospitalized 10 times or more, two points for 5 through 9 times, three points for 3 times, four points for no more than 1 time, five points if they have never been hospitalized for any reason (pregnancy should not be counted).

J. *Health—II.* Ask subjects to carefully remember how many times they have visited a doctor within the past year. Give one point for 4 or more times, two points for 3 times, three points for 2 times, four points for 1 time, five points for no visits at all.

Compare the scores for each test for persons within the age groups you have chosen. Do you see any patterns? Are the results of aging evident? What other conclusions can you draw?

Cognitive Development

In Chapter 15, we described the changes in intelligence that develop across the adult lifespan, focusing on middle age. In this chapter we take a closer look at old age. The major question is whether a significant decline in cognitive competence tends to occur as we become elderly. A review of the research on this question reveals a serious conflict. Salthouse (1990) stated it well:

Results from psychometric tests and experimental tasks designed to assess cognitive ability frequently reveal rather substantial age-related declines in the range from 20 to 70 years of age.... On the other hand, adults in their 60s and 70s are seldom perceived to be less cognitively competent than adults in their 20s and 30s, and in fact, many of the most responsible and demanding leadership positions in society are routinely held by late middle-aged or older adults. (p. 310)

Cognitive Ability in the Elderly: Tests versus Observations

So wherein lies the truth—in the results of tests, or in our observations of actual performance? As we said, the answer is not simple. What factors could account for this discrepancy? Currently there are four hypotheses, each of which play a part (Salthouse, 1990):

- *Differences in type of cognition.* Intelligence tests tend to measure specific bands of cognitive ability, whereas assessments of real-life activities probably also include noncognitive capacities, such as personality traits. Thus some aspects of IQ may decline without causing lowered performance on the job, for example.

- *Differences in the representativeness of the individuals or observations.* Many examples exist of elderly persons who can perform admirably even into their nineties, but do these individuals really represent the average elderly person? Probably not. It is also probable that only the most competent individuals are able to survive in such demanding situations. Those who are less competent will have dropped out of the competition at an earlier age. Therefore, when we examine the abilities of successful older persons, we may be studying only the "cream of the crop." Finally, it seems likely that observed competence represents only one type of cognitive ability (balancing the company's books, reading music), whereas intelligence testing involves several (verbal, math, reasoning, and other abilities).

- *Different standards of evaluation.* Most cognitive tests tend to push individuals to their limits of ability. Assessments of real-life tasks, those with which people are quite familiar (such as reading the newspaper), may require a lower standard of testing.

- *Different amounts of experience.* Doing well on an intelligence test requires one to employ traits that are not used every day, such as assembling blocks so that they resemble certain patterns. The skills assessed in real-life situations are more likely to be those the individual has practiced for years. For example, driving ability may remain high if the person continues to drive regularly as she ages.

Each of these hypotheses seeks to explain the discrepancy between tested ability and actual performance as being the result of faulty research techniques. Many other writers have suggested that perhaps the elderly really are inferior in cognitive competence to younger persons but that they find ways to compensate for their lost cognitive abilities. Thus older persons are able to maintain performance levels even as ability is waning. Unfortunately, no one has suggested how such compensation might be achieved, so this hypothesis is doubtful.

Another question about the decline of cognitive ability in the elderly is, can lowered capacity be recovered through training? Here there is good news. Numerous methods have been successful in improving elderly cognitive skills. For example, important improvements have been demonstrated in:

- Spatial orientation and inductive reasoning (Willis & Schaie, 1986)

- The flexibility of fluid intelligence and problem-solving strategies (Baltes & others, 1989)

- Cognitive plasticity of memory skills (Kliegl & others, 1989, 1990)

- Long-term effects of fluid ability (in the old-old) (Willis & Nessleroade, 1990)

It seems likely that, through the use of new training techniques and possibly through new drugs, the decline in cognitive ability in old age (whatever it may actually be) will submit to reductions and even reversals in the years to come.

Another aspect of cognitive decline has proven of great interest to psychologists. It is referred to as terminal drop.

Terminal Drop

Researchers have come to several different conclusions concerning the effect of age on intelligence level.

Birren was the first to discuss **terminal drop** (1964). He defined it as the period preceding the person's death, from a few weeks up to two years prior. This research looks at the relationship, not between intelligence and age (which is the number of years from birth till the time of testing), but between intelligence and survivorship (which is the number of years from the time of testing until death). The hypothesis is that the person's perception, consciously or unconsciously, of impending death may cause the decline in intelligence. This perception causes the person to begin withdrawing from the world. Consequently, performance on an intelligence test drops markedly.

According to Birren,

> The individual himself may or may not be aware in himself of diffuse changes in mood, in mental functioning, or in the way his body responds. Terminal [drop] may be paced by a disease initially remote from the nervous system, such as a cancer of the stomach. Thereafter, over a series of months, a rapid sequence of changes might be observed in overt behavior or in measured psychological characteristics of the individual. It is as though at this point the physiology of the individual had started on a new phase, that the organism is unable to stop. (p. 280)

The terminal drop hypothesis has had considerable support over the years. For example, Siegler (1975) reviewed eight studies of the phenomenon and discovered a strong positive relationship between the length of survivorship and high level of intellectual ability. That is, the higher the intelligence, the longer the person is likely to live after the time of testing.

Some researchers have questioned whether terminal drop pervades all cognitive abilities or is restricted to specific ones. In a study designed to answer this question, White and Cunningham (1988) found terminal drop to apply to a shorter period than five years and to be more restricted than was previously thought. They reached the following conclusions:

> Only vocabulary scores for those who died at age 70 or less and within two years of testing were affected by terminal drop. . . . Thus the terminal drop phenomenon may be limited to abilities that typically are relatively unaffected by age, such as vocabulary or other verbal abilities. Furthermore, the effects may be restricted to a time period much closer to death than had been originally proposed. (p. 141)

Small and Backman (1997) studied the effects of terminal drop among the very old (ages 75 to 95). They found that ". . . episodic memory and verbal skill may be particularly sensitive in predicting such effects" (p. 309).

One final warning: Although virtually all studies described here use IQ tests to measure intelligence, the two are not identical. IQ involves school-related abilities, whereas intelligence is made up of these and many other abilities (e.g., spatial ability and "street smarts"). It is not possible at present to discern how much this discrepancy affects the research. Another mental trait that is hard to study, but is even more vital to understand and cultivate, is creativity.

An Applied View

Ways to Keep Memory Functioning

Memory loss is one of the signs of aging that causes people the most concern. A 50-year-old may worry about forgetfulness, whereas a 70-year-old may fear that this forgetfulness is actually a sign of Alzheimer's disease. In a society that is full of information, such as written words, television, and computer technology, it is not surprising that people feel a sense of overload, and a sense of fear when they can't remember where they parked their car. What may be surprising, however, are the recent findings that memory doesn't really diminish over the years.

Although brain changes do occur with age, these changes do not necessarily mean that memory loss will be the result. Rather, it simply takes older people longer to learn, and requires more effort to store memory for quick recall later. It is the stresses and distractions in the environment that keep people from retrieving details more easily. In the right environment, one that includes physical and mind-stimulating activities and reduced stress, the memory of healthy people in their seventies and eighties can expand.

Photographs can aid memory, but also can induce false memory in older adults (ages 60 to 75). Angell and associates (1997) found that viewing photographs can prompt better recall in both older and younger adults (ages 16 to 22). However, older adults were more likely to "remember" an event in which they had not participated but only had viewed in a photograph.

Studies have shown that people who feel good about themselves and who feel a sense of control in their lives are better prepared to maintain their mental abilities. Self-help classes for memory improvement are one way in which older people can take an active role in strengthening their memory capacities. Although some people believe that drugs or herbs can improve memory, there is no convincing proof that substances work. Taking the initiative to exercise their minds, older people may still occasionally forget where they put their slippers, but they won't soon forget the essentials.

Creativity

In Chapter 15, we concluded that quantity of creative production probably drops in old age but that quality of production may not. This is based on studies of actual productivity. But what about potential for production? Might it be that the elderly are capable of great creativity but that, as with IQ, factors like motivation and opportunity prevent them from fulfilling this ability? That is the question addressed by the next set of studies we'll discuss.

Cross-Sectional Studies of Creative Productivity

The first large-scale study to look at the creative productivity of typical people at various ages who are still alive was completed by Alpaugh and associates (1976; see also Alpaugh & Birren, 1977). They administered two batteries of creativity tests to 111 schoolteachers aged 20 to 83. Their findings supported the idea that creativity does decline with age. One major criticism of their research is that the tests they used are probably not equally valid for all age groups. The younger subjects are more likely to have had practice with these types of materials than the older ones. For example, the study of creativity is relatively new, so the tests used to measure it have been designed recently. Thus those who attended school more recently are more likely to have encountered such tests than those who graduated many years ago. Such familiarity would provide an advantage to the younger subjects in the study.

Jaquish and Ripple (1980) attempted to evaluate the effects of aging while avoiding the problem of using age-related materials. These researchers gathered data on six age groups across the lifespan: 10 to 12 years (61 people); 13 to 17 years (71 people); 18 to 25 years (70 people); 26 to 39 years (58 people); 40 to 60 years (51 people); and 61 to 84 years (39 people). The study had a total of 350 subjects.

The definition of creativity in this study was restricted to the concepts of fluency, flexibility, and originality; these are collectively known as divergent thinking

Research indicates that the time right after retirement can be a period of creative growth, as the individual turns from the demands of a work schedule to the opportunities offered by an artistic endeavor.

abilities. These three traits were measured through the use of an auditory exercise, which was recorded on cassette. Known as the Sounds and Images Test, it elicits responses to the "weird" sounds presented on the tape. Responses are then scored according to the three traits of divergent thinking. The researchers believe that this test is so unusual that no age group is likely to have had more experience with it than any other.

A number of interesting findings have resulted from this study, as you can see in Table 17.2. On all three measures of divergent thinking, the scores generally increased slightly across the first five age groups. Scores for the 40- to 60-year-old group increased significantly, whereas scores for the 61- to 84-year-old group decreased significantly below the scores of any of the younger age groups. Furthermore, when decline in divergent thinking did occur, it was more pronounced in quantity than in quality. That is, greater age differences occurred in fluency (a measure of quantity) than in originality (a measure of quality). Finally, it is not known to what extent the oldest subjects were affected by hearing loss, particularly of high and low tones. Obviously, this could be an alternative explanation of the findings for this oldest group.

Probably the most important finding of the study had to do with the relationship between divergent thinking and self-esteem, which was measured by the Coopersmith Self-Esteem Inventory. Table 17.2 indicates that self-esteem follows a pattern quite similar to the other three traits.

TABLE 17.2 MEANS FOR DIVERGENT THINKING AND SELF-ESTEEM SCORES

Age Group	Fluency	Flexibility	Originality	Self-Esteem
	Mean	Mean	Mean	Mean
18–25	31	19	19	34
26–39	30	18	19	37
40–60	36	21	20	38
61–84	22	15	15	32

From G. Jaquish and R. E. Ripple, "Cognitive Creative Abilities Across the Adult Life Span" in *Human Development*. Copyright ©1980 S. Karger AG, Basel, Switzerland. Reprinted by permission of the publisher.

Of special interest is the relationship between self-esteem and divergent thinking for the oldest group: The correlations were moderately high in every case. This indicates that self-esteem may have a positive effect on creative abilities over the years, or that creativity may enhance self-esteem, or both. Jaquish and Ripple (1980) concluded that

> There is much more plasticity in adult development than has been traditionally assumed. Such an interpretation should find a hospitable audience among those people concerned with educational intervention. If the creative abilities of older adults were to be realized in productivity, it would be difficult to overestimate the importance of the formation of new attitudes of society, teachers in continuing adult education programs, and in the older adults themselves. (p. 152)

The Stages of Life during Which Creativity May Best Be Cultivated

In this final section we present Dacey's theory (1989b) that there are certain critical periods in life during which creative ability can be cultivated most effectively. Its relevance to the study of late adulthood will be obvious. Table 17.3 presents a list of these periods for males and females.

The basic premise of this theory is that a person's inherent creativity can blossom best during a period of crisis and change (Esquivel, 1995; Freedman, 1993; Hennessey, 1995; Litterst & Eyo, 1993; Moukwa, 1995; Tavalin, 1995; Zerbe, 1992). The six periods chosen in table 17.3 are ages at which most people experience stress due to life changes.

TABLE 17.3	PEAK PERIODS OF LIFE DURING WHICH CREATIVITY MAY MOST READILY BE CULTIVATED	
For Males	**For Females**	
1. 0–5 years old	0–5 years old	
2. 11–14 years old	10–13 years old	
3. 18–20 years old	18–20 years old	
4. 29–31 years old	29–31 years old	
5. 40–45 years old	40 (37?)–45 years old	
6. 60–65 years old	60–65 years old	

Reprinted with the permission of Lexington Books, an imprint of The Free Press, a Division of Simon & Schuster, Inc., from *Fundamentals of Creative Thinking* by John S. Dacey. Copyright © 1989 by Lexington Books.

The table presents a new theory, and thus it must be considered speculative. Nevertheless some direct evidence supports it. Some excellent research from the fields of personality and cognitive development also indicates that these periods are more volatile than any others.

Included in the theory is the concept that major gains in creative performance are less likely with each succeeding period. That is, what happens to the person in the early years is far more influential than what happens in the later years. The older people become, the less likely they are to have a sudden burst of highly creative production.

The Sixth Peak Period

Evidence for the first five peak periods has been presented earlier in this book. The first period is mentioned in Chapter 7 (although not called creativity per se), the second and third in Chapter 12, the fourth in Chapter 14, and the fifth in Chapter 16. The rationale for the sixth period, from 60 to 65, is reviewed here.

For most men and for a growing number of women, this is the period in which retirement occurs. Even if a woman has not been in the labor force, she has many adjustments to make because of her husband's retirement. Thus most adults are faced with a major adjustment of self-concept at this time in their lives.

Although some do not adjust well and begin withdrawing from society, others take advantage of the change to pursue creative goals that had previously been impossible for them. Obviously a majority of the "young old" (the new term for those who are aged 60 to 70) do not suddenly become creative, but a substantial number do. Of the several thousand highly productive people he studied, Lehman (1953, 1962) found more than 100, or almost 5 percent, whose major productivity began in the years after 60.

In addition to highly visible contributions, many of the elderly become creative in less newsworthy ways. Gerontologist Jack Botwinick, who presents an excellent analysis of this topic in his book *Aging and Behavior* (1984), suggested that many elderly persons exercise a newfound creativity by mentoring younger people. Though largely unheralded, such guidance and encouragement of younger creators unquestionably has invaluable benefits for society.

This is not to say that maintaining or increasing creative performance in one's later years is easy. There are inherent problems that are not readily overcome. Psychologist B.F. Skinner (1983), who had a 60-year-long career of highly creative achievement, stated that productivity is difficult for the elderly because they tend to lose interest in work, find it hard to start working, and work more slowly:

> It is easy to attribute this change to them, but we should not overlook a change in their world. For motivation, read reinforcement. In old age, behavior is not so strongly reinforced. Biological aging weakens reinforcing consequences. Behavior is more and more likely to be followed by aches and pains and quick fatigue. Things tend to become "not worth doing" in the sense that the aversive consequences exact too high a price. Positive reinforcers become less common and less powerful. Poor vision closes off the world of art, faulty hearing the enjoyment of highly fidelitous music. Foods do not taste as good, and erogenous tissues grow less sensitive. Social reinforcers are attenuated. Interests and tastes are shared with a smaller number of people. (p. 28)

It is increasingly clear that creativity may blossom at any age. This theory of "the peak periods of creative growth" is not meant to disparage that fact. Solid evidence indicates, however, that the best opportunities lie in the six periods identified by the theory. Are there also periods in the development of gender roles in later life that have special importance? of sexuality? of family relations? of work and retirement? We'll examine these questions in the next chapter.

One final point: What is the relationship between intelligence and creativity, and how do they relate to the highest level of human cognition, wisdom? In Table 17.4, Robert Sternberg's (1990) comparison of the three is presented.

As you can see in Table 17.4, the phrase "going beyond" typifies the concept of creativity. Robert Kegan, in his groundbreaking book, *In Over Our Heads* (1994), suggests that as the average life span continues to increase, we will be "going beyond" more and more, simply because more people live to old age:

> A hundred years ago the average American lived to an age we today call "mid-life," the middle forties. Today the average American lives more than twenty years longer, an entire generation longer for each individual life. What might the individual generate given an additional generation to live? My candidate: a qualitatively new order of consciousness. I suggest we are gradually seeing more adults working on a qualitatively different order of consciousness than did adults one hundred years ago because we live twenty or more years longer than we used to. (p. 352)

📖 Two books that delve into how changes in cognitive functioning are experienced in old age are: (1) Sarton's *As we are now.* New York: Norton. A novel in the form of the diary of a retired schoolteacher, this is a powerful portrayal of her experiences when she is put in a nursing home by her relatives. (2) Skinner and Vaughan's *Enjoy old age: A program of self-management.* New York: Norton. In this book, the grandfather of behaviorism explains how to use behavior modification to better handle the problems of aging. A good read, whether you are elderly or plan to help someone who is.

TABLE 17.4   SUMMARY, SIMPLIFIED COMPARISON AMONG WISDOM, INTELLIGENCE, AND CREATIVITY

	Construct		
Aspect	Wisdom	Intelligence	Creativity
Knowledge	Understanding of its presuppositions and meanings and as well as its limitations	Recall, analysis, and use	Going beyond what is available
Processes	Understanding of what is automatic and why	Automatization of procedures	Applied to novel tasks
Primary intellectual style	Judicial	Executive	Legislative
Personality	Understanding of ambiguity and obstacles	Eliminating ambiguity and overcoming obstacles within conventional framework	Tolerance of ambiguity and redefinition of obstacles
Motivation	To understand what is known and what it means	To know and to use what is known	To go beyond what is known
Environmental context	Appreciation in environment of depth of understanding	Appreciation in environment of extent and breadth of understanding	Appreciation in environment of going beyond what is currently understood

From R. J. Sternberg, *Wisdom.* Copyright ©1990, Cambridge University Press, New York. Reprinted with the permission of Cambridge University Press.

Guided Review

12. Discrepancies between the results of tests and our observations of cognitive abilities may be due to differences in type of cognition, differences in the representation of the individuals or observations, different standards of _____, and different amounts of experience.
13. Training can increase abilities in older adults. However, about two years before death, a _____ _____ in mental functioning often occurs.
14. It is suggested that a decline in intelligence in the later years may be caused by the person's _____ of impending death.
15. Jaquish and Ripple found in their studies on creativity that there is a correlation between _____ and creativity.
16. Dacey sees creativity as blossoming during periods of _____ and _____.
17. Wisdom is different from both creativity and intelligence, in that it has a focus on _____.

CONCLUSION

At the beginning of this chapter we asked, "Must growing old mean decline?" The answer is that some decline is inevitable, but the picture is much less gloomy than we have been led to believe. The loss of mental and physical abilities is, on the average, relatively slight; some individuals experience only moderate physical loss and no cognitive loss at all. For many older adults, compensatory skills and abilities may replace lost capacities. The same is true for personal and social development.

Here once again we run into the bugaboo of all human development: the

Answers

12. evaluation (or testing)   13. terminal drop   14. perception   15. self-esteem   16. crisis, change   17. understanding

self-fulfilling prophecy. Because American society has been changing rapidly for many decades, older adults are frequently viewed as incompetent—their experience appears to have little relevance in "modern times." Yet carefully controlled laboratory measurements of their abilities make clear that their losses may be relatively slight.

Perhaps as we learn to understand the aging process, and as the process is better understood by the public in general, the majority of adults will not assume that their abilities must undergo severe decline. In such a situation, the quality of life of the elderly surely will improve greatly, and because we could reasonably expect an increase in the productive contributions of seniors, all of society would benefit!

In summary:

Must We Age and Die?

- A variety of physiological theories regarding aging and death exist. These include aging by program, homeostatic imbalance, and cross-linkage theories.
- Gene theory also suggests that aging is programmed but says that the program exists in certain harmful genes.

- The natural environment is also an important factor in mortality (e.g., now fewer elderly mortalities are due to the spread of influenza).
- Major modifiers of ability such as training, nutrition, illness, stress level, and personality type also affect one's rate of aging.

Physical Development

- Although reaction time appears to decline with age, Elias and others have pointed to several reasons for this decline.
- We may conclude that variables other than sheer neural or motor activities account for most change in physical skills over time. These include ageism, motivation, depression, anxiety, response strategies, and response style.
- Changes in sensory abilities, the skeletal system, skin, teeth, hair, and locomotion are noticeable in late adulthood.
- Even though hormone production slows down during late adulthood, a detriment in one area is often compensated for by some other gland.
- Probably the single greatest scourge of the elderly, and in many ways the

most debilitating, is Alzheimer's disease.
- A strong relationship exists between physical and mental health.

Cognitive Development

- A number of factors have been suggested as explaining the difference between tested and observed changes in elderly cognition. These include differences in type of cognition, the representativeness of the individuals or observations, standards of evaluation, and amounts of experience.
- The person's perception, consciously or unconsciously, of impending death may cause a decline in intelligence in the later years. This is called terminal drop.
- Creativity is evidenced in late adulthood and in some cases may be strongest during this time. Although quantity of creative production probably drops in old age, the quality of creative production and potential ability probably do not.

KEY TERMS

Accumulation of errors
Accumulation of metabolic waste
Ageism
Aging by program

Antigens
Autoimmunity
Collagen
Cross-linkage theory

Gene theory
Homeostatic imbalance
Terminal drop
Wear and tear theory

WHAT DO YOU THINK?

1. Which of the explanations of why we age and die do you find most persuasive?
2. Which factors do you believe most strongly affect aging: physiological, genetic, environmental, or some others?
3. Regarding the decline of physical systems, which has the greatest impact on the person's life: reaction time, sensory abilities,

other body systems, hormonal balance, health, or appearance? Why?
4. Johnny Kelly of Boston ran the Boston Marathon every year until he was well into his eighties. Why do some people seem to age so much better than others?
5. Regarding the decline of cognitive systems, which has the greatest impact on the person's life:

intelligence, creativity, memory, or learning? Why?
6. Programs in which young people meet regularly with elderly adults seem to have rewards for all involved. By what other means might we better tap the knowledge and creativity of the elderly?
7. What is the nature of wisdom?

CHAPTER REVIEW TEST

1. The counterpart theory holds that
   a. the aging process is programmed.
   b. factors in human existence useful in earlier years become counterproductive in later years.
   c. early deterioration is due to hard work and a stressful lifestyle.
   d. the aging process is due to alterations in cell proteins.

2. One explanation of aging is that the various life-support systems gradually weaken and that death comes about as a cumulative result of these various weaknesses. This refers to which aspect of aging?
   a. Genetic
   b. Environmental
   c. Physiological
   d. Human abilities

3. According to the cross-linkage theory, what happens to collagen, the major connective tissue in the body that provides elasticity in our skin, as we grow older?
   a. it becomes a waste product as a result of a metabolism build-up in the body
   b. it causes early aging
   c. it contributes to our body's tissues becoming more self-rejecting
   d. our skin wrinkles because the proteins of collagen are altered

4. A failure in the body's systems to regulate the proper interaction of organs is known as
   a. cross-linkage theory.
   b. autoimmunity.
   c. homeostatic imbalance.
   d. counterpart theory.

5. Studies of monozygotic twins showing that they have more similar lengths of life than do dizygotic twins are evidence of which aspect of aging?
   a. Human ability

   b. Environmental
   c. Physiological
   d. Genetic

6. In examining the effects of the environment on aging, one factor that has contributed to lower mortality rates in Western culture is
   a. better diet.
   b. changes in the evolutionary process.
   c. the increased use of vaccines in early childhood.
   d. None of the above.

7. Stress level, educational level, motivation, and personality type are examples of
   a. genetic factors.
   b. physiological factors.
   c. environmental factors.
   d. modifiers of ability.

8. Ageism can be defined as
   a. the study of late adulthood.
   b. the study of human development as one ages.
   c. a type of prejudice toward older adults.
   d. physical changes from middle to older adulthood.

9. A breakdown in the system in the brain that produces acetylcholine results in
   a. Huntington's chorea.
   b. Alzheimer's disease.
   c. terminal drop.
   d. lowered intelligence.

10. Relatively few symptoms of Alzheimer's respond to any treatment, with the exception of
    a. anxiety.
    b. long-term memory loss.
    c. short-term memory loss.
    d. depression.

11. Research indicating that there is a strong positive relationship between the length of survivorship and high level of intellectual ability is known as the

    a. terminal drop theory.
    b. cross-linkage theory.
    c. homeostasis theory.
    d. the aging by program theory.

12. According to terminal drop theory, a person's perception of _____ causes the person to begin withdrawing from the world and, consequently, performance on an IQ test drops markedly.
    a. personal health
    b. impending death
    c. intellectual abilities
    d. interpersonal abilities

13. Jaquish and Ripple (1980) found a positive relationship between self-esteem and _____ for the oldest group of subjects.
    a. divergent thinking
    b. originality
    c. flexibility
    d. fluency

14. Jaquish and Ripple defined creativity using the concepts of fluency, flexibility, and originality—collectively known as
    a. divergent thinking.
    b. congruent thinking.
    c. a measure of intelligence.
    d. None of the above.

15. Dacey (1989b) proposed that there are certain _____ in life during which creative ability can be cultivated most effectively.
    a. work-related experiences
    b. critical periods
    c. ages
    d. educational experiences

16. During the sixth peak period, many people exercise a newfound creativity by
    a. relieving themselves from the stresses of life.
    b. retiring.
    c. increasing their cognitive abilities.
    d. mentoring younger people.

Psychosocial Development in Late Adulthood

Getting married in 1948 I married into a world that had a very definite definition of marriage. I married into a man-oriented society, where the man was the provider, the center, the whatnot, and the woman circled around the man. But I married Ruby Dee; Ruby had some other ideas about marriage. [Laughs.] There were one or two other extra things on her agenda that I didn't know about, but when they came up I saw no reason to challenge her. For example, after our first baby was born and we moved down to Mount Vernon, New York, I remember Ruby standing washing dishes one day and saying to me, quite confidently, "You know, I'm not going to do this the rest of my life." I said, "No? What are you going to do?" She said, "Well, I'm going to be an actor. I'm still going to act." I said, "Yes." She said, "I'm going to go to acting school." And I said, "Well, okay." And at that time we didn't have much money, so we decided that Ruby would go to acting school and I would stay home and sometimes wash the dishes and take care of the baby. And when Ruby came home she would teach me what she learned at the acting class.

Now, when I stepped into the marriage I didn't think of that, but that happened. And over the years I think the central thing that I've learned is how to more easily open my life and let Ruby in. I think women are much more generous in letting people into their lives than men—although I might be wrong. I think that men come with a sense that they are the complete embodiment of what God intended should represent value, virtue, power, and all that sort of thing, and that women, to some degree, are there to service and serve them—that's how women fulfill themselves. Gradually my wife and the circumstances of the time led me to a different understanding, and I'm glad for that, because it made me a broader and a deeper and a much richer person. It has enriched my spirit, my spirituality. It means also—and this is the best part of it all—that I learned a lesson a long time ago, and the lesson is, "The way to make a man rich is to decrease his wants." I learn more and more every day what not to want and how not to want it. To me that is the regimen of the spirit.

Actor and biographer Ossie Davis, age 75, and wife, Ruby Dee ✪

When you finish reading this chapter, you should be able to

- Define what is meant by "crossover" regarding gender roles in late adulthood.
- Contrast the social, emotional, and physical aspects of sexuality for men and women in late adulthood.
- Analyze White's summary comments regarding sexuality in late adulthood.
- Identify the four basic phases through which most adults pass in relation to their families.
- Describe characteristics of the older worker.
- Assess the relationship between retirement and leisure.
- Summarize Neugarten's findings regarding the effects of aging on personal development.
- Contrast activity theory with disengagement theory.
- Appraise Erikson's final stage of human development: integrity versus despair.

Research on the aging process got an encouraging boost from the American Psychological Association recently. This parent organization for psychologists formed the Continuing Committee on Aging (Abeles, 1997). The purpose of the committee is to foster ". . . research on normal and pathological aging; foster the development of a science of gender, ethnicity and aging; support psychological practice in nursing homes . . ." (p. 2), as well as other elderly concerns such as memory (Murray, 1997a), depression (DeAngelis, 1997), social priorities (Murray, 1997b), and the stress of caregiving to ill spouses (Murray, 1997c). In 1997, the keynote address to the A. P. A. annual convention was given by Nobel Laureate Elie Weisel, who emphasized the need for gratitude to the elderly for their role in helping us remember the lessons of the past, such as has been the case with the Holocaust (Sleek, 1997). He defended the right of the elderly and other often-victimized populations. These efforts by the A. P. A. to focus on elderly issues should help us deal with the problems caused by the mushrooming of the numbers of those in this age group, particularly in the area of social development.

Social Development

This section is devoted to five aspects of social development: gender roles, sexuality, families, the older worker, and retirement.

Gender Roles

You might think that when people reach old age, their gender roles will have become pretty well fixed. In fact, researchers have known for some time that this is not so.

> When people enter their sixties, they enter a new and final stage in the life cycle. At this point they confront the loss of many highly valued roles, the need to establish a new life structure for the remaining years, and the undeniable fact of life's termination. Widowhood and retirement are the central role transitions likely to occur at this time, but the death of friends and relatives also diminishes one's social network. Although people are aware of the inevitability of these role losses as they enter old age, their often abrupt reality may result in severe role discontinuity. (Sales, 1978, p. 185)

To sum up, the major concern for gender roles among the elderly is **role discontinuity.** See the accompanying box for several questions you should keep in mind as you read the theories and research summaries that follow.

The "crossover effect" concerns the tendency of men to do more things that are considered feminine, such as washing the dishes, and for women to do more things that are considered masculine, such as taking charge of repairs to the home.

What's Your VIEW?   Is Role Discontinuity Inherent in Growing Old?

Role discontinuity occurs when people experience an abrupt change in their style of life and their role in it. Is this a natural part of growing old? Should we expect our world to shrink and our power to erode? Or is this just a stereotype of old age?

Is role discontinuity a problem only for the poor, who have less control over their lives than the wealthy? Does high intelligence make a difference? How about gender? What's your view?

A number of gerontologists have noted that people in late adulthood experience a **crossover** in gender roles. Older men become more like women, and older women become more like men. They do not actually cross over—they just become more like each other. For example, this is what Neugarten (1968) found in her groundbreaking studies of aging men and women. She stated that "women, as they age, seem to become more tolerant of their own aggressive, egocentric impulses; whereas men, as they age, [become more tolerant] of their own nurturative and affiliative impulses" (p. 71). In Gutman's terms (1973), men pass from "active to passive mastery," and women do just the opposite.

The differences between men and women, so many of which seem to be based on sexuality, are no longer as important. With the barriers breaking down, older men and women seem to have more in common with each other, and thus may be more of a solace to each other as they deal with the disruptive changes of growing old. This is not to say that men and women reverse gender roles. Rather, they move toward androgyny (see Chapter 14), accepting whatever role, male or female, is appropriate in the situation.

On the basis of data obtained by University of California at Berkeley, Norma Haan (1976, 1981, 1989) concluded that the gender-role changes that result from aging generally lead toward greater candor with others and comfort with one's self. For the most part, she said, "people change, but slowly, while maintaining some continuity" (1989, p. 25).

Friendships among the elderly also show gender-role differences (A. A. R. P., 1997). Although older men and women are alike in that they rarely terminate friendships, they differ in several ways:

- Men tend to trust their best friend more.

- On the other hand, men have less personal conversations with their male friends than do women with their female friends.

- Women place relationships at the top of their list, whereas for men, topical subjects such as sports, politics, and career are most important.

Sexuality

Prior to the 1980s, most reports on sex among the elderly agreed that sexual practices drop off sharply in old age. For example, Pearlman (1972) reported that only 20 percent of elderly males have sex two times or more per month. Serious doubts exist, however, about the reliability of these reports. Society disapproves of the idea of sex among the elderly, so it may be that many do not report what actually goes on.

Although perceptions about sexuality among the elderly may be somewhat distorted by such reports, a recent study conducted by Hillman and Stricker (1996) revealed another factor that influences attitudes toward elderly sexuality. People with close contact to their grandparents tend to have a more permissive attitude toward

The question of whether to allow residents of nursing homes to engage in sex has been a growing problem as elders' attitudes toward sex change.

elderly sexuality than those who are less involved with their grandparents. Further, the older the subjects in this study, the greater their overall knowledge about elderly sexuality, which, in turn, was linked to acceptance of this sexuality. Close contact with elderly relatives and others may disprove commonly held assumptions about sex and aging.

The Janus Report

An investigation that collected data on frequency of sexual activity among the elderly, the Janus Report (Janus & Janus, 1993) gives a picture that weakens the stereotype of the sexually inactive elder even more. According to this research, in the last decade of this century, there is little difference in the practices of young adults and elderly adults! In fact, this study found rather minor differences among any of its four age groups. Either the adults in the Janus study were more honest in reporting what they actually do, or some great changes in sexual attitudes among older Americans have occurred in recent years.

Sex and the "Old-Old"

In a fascinating study restricted to people 80 to 102 years old by Bretschneider and McCoy (1988), we get a look at the sexual activities of those elderly who used to be thought totally inactive. Table 18.1 gives us some surprises. In previous years (the "past " in Table 18.1), the men claim to have engaged in intercourse more than the women, but no difference occurred in enjoyment. In their present lives, 63 percent of the men and 30 percent of the women say they have intercourse at least sometimes, and 76 percent of the men and 39 percent of the women say they enjoy it at least mildly. Another interesting finding of this study is that the men re-

TABLE 18.1   REPORTED FREQUENCY AND ENJOYMENT OF SEXUAL INTERCOURSE BY 80- TO 102-YEAR-OLD MEN AND WOMEN IN THE PAST (YOUNGER YEARS) AND IN THE PRESENT

	Entire Sample		Frequency							
			Never		Sometimes		Often		Very often	
	N	%	n	%	n	%	n	%	n	%
Past										
Men	92	92	3	3	3	3	60	65	26	28
Women	90	88	2	2	10	11	70	78	8	9
Present										
Men	80	80	30	38	27	34	21	26	2	3
Women	80	78	56	70	16	20	8	10	0	0
	Entire Sample		Enjoyment							
			None		Mild		Moderate		Great	
	N	%	n	%	n	%	n	%	n	%
Past										
Men	91	91	3	3	5	6	23	25	60	66
Women	92	90	5	5	9	10	34	37	44	48
Present										
Men	79	79	19	24	11	14	21	27	28	35
Women	82	80	50	61	10	12	13	16	9	11

From J. G. Bretschneider and N. L. McCoy, "Sexual Interest and Behavior in Healthy 80- to 102-Year-Olds" in *Archives of Sexual Behavior,* 17(2):117. Copyright ©1988 Plenum Press, New York, NY. Reprinted by permission.

ported having their first intercourse at an average age of 22 and women at age 25. What a difference from today's figures (see Chapter 13)!

Widowhood and Sexuality

A number of factors account for gender differences in attitudes and interest in sex. For example, women outlive men by approximately seven years. Most married women will become widows because they marry men nearly four years older than themselves. In contrast, most men in society will not become widowers unless they reach age 85 (National Center for Health Statistics, 1992). Due to this imbalance of elderly males and females, it is more difficult for women to find sexual partners in their aging years.

Whether or not a woman is sexually active depends mainly on her marital status. Men have generally had more opportunity for extramarital sexual relations than women, due to the **differential opportunity structure.** This means that due to social disapproval and more rigid rules enforced by parents, peers, and the legal system, women have not had the same access to sex as men have had.

Impotency

One of the biggest fears in males of increasing age is **impotency.** Physical changes, nonsupportive partners and peers, and internal fears may be enough to inhibit or terminate sexual activity in males. It may become a self-fulfilling prophecy.

Sleep laboratory experiments have shown that many men in their sixties to eighties who have labeled themselves as impotent regularly experience erections in their sleep. In many cases a man is capable of having intercourse, but a physical condition such as diabetes impedes it. New types of prosthetic devices can remedy a variety of psychological and physical problems. Although recent findings have hastened the pursuit of wonder drugs, prosthetic devices may be the best solution (Benson, 1996). The newest drug, Viagra, may change this.

One pervading myth is that surgery of the prostate gland inevitably leads to impotency. Many elderly men experience pain and swelling of this small gland, and a **prostatectomy** (removal of all or a part of this gland) is sometimes necessary. Most impotency that results from the removal of this gland is psychological rather than physical.

Most sexual problems that women experience are due to hormonal changes. The vaginal walls begin to thin, and intercourse may become painful, with itching and burning sensations. Estrogen pills and hormone creams relieve many of these symptoms. Further, if women believe that sexual activity ceases with menopause and aging, it probably will. Although women have fewer concerns about sex, they are often worried about losing their attractiveness, which can also have a negative effect on their sex lives.

At any rate, it is quite likely that there is a real decline in sexual activity among the elderly. Men are often concerned about their ability to consummate intercourse. They also worry about their loss of masculinity, in terms of looks and strength. However, the literature on sex among the elderly shows a new attitude emerging. Datan and colleagues (1987) described very well a difference between **generative love** and **existential love:**

> We believe that existential love, the capacity to cherish the present moment, is one of the greatest gifts of maturity. Perhaps we first learn this love when we first confront the certainty of our own personal death, most often in middle adulthood. Generative love is most characteristic of parenthood, a time during which sacrifices are gladly made for the sake of the children. However, it is existential love, we feel, that creates the unique patience and tenderness so often seen in grandparents, who know how brief the period of childhood is, since they have seen their own children leave childhood behind them.

An Applied View

Decisions Most Older Couples Must Make

Most older couples need to make a number of decisions that will be vital to their family lives (Cox, 1988), including whether or not to

- remain in their current home with its history and memories, or move to a new home or apartment.
- remain in the same community or move to a different one, or perhaps move to a retirement community.
- remain active in current organizations, join new ones, or simply not be bothered with organizational affiliations.

- try to locate near children and close friends or move to a different section of the country.
- seek activities satisfying to both husband and wife, or participate independently.

Obviously the decisions they make can have a major impact on their families and themselves. Each of these decisions has the capacity to cause considerable stress for all the family's members. Being aware of them, and confronting them openly, perhaps with a counselor, can greatly reduce the stress.

We have not yet awakened to the potential for existential love between old women and old men, just as we are not yet prepared to recognize the pleasures of sexuality as natural to the life span, particularly to the postparental period.

Those old people who have had the misfortune of spending their last days in nursing homes may learn that love can be lethal. We have been told of an old woman and an old man who fell in love. The old man's children thought this late flowering was "cute"; however, the old woman's children thought it was disgraceful, and over her protests, they removed her from the nursing home. One month later she registered her final protest: she died. (p. 287)

Out of all the hundreds and hundreds of studies of monkeys, one finding applies to every type: From the largest gorilla to the tiniest spider monkey, they all spend about four hours a day in "grooming." Grooming refers to their different ways of touching—stroking, removing bugs, hugging, sex. It is obviously genetic. It seems likely that we humans have something in common with them. We all need to be touched, too. The elderly get less touching than the rest of us, perhaps because they are not seen as being attractive. But they need physical contact just as much as everyone else. It is hoped that a new attitude will spread and make their lives that much happier (Wacks, 1994).

The Elderly and Their Families

The familial relationship undergoes changes in membership, organization, and role during the aging process. Due to improved health care, individuals can expect to live longer, which means that married couples will have more years together after their children leave home. Though exceptions (those who are divorced, childless, or who never married) occur, most middle-aged couples go through similar stages in the life cycle. Following are the four basic phases:

1. The child-raising stage

2. The stage of childlessness before retirement

3. The retirement stage

4. Widowhood and widowerhood

The duration of each stage in the life cycle, and the ages of the family members for each stage, vary from family to family. Childbearing patterns have a lot to do with life in the late stages of life. Couples who complete their families in their early years will have a different lifestyle when their last child leaves home than couples with "change of life" babies, who may have a dependent child at home when they are ready to retire. This can pose serious economic problems for those retirees on fixed incomes, trying to meet the staggering costs of education. In addition, with children in the home, saving for retirement is difficult.

Retirement may bring about changes for both spouses, but wives who have not properly prepared themselves emotionally and financially for retirement may find it particularly stressful. Retirement generally signifies a decrease in income and a lowering of the standard of living, but it may take a while before some of these problems are noticed. Household duties may change, with the husband generally helping more.

Although many changes affect the elderly family, in some marriages it may be true that the more things change the more they stay the same. Studies have shown that among elderly married couples, certain factors contribute to the well-being of the relationship that, in turn, promote a stable, satisfying marriage. Lauer and associates (1990) studied the benefits of marriage for both men and women, and found the following variables to be of most importance to the durability of a marriage: being married to someone they liked as a person and enjoyed being with; commitment to the spouse and the marriage; a sense of humor; and consensus on specific matters (examples are aims and goals in life, friends, decision making).

Other studies that have examined elderly couples in long-term marriages have determined that positive attributes (e.g., trust, open communication) at the beginning of the relationship will foster a strong foundation for the increasing interdependencies that couples experience throughout their marriage (Levenson & others, 1993). Elderly couples in long-term marriages tend to resolve emotional conflicts with less negative behavior than younger married couples (Carstensen & others, 1995). It has been found, however, that those situations in which one spouse suffers a long-term illness do tend to have more problems (Wickrama & others, 1997). As couples change over time, it will be interesting to see whether the interactional processes in the long-term marriage also change, or if they remain stable despite individual development.

Widowhood

With women outliving men by large margins, the wife is most often the survivor. Only half of women over 65 are living with a partner. Many widows have to take on additional duties, including managing household finances and janitorial tasks, and some will have to seek employment. Widowhood affects social relationships with family and friends. Often a widow is the "fifth wheel" in social settings, and former relationships may dissipate. Fortunately, new social activities and friends emerge and replace the old ones. Many of the widows in Lopata's study (1973) came to realize some compensations in widowhood, including increased independence and a decline in their workload.

Howie (1992–1993) suggested that we consider widowhood to be a normal part of aging for women. Thus the ideal focus is shifted from bereavement to concern with the social implications of the extended years of widows' lives. Women should regard widowhood with the understanding that it is yet another passage in the process of aging and dying.

Remarriage is an alternative to the loneliness that most widows and widowers feel after losing their spouse. However, remarriage rates for senior citizens are low, and it is not an option for most. The reasons for not remarrying include the following:

- Many of the elderly view it as improper.

- Children may oppose remarriage.

- Social Security laws penalize widows who remarry.

- There are three single women for every single man over age 65.

Seniors who choose to remarry, however, enjoy much success if the ingredients of love, companionship, financial security, and offspring consent are present.

An important aspect of happiness in the elderly person's family life is whether he or she is living with a spouse, with children, or with another relative. The first has been more common in recent years (Turner & Helms, 1989), probably as a result of better health care among the elderly, and better support systems for them. In most cases, living with one's spouse is preferred, so this is probably contributing to an increase in happiness in our senior citizens.

A Sociocultural View — Caregiving for Elderly in Swarthmore, Pennsylvania, and Botswana, Africa

Draper and Keith (1992) were perplexed by the question, "Why is care for the elderly such a problem for Americans?" Draper had recently returned from studying the lifestyle of the !Kung people of Botswana and decided to do a comparison study with Keith of elder care in Swarthmore, a Philadelphia suburb.

Older residents of Swarthmore are extremely worried about their care, especially with regard to loss of health, which generates feelings of fear. The researchers learned that for many of the elders, need for care is a primary reason for moving into Swarthmore. They do so to be near a child or relative who could supervise their eventual move into a retirement home should professional care prove necessary. The problem is that whether they moved into Swarthmore (to be near relatives), or moved out of

Swarthmore (to enter a retirement community), the costs to the older person usually involve loss of ties to their communities.

In contrast, elders of the !Kung villages "age in place." They do not retire, relocate, or enter age-graded elder care institutions. Indeed, they have no other place to go. The !Kung were asked, "For an old person, what makes a good life?" One-third responded, "If you have a child to take care of you, you have a good life." Care is almost always provided by one's children and community.

For the people of Swarthmore, technologically superb care is available, but its benefits must be weighed against the loss of community ties and personal autonomy. For the !Kung, social needs and physical care are compatible.

Care of Elderly Parents

Developmental psychologists have become much more interested in caregiving to elders in recent years. Variables studied have included stress caused by living alone or in nursing homes (Fingerman, 1995; Malonebeach & others, 1995; Naleppa, 1996; Ponder & Pomery, 1996; Stephens & Townsend, 1997; Territo, 1996; Townsend & Franks, 1995), abuse (Hwalek & others, 1996; Neale & others, 1996), and coping strategies (Devries & others, 1997; Mok & Mui, 1996).

Elderly people identify their adult children, when they have them, as the primary helpers in their lives. When these people have both an adult son and an adult daughter, elderly people most often name the son as the primary helper (Stoller & others, 1992). This is surprising, because as we pointed out in Chapter 16, care of elderly parents is almost always undertaken by daughters, if the elderly persons have any.

In the past, elder care was most often done by unmarried daughters, if there were any. They were expected to do this because it was assumed that the work would be easier for them, because they had no responsibilities for husband or children. In fact, married women report that their married status makes caregiving for their elderly parents easier. They have less depression, higher incomes, and other forms of socioeconomic support than unmarried women (Brody & others, 1992).

What about the situation in which the elders have no children, or at least none

For those who want to work with older adults, put *Promoting successful aging* at the top of your list. Roth and Atherton have written a readable book that is half about theory and research and half about the specific strategies for dealing with the needs of the elderly.

Do You Know Your Grandparents?

Are your grandparents still alive? Even though you have probably known them for many years, you may not know them very well. Try answering the questions below for one set of your grandparents, and if possible, check your answers with them to get your GKQ (Grandparent Knowledge Quotient).

1. What's your grandmother's favorite activity?
2. In total, how many rings do your grandparents wear?
3. What color are your grandfather's eyes?
4. Where does your grandfather eat lunch?
5. What is your grandmother's favorite TV show?
6. In what year did your grandparents meet?

7. For whom did your grandmother vote for president in 1996?
8. Does your grandfather know how to prepare asparagus?
9. Who is your grandfather's favorite relative?
10. Name some of either of your grandparents' favorite movie stars.

You might try making up a test like this about yourself and asking your grandparents, parents, siblings, and friends to respond to it. It should be interesting to see which of them knows you best.

who are willing or able to care for them? Research indicates that elderly individuals who have no kin tend to substitute a close friend whom they persuade to take the place of the absent relative. Nearly 40 percent of a group of elders surveyed could actually identify such a person who filled this role (MacRae, 1992).

Clearly, most family and close friends still feel that they ought to take care of the elderly in their own homes if possible. In their study of the outcome of several types of elder care, however, Strawbridge and Wallhagen (1992) concluded: "While important, family care for frail elders is not always appropriate and should be but one option in long-term care" (p. 92).

The Changing Role of the Grandparent

In today's world, with increased life expectancy, grandparenthood has become a unique experience within the family system (Smith, 1989). Grandparenthood is positively linked to the mental health and morale of elderly persons. In a classic study, Neugarten and Weinstein (1964) examined styles of grandparenting and created categories for five general styles: "formal," "the fun seeker," "the surrogate parent," "the reservoir of family wisdom," and "the distant figure." An interesting finding was that the fun seeker and the distant figure emerged as the most popular styles of grandparenting. Both exclude an emphasis on authority. Many grandparents preferred a grandparent-grandchild relationship in which their role was simply to enjoy being with their grandchildren rather than feeling responsible as coparents with their adult children.

In the American culture of today, the importance of grandparents is intensified, due to the many roles they feel they must play: providing emotional support and financial assistance to their children and grandchildren in divorce and substance abuse situations (Smith, 1989) and acting as gender-role socialization agents. Bengston and Robertson (1985) included some "symbolic functions" of the grandparent role: acting as the "family watchdog"; behaving as arbitrators; and merely "being there." Although grandparents tend to find these roles emotionally rewarding, studies have shown that they often have psychological, physical, and economic costs (Burton, 1992). For example, arbitrators sometimes find that their efforts go unappreciated by both parties, leaving everybody angry at everyone else!

Erikson (1963) explained, in his stage of generativity, the significance of grandchildren to grandparents. Erikson believed that generativity referred to providing a

Grandfather-Grandchild Relations among White and African American Men

What causes grandfathers to be close to their grandchildren? Kivett (1991) found that a number of factors make important differences. For both whites and African Americans, relationship with the grandchild is more warm and loving when: they live near each other (most lived within 10 minutes of each other); the grandchild is a grandson; both grandfather and grandchildren are younger (most grandchildren were 15 years or younger); and health of the grandfather is good. The closeness of the relationship also increases with the number of grandchildren and the educational and income levels of the grandfather. Both groups rated the grandfather role as third in importance to other roles (spouse first, then father).

The grandfather role assumed more importance among African American than white men, however. African American grandfathers had more levels of kin in their households, more associations with grandchildren, and greater expectations for assistance. They also reported getting along better with grandchildren and felt closer to them than white grandfathers. Differences appear to be a function of ethnic background rather than economic factors. Kivett observed that African American grandfathers see children as holding the key to the future, whereas white grandfathers seemed to emphasize the past and hold themselves up as models, seeing their role as passing on customs to the young.

better life for future generations and that not having reached the stage of generativity would cause stagnation and self-absorption in the individual (see Chapter 16). The personal development of grandparents is furthered by their close rapport with younger generations and vice versa. When this vital relationship is disrupted, as it usually is in the case of divorce, the suffering of grandparents can be agonizing (Gray & Geron, 1995).

The Older Worker

Only a small percentage of all older adults are in the labor force—about 11 percent. Many of these retirements were due to forced retirement. Today, only airline pilots and public safety workers such as fire fighters and police can be forced to retire because of their age. However, not many people want to continue working past 65. For example, a large steel corporation that has never had mandatory retirement finds that less than 1 percent of their 40,000 workers stay on past 65. The average age of retirement at this company is below 62. Of those who do wish to stay on, most seem able to do a good job of meeting their requirements (Clay, 1996).

Interest in Work

Older people clearly care less about working than younger people. For example, Cohn (1979) reported: "Toward the end of the period of labor force participation, the satisfactions men derive from work are transferred from the actual experience of work to its consequences" (p. 264). These percentages likely are even lower today. That is, no more than half of older workers may be willing to work for its own sake. Of course, many younger workers do it only for the pay, too. The social value of the work itself is probably the most significant differential.

Performance

As this society ages through greater longevity, the aging of the baby boom generation, and decreased birth rates, some of the stereotypes about aging are coming under closer scrutiny. One stereotype is that work performance necessarily declines with age (Rhodes, 1983). An excellent series of longitudinal studies performed by Erdman and associates (1985), which yielded a sample of more than 7,000 subjects, has provided an in-depth look at this and other aspects of the relationships between old age and work. The stereotype that age equals declining performance is getting more research attention because the number of workers in the last two decades of their careers will grow 41 percent while the number of workers 16 to 35 years old will decline slightly (Johnston, 1987).

The stereotype is bolstered by research on aging that demonstrates a decline in abilities such as dexterity, speed of response, agility, hearing, and vision. If all these abilities decline, then surely job performance must decline with age. However, McEvoy and Cascio (1989) conducted an extensive meta-analysis (a study that compiles the results of many other studies) of 96 studies and found no relationship between age and job performance. It made no difference whether the performance measure was ratings or productivity measures, nor whether the type of job was professional or nonprofessional.

What explanation is there for these results? How does the older worker deal with the mild decline of physical abilities that affects most elderly persons? Experience is one answer. There is said to be no substitute for it, and it is certainly valued by employers. Other reasons cited are that older workers have lower absenteeism, turnover, illness, and accident rates (Kacmar & Ferris, 1989; Martocchio, 1989). They also tend to have higher job satisfaction and more positive work values than younger workers. These qualifications seem to offset any decreases in physical ability that increasing age causes.

A number of new programs are being set up to help more older workers achieve as much as they can on the job (Brady & Gray, 1988). When older workers are adequately advised, they can remain a useful and satisfied part of the workforce (Bornstein, 1986; Cahill & Salomone, 1987). More and more, we find that counselors in this field employ the biopsychosocial model in their work. Can you see how?

Retirement

"I just don't want to retire," said Charlie, a 65-year-old shipping clerk. "But you've worked hard, and you should get the fruits of your labor," said his boss. "Fruits of my labor, my backside! I know lots of guys, as soon as they retire, they get sick or something and then they die. I know if I retire I'm gonna die. I'm gonna die!" Despite his protestations, Charlie was retired. Three months later he was dead.

For many people, retirement is a welcome relief from a frustrating and boring job. For others, it is just as difficult as being unemployed. Retirement requires changing the habits of an adult lifetime. This probably explains why more than 11 percent of those 65 and over are employed.

Nevertheless, the great majority of the elderly do not choose to work. Money is probably not the major factor in that decision (Hayward, 1986). The decision is a complicated one, but most people now feel they have enough financial security so that they need not work. Health may be the biggest factor. Crowley (1986) found that the well-being of 1,200 retirees was highly dependent on the state of their health at the time of retirement.

Retirement seems to be harder on males than females. Many feel that they have nothing to do, although their wives still have a job. The home still must be taken care of, the meals cooked, the clothes cleaned. Most older wives have already adjusted to a reduction in their roles because their children have left home. For men, the change usually comes all at once.

Retirement and Leisure

How you view retirement depends on the work and leisure experiences you have had up to the point of retirement. The leisure activities pursued throughout life play a crucial role in your social adjustment later on. The relationships among work, retirement, and leisure can be seen in Figure 18.1.

Figure 18.1

The interrelatedness of work, leisure, and retirement. Solid lines denote the direct influence of (1) work on leisure, and (2) work and leisure upon retirement. Broken lines suggest a possible feedback influence whereby preferences for uses of leisure time may affect choice of jobs, and the availability of more time in retirement may affect content of leisure activities.

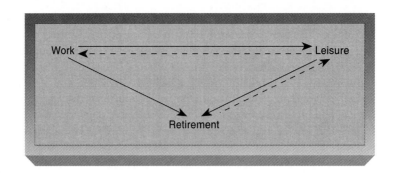

The type of work you do directly affects how you spend leisure time, in two ways. The scheduling of work affects when leisure time is available. A person who works second or third shift might be unable to take part in activities that are often thought of as evening activities, such as dining and dancing. Second, the content of work may influence how much time will be left over for leisure activities. Persons with physically draining positions may be too tired to do anything but nap after work. On the other hand, a person with a desk job may choose physically challenging activities during leisure hours.

When leisure is no more than an extension of work experiences and attitudes, it performs what leisure theorists call a spillover function. For example, some people try to relax by performing some of their easier tasks at home—the "stuffed briefcase" syndrome. Conversely, when leisure time is engaged in to make up for disappointment and stress at work, it is described as a compensatory function. An example would be excessive partying at the end of the workday or week. An overabundance of compensatory leisure will leave one as unprepared to face retirement as an overabundance of work-related activities.

Making Retirement More Enjoyable

The belief is growing that retired persons are an important resource to the community. Numerous efforts have been made in recent years to tap this powerful re-

Pet Ownership by Elderly People

Most pets are important to their families, and they have proven especially important to older people. Pets play a role in the lives of elderly people who find retirement boring or are lonely because of the death of family and friends. In a recent study, a sample of older people indicated that their pets were a factor in their choice of housing (Smith & others, 1992). Unfortunately, past practices often discriminated against pet owners, who often were forced either to give up their pet or seek alternative housing. Younger people usually have more housing options, but those options for older people are often limited, due to reduced incomes or health concerns.

Fortunately, things are changing. In 1983 President Reagan signed a law prohibiting discrimination against elderly and handicapped pet owners in federally assisted housing (Public Law 98–181). This law has been enforced unequally because of clumsy state guidelines. Nevertheless, several private housing facilities for semi-independent elderly people in the Chicago area have recently changed their policies to permit pet ownership. This, along with other similar actions across the country, is encouraging.

Because pets are often vital companions for older people, can you think of other things that might be done to help the elderly obtain pets, and to help make ownership easier?

A Sociocultural View

Western and Eastern Views of Retirement

According to Thomas Cole (1991), the Western view of life divides it into three stages: becoming educated, working, and retiring. Those who get a good education and who rise to the upper ranks in their career path can afford to have many choices in their retired years. Those who are not so successful, and they are by far the majority, will have meager retired financial status or will depend on public funds for their sustenance. In either case, they will lose power, respect, and options in their elder years because Westerners see them as weak.

As a result, Cole asserts, many seek to alter, reverse, or somehow control the biological process of aging. In so doing, they fail to appreciate being old as part of human existence. In the view of many Easterners, as physical strength is lost, the wisdom of age takes its place. The elderly grow in respect and thus their role is changed but not diminished. Perhaps we in the West need to become more aware of and rethink our life course perspective.

An excellent source of information on the elderly is the American Association of Retired Persons (A.A.R.P.). With about 30 million members, this powerful group publishes materials that may interest you. Write to them at National Headquarters, 601 E Street NW, Washington, DC 20049.

source. A number of national programs now make an effort to involve retired persons in volunteer and paid work of service to society.

Recent surveys seem to indicate that the "golden years" are not so golden for many retired persons. But with improving health conditions (see Chapter 17), improved understanding of the nature of life after 65, and a considerable increase in government involvement, the lives of retirees have a far better chance of being fruitful.

Contrary to the stereotype, getting old need not, and usually does not, mean being lonely. In fact, the elderly, most of whom have a good deal of free time, often use it to develop their social lives. We now move to a discussion about their personal development.

Guided Review

1. Many changes occur in late adulthood, including role _____ (an abrupt and disruptive change in role) and "crossover" of sex roles.
2. In late adulthood, the gender role of older men becomes _____ like that of women, and women's role becomes _____ like that of men.
3. The child-launching phase, the childless preretirement period, the retirement phase, and _____ are stages most middle-aged and aged couples can anticipate.
4. Five general styles of grandparenting have been identified by Neugarten and Weinstein (1964): formal, fun seeking, _____ _____, reservoir of family wisdom, and distant figure.
5. Although some decline in dexterity, speed, and agility occurs in older workers, _____ may be one of the reasons that job performance does not generally decline among these workers.
6. Leisure theorists write about two functions for leisure: a spillover function and a _____ function.
7. Retirement is _____ difficult for females than for males.

Answers

1. discontinuity 2. more, more 3. widowhood 4. surrogate parent 5. experience 6. compensatory 7. less

Personal Development

Two points of view have received most interest in the field of personality development in the elderly: those of the Committee on Human Development and those of Erik Erikson. Although dated, these two bodies of research are still respected by personality experts and so must be included in this chapter.

Personal Development: Committee on Human Development

What are the effects of aging on personal development? The Committee on Human Development, consisting of gerontologist Bernice Neugarten and her associates at the University of Chicago have been responsible for some of the most highly respected research on this topic (e.g., Havighurst & others, 1968; Neugarten, 1968).

Adults between the ages of 54 and 94 who were residents of Kansas City were asked to participate in a study of change across the adult lifespan. The sample is somewhat biased in that it represents only white persons who were living on their own (i.e., not institutionalized) at the time of the study. They were somewhat better educated and of a higher socioeconomic group than is typical for this age group. Nevertheless, the sample is reasonably well balanced, and because of the thoroughness with which these persons were studied, this research has become a classic in the field of adult psychology. Neugarten summarized the findings:

- In the middle years (especially the fifties), a change occurs in the perception of time and death and the relationship of the self to them. Introspection, contemplation, reflection, and self-evaluation become important aspects of life. People at this age become more interested in their "inner selves."

- Perception of how well one can control the environment undergoes a marked change:

> Forty-year-olds, for example, seem to see the environment as one that rewards boldness and risk-taking, and to see themselves as possessing energy congruent with the opportunities perceived in the outer world. Sixty-year-olds, however, perceive the world as complex and dangerous, no longer to be reformed in line with one's wishes, and the individual as conforming and accommodating to outer-world demands. (1968, p. 140)

Erikson believes that the character of the old Swedish doctor in Ingmar Bergman's famous film, *Wild Strawberries,* excellently reflects the eight stages he proposes.

- **Emotional energy** declines with age. Tests showed that intensity of emotion invested in tasks undergoes a definite decline in the later years.

- **Gender-role reversals** also occur with age (discussed earlier in this chapter).

- **Age-status** becomes more rigid with development. Age-status refers to society's expectations about what is normal at various ages. These expectations change not only with advancing years, but according to the particular society and to the historical context. For example, in 1940 a woman who was not married by age 22 was not considered unusual, but if she had not married by the time she was 27, people began to worry. In the late 1980s, the expected age of marriage is much less rigid. This holds only for the United States; in Samoa, for example, concern arises if a person is not married by age 15.

What is the optimum pattern of aging in terms of our relationships with other people? The Committee on Human Development has also investigated this question. For many years, there have been two different positions on this question, known as the activity theory and the disengagement theory.

According to the **activity theory,** human beings flourish through interaction with other people and through keeping physically active. They are unhappy when, as they reach the older years, their contacts with others shrink as a result of death, illness, and societal limitations. Those who are able to keep up the social activity of their middle years are considered the most successful.

Disengagement theory contradicts this idea. According to this position, the belief that activity is better than passivity is a bias of the Western world. This was not always so; the Greeks, for example, valued their warriors and athletes but reserved the highest distinction for such contemplative philosophers as Sophocles, Plato, and Aristotle. Many people in the countries of the Eastern Hemisphere also hold this view. According to disengagement theory, the most mature adults are likely to gradually disengage themselves from their fellow human beings in preparation for death. They become less interested in their interactions with others and more absorbed in internal concerns. They accept the decreasing attention of a society that views them as losing power.

Does this mean that the tendency toward disengagement is more normal than the tendency toward activity? Researchers no longer think so (Achenbaum & Bengston, 1994). It is now believed that what has appeared to be disengagement is

Clearly the group on the left is enjoying itself more than the woman on the right, but does that mean that the disengagement theory is wrong? Isn't it only natural for people to slowly disengage from society as they approach death?

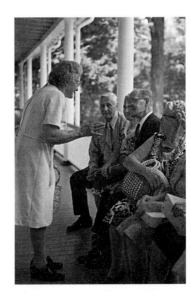

An Applied View

Getting Perspective on Your Thinking

If you hope to be the kind of person who ends his or her life with a sense of integrity, the time to begin is right now. You don't get to be a happy elderly person unless you plan and work for it. You can do this in many ways, but we have some suggestions to pass along to you.

Whenever you are about to make an important decision, follow these four steps:

1. Come to some tentative conclusion about what you should do.

2. Close your eyes and picture yourself as a 75-year-old woman or man.

3. Imagine yourself explaining your decision to that old person, and try to picture her or him telling you what she or he thinks about what you have decided.

4. If you don't like what you hear, rethink the decision and go through this process again.

Use this technique to get a better perspective on your thinking; you will be surprised by how much wisdom you already have.

instead a temporary transition from the highly active role of the middle-aged adult to the more sedate, spiritually oriented role of the elderly person. Most humans are social animals, so real disengagement from one's fellows may be the result of traumatic experience or a physiologically caused mental disturbance such as clinical depression. On the other hand, activity theory, with its emphasis on social involvement, is now considered too general (Marshall, 1994). For example, many people may reduce social contacts, but keep active with solitary hobbies. Activity per se has not been found to correlate with a personal sense of satisfaction with life. Carstensen (1995, 1996) offered a resolution of the debate with her **socio-emotional selectivity theory.** She suggested that humans use social contact to obtain physical survival, information they need, the maintenance of a sense of self and pleasure and comfort. These goals exist throughout life, but the importance of each shifts with age. For the elderly, the need for physical survival so important in infancy and the need for information from others in younger adulthood become less important. The need for emotional support grows. They tend to get this support from relatives and close friends (their "social convoys," as they have been called) more and more, and less and less from casual acquaintances such as coworkers. In fact, this is true of anyone who is threatened, such as terminally ill young people. Joseph Cardinal Bernardin, when dying of cancer, expressed it this way:

> I now realized that when I asked my doctor for the test results, I had to let go of everything. . . . One of the things I have noticed about illness is that it draws you inside yourself. When we are ill, we tend to focus on our own pain and suffering. We may feel sorry for ourselves or become depressed. (p. 21)

In three words I can sum up everything I've learned about life. It goes on.

Further, the challenges faced in later life can be quite different. For example, Kling and associates (1997) have investigated elderly coping with loss of home, community relocation, and caring for a mentally ill adult child. Other research that has evaluated altered coping skills of the late adult population (and ways to improve these skills) have been completed by Heckhausen (1997) and Tabourse (1995). Thus the elderly appear to be disengaging, but in fact they are simply becoming more selective about with whom they wish to spend their social time. Carstensen's socio-emotional selectivity theory appears to explain the changes that occur better than either disengagement or activity theory.

Personal Development: Erikson

Erikson believed that resolution of each of the first seven crises in his theory should lead us to achieve a sense of personal **integrity.** Older adults who have a sense of integrity feel their lives have been well spent. The decisions and actions they have taken seem to them to fit together—their lives are integrated. They are saddened by the sense that time is running out and that they will not get many more chances to make an impact, but they feel reasonably well satisfied with their achievements. They usually have a sense of having helped to achieve a more dignified life for humankind.

The acceptance of human progress, including one's own, is essential for this final sense of integrity. This is the path to wisdom, which Erikson defined as "the detached and yet active concern with life itself in the face of death itself" (1978, p. 26). An example of such active concern with life is the life review (Wallace, 1992), when elderly people think about and tell stories about days gone by, and of past experiences. Such storytelling can help the elderly find new meaning in the face of imminent death.

When people look back over their lives and feel that they have made many wrong decisions, or more commonly, that they have frequently not made any decisions at all, they tend to see life as lacking integrity. They feel **despair,** which is the second half of this last stage of crisis. They are angry that there can never be another chance to make their lives make sense. They often hide their fear of death by appearing contemptuous of humanity in general, and those of other religions and races in particular. As Erikson put it, "Such despair is often hidden behind a show of disgust" (1968, p. 140).

Erikson (1978) provided a panoramic view of his life-cycle theory in an analysis of Swedish film director Ingmar Bergman's famous film *Wild Strawberries*. In this picture, an elderly Swedish doctor goes from his hometown to a large city, where he is to be honored for 50 years of service to the medical profession. On the way, he stops by his childhood home and, resting in an old strawberry patch, begins an imaginary journey through his entire life, starting with his earliest memories. In the ruminations of this old man, Erikson saw clear and specific reflections of the eight stages he proposed.

Erikson demonstrated through Bergman's words that, like his other seven stages, this last stage involves a life crisis. Poignantly, the old doctor struggles to make sense out of the events of his life. He is ultimately successful in achieving a sense of integrity. The film is well worth seeing, and Erikson's analysis makes it an even more meaningful experience.

To better understand what if feels like for an individual to reach late adulthood, you may want to read the following books: (1) Cowley's *The view from 80* (New York: Penguin) is a personal account the author wrote when he was 82 years old. Critic Donald Hall describes this book as "Eloquent on the felt disparity between an unchanged self and the costume of altered flesh"; (2) *Coming of age,* written by de Beauvoir, is a magnificent psychological study that provides an intense look at what it means, rather than how it feels, to become old.

Guided Review

8. Researchers with the Committee on Human Development found that adults between the ages of 54 and 94 changed their perception of how well they could control the environment and that there was a marked decline in the _____ _____ they invested in tasks as they aged.
9. _____ theory and _____ theory offer explanations of ways in which people cope with aging.
10. According to the disengagement theory, most adults will disengage themselves from their fellow human beings in preparation for _____.
11. According to Carstensen's socio-emotional selectivity theory, humans use social contact for four reasons: to obtain physical survival, to get information they need, to maintain a _____ _____ _____, and to acquire pleasure and comfort.
12. Erikson suggests that as we look back over our lives, if we see our lives as having been _____, we have achieved the goal of his final stage of life.

Answers

8. emotional energy 9. Activity, disengagement 10. death 11. sense of self 12. integrated

CONCLUSION

Many changes happen during later adulthood. A "crossover" effect in gender roles occurs, sexual activity changes, and the nature of family relationships undergoes several alterations.

As we leave the industrial age and enter the age of information processing, the nation's older workers experience an incredibly different environment from that of their predecessors of 50 years ago. Even retirement is a much-changed adventure. As in each of the preceding chapters, life appears as never-ending change but change with discernible patterns. Perhaps more stress takes place in old age than before, but more effective techniques are also available for dealing with it.

In summary:

Social Development

- A number of gerontologists have noted that people in late adulthood experience a "crossover" in gender roles: Older men become more like women, and older women become more like men.
- White summarizes that in late adulthood males are generally more sexually active than females but that declining activity in the female is usually attributable to declining interest or illness in the male partner.
- Research suggests four basic phases through which most middle-aged and aged couples pass: child-launching, childless preretirement, retirement, and widowhood.
- Although older people show less interest in working than younger people, discrimination and stereotypes about older workers underestimate their desire to help.
- Men usually find retirement more difficult than do women.

Personal Development

- Neugarten's work on the effects of aging on personal development reveals that elderly people become more interested in their "inner selves," perceptions of the environment change, psychic energy declines, gender-role reversals occur, and age-status becomes more rigid.
- The Committee on Human Development investigated patterns of aging, including activity theory and disengagement theory. Today, the more accepted explanation of elderly social behavior is Carstensen's socio-emotional selectivity theory.
- For Erikson, resolution of each of the first seven stages in his eight-stage theory should lead people to achieve a sense of integrity in the last stage. If not, they experience despair.

KEY TERMS

Activity theory
Age-status
Crossover
Despair
Differential opportunity structure

Disengagement theory
Emotional energy
Existential love
Gender-role reversals
Generative love

Impotency
Integrity
Prostatectomy
Role discontinuity
Socio-emotional selectivity theory

WHAT DO YOU THINK?

1. Traditionally in Western society, elderly men marrying young women has been more accepted than elderly women marrying young men. Why do you believe these attitudinal differences arose?
2. What is your position on sex in old-age institutions? Should there be any restrictions at all?
3. Which aspect of your family life do you most fear change in as you get old?
4. What are some ways that the experience of older workers facing mandatory retirement could best be used in our society?
5. Some have said that whereas Erikson's first seven stages describe crises in which action should be taken, the last stage, integrity versus despair, is merely reactive. All he has the elderly doing is sitting in a rocking chair and looking back over their lives. Do you believe that this criticism is valid?

CHAPTER REVIEW TEST

1. **In late adulthood, crossover in sex roles means that**
   a. older men and women identify with each other more.
   b. older men become more like women, and older women become more like men.
   c. older men take on roles most often associated with women.
   d. older women take on roles most often associated with men.
2. **Whether or not an older woman is sexually active depends mainly on her**
   a. level of interest.

b. marital status.

c. perception of her children's attitudes.

d. number of interpersonal relationships.

3. **Examples of experiences that may inhibit or terminate sexual activity in adult men include**

a. physical changes.

b. nonsupportive partners and peers.

c. internal fears.

d. All of the answers are correct.

4. **What is the first phase of the life cycle most middle-aged couples go through?**

a. Widowhood

b. The retirement phase

c. The child-launching phase

d. The childless preretirement period

5. **John and Sarah are the parents of three children and provide an example of generative love. They**

a. gladly make many sacrifices for the sake of the children.

b. cherish the time they have with their children at present.

c. expose their children to the culture and traditions of their ancestry.

d. are committed to spending all their time with the children.

6. **In Helena Lopata's study of changes that occur with the death of a spouse, many widows reported that a compensation of widowhood is**

a. managing household finances.

b. employment.

c. increased independence.

d. increased economic well-being.

7. **When children supplant the deceased father as the mother's center of attention, they are**

a. preventing their mother from becoming independent.

b. prolonging their mother's grief.

c. helping their mother adjust to widowhood.

d. not allowing their mother to remarry.

8. **Older workers make valued employees for all of the following reasons, except lower**

a. absenteeism.

b. turnover.

c. accident rates.

d. health-care costs.

9. **From research on 1,200 retirees, Crowley (1986) found that a person's state of health was highly dependent upon**

a. whether they were still married.

b. their financial stability.

c. their well-being.

d. their level of education.

10. **Retirement may be most stressful for wives who have not properly prepared themselves for retirement financially and**

a. physically.

b. emotionally.

c. spiritually.

d. legally.

11. **According to leisure theorists, a spillover function refers to**

a. when leisure is no more than an extension of work experiences and attitudes.

b. when leisure time is engaged in to make up for disappointment and stress at work.

c. when leisure time is spent worrying about stressful events at work.

d. when leisure time takes away from time to be spent at work.

12. **The idea that there are societal expectations about what is normal at various stages refers to**

a. gender roles.

b. socialization.

c. age-status.

d. role continuity.

13. **According to Carstensen socio-emotional selectivity theory, humans use _____ _____ to obtain physical survival, information they need, the maintenance of a sense of self and pleasure and comfort.**

a. psychological engagement

b. social contact

c. emotional reflection

d. social love

14. **When adults distance themselves from other human beings in preparation for death and become less interested in their interactions with others, it is referred to as**

a. disengagement theory.

b. separation theory.

c. distantiation.

d. personal engagement theory.

15. **For Erik Erikson, we are led to a sense of personal integrity by**

a. personal well-being.

b. a sense of self-control.

c. achievement.

d. a sense that life has been well spent.

16. **According to Erikson, people who are contemptuous of humanity**

a. have psychologically disengaged.

b. have been socially rejected.

c. are preparing for an attack.

d. are looking back over their lives and hiding their fear of death.

Answers

1. b 2. b 3. d 4. c 5. a 6. c 7. c 8. d 9. c 10. b 11. a 12. c 13. b 14. a 15. d 16. d

Dying and Spirituality

As I said, you got to check out some time; you can't stay here forever. . . . Well, you just hope you go with a little dignity, that you don't have to suffer from Alzheimer's or die slowly in a rest home alone somewhere. I thought it was very interesting when I was in Bora Bora for six months. I was down there making a movie. . . . I did not live with the company, but found a house by myself up a road. There was a family next door—Polynesian natives—and the old lady of the house was there and she was dying. She suddenly said, "I'm going to die," and went to bed for three days and died. I remember at her funeral that everybody was dressed in white; it was like a wedding almost. And I was talking to them about it and they said, "Oh, yes, the fathers and the mothers are the most respected. They just go and die when they're ready." I said, "Geez, does that really go on like this all the time?" They said, "That's the way this society works." There are no old age homes, no old people wandering around, you know, suffering to death. Isn't it a strange thing, I thought to myself. What a respect for age that we don't have. . . . Like I say, life is like a hotel. We all check in and we all check out. Seems to me that the Polynesian approach to checking out is a great deal better than ours.

Actor Jason Robards, age 72 ✹

When you finish reading this chapter, you should be able to

- Explain the four types of death.

- Give the legal definition of death.

- Explain what is meant by grief work and its place in Lindemann's stages.

- Explain what is meant by "pathological grieving" and how it prevents successful conclusion of a life crisis.

- Discuss the positive effects of grief and the funeral on dealing with another's death.

- Discuss suicide among the elderly along with the influence of race, residence, and gender.

- Evaluate information on alternative ways of dying "successfully."

- Present reasons for the growth in religious participation among adults.

- Compare the theories of spirituality presented by Frankl, Jung, and Wilson.

- List and describe Fowler's six stages of faith development.

The Role of Death in Life

Americans, who have long been accused of abhorring the subject of death, are now giving it considerable attention. From the ways we teach the young about death (Stambrook & Parker, 1987) to the ways in which we bury our dead (Marshall &

Since the first historian, Homer, began recording the lives of the Greeks, the meaning of death has been a central issue.

Levy, 1990), we seem to have switched to an eager confrontation of the problem.

In this section, we review research and theory from the social and physical sciences to examine three major concerns: What is death? How do we deal with the death of others? How do we deal with our own death?

What Is Death?

> The matter of my friend rests heavy upon me.
> How can I be salved?
> How can I be stilled?
> My friend, who I loved, has turned to clay.
> Must I, too, lie me down
> Not to rise again for ever and ever?
>
> Gilgamesh, c. 2000 B.C.E.

In the movies, death is almost invariably portrayed in the same sequence: Dying people make a final statement, close their eyes, fall back on the pillow or into the arms of a loved one, and are pronounced dead. In fact, death rarely occurs that way. In most cases, the person dies gradually. Death is a state, but dying is a process.

Ascertaining when people are truly and finally dead has been a medical problem for centuries. For example, in the early 1900s, Franz Hartmann claimed to have collected approximately 700 cases of premature burial or "close calls." In 1896 the "Society for the Prevention of Premature Burial" was founded. Fear of premature burial was so strong that in 1897 in Berlin, a patent was granted for a life signal device that sent up a warning flag and turned on a light if movement was detected inside the coffin.

The more absolute death seems, the more authentic life becomes.
John Fowles

We no longer have any serious problem in determining whether a person is dead. But determining exactly when death occurred has come to be of even greater importance because of organ donations. All the body's systems do not cease simultaneously, so disagreements exist over which system is most significant in judging whether a person is dead.

The Leading Causes of Death in the United States

In Figure 19.1, we see listed the nine major causes of death for persons of all ages. The rates are given for males and females, and some of the differences in rates between the two are interesting. Are you familiar with each of these causes of death? If not, you may want to look up the ones you don't know in a dictionary.

Four Types of Death

Today, four types of death are recognized: clinical death, brain death, biological or cellular death, and social death.

Clinical Death

In one sense, the individual is dead when his or her respiration and heartbeat have stopped. This is the aspect of dying referred to in the movies when the doctor turns and sadly announces, "I'm sorry, but he's gone." Actually, **clinical death** is the least useful to the medical profession and to society at large because it is unreliable.

Due to the advent of **cardiopulmonary resuscitation (CPR),** many individuals whose lungs and heart had ceased to function have been saved. In other cases, spontaneous restarting of the heart and lungs has occurred after failure.

Figure 19.1

Death rates by cause and sex, United States

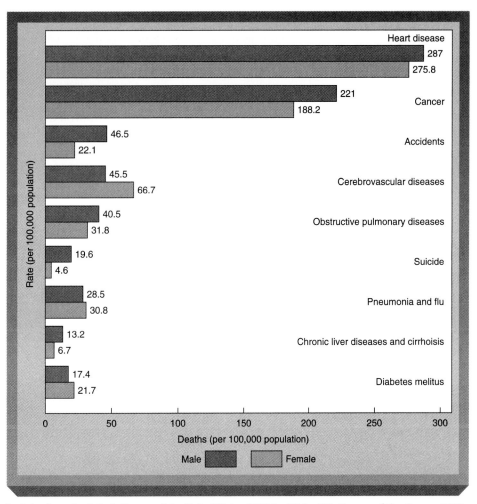

Statistics from *Statistical Abstract of the United States, 1995* (p. 95) by U.S. Bureau of the Census, 1995, Washington, DC: U.S. Government Printing Office.

Brain Death

Death of the brain occurs when it fails to receive a sufficient supply of oxygen for a short period of time (usually 8 to 10 minutes). The cessation of brain function occurs in three stages: First the cortex stops, then the midbrain fails, and finally the brain stem ceases to function. When the cortex and midbrain stop operating, **brain death** has occurred, and the person enters an irreversible coma. The body can remain alive in this condition for a long time, because the autonomic processes are governed by the brain stem. Consciousness and alertness, however, will never be regained (Kammerman, 1988).

Biological Death

The cells and the organs of the body can remain in a functioning condition long after the failure of the heart and lungs. **Biological death** occurs when it is no longer possible to discern an electrical charge in the tissues of the heart and lungs.

Social Death

It is possible to ensure that all or part of your body will be donated for use after your death, usually by a designation on your driver's license. Have you done this? If not, what are your reasons for refraining?

Sudnow (1967) was the first to suggest the concept of **social death,** which, "within the hospital setting, is marked at that point at which a patient is treated essentially as a corpse although perhaps still 'clinically' or 'biologically' alive" (p. 74). He cites cases in which body preparation (e.g., closing the eyes, binding the feet) were started while the patient was still alive, to make things easier for the staff. Also, in some cases, family members have signed autopsy permissions while the patient was still alive.

So when is a person really dead? If a person has suffered brain death, but the heart is still beating, should the heart be removed and used for a transplant operation?

One complex case (Goldsmith, 1988) involved the Loma Linda University Medical Center, famous for its work in the area of organ transplants. They attempted to initiate a program that would provide scarce organs for transplants. In this program, healthy hearts and other organs would be taken from babies born with anencephaly, a condition in which part or all of the brain is missing at birth. Ninety-five percent of these babies die within one week. When the anencephalic infants were born, they were flown to Loma Linda and given traditional "comfort care" (warmth, nutrition, and hydration). In addition, they were put on artificial breathing support for a maximum of seven days. The hospital maintained that they were put on respirators until a technical definition of brain death could be ascertained. But critics contended that this was done because the organs needed the time to mature for a successful transplant to occur. A storm of controversy ended the program before any donations could be made. Critics accused the hospital of "organ farming." The hospital argued that it was not only trying to increase the number of organ donors for infants but also giving the families of anencephalic babies an opportunity to "turn their tragedy into something good." With the advent of more advanced technology, the distinction between life and death becomes blurred, and the ethical considerations grow increasingly complex.

The Legal Definition of Death

In 1968 the Harvard Ad Hoc Committee to Examine the Criteria of Brain Death suggested the following criteria for **legal death:** "Unreceptivity and unresponsivity, no movements or breathing, no reflexes, and a flat **electroencephalogram (EEG)** reading that remains flat for 24 hours."

Such criteria preclude the donation of organs in most cases, because the organs would probably suffer irreparable damage in the 24 hours needed to check the EEG. Others have suggested that the time at which the cerebral cortex has been irreparably damaged should be accepted as the time when organs can be removed from the body (Jefko, 1980).

Organ donation is not the only difficulty involved. An increasing number of cases illustrate the ethical problem created by maintaining the life of comatose individuals with the support of technical equipment. A number of medical personnel, philosophers, and theorists have suggested that maintaining life under these conditions is wrong. What do you think?

Although scientists may disagree on the exact nature of death itself, we have been learning a great deal about how people deal, and how they should deal, with the death of their loved ones. We turn to that subject now.

Dealing Successfully with the Death of Others

Until this century, people were used to seeing death. It was considered a normal part of life. Half of all children died before their tenth birthday, one-third within their first year. Only in recent decades have the rates of death from all causes declined so much. Even the number of deaths from the scourge of AIDS are decreasing (CDC, 1996).

In modern Western societies, death comes mostly to the old. For example, 55 percent of all males are 65 or over when they die, and almost a third are past 75. The mortality rate has declined in our country from 17 per 1,000 population in 1900 to slightly less than 9 per 1,000 today (U. S. Census, 1996). For the first time in history, a family may expect to live 20 years (on the average) without one of its members dying.

An important exception should be noted: the huge number of children who are losing their mothers to AIDS (Callan, 1995). As of 2000, 125,000 children and 21,000 adolescents will have suffered this fate. Four out of five of them are from African American or Latino families.

The causes of overall lower mortality are clear: virtual elimination of infant and child mortality, and increasing control over the diseases of youth and middle age. For this reason, the subject of death became more and more taboo in the first half of this century. Probably as a result, social scientists spent little time studying our reactions to it or trying to find better ways to help us deal with it. Fortunately, in recent decades, this has changed.

Grief Work

> No one ever told me that grief felt so like fear. I am not afraid, but the sensation is like being afraid. The same fluttering in the stomach, the same restlessness, the yawning. I keep on swallowing. (C. Lewis)

Grief has a great deal in common with fear, and most grieving people really are afraid, at least unconsciously. They are frightened by the strength of their feelings, and they often fear that they are losing their sanity. They feel that they cannot go on, that their loss is so great that their own lives are in danger.

Grief not only follows death; when there is advance warning, it frequently precedes it. Fulton (1977) found that anticipatory grief has four phases: depression, a heightened concern for the ill person, rehearsal of death, and finally an attempt to adjust to the consequences that are likely to occur after the death.

The topic of anticipatory grief has received increasing attention lately. Major debates have occurred about its exact nature. For example, Hill and associates (1988) found that those widows who had anticipated their husband's death reported a higher level of mental health than those who had not. Most researchers agree that a forewarning of the impending death of a loved one can have therapeutic consequences:

• Avoiding the shock and fear that often accompanies sudden death

• Being able to make plans for the future that won't be regarded as betrayals

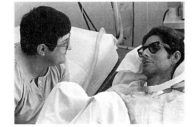

Anticipatory grief, which precedes the sick person's death, is usually very difficult. It often provides a number of benefits to the grieving, however.

- Expressing thoughts and feelings to the dying loved ones, thereby avoiding a sense of lost opportunity

- A time to prepare for the changes ahead

Pathological Grieving

The process of grieving, painful as it is, is experienced and resolved by most individuals. In some cases, however, morbid grief reactions occur that prevent the successful conclusion of this life crisis. Three types of these grief reactions are: delayed reaction, distorted reaction, and pathological mourning.

Delayed Reaction

In some cases, the intense reaction of the first stage is postponed for days, months, and in some cases years. In these cases, it is common for some seemingly unrelated incident to bring to the surface an intense grieving, which the individual does not even recognize as grief. Take, for example, the case of a 42-year-old man who underwent therapy to deal with an unaccountable depression. It was soon discovered that when he was 22, his 42-year-old mother committed suicide. Apparently, the occurrence of his own 42nd birthday brought to the surface all the feelings that he had managed to repress since that time.

 *An Applied View* | *A Personal Experience of One of the Authors with Delayed Reaction*

I am stepping out of my role as an author to relate an experience of mine that is relevant to this discussion of the function of grief. In April 1957 I joined the U. S. Navy and sailed to the Mediterranean for a six-month tour of duty on an oil supply ship. In early November I returned home to a joyful reunion with my family. After this wonderful weekend at home, I returned to my ship. Two days later I received a telegram informing me of a tragedy: My mother, two younger brothers, and two younger sisters had been killed in a fire that had destroyed our house. My father and three younger brothers and a sister had escaped with serious burns.

On the long train ride home from the naval port, I recall thinking that, as the oldest, I should be especially helpful to my father in the terrible time ahead. I was also aware of a curious absence of dismay in myself.

In our medium-sized upstate New York town, the catastrophe was unprecedented, and expressions of grief and condolences were myriad. People kept saying to me, "Don't try to be so brave. It's good for you to let yourself cry." And I tried to, but tears just wouldn't come.

At the funeral, the caskets were closed, and I can remember thinking that maybe, just maybe, this was all just a horrible dream. I distinctly remember one fantasy about my brother Mike. He was born on my first birthday and in the several years before the fire, I had become especially close to him. I imagined that he had actually hit his head trying to escape and had wandered off to Chicago with a case of amnesia and that no one was willing to admit that

they didn't know where he was. I knew this wasn't true, but yet I secretly clung to the possibility. After a very difficult period of time, our family gradually began a new life. Many people generously helped us, and eventually the memories faded.

Several times in the years that followed, I went to doctors because of a stomachache, a painful stiff neck, or some other malady that couldn't be diagnosed physically. One doctor suggested that I might be suffering from an unresolved subconscious problem, but I doubted it.

Then one night in 1972, 15 years after the fire, I was watching "The Walton's Christmas," a television show in which the father of a close family is lost and feared dead. Although dissimilar from my own experience, this tragedy triggered an incredible response in me. Suddenly and finally it occurred to me: "My God, half my family is really gone forever!" I began sobbing and could not stop for more than three hours. When I finally stopped, I felt weak and empty, relieved of an awful burden. In the days that followed I believe I went through a clear-cut "delayed grief" reaction.

Therefore, the answer to the question, at least in my experience, is clear: Grief work really is essential, and we avoid it only at the cost of even greater pain. My father died some years ago, and my grief was immediate and intense. I cannot help but feel that my emotional response that time was considerably more appropriate and healthy.

John Dacey

Dealing with Grief and Associated Anger

Many people suffering from grief and the anger that often accompanies it believe that their only option is to "wait it out" and "just get through it." As one client we know put it, "I can't believe I'm so weak that I can't get past this!" In fact, grief sufferers have a number of options; most of these activities can provide relief from their pain, often by turning it to some good:

• Join a volunteer program. For example, those who have lost a loved one in a drunk driving incident can join Mothers Against Drunk Driving.
• Volunteer to do work for a friend or neighbor who needs the help.
• Find physical outlets for painful feelings — any-

thing from an exercise club to beating the carpets with a broom.
• Talk about feelings with a trusted friend or relative.
• Seek psychotherapeutic help. There are specialists who are trained to help with grief and anger.
• Join a support group. In addition to groups that deal generally with grief or anger, there are specialty groups such as groups for those who have lost a child or are related to a suicide victim.
• Work for a hotline such as those operated by the Good Samaritans.
• Learn to meditate.
• Join a yoga class.

To learn more about dealing with death, you may want to read one of the following books: (1) A Pulitzer Prize–winning novel related to this topic is Agee's, *A death in the family.* This novel focuses on the effect of a man's death on his young son; (2) Becker's, *The denial of death* provides a brilliant analysis of the human failure to acknowledge death, and explores the theories of Freud, Rank, Jung, Fromm, and others. Becker was awarded the Pulitzer Prize for this work; (3) One of Freud's most famous works, *Totem and taboo,* explains how psychoanalysis looks at death and dying.

Distorted Reactions

In most cases, distorted reactions are normal symptoms carried to an extreme degree. They include adopting the behavior traits of the deceased, such as aspects of the deceased's fatal illness and other types of psychosomatic ailments, particularly colitis, arthritis, and asthma.

An example we know of is a young man whose mother died of lymphomic cancer. At her death, she had large boils on her neck. Some weeks after she died, her son discovered lumps on his neck that quickly developed into boils. On examination, they were found to be benign. In fact, it was determined that they were entirely psychosomatic. That is, the doctors decided that the only explanation of their existence was the great stress in the young man's mind over the loss of his mother.

The ultimate distorted reaction is depression so deep that it causes the death of a surviving loved one. This is especially likely to happen to widowers (Martikainen & Valkonen, 1996).

Pathological Mourning

In pathological mourning the process is not skipped but is prolonged and intensified to an abnormal degree (disabling distress is experienced for more than a few years) (Wortman & Davis, 1997). Frequently, the person suffering from pathological mourning tries to preserve every object of the deceased in perpetual memory.

An example of this illness is the man who worked hard with his wife to renovate an old cottage they had bought in order to live by a lake not far from their home. A few days before they were going to move in, she died of a heart attack. Many months later, friends noticed that he would disappear for several days at a time. One friend followed him to the cottage and found that he had created a shrine to her memory in it. Her clothes and other possessions were laid out in all the rooms, and her picture was on all the walls. Only after extensive therapy was he able to go through a more normal grief, give up the shrine, and move on with his life.

The Role of Grief

Most psychologists who have examined the role of grief have concluded that it is an essential aspect of a healthy encounter with the crisis of death. They believe that open confrontation with the loss of a loved one is essential to accepting the reality of a world in which the deceased is no longer present. Attempts to repress or avoid thoughts about the loss are only going to push them into the subconscious, where they will continue to cause problems until they are dragged out and accepted fully.

And yet, dealing with grief is also costly. For example, the mortality rate among grieving persons is seven times higher than a matched sample of nongrieving persons. Anthropologist Norman Klein (1978) made the point that psychologists may be too insistent that our grief be public and deep:

> In our own society, faddish therapies stress the idea that expressing sorrow, anger, or pain is a good thing, and the only means for "dealing with one's feelings" honestly . . . yet it is surely conceivable that some Americans can work through grief internally and privately, without psychological cost. It is even more conceivable that whole cultural subgroups may have different ways of conceding and responding to such experience. (p. 122)

Klein went on to cite the Japanese, who are most reticent about public grief and yet seem to suffer no ill effects from this reticence. The Balinese frequently laugh at the time of death, because, they say, they are trying to avoid crying; yet they seem to be psychologically healthy. Some cultures employ "keeners" who wail loudly so that the bereaved will not have to do so themselves.

His position has been reinforced by more recent research (Wortman & Davis, 1997). On the basis of their review of research on the grief response, they argued that a number of widely held beliefs are not supported by the evidence. They concluded that:

- A significant proportion of those who report little or no distress or depression after the death of a loved one also did not experience physical maladies as a result.

- Delayed grief does exist but it is extremely rare.

- Many physicians refrain from prescribing antidepressants and anti-anxiety drugs, believing that loss must equal suffering. The researchers referred to this attitude as "pharmacological Calvinism."

- Arriving at some philosophical reason for the loss of a loved one only rarely results in a lessening of distress. People who struggle to learn "Why me?" tend to have more distress than those who do not look for answers.

- The idea that grieving normally ends after one year is false; there is wide variation in the length of time people need to recover from loss.

- People often feel that they should cover up their grief if it goes on over a year, because others are made uncomfortable by it. This attitude of "grin and bear it" often prevents sufferers from getting the psychological help that can ease their burden.

The Role of the Funeral

One of the hardest aspects of dealing with the death of a loved one is deciding how the funeral (if there is to be one) is to be conducted. Funerals have always been an important part of American life, whether the elaborate burial rituals practiced by Native Americans, or the simple funerals of our colonial forbearers. Some research indicates that the rituals surrounding funerals have a therapeutic benefit that facilitates the grieving process (Marshall & Levy, 1990).

Once the intimate responsibility of each family, care for the dead in the United States has been transferred to a paid service industry. The need for this new service was brought about by changes in society during the first part of this century. The more mobile, urbanized workforce had less family support and less time to devote to the task of caring for the dead. In a relatively short time, funeral homes and

In your opinion, what are the appropriate arrangements for a funeral? Are you in favor of formal religious services? Why or why not?

A Sociocultural View

The Funeral in Other Times and Countries

Looking at the funeral practices of former cultures shows us not only how they buried their dead but also something about their values.

Ancient Egypt

Upon the death of the head of the house in ancient Egypt, women would rush frantically through the streets, beating their breasts from time to time and clutching their hair. The body of the deceased was removed as soon as possible to the embalming chambers, where a priest, a surgeon, and a team of assistants proceeded with the embalming operation. (The Egyptians believed in the life beyond; embalming was intended to protect the body for this journey.) While the body was being embalmed, arrangements for the final entombment began. When the mummified corpse was ready for the funeral procession and installation in its final resting place, it was placed on a sledge drawn by oxen or men and accompanied by wailing servants, professional mourners simulating anguished grief, and relatives. It was believed that when the body was placed in an elaborate tomb (family wealth and prestige exerted an obvious influence on tomb size), its spirits would depart and later return through a series of ritualistic actions.

Ancient Greece

Reverence for the dead permeated burial customs during all phases of ancient Greek civilization. Within a day after death the body was washed, anointed, dressed in white, and laid out in state for one to seven days, depending on the social prestige of the deceased. Family and friends could view the corpse during this time. For the funeral procession, the body was placed on a bier carried by friends and relatives and followed by female mourners, fraternity members, and hired dirge singers. Inside the tomb were artistic ornaments, jewels, vases, and articles of play and war. Like the Egyptians, the ancient Greeks prepared their tombs and arranged for subsequent care while they were still alive. About 1000 B.C.E. the Greeks began to cremate their dead. Although earth burial was never entirely superseded, the belief in the power of the flame to free the soul acted as a strong impetus to the practice of cremation. A choice of burial or cremation was available during all the late Greek periods.

The Roman Empire

Generally speaking, the Romans envisioned some type of afterlife and, like the Greeks, practiced both cremation and earth burial. When a wealthy person died, the body was dressed in a white toga and placed on a funeral couch, feet to the door, to lie in state for several days. For reasons of sanitation, burial within the walls of Rome was

prohibited; consequently, great roads outside the city were lined with elaborate tombs erected for the well-to-do. For the poor, there was no such magnificence; for slaves and aliens, there was a common burial pit outside the city walls.

Anglo-Saxon England

In Anglo-Saxon England (approximately the time when invading Low German tribes conquered the country in the fifth century), the body of the deceased was placed on a bier or in a hearse. On the corpse was laid the book of the Gospels as a symbol of faith and the cross as a symbol of hope. For the journey to the grave, a pall of silk or linen was placed over the corpse. The funeral procession included priests bearing lighted candles and chanting psalms, friends who had been summoned, relatives, and strangers who deemed it their duty as a corporal work of mercy to join the party. Mass was then sung for the dead, the body was solemnly laid in the grave (generally without a coffin), the mortuary fee was paid from the estate of the deceased, and liberal alms were given to the poor.

Colonial New England

Burials and funeral practices were models of simplicity and quiet dignity in eighteenth century New England. Upon death, neighbors (or possibly a nurse if the family was well-to-do) would wash and lay out the body. The local carpenter or cabinetmaker would build the coffin, selecting a quality of wood to fit the social position of the deceased. In special cases, metal decorations imported from England were used on the coffin. In church, funeral services consisted of prayers and sermons said over the pall-covered bier. Funeral sermons often were printed (with skull and crossbones prominently displayed) and circulated among the public. The funeral service at the grave was simple, primarily a brief prayer followed by the ritual commitment of the body to the earth. The filling of the grave, with neighbors frequently supplying the necessary labor because there were no professional gravediggers, marked the formal end of the early-colonial funeral ceremony.

Let's hope it won't happen, but what would you do if you were called upon to organize a funeral tomorrow? Would you know whom to notify? How would you arrange for the preparation and disposition of the body? What kind of ceremony, religious or otherwise, would you ask for? What would you do about a funeral home, a cemetery plot, and the will and death benefits of the deceased?

Perhaps you could discuss this with some of your friends or classmates, to see how they would feel. Notice how you feel about opinions that differ from yours.

Source: Turner & Helms (1989, pp. 492–93).

funeral directors became the accepted form of care for one's dead relatives (Fulton & Owen, 1988).

This commercialization of care for the dead has had mixed results. During the 1950s and 1960s, funeral homes came under stinging criticism for their expense and their lack of sensitivity to the needs of the surviving family members. The bereaved often felt that the funeral directors were more interested in dramatic and expensive presentations of the body than in what might be best for the family members.

A more current survey has revealed that only about 42 percent of funeral directors have had any formal education in the physical and psychological effects of the death of a loved one, and most of those who had some education felt it was inadequate (Weeks, 1989). Recent trends such as cremations and memorial services without the body (often because some body parts have been donated for transplants or science research) have relieved people of the more unpleasant and expensive aspects of funeral services (Marshall & Levy, 1990). Some families are now involving a professional grief counselor in the process.

Dealing Successfully with One's Own Death

> Having nearly died, I've found death like that sweet feeling that people have that let themselves slide into sleep. I believe that this is the same feeling that people find themselves in whom we see fainting in the agony of death, and I maintain that we pity them without cause. If you know not how to die, never trouble yourself. Nature will in a moment fully and sufficiently instruct you; she will exactly do that business for you; take you no care for it. Michel de Montaigne

Why is the acceptance of death so painful to so many of us? Why does it come up in every developmental stage, only to be partially resolved and partially denied?

Many people find dying a much harder experience than Montaigne would have us believe it is. Many dying patients feel seriously depressed before their deaths, and a large number have suicidal feelings. Among the reasons for these depressions are the following:

• Medication-induced mood alterations

• Awareness of how little time is left

• Feelings of isolation from relatives and friends who are withdrawing

• Feelings of grief for the losses that are close at hand

• Feelings of disillusion and resentment over injustice

Depression is sometimes described as cognitive withdrawal, because many patients have a decreasing ability and motivation to process stimuli as death nears (see terminal drop, Chapter 17). Also common is a strong sense of fear and a deep sense of sorrow (Sanders, 1989).

Must dying, then, always be such an unhappy experience? European psychiatrist Elisabeth Kübler-Ross is the most famous student of the process of death. Her three books on the subject have all been best sellers: *On Death and Dying* (1969), *Death—The Final Stage of Growth* (1975), and *To Live Until We Say Good-bye* (1978). Kübler-Ross discovered that, far from wanting to avoid the topic of death, many dying patients have a strong urge to discuss it. She interviewed hundreds of terminally ill persons. On the basis of these interviews, she developed a five-stage theory, describing the emotions that underlie the process of dying. The stages in her theory are flexible, in that people can move through them quickly, slowly, or not at all. Some fluctuation occurs between the stages, but by and large people tend to move through them in sequential order. They are portrayed in Figure 19.2.

Kübler-Ross's stage theory was the first to counter the common assumption that

Figure 19.2

Kübler-Ross's stages of dying

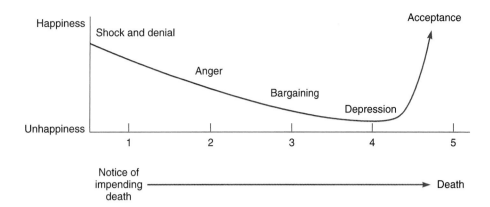

it is abnormal to have strong emotions during the dying process. However, no empirical confirmation that this particular sequence of stages is universal exists. Her theory overlooks the effects of personality, ethnic, or religious factors. It also does not take into account the influence of the specific illness and treatment, nor the availability of social support (Kastenbaum & Kastenbaum, 1989). So, should we accept Kübler-Ross's model or not? The biological, psychological, and social aspects of the process of dying are obviously very complex. We will need to know much more—knowledge gained through careful research—before we can answer this question. We can say that her theory, like all good theories, has at least provided us with five constructs (the five stages) to help guide that research.

Another theory, also based on observation and also describing five stages, is that of Saunders (1989). Her suggested stages are shock, awareness of loss, with-

Guided Review

1. Currently four different definitions of death exist: clinical death (stoppage of respiration and heart), brain death (cessation of cortex and midbrain activity), _____ death (not possible to discern electrical changes in tissues of heart and lungs), and _____ death (person treated essentially as dead).
2. The criteria for legal death is unreceptivity, no movements or breathing, no reflexes, and a flat _____ reading that remains flat for 24 hours.
3. The causes in Western society for lower mortality rates are the reduction of infant and child mortality and increasing control over the _____ of youth and middle age.
4. In addition to normal grief, there are three types of morbid grief reactions: _____ grief, distorted reactions, and _____ mourning.
5. Anticipatory grief is characterized by four phases: _____, a heightened concern for the ill person, _____ of death, and an attempt to adjust to the consequences that will occur after death.
6. Most psychologists believe that grief is essential as a part of a _____ encounter with death, but the forms that healthy grief might take have not yet been studied well empirically.
7. People may feel depressed before their own death because they are experiencing feelings of loss for friends and family, as well as feeling a sense of _____ over injustice.
8. Elisabeth Kübler-Ross argues that dying has five stages. These stages are shock and denial, anger, _____, depression, and acceptance.

Answers

1. biological, social 2. electroencephalogram (EEG) 3. diseases 4. delayed, pathological 5. depression, rehearsal 6. healthy 7. resentment 8. bargaining

drawal, healing, and renewal. The similarities with Kübler-Ross's stages are noteworthy. Wortman & Silver (1989) agree with the themes presented by Kübler-Ross and Saunders but urge that they do not occur in set stages in all individuals. Rather, these studies find that the themes are intermingled, ending with some people on a positive note and others react finally with anger and/or depression. As to the latter, some have urged that it is the right reaction. We are reminded of Dylan Thomas's famous lines of poetry, addressed to his father:

No matter how well prepared we are, death is always sad and stressful. Most of the time, though, we know that we can do nothing about it, and so we must accept the inevitable. How different it is when the death was not inevitable but was chosen by the person because life had become no longer worth living.

Suicide: The Rejection of Life

As you will see, we are beginning to learn more about how and why suicides happen. This information will surely help us in our efforts to prevent such unfortunate deaths.

The Overall Picture

Suicide and attempted suicide among adolescents are growing national problems (Holinger & others, 1987) and an increasingly common response to stress and depression among young persons (Dempsey, 1994). Suicide now ranks as the second leading cause of death among persons age 15 to 19, and many experts believe that if no suicides were "covered up," it would be the leading cause. In 1995, nearly 31,000 persons died by their own hands (Rosenberg & others, 1996). The rates were higher for whites than for non-whites (USDHHS, 1996). Younger adults today have generally higher rates of suicide than their grandparents did at that age (Conwell, 1995; Centers for Disease Prevention and Control, 1996). Teenagers have become not only more suicidal but apparently more reckless and self-destructive in general. As the suicide rate has risen steadily over the past 20 years, so too has the rate for motor vehicle accidents (the leading cause of death), accidents of other types, and homicides (U.S. Bureau of the Census, 1992).

Although suicide rates for teenagers have risen 72 percent since 1988, the rate for most other age groups has decreased. It would be safe to say that although the United States as a whole has become slightly less suicidal, teenagers and young people in general (age 30 and under) have become dramatically more suicidal. The increase has risen most steadily and most consistently among teenagers. It should be noted, however, that teen suicidal deaths rank high because teens have a relatively low rate of death from other causes (Swedo & others, 1991).

To better understand how we, as individuals, handle our own death, read: (1) Kübler-Ross's On death and dying, *a classic in this field; (2) Tolstoy's* The death of Ivan Illich, *a novel about a man who learns that he has terminal cancer, and his lonely journey into understanding the meaning of life and the ability to accept his own death.*

Do not go gentle into that good night—

Rage, rage, against the dying of the light.

Males are three to four times more likely to die of suicide attempts than are females.

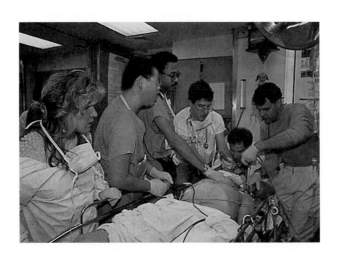

The Danger Signs of Suicide

- Sudden changes in mood or behavior.
- Pulling away from family and friends.
- Marked increase or decrease in sleeping.
- Becoming "accident prone."
- Talking about death or suicide, or heightened interest in reading about them.
- Heightened interest in music or art that deals with death.
- Giving away favorite possessions.
- Impetuous desire to get affairs in order.
- Abrupt drop in school or work performance.
- Impulsive drug and alcohol abuse.
- Changes in personal hygiene.

- Lack of interest in food.
- Unusual anger, anxiety, or apathy.
- Hypochondria.
- Inability to concentrate.
- Experience of serious personal loss.
- Previous history of suicide attempts.
- No single one of these signs is in itself a clear indication of suicidal ideation. Several of them, however, is cause for concern. Anyone talking about committing suicide should be taken seriously and a mental health professional should be consulted, even when you feel sure the person is "only talking about it to get attention or sympa-

Two other groups are much more prone to suicide, however: the so-called middle-old and old-old groups. Although the suicide rate for 15- to 24-year-olds is high—12.5 per 100,000—the rate for those 75 and older is almost double that, with males accounting for almost all the difference (U. S. National Center for Health Statistics, 1996). In fact, the older single white male is by far the person most likely to die of suicide (USDHHS, 1996). Accordingly, since older people make up the fastest growing portion of the population, the number of suicides among the elderly will continue to rise (Conwell & others, 1990). Glass and Reed (1993) stated that although teenage suicides receive significantly more media attention, elderly people are at higher risk for suicide than any other age group.

For the elderly, poor health is often both a cause of suicide and a way of covering it up. Loneliness is a second major factor. Effects of factors and forces on the behavior of people are important to understanding the development of the suicidal process (Mishara, 1996). It should be noted that for unstable individuals, even minor changes in their life patterns can push them either toward committing suicide or inhibit their tendency to do so.

Woodruff-Pak relates the story of an elderly retiree from the police force who had made an excellent adjustment to leaving the force. When he discovered that he had a large brain tumor, however, he became very depressed at the thought of leaving his wife, children, and nine grandchildren, to all of whom he was deeply attached. One day, after asking his wife to go to the store for his favorite candy, he shot himself. His wife discovered him and threw away his pistol. She told the paramedics she saw a man fleeing from her house. The "case" remained unsolved, and she was able to bury her husband in a Catholic cemetery.

The Influence of Gender on Suicide

At all ages, major gender differences exist. The rate for males is much higher due to the type of suicidal behavior engaged in, the methods used, the lethality of the attempt, and the degree of psychiatric disturbance present. Males and females are two very different suicidal types. Universally, males are about four times more likely to die of suicide than females (statistical abstract of the U.S., 1995). Attempt rates show even more dramatic gender differences, but in the opposite direction. Failed attempts at suicide among females are much higher than for males (Woodruff-Pak,

An Applied VIEW

My Attempts at Suicide (by Anonymous)

My first psychiatrist told my parents that my psychological tests indicated that I was potentially suicidal. I was 14 then. At 22, I had made five suicide attempts and had been in six mental institutions, which add up to 29 months as a mental patient and five years of intensive therapy. My diagnosis was borderline schizophrenia, chronic depression, and sadomasochism. Why? How had I become so obsessed with suicide?

When I flash back on my adolescent days, I remember feeling ugly, socially awkward, stuck away in an all-girls' boarding school reading Camus and Hesse, unpopular, and stupid! In fact, I was not quite as dreadful as all that, but in my mind I was. I felt different. I once wrote, "I'm at the bottom of an upside-down garbage can and it's so ugly." The world was horrible, but I was the worst part of it.

Suicide was my escape. Unsuccessful suicide attempts put me in the care of others who delicately forced me to confront my feelings of sadness and anger. I had to learn to share with others and sometimes that was what I secretly wanted. Two of my attempts, however, were calculated, purposeful acts. Despite what shrinks may say, I wanted to be dead, not taken care of.

What did death mean to me? One of my earliest memories is sitting on moss-covered ground in a grove of pines, reading *The Prayer for the Dead* with my basset hound curled up beside me. Suicide meant escape from hell on earth. No other purgatory could be worse than this one. Even if I were reincarnated, I would end up being some "lowly animal" with the kind of mind that could not

plague me with frightening, lonely, depressing thoughts. I clung to my friends and family, but it only increased my anger and self-contempt. I treated those people as my keepers who temporarily saved me from being left alone with my tormenting mind.

The final blow hit in Boston. I gradually withdrew from the few friends I had as well as my family. Death had grown so close that I no longer felt that I had much time. It was impossible to commit myself to anyone or anything. I was reserved, yet few people could sense how obsessed I was with death. Signs of affection terrified me because I knew I could not let anyone count on me. I needed death if life became too unbearable.

It finally did. I had become so passive that I no longer made contact with people. They had to call me. So much time had elapsed since I had felt close to someone that it seemed my "disappearance" would not really upset anyone. In addition to this, I was convinced that I was too stupid to handle academics or even a menial job (even though I had two jobs at the time). On a day when I knew no one would try and reach me, I took three times the lethal dosage of Seconal.

I was found 24 hours later and came out of a coma after 48 more. My arm was paralyzed. This time, I was placed in a long-term hospital. Another try at life began. With the help of an excellent therapist and the patient love of those whom I had thus far rejected, I have started once more. It has been two years since I took the pills. I think I know why people bother to live now.

1988). A major reason for the high survival rate among females is the method used. Whereas males often resort to such violent and effective means as firearms and hanging, females tend to choose less violent and less deadly means, such as pills. Male suicide attempters are considered significantly more disturbed than female attempters (Blum & others, 1992). Males are usually more committed to dying and therefore succeed far more often.

In light of the increase of suicides among the elderly, the prevention of suicide is gaining more attention (Cattell & Jolley, 1995). Health care professionals can play an important role in suicide prevention. Examining the practical role of the community in the lives of the elderly is a good beginning in these prevention efforts.

It should be noted, however, that although some elderly people may contemplate suicide, many have successfully resisted the urge to commit it. Older adults have certain coping abilities and reasons for living that enable them to face many demands of advanced age (Range & Stringer, 1996). One possible reason that more men than women die by their own hands is that older women are able to list more reasons for living than are men. In fact, Range and Stringer reported that older women often have greater ability to cope than they even realize. The authors suggest that suicide prevention strategies target men and encourage the development of deterrents to suicide.

Guided Review

9. Suicide and attempted suicide is an increasingly common response to _____ and depression among young people.
10. The suicide rate for men and women over 70 years of age is almost _____ as high as for men and women between the ages of 15 and 24 years.
11. The African American suicide rate is about the same as whites until age 24, then African American rates are generally _____ than those of whites.
12. In recent decades, suicidal behavior remains a behavior in which whites and the _____ _____ are overrepresented.

"Successful" Dying

Death and dying, by whatever means, are not one of our favorite topics, but they do have an important place in our study of life. In the next section of this chapter, we will discuss two of the ways we humans have to deal with death in a mature and satisfying way.

Death with Dignity

> So, my judges, face death with good hope, and know for certain that no evil can happen to a good man, either in life or after death. Socrates

No doubt most people would rather not suffer serious physical pain when they die, and many would prefer to avoid the emotional pain that often attends death. Until recently, however, only a few had any choice. Today, great debates have formed around two alternatives, both of them a form of **euthanasia.** There are two types of euthanasia (which means a "good death"). Passive euthanasia refers to refraining from continuing efforts to sustain a faltering life, such as turning off life-support systems. These methods are either covered by a living will, or are determined by the patient's legal representative. Active euthanasia means actively ending a life, either through directly killing the patient or by physician-assisted suicide.

On 30 September 1976, Governor Edmund Brown, Jr., of California signed the "Natural Death Act," the first death with dignity law in the nation. The statute states the right of an adult to sign a written directive instructing her or his physician to withhold or withdraw life-sustaining procedures in the event of a terminal condition. The law contains specific definitions for "terminal condition," "life-sustaining procedure," and "qualified patient." The directive must be drawn up in the form set forth by the statute. It must be signed and dated by an adult of sound mind and witnessed by two persons not related by blood or entitled to the estate of the declarant.

Since then all but 10 states have established such procedures. In June 1990 the Supreme Court ruled that because the desires of a Missouri woman who has been lying in a coma since 1983 had not been made explicit through a living will, she could not be allowed to die despite her parents' wishes. However, the Court has ruled that when procedures established within each state are followed, the "right to die" would be constitutional.

Almost 80 percent of Americans die in hospitals, and 70 percent of those deaths involve some aspect of medical technology such as breathing, feeding, and waste elimination equipment. Hence it is essential that those who do not want to be maintained on life-support systems if they become terminal put their wishes in writing

Answers

according to their state's laws. Open communications with one's doctor is also essential (Lynn & others, 1996).

What's Your View?

Is the Living Will Concept Fair to All?

Many things spread in popularity even if they are not always good for people. Although the living will concept does grant greater control over life to the person whose life it is, it has been argued that many individuals will invoke the law only when they believe they are dying. But is this right?

When people know they are likely to die, they are frequently in a depressed state. They may feel that now they are becoming worthless and so should not be a burden on those around them. They may feel that they "just want to get it over with." Opponents of the law say that this is no time for a person to be making judgments about what should happen if death appears imminent. Their judgment is impaired by the depression. As Attorney Thomas Marzen has remarked, "People who are not dying are being denied treatment. The family doesn't object, the doctor doesn't object, and no one seems to care" (Gest, 1989, p. 36). What do you think? What would you want for your parents? For yourself? For your children?

Physician-Assisted Suicide

Whatever you want to do, do it now. There are only so many tomorrows.

Today there is also a serious debate taking place over the appropriateness of physician-assisted suicide (Foreman, 1996). In this case, someone on the medical team typically injects an overdose of morphine, which quickly brings on unconsciousness and death. Those who support it claim a number of advantages for it: time of death is up to the patient; it can be used by those for whom the hospice or hospital is inappropriate; and death is painless if the patient is given a high enough dose of morphine. Others suggest that its limitations are: it is an extreme way to end suffering; some family members may be made to feel guilty; it may interfere with healing in relationships; it is opposed by most major religions; and it could be abused in order to save money. In a letter to the Supreme Court from his deathbed (Woodward & McCormick, 1996, p. 62), Cardinal Bernardin wrote, "As one who is dying, I have especially come to appreciate the gift of life. Creating a new right to assisted suicide will endanger society and send a false signal that a less than 'perfect' life is not worth living."

At this time, the American public seems to favor physician-assisted suicide. Dr. Jack Kevorkian has assisted at over three dozen suicides, and has not been convicted (Kolata, 1996). Polls have found that two-thirds of the American public wants legislation permitting some form of the practice (Taylor, 1995). The American Medical Association has established a task force to attempt to establish clearer ethical guidance for patients, their families, and their doctors (Simpson, 1996).

The Hospice: "A Better Way of Dying"

The "death ward" in most hospitals is not a nice place to be. The atmosphere is one of hushed whispers and fake smiles. No children below the age of 12 are allowed. Medications to control the pain are usually given on a schedule rather than as needed. Machines are used to continue life at all costs, though the patient may desire death. Viewing a typical American death ward made British historian Toynbee conclude that "Death is un-American."

In reaction to this, some have reached back to the Middle Ages, when religious orders set up havens in which dying pilgrims could come to spend their last days. The modern **hospice** was established to provide for a more "natural" death for

The modern hospice is organized to afford a more "natural death" to the dying. Although this woman knows she does not have long to live she is able to maintain a positive attitude with the help of the hospice staff.

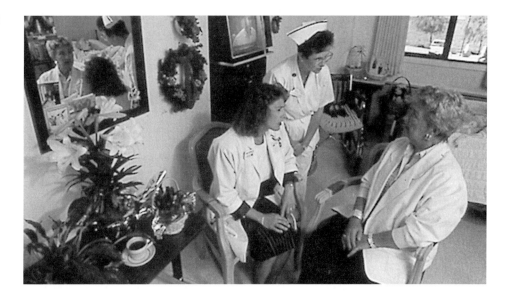

those who are terminally ill. The first U. S. hospice opened in New Haven, Connecticut, in 1971. Since then the National Hospice Organization has been formed to help promulgate this movement.

The hospice is not a new type of facility; it is a new philosophy of patient care in the United States (although not new in Europe). Hospices do pioneering work in such neglected areas as the easing of pain and psychological counseling of patients and their families. Even before patients begin to suffer pain, which in diseases such as cancer can be excruciating, they are given a mixture of morphine, cocaine, alcohol, and syrup so they come to realize that pain can be controlled. Known as "Brompton's Mixture," this concoction is used only when the patient's need is severe; it is very effective in alleviating both pain and the fear accompanying it. A major goal of the hospice is to keep the person's mind as clear as possible at all times.

Whenever advisable, the hospice allows the patient to remain at home and provides daily visits by staff nurses and volunteers. Jane Murdock, a California schoolteacher,

> recalls how her dying mother at first refused to see her grandchildren after she was brought home from the hospital. But when the visiting hospice team began reducing her pain and reassuring her and her family in other ways, a new tranquillity set in. Finally the woman even let the youngsters give her medication, and assist her about the house. Says Murdock: "I felt when she died that it was a victory for all of us. None of us had any guilt."
> ("A Better Way of Dying," Alban, 1978, p. 66)

The hospice program movement has now grown to the point that it supports its own journal. Articles in the *Hospice Journal* often provide supplementary information about special issues concerning the terminally ill. For example, an article on hospice care for patients with AIDS (Schofferman, 1987) delved into additional issues of concern: irrational fear of contagion, homophobia (fear of homosexuals) by friends and relatives, and special difficulties in caring for substance abusers.

One of the major questions now being considered is whether the hospice should continue as a separate facility run solely for that purpose or become a standard part of all major hospitals. Currently, hospice programs in the United States are primarily home-based care, with the sponsorship of such programs evenly divided between hospitals and community agencies. Many insurance programs now cover hospice care (Bulkin & Lukashok, 1988). Although many assume hospices deal only

Figure 19.3

Growth of hospices in the United States

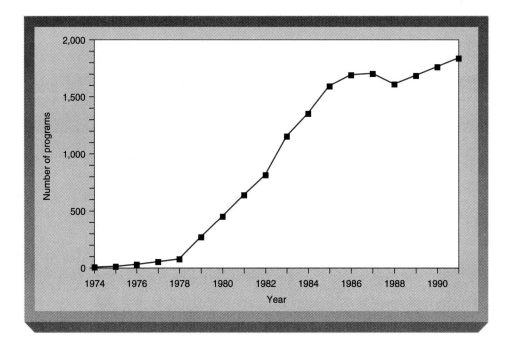

with the elderly, as can be seen in Figure 19.3, nearly one-third of the patients are younger than 65.

Whatever the case, for most of us, dying is frightening and, ultimately, very hard to understand. To come to terms with it, we almost always rely on our spiritual rather than our cognitive powers.

Guided Review

13. A law was passed in California in 1976 that allows death with dignity, which means that adults have the right to legally state their rejection of _____ procedures when they are in a terminal condition.
14. The hospice was established to provide a more _____ death for people who are terminally ill.
15. The hospice movement contributes to the death with dignity movement by providing relief from distressing symptoms and providing a _____ _____ for the terminal patient.
16. One of the major goals of the hospice is to keep the patient's _____ as clear as possible.

Spirituality

> There is but one true philosophical problem, and this is suicide: Judging whether life is or is not worth living amounts to answering the fundamental question of philosophy. Albert Camus

Spirituality is concerned not only with whether life is worth living but why it is worth living. It may involve the attempt to better understand the reasons for living, through striving to know the intentions of a Supreme Being. An example is reading

Answers

13. life-sustaining 14. natural 15. caring environment 16. mind

An Applied View

If You Had Your Life to Live Over Again, What Would You Do Differently?

This question was recently asked of 122 retired persons by DeGenova (1992). She discovered that her sample chose the pursuit of education more than any other area. This emphasis on education among retirees may be because they feel their lack of education led to missed or limited opportunities. Although these people indicated they would have spent more time doing a variety of things, they said that they would have spent less time worrying about work.

This poem describes the feelings of one 81-year-old lady, Nadine Stair, on the topic:

If I had my life to live over,
I'd like to make more mistakes next time.
I'd relax, I would limber up. I would be sillier
than I have been this trip. I would take fewer
things seriously. I would take more chances.
I would climb more mountains and swim more
rivers. I would eat more ice cream and less

beans. I would perhaps have more actual troubles,
but I'd have fewer imaginary ones.
You see, I'm one of those people who live sensibly
and sanely hour after hour, day after day. Oh, I've
had my moments, and if I had it to do over again,
I'd have more of them. In fact, I'd try to have
nothing else. Just moments, one after another,
instead of living so many years ahead of each day.
I've been one of those persons who never goes
anywhere without a thermometer, a hot water
bottle, a raincoat, and a parachute. If I had to do
it again, I would travel lighter than I have.
If I had my life to live over, I would start
barefoot earlier in the spring and stay that way later
in the fall.
I would go to more dances.
I would ride more merry-go-rounds.
I would pick more daisies!

inspired books such as the Bible. Another is trying to discern the purposes and goals of some universal life force by, for example, examining historical trends in biological changes of species. In any case, spirituality includes all of our efforts to gain insight into the underlying, overriding forces of life. For many, it is the only justification for morality.

How important a role does spirituality play in the lives of typical American adults? One way this question has been investigated is through looking at religious participation and at religious attitudes. These factors are sometimes misleading, but together they offer one fairly reliable answer to the question.

Religious Participation

Americans have always been highly religious. This statement is supported by numerous Gallup polls (Gallup, 1988). A majority of the elderly consider religious practice to be of major importance in their lives. According to surveys, 96 percent of those over 65 believe in God, and 82 percent report that religion plays a significant role in their lives.

Religious life is of great importance to many of the elderly.

What's Your View?

Some Questions about Religious Preference

Religious Preference, Church Membership, and Attendance: 1957 to 1989 (in percent)

The following chart lists a number of facts about American religious practices.

| Year | Religious Preference | | | | | Church/synagogue members | Persons attending church/synagogue | Age and Region | Church/synagogue members, 1989 |
	Protestant	Catholic	Jewish	Other	None				
1957......	66	26	3	1	3	73	47	18–29 years old	61
1967......	67	25	3	3	2	73	43	30–49 years old	66
1975......	62	27	2	4	6	71	41	50 years and over	76
1980......	61	28	2	2	7	69	40	East	69
1985......	57	28	2	4	9	71	42	Midwest	72
1988......	56	28	2	2	9	65	42	South	74
1989......	56	28	2	4	10	69	43	West	55

Source: Bureau of the Census (1992).

These facts suggest a number of interesting questions. For example:

- The percentage of our population who belong to Protestant religions has been dropping, and the number who say they have no religious preference has been growing. Is this a real change, or are people becoming more honest? If the latter, why?

- Church/synagogue membership was dropping but has recently rebounded. Why?
- Older people participate more in religious services than younger people. Why?
- The West has the least religious participation, the South the most. Why?

What are your opinions on these questions?

Religious values become stronger with age. For example, the percentage of people who express strong religious beliefs increases from 35 percent among young adults to 47 percent in middle age to 66 percent among the elderly. Attending services once or more each month grows among these three age groups from 50 percent to 67 percent to nearly 75 percent (Russell, 1989). Furthermore, the influence of religion appears to be highly related to a sense of well-being in elderly persons.

In their study of 836 elderly persons, Koenig and associates (1988) attempted to clear this up. They looked at nonorganizational practices (prayer, Bible reading, etc.) and subjective religious feelings, as well as organized religious practices. They found moderately strong correlations between morale and all three religious measures. The relationships were especially strong for women and for those over 75.

Spirituality does appear to develop with age. A number of theories have been offered as to how and why this is so. Among them, four views have come to receive highest regard: those of Viennese psychoanalysts Viktor Frankl and Carl Jung, sociobiologist E. O. Wilson, and theologian James Fowler.

Frankl's Theory of Spirituality

Frankl (1967) described human life as developing in three interdependent stages according to the predominant dimension of each stage.

Dr. Victor Frankl, survivor of six years in a Nazi concentration camp, has made many contributions to the field of psychology and spirituality.

1. The **somatic** (physical) **dimension.** According to the somatic dimension, all persons are motivated by the struggle to keep themselves alive and to help the species survive. This intention is motivated entirely by instincts. It exists at birth and continues throughout life.

2. The **psychological dimension.** Personality begins to form at birth and develops as a result of instincts, drives, capacities, and interactions with the environment. The psychological dimension and the somatic dimension are highly developed by the time the individual reaches early adulthood.

3. The **noetic dimension.** The noetic dimension has roots in childhood but primarily develops in late adolescence. It is spiritual not only in the religious sense but also in the totality of the search for the meaningfulness of life. This aspect distinguishes humans from all other species. The freedom to make choices is the basis of responsibility. Reason exists in the noetic realm. Conscience, which greatly affects the meaningfulness that we discover in life, resides in the noetic.

Frankl believed that development in the physical and personality dimensions results from the total sum of the influences bearing upon an individual. The noetic, on the other hand, is greater than the sum of its parts. This means that we as adults are responsible for inventing (or reinventing) ourselves! Whatever weaknesses our parents may have given us, we can and should try to overcome them. They need not govern our lives.

Jung's Theory of Spirituality

Jung (1933, 1971), a student of Freud's, agreed to a large extent with his mentor's description of development in the first half of the human life. But he felt that Freud's ideas were inadequate to describe development during adulthood. Jung saw spiritual development as occurring in two stages.

The First Half of Life

In each of the Jungian functions of thinking, feeling, sensing, and intuiting, the personality develops toward individuation (see Chapter 14). Most people are well in-

Dr. Carl Jung, a student of Freud's, introduced many concepts into psychology, including the anima and animus.

dividuated by the middle of life, at approximately age 35; that is, we are most different from each other at this age.

The Second Half of Life

The goal of human development in the second half of life is just the opposite. Here a movement toward wholeness or unity of personality is the goal. Somewhere around mid-life, the individual should begin to assess the various systems of his or her personality and come to acknowledge the disorganized state of these systems. There should be a turning inward or self-inspection that marks the beginning of true adult spirituality. The goals of this introspection are:

- discovering a meaning and purpose in life;

- gaining a perspective on others, determining values and activities in which one is willing to invest energy and creativity; and

- preparing for the final stage of life—death.

Spirituality in the second half of life develops as a complement to the first half of life. By nourishing one's undeveloped side of life, one comes to a recognition of the spiritual and supernatural aspects of existence. For men, this means developing the **anima,** and for females the **animus.**

In contrast to the self-determination of spirituality seen in Frankl's and Jung's psychological points of view, sociobiology sees spirituality as determined almost entirely by instinct, that is, as a function of the genes.

Once we truly know that life is difficult—once we truly understand and accept it—then life is no longer difficult. Because once it is accepted, the fact that life is difficult no longer matters. M. S. Peck

Wilson's Theory of Spirituality

The predisposition to religious belief is the most complex and powerful force in the human mind and in all probability an ineradicable part of human nature. Edward Wilson

Harvard sociobiologist Edward O. Wilson, the leading spokesperson for the sociobiological point of view (see Chapter 13), argued that religion and spirituality are inseparable. Together they grant essential benefits to believers. He argued that all societies, from hunter-gatherer bands to socialist republics, have religious practices with roots that go back at least as far as the Neanderthal period.

For example, he argued that even modern Russian society, which is still largely anticlergy and pro-socialism, is as much a religious society as any other. Wilson (1978) cited one of Lenin's closest disciples, Grefori Pyatakov, who describes what it is to be "a real Communist"—one who

will readily cast out from his mind fears in which he has believed for years. A true Bolshevik has submerged his personality in the collectivity, the "Party," to such an extent that he can make the necessary effort to break away from his opinions and convictions and can honestly agree with the "Party"—that is the test of a true Bolshevik. (p.184)

Wilson said that in this statement we see the essence of religious spirituality. Humans, he argued, have a need to develop simple rules for handling complex problems. We also have a strong need for an unconscious sense of order in our daily lives. We strongly resist attempts to disrupt this order, which religion almost always protects.

Religion is one of the few uniquely human behaviors. Rituals and beliefs that make up religious life are not seen among any other animals. Some scientists, notably Lorenz and Tinbergen, argued that animal displays, dances, and rituals are similar to human religious ceremonies. Wilson believed this comparison was wrong;

animal displays are for the purpose of communicating (sexual desire, etc.), but religious ceremonies intend far more than mere communication.

Their goal is to "reaffirm and rejuvenate the moral values of the community" (Wilson, 1978, p. 179). Furthermore, religious learning is almost entirely unconscious. Most religious tenets are taught and deeply internalized early in life. Early teaching is a necessity if children are to learn to subvert their natural self-interests to the interest of society.

The sociobiological explanation of spirituality, then, is that through religious practice, the survival of practitioners is enhanced. Those who practice religion are more likely to stay alive (or at least they were in the past) than those who do not practice religion.

Wilson believed that even a person's willingness to be controlled may be genetic. Although all societies need some rebels, they also require that the vast majority of people be controllable, typically through religious and political beliefs. Therefore, Wilson believed that over the long run genes that favor willingness to be controlled have been favored by natural selection.

The potential for self-sacrifice can be strengthened in this manner, because the willingness of individuals to relinquish rewards or even surrender their own lives will favor group survival. The Jonestown mass suicide, for example, appears to have occurred because of the group's hope to remain united in afterlife. This concept of self-sacrifice is also the basis for Weinrich's (1987) assertion that homosexuality is an altruistic behavior (see Chapter 13).

Religions usually favor survival of their believers. This is not always true, though, and is true to differing degrees. It has been estimated that there have been more than 100,000 different religious faiths since humankind began. Obviously most have failed.

Some religions are even contrary to the survival needs of their believers. The Shaker religion, which disallows sexual intercourse to any of its participants, is an example. Shakerism lasted in this country for no more than two centuries. It flourished in the nineteenth century, but only a very few believers exist today. With no new recruits, it seems doomed to extinction. This, Wilson argued, is always the case for those religions that do not somehow enhance the vitality and hardiness of the groups that support them. The constant pursuit of a better chance for survival is why new ones are started.

Religions, according to the sociobiological point of view, develop through three steps:

1. **Objectification.** First, a perception of reality is described. Objectification occurs, which includes images and definitions that are easy to understand. Examples are good versus evil, heaven versus hell, and the control of the forces of nature by a god or gods.

2. **Commitment.** People devote their lives to these objectified ideas. Out of this commitment, they are willing under any circumstances to help those who have done the same.

3. **Mythification.** In mythification, stories are developed that tell why the members of the religion have a special place in the world. These stories are rational and enhance the person's understanding of the physical as well as spiritual world. The stories include explanations of how and why the world, as well as the religion, came to be. In earlier, less sophisticated religions, the faith is said to have been founded at the same time as the beginning of the race. These rarely include all-powerful or all-knowing gods. In less than one-third of the known religions is there a highly placed god, and in even fewer is there a notion of a moral god who has created the world. In the later religions, God is always seen as male, and almost always as the shepherd of a flock.

Not surprisingly, Wilson saw science as taking the place of theology today, because science has explained natural forces more effectively than theology. In fact, he asserted that science has explained theology itself. Although he saw theology as being phased out, he argued that the demise of religion is not at all likely. As long as religions make people more likely to survive and propagate themselves, Wilson suggested, they will enjoy worldwide popularity.

Wilson's theory attempted to explain spiritual development within societies. Theologian James Fowler has offered a description of the development of faith throughout the life cycle of individuals, without regard to the culture in which faith forms.

Fowler's Theory of Spirituality

James Fowler (1974, 1975a, 1975b, 1991, 1993) offered a theoretical framework built on the ideas of Piaget, Erikson, and Kohlberg. He believed strongly that cognitive and emotional needs are inseparable in the development of spirituality. Spirituality cannot develop faster than intellectual ability, and also depends on the development of personality. Thus Fowler's theory of faith development integrates the role of the unconscious, of needs, of personal strivings, and of cognitive growth. As he described it (1993):

> Faith develops with the establishment of new centers of value, new images of power, and new master stories that coalesce in stages and advance toward a point where there is maximal individuation of the self and corresponding minimization of the personal ego as the point from which evaluations are made. (p. 27)

Fowler saw faith developing in six steps. He said that the stages in faith development can be delayed indefinitely, but the person must have reached at least a certain minimal age at each stage in order to move on to a succeeding stage. His six stages are as follows:

1. **Intuitive-projective faith.** For intuitive-projective faith, minimal age is 4 years. In this stage, the individual focuses on surface qualities, as portrayed by adult models. This stage depends to a great extent on fantasy. Conceptions of God or a supreme being reflect a belief in magic.

2. **Mythical-literal faith.** For mythical-literal faith, minimal age is 5 to 6 years. Fantasy ceases to be a primary source of knowledge at this stage, and verification of facts becomes necessary. Verification of truth comes not from actual experience but from such authorities as teachers, parents, books, and tradition. Faith in this stage is mainly concrete, and depends heavily on stories told by highly credible storytellers. For example, the traditional story of Adam and Eve is taken quite literally.

3. **Poetic-conventional faith.** For poetic-conventional faith, minimal age is 12 to 13 years. The child is entering Piaget's codification stage. Faith is still conventional and depends on a consensus of opinion of other, more authoritative persons. Now the person moves away from family influence and into new relationships. Faith begins to provide a coherent and meaningful synthesis of these relationships.

   Individuals become aware of symbolism and realize that there is more than one way of knowing truth. Learned facts are still taken as the main source of information, but individuals in Stage 3 begin to trust their own judgment and the quality of selected authorities. Nevertheless, they do not yet place full confidence in their own judgment.

4. **Individuating-reflective faith.** For individuating-reflective faith, minimal age is 18 to 19 years. Youths in stage 3 are unable to synthesize new areas of experience, because depending on others in the community does not always solve problems. Individuals in Stage 4 begin to assume responsibility for their own beliefs, attitudes, commitments, and lifestyle. The faith learned in earlier stages is now disregarded, and greater attention is paid to one's own experience. Those individuals who still need authority figures have a tendency to join and become completely devoted to clubs and cults.

5. **Paradoxical-consolidation faith.** For paradoxical-consolidation faith, minimal age is 30. In this stage such elements of faith as symbols, rituals, and beliefs start to become understood and consolidated. The person begins to realize that other approaches to dealing with such complex questions as the supernatural and supreme being can be as valid as her or his own. The individual at this stage considers all people to belong to the same universal community and has a true regard for the kinship of all people.

6. **Universalizing faith.** For universalizing faith, minimal age is 40 years. As with Kohlberg's final stage, very few people ever reach this level. Here the individual lives in the real world but is not of it. Such persons do not merely recognize the mutuality of existence; they act on the basis of it. People at this stage appear to be truly genuine and lack the need to "save face" that exists at the lower stages.

Fowler (1991, 1993) summarizes his position: "Faith develops with the establishment of new centers of value, new images of power, and new master stories that coalesce in stages . . ." (1991, p. 27). This development simultaneously produces a more individualized self and a less egocentric view of the world. As a result of this process, moral decision making is enhanced.

Stage 6, as described by Fowler, compares closely with a hypothetical Stage 7 of morality proposed by Kohlberg (see Chapter 9). Although he never found anyone at a Stage 7 level of morality, Kohlberg believed that theoretically there should be a stage for those few persons who rise above the purely cognitive and achieve a place where they transcend logic. These individuals, who are rare indeed, come to understand why one should be just and ethical in a world that is unjust. A burning love of universal humankind presses them always to act in truly moral ways.

The development of spirituality and morality appears to be parallel all along the sequence, especially in the Kohlberg and Fowler models. At the early levels, the orientation is basically selfish; ethical thinking and behavior are virtually nonexistent. The child is "good" only to please more powerful persons.

At the second two levels, concern for the opinion of the community in general takes over. "What will people think!" is uppermost in religion as well as in moral decisions. Only if and when the highest levels are reached do true spirituality and morality emerge. And for a few individuals at the highest level, the distinction between the moral and the spiritual no longer exists.

In an extension of this view of spirituality too complex to be covered here, Eugene and associates (1993) discussed Wilbur's nine-stage developmental model of consciousness. This theory draws equally from Western and Eastern approaches and expands on Piaget's work. The last three stages deal with transpersonal development, in which perceptual power arises from inner sight rather than from thought. Cross-cultural similarities at the higher levels of spiritual development reported in the study support the claim that there is deep mystical unity of the world's spiritual traditions.

Why do people vary so much in level of spirituality? Can the biopsychosocial

Religion is for those who are afraid to go to Hell. Spirituality is for those who have already been there.

An elderly recovering alcoholic

model help us answer this question? Do you believe that Fowler's ideas would apply to Eastern cultures? What's your opinion?

Guided Review

17. _____ is concerned with whether life is worth living and why it is worth living.
18. For many Americans religion is connected to spirituality. The influence of religion appears to be highly related to a sense of _____ in elderly persons.
19. Victor Frankl looks at spirituality, and especially the third or _____ dimension, as directed toward transcending training and aspiring to higher levels of thought and behavior.
20. Carl Jung sees life in two halves, with the _____ second half of life directed toward finding meaning and _____, and preparing for death.
21. Wilson argues that the evolutionary or survival value of spirituality develops in three stages. These stages are objectification, commitment, and _____.
22. Fowler, like Piaget, Erikson, and Kohlberg, includes stages of development and a _____ age for each stage in his theory of faith development.
23. Fowler sees faith developing in six stages: intuitive-projective, _____ poetic-conventional, individuating-reflective, paradoxical-consolidation, and _____.

CONCLUSION

"The distinction between the moral and the spiritual no longer exists." What a wonderful goal to choose as a means of living the good life. It is probably also the best way to ensure a successful death. We sincerely hope that having read this book will contribute in some small way to your achievement of those two preeminent goals!

In summary:

The Role of Death in Life

- Today, four types of death are recognized: clinical death, brain death, biological or cellular death, and social death.
- In modern Western societies, death comes mostly to the old.
- Grief both follows and can precede the death of a loved one.
- In some cases, morbid grief reactions occur that prevent the successful conclusion of the life crisis. These are known as delayed reactions,

distorted reactions, and pathological reactions.
- Most psychologists who have examined the role of grief have concluded that it is a healthy aspect of the crisis of death.
- Funerals have always been an important part of American life. Research has indicated that the rituals surrounding funerals have therapeutic benefits that facilitate the grieving process.
- Kübler-Ross has offered five stages of dying: shock and denial, anger, bargaining, depression, and acceptance.

Suicide: The Rejection of Life

- Suicide rates for those over 75 is double that of adolescents, with the older white male most likely to take his life.
- Males and females are very different regarding suicide, with men

being more likely to die than women.

"Successful" Dying

- The hospice movement and "death with dignity" legislation have provided people with more control over their own death, making it a bit easier to accept.

Spirituality

- In recent decades, participation in religious activities has been changing in a number of ways.
- The elderly practice their religions to a greater degree than other adults.
- Theories of spirituality have been presented by Frankl, Jung, Wilson, and Fowler.
- Fowler has incorporated the work of Erikson, Piaget, and Kohlberg in his theory of the development of faith, which proceeds through six stages.

Answers

17. Spirituality 18. well-being 19. noetic 20. spiritual, purpose 21. mythification 22. minimal 23. mythical-literal, universalizing

KEY TERMS

Anima
Animus
Biological death
Brain death
Cardiopulmonary resuscitation (CPR)
Clinical death
Commitment
Electroencephalogram (EEG)

Euthanasia
Hospice
Individuating-reflective faith
Intuitive-projective faith
Legal death
Mythical-literal faith
Mythification
Noetic dimension

Objectification
Paradoxical-consolidation faith
Poetic-conventional faith
Psychological dimension
Social death
Somatic dimension
Universalizing faith

WHAT DO YOU THINK?

1. It has been suggested that people in Western society typically are more fearful of death than are members of Eastern cultures. If so, what factors contribute to our more frightened attitude?
2. Most of us think of grief as something that happens to us. Do you think it makes sense to describe it as "work"?
3. How do you feel about the idea of "successful death"?

4. Are there some old people—those who have lost their spouse and all their friends, or those who are undeniably terminal—who should be allowed to take their own lives? Should these people be helped to have a "ceremony of death"?
5. In this chapter we have suggested two ways of making death more dignified. Can you think of any others?
6. Are you satisfied with your own

level of religious participation? What do you think you should do differently?
7. How would you define your own spirituality?
8. Fowler states that there is a certain minimal age for each of his stages of spiritual development. What kinds of experience do you think would move a person from one stage to the next?

CHAPTER REVIEW TEST

1. **If brain death occurs, a person still remains alive in this condition because**
   a. autoplasia stimulates the autonomic processes.
   b. neuroplasia stimulates the autonomic processes.
   c. the autonomic processes are governed by the brain stem.
   d. the autonomic processes are governed by the cortex.

2. **Legal death occurs when**
   a. respiration and heartbeat have stopped.
   b. the brain fails to receive sufficient amount of oxygen.
   c. there is an unreceptivity and unresponsivity, no movements or breathing, no reflexes, and a flat electroencephalogram reading that remains flat for 24 hours.
   d. it is no longer possible to discern an electrical charge in the tissues of the heart and lung.

3. **The phases of anticipatory grief are**
   a. depression, a heightened concern for the ill person, rehearsal of death, and an attempt to adjust to the consequences that are likely to occur after the death.
   b. depression and rehearsal of death.
   c. a heightened concern for the ill person, rehearsal of death, and an attempt to adjust to the consequences that are likely to occur after the death.
   d. depression, a heightened concern for the ill person, and rehearsal of death.

4. **Knowledge of the impending death of a loved one can have which therapeutic consequences?**
   a. Avoidance of shock
   b. Ability to plan for the future
   c. Time to prepare for impending changes
   d. All of the answers are correct.

5. **According to Kübler-Ross, many dying people want to discuss**
   a. plans for the family.
   b. burial arrangements.
   c. feelings and emotions about their death.
   d. anything but their death.

6. **A young man, whose father died from lung cancer, is displaying grief known as distorted reaction. He has**
   a. experienced grieving stages that are prolonged and intensified to an abnormal degree.
   b. developed some of the same symptoms his father had, which his doctor determined were entirely psychosomatic.
   c. created a shrine in memory of his father.
   d. experienced anticipatory grief.

7. **Why do many dying patients feel depressed before their deaths?**
   a. Medication-induced mood alterations
   b. Feelings of isolation from

relatives and friends who are withdrawing

c. Awareness of how little time is left

d. All of the answers are correct.

8. Older single white males are most likely to die of

a. cancer.

b. heart disease.

c. accident.

d. suicide.

9. The law that grants an adult the right to instruct his or her physician to withhold or withdraw life-sustaining procedures in the event of a terminal condition is known as the

a. "right to life" law.

b. "living will" law.

c. "death with dignity" law.

d. None of the answers are correct.

10. Home-based care for the dying is known as the

a. Visiting Nurses program.

b. hospice program.

c. behavioral medicine program.

d. home-health program.

11. Whether life is worth living and why it is worth living is the major premise of

a. spirituality.

b. religion.

c. separation anxiety.

d. None of the answers are correct.

12. In what stage in Frankl's theory of spirituality are persons motivated by the struggle to keep themselves alive and to help the species survive?

a. Somatic dimension

b. Psychological dimension

c. Noetic dimension

d. None of the answers are correct.

13. In Fowler's theory of spirituality, stages in _____ can be delayed indefinitely, but the person must have reached a certain minimal age at each stage to move on to a succeeding stage.

a. psychological growth

b. spiritual belief

c. faith development

d. commitment

14. According to Fowler, what is the minimal age at which a person can gain universalizing faith?

a. 12 to 13 years old

b. 18 to 19 years old

c. 30 years old

d. 40 years old

15. According to Jung, by the age of 35, most people are well

a. established.

b. prepared for life's work.

c. individuated.

d. on their way to developing a wholeness of personality.

16. The sociobiological point of view states that we develop religion through what steps?

a. Objectification, commitment, mythification

b. Commitment and mythification

c. Objectification and mythification

d. Objection and commitment

Answers

1. c, 2. c, 3. a, 4. d, 5. d, 6. b, 7. d, 8. d, 9. c, 10. b, 11. a, 12. a, 13. c, 14. d, 15. c, 16. a

A

Absorbent mind   Montessori's term for a child's ability to absorb experiences from the environment (0 to 6 years) (Ch. 7).

Accommodation   Piaget's term to describe the manner by which cognitive structures change (Ch. 2).

Accumulation-of-errors theory   As cells die, they must synthesize new proteins to make new cells. As this is done, occasionally an error occurs. Over time, these errors mount up and may finally grow serious enough to cause organ failure (Ch. 17).

Accumulation of metabolic waste   Waste products resulting from metabolism build-up in various parts of the body, contributing greatly to the decreasing competence of those parts (Ch. 17).

Activity theory   Human beings flourish through interaction with other people. They are unhappy when, as they reach the older years, their contacts with others shrink as a result of death, illness, and societal limitations. Those who are able to keep up the social activity of their middle years are considered the most successful (Ch. 18).

Adaptation   One of the two functional invariants in Piaget's theory (Ch. 2).

Adhesion   The time during which the prepared surface of the uterus and the outer surface of the fertilized egg, now called the trophoblast, touch and actually "stick together" (Ch. 4).

Adolescent egocentrism   The reversion to the self-centered thinking patterns of childhood that sometimes occurs in the teen years (Ch. 11).

Adoption   To take a child of other parents voluntarily as one's own (Ch. 3).

Adult Attachment Interview (AAI)   Evaluates adults' responses to questions about attachment (Ch. 6).

Afterbirth   Stage three of the birth process during which the placenta and other membranes are discharged (Ch. 4).

Ageism   The prejudice that the elderly are inferior to those who are younger (Ch. 17).

Age-status   Refers to society's expectations about what is normal at various ages (Ch. 18).

Aggression   Hostile or destructive behavior directed at another (Ch. 10).

Aging by program   The theory that all animals seem to die when their "program" dictates (Ch. 17).

AID   Artificial insemination by donor (Ch. 3).

AIDS (Acquired Immune Deficiency Syndrome)   A condition caused by a virus that invades the body's immune system, making it vulnerable to infections and life-threatening illnesses (Chs. 4 and 12).

Alarm reaction   Selye's term for a "call to arms" of the body's defensive forces (Ch. 16).

Alleles   Different forms of a gene (Ch. 3).

Amniocentesis   A process that entails inserting a needle through the mother's abdomen, piercing the amniotic sac and withdrawing a sample of the amniotic fluid (Ch. 4).

Anal stage   Freud's belief that the anus is the main source of pleasure during the age 1½ to 3 years (Ch. 2).

Androgogy   The science of teaching adults (Ch. 15).

Androgyny   Functional level of gender-role identifications that incorporate male and female qualities (Ch. 14).

Anima   The female side of the personality. Males tend to repress it until later in life (Ch. 19).

Animism   Children consider objects as alive and conscious that adults consider inert (Ch. 7).

Animus   The male side of the personality. Females tend to repress it until later in life (Ch. 19).

Anticipatory images   Piaget's term for images (including movements and transformation) that enable the child to anticipate change (Ch. 7).

Anorexia nervosa   A syndrome of self-starvation that mainly affects adolescent and young adult females (Ch. 11).

Anoxia (lack of oxygen)   A condition that possibly can cause brain damage or death if it occurs during the birth process (Ch. 4).

Antigens   The substances in the blood that fight to kill foreign bodies (Ch. 17).

Apgar   A scale to evaluate a newborn's basic life signs administered one minute after birth and repeated at three-, five- and ten-minute intervals; it uses five life signs—heart rate, respiratory effort, muscle tone, reflex irritability, and skin color (Ch. 5).

Apnea   Brief periods when breathing is suspended (Ch. 5).

Apposition   The fertilized egg, now called a blastocyst, comes to rest against the uterine wall (Ch. 4).

Artificialism   Children attribute human life to inanimate objects (Ch. 7).

Assimilation   Piaget's term to describe the manner in which we incorporate data into our cognitive structures (Ch. 2).

Attachment   Behavior intended to keep a child (or adult) in close proximity to a significant other (Ch. 6).

Autonomy   Infants realize that they have a share in controlling their interactions with others (Ch. 6).

Authoritarian parenting style   Parents strive for complete control over their children's behavior by establishing complex sets of rules (Ch. 12).

Authoritarian parents   Baumrind's term for parents who are demanding and want instant obedience as the most desirable child trait (Ch. 8).

Authoritative parenting style   The most common parenting style, in which parents are sometimes authoritarian and sometimes permissive, depending to some extent on the parents' mood. Parents believe that both parents and children have rights but that parental authority must predominate (Ch. 12).

Autoimmunity   The process by which the immune system in the body rejects the body's own tissue (Ch. 17).

Autosexuality The love of oneself; the stage at which the child becomes aware of himself or herself as a source of sexual pleasure, and consciously experiments with masturbation (Ch. 12).

B

Babbling Infant produces sounds approximating speech between 5 and 6 months (Ch. 5).

Basal metabolism rate (BMR) The minimum amount of energy an individual tends to use when in a resting state (Ch. 15).

Battered Child Syndrome Classic physical abuse (Ch. 10).

Bilingualism Students are taught partly in English and partly in their own language (Ch. 7).

Binocular coordination Three-dimensional vision, appears around 4 months (Ch. 5).

Biological death Death occurs when it is no longer possible to discern an electrical charge in the tissues of the heart and lungs (Ch. 19).

Biopsychosocial interactions A term for the idea that development proceeds by the interaction of biological, psychological, and social forces (Chs. 1 and 14).

Biopsychosocial theory of homosexuality The theory that homosexuality is caused by some factor in a person's DNA that affects temperament, which in turn interacts with psychological and social factors to determine sexual orientation (Ch. 12).

Blastocyst When the fertilized egg reaches the uterus (about 7 days), it's known as a blastocyst (Ch. 4).

Brain death Death of the brain occurs when it fails to receive a sufficient supply of oxygen for a short period of time (usually eight to ten minutes) (Ch. 19).

Breech birth A birth in which the baby is born feet first, buttocks first, or in a crosswise position (transverse presentation) (Ch. 4).

Bullies Those who have aggressive reaction patterns and have considerable physical strength (Ch. 10).

Bulimia nervosa This disorder is characterized by "episodic binge-eating accompanied by an awareness that the eating pattern is abnormal, fear of not being able to stop eating voluntarily, and depressed mood and self-deprecating thoughts following the eating binges" (Ch. 11).

C

Capacitation Removal of layer surrounding sperm (Ch. 3).

Cardiopulmonary resuscitation (CPR) A technique for reviving an individual's lungs and/or heart that have ceased to function (Ch. 19).

Caretaker speech (See also motherese.) A high-pitched voice and simple words are used with children (Ch. 7).

Cellular differentiation Embryonic cells are destined for specific functions (Ch. 4).

Centration A feature of preoperational thought—the centering of attention on one aspect of an object and the neglecting of any other features (Ch. 7).

Cesarean section A surgery performed to deliver the baby through the abdomen if for some reason the child cannot come through the birth canal (Ch. 4).

Child abuse Commonly includes physical abuse, sexual abuse, emotional abuse, physical neglect, emotional neglect, and educational neglect (Ch. 10).

Children at risk Children who give early signs of physical or psychological difficulties; unless helped by appropriate intervention, may continue to experience problems, perhaps with increasing intensity, throughout the lifespan (Ch. 4).

Chlamydia Bacterial infection that may cause infertility; now the most common STI, with about 5 to 7 million new cases each year. There often are no symptoms; it is diagnosed only when complications develop (Chs. 3 and 12).

Cholesterol A substance in the blood that adheres to the walls of the blood vessels, restricting the flow of blood and causing strokes and heart attacks (Ch. 13).

Chorionic villi sampling (CVS) A procedure in which a catheter (small tube) is inserted through the vagina to the villi and a small section is suctioned into the tube (Ch. 4).

Chromosome failure Biological changes such as enlarged breasts in males and abnormal body hair in females (Ch. 14).

Classification The process by which concrete operational children can group objects with some similarities within a larger category (Chs. 7 and 9).

Climacteric Refers to a relatively abrupt change in the body, brought about by changes in hormonal balances (Ch. 15).

Climacterium Refers to the loss of reproductive ability (Ch. 15).

Clinical death The individual is dead when his or her respiration and heartbeat have stopped (Ch. 19).

Closed adoption Natural parents know nothing about the adopting parents (Ch. 3).

Cognitive structures Piaget's term to describe the basic tools of cognitive development (Ch. 2).

Collagen The major connective tissue in the body; it provides the elasticity in our skin and blood vessels (Ch. 17).

Commitment The third phase in Perry's theory, in which the individual realizes that certainty is impossible but that commitment to a certain position is necessary, even without certainty; For Fowler, the third step in the birth of a religion, in which people devote their lives to objectified ideas. They are willing under any circumstances to help those who have done the same (Chs. 13 and 19).

Competence Children's sense of self-esteem related to athletic competence, likability by peers, physical appearance, and behavioral conduct (Ch. 10).

Concrete operational period Piaget's third stage of cognitive development during which children begin to employ logical thought processes with concrete material (Ch. 9).

Conservation Children conserve the essence of something even though surface features change (Chs. 7 and 9).

Constructed knowledge Belenky's fifth phase of women's thinking; characterized by an integration of the subjective and procedural ways of knowing (types 3 and 4) (Ch. 13).

Continuity The lasting quality of experiences; development proceeds steadily and sequentially (Ch. 1).

Controlled scribbling Drawing in which children carefully watch what they are doing, whereas before they looked away (Ch. 7).

Convergent thinking Thinking used to find one correct answer (Ch. 11).

Cooing Early language sounds that resemble vowels (Ch. 5).

Coordination of secondary schemes Infants combine secondary schemes to obtain a goal (Ch. 5).

Coregulation A sharing of decision making between parent and child (Ch. 8).

Crawling Locomotion in which the infant's abdomen touches the floor and the weight of the head and shoulders rests on the elbows (Ch. 5).

Creeping Movement is on hands and knees and the trunk does not touch the ground; creeping appears from 9 months in most youngsters (Ch. 5).

Critical thinking Those mental processes that help us to solve problems and make decisions (Ch. 9).

Cross-linkage theory A theory of aging stating that the proteins that make up a large part of cells are composed of peptides. When cross-links are formed between peptides (a natural process of the body), the proteins are altered, often for the worse (Ch. 17).

Crossover Older men become more like women, and older women become more like men (Ch. 18).

Cross-sectional studies This method compares groups of individuals of various ages at the same time in order to investigate the effects of aging (Ch. 1).

Crowds Groups known for certain values, attitudes, or activities (Ch. 12).

Cryopreservation Freezing embryos for future use (Ch. 3).

Crystallized intelligence Involves perceiving relationships, educing correlates, reasoning, abstracting, concept of attainment, and problem solving, as measured primarily in unspeeded tasks involving various kinds of content (semantic, figural, symbolic) (Ch. 15).

Cultural constructivism When children use the particular environment around them, they construct their own world view (Ch. 1).

Culture Those values, beliefs, and behaviors characteristic of a large group of people, for example, those of Hispanic origin (Ch. 1).

Cumulative continuity When a person's interactional style is reinforced by the environment, thus sustaining it across the lifespan (Ch. 16).

Cystic fibrosis Chromosomal disorder producing a malfunction of the exocrine glands (Ch. 3).

Cytogenetics The study of chromosomes (Ch. 3).

Cytomegalovirus (CMV). A virus that can cause damage ranging from mental retardation, blindness, deafness, and even death. One of the major difficulties in combatting this disease is that it remains unrecognized in pregnant women (Ch. 4).

D

Day care Locations providing services and care for children (Ch. 8).

Decentering The process by which concrete operational children can concentrate on more than one aspect of a situation (Ch. 9).

Decoding The technique by which we recognize words (Ch. 9).

Deferred imitation Imitative behavior that continues after the disappearance of the model to be imitated (Ch. 7).

DES (diethylstilbestrol) In the late 1940s and 1950s, DES (a synthetic hormone) was administered to pregnant women supposedly to prevent miscarriage. It was later found that the daughters of the women who had received this treatment were more susceptible to vaginal and cervical cancer (Ch. 4).

Descriptive studies Information is gathered on subjects without manipulating them in any way (Ch. 1).

Despair The counterpart to integrity in the last stage of Erikson's theory. When people look back over their lives and feel that they have made many wrong decisions, or more commonly, that they have not made any decisions at all (Ch. 18).

Developing readers Children who are beginning to understand the relationship between sound and symbol and pay close attention to the print in their efforts at decoding (Ch. 9).

Developmental biodynamics A new method of studying motor development; stresses the relationship between perception and action (Ch. 5).

Developmental contextualism Focuses not only on the interactions between heredity and environment but the changes resulting from the interactions (Ch. 1).

Developmental risk Children who may be susceptible to problems because of some physical or psychological difficulty ("at-risk" children) (Ch. 4).

Developmentally delayed A term that describes children who experience a developmental lag because of either physical or psychological causes; these children usually "catch up" (Ch. 7).

Diethylstilbestrol Drug administered to pregnant women to help them hold embryo or fetus; later found to increase the risk of genital cancer in the daughters of these women (Ch. 4).

Difficult children Term to describe restless, irritable children; associated with Chess and Thomas (Ch. 6).

Differential opportunity structure Due to social disapproval and more rigid rules enforced by parents, peers, and the legal system, women have not had the same access to sex that men have had (Ch. 18).

Dilation Stage one of the birth process during which the cervix dilates to about 4 inches in diameter (Ch. 4).

Discontinuity Behaviors that are apparently unrelated to earlier aspects of development (Ch. 1).

Disengagement theory According to this position, the most mature adults are likely to gradually disengage themselves from their fellow human beings in preparation for death. They become less interested in their interactions with others, and more concerned with internal concerns (Ch. 18).

Distantiation The readiness of all of us to distance ourselves from others when we feel threatened by their behavior (Ch. 14).

Divergent thinking Thinking used when a problem to be solved has many possible answers. What are some ways that a school curriculum can enhance creative thinking at the junior and senior high school levels? (Ch. 11).

DNA Deoxyribonucleic acid; the chemical structure of the gene that accounts for our inherited characteristics (Ch. 3).

Dominant The tendency of a gene to be expressed in a trait (Ch. 3).

Down syndrome Genetic abnormality caused by a deviation on the twenty-first pair of chromosomes (Ch. 3).

Drawing Piaget's use of the term to indicate a growing symbolic ability (Ch. 7).

Dual-career family A family in which both the mother and the father are working, usually full time (Ch. 13).

Dualism Perry's initial phase of ethical development, in which "things are either absolutely right or absolutely wrong" (Ch. 13).

Dual-process model A model of intelligence that says there may be a decline in the mechanics of intelligence, such as classification skills and logical reasoning, but that the pragmatics are likely to increase (Ch. 15).

DUPE   Problem-solving model (Determine a problem exists, Understand its nature, Plan for its solution, and Evaluate the solution) (Ch. 9).

E

Easy children   Term used to describe calm, relaxed children; associated with Chess and Thomas (Ch. 6).

Ectoderm   The outer layer of the embryo that will give rise to nervous system, among other developmental features (Ch. 4).

Ectopic pregnancy   A pregnancy in which the fertilized egg attempts to develop in one of the fallopian tubes; this is sometimes referred to as a *tubal pregnancy* (Ch. 4).

Egg donor   Woman either donates or sells eggs (Ch. 3).

Ego   One of the three structures of the psyche according to Freud; mediates between the id and the superego (Ch. 2).

Egocentric speech   Piaget's term to describe children's speech when they do not care to whom they speak (Ch. 5).

Egocentrism   Child focuses on self in early phases of cognitive development; term associated with Piaget (Chs. 5 and 7).

Electroencephalogram (EEG)   A graphic record of the electrical activity of the brain (Ch. 19).

Embryo transfer   A form of assisted reproduction (GIFT) (Ch. 3).

Embryonic period   Third through the eighth week following fertilization (Ch. 4).

Emergent readers   Children who can identify letters and recognize some common words; they know what books "do" and they attempt to read by using semantic and syntactic cues (Ch. 9).

Emotional divorce   Sometimes a couple learns to "withstand" each other, rather than live with each other. The only activities and interests that they shared were ones that revolved around the children. When the children leave, they are forced to recognize how far apart they have drifted; in effect, they are emotionally divorced (Ch. 16).

Emotional energy   The emotional feelings invested in various life tasks (Ch. 18).

Empty nest syndrome   Refers to the feelings parents may have as a result of their last child leaving home (Ch. 16).

Encoding   Translating speech sounds into meaningful language (Ch. 9).

Endoderm   The inner layer of the embryo that will give rise to the lungs, liver, and pancreas, among other developmental features (Ch. 4).

Endometriosis   A condition in which tissue normally found in the uterus grows in other areas, such as the fallopian tubes (Ch. 3).

Entrainment   Term used to describe the rhythm that is established between a parent's and an infant's behavior (Ch. 6).

Equilibration   Piaget's term to describe the balance between assimilation and accommodation (Ch. 2).

Escape   Perry's term for refusing responsibility for making any commitments. Because everyone's opinion is "equally right," the person believes that no commitments need be made, and so escapes from the dilemma (Ch. 13).

ESL   English as a second Language (Ch. 7).

Esteem needs   Maslow's term that refers to the reactions of others to us as individuals; it also refers to our opinion of ourselves (Ch. 2).

Estrogen replacement therapy (ERT)   A process in which estrogen is given in low levels to a woman experiencing severe problems with menopause (Ch. 15).

Ethology   The study of behavior in natural settings (Ch. 6).

Euthanasia   Means a "good death." There are two types: passive euthanasia, in which the patient's legal instructions are carried out by the medical team, and active euthanasia, in which the patient's life is ended in ways that are now illegal (Ch. 19).

Existential love   The capacity to cherish the present moment, perhaps first learned when we confront the certainty of our own personal death (Ch. 18).

Explicit memory   Those events that we consciously remember (Ch. 5).

Expressive language   Language that children use to express their own ideas and needs (Ch. 7).

Expulsion   Stage two of the birth process during which the baby passes through the birth canal (Ch. 4).

External fertilization   Fertilization occurs outside of the woman's body (Ch. 3).

Extinction   Refers to the process by which conditioned responses are lost (Ch. 2).

Extrinsic motivation   Children react to external pressures (Ch. 9).

F

Failure-to-thrive (FTT)   A condition in which the weight and height of infants consistently remain far below normal (the bottom 3 percent of height and weight measures) (Ch. 5).

Fallopian tubes   Passageway for the egg once it is discharged from the ovary's surface (Ch. 3).

False beliefs   Failure to understand the reasoning of others (Ch. 9).

Fastmapping   Techniques to help children detect word meanings (Ch. 7).

Fetal alcohol syndrome (FAS)   Refers to babies when their mothers drink alcohol during pregnancy; they manifest four clusters of symptoms: psychological functioning, growth factors, physical features, and structural effects (Ch. 4).

Fetal period   The period extending from the beginning of the third month to birth (Ch. 4).

Fetoscopy   A procedure in which a tiny instrument called a fetoscope is inserted into the amniotic cavity, making it possible to see the fetus (Ch. 4).

Fluid intelligence   Involves perceiving relationships, educing correlates, maintaining span of immediate awareness in reasoning, abstracting, concept formation, and problem solving, as measured in unspeeded as well as speeded tasks involving figural, symbolic, or semantic content (Ch. 15).

Forceps delivery   A procedure in which the physician, for safety, will withdraw the baby with forceps during the first phase of birth (Ch. 4).

Fragile X syndrome   A sex-linked inheritance disorder in which the bottom half of the X chromosome looks as if it is ready to fall off; causes mental retardation in 80 percent of the cases (Ch. 3).

Friend   A nonfamilial relationship that offers feelings of warmth and support (Ch. 10).

Functional invariants   In Piaget's theory, functional invariants refer to the psychological mechanisms of adaptation and organization (Ch. 2).

G

Gender identity   The conviction that one belongs to the sex of birth (Ch. 1).

Gender revolution   Levinson's term; the meanings of gender are changing and becoming more similar (Ch. 16).

Gender role   Culturally acceptable sexual behavior (Ch. 1).

Gender-role reversals Older men see themselves and other males as becoming submissive and less authoritative with advancing years. Conversely, older women see themselves and other women as becoming more dominant and self-assured as they grow older (Ch. 18).

Gender-role stereotypes Stereotypes that associate males and females with rigid categories of behavior and/or appearance (Ch. 14).

Gender splitting Levinson's term; all societies support the idea that there should be a clear difference between what is considered appropriate for males and for females; gender splitting appears to be universal (Ch. 16).

Gender stereotypes Beliefs about the characteristics associated with male or female (Ch. 1).

Gene theory The theory that aging is due to certain harmful genes (Ch. 17).

General adaptation syndrome Refers to a set of reactions that occur in animals in response to all toxic substances, regardless of their source. Involves three stages: alarm, resistance and exhaustion (Ch. 16).

Generative love Most characteristic of parenthood, a time during which sacrifices are gladly made for the sake of the children (Ch. 18).

Generativity Erikson's term for the ability to be useful to ourselves and to society (Ch. 16).

Genital herpes An incurable sexually transmitted infection, with about 500,000 new cases every year (Ch. 12).

Genital stage Freud's belief in a resurgence of a strong sex drive from 12 years and beyond (Ch. 2).

Genotype An individual's genetic composition (Ch. 3).

German measles (rubella) A typically mild childhood disease caused by a virus; pregnant women, who contract this disease may give birth to a baby with a defect: congenital heart disorder, cataracts, deafness, mental retardation. The risk is especially high if the disease appears early in the pregnancy (Ch. 4).

Germinal period The first two weeks following fertilization (Ch. 4).

Glaucoma Results from a buildup of pressure inside the eye due to excessive fluid. The resulting damage can destroy one's vision (Ch. 15).

Gonorrhea Well-known venereal infection accounting for between 1.5 and 2 million cases per year (Ch. 12).

Goodness of fit Compatibility between parental and child behavior; how well parents and their children get along (Ch. 6).

Group marriage A marriage that includes two or more of both husbands and wives, who all exercise common privileges and responsibilities (Ch. 14).

H

Habituation A process in which stimuli that are presented frequently cause a decrease in an infant's attention (Ch. 5).

Handedness Children's preference for using one hand over the other (Ch. 7).

Head Start Early intervention program intended to provide educational and developmental services to disadvantaged children (Ch. 7).

Hemophilia A genetic condition causing incorrect blood clotting; called the "bleeder's disease" (Ch. 3).

Hepatitis B A viral infection transmitted through sex or shared needles (Ch. 12).

Herpes simplex An infection that usually occurs during birth; a child can develop the symptoms during the first week following the birth. The eyes and nervous system are most susceptible to this disease (Ch. 4).

Heterosexuality Love of members of the opposite sex (Ch. 12).

Heterozygous Different alleles for a trait (Ch. 3).

Holophrase Children's first words that usually carry multiple meanings (Ch. 5).

Holophrastic speech The use of one word to communicate many meanings and ideas (Ch. 5).

Homelessness Those who live in shelters, or on the street, or parks (Ch. 8).

Homosexuality Love of members of one's own sex (Ch. 12).

Homeostatic imbalance The theory that aging is due to a failure in the systems that regulates the proper interaction of the organs (Ch. 17).

Homosexual marriage Though not accepted legally, the weddings of homosexuals are now accepted by some religions (Ch. 14).

Homozygous Identical alleles for a trait (Ch. 3).

Hormonal balance One of the triggering mechanisms of puberty that may be used to indicate the onset of adolescence (Ch. 11).

Hospice A facility and/or program dedicated to assisting those who have accepted the fact that they are dying and desire a "death with dignity." Provides pain control and counseling but does not attempt to cure anyone (Ch. 19).

Human Genome Project The attempt to identify and map the 50,000 to 100,000 genes that constitute the human genetic endowment (Ch. 3).

Human immunodeficiency virus (HIV) The virus that leads to AIDS (Ch. 12).

I

Id One of the three structures of the psyche according to Freud; the source of our instinctive desires (Ch. 2).

Identity crisis Erikson's term for those situations, usually in adolescence, that cause us to make major decisions about our identity (Chs. 2 and 11).

Individuation Refers to the fullest development of one's self (Ch. 8).

Imaginary audience Adolescents' perception that the world is constantly scrutinizing their behavior and physical appearance (Ch. 11).

Imitative behavior The tendency of infants to mimic the behavior of others (Ch. 5).

Implantation Fertilized egg attaches and secures itself to uterine wall (Chs. 3 and 4).

Implicit memory Memory that affects our behavior without our being aware of it (Ch. 5).

Impotency The inability to engage in the sexual act (Ch. 18).

Impulsivity A child's lack of ability to delay gratification (Ch. 10).

Independent readers Children who can read ably and without assistance using all of the cueing systems (Ch. 9).

Individuating-reflective faith The fourth developmental step of Fowler's theory of faith. Individuals in stage four begin to assume responsibility for their own beliefs, attitudes, commitments, and lifestyle (Ch. 19).

Individuation Refers to our becoming more individual; we develop a separate and special personality, derived less and less from our parents and teachers and more from our own behavior (Ch. 14).

Infantile amnesia Our inability to recall events from early in life (Ch. 5).

Infertility An inability to achieve pregnancy after two years (Ch. 3).

Inner speech Serves to guide and plan behavior (Ch. 5).

Insecure parents Those parents who believe everything they do inevitably influences their child's destiny; they feel overwhelmed by the difficulties of parenting (Ch. 8).

Instrumental conditioning Skinner's form of conditioning in which a reinforcement follows the desired response; also known as operant conditioning (Ch. 2).

Integrity The resolution of each of the first seven crises in Erikson's theory should lead us to achieve a sense of personal integrity. Older adults who have a sense of integrity feel their lives have been well spent. The decisions and actions they have taken seem to them to fit together (Ch. 18).

Interaction Behaviors involving two or more people (Ch. 6).

Interactional continuity Exists when a person's style evokes reciprocal responses from others in ongoing social interaction, thereby sustaining the behavior pattern across the lifespan when a similar interactive event occurs (Ch. 16).

Interactive errors Interactions between a mother and child that result in a miscoordination (Ch. 6).

Interactive repair Correcting negative interactions and returning them to a positive state (Ch. 6).

Intergenerational continuity Term used to describe the connection between childhood experiences and adult behavior (Ch. 6).

Internal fertilization A natural process in which fertilization occurs within the woman (Ch. 3).

Intimacy Erikson's stage that represents the ability to relate one's deepest hopes and fears to another person and to accept another's need for intimacy in turn (Ch. 14).

Intimidated parents Those parents who lack the ability to be firm with their child (Ch. 8).

Intrauterine device Usually a plastic loop inserted into the uterus as a contraceptive device (Ch. 3).

Intrinsic motivation Children do something because they want to (Ch. 9).

Intuitive-projective faith The first developmental step of Fowler's theory of faith. In this stage, the individual focuses on surface qualities, as portrayed by adult models (Ch. 19).

Invasion Period during which the trophoblast digs in and begins to bury itself in the uterine lining (Ch. 4).

In vitro fertilization Fertilization that occurs "in the dish"; an external fertilization technique (Ch. 3).

Irreversibility The inability to reverse thinking, that is, to solve a problem and then proceed in reverse, tracing the steps back to the original question or premise (Ch. 7).

Isolation The readiness all of us have to isolate ourselves from others when we feel threatened by their behavior (Ch. 14).

IUGR Intrauterine growth retardation, a condition that can occur when the mother's nutrient supply during pregnancy is too low (Ch. 4).

K

Klinefelter syndrome Males with the XXY chromosomal pattern (Ch. 3).

Knowledge-acquisition components Sternberg's term for those components that help us to learn how to solve problems in the first place (Ch. 9).

L

Language acquisition support system (LASS) Bruner's term for the support children get in acquiring their language (Ch. 5).

Language explosion Rapid acquisition of words beginning at 18 months (Ch. 5).

Latency Freud's belief that the sex drive becomes dormant 5 to 12 years (Ch. 2).

Lateralization Refers to a preferred side of the brain for a particular activity (Ch. 7).

Legal death Condition defined as "unreceptivity and unresponsivity, no movements or breathing, no reflexes, and a flat electroencephalogram (EEG) reading that remains flat for 24 hours" (Ch. 19).

Learning theory of homosexuality The belief that homosexuality is the result of learned experiences from significant others (Ch. 12).

Life course Levinson's term. Life refers to all aspects of living—everything that has significance in a life; course refers to the flow or unfolding of an individual's life (Ch. 14).

Life cycle Levinson's term. The life cycle is a general pattern of adult development, whereas the life course is the unique embodiment of the life cycle by an individual (Ch. 14).

Life structure Levinson's term. The underlying pattern or design of a person's life at a given time (Ch. 14).

Longitudinal studies The experimenter makes several observations of the same individuals at two or more times in their lives. Examples are: determining the long-term effects of learning on behavior; the stability of habits and intelligence; and the factors involved in memory (Ch. 1).

Love and belongingness needs Maslow's term that refers to the need for family and friends (Ch. 2).

M

Macrosystem The blueprint of any society (Ch. 1).

Male change of life Change in hormonal balance and sexual potency (Ch. 15).

Manipulative experiments The experimenter attempts to keep all variables (all the factors that can affect a particular outcome) constant except one, which is carefully manipulated (Ch. 1).

Maturation The process of physical and mental development due to physiology (Ch. 11).

Maximum growth spurt The period of adolescence when physical growth is at its fastest (Ch. 11).

Meiosis Cell division in which the number of chromosomes is halved (Ch. 3).

Menarche Onset of menstruation (Ch. 11).

Mentoring The act of assisting another, usually younger, person with his or her work or life tasks (Ch. 14).

Menopause The cessation of menstruation (Ch. 15).

Mesoderm The middle layer of the embryo that gives rise to muscles, skeleton, excretory system (Ch. 4).

Mesosystem The relationship among microsystems (Ch. 1).

Metacognition The theory of mind that refers to children's ability to construct their own ideas of how their minds work (Ch. 7).

Metacognitive experiences Responses to cognitive stimuli (Ch. 7).

Metacognitive knowledge A child's knowledge and beliefs, gained from experience, about cognitive matters (Ch. 7).

Metacomponents Sternberg's term for those components that help us to plan, monitor, and evaluate our problem-solving strategies (Ch. 9).

Metalinguistic awareness A capacity to think about and talk about language (Ch. 9).

Microsystem The home or school (Ch. 1).

Midcareer crisis A stage that some persons go through in middle age during which they come to question their career goals, discover that their dreams for advancement may be unrealistic, and their relations with fellow employees are changing (Ch. 15).

Mid-life transition Levinson's term for the phase that usually lasts for five years and generally extends from age 40 to 45 (Ch. 16).

Miscarriage The term that describes when a pregnancy ends spontaneously before the twentieth week (Ch. 4).

Mitosis Cell division in which the number of chromosomes remains the same (Ch. 3).

Modeling Bandura's term for observational learning (Ch. 2).

Monogamy The standard marriage form in the United States and most other nations, in which there is one husband and one wife (Ch. 14).

Moral dilemma A modified clinical technique used by Kohlberg in which a conflict is posed for which subjects justify the morality of their choices (Ch. 9).

Motherese Using simple words when talking to children (Chs. 5 and 7).

Motor skills Skills (both gross and and fine) resulting from physical development enabling children to perform smooth and coordinated physical acts (Ch. 7).

Multiple intelligence Gardner's theory that attributes seven types of intelligence to humans (Ch. 9).

Mutations Abrupt hereditary changes (Ch. 3).

Mythical-literal faith The second developmental step of Fowler's theory of faith. Fantasy ceases to be a primary source of knowledge at this stage, and verification of facts becomes necessary (Ch. 19).

Mythification Stories are developed that tell why members of a religion have a special place in the world. These stories are rational and enhance the person's understanding of the physical as well as the spiritual world (Ch. 19).

N

Naturalistic experiments In these experiments, the researcher acts solely as an observer and does as little as possible to disturb the environment. "Nature" performs the experiment, and the researcher acts as a recorder of the results (Ch. 1).

Negative reinforcement Refers to those stimuli whose withdrawal strengthens behavior (Ch. 2).

NEO model of personality McCrae and Costa's theory that there are three major personality traits, which they feel govern the adult personality (Ch. 16).

Neonate The term for an infant in the first days and weeks after birth (Ch. 5).

Neurological assessment Identifies any neurological problem, suggests means of monitoring the problem, and offers a prognosis about the problem (Ch. 5).

New York Longitudinal Study Long-term study by Chess and Thomas of the personality characteristics of children (Ch. 6).

Noetic dimension Frankl's third stage of human development has roots in childhood but primarily develops in late adolescence. It is spiritual, not only in the religious sense but in the totality of the search for the meaningfulness of life (Ch. 19).

No-fault divorce The law that lets people get divorced without proving some atrocious act by one of the spouses. In legal language, this is known as an irretrievable breakdown of a marriage (Ch. 16).

Normal range of development The stage of pubertal change occur at times that are within the normal range of occurrence (Ch. 11).

Novice phase Period of ages 17–33 that includes early adult transition, according to Levinson (Ch. 14).

Numeration The process by which concrete operational children grasp the meaning of number, the oneness of one (Ch. 9).

Nurturing parenting style The style of parenting in which parents use indirect methods such as discussion and modeling rather than punishment to influence their child's behavior. Rules are kept to a minimum (Ch. 12).

O

Object permanence Refers to children gradually realizing that there are permanent objects around them, even when these objects are out of sight (Ch. 5).

Objectification Fowler's term for the first step in the birth of a religion in which a perception of reality is described (Ch. 19).

Observational learning A term associated with Bandura, meaning that we learn from watching others (Ch. 10).

Olfactory sense The sense of smell, which uses the olfactory nerves in the nose and tongue (Ch. 15).

One-time, one-group studies Studies carried out only once on one group of studies (Ch. 1)

Open adoption Natural parent has considerable input into the adoption process (Ch. 3).

Operant conditioning Skinner's form of conditioning in which a reinforcement follows the desired response; also known as instrumental conditioning (Ch. 2).

Oral stage Freud's belief that the mouth is the main source of pleasure from age 0 to 1½ years (Ch. 2).

Organ reserve Refers to that part of the total capacity of our body's organs that we do not normally need to use (Ch. 13).

Organization One of the two functional invariants in Piaget's theory (Ch. 2).

Organogenesis The formation of organs during embryonic period (Ch. 4).

Overextensions Children's tendency to apply a word too widely (Ch. 7).

Overinterpretive parents Those parents who feel they must explore in depth the complex psychological meanings behind their child's behavior (Ch. 8).

Overregulation Children's inappropriate use of language rules they have learned (Ch. 7).

Ovulation Egg bursts from the surface of the ovary (Ch. 3).

P

Paradoxical-consolidation faith The fifth developmental step of Fowler's theory of faith. In this stage, such elements of faith as symbols, rituals, and beliefs start to become understood and consolidated (Ch. 19).

Pathological parents Those parents who actually suffer from a form of mental illness, which does not necessarily mean that their child will be subject to psychological disturbances (Ch. 8).

Pedagogy The science of teaching children (Ch. 15).

Peer Refers to youngsters who are similar in age to other children, usually within 12 months of one another (Ch. 10).

Peer victimization A form of abuse in which a child is frequently the target of peer aggression (Ch. 10).

Pelvic inflammatory disease (PID) Infection that often results from chlamydia or gonorrhea, and frequently causes prolonged problems, including infertility (Chs. 3 and 12).

Performance components Sternberg's term for those components that help us to execute the instructions of the metacomponents (Ch. 9).

Permissive parenting style Parents have little or no control over their children and refrain from disciplinary measures (Chs. 8 and 12).

Personal fable Adolescents' tendency to think of themselves in heroic or mythical terms (Ch. 11).

Phallic stage Freud's belief that the sex organs become the main source of pleasure from age 3 to 5 years (Ch. 2).

Phenotype The observable expression of gene action (Ch. 3).

Phenylketonuria (PKU) Chromosomal disorder resulting in a failure of the body to break down the amino acid phenylalanine (Ch. 3).

Phonological cues Using sounds to form words (Ch. 9).

Phonology Describes how to put sounds together to form words (Ch. 7).

Physiological needs Maslow's term to indicate the importance of satisfying basic needs such as hunger, thirst, and sleep (Ch. 2).

Placenta The placenta supplies the embryo with all its needs, carries off all its wastes, and protects it from danger (Ch. 4).

Play An activity that children engage in because they enjoy it for its own sake (Ch. 8).

Poetic-conventional faith The third developmental step of Fowler's theory of faith. Faith is still conventional and depends on a consensus of opinion of other, more authoritative persons (Ch. 19).

Polyandry A marriage in which there is one wife but two or more husbands (Ch. 14).

Polygamy A marriage in which there is one husband but two or more wives (Ch. 14).

Polygenic inheritance Many genes contribute to the formation of a particular trait (Ch. 3).

Positive reinforcement Refers to those stimuli whose presentation as a consequence of a response strengthens or increases the rate of the response (Ch. 2).

Postnatal depression The low or "down" feeling many women experience a few days after giving birth (Ch. 4).

Pragmatic cues Practical signals used to discover meaning (Ch. 9).

Pragmatics Describes how we learn to take part in a conversation (Ch. 7).

Precociousness The ability to do what others are able to do, but at a younger age (Ch. 11).

Prematurity A condition that occurs less than 37 weeks after conception and is defined by low birth weight and immaturity (Ch. 4).

Prenatal learning Possibility that the fetus learns while in the womb (Ch. 4).

Preoperational Piaget's second stage of cognitive development, extending from about 2 to 7 years (Ch. 7).

Prepared childbirth Combination of relaxation techniques and information about the birth process; sometimes called the Lamaze method after its founder (Ch. 4).

Prepared environment Use of age-appropriate materials to further cognitive development (Ch. 7).

Primary circular reactions Infants repeat some act involving their bodies; term associated with Piaget's theory (Ch. 5).

Procedural knowledge Belenky's fourth phase of women's thinking; characterized by a distrust of both knowledge from authority and the female thinker's own inner authority or "gut" (Ch. 13).

Prodigiousness The ability to do qualitatively better than the rest of us are able to do; such a person is referred to as a prodigy (Ch. 11).

Project Head Start Programs intended to provide educational and developmental services to preschool children from low-income families (Ch. 7).

Prosocial behavior Refers to such behaviors as friendliness, self-control, and being helpful (Ch. 10).

Prostatectomy The removal of all or part of the male prostate gland (Ch. 18).

Protective factors Characteristics of resilient individuals that protect them from stress (Ch. 16).

Psychoanalytic theory Freud's theory of the development of personality (Ch. 2).

Psychoanalytic theory of homosexuality Freud's theory suggests that if the child's first sexual feelings about the parent of the opposite sex are strongly punished, the child may identify with the same-sex parent and develop a permanent homosexual orientation (Ch. 12).

Psychological dimension The second stage of Frankl's theory of human development, in which personality begins to form at birth and develops as a result of instincts, drives, capacities, and interactions with the environment (Ch. 19).

Puberty A relatively abrupt and qualitatively different set of physical changes that normally occur at the beginning of the teen years (Ch. 11).

Punishment Usually refers to a decrease in the frequency of a response when certain unpleasant consequences immediately follow it (Ch. 2).

R

Random scribbling Drawing in which children use dots and lines with simple arm movements (Ch. 7).

Realism Refers to when children learn to distinguish and accept the real world (Ch. 7).

Received knowledge Belenky's second phase of women's thinking; characterized by being awed by the authorities but far less affiliated with them (Ch. 13).

Receptive language Language that children use to show an understanding of words without necessarily producing them (Ch. 7).

Recessive A gene whose trait is not expressed unless paired with another recessive gene, for example, both parents contribute genes for blue eyes (Ch. 3).

Reciprocal interactions Similar to transactional model; recognizes the child's active role in its development; I do something to the child, the child changes; as a result of the changes in the child, I change (Chs. 1 and 5).

Reconciliation fantasies Children who wish their parents could get together again following divorce (Ch. 8).

Reflective listening A method of talking to others; you rephrase the person's comments to show you understand (Ch. 12).

Reflex   When a stimulus repeatedly elicits the same response (Ch. 5).

Reinforcement   Usually refers to an increase in the frequency of a response when certain pleasant consequences immediately follow it (Ch. 2).

Relativism   The second phase in Perry's theory. An attitude or philosophy that says anything can be right or wrong depending on the situation; all views are equally right (Ch. 13).

Representation   Child's growing ability to engage in abstract thinking (Ch. 7).

Reproductive images   Mental images that are faithful to the original object or event being represented; Piaget's term for images that are restricted to those sights previously perceived (Ch. 7).

Repudiation   Striving toward a state of identity means committing to one life style and repudiating (giving up) all the other possibilities, at least for the present (Ch. 11).

Resiliency   The ability to recover from either physiological or psychological trauma and return to a normal developmental path (Ch. 1).

Resilient children   Children who sustain some type of physiological or psychological trauma yet remain on a normal developmental path (Ch. 10).

Respiratory distress syndrome (RDS)   A problem common with premature babies that is caused by the lack of a substance called surfactant, which keeps the air sacs in the lungs open (Ch. 5).

Retreat   According to Perry's theory of ethical development, when someone retreats to an earlier ethical position (Ch. 13).

Rh factor   An incompatibility between the blood types of mother and child; if the mother is Rh-negative and the child is Rh-positive, miscarriage or even infant death can result (Ch. 4).

Risk factors   Stressors that individuals experience (Ch. 16).

Role discontinuity   Abrupt and disruptive change caused by conflicts among one's various roles in life (Ch. 18).

S

Safety needs   Maslow's term to represent the importance of security, protection, stability, freedom from fear and anxiety, and the need for structure and limits (Ch. 2).

Scaffolding   Helping children move from initial difficulties with a topic to a point where, with help, they gradually learn to perform the task independently (Chs. 2 and 5).

Scheme   Piaget's term to describe the patterns of behavior that infants use to interact with their environment (Ch. 2).

Secondary circular reactions   Infants direct their activities toward objects and events outside themselves (Ch. 5).

Secular trend   The phenomenon (in recent centuries) of adolescents entering puberty sooner and growing taller and heavier (Ch. 11).

Secure parents   Those parents who are confident of their techniques; they assume they will cope successfully and look on parenting as an exciting challenge (Ch. 8).

Self-actualization   Maslow's term that means we use our abilities to the limit of our potentialities (Ch. 2).

Self-concept   Children know who they are and what makes them different from everyone else (Chs. 8 and 10).

Self-control   Restraint exercised over impulses, emotions, and desires (Ch. 10).

Self-esteem   Children possess feelings of confidence and satisfaction with one's self (Ch. 8 and 10).

Self-fulfilling prophecy   Making an idea come true simply by believing it will (Ch. 15).

Semantic cues   Readers relate words to what they signify (Ch. 9).

Semantics   Describes how to interpret the meaning of words (Ch. 7).

Senile macular degeneration   This disease of the retina is a leading cause of blindness, beginning as blurred vision and a dark spot in the center of the field of vision (Ch. 15).

Sensitive periods   Certain times in the lifespan when a particular experience has a greater and more lasting impact than at another time (Chs. 1 and 7).

Sensitive responsiveness   Refers to the ability to recognize the meaning of a child's behavior (Ch. 6).

Sensorimotor period   Piaget's term for the first of his cognitive stages of development (0 to 2 years) (Ch. 5).

Sequential (longitudinal/cross-sectional) studies   A cross-sectional study done at several times with the same groups of individuals (Ch. 1).

Seriation   The process by which concrete operational children can arrange objects by increasing or decreasing size (Ch. 9).

Sex cleavage   Youngsters of the same sex tend to play and do things together (Ch. 8).

Sexual abuse   Any sexual activity between a child and adult, whether by force or consent (Ch. 10).

Sexually transmitted diseases (STD)   Class of diseases that may cause infertility (Ch. 3).

Sexually transmitted infections   A class of infections that are transmitted through sexual behavior (Ch. 12).

Sickle-cell anemia   A chromosomal disorder resulting in abnormal hemoglobin (Ch. 3).

Silence   Belenky's first phase of women's thinking, characterized by concepts of right and wrong (Ch. 13).

Sleeping disorder   A child who does not sleep readily and wakes repeatedly (Ch. 5).

Slow-to-warmup children   Term used to describe children with low intensity of reactions; may be rather negative when encountering anything new (Ch. 6).

Social death   The point at which a patient is treated essentially as a corpse, although perhaps still "clinically" or "biologically" alive (Ch. 19).

Social (cognitive) learning theory   Bandura's theory that refers to the process whereby the information we glean from observing others influences our behavior (Ch. 2).

Social perspective-taking   The idea that children's views on how to relate to others emerge from their personal theories about the traits of others (Ch. 10).

Socialization   Refers to the need to establish and maintain relations with others and to regulate behavior according to society's demands (Ch. 8).

Socialized speech   Piaget's term for the time when children begin to exchange ideas with each other (Ch. 5).

Socio-emotional selectivity theory   According to this theory, humans use social contact for four reasons: to obtain physical survival, to get information they need, to maintain a sense of self, and to acquire pleasure and comfort. For the elderly the last two are most important (Ch. 18).

Solidarity   Erikson's term for the personality style of persons who are able to commit themselves in concrete affiliations and partnerships with others and have developed the "ethical strength to abide by such commitments, even though they may call for significant sacrifices and compromises" (Ch. 14).

Somatic dimension   The first stage of Frankl's theory of human development, in which all persons are motivated by the struggle to keep themselves alive and to help the species survive (Ch. 19).

Sperm   The germ cell that carries the male's 23 chromosomes (Ch. 3).

Sperm donor   Male either donates or sells sperm (Ch. 3).

Spina bifida   A genetic disorder resulting in the failure of the neural tube to close (Ch. 3).

Stability   A belief that children's early experiences affect them for life (Ch. 1).

Stage of exhaustion   Selye's term for the body's physiological responses that revert to their condition during the stage of alarm (Ch. 16).

Stage of resistance   Selye's term for the body's reaction that is generally a reversal of the alarm reaction (Ch. 16).

Stage theorists   Researchers who believe that research based on personality traits is too narrow in focus and that we must also look at the stages of change each person goes through (Ch. 16).

Stagnation   According to Erikson, the seventh stage of life (middle-aged adulthood) tends to be marked either by generativity or by stagnation—boredom, self-indulgence, and the inability to contribute to society (Ch. 16).

State of identity   If individuals were in a state of identity (an ideal circumstance), the various aspects of their self-image would be in agreement with each other; they would be identical (Ch. 11).

Stillbirth   The term used to describe, after the twentieth week, the spontaneous end of a pregnancy is called a stillbirth if the baby is born dead (Ch. 4).

Stress   Anything that upsets our equilibrium—both psychological and physiological (Ch. 10).

Structure building   Levinson's term. During structure-building periods, individuals face the task of building a stable structure around choices they have made (Ch. 14).

Structure changing   Levinson's term. A process of reappraising the existing life structure and exploring the possibilities for new life structures characterizes the structure-changing period (Ch. 14).

STD (sexually transmitted diseases)   A major cause of infertility (Ch. 3).

Subculture   A subgroup within a culture, in this case a social culture (Ch. 12).

Subjective knowledge   Belenky's third phase of women's thinking; characterized by some crisis of male authority that sparked a distrust of outside sources of knowledge, and some experience that confirmed a trust in women thinkers themselves (Ch. 13).

Sudden infant death syndrome (SIDS)   Death of an apparently healthy infant, usually between 2 and 4 months of age; thought to be a brain-related respiratory problem (Ch. 5).

Superego   One of the three structures of the psyche according to Freud; acts as a conscience (Ch. 2).

Surrogacy motherhood   One woman carries another woman's embryo (Ch. 3).

Symbolic play   The game of pretending; one of five preoperational behavior patterns (Ch. 7).

Symmetry   An infant's capacity for attention; style of responding influences interactions (Ch. 6).

Synchrony   The ability of parents to adjust their behavior to that of an infant (Ch. 6).

Syntactic cues   Using language rules to combine words into sentences (Ch. 9).

Syntax   Describes how we learn to put words together to form sentences (Ch. 7).

Syphilis   A sexually transmitted infection that presents a great danger in that in its early stage there are no symptoms. If untreated, it can be fatal (Chs. 4 and 12).

T

Telegraphic speech   Initial multiple-word utterances, usually two or three words (Ch. 5).

Temperament   A child's basic personality that is now thought to be discernible soon after birth; how a child interacts with the environment (Chs. 6 and 10).

Temporizing   An aspect of Perry's theory of ethical development, in which some people remain in one position for a year or more, exploring its implications but hesitating to make any further progress (Ch. 13).

Teratogens   Any agents that can cause abnormalities, including drugs, chemicals, infections, pollutants, and the mother's physical state (Ch. 4).

Terminal drop   The period of from a few weeks up to two years before a person's death, during which his or her intelligence is presumed to decline rapidly (Ch. 17).

Tertiary circular reaction   Repetition with variation; the infant is exploring the world's possibilities (Ch. 5).

Thalidomide   A popular drug prescribed during the early 1960s that was later found to cause a variety of birth defects when taken by women early in their pregnancy (Ch. 4).

Theory of mind   Children's realization that others' thoughts affect their behavior (Ch. 7).

Toxoplasmosis   Caused by a protozoan, it may cause damage to the nervous system; transmitted by animals, especially cats (Ch. 4).

Traditional marriage enterprise   Levinson's term. The main goal of this type of marriage is to form and maintain a family (Ch. 16).

Trait theorists   Researchers who look at pieces of the personality (personality traits), as measured by detailed questionnaires (Ch. 16).

Transformation   Children learn to think about what they shouldn't do in different terms (Ch. 10).

Transition   Levinson's concept that each new era begins as an old era is approaching its end. That "in-between" time is a transition (Ch. 14).

Transition-linked turning points   The precursors and outcomes of a variety of transitions. A constellation of events that define the transition period or the timing and sequence of events that occur within a transitional period. For example, puberty and school events are frequently studied as key transitions signaling the entry into adolescence (Ch. 11).

Treatment   The variable that the experimenter manipulates (Ch. 1).

Triarchic model of intelligence   A three-tier explanation of intelligence proposed by Robert Sternberg (Ch. 9).

Trophoblast   The outer surface of the fertilized egg (Ch. 4).

Turner syndrome   Females with the XO chromosomal pattern (Ch. 3).

U

Ultrasound   The use of sound waves to produce an image that enables a physician to detect structural abnormalities (Ch. 4).

Umbilical cord   Contains blood vessels that go to and from the mother through the arteries and veins supplying the placenta (Ch. 4).

Uniform growth   Montessori's term to describe the developmental period in which children show considerable stability (Ch. 7).

Universalizing faith The final developmental step of Fowler's theory of faith. Here the individual lives in the real world but is not of it. Such persons do not merely recognize the mutuality of existence; they act on the basis of it (Ch. 19).

Use of metaphor The ability to think of a word or phrase that by comparison or analogy can be used to stand for another word or phrase (Ch. 11).

V

Validation Fromm's term for the reciprocal sharing of deep secrets and feelings that allows people to feel loved and accepted (Ch. 14).

Variable accommodation Focusing on objects at various distance; appears at about 2 months (Ch. 5).

Victimized parents Those parents who believe it just isn't fair if their child shows any sign of a problem after all they have done for the child (Ch. 8).

Vocables Consistent sound patterns to refer to objects and events (Ch. 5).

W

Wear and tear theory The theory that aging is due to the cumulative effects of hard work and lifelong stress (Ch. 17).

Whole Language A method in which students learn to read by obtaining the meaning of words, with phonics being introduced when needed from context (Ch. 7).

Z

Zone of proximal development The distance between a child's actual developmental level and a higher level of potential development with adult guidance (what children can do independently and what they can do with help) (Ch. 2).

Zygote The fertilized egg (Ch. 3).

Zygote intrafallopian transfer (ZIFT) The fertilized egg (the zygote) is transferred to the fallopian tube (Ch. 3).

References

A. A. R. P. (September-October, 1997). Friendship facts. *Modern Maturity, 41.*

Abeles, N. (1997). A victory for the aging community. *APA Monitor, 28* (10), 2.

Abeshouse, R. P. (1987). *Lifelong learning, Part I: Education for a competitive economy.* Washington, DC: Roosevelt Center for American Policy Studies.

Abravanel, E. & DeYoung, N. (1991). Does object modeling elicit imitative like gestures prom young infants? *Journal of Experimental Child Psychology, 52,* 22–40.

Adams, G., Montemayor, R., & Gullotta, T. (1996). Psychosocial development during adolescence: The legacy of John Hill. In G. Adams, R. Montemayor, & T. Gullotta (Eds.), *Psychosocial development during adolescence.* Thousand Oaks, CA: Sage.

Adams, H.E., Wright, L.W., & Lohr, B.A. (1996). Is homophobia associated with homosexual arousal? *Journal of Abnormal Psychology, 105* (3), 440–445.

Ahrons, C. (1994). The effects of the postdivorce relationship on paternal involvement: A longitudinal view. *American Journal of Orthopsychiatry,* 63, 441–450.

Akhtar, N., Carpenter, M., & Tomasello, M. (1996). The role of discourse novelty in early word learning. *Child Development, 67,* 635–645.

Alexander, G. & Korenbrot, C. (1995). The role of prenatal care in preventing low birth weight. *The Future of Children, 5* (1), 103–120.

Allen, B.P. (1995). Gender stereotypes are not accurate: A replication of Martin (1987) using diagnostic vs. self-report and behavioral criteria. *Sex Roles, 32* (9/10), 583–600.

Al-Mabuk, C. P. A. & Enright, R. D. (1995). Forgiveness education with parentally love-deprived late adolescents. *Journal of Moral Education, 24,* 427–444.

Al-Mateen, C.S., Brookman, R., Best, A.M., & Singh, N. (1996). Inquiring about sexual abuse. *Journal of the American Academy of Child and Adolescent Psychiatry, 35* (4), 407–408.

Alpaugh, P., Renner, V., & Birren, J. (1976). Age and creativity. *Educational Gerontology, 1,* 17–40.

Alsaker, F. (1995). Is puberty a critical period for socialization? *Journal of Adolescence, 18,* 427–444.

Alsaker, F. (1996). Annotation: The impact of puberty. *Journal of Child Psychology and Psychiatry and Allied Disciplines, 37* (3), 249–258.

Alva, S. A. & Jones, M. (1994). Psychosocial adjustment and self-reported patterns of alcohol use among Hispanic adolescents. *Journal of Early Adolescence, 14,* 432–448.

Alves, J. (1993). Transgressions and transformations: Initiation rites among urban Portuguese boys. *American Anthropologist, 95* (4), 894–928.

Alzheimer's Association Annual Report. (1996). *A world without Alzheimer's.* Washington, DC: Alzheimer's Association.

American Association of Retired Persons. (1990a, January). FDA warns against dietary supplement. *A.A.R.P., 31* (1), 7.

American Association of Retired Persons. (1990b, January). Study links alcohol to heart damage. *A.A.R.P., 31* (1), 7.

American Heart Association. (1984). *Eating for a healthy heart: Dietary treatment of hyperlipidemia.* Dallas: American Heart Association.

American Psychiatric Association. (1994). *Diagnostic and statistical manual mental disorders* (4th ed.), Washington, DC: author.

Anderson, E.G. (1996). Worrying about health: A uniquely American pastime? *Geriatrics, 51* (9), 56–60.

Anderson, J., Crawford, C., Nadeau, J., & Lindberg, T. (1992). Was the Duchess of Windsor right? A cross cultural review of the socioecology of ideals of female body shape. *Ethology and Sociobiology, 13* (3), 197–227.

Angell, K. E., Gross, W., Johnson, M. S., Koutstaal, W., & Schacter, D. L. (1997). False recollection induced by photographs: A comparison of older and younger adults. *Psychology and Aging, 12* (2) 203–215.

Annie E. Casey Foundation. (1995). State profiles of child well-being. *Kids Count Data Book.* Boston, MA.

Arcus, D., Gardner, S., & Anderson, C. (1992). Infant reactivity, maternal style, and the development of inhibited and uninhibited behavioral profiles. *Temperament and environment.* Symposium at the biennial meeting of the International Society for Infant Studies.

Arnett, J. (1996). What it means to be an adult. *Journal of Adult Development. 3* (1), 38–47.

Avery, M. E. & Litwack, G. (1983). *Born early.* New York: Little, Brown.

Azar, B. (1996). Project explores landscape of midlife. *APA Monitor, 27* (11), 26.

Azar, B. (1996) Some forms of memory improve as people age. *APA Monitor, 27* (11), 27.

Azar, B. (1997a). More research needed on the leading causes of death. *APA Monitor, 28* (10), 31.

Azar, B. (1997b). Be careful how you define intelligence. *APA Monitor, 28* (10), 37.

Bailey, J. (1991). A genetic study of male sexual orientation. *Archives of General Psychiatry, 48,* 1089–1096.

Bailey, J.M. & Pillard, R.C. (1991). A genetic study of male sexual orientation. *Archives of General Psychiatry, 48,* 1089–1096.

Bailey, J. M., Pillard, R.C., Neale, M.C., & Agyei, Y. (1993). Heritable factors influence sexual orientation in women. *Archives of General Psychiatry, 50,* 217–223.

Baltes, P. B. (1993). The aging mind: Potential and limits. *The Gerontologist, 33* (5), 580–594.

Baltes, P. B. & Blates, M.M. (Eds.) (1990). *Successful aging: Perspectives from the behavioral sciences.* Cambridge: Cambridge University Press.

Baltes, P. B., Sowarka, D., & Kliegl, R. (1989). Cognitive training research on fluid intelligence in old age: What can older adults achieve by themselves. *Psychology and Aging, 4* (2), 217–221.

Baltimore, D. (1994). What is the Genome project? In N. Cooper (Ed.), *The human genome project*. Mill Valley, CA: University Science Books.

Bandura, A. (1997). *Self-efficacy: The exercise of control*. New York: Freeman.

Banks, J. (1993). Multicultural education: Development, dimensions, and challenges. *Phi Delta Kappan* (September), 22–28.

Banks, J. & Banks, C. A. (Eds.). (1993). *Multicultural education: Issues and perspectives*. Boston: Allyn and Bacon.

Barnes, G. M., Farrell, M. P., & Banerjee, S. (1994). Family influences on alcohol abuse and other problem behaviors among black and white adolescents in a general population sample. *Journal of Research on Adolescence, 4,* 183–201.

Barry, D. (1993). Screen violence and America's children. *Spectrum, 66* (3), 37–42.

Bartlett, S. (1997). No place to play: Implications for the interactions of parents and children. *Journal of Children and Poverty, 3* (1).

Baumrind, D. (1986). *Familial antecedents of social competence in middle childhood*. Unpublished manuscript.

Baumrind, D. (1991). The influence of parenting style on adolescent competence and substance use. Special Issue: The work of John P. Hill: I. Theoretical, instructional, and policy contributions. *Journal of Early Adolescence, 11,* (1), 56–95.

Baumrind, D. (1993). The average expectable environment is not good enough: A response to Scarr. *Child Development, 64* (5), 1299–1317.

Baumrind, D. (1995). Commentary on sexual orientation: Research and social policy implications. Special Issue: Sexual orientation and human development. *Developmental Psychology, 31* (1), 130–136.

Beaty, L.A. (1995). Effects of paternal absence on male adolescents' peer relations and self-image. *Adolescence, 30* (120), 873–880.

Becoming a nation of readers: The report of the commission on reading. (1984). Washington, DC: National Academy of Education, National Institute of Education, and Center for the Study of Reading.

Belenky, M., Clinchy, B., Goldberger, N., & Tarule, J. (1986). *Women's ways of knowing*. New York: Basic Books.

Belsky, J. (1996). Parent, infant, and social-contextual antecedents of father-son attachment security. *Developmental Psychology, 32* (5), 905–913.

Bem, S. (1975). Androgyny vs. the light little lives of fluffy women and chesty men. *Psychology Today, 9* (4), 58–59, 61–62.

Bem, S. (1995). Dismantling gender polarization and compulsory heterosexuality: Should we turn the volume down or up? *Journal of Sex Research, 32* (4), 329–334.

Bem, S. (1996). Exotic becomes erotic. *Psychological Review, 103* (2), 320–335.

Bengston, V. L. & Robertson, J. L. (Eds.). (1985). *Grandparenthood*. Beverly Hills, CA: Sage.

Benson, G.S. (1996). Editorial: Male sexual dysfunction—pitfalls, pills and prostheses. *The Journal of Urology, 156,* 1636.

Bergman, S. (1991). Men's psychological development. *Work in Progress:* No. 48. Wellesley, MA: The Stone Center, Wellesley College, 1–13.

Berk, L. (1997). *Child development* (4th ed.). Needham Heights, MA: Allyn & Bacon.

Bingham, C.R. & Crockett, L.J. (1996). Longitudinal adjustment patterns of boys and girls experiencing early, middle, and late sexual intercourse. *Developmental Psychology, 32* (4), 647–658.

Birren, J. (1960). Behavioral theories of aging. In N. Shock (Ed.), *Aging*. Washington, DC: American Association for the Advancement of Science.

Birren, J. (1964). *The psychology of aging*. Englewood Cliffs, NJ: Prentice-Hall.

Bito, H., Tsien, R.W., & Deisseroth, K. (1996). Signaling from synapse to nucleus: Postsynaptic CREB phosphorylation during multiple forms of hippocampal synaptic plasticity. *Neuron,* Jan. 16 (1), 89–101.

Bjorklund, D. (1997). In search for a metatheory for cognitive development (or, Piaget is dead and I don't feel so good myself). *Child Development, 68* (1), 144–148.

Blackman, J. (1997). *Medical aspects of developmental disabilities in children birth to three*. Gaithersburg, MD: Aspen Publications.

Blum, R. W., Harmon, B., Harris, L., Bergeisen, L., & Resnick, M. (1992). American-Indian-Alaska native youth health. *Journal of the American Medical Association, 267,* 1637–1644.

Blumenkrantz, D. & Gavazzi, S. (1993). Guiding transitional events for children and adolescents through a modern day rite of passage. *Journal of Primary Prevention, 13* (3), 199–212.

Blumenkrantz, D. (1992a). *Fulfilling the promise of children's services*. San Francisco: Jossey-Bass.

Blumenkrantz, D. (1992b). *Rite of passage experience*. Glastonbury, CT: R.O.P.E.

Blumenkrantz, D. (1996). *The rite way: Guiding youth to adulthood and the problem of communitas*. Michigan: University of Michigan Press.

Bly, Robert. (1990). *Iron John*. Reading, MA: Addison-Wesley.

Bodmer, W. & McKie, R. (1995). *The book of man*. New York: Scribner.

Boivin, M. & Hymel, S. (1997). Peer experiences and social self-perceptions: A sequential model. *Developmental Psychology, 33* (1), 135–145.

Booth, D. (1994). *Classroom voices: Language-based learning in the elementary school*. New York: Harcourt Brace.

Bornstein, M. (1992). Perception across the life cycle. In M. Bornstein & M. Lamb (Eds.), *Developmental psychology: An advanced textbook* (3rd ed.). Hillsdale, NJ: Erlbaum.

Bornstein, M. (1995). Parenting infants. In M. Bornstein (Ed.), *Handbook of parenting* (Vol. 3). Hillsdale, NJ: Erlbaum.

Botwinick, J. (1984). *Aging and behavior* (3rd ed). New York: Springer.

Bouchard, T. (1994). Genes, environment, and personality. *Science, 264,* 1700–1791.

Bowlby, J. (1969). *Attachment,* New York: Basic Books.

Bowlby, J. (1982). Attachment and loss: retrospect and prospect. *American Journal of Orthopsychiatry, 52,* 664–678.

Bowlby, J. (1988). *A secure base*. New York: Basic Books.

Bornstein, J. M. (1986). Retraining the older worker: Michigan's experience with senior employment services. Special issue: Career counseling of older adults. *Journal of Career Development, 13* (2), 14–22.

Borgman, R. (1986). "Don't come home again:" Parental banishment of delinquent youths. *Child Welfare, 65* (3), 295–304.

Borum, R. (1996). Improving the clinical practice of violence risk assessment. *American Psychologist, 51,* 945–956.

Botwinick, J. (1977). Intellectual abilities. In J. E. Birren & K. W. Schaie (Eds.), *Handbook of the psychology of aging*. New York: Van Nostrand Reinhold.

Boyer, E. (1990). Giving dignity to the

teaching profession. In D. Dill & Associates (Eds.). *What teachers need to know*. San Francisco: Jossey-Bass.

Brabeck, M. (1983). Moral judgment: Theory and research on differences between males and females. *Developmental Review, 3,* 274–291.

Bransford, J. & Stein, B. (1993). *The IDEAL problem solver*. New York: Freeman.

Bradway, K., Thompson, C., & Graven, S. (1958). Preschool IQs after 25 years. *Journal of Educational Psychology, 49,* 278–281.

Brady, B. A. & Gray, D. D. (1988). Employment services for older job seekers. *The Gerontologist, 27,* 565–568.

Braverman, S. & Paris, J. (1993). The male mid-life crisis in the grown-up resilient child. *Psychotherapy, 30,* 651–656.

Brazelton, T. B. & Nugent, K. (1995). *Neonatal behavioral assessment scale*. London: Heinemann.

Bredekamp, S. & Copple, C. (Eds.). (1997). *Developmentally appropriate practice in early childhood programs*. Washington, DC: National Association for the Education of Young People.

Bretschneider, J. G. & McCoy, N. L. (1988). Sexual interest and behavior in healthy 80 to 102 year olds. *Archives of Sexual Behavior, 17* (2), 109–129. New York: Plenum Press.

Broberg, A., Wessels, H., Lamb, M., & Hwang, C. (1997). Effects of daycare on the development of cognitive abilities in 8-year-old: A longitudinal study. *Developmental Psychology, 33* (1), 62–69.

Brody, G., Stoneman, Z., & McCoy, J. (1992). Associations of maternal and paternal direct and differential behavior with sibling relationships: Contemporaneous and longitudinal analyses. *Child Development, 63,* 82–92.

Brody, G.H., Stoneman, Z., & Flor, D. (1996). Parental religiosity, family processes, and youth competence in rural, two-parent African American families. *Developmental Psychology, 32* (4), 696–706.

Brodzinsky, D., Lang, R., & Smith, D. (1995). Parenting adopted children. In M. Bornstein (Ed.). *Handbook of parenting* (Vol. 3). Hillsdale, NJ: Erlbaum.

Bronfenbrenner, U. (1978). *The ecology of human development*. Cambridge, MA: Harvard University Press.

Bronson, M. (1995). *The right stuff for children birth to 8*. Washington, DC: National Association for the Education of Young People.

Brooks-Gunn, J. (1987). Pubertal processes. In V. B. Van Hasselt & M. Hersen (Eds.), *Handbook of adolescent psychology*. New York: Pergamon.

Brooks-Gunn, J., Peterson, A., & Eichorn, D. (1985). The study of maturational timing effects in adolescence. *Journal of Youth and Adolescence, 14* (3), 149–161.

Brown, B. B. (1990). Peer groups and peer cultures. In S. Feldman & G. Elliot (Eds.), *At the threshold: The developing adolescent*. Cambridge, MA: Harvard University Press.

Brown, B.R., Baranowski, M.D., Kulig, J.W., & Stephenson, J.N. (1996). Searching for the Magic Johnson effect: AIDS, adolescents, and celebrity disclosure. *Adolescence, 31* (122), 253–264.

Brown, J. K. (1982). Cross-cultural perspectives on middle-aged women. *Current Anthropology, 23* (2), 143–156.

Brown, J. & Dunn, J. (1996). Continuities in emotion understanding from three to six years. *Child Development, 67,* 789–802.

Brown, R. (1973). *A first language: The early stages*. Cambridge, MA: Harvard University Press.

Brown, S.L. & Booth, A. (1996). Cohabitation versus marriage: A comparison of relationship quality. *Journal of Marriage and Family, 58* (8), 668–678.

Bruner, J. (1966). *Toward a theory of instruction*. Cambridge, MA: Harvard University Press.

Brunstein, J.C., Dangelmayer, G., & Schultheiss, O.C. (1996). Personal goals and social support in close relationships: Effects on relationship mood and marital satisfaction. *Journal of Personality and Social Psychology, 71* (5), 1006–1019.

Buchanan, D. (1992). Outward Bound goes to the inner city. *Educational Leadership, 50* (4), 38–39.

Bulkin, W. & Lukashok, H. (1988). Rx for dying. *New England Journal of Medicine, 318,* 376–378.

Bureau of the Census. (1996). *Statistical Abstract of the United States*. Washington, DC: Author.

Burke, J. & Hagedorn, J. M. (1995). Are gangs created by a need for family? In R. Del Campo and D.S. Del Campo (Eds.), *Taking sides: Clashing views on controversial issues in childhood and society* (pp. 360–376). Guilford, CT:

The Dushkin Publishing Group, Inc.

Burkhardt, S. & Rotatori, A. (1995). *Treatment and prevention of childhood sexual abuse*. Washington, DC: Taylto & Francis.

Bursik, K. (1995). Gender-related personality traits and ego development: Differential patterns for men and women. *Sex Roles, 32* (9/10), 601–615.

Burton, L.M. (1992). Black grandparents rearing children of drug-addicted parents: Stressors, outcomes, and social service needs. *The Gerontologist, 32* (6), 744–751.

Butler, R., Walker, W., Skowronski, J., & Shannon, L. (1995). Age responses to the love structures scale. *International Journal of Aging and Human Development, 40* (4), 281–296.

Byne, W. (1994, May). The biological evidence challenged. *Scientific American,* 50–55.

Cahill, M. & Salomone, P. R. (1987). Career counseling for work life extension: Integrating the older worker into the labor force. *Career Development Quarterly, 35* (3), 188–196.

Call, V., Sprecher, S., & Schwartz, P. (1995). The incidence and frequency of marital sex in a national sample. *Journal of Marriage and the Family, 57* (3), 639–652.

Callow, R. (1994). Classroom provision for the able & the exceptionally able. *Journal on Support-for-Learning, 9* (4), 151–154.

Cameron-Jones, M. & O'Hara, P. (1995). Mentors' perceptions of their roles with students in initial teacher training. *Cambridge Journal of Education, 25* (2), 189–199.

Campbell, B. & Gaddy, J. (1987). Rates of aging and dietary restrictions: Sensory and motor function in the Fischer 344 rat. *Journal of Gerontology, 42* (2), 154–159.

Cancian, M. & Meyer, D.R. (1996). Changing policy, changing practice: Mothers' incomes and child support orders. *Journal of Marriage and the Family, 58* (8), 618–627.

Capacchione, L. (1989). *The creative journal for children*. Boston: Shambhala.

Carnegie Corporation of New York. (1995). *Great Transitions: Preparing Adolescents for a New Century*. Carnegie Council on Adolescent Development.

Carnevali, D. L. & Patrick, M. (Eds.). (1986). *Nursing management for the elderly* (2nd ed.). Philadelphia: J. B. Lippincott.

Carney, J. (1993). "Is it really so terrible here?" Karl Menninger's pursuit of Erik Erikson. Special Issue: Erik H. Erikson. *Psychohistory-Review, 22* (1), 119–153.

Carstensen, L. (1992). Social and emotional patterns: Support for socioemotional selectivity theory. *Psychology and Aging, 7* (3), 331–338.

Carstensen, L. L. (1995). Evidence for a life-span theory of socioemotional selectivity. *Current Directions in Psychological Science, 4* (5), 151–156.

Carstensen, L.L., Gottman, J.M., & Levensen, R.W. (1995). Emotional behavior in long-term marriage. *Psychology and Aging, 10* (1), 140–149.

Casas, J. & Pytluk, S. (1995). Hispanic identity development: Implications for research and practice. In J. Ponterotto, J. Casas, L. Suzuki, & C. Alexander (Ed.), *Handbook of Multicultural counseling.* Thousand Oaks, CA: Sage.

Caserta. M.S., Lund, D.A., & Wright, S.D. (1996). Exploring the caregiver burden inventory (CBI): Further evidence for a multidimensional view of burden. *International Journal of Aging and Human Development, 43* (43), 21–34.

Casey, M. B., Nuttall, R., & Pezaris, E. (1997). Mediators of gender differences in mathematics college entrance test scores. *Developmental Psychology, 33* (4), 669–680.

Caspi, A., Bem, D.J., & Elder, G.H. Jr. (1989). Continuities and consequences of interactional styles across the life course. *Journal of Personality, 57* (2), 375–406.

Caspi, A., Belsky, J., & Silva, P. (1992). Childhood experience and the onset of menarche: A test of a sociobiological model. *Child Development* 63 (1), 47–58.

Cassidy, J., Kirsch, S., Scolton, K., & Parke, R. (1996). Attachment and Representations of peer relationships. *Developmental Psychology, 32* (5), 892–904.

Cattell, H. & Jolley, D.J. (1995). One hundred cases of suicide in elderly people. *British Journal of Psychiatry, 166,* 451–457.

Cauffman, E., & Steinberg, L. (1996). Interactive effects of menarcheal status and dating on dieting and disordered eating among adolescent girls. *Developmental Psychology, 32* (4), 631–635.

CDC (Centers for Disease Control). (1997). AIDS and HIV in the United States. Atlanta, GA: Monthly report.

Ceci, S. (1996). *On intelligence.* Cambridge, MA: Harvard University Press.

Checkley, K. (1997). The first seven . . . and the eighth. *Educational Leadership, 5* (1), 8–13.

Chamberlain, P. & Patterson, G. (1995). Discipline and child compliance in parenting. In M. Bornstein (Ed.), *Handbook of parenting.* Hillsdale, NJ: Erlbaum.

Chen, X., Rubin, K., & Li, D. (1997). Relation between academic achievement and social adjustment: Evidence from Chinese children. *Developmental Psychology, 33* (3), 518–525.

Cherlin, A., Furstenberg, F. Chase-Lansdale, P., Kiernan, K., Robins, P., Morrison, D., & Teitler, J. (1991). Longitudinal studies of effects of divorce in Great Britain and the United States. *Science, 252,* 1386–1389.

Children's Defense Fund (1989). *A day in the lives of some teens.* Washington, DC: Children's Defense Fund.

Children's Defense Fund. (1995). *The state of America's children yearbook.* Washington, DC: Children's Defense Fund.

Children's Defense Fund. (1996). *The state of America's children yearbook.* Washington, DC: Children's Defense Fund.

Chiriboga, D. A. (1989). Mental health at the midpoint. In S. Hunter & M. Sundel (Eds.), *Midlife myths.* Newbury Park, CA: Sage.

Cigarette smoking among adults. (June 15, 1992). *Journal of the American Medical Association, 267* (3), 3133.

Clay, R. (1996, December). Some elders thrive on working into late life. *A. P. A. Monitor,* 35.

Clay, R. (1997). Laughter may be no laughing matter. *APA Monitor,* 28 (9), p. 18.

Clifford, B., Gunter, B., & McAleer, J. (1995). *Television and children.* Hillsdale, NJ: Erlbaum.

Clifford, P., Tan, S., & Gorsuch, R. (1991). Efficacy of a self-directed behavioral health change program: Weight, body, composition, cardiovascular fitness, blood pressure, health risk and psychological mediating variables. *Journal of Behavioral Medicine, 14* (3), 303–323.

Clyman, B.B. & Pompei, P. (1996a). Osteoarthritis: New roles for drug therapy and surgery. *Geriatrics, 51* (9), 32–36.

Clyman, B.B. & Pompei, P. (1996b). Osteoarthritis: What to look for, and

when to treat it. *Geriatrics, 51* (8), 36–41.

Cochran, S.V. & Rabinowitz, F.E. (1996). Men, loss, and psychotherapy. *Psychotherapy, 33* (4), 593–600.

Coffey, P., Leitenberg, H., Henning, K., & Turner, T. (1996). Mediators of the long-term impact of child sexual abuse: Perceived stigma, betrayal, powerlessness, and self-blame. *Child Abuse and Neglect, 20* (5), 447–455.

Coffey, P., Leitenberg, H., Henning, K., & Turner, T. (1996). The relation between methods of coping during adulthood with a history of childhood sexual abuse and current psychological adjustment. *Journal of Consulting and Clinical Psychology, 64* (5), 1090–1093.

Cohen, J. (Feb. 7, 1997). The genomics gamble. *Science, 275,* 767–772.

Cohen-Mansfield, J. & Marx, M. S. (1992). The social network of the agitated nursing home resident. *Research on Aging, 14* (1), 110–123.

Cohn, R. (1979). Age and the satisfactions from work. *Journal of Gerontology, 34,* 264–272.

Col, N.F., Eckman, M.H., Kara, R.H., Pauker, S.G., Goldberg, R.J., Ross, E.M., Orr, R.K., & Wong, J.B. (1997, April 9). Patient-specific decisions about hormone replacement therapy in postmenopausal women. *Journal of the American Medical Association, 277,* (14), 1140–1147.

Cole, E. & Rothblum, E. (1990). Commentary on "Sexuality and the midlife woman." *Psychology of Women Quarterly, 14* (4), 509–512.

Cole, M. (1996). *Cultural psychology.* Cambridge, MA: Harvard University Press.

Cole, M. & Cole, S. (1996). *The development of children.* New York: Freeman.

Cole, T. (1991). The specter of old age: History, politics, and culture in an aging America. In B. Hess and E. Markson (Eds.), *Growing old in America* (pp. 23–38). New Brunswick, NJ: Transaction.

Coles, R. (1970). *Erikson Erikson: The growth of his work.* Boston: Little, Brown.

Coles, R. (1997). *The moral intelligence of children.* Boston: Random House.

Collins, M.F. & Weatherburn, D. (1995). Unemployment and the dynamics of offender populations. *Journal of Quantitative Criminology, 11* (3), 231–245.

Collins, N.L., Dunkel-Schetter, C., Lobel, M., & Scrimshaw, S.C.M. (1993). Social support in pregnancy: Psychosocial correlates of birth outcomes and postpartum depression. *Journal of Personality and Social Psychology, 65* (6), 1243–1258.

Collins, P. (1993). The interpersonal vicissitudes of mentorship: An exploratory study in the field of supervisor-student relationship. *Clinical Supervisor, 11* (1), 121–135.

Coltrane, S. & Ishii-Kuntz, M. (1992). Men's housework: A life course perspective. *Journal of Marriage & Family, 54,* 43–57.

Compas, B., Hinden, B. R., & Grehardt, C. (1995). Adolescent development: Pathways and processes of risk and resilience. *Annual Review of Psychology, 46,* 265–293.

Comstock, G. (1993). The medium and society: The role of television in American society. In G. Berry & Asamen, J. (Eds.). *Children and television.* Newbury Park, CA: Sage.

Comstock, G. & Paik, H. (1991). *Television and the American child.* New York: Academic.

Comstock, G. & Paik, H. (1994). The effects of television violence on antisocial behavior: A meta-analysis. *Communication Research, 21,* 269–277.

Conwell, Y. (1995). Suicide among elderly persons. *Psychiatric Services, 46* (6), 563–572.

Conwell, Y., Rotenberg, M., & Caine, E.D. (1990). Completed suicide at age 50 and over. *Journal of the American Geriatrics Society, 38,* 640–644.

Cook-Deegan, R. (1995). *The gene wars: Science, politics, and the human genome.* New York: Norton.

Cooksey, E.C. & Fondell, M.M. (1996). Spending time with his kids: Effects of family structure on fathers' and children's lives. *Journal of Marriage and the Family, 58* (8), 693–707.

Cooksey, E.C., Rindfuss, R.R., & Guilkey, D.K. (1996). The initiation of adolescent sexual and contraceptive behavior during changing times. *Journal of Health and Social Behavior, 37* (1), 59–74.

Cooper, N. (Ed.). (1994). *The human genome project.* Mill Valley, CA: University Science Books.

Coronary disease attributable to sedentary lifestyle. (September 19, 1990). *Journal of the American Medical Association, 328* (8), 574–578.

Costa, F. M., Jessor, R., Donovan, J. E., & Fortenberry, J. D. (1995). Early initiation of sexual intercourse: The influence of psychosocial unconventionality. *Journal of Research on Adolescence, 5* (1), 71–91.

Costa, P.T. & McCrae, R.R. (1995). Domains and facets: Hierarchical personality assessment using the revised NEO Personality Inventory. *Journal of Personality Assessment, 64* (1), 21–50.

Cote, J. E. & Levine, C. (1988). The relationship between ego identity status and Erikson's notions of institutionalized moratoria, value orientation stage, and ego dominance. *Journal of Youth and Adolescence, 17* (1), 81–100.

Cowart, B.J., Yokomukai, Y., & Beauchamp, G.K. (1994). Bitter taste in aging: Compound-specific decline in sensitivity. *Physiology and Behavior, 56* (4), 1237–1241.

Cox, H. (1988). *Later life.* Englewood Cliffs, NJ: Prentice-Hall.

Craig, T.K.J. (1996) Adversity and depression. *International Review of Psychiatry, 8* (4), 341–353.

Craig-Bray, L., Adams, G. R., & Dobson, W. R. (1988). Identity formation and social relations during late adolescence. *Journal of Youth and Adolescence, 17* (2), 173–188.

Creeden, J.E. (1990). Environmental and behavioral factors affecting fraternity drinking. *Journal of College Student Development, 31,* 465–467.

Crick, N. (1996). The role of overt aggression, relational aggression, and prosocial behavior in the prediction of children's future social adjustment. *Child Development, 67,* 2317–2327.

Crick, N., Casas, J., & Mosher, M. (1997). Relational and overt aggression in preschool. *Developmental Psychology, 33* (4), 579–588.

Criqui, M. H. (1990). Comment on Shaper's "Alcohol and mortality." *British Journal of Addiction, 85* (7), 854–857.

Crohan, S. E., Antonucci, T. C., Adelman, P. K., & Coleman, L. M. (1989). Job characteristics and well-being at mid-life: Ethnic and gender comparisons. *Psychology of Women Quarterly, 13,* 223–235.

Crouter, A. C., Perry-Jenkins, M., Huston, T. L., & McHale, S. M. (1987). Processes underlying father involvement in dual-earner and single-earner families. *Developmental Psychology, 23,* 431–440.

Crowley, J. E. (1986). Longitudinal effects of retirement on men's well-being & health. *Journal of Business and Psychology, 1* (2), 95–113.

Culp, M., Clyman, M., & Culp, R. (1995). Adolescent depressed mood, reports of suicide attempts, and asking for help. *Adolescence, 30,* 827–837.

Curtis, H. & Barnes, N.S. (1994). *Invitation to biology.* New York: Worth.

Curtis, J.M. & Curtis, M.J. (1993). Factors related to susceptibility and recruitment by cults. *Psychological Reports, 73,* 451–460.

Cutler, W., Schleidt, W., & Friedmann, E. (1987). Lunar influences on the reproductive cycle in women. *Human Biology, 59,* 959–972.

D'Augelli, A. & Patterson, C. (1995). Lesbian, gay, and bisexual identities over the lifespan. *Psychological Perspectives.* New York: Oxford University Press.

Dacey, J. S. (1986). *Adolescents today* (3rd ed.). Glenview, IL: Scott, Foresman.

Dacey, J. S. (1989a). *Fundamentals of creative thinking.* Lexington, MA: D.C. Heath/Lexington Books.

Dacey, J. S. (1989b). Peak periods of creative growth across the life span. *The Journal of Creative Behavior, 24* (4), 224–247.

Dacey, J. S. (1989c). Discriminating characteristics of the families of highly creative adolescents. *The Journal of Creative Behavior, 24* (4), 263–271.

Dacey, J. (1993). Reducing dropout rate in inner city middle school students through instruction in self-control. *Journal of Research in Middle Level Education,* Fall, 109–116.

Dacey, J. (1998). A history of the concept of creativity. In H. Gardner & R. Sternberg, (Eds.), *Encyclopedia of creativity.* San Francisco: Academic Press.

Dacey, J. & Kenny, M. (1997). *Adolescent development* (2nd ed.). Boston: McGraw-Hill.

Dacey, J. & Lennon, K. (1998). *Understanding creativity: The interplay of biological, psychological and social forces.* San Francisco: Jossey-Bass.

Dacey, J. S. & Packer, A. (1992). *The nurturing parent: How to raise a creative, loving, responsible child.* New York: Fireside/Simon & Schuster.

Dacey, J., deSalvatore, L., & Robinson, J. (1996). The results of teaching middle school students two relaxation techniques as part of a conflict prevention program. *Research in Middle Level Education,* Fall.

Dancer, L. & Gilbert, L. (1993). Spouses' family work participation and its relation to wives' occupational level. *Sex Roles, 28* (3/4), 127–145.

Darkenwald, G., & Novak, R. (1997). Classroom age competition and academic achievement in college. *Adult Education Quarterly, 47* (3/4), 108.

Darrach, B. (1992). The war on aging. *Life, 15* (10), 32–45.

Datan, N., Rodeheaver, D., & Hughes, F. (1987). Adult development and aging. *Annual Review of Psychology, 38,* 153–180.

Davidson, J.M. (1989). Sexual emotions, hormones, and behavior. *Advances, 6* (2), 56–58.

Davis, C., Lovie-Kitchin, J., & Thompson, B. (1995, January-February). Psychosocial adjustment to age-related macular degeneration. *Journal of Visual Impairment and Blindness,* 16–27.

Deacon, S., Minichiello, V., & Plummer, D. (1995). Sexuality and older people: Revisiting the assumptions. *Educational Gerontology, 21,* 497–513.

DeAngelis, T. (1997). Elderly may be less depressed than the young. *APA Monitor, 28* (10), 25.

De Casper, A., Lecanuet, J., Busnel, M., & Granier-Deferre, C. (1994). Fetal reactions to recurrent maternal speech. *Infant Behavior and Development, 17* (2), 159–164.

DeGenova, M. K. (1992). If you had your life to live over again, What would you do differently? *International Journal of Aging and Human Development, 34* (2), 135–143.

Del Vecchio, M., Zhou, H., Tully, T., & Yin, J.C. (1995). CREB as a memory modulator: Induced expression of a dCREB2 activator insoform enhances long-term memory in drosophila. *Cell, 81* (1), 107–215.

Darling-Hammond, L. (1994). Performance-based assessment and educational equity. *Harvard Educational Review, 64* (1), 5–30.

Dekovic, M. & Janssens, J. (1992). Parents' child-rearing style and child's sociometric status. *Developmental Psychology, 28,* 925–932.

Dellman-Jenkins, M., Lambert, D., Fruit, D., & Dinero, T. (1986). Old and young together. *Childhood Education,* 206–212.

DeVries, H. M., Hamilton, D. W., Lovett, S., & Gallagher-Thompson, D. (1997). Patterns of coping preferences for male and female caregivers of frail older adults. *Psychology & Aging, 12,* 263–267.

di Mauro, D. (1995). *Sexuality research in the United States: An assessment of social and behavioral sciences.* New York: The Social Science Research Council.

Diamant, L. & McAnulty, R. D. (1995).

The psychology of sexual orientation behavior & identity. Westport, CT: Greenwood Press.

Diehl, M., Willis, S. L., & Schaie, K. W. (1995). Everyday problem solving in older adults. *Psychology and Aging, 10* (3), 478–491.

Dinnerstein, M. (1992). *Women between two worlds: Reflections on work and family.* Philadelphia: Temple University Press.

DiPietro, J., Hodgson, D., Costiga, K., & Johnson T. (1996). Fetal antecedents of infant temperament. *Child Development, 67,* 2568–2583.

Dishion, T. J., Andrews, D. W., & Crosby, L. (1995). Antisocial boys and their friends in early adolescence: Relationship characteristics, quality, and interactional process. *Child Development, 66,* 139–151.

Donner, M. (Feb., 1997). A genetic basis for the sudden infant death sex ratio. *Med Hypotheses, 2,* 137–142.

Dranoff, S. M. (1974). Masturbation and the male adolescent. *Adolescence, 9* (34), 16–176.

Draper, P. & Keith, J. (1992). Cultural contexts of care: Family caregiving for elderly in America and Africa. *Journal of Aging Studies, 6* (2), 113–134.

Duncan, G., Brooks-Gunn, J., & Klebanov, P. (1994). *Child Development, 65,* 296–318.

Dunn, J. (1994). Experience and understanding of emotions, relationships, and membership in a particular culture. In Paul Ekman & Richard Davidson (Eds.). *The nature of emotion.* New York: Oxford University Press.

Dunn, J., Brown, J., & Maguire, M. (1995). The development of children's moral sensibility: Individual differences and emotion understanding. *Developmental Psychology, 31,* 649–659.

Dunn, J., Slomkowski, C., & Beardsall, L. (1994). Sibling relationships from the preschool period through middle childhood and early adolescence. *Developmental Psychology, 30* (3), 315–324.

Duvall, E. (1971). Family development. Philadelphia: Lippincott.

Eakes, G. (1995). Chronic sorrow: The lived experience of parents of chronically mentally ill individuals. *Archives of Psychiatric Nursing, 9* (2), 77–84.

Eastman, P. (1997). Slowing down Alzheimer's. *American Association of Retired Persons Bulletin, 38,* 1–6.

Edwards, C. (1995). Parenting toddlers. In M. Bornstein (Ed.), *Handbook of parenting.* Hillsdale, NJ: Erlbaum.

Edwards. R. & Usher, R. (1997). University adult education in the postmodern moment. *Adult Education Quarterly, 47,* (3/4), 153.

Eilenberg, J., Fullilove, M., Goldman, R.G., & Mellman, L. (1996). Quality and use of trauma histories obtained from psychiatric outpatients through mandated inquiry. *Psychiatric Services, 47* (2), 165–169.

Eisdorfer, C. & Wilkie, F. (1973). Intellectual changes and advancing age. In L. Jarvik (Ed.), *Intellectual functioning in adults.* New York: Springer.

Elias, M., Elias, P., & Elias, J. (1977). *Basic processes in adult developmental psychology.* St. Louis: Mosby.

Elkind, D. (1978). *The child's reality: Three developmental themes.* Hillsdale, NJ: Erlbaum.

Elkind, D. & Bowen, R. (1979). Imaginary audience behavior in children and adolescents. *Developmental Psychology, 15,* 38–44.

Ekman, P. & Davidson, R. (Eds.). (1994). *The nature of emotions.* New York: Oxford University Press.

Eisenberg, Fabes, R., Murphy, M., Karbon, K., & Smith, M. The relation of children's dispositional empathy-related responding to their emotionality, regulation, and social functioning. *Developmental Psychology, 32* (2), 195–209.

Eliason, M.J. (1995). Accounts of sexual identity formation in heterosexual students. *Sex Roles, 32* (11/12), 821–834.

Elliott, S., Kratochwill, T., Littlefield, J., & Travers, J. (1996). *Educational psychology: Effective teaching, effective learning.* Dubuque, IA: Brown/Benchmark.

Eng, T.R. & Butler, W.T. (Eds.) (1997). *The hidden epidemic: Confronting sexually transmitted diseases.* Washington, DC: National Academy Press.

Engstrom, P. F. (1986). Cancer control objectives for the year 2000. In L. E. Mortenseon, P. F. Engstrom, & P. N. Anderson (Eds.), *Advances in cancer control.* New York: Alan R. Liss.

Enright, R. D., Levy, V. M., Harris, D., & Lapsley, D. K. (1987). Do economic conditions influence how theorists view adolescents? *Journal of Youth and Adolescence, 16* (6), 541–560.

Erikson, E. (1958). *Young man Luther: A study in psychoanalysis and history.* New York: Norton.

Erikson, E. (1959). Growth and crises of the healthy personality. *Psychological Issues, 1.*

Erikson, E. (1963). *Childhood and society* (2nd ed.). New York: Norton.

Erikson, E. (1968). *Identity: Youth and crisis.* New York: Norton.

Erikson, E. (1969). *Gandhi's truth: On the origins of militant nonviolence.* New York: Norton.

Erikson, E. (1975). *Life, history, and the historical movement.* New York: Norton.

Erikson, E. (1978). *Adulthood.* New York: Norton.

Escarce, M. (1995). A cross-cultural study of Nepalese neonatal behavior. In K. Nugent, B. Lester, & T. B. Brazelton, (Eds.), *The cultural context of infancy.* Norwood, NJ: Ablex.

Esquivel, G.B. (1995). Teacher behaviors that foster creativity. Special Issue: Toward an educational psychology of creativity: I. *Educational Psychology Review, 7* (2), 185–202.

Ewert, A. & Heywood, J. (1991). Group development in the natural environment: Expectations, outcomes, and techniques. *Environment and Behavior, 23* (5), 592–615.

Exploring the environment. (Spring, 1996). *Alzheimer's Association National Newsletter, 16* (1), 4a.

Fagerstrom, R. (1994). Correlation between depression and vision in aged patients before and after cataract operations. *Psychological Reports, 75,* 115–125.

Fagot, B. (1995). Parenting boys and girls. In M. Bornstein (Ed.), *Handbook of parenting.* Hillsdale, NJ: Erlbaum.

Fagot, B., Leinbach, M., & O'Boyle, C. (1992). Gender labeling, gender stereotyping, and parenting behaviors. *Developmental Psychology, 28,* 225–230.

Farrell, M. & Strang, J. (1991). Substance use and misuse in childhood and adolescence. *Journal of Child Psychology and Psychiatry and Allied Disciplines, 32* (1), 109–128.

Feldman, B. (1995). The search for identity in late adolescence. In M. Sidoli & G. Bovensiepen (Eds.), *Incest fantasies and self-destructive acts: Jungian and post-Jungian psychotherapy in adolescence.* New Brunswick, NJ: Transaction Publishers.

Feldman, D. (1979). The mysterious case of extreme giftedness. In A. H. Passow (Ed.), *The gifted and the talented: Their education and development.* Chicago: Univ. of Chicago Press (NSSE).

Feldman, S. S., Fisher, L., Ranson, D. C., & Dimiceli, S. (1995). Is "what is good for the goose good for the gander?" Sex differences in relations between adolescent coping and adult adaptation. *Journal of Research on Adolescence, 5,* 333–359.

Feldman, S. S., Rosenthal, D. R., Brown, N. L., & Canning, R. D. (1995). Predicting sexual experience in adolescent boys from peer rejection and acceptance during childhood. *Journal of Research on Adolescence, 5,* 387–411.

Fergusson, D. M. & Lynskey, M. T. (1996). Adolescent resiliency to family adversity. *Journal of Child Psychology and Psychiatry and Allied Disciplines, 37* (3) 281–292.

Fingerman, K. (1995). Aging mothers' and their adult daughters' perceptions of conflict behaviors. *Psychology & Aging, 10,* 639–649.

Finkelhor, D. (1996, August). *Keynote Address.* Presented at the International Congress on Child Abuse and Neglect. Dublin, Ireland.

Firstman, R. & Talan, J. (1997). *The death of innocents.* New York: Bantam.

Fiske, S.T. & Glick, P. (1995). Ambivalence and stereotypes cause sexual harassment: A theory with implications for organizational change. *Journal of Social Issues, 51* (1), 97–115.

Flannery, D. J., Vazsonyi, A. T., & Rowe, D. C. (1996). Caucasian and Hispanic early adolescent substance use: Parenting, personality, and school adjustment. *Journal of Early Adolescence, 16,* 71–89.

Fodor, I. & Franks, V. (1990). Women in midlife and beyond: The new prime of life? *Psychology of Women Quarterly, 14,* 445–449.

Ford, K. & Norris, A.E. (1995). Factors related to condom use with casual partners among urban African-American and Hispanic males. *AIDS Education and Prevention, 7* (6), 494–503.

Fordham, S. & Ogbu, J. U. (1986). Black students' school success: Coping with the burden of "acting white." *Urban Review, 18,* 176–206.

Foreman, J. (1996 June). Doctors and patients at the end of life. *The Boston Globe, 23.*

Forthofer, M.S., Markman, H.J., Cox, M., Stanley, S., & Kessler, R.C. (1996). Associations between marital distress and work loss in a national sample. *Journal of Marriage and the Family, 58* (8), 597–605.

Fowler, J. (1974). Toward a developmental perspective on faith. *Religious Education, 69,* 207–219.

Fowler, J. (1975a). *Stages in faith: The structural developmental approach.* Harvard Divinity School Research Project on Faith and Moral Development.

Fowler, J. (1975b, October). *Faith development theory and the aims of religious socialization.* Paper presented at annual meeting of the Religious Research Association, Milwaukee, WI.

Fowler, J. (1993). Response to Helmut Reich: Overview or apologetic? *International Journal for the Psychology of Religion, 3* (3), 173–179.

Fowler, J.W. (1991). Stages in faith consciousness. *New Directions for Child Development, 52,* 27–45.

Fox, J. (1997). *Primary health care of children.* St. Louis: Mosby.

Fraiberg, S., Adelson, E., & Shapiro, V. (1987). Ghosts in the nursery: A psychoanalytic approach to the problems of impaired mother-infant relationships. In L. Fraiberg (Ed.), *Selected writings of Selma Fraiberg* (pp. 100–136). Columbus: Ohio State University Press.

Frankl, V. (1967). *Psychotherapy and existentialism.* New York: Simon & Schuster.

Frankland, P.W., Blendy, J.A., Coblentz, J., Marowitz, Z., Scheutz, G., Silva, A.J., & Kogan, J.H. (1997). Spaced training induces normal long-term memory in CREB mutant mice. *Current Biology, 17* (1), 1–11.

Freedman, L.D. (1993). TA tools for self-managing work teams. Special Issue: TA in organizations. *Transactional Analysis Journal, 23* (2) 104–109.

Freitag, M., Belsky, J., Grossman, K., Grossman, K., & Scheuerer, H. Continuity in parent-child relationships from infancy to middle childhood and relationships with friendship competence. *Child Developmet, 67,* 1437–1454.

Freud, A., & Dann, S. (1951). An experiment in group upbringing. *Psychoanalytic Study of the Child, 6,* 127–168.

Freud, A. (1968). Adolescence. In A. E. Winder & D. L. Angus (Eds.), *Adolescence: Contemporary studies.* New York: American Book.

Freud, S. (1955). Totem and taboo. In J. Strachey (Ed. and Trans.), *The standard edition of the complete psychological works of Sigmund Freud*

(Vol. 13). London: Hogarth Press (Original work published 1914).

Freud, S. (1966). *The complete introductory lectures on psychoanalysis*. Translated and edited by James Strachey. New York: Norton.

Friedan, B. (1963). *The feminine mystique*. New York: W. W. Norton.

Friedman, S. (1996). Reproductive conflicts in incest victims: An unnoticed consequence of childhood sexual abuse. *Psychoanalytic Quarterly, 65* (2), 383–388.

Fricker, H., Hindermann, R., & Bruppacher, R. (1995). The Aarau study on pregnancy and the newborn: An epidemiologic investigation of the course of pregnancy in 996 Swiss women, and its influence on newborn behavior using the Brazelton scale. In K. Nugent, B. Lester, and T. B. Brazelton (Eds.), *The cultural context of infancy*. Norwood, NJ: Ablex.

Frisch, R. E. (1988). Fatness and fertility. *Scientific American, 258* (3), 88–95.

Fromm, E. (1955). *The sane society*. New York: Holt, Rinehart & Winston.

Fromm, E. (1968). *The art of loving*. New York: Harper & Row.

Fulton, R. (1977). General aspects. In N. Linzer (Ed.), *Understanding bereavement and grief*. New York: Yeshiva University Press.

Funk, J. B. (1993). Reevaluating the impact of video games. *Clinical Pediatrics, 32* (2) 86–90.

Furnham, A. & Weir, C. (1996). Lay theories of child development. *Journal of Genetic Psychology, 157* (2), 211–226.

Furstenberg, F. F. (1990). The new extended family. In K. Pasley & M. Ihinger-Tallman (Eds.), *Remarriage and stepparenting*. New York: Guilford.

Gabriel, T. (1997, January 5). Pack dating: For a good time, call a crowd [New York Times Magazine]. *The New York Times*, pp. 22–23, 38.

Gagnon, J. H. & Simon, W. (1969). They're going to learn on the street anyway. *Psychology Today, 3* (2), 46 ff.

Gagnon, J. H. & Simon, W. (1987). The sexual scripting of oral genital contacts. *Archives of Sexual Behavior, 16* (1), 1–25.

Galen, B. & Underwood, M. (1996). A developmental investigation of social aggression among children. *Developmental Psychology, 33* (4), 589–600.

Gallup, G. (1988). *The Gallup poll*. New York: Random House.

Galton, F. (1870). *Hereditary genius*. New York: Appleton.

Galton, F. (1879). Psychometric experiments. *Brain, 2,* 148–162.

Garcia Coll, C. (1990). Developmental outcome of minority infants: A process-oriented look into our beginnings. *Child Development, 61* (2), 270–289.

Garcia Coll, C., Lamberty, G., Jenkins, R., McAdoo, H., Crnic, K., Wasik, B., & Garcia, H. (1996). An integrative model for the study of developmental competencies in minority children. *Child Development, 67,* 1891–1914.

Gardner, H. (1982). *Art, mind and brain*. New York: Basic.

Gardner, H. (1991). *The unschooled mind*. New York: Basic.

Gardner, H. (1993). *Frames of mind: The theory of multiple intelligences*. New York: Basic Books.

Gardner, H. (1995). *Leading minds: An anatomy of leadership*. New York: Basic Books.

Gardner, H. (1997). *Extraordinary minds*. New York: Basic.

Gardner, H. & Winner, E. (1982). Children's conceptions (and misconceptions) of the arts. In H. Gardner, *Art, mind, and brain*. New York: Basic Books.

Garvey, C. (1990). *Play*. Cambridge, MA: Harvard University Press.

Garfein, A. J. & Herzog, A.R. (1995). Robust aging among the young-old, old-old, and oldest-old. *Journal of Gerontology: Social Sciences, 50B* (2), S77–S87.

Garland, A. F. & Zigler, E. (1993, February). Adolescent suicide prevention: Current research and social policy implications. *American Psychologist,* 169–182.

Garner, R. (1992). Learning from school texts. *Educational Psychologist, 27* (1), 53–64.

Garratt, D., Roche, J., & Tucker, S. (1997). *Changing experiences of youth*. London: Sage.

Garrod, A., Smulyan, L., Power, S., & Kilkenny, R. (1995). *Adolescent portraits*. Needham Heights, MA: Allyn & Bacon.

Garvey, M.J. & Schaffer, C.B. (1994). Are some symptoms of depression age dependent? *Journal of Affective Disorders, 32,* 247–251.

Gary, F., Moorhead, J., & Warren, J. (1996). Characteristics of troubled youths in a shelter. *Archives of Psychiatric Nursing, 10* (1), 41–48.

Gavazzi, S. & Blumenkrantz, D. (1993). Facilitating clinical work with adolescents and their families through the rite of passage experience program. *Journal of Family Psychotherapy, 4* (2), 47–67.

Ge, X., Best, K.M., Conger, R.D., & Simons, R.L. (1996). Parenting behaviors and the occurrence and co-occurrence of adolescent depressive symptoms and conduct problems. *Developmental Psychology, 32* (4), 717–731.

Ge, X., Conger, R.D., Cadoret, R.J., Neiderhiser, J.N., Yates, W., Troughton, E., & Stewart, M.A. (1996). The developmental interface between nature and nurture: A mutual influence model of child antisocial behavior and parent behaviors. *Developmental Psychology, 32* (4), 574–589.

Geary, D., Bow-Thomas, C., Lin, F., & Siegler, R. (1996). Development of arithmetical competencies in Chinese and American children: Age, language, and schooling. *Child Development, 67,* 2022–2044.

Geis, J.A. & Klein, H.A. (1989). The relationship of life satisfaction to life change among the elderly. *The Journal of Genetic Psychology, 151* (2), 269–271.

Gelfand, M.J., Fitzgerald, L.F., & Drasgow, F. (1995). The structure of sexual harassment: A confirmatory analysis across cultures and settings. *Journal of Vocational Behavior, 47,* 164–177.

Gerson, L. W., Jarjoura, D., & McCord, G. (1987). Factors related to impaired mental health in urban elderly. *Research on Aging, 9* (3), 356–371.

Gfellner, B. B. (1994). A matched group comparison of drug use and problem behavior among Canadian Indian and white adolescents. Special Issue: Canadian research on early adolescence. *Journal of Early Adolescence, 14,* 24–48.

Giles, H., Coupland, N., Coupland, J., Williams, A., & Nussbaum, J. (1992). Intergenerational talk and communication with older people.

Gilligan, C. (1982). *In a different voice*. Cambridge, MA: Harvard University Press.

Gilligan, C., Lyons, N., & Hanmer, T. (1990). *Making connections*. Cambridge, MA: Harvard University Press.

Gilligan, C., Lyons, N., & Hanmer, T. (1990). *Making connections: The relational worlds of adolescent girls at Emma Willard School*. Cambridge, MA: Harvard University Press.

Gilovich, K.D. & Miller, L. (1994). Combining adult and adolescent female incest survivors in a weekend retreat. *Journal of Child Sexual Abuse, 3* (2), 15–30.

Gitlin, T. (1987). *Years of hope, days of rage.* New York: Bantam Books, Inc.

Glass, J.C., Jr. & Reed, S.E. (1993). To live or die: A look at elderly suicide. *Educational Gerontology, 19,* 767–778.

Gleick, J. (1992). *Genius: The life and science of Richard Feynman.* New York: Partheon.

Gold, P. E., Jones, M. G., Korol, D. L., Manning, C. A., & Wilkniss, S. M. (1997). Age-related differences in an ecologically based study of rote learning. *Psychology and Aging, 12* (2) 372–375.

Goldsmith, M. F. (1988). Anencephalic organ donor program suspended; Loma Linda report expected to detail findings. *Journal of the American Medical Association, 260,* 1671–1672.

Goleman, D. (1985). *Vital lies, simple truths: The psychology of self-deception.* New York: Simon & Schuster.

Goleman, D. (1995). *Emotional intelligence.* New York: Bantam.

Gosse, G.H. & Barnes, M.J. (1994). Human grief resulting from the death of a pet. *Anthrozoos, 7* (2), 103–112.

Gottman, J. M. & Krokoff, L. J. (1989). Marital interaction and satisfaction: A longitudinal view. *Journal of Consulting and Clinical Psychology, 57,* 47–52.

Graber, J.A. & Brooks-Gunn, J. (1996). Transitions and turning points: Navigating the passage from childhood through adolescence. *Developmental Psychology, 32* (4), 768–776.

Graham, B. (1994). Mentoring and professional development in careers services in higher education. *British Journal of Guidance and Counselling, 22* (2), 261–271.

Graham, S. (1994). Motivation in African-Americans. *Review of Educational Research, 64* (1), 55–117.

Graham, S. & Hudley, C. (1994). Attributions of aggressive and nonaggressive African American male early adolescents: A study of construct accessibility. *Developmental Psychology, 30,* 365–373.

Gray, C.A. & Geron, S.M. (1995). The other sorrow of divorce: The effects on grandparents when their adult children divorce. *Journal of Gerontological Social Work, 23* (3/4), 139–159.

Green, A.H. (1995). Comparing child victims and adult survivors: Clues to the pathogenesis of child sexual abuse. *Journal of the American Academy of Psychoanalysis, 23* (4), 655–670.

Green, C.P. (1991). Clinical considerations: Midlife daughters and their aging parents. *Journal of Gerontological Nursing, 17* (11), 6–12.

Greenberger, E. & Chen, C. (1996). Perceived family relationships and depressed mood in early and late adolescence: A comparison of European and Asian Americans. *Developmental Psychology, 32* (4), 707–716.

Greene, K., Rubin, D. L., Hale, J. L., &Walters, L. H. (1996). The utility of understanding adolescent egocentrism in designing health promotion messages. *Health Communication, 8* (2), 131–152.

Greenspan, S. (1995). *The challenging child.* Reading, MA: Addison-Wesley.

Greenspan, S. & Benderly, B. (1997). *The growth of the mind.* Reading, MA: Addison-Wesley.

Greenstein, T.N. (1996). Husbands' participation in domestic labor: Interactive effects of wives' and husbands' gender ideologies. *Journal of Marriage and the Family, 58* (8), 585–595.

Grisso, T. & Tomkins, A. (1996). Communicating violence risk assessment. *American Psychologist, 51* (9), 928–930.

Grossman, H. Y. & Chester, N. L. (1990). *The experience and meaning of work in women's lives.* Hillsdale, NJ: Erlbaum.

Grusec, J., Goodnow, J., & Cohen, L. (1996). Household work and the development of concern for others. *Developmental Psychology, 32* (6), 999–1007.

Guberman, S. (1996). The development of everyday mathematics in Brazilian children with limited formal education. *Child Development, 67,* 1609–1623.

Guelzow, M. G., Bird, G. W., & Koball, E. H. (1991). An exploratory path analysis of the stress process for dual career men and women. *Journal of Marriage and the Family, 53,* 151–164.

Guilford, J. P. (1975). Creativity: A quarter century of progress. In I. A. Taylor & J. W. Getzels (Eds.), *Perspectives in creativity.* Chicago: Aldine.

Gutman, D. (1973, December). Men, women and the parental imperative. *Commentary,* 59–64.

Gyulay, J. (1989). What suicide leaves behind. Special Issue: The death of a child. *Counseling and Values, 35* (2), 104–113.

Haan, N. (1976). ". . . change and sameness . . ." reconsidered. *International Journal of Aging and Human Development, 7,* 59–65.

Haan, N. (1981). Common dimensions of personality development. In D. M. Eichorn (Ed.), *Present and past in middle life.* New York: Academic Press.

Haan, N. (1989). Personality at midlife. In S. Hunter & M. Sundel (Eds.), *Midlife myths.* Newbury Park, CA: Sage.

Hack, M., Klein, N., & Taylor, H. (1995, Spring Issue), Long-term developmental outcomes of low birth weight infants. *Future of Children, 5* (1), 176–196.

Haignere, C.S., Culhane, J.F., Balsley, C.M., & Legos, P. (1996). Teachers' receptivenessand comfort teaching sexuality education and using non-traditional teaching strategies. *Journal of School Health, 66* (4), 140–144.

Hajcak, F. & Garwood, P. (1989). Quick-fix sex: Pseudosexuality in adolescents. *Adolescence, 23* (92), 75–76.

Hakuta, K. (1986). *Mirror of language: The debate of bilingualism.* New York: Basic Books.

Hakuta, K. & McLaughlin, B. (1996). Bilingualism and second language learning: Seven tensions that define the research. In D. Berliner & R. Calfee (Eds.). *Handbook of Educational Psychology.* New York: Macmillan.

Halford, G. S. (1989). Reflection on 25 years of Piagetian cognitive psychology, 1963–1988. *Human Development, 32,* 325–357.

Hall, G. S. (1904). *Adolescence.* (2 vols.) New York: Appleton-Century-Crofts.

Hallman, R. (1967). Techniques for creative teaching. *Journal of Creative Behavior, 1* (3), 325–330.

Hamer, D. (1993). A linkage between diva markers on x chromosome & male sexual orientation. *Science, 261,* 321–327.

Hammond, W.A. & Romney, D.M. (1995). Cognitive factors contributing to adolescent depression. *Journal of Youth Adolescence, 24,* 667–682.

Hammond, W. R. & Yung, B. (1993). Psychology's role in the public health response to assaultive violence among young African-American men. Special

Issue: Adolescence. *American Psychologist, 48* (2), 142–154.

Harris, A.C. (1994). Ethnicity as a determinant of sex role identity: A replication study of item selection for the Bem Sex Role Inventory. *Sex Roles, 31* (3/4), 241–273.

Harris, D.K., Changas, P.S., & Palmore, E.B. (1996). Palmore's first facts on aging quiz in a multiple-choice format. *Educational Gerontology, 22,* 575–589.

Harris, J. & Fiedler, C. (1988). Preadolescent attitudes toward the elderly. *Adolescence, 23,* 335–340.

Harry, J. (1986). Sampling gay men. *Journal of Sex Research, 22,* 21–34.

Hart, D., Hofmann, V., Edelstein, W., & Keller, M.(1997). The relation of childhood personality types to adolescent behavior and development. A longitudinal study of Icelandic children. *Developmental Psychology, 33* (2), 195–205.

Harter, S. (1993). Visions of self: Beyond the Me in the mirror. In J. Jacobs, (Ed.), *Developmental perspectives on motivation.* Lincoln, NE: University of Nebraska Press.

Hartup, W. (1996). The company they keep: Friendships and their developmental significance. *Child Development, 67,* 1–13.

Harvard Health Letter. (1991). *Elderly drivers.* Cambridge, MA: Harvard University Press.

Harvard Men's Health Watch. (1997, October). Prudence and the prostate. *Harvard Men's Health Watch, 2* (3), 5–7.

Hauser, S. T. & Bowlds, M. K. (1990). In S. Feldman & G. Elliot (Eds.), *At the threshold: The developing adolescent.* Cambridge, MA: Harvard University Press.

Havighurst, R., Neugarten, B., & Tobin, S. (1968). Disengagement and patterns of aging. In B. Neugarten (Ed.), *Middle age and aging.* Chicago: University of Chicago Press.

Hawkins, R. D., Kandel, E. R., & Siegelbaum, S. A. (1993). Learning to modulate transmitter release: Themes and variations in synaptic plasticity. *Annual Review of Neuroscience, 16,* 625–665.

Hawkins, R.D. & Kandel, E.R. (1996). Long-term potentiation is reduced in mice that are doubly mutant in endothelial and neuronal nitric oxide synthase. *Cell, 87,* 6.

Hayne, H. & Rovee-Collier, C. (1995). The organization of reactivated memory in infancy. *Child Development, 66,* 893–906.

Hayward, M. D. (1986). The influence of occupational characteristics on men's early retirement. *Social Forces, 64* (4), 1032–1045.

Heckhausen, J. (1997). Developmental regulation across adulthood: Primary & secondary control of age-related challenges. *Developmental Psychology, 33* (1), 176–187.

Heimann, B. & Pittenger-Khushwant, K. (1996). The impact of formal mentorship on socialization and commitment of newcomers. *Journal of Managerial Issues, 8* (1), 108–117.

Hennessey, B. A. (1995). Social, environmental, and developmental issues and creativity. Special Issue: Toward an educational psychology of creativity: I. *Educational Psychology Review, 7* (2), 163–183.

Henning, K., Leitenberg, H., Coffey, P., & Turner, T. (1996). Long-term psychological and social impact of witnessing physical conflict between parents. *Journal of Interpersonal Violence, 11* (1), 35–51.

Henry, B., Caspi, A., Moffit, T.E., & Silva, P.A. (1996). Temperamental and familial predictors of violent and nonviolent criminal convictions: Age 3 to age 18. *Developmental Psychology, 32* (4), 614–623.

Herman-Giddens, M., Slora, E., Wasserman, R., Bourdony, C., Koch, G., & Hasemeier, C. (1997). Secondary sexual characteristics and menses in young girls in office practice: A study from the pediatric research office settings network. *Pediatrics, 99* (4), 505–518.

Hersch, P. (1991a, April). Teen epidemic. *American Health,* 42–45.

Hersch, P. (1991b, May). Sexually transmitted diseases are ravaging our children. *American Health,* 42–52.

Hertz, R. (1989). Dual-career corporate couples: Shaping marriages through work. In B. Risman & P. Schwartz, (Eds.), *Gender in intimate relationships.* Belmont, CA: Wadsworth.

Hertz, R. (1991). Dual career couples and the American dream: Self-sufficiency and achievement. *Journal of Comparative Family Studies, 22* (2), 247–262.

Hertzog, C. (1989). Influences of cognitive slowing on age differences in intelligence. *Developmental Psychology, 25,* 636–651.

Hertzog, C., Kidder, D. P., Mayhorn, C. B., Morrell, R. W., & Park, D. C. (1997). Effect of age on event-based and time-based prospective memory. *Psychology and Aging, 12* (2) 314–327.

Hetherington, E. M., Staney-Hagan, M., & Anderson, E. (1989). Marital transitions: A child's perspective. *American Psychologist, 44,* 303–312.

Hetherington, M. & Stanley-Hagan, M. (1995). Parenting in divorced and remarried families. In M. H. Bornstein (Ed.), Children and parenting (Vol. 4) Hillsdale, NJ: Erlbaum.

HHS News. (1997). *Teen sex down, new study shows.* Washington, DC: U. S. Department of Health and Human Services.

Hill, C. D., Thompson, L. W., & Gallagher, D. (1988). The role of anticipatory bereavement in older women's adjustment to widowhood. *The Gerontologist, 28* (6), 7–12.

Hill, J. P. & Holmbeck, G. N. (1986). Disagreements about rules in families with seventh-grade girls and boys. *Journal of Youth and Adolescence, 16* (3), 221–246.

Hill, J. P. (1987). Central changes during adolescence. (Society for Research on Adolescence) Research on Adolescents and their families. In W. Damon (Ed.), *New Directions in Child Psychology.* San Francisco: & Jossey-Bass.

Hillman, J.L. & Stricker, G. (1996). Predictors of college students' knowledge of and attitudes toward elderly sexuality: The relevance of grandparental contact. *Educational Gerontology, 22,* 539–555.

Hinde, R. (1991). Relationships, attachment, and culture: A tribute to John Bowlby. The effects of relationships on relationships. *Infant Mental Health Journal, 12* (3), 154–163.

Hinde, R. (1993). A comparative study of relationship structure. *British Journal of Social Psychology, 32* (3), 191–207.

Hines, A.M. (1997). Divorce-related transitions, adolescent development, and the role of the parent-child relationship: A review of the literature. *Journal of Marriage and the Family, 59* (2), 375–388.

Hoffman, K. & Stage, E. (1993). Science for all: Getting it right for the 21st century. *Educational Leadership, 50* (5), 27–31.

Hoffman, S. & Duncan, G. (1988). What are the economic consequences of divorce? *Demography, 25,* 641–645.

Holden, C. (1987). Alcoholism and the medical cost crunch. *Science, 235,* 1132–1133.

Holinger, P. C., Offer, D., & Ostrov, E. (1987). Suicide and homicide in the United States: An epidemiologic study of violent death, population changes, and the potential for prediction. *American Journal of Psychiatry, 144* (2), 215–219.

Holland, J. L. (1973). *Making vocational choices: A theory of careers.* Englewood Cliffs, NJ: Prentice-Hall.

Honan, W.H. (1997, March 16). Drug arrests rise 18% on major college campuses, survey finds. *The New York Times,* p. 25.

Horn, J. L. (1975). *Psychometric studies of aging and intelligence.* New York: Raven Press.

Horn, J. L. (1978). Human ability systems. In P. B. Baltes (Ed.), *Life-span development and behavior* (Vol. 1). New York: Academic Press.

Horn, J. L., Donaldson, G., & Engstrom, R. (1981). Apprehension, memory, and fluid intelligence decline in adulthood. *Research on Aging, 3,* 33–84.

Horwitz, A., White, H., & Howell-White, S. (1996). Becoming married and mental health. *Journal of Marriage and the Family, 58,* 895–907.

Howe, P. (1997, October). Study of elders favors calcium, vitamin D. Boston, MA: *The Boston Globe,* A12.

Howie, L. (1992–93). Old women and widowhood: A dying status passage. *Omega, 26* (3), 223–233.

Hu, S. (1995). Xq28 linkage between sexual orientation in males but not females. *Nature Genetics, 11,* 248–256.

Huerta, R., Mena, A., Malacara, J.M., & De Leon, J.D. (1995). Symptoms at perimenopausal period: Its association with attitudes toward sexuality, life-style, family function, and FSH levels. *Psychoneuroendocrinology, 20* (2), 135–148.

Hurwitz, A. (1997). *The Journal of the American Medical Association.*

Hulit, L. & Howard, M. (1997). *Born to talk.* Needham Heights, MA: Allyn & Bacon.

Hulicka, I. (1967). Short-term learning and memory. *Journal of the American Geriatrics Society, 15,* 285–294.

Hunt, T. & Lindley, C. J. (1989). *Testing older adults.* Washington, DC: Center for Psychological Services.

Hunter, S. & Sundel, M. (1989). *Midlife myths.* Newbury Park, CA: Sage.

Huttenlocher, P. (1994). Synaptogenesis in the human cerebral cortex. In G. Dawson & K. Fischer (Eds.), *Human behavior and the developing brain.* New York: Guilford.

Hwalek, M., Neale, A., Goodrich, C. & Quinn, K. (1996). The association of elder abuse and substance abuse in the Illinois elder abuse system. *The Gerontologist, 36* (5), 694–700.

Hyde, J.S. & DeLamater, J. (1997). *Understanding human sexuality* (6th ed.). New York: McGraw-Hill.

Igoa, C. (1995). *The inner world of the immigrant child.* Mahwah, NJ: Erlbaum.

Isaacs, T.C. (1994). The archetypal nature of Christian initiation. *Pastoral Psychology, 42* (3), 163–170.

Iwanir, S. & Ayal, H. (1991). Midlife divorce initiation. *Contemporary Family Therapy, 13* (6), 609–623.

Izard, C. (1994), Intersystems connections. In Paul Ekman & Richard Davidson (Eds.). *The nature of emotion.* Oxford University Press, 1994.

Jackson, H. & Nuttall, R. (1997). *Childhood abuse: Effects on clinicians' personal and professional lives.* Thousand Oaks, CA: Sage.

Jackson, J. S. & Gibson, R. C. (1985). Work and retirement among the black elderly. In Z. S. Blou (Ed.), *Current perspectives on aging and the life cycle: Vol. 1: Work, retirement, and social policy.* Greenwich, CN: JAI Press.

Jacobsen, T. & Hofmann, V. (1997). Children's attachment representations: Longitudinal relations to school behavior and academic competency in middle childhood and adolescence. *Developmental Psychology, 33* (4), 703–710.

Jacobvitz, D.B. & Bush, N.F. (1996). Reconstructions of family relationships: Parent-child alliances, personal distress, and self-esteem. *Developmental Psychology, 32* (4), 732–743.

James, M. (1990). Adolescent values clarification: A positive influence on perceived locus of control. *Journal of Alcohol and Drug Education, 35* (2), 75–80.

Janus, S. & Janus, C. (1993). *The Janus report on sexual behavior.* New York: Wiley.

Jaquish, G. & Ripple, R. E. (1980). Cognitive creative abilities across the adult life span. *Human Development, 34,* 143–152.

Jefko, W. (1980). Redefining death. In E. Schneiderman (Ed.), *Death: Current perspectives.* Palo Alto, CA: Mayfield.

Jenkins, J. & Astington, J. (1996). Cognitive factors and family structure associated with theory of mind development in young children.

Developmental Psychology, 32 (1), 70–78.

Jennings, J. & Kamarck, T. (1997). Aging or disease? *Psychology and Aging, 2,* 239.

Jennings, J. R., Kamarck, T., Manuck, S., & Everson, S. A. (1997). Aging or disease? Cardiovascular reactivity in Finnish men over the middle years. *Psychology and Aging, 12* (2), 225–238.

Jessor, R., Van Den Boss, J., Vanderryn, J., Costa, F. M., et al. (1995). Protective factors in adolescent problem behavior: Moderator effects and developmental change. *Developmental Psychology, 31,* 923–933.

Jezel, D.R., Molidor, C.E., & Wright, T.L. (1996). Physical, sexual, and psychological abuse in high school dating relationships: Prevalence rates and self-esteem issues. *Child and Adolescent Social Work Journal, 13* (1), 69–87.

Johnson, B., Shulman, S., & Collins, W. A. (1991). Systemic patterns of parenting as reported by adolescents: Developmental differences and implications for psychosocial outcomes. *Journal of Adolescent Research, 6* (2), 235–252.

Johnson, C.C., Myers, L., Webber, L.S., Hunter, S.M., & Srinivasan, S.R., & Berenson, G.S. (1995). Alcohol consumption among adolescents and young adults: The Bogalusa heart study, 1981 to 1991. *American Journal of Public Health, 85* (7), 979–982.

Johnson, T.P., Aschkenasy, J.R., Herbers, M.R., & Gillenwater, S.A. (1996). Self-reported risk factors for AIDS among homeless youth. *AIDS Education and Prevention, 8* (4), 308–322.

Johnston, L., O'Malley, P. M., & Bachman, J. G. (1996). *National survey results on drug use from the monitoring the future study, 1975–1994.* Vol. II: College students and young adults. Washington, DC: National Institute on Drug Abuse.

Johnston, W. B. (1987). *Workforce 2000: Work and workers for the 21st century.* Indianapolis, IN: Hudson Institute.

Jones, S. (1993). *The language of genes.* New York: Anchor Books.

Jones, S. (1996). Imitation or exploration: Young infants' matching of adults' oral gestures. *Child Development, 67,* 1952–1969.

Julian, T., Mc Kenry, P., & McKelvey, M. (1992). Components of men's well-being at mid-life. *Issues in Mental Health Nursing, 13* (4), 285–299.

Jung, C. G. (1933). *Modern man in*

search of a soul. New York: Harcourt, Brace & World.

Jung, C. G. (1971). *The portable Jung.* (Joseph Campbell, Ed.). New York: Viking Press.

Kacmar, K. M. & Ferris, G. R. (1989). Theoretical and methodological considerations in the age-job satisfaction relationship. *Journal of Applied Psychology, 74,* 201–207.

Kaestner, K.H., Schmid, W., Gass, P., Schutz, G., & Blendy, J.A. (1996). Targeting of the CREB gene leads to up-regulation of a novel CREB mRNA insoform. *EMBO Journal, 15* (5), 1098–1106.

Kagan, J. (1994). *Galen's prophecy.* New York: Basic.

Kagan, J. (1997). Temperament and the reactions to unfamiliarity. *Child Development, 68* (1), 139–143.

Kakuchi, S. (1997, September 27). Graying of Japan. *The Boston Globe,* A3.

Kallman, F. & Jarvik, L. (1959). Individual differences in constitution and genetic background. In J. Birren (Ed.), *Handbook of aging and the individual.* Chicago: Univ. of Chicago Press.

Kamino, K., Tateishi, K., Satoh, T., Nishiwaki, Y., Yoshiiwa, A., Miki, T., & Ogihara, T., & Sato, N. (1997). Elevated amyloid beta protein (1–40) level induces CREB phosphorylation at serine-133 via p44/42 MAP kinanse (Erk1/2)-research, *Biochemical and Biophysical Research Communications, 232* (3), 637–645.

Kammerman, J. B. (1988). *Death in the midst of life.* Englewood Cliffs, NJ: Prentice-Hall.

Kangas, J. & Bradway, K. (1971). Intelligence at midlife: A 38-year follow-up. *Developmental Psychology, 5,* 333–337.

Karp, S.A., Holmstrom, R.W., Silber, D.E., & Stock, L.J. (1995). Personalities of women reporting incestuous abuse during childhood. *Perceptual and Motor Skills, 81* (3), 955–965.

Kart, C. S., Metress, E. K., & Metress, S. P. (1988). *Aging, health and society.* Boston: Jones & Bartlett Publishers, Inc.

Kastenbaum, R. & Kastenbaum, B. (1989). *The encyclopedia of death.* Phoenix: Oryx Press.

Kaufman, A., & Wang, J. (1992). Gender, race, and education differences on the K-BIT at ages 4 to 90 years. *Journal of Psychoeducational Assessment, 10* (3), 219–229.

Kaufman, A.S., Reynolds, C.R., & McLean, J.E. (1989). Age and WAIS-R intelligence in a national sample of adults in the 20- to 74-year age range: A gross-sectional analysis with education level controlled. *Intelligence, 13* (3), 235–253.

Kaufman, J.C., McLean, J.E., Kaufman, A.S., & Kaufman, N.L. (1994). White-black and white-hispanic differences on fluid and crystallized abilities by age across the 11- to 94-year range. *Psychological Reports, 75,* 1279–1288.

Kazdin, A. (1993). Adolescent mental health. *American Psychologist, 48* (2), 127–141.

Kazdin, A.E. (Ed.). (1997). *Encyclopedia of psychology.* Washington, DC: American Psychological Association.

Kegan, R. (1994). *In over our heads.* Cambridge, MA: Harvard University Press.

Kelly, J. & Hansen, D. (1990). Social interactions and adjustment. In V. VanHasselt & M. Herson (Eds.). *Handbook of adolescent psychology.* New York: Pergamon, 131–146.

Kendall-Tackett, K., Williams, L., & Finkelhor, D. (1993). Impact of sexual abuse on children: A review and synthesis of recent empirical studies. *Psychological Bulletin, 113,* 164–180.

Kendig, H., Hashimoto, A., & Coppard, L. (Eds.). (1992). *Family support for the elderly: The international experience.* Oxford: Oxford University Press.

Kerns, K., Klepac, L., & Cole, A. (1996). Peer relationships and preadolescents' perceptions of security in the child-mother relationship. *Developmental Psychology, 32* (3), 457–466.

Kidder, L.H., Lafleur, R.A., & Wells, C.V. (1995). Recalling harassment, reconstructing experience. *Journal of Social Issues, 51* (1), 53–67.

Kiebler, M., Lee, C.J., Lev-Ram, V., Tsien, R.Y., Kandel, E.R., Hawkins, R.D., & Arancio, O. (1996). Nitric oxide acts directly in the presynaptic neuron to produce long-term potentiation in cultured hippocampal neurons. *Cell, 87* (6), 1025–1035.

Kielsmeier, J.C. (1996). Walkabout: More than summer school. *Education and Urban Society, 28* (2), 167–175.

Kim, K., Smith, P., & Palermitti, A. (1997). Conflict in childhood and reproductive development. *Evolution and Human Behavior, 18* (2),109–142.

Kimmel, D. (1974). *Adulthood and aging.* New York: Wiley.

Kimmel, D. C. & Weiner, I. B. (1985). *Adolescence: A developmental transition.* Hillsdale, NJ: Erlbaum.

King, I. (1914). *The high school age.*

Indianapolis: Bobbs-Merrill.

King, V. (1994). Nonresident father involvement and child well-being. *Journal of Family Issues, 15* (1), 78–96.

Kinsey, A., Pomeroy, W., Martin, C., & Gebhard, P. (1948). *Sexual behavior in the human male.* Philadelphia: Saunders.

Kinsey, A., Pomeroy, W., Martin, C., & Gebhard, P. (1953). *Sexual behavior in the human female.* Philadelphia: Saunders.

Kivett, V. R. (1991). Centrality of the grandfather role among older rural black and white men. *Journal of Gerontology, 46* (5), 250–258.

Klassen, A. D., Williams, C. J., & Levitt, E. E. (1989). *Sex and morality in the U.S.: An empirical enquiry under the auspices of the Kinsey Institute.* Middletown, CT: Wesleyan University Press.

Klein, N. (1978, October). Is there a right way to die? *Psychology Today, 12,* 122.

Klein, R. (1991). Age-related eye disease, visual impairment, and driving in the elderly. *Human Factors, 33* (5), 521–525.

Kliegl, R., Smith, J., & Baltes, P. (1989). Testing-the-limits and the study of adult age differences in cognitive plasticity of a mnemonic skill. *Developmental Psychology, 25* (2), 247–256.

Kliegl, R., Smith, J., & Baltes, P. (1990). On the locus and process of magnification of age differences during mnemonic training. *Developmental Psychology, 26* (6), 894–904.

Kling, K., Seltzer, M., & Ryff, C. (1997). Distinctive late-life challenges. *Psychology & Aging, 12* (2), 288–295.

Klonof-Cohen, H. (May, 1997). Sleep position and sudden infant death in the United States. *Epidemiology, 3,* 327–329.

Kneisl, C. R. & Ames, S. W. (1986). *Adult health nursing: A biopsychosocial approach.* New York: Addison-Wesley.

Knopf, M. (1993). Having shaved a kiwi fruit. *Psychological Research, 53* (3), 203–224.

Knopf, M. & Neidhardt, E. (1989). Aging and memory for action events. *Developmental Psychology, 25* (5), 780–786.

Knowles, M. (1989). *The adult learner: A neglected species.* Houston: Gulf.

Knox, R. A. (1997, February 10). Growing older. Boston, MA: *The Boston Globe,* C1.

Koberg, C., Boss, R., Chappell, D., & Ringer, R. (1994). Correlates &

consequences of protege mentoring in a large hospital. *Group & Organization Management, 19* (2), 219–239.

Kochanska, G. Mutually responsive orientation between mothers and their young children: Implications for early socialization. *Child Development, 68* (1), 94–11.

Koenig, H. G., Kvale, J. N., & Ferrell, C. (1988). Religion and well-being in later life. *The Gerontologist, 28* (1), 18–20.

Kogan, N. (1983). Stylistic variation in childhood and adolescence: Creativity, metaphor, cognitive styles. In P. H. Mussen (Ed.), *Handbook of child psychology* (Vol. 3). New York: Wiley.

Koss, M., Gidycz, C., & Wisniewski, N. (1987). The scope of rape: Incidence and prevalence of sexual aggression and victimization in a national sample of higher education students. *Journal of Consulting and Clinical Psychology, 55,* 162–170.

Kowal, K., & Kramer, I. (1997). Children's understanding of parental differential treatment. *Child Development, 68* (1), 113–126.

Krause, N. & Wray, L. (1991). Psychosocial correlates of health and illness among minority elders. *Generations, 15,* 25–30.

Kruger, A. (1994). The midlife transition: Crisis or chimera? *Psychological Reports, 75,* 1299–1305.

Kübler-Ross, E. (1969). *On death and dying.* New York: Macmillan.

Kübler-Ross, E. (1975). *Death: The final stage of growth.* Englewood Cliffs, NJ: Prentice-Hall.

Kübler-Ross, E. & Warshaw, W. (1978). *To live until we say goodbye.* Englewood Cliffs, NJ: Prentice-Hall.

Labouvie-Vief, G. & Lawrence, R. (1985). Object knowledge, personal knowledge, and processes of equilibration in adult cognition. *Human Development, 28,* 25–39.

Lachman, M. E. (1992). Improving memory and control beliefs through cognitive restructuring and self-generated strategies. *Journal of Gerontology, 47* (5), 293–299.

Lamb, M. E. (1987). *The father's role: Cross-cultural perspectives.* Hillsdale, NJ: Erlbaum.

Langer, E. (1993). A mindful education. *Educational Psychologist, 28* (1), 43–50.

Langlois, J., Ritter, J., Casey, R., & Sawin, D. (1995). Infant attractiveness predicts maternal behaviors and attitudes. *Developmental Psychology, 31,* 464–472.

Larson, R.W., Richards, M.H., Moneta, G., Holmbeck, G., & Duckett, E. (1996). Changes in adolescents' daily interactions with their families from ages 10 to 18: Disengagement and transformation. *Developmental Psychology, 32* (4), 744–754.

Lauer, R.H., Lauer, J.C., & Kerr, S.T. (1990). The long-term marriage: Perceptions of stability and satisfaction. *International Journal of Aging and Human Development, 31* (3), 189–195.

Lauman, E.O., Gagnon, J.H., Michael, R.T., & Michaels, S. (1994). *The social organization of sexuality: Sexual practices in the United States.* Chicago, IL: The University of Chicago Press.

Lease, K. P. & Robbins, S. B. (1994). Relationships between goal attributes and the academic achievement of Southeast Asian adolescent refugees. *Journal of Counseling Psychology, 41* (1), 45–52.

LeBlanc, A.N. (1994, August 14). While Manny's locked up [The New York Times Magazine]. *The New York Times,* pp. 26–33, 46, 49, 53.

Leeming, F., Dwyer, W., & Oliver, D. (1996). *Issues in adolescent sexuality.* Needham Heights, MA: Allyn & Bacon.

Lehman, H. C. (1953). *Age and achievement.* Princeton, NJ: Princeton University Press.

Lehman, H. C. (1962). The creative production rates of present versus past generations of scientists. *Journal of Gerontology, 17,* 409–417.

Lehman, H. C. (1964). The relationship between chronological age and high level research output in physics and chemistry. *Journal of Gerontology, 19,* 157–164.

Leiblum, S. R. (1990). Sexuality and the midlife woman. *Psychology of Women Quarterly, 14* (4), 495–508.

Leitenberg, H., Detzer, M., & Srebnik, D. (1993). Gender differences in masturbation and the relation of masturbation experience in preadolescence and/or early adolescence to sexual behavior and sexual adjustment in young adulthood. *Archives of Sexual Behavior, 22* (2), 87–98.

Leonard, M. (1997, March 23). Fleeting memories. *The Boston Globe,* pp. E1–E2.

Lerner, R. (January, 1991). Changing organism—context relations as the basic process of development: A developmental contextual perspective. *Developmental Psychology,* Vol. 27 (1), 27–32.

Lerner, R.M. (1995). *America's youth in crisis: Challenges and options for programs and policies.* Thousand Oaks, CA: Sage.

Lerner, R.M. (1996). Relative plasticity, integration, temporality, and diversity in human development: A developmental contextual perspective about theory, process, and method. *Developmental Psychology, 32,* 781–786.

Lerner, R.M. (Ed.). (1998). Theoretical models of human development. *Handbook of Child Psychology* (5th ed.), Vol. 1.

Lerner, R.M. & Korn, M.E. (1997). Developmental psychology: Theories. In A.E. Kayolin (Ed.), *Encyclopedia of Psychology.* Washington, DC: A.P.A.

Lerner, R. M. & Simi, N. L. (1997). A holistic, integrated model of risk and protection in adolescence: A developmental contextual perspective about research, programs, and policies. Paper presented at a conference on "Developmental science and the holisitic approach: A symposium followed up at the Royal Swedish Academy of Sciences," Wiks Castle, Sweden, May 24–27.

Lesesne, T., Chance, R., & Buckman, L. (1995). Pasages: Young adults coming of age. *Journal of Reading, 38* (5), 406–410.

LeVay, S. (1993). *The sexual brain.* Cambridge, MA: The MIT Press.

LeVay, S. & Hamer, D. (1994). Evidence of a biological influence in male homosexuality." *Scientific American, 270* (5), 43–49.

Levinson, D. (1978). *The seasons of a man's life.* New York: Knopf.

Levinson, D. (1986). A conception of adult development. *American Psychologist, 41* (1), 3–13.

Levinson, D. (1990a). A theory of life structure development in adulthood. In C. N. Alexander & E. J. Langer (Eds.), *Higher states of human development* (pp. 35–54). New York: Oxford University Press.

Levinson, D. (1990b). *Seasons of a woman's life.* Presented at the 98th annual convention of the American Psychological Association, Boston.

Levensen, R.W., Carstensen, L.L., & Gottman, J.M. (1993). Long-term marriage: Age, gender, and satisfaction. *Psychology and Aging, 8* (2), 301–313.

Lewis, C. (1963). *A grief observed*. New York: Seabury Press.

Lewis, K.G. & Moon, S. (1997). Always single and single again women: A qualitative study. *Journal of Marital and Family Therapy, 23* (2), 115–134.

Lewkowicz, D. (1996). Infants' response to the audible and visual properties of the face: 1. Role of lexical-syntactic content, temporal synchrony, gender, and manner of speech. *Developmental Psychology, 32* (2), 347–366.

Li, W., Tully, T., & Kalderon, D. (1996). Effects of a conditional drosophila PKA mutant on olfactory learning and memory. *Learning and Memory, 2* (6), 320–333.

Lickona, T. (1996). Eleven principles of effective character education. *Journal of Moral Education, 25,* 93–100.

Liebert, R. M., Sprafkin, J. N., & Davidson, E. (1988). *The early window*. New York: Pergamon.

Lindenberger, U. & Baltes, P.B. (1994). Sensory functioning and intelligence in old age: A strong connection. *Psychology and Aging, 9* (3), 339–355.

Litterst, J.K. & Eyo, B.A. (1993). Developing classroom imagination: Shaping and energizing a suitable climate for growth, discovery, and vision. *Journal of Creative Behavior, 27* (4), 270–282.

Little, T. & Lopez, D. (1997). Regularities in the development of children's causality beliefs about school performance across six sociocultural contexts. *Developmental Psychology, 33* (1), 165–175.

Lutz, C. & Przytulski, K. (1997). *Nutrition and diet therapy*. Philadelphia: F. A. Davis Co.

Lytton, H., Singh, J., & Gallagher, L. (1995). Parenting twins. In M. Bornstein (Ed.), *Handbook of parenting* (Vol. 1). Hillsdale, NJ: Erlbaum.

MacRae, H. (1992). Fictive kin as a component of the social networks of older people. *Research on Aging, 14* (2), 226–247.

Main, M. (April, 1996). Introduction to the special section on attachment and psychopathology: Overview of the field of attachment. *Journal of Consulting and Clinical Psychology, 64* (2), 237–242.

Malonebeach, E., Zarit, S., & Farbman, D. (1995). Variability in daily events & mood of family caregivers to cognitively impaired elders.

International Journal of Aging & Human Development, 41, 151–167.

Malowald, M. (1992). To be or not to be a woman: Anorexia nervosa, normative gender roles, and feminism. *Journal of Medicine and Philosophy, 17* (2), 233–251.

Manchester, W. (1983). *The last lion: Winston Spencer Churchill*. Boston: Little Brown.

Manning, M. & Baruth, L. (1996). *Multicultural education of children and adolescents*. Needham Heights, NJ: Allyn and Bacon.

Marcia, J. E. (1980). Identity in adolescence. In J. Adelson (Ed.), *Handbook of adolescent psychology*. New York: Wiley.

Marcia, J. E. (1983). Some directions for the investigation of ego development in early adolescence. *Journal of Early Adolescence, 3* (3), 215–223.

Marrs, R., Bloch, L., & Silverman, K. (1997). *Dr. Richard Marrs fertility book*. New York: Delacorte.

Marrs, R., Bloch, L., & Silverman, K. (1997). *Fertility book*. New York: Delacorte.

Marsh, H.W. & Richards, G.E. (1988). The outward bound bridging course for low-achieving high school males: Effect on academic achievement and multidimensional self-concepts. *Australian Journal of Psychology, 40* (3), 281–298.

Marshall, E. (Nov. 29, 1996). The human genome hunt scales up. *Science, 274,* 1456.

Marshall, L. (1981). Auditory processing in aging listeners. *Journal of Speech and Hearing Disorders, 46,* 226–240.

Marshall, V. & Levy, J. (1990). Aging and dying. In R. Binstock & L. George, (Eds.), *Handbook of aging and the social sciences*. San Diego, CA: Academic Press.

Marsiglio, W. (1992). Stepfathers with minor children living at home. *Journal of Family Issues, 13* (2), 195–214.

Martin, D. H., Mroczkowski, T. F., Dalu, Z. A., McCarty, J., Jones, R. B., & Hopkins, S. J. Azithromycin for Chlamydial Infections Study Group (1992). A controlled trial of a single dose of Azithromycin for the treatment of chlamydial urethritis and cervicitis. *New England Journal of Medicine, 327* (13), 921–925.

Martocchio, J. J. (1989). Age-related differences in employee absenteeism: A meta-analysis. *Psychology and Aging, 4,* 409–414.

Maslow, A. (1987). *Motivation and personality*. (Revised by R. Frager, J,

Fadiman, C. McReynolds, & R. Cox.) New York: Harper & Row.

Masoro, E. J. (1984). Nutrition as a modulator of the aging process. *Physiologist, 27* (2), 98–101.

Massachusetts Department of Public Health (1991). *Adolescents at risk 1991: Sexually transmitted diseases*. Boston, MA: Author.

Masters, W. & Johnson, V. (1966). *Human sexual response*. Boston: Little, Brown.

Masters, W. & Johnson, V. (1970). *Human sexual inadequacy*. Boston: Little, Brown.

Masters, W. H., Johnson, V. E., & Kolodny, R. C. (1986). *Masters and Johnson on sex and human loving*. Boston: Little, Brown.

Masters, W.H., Johnson, V.E., & Kolodny, R.C. (1995). *Human sexuality* (5th ed.). New York: HarperCollins College Publishers.

Matthews, K., Wing, R., Kuller, L., Meilahn, E., Kelsey, S., Costello, E., & Caggiula, A. (1990). Influences of natural menopause on psychological characteristics and symptoms of middle-aged healthy women. *Journal of Consulting and Clinical Psychology, 58* (3), 345–351.

Matusow, A. J. (1984). *The unraveling of America*. New York: Harper & Row.

Mazess, R. B. (1982). On aging bone loss. *Clinical Orthopaedics and Related Research, 165,* 239–252.

McAdams, D.P., de St. Aubin, E., & Logan, R.L. (1993). Generativity among young, midlife, and older adults. *Psychology and Aging, 8* (2), 221–230.

McCandless, B. & Bardarah, J. (1991). The church confronting adult depression: A challenge. Special issue: Depression and religion. *Counseling and Values, 35* (2), 104–113.

McCary, J. (1978). *McCary's human sexuality*. New York: Van Nostrand Reinhold.

McClintock, M. & Herdt, G. (1996). Rethinking puberty: The development of sexual attraction. *Current Directions in Psychological Science, 5,* 178–183.

McCrae, R. & Costa, P. T., Jr. (1984). *Emerging lives, enduring dispositions: Personality in adulthood*. Boston: Little, Brown.

McEvoy, G. M. & Cascio, W. F. (1989). Cumulative evidence of the relationship between employee age and job performance. *Journal of Applied Psychology, 74,* 11–17.

McGaugh, J. L., Coleman-Mesches, K., & West, M. A. (1997). Opposite effects on two different measures of retention following unilateral inactivation of the amygdala. *Behavioral Brain Research, 86* (1), 17–23.

McGaugh, J.L. & Guzowski, J.F. (1997). Antisense oligodeoxynucleotide-mediated disruption of hippocampal cAMP response element binding protein levels impairs consolidation of memory for water maze training. *Proceedings of the National Academy of Sciences, 94* (6), 2693–2698.

McGhee, P. & Panoutsopoulou, T. (1995). The role of cognitive factors in children's metaphor and humor comprehension. *International Journal of Humor Research, 3* (2), 119–146.

McGue, M., Sharma, A., & Benson, P. (1996). The effect of common rearing on adolescent adjustment: Evidence from a U.S. adoption cohort. *Developmental Psychology, 32* (4), 604–613.

McKusick, V. (1992). *Mendelian inheritance in man: Catalogs of autosomal dominant, autosomal recessive, and X-linked phenotypes* (10th ed.). Baltimore: Johns Hopkins University Press.

McNeill, J. (1995). *Freedom, glorious freedom.* Boston: Beacon.

Mead, M. (1972, April). *Long living in cross-sectional perspective.* Paper presented to the Gerontological Society, San Juan, Puerto Rico.

Mech, E., Pryde, J., & Rycraft, J. R. (1995). Mentors for adolescents in foster care. *Child & Adolescent Social Work Journal, 12* (4), 317–328.

Menyuk, P., Liebergott, J., & Schultz, M. (1995). *Early language development in full-term and premature infants.* Hillsdale, NJ: Erlbaum.

Meshot, C. & Leitner, L. (1992–93). Adolescent mourning and parental death. *Death Studies, 17* (4), 319–332.

Meston, C.M., Trapnell, P.D., & Gorzalka, B.B. (1996). Ethnic and gender differences in sexuality: Variations in sexual behavior between Asian and non-Asian university students. *Archives of Sexual Behavior, 25* (1), 33–72.

Michael, R., Gagman, J., Laumann, E., & Kolata, G. (1994). *Sex in America.* Boston: Little, Brown.

Mintz, B. I. & Betz, N. E. (1988). Prevalence and correlates of eating disordered behaviors among undergraduate women. *Journal of Counseling Psychology, 35,* 463–471.

Mischel, H. & Mischel, W. (1983). The development of children's knowledge of self-control strategies. *Child Development, 54,* 603–619.

Mishara, B.L. (1996). A dynamic developmental model of suicide. *Human Development, 39,* 181–194.

Mitchell, C. M., O'Neil, T. D., Beals, J., Dick, R. W., Keane, E., & Manson, S. M. (1996). Dimensionality of alcohol use among American Indian adolescents: Latent structure, construct validity, and implications for developmental research. *Journal of Research on Adolescence, 6,* 151–180.

Mok, B. & Mui, A. (1996). Empowerment in residential care for the elders: The case of an aged home in Hong Kong. *Journal of Gerontological Social Work, 27* (1/2).

Molina, B. S. G., & Chassin, L. (1996). The parent-adolescent relationship at puberty: Hispanic ethnicity and parent alcoholism as moderators. *Developmental Psychology, 32* (4) 675–686.

Montero, I., Ruiz, I., & Hernandez, I. (1993). Social functioning as a significant factor in women's help-seeking behavior during the climacteric period. *Social Psychiatry and Psychiatric Epidemiology, 28,* 178–183.

Montgomery, R., Haemmerlie, F., & Zoellner, S. (1996). The "imaginary audience," self-handicapping and drinking patterns among college students. *Psychological Reports, 79,* (3), 783–785.

Moore, B. N. & Parker, R. (1986). *Critical thinking.* Mountain View, CA: Mayfield Publishing Co.

Moore, E. W., McCann, H., & McCann, J. (1985). *Creative and critical thinking.* Boston, MA: Houghton Mifflin.

Moore, K. & Persaud, T. (1998). *Before we are born: Essentials of embryology and birth defects.* Philadelphia: Saunders.

Moore, K. & Persaud, T. (1998). *Before we are born* (4th ed.). Philadelphia: Saunders.

Moore, M. (1997). *Nutritional care.* St. Louis: Mosby.

Moore, R. (1995). Psychological factors and the etiology of binge eating. *Addictive Behaviors, 20* (6), 713–723.

Morgan, L. A. (1991). *After marriage ends: Economic consequences for midlife women.* London: Sage.

Morris, J. (1974, July). Conundrum. *Ms.,* 57–64.

Moukwa, M. (1995). A structure to foster creativity: An industrial experience. *Journal of Creative Behavior, 29* (1), 54–63.

Muller, C. F. & Boaz, R. F. (1988). Health

as a reason or a rationalization for being retired? *Research on Aging, 10* (1), 37–55.

Murphy, S.A. (1996). Parent bereavement stress and preventive intervention following the violent deaths of adolescent or young adult children. *Death Studies, 20* (5), 441–452.

Murray, B. (1997a). Our 20s appear to be the age we can't forget. *APA Monitor, 28* (10), 24.

Murray, B. (1997b). Elderly people alter their social priorities as they age. *APA Monitor, 28* (10), 25.

Murray, B. (1997c). Psychologist help ease caregivers' stress. *APA Monitor, 28* (10), 26.

Murrell, A.J., Olson, J.E., & Frieze, I.H. (1995). Sexual harassment and gender discrimination: A longitudinal study of women managers. *Journal of Social Issues, 51* (1), 139–149.

Muuss, R. E. (1996). *Theories of Adolescence* (7th ed). New York: McGraw-Hill.

Nakonezny, P.A., Shull, R.D., & Rodgers, J.L. (1995). The effect of no-fault divorce law on the divorce rate across the 50 states and its relation to income, education, and religiosity. *Journal of Marriage and the Family, 57* (2), 477–488.

Naleppa, M. (1996). Families and the institutionalized elderly. *Journal of Gerontological Social Work, 27* (1/2).

National Center for Education Statistics. (1992). *American education at a glance.* Washington, DC: Office of Educational Research and Improvement.

National Center for Health Statistics. (1995). *Healthy people 2000.* Hyattsville, MD: Public Health Service.

National Council of Teachers of Mathematics. (1989). Curriculum and evaluation standards for school mathematics. Reston, VA.

National Institute for Health Statistics. (1994). *Obesity in the American population.* Washington, DC: U.S. Government Printing Office.

National Institute of Allergy and Infectious Diseases. (1987). *STDA.* Atlanta: Centers for Disease Control.

National Institute on Aging. (1993). Forgetfulness in old age: It's not what you think. *Age page.* U.S. Department of Health and Human Services.

Neale, A., Hwalek, M., Goodrich, C., & Quinn, K. (1996). The Illinois elder abuse system: Program description &

administrative findings. *The Gerontologist, 36,* 502–511.

Neugarten, B. (Ed.). (1968). *Middle age and aging.* Chicago: University of Chicago Press.

Neugarten, B. & Moore, J. (1968). The changing age-status system. In B. Neugarten (Ed.), *Middle age and aging.* Chicago: Univ. of Chicago Press.

Neugarten, B. L. & Weinstein, K. K. (1964). The changing American grandparent. *Journal of Marriage and the Family, 26,* 199–206.

Newcomb, M., Bukowski, W., & Pattee, L. (1993). Children's peer relations: A meta-analytic review of popular, rejected, neglected, controversial, and average sociometric status. *Psychological Bulletin, 113,* 99–128.

Newman, D., Caspi, A., Moffitt, T., & Silva, P. (1997). Antecedents of adult interpersonal functioning: Effects of individual differences in age 3 temperament. *Developmental Psychology, 33* (2), 206–217.

Nilsson, L., Furuhjelm, M., Ingleman-Sundberg, A., & Wirsen, C. (1993). *A child is born.* New York: Delacorte.

Niijhuis, J. (Ed.) (1992). *Fetal behavior: Developmental and perinatal aspects.* New york: Oxford University Press.

Nilsson, L. G. (1995). Dissociated effects of elaboration on memory of enacted and non-enacted events. *Psychological Research, 36* (2), 225–233.

Nolinske, T. (1995). Multiple mentoring relationships facilitate learning during fieldwork. *American Journal of Occupational Therapy, 49* (1), 39–43.

Nugent, K., Lester, B., & Brazelton, B. (1995). *The cultural context of infancy.* Norwood, NJ: Ablex.

Nurmi, J. (1992). Age differences in adult life goals, concerns, and their temporal extension: A life course approach to future-oriented motivation. *International Journal of Behavioral Development, 15* (4), 487–508.

O'Connor, D. & Wolfe, D.M. (1991). From crisis to growth at midlife: Changes in personal paradigm. *Journal of Organizational Behavior, 12,* 323–340.

O'Conor, A. (1995). Breaking the silence. In G. Unks (Ed.), *The gay teen.* New York: Routledge.

Olds, S., London, M., & Ladewig, P. (1996). *Maternal-newborn nursing.* Reading, MA: Addison-Wesley.

Olweus, D. (1982). Development of stable aggression reaction patterns in males. In R. Blanchard & C. Blanchard (Eds.). *Advances in the study of aggression.* Vol. 1 New York: Academic.

Olweus, D. (1993). *Bullying at school: What we know and what we can do.* Cambridge, England: Oxford.

Olweus, D. (1995). Bullying or peer abuse at school: Facts and interventions. (1995). *Current directions in psychological science. 4* (6), 196–200.

Ornstein, R. & Sobel, D. (1987). *The healing brain.* New York: Simon & Schuster.

Ossip-Klein, D. J., Doyne, E. J., Bowman, E. D., Osborn, K. M., McDougall-Wilson, I. B., & Neimeyer, R. A. (1989). Effects of running or weight lifting on self-concept in clinically depressed women. *Journal of Consulting and Clinical Psychology, 57,* 158–161.

Ottesen, C. C. (1993). *L. A. Stories.* Yarmouth, ME: Intercultural Press.

Owens, W. (1953). Aging and mental abilities. *Genetic Psychology Monographs, 48,* 3–54.

Oyserman, D. & Markus, H. (1990). Possible selves in balance: Implications for delinquency. *Journal of Social Issues, 46* (2), 141–157.

Palmer, C.T. & Tiller, C.F. (1995). Sexual access to females as a motivation for joining gangs: An evolutionary approach. *The Journal of Sex Research, 32,* 213–217.

Palmore, E. (1985). How to live longer and like it. *Journal of Applied Gerontology 4,* (2) 1–8.

Park, S., Belsky, J., Putnam, S., & Crnic, K. (1997). Infant emotionality, parenting, and 3-year inhibition: Exploring stability and lawful discontinuity in a male sample. *Developmental Psychology, 33* (2), 218–227.

Parke, R. (1996). *Fatherhood.* Cambridge, MA: Harvard University Press.

Patterson, C. (1995). Special section: Sexual orientation & human development. *Developmental Psychology, 31,* 3–140.

Paul, R. W. (1987). Dialogical thinking. In J. B. Baron & R. J. Sternberg (Eds.), *Teaching thinking skills.* New York: W. H. Freeman.

Pearlman, C. (1972, November). Frequency of intercourse in males at different ages. *Medical Aspects of Human Sexuality,* 92–113.

Perkins, D., Jay, E., & Tishman. (1993).

Introduction: New conceptions of thinking. Educational Psychologist, 28, 67–85.

Perry, W. (1968a). *Forms of intellectual and ethical development in the college years.* New York: Holt, Rinehart & Winston.

Perry, W. (1968b, April). *Patterns of development in thought and values of students in a liberal arts college: A validation of a scheme.* Washington, DC: U.S. Department of Health, Education, and Welfare, Office of Education, Bureau of Research. Final report.

Perry, W. (1981). Cognitive and ethical growth. In A. Chickering (Ed.), *The modern American college.* San Francisco: Jossey-Bass.

Peters, J. (1997). *When mothers work.* Reading, MA: Addison-Wesley.

Petersen, A. C., Crockett, I., Richards, M., & Boxer, A. (1988). A self-report measure of pubertal status. *Journal of Youth and Adolescence, 17,* 117–134.

Petersen, A., Leffert, N., & Graham, B. (1995). Adolescent development and the emergence of sexuality. *Suicide and Life Threatening Behavior, 25,* 4–17

Petersen, A.C., Compas, B.E., Brooks–Gunn, J., Stemmler, M., Ey, S., & Grant, K.E. (1993, February). Depression in adolescence. *American Psychologist,* 155–168.

Petherbridge, J. (1996). Debriefing work experience: A reflection on reflection? *British Journal of Guidance & Counseling, 24* (2), 243–257.

Pfaff, W. (1997). *The future of the U.S. as a great power.* Pittsburgh: Carnegie Council on Ethics and International Affairs.

Phinney, J.S. (1996). When we talk about American ethnic groups, what do we mean? *American Psychologist, 51* (9), 918–927.

Phinney, J.S. & Alipuria, L.L. (1990). Ethnic identity in college students from four ethnic groups. *Journal of Adolescence, 13,* 171–183.

Piaget, J. (1926). *The language and thought of the child.* New York: Harcourt, Brace, and World.

Piaget, J. (1932). *The moral judgment of the child.* New York: Macmillan.

Piaget, J. (1952). *The origins of intelligence in children.* New York: International Universities Press.

Piaget, J. (1966). *Psychology of intelligence.* Totowa, NJ: Littlefield, Adams, & Co.

Piaget, J. (1967). *Six psychological studies.* New York: Random House.

Piaget, J. (1973). *The child and reality.* New York: Viking.

Piaget, J., and Inhelder, B. (1969). *The psychology of the child.* New York: Basic.

Pike, A., McGuire, S., Hetherington, E.M., Reiss, D., & Plomin, R. (1996). Family environment and adolescent depressive symptoms and antisocial behavior: A multivariate genetic analysis. *Developmental Psychology, 32* (4), 590–603.

Pipher, M. (1994). *Reviving Ophelia.* New York: Ballantine.

Pipp-Siegel, S. & Foltz, C. (1997). Toddlers' acquisition of self/other knowledge: Ecological and interpersonal aspects of self and other. *Child Development, 68* (1), 69–79.

Pi-Sunyer, F. X. (1994). The fattening of America. *The Journal of the American Medical Association, 272* (3), 238.

Pizer, H. (Ed.). (1983). *Over fifty-five, healthy and alive.* New York: Van Nostrand Reinhold.

Plomin, R., DeFries, J., McClearn, G., & Rutter, M. (1997). *Behavioral genetics: A primer* (3d ed.). New York: Freeman.

Plomin, R., Reiss, D., Hetherington, E. M. & Howe, G. (1994). Nature and nurture: Genetic contributions to measures of the family environment. *Developmental Psychology, 30* (1), 32–43.

Pohl, J. M., Given, C. W., Collins, C.E., & Given, B.A. (1994). Social vulnerability and reactions to caregiving in daughters and daughters-in-law caring for disabled aging parents. *Health Care for Women International, 15,* 385–395.

Pollock, R. (1995). A test of conceptual models depicting the developmental course of informal mentor protege relationships in the work place. *Journal of Vocational Behavior* (46) 146–162.

Ponder, R. & Pomeroy, E. (1996). The grief of caregivers. *Journal of Gerontological Social Work, 27* (1/2). The Haworth Press, Inc.

Popenoe, D. (1996). *Life without father.* New York: Martin Kessler Books.

Powell, C. (1996). *My American journey.* New York: Random House.

Pritham, U., & Sammaons, L. (1993). Korean's women's attitudes toward pregnancy and prenatal care. *Health Care, Women Int, 14,* 145.

Prosser, J. & McArdle, P. (1996). The changing mental health of children and adolescents: Evidence for a deterioration? *Psychological Medicine, 26* (4) 715–725.

Range, L. M. & Stringer, T.A. (1996). Reasons for living and coping abilities among older adults. *International Journal of Aging and Human Development, 43* (1), 1–5.

Raymo, C. (1996). Searching for a metaphor for the miraculous. *The Boston Globe,* January 15.

Reed-Victor, E. & Stronge, J. (1997). Building resiliency: Constructive directions for homeless education. *Journal of Children and Poverty, 3* (1), 67–91.

Reimer, M. (1996). "Sinking into the ground": The development and consequences of shame in adolescence. *Developmental Review, 16* (4), 321–357

Reinke, B., Ellicott, A., Harris, R., & Hancock, E. (1985). Timing of psychosocial change in women's lives. *Human Development, 28,* 259–280.

Remafedi, G. (1988). Homosexual youth. *Journal of the American Medical Association, 258* (2), 222–225.

Restak, R. (1991). *The brain has a mind of its own.* New York: Crown.

Reyes, B. (1997, October 13). More marrying outside of racial group, data show. Boston: *The Boston Globe* (Associated Press), p. A1.

Rhodes, S. (1983). Age-related differences in work attitudes and behavior: A review and conceptual analysis. *Psychological Bulletin, 93,* 328–367.

Rierdan, J., Koff, E., & Stubbs, M. (1988). *A longitudinal analysis of body image as a predictor of the onset and persistence of adolescent girls' depression.* Working Paper No. 188, Wellesley College Center for Research on Women.

Robak, R.W. & Weitzman, S.P. (1994–95). Grieving the loss of romantic relationships in young adults: An empirical study of disenfranchised grief. *Omega Journal of Death and Dying, 30* (4), 269–281.

Roche, J. & Ramsbey, T.W. (1993). Premarital sexuality: A five-year follow-up study of attitudes and behavior by dating stage. *Adolescence, 28* (109), 67–80.

Roche, J. & Tucker, S. (1997). *Youth in society.* London: Sage.

Rodgers, J., Harris, D.F., & Vickers, K.B. (1992). Seasonality of first coitus in the United States. *Social Biology, 39* (1/2), 1–14.

Rogoff, B. (1990). *Apprenticeship in thinking: Cognitive development in social context.* New York: Oxford University Press.

Rogosh, F., Cicchetti, D., Shields, A., & Toth, S. (1995). Parenting dysfunction in child maltreatment. In Bornstein, M. (Ed.), *Handbook of parenting.* Mahwah, NJ: Erlbaum.

Rose, L. (Sept., 1995). The 27th Annual Phi Delta Kappa/Gallup Poll of the Public's Attitudes Towards the Public Schools. *Phi Delta Kappan, 77* (1), 41–59.

Rose, S. (1990). *Neurobiology of learning and memory.* NJ: World Scientific.

Rosen, E. I. (1987). *Bitter choices: Blue-collar women in and out of work.* Chicago: Univ. of Chicago Press.

Rosenthal, S. (1996, July). Identifying risk-taking in teen girls. *Ob.Gyn. News,* p. 12.

Rosin, H. M. (1990). The effects of dual career participation on men: Some determinants of variation in career and personal satisfaction. *Human Relations, 43* (2), 169–182.

Ross, H. (1996). Negotiating principles of entitlement in sibling property disputes. *Developmental Psychology, 32* (1), 90–101.

Ross, H.M. (1994). "Meanings adult daughters attach to a parent's death": Comment. *Western Journal of Nursing Research, 16* (4), 361–362.

Rossi, A.S. (Ed.) (1994). *Sexuality across the life course.* Chicago: The University Chicago Press.

Rothbart, M. (1994). Emotioanl development: Changes in reactivity and self-regulation. In Paul ekman & Richard Davidson (Eds.). *The nature of emotion.* Oxford University Press, 1994.

Rowland, D.L., Greenleaf, W.J., Dorfman, L.J., & Davidson, J.M. (1993). Aging and sexual function in men. *Archives of Sexual Behavior, 22* (6), 545–557.

Rubin, R. (1995). *Maternal identity and maternal experience.* New York: Springer.

Rubin, S.S. & Schechter, N. (1997). Exploring the social construction of bereavement: Perceptions of adjustment and recovery in bereaved men. *American Journal of Orthopsychiatry, 67* (2), 279–289.

Ruffman, T. & Keenan, T. (1996). The belief-based emotion of surprise: The case for a lag in understanding relative to false belief. *Developmental Psychology, 32* (1), 40–49.

Rushton, J. & Ankney, C. D. (1997). Brain size and cognitive ability. *Psychonomic Bulletin and Review, 3,* (1), 21–36.

Russell, C. H. (1989). *Good news about aging*. New York: Wiley.

Rutter, M. (1981). *Maternal deprivation reassessed*. New York: Penguin.

Rutter, M. (1983). School effects on pupil progress: Research findings and policy implications. *Child Development, 54*, 1–29.

Rutter, M. (1996). Maternal deprivation. In Marc Bornsteinn (ED.), *Handbook of Parenting*, Vol. 4: Applied and Practical Parenting. Mahwah, NJ: Lawrence Erlbaum.

Rutter, M. (1997). Nature-nurture integration: The example of antisocial behavior. *American psychologist, 52* (4), 390–398.

Ryan, G. & Lane, S. (1997). *Juvenile sexual offending*. San Fransisco: Jossey-Bass.

Rymer, R. (1993). *Genie: A scientific tragedy*. New York: Harper.

Sales, E. (1978). Women's adult development. In I. Fieze (Ed.), *Women and sex roles*. New York: W. W. Norton.

Salthouse, T. (1990). Cognitive competence and expertise in aging. In *Handbook of the psychology of aging*. New York: Academic Press.

Saluter, A. F. (1991). *Marital status and living arrangements: March 1991*. Current Population Reports, P-20 (No. 461). Washington, DC: Bureau of the Census.

Sanday, P.R. (1990). *Fraternity gang rape: Sex. brotherhood, and privilege on campus*. New York: New York University Press.

Sanders, G. F. & Mullis, R. L. (1988). Family influences on sexual attitudes and knowledge as reported by college students. *Adolescence, 23* (92), 837–846.

Sansavini, A., Bertoncici, J., & Giovanelli, G. (1997). Newborns discriminate the rhythm of multisyllabic words. *Developmental Psychology, 33* (1), 3–11.

Sanyika, D. (1996). Gang rites and rituals of initiation. In L.C. Mahdi, N.G. Christopher, & M. Meade (Eds.), *Gang behavior*. Chicago: Open Court.

Saul, J. (1997). Adult education and religion. *Adult Education Quarterly, 47* (3/4), 169.

Saunders, J. B. (1989). The efficacy of treatment for drinking problems. Special issue: Psychiatry and the addictions. *International Review of Psychiatry, 1*, 121–137.

Savin-Williams, R. C. (1995). An exploratory study of pubertal maturation timing and self-esteem among gay and bisexual male youths. Special Issue: Sexual orientation and human development. *Developmental Psychology, 31*, 56–64.

Savin-Williams, R. C. & Berndt, T. J. (1990). Friendship and peer relations. In S. Feldman & G. Elliot (Eds.), *At the threshold: The developing adolescent*. Cambridge, MA: Harvard University Press.

Schacter, D. (1996). *Searching for memory*. New York: Basic Books.

Schaie, K. W. & Hertzog, C. (1983). Fourteen-year cohort-sequential analyses of adult intellectual development. *Developmental Psychology, 19*, 531–543.

Scharlach, A.E. & Fuller-Thomson, E. (1994). Coping strategies following the death of an elderly parent. *Journal of Gerontological Social Work, 21* (3/4), 85–100.

Scheidlinger, S. (1994). A commentary on adolescent group violence. *Child Psychiatry and Human Development, 25*, 3–11.

Schoem, D. (1991). *Inside separate worlds: Life stories of young Blacks, Jews, and Latinos*. Ann Arbor: University of Michigan Press.

Schofferman, J. (1987). Hospice care of the patient with AIDS. *The Hospice Journal, 3*, 51–84.

Schroedel, J. R. (1990). Blue-collar women: Paying the price at home on the job. In H. Y. Grossman & N. L. Chester (Eds.), *The experience and meaning of work in women's lives*. Hillsdale, NJ: Erlbaum.

Schulenberg, J., Wadsworth, K. N., O'Malley, P. M., Bachman, J. G., & Johnston, L.D. (1996). Adolescent risk factors for binge drinking during the transition to young adulthood: Variable- and pattern-centered approaches to change. *Developmental Psychology, 32,* (4), 659–673.

Schulz, R. & Ewen, R. B. (1988). *Adult development and aging: Myths and emerging realities*. New York: Macmillan.

Schwartz, D., Dodge, K., & Coie, J. (1993). The emergence of chronic peer victimization in boys' play groups. *Child Development, 64*, 1755–1772.

Scott, D. (Ed.). (1988). *Anorexia and bulimia*. New York: New York University Press.

Sears, W. & Sears, M. (1994). *The birth book*. Boston: Little, Brown.

Sebald, H. (1977). *Adolescence: A social psychological analysis* (2nd ed.). Englewood Cliffs, NJ: Prentice-Hall.

Seifer, R., Schiller, M., & Sameroff, A. (1996). Attachment, maternal sensitivity, and infant temperament during the first year of life. *Developmental Psychology, 32* (1), 12–25.

Selman, R. L. & Schultz, L. H. (1990). *Making a friend in youth: Developmental theory and pair therapy*. Chicago: University of Chicago Press.

Selye, H. (1956). *The stress of life*. New York: McGraw-Hill.

Selye, H. (1975, October). Implications of stress concept. *New York State Journal of Medicine*, 2139–2145.

Selye, H. (1982). History and present status of the stress concept. In L. Goldberger & S. Breznitz (Eds.), *Handbook of stress: Theoretical and clinical aspects*. New York: The Free Press.

Seppa, N. (1996). Rwanda starts its long healing process. *The APA Monitor* (August, 1996), 14.

Seppa, N. (1997, March). What defines a man today? *APA Monitor,* pp. 1, 12.

Serakan, U. (1989). Understanding the dynamics of self-concept of members in dual-career families. *Human Relations, 42* (2), 97–116.

Shade, B. (1987). Ecological correlates of the educative style of Afro-American children. *Journal of Negro Education, 56*, 88–99.

Shahtahmasebi, S., Davies, R., & Wenger, G. C. (1992). A longitudinal analysis of factors related to survival in old age. *The Gerontologist, 32* (3), 404–413.

Shanker, A. (1995). *Where we stand*. New York Times.

Shapiro, B. (1997). Researchers questions the way society grieves. *APA Monitor, 28* (10), 36.

Shatz, C. (1996). Emergence of order in visual system development. *Journal of Physiology, 90* (3–4), 141–150.

Sheehy, G. (1992). *The silent passage: Menopause*. New York: Random House.

Shek, D.T.L. (1995). Gender differences in marital quality and well-being in Chinese married adults. *Sex Roles, 32* (11/12), 699–715.

Shek, D.T.L. (1995). Marital quality and psychological well-being of married adults in a Chinese context. *The Journal of Genetic Psychology, 156* (1), 45–56.

Siegel, J. & Shaughnessy, M. (1995). There is a first time for everything: Understanding adolescence. *Adolescence, 30* (117), 217–221.

Siegler, I. (1975). The terminal drop

hypothesis: Fact or artifact? *Experimental Aging Research, 1,* 169.

Sigelman, C.K., Estrada, A.L., Derenowski, E.B., & Woods, T.E. (1996). Intuitive theories of human immunodeficiency virus transmission: Their development and implications. *Journal of Pediatric Psychology, 21* (4), 555–572.

Silverstein, L.B. (1991). Transforming the debate about child care and maternal employment. *American Psychologist, 46 (10),* 1025–1032.

Simonton, D. K. (1975). Age and literary creativity. *Journal of Cross-Cultural Creativity, 6,* 259–277.

Simonton, D. K. (1976). Biographical determinants of achieved eminence. *Journal of Personality and Social Psychology, 33,* 218–276.

Simonton, D. K. (1977a). Creativity, age and stress. *Journal of Personality and Social Psychology, 35,* 791–804.

Simonton, D. K. (1977b). Eminence, creativity and geographical marginality. *Journal of Personality and Social Psychology, 35,* 805–816.

Simonton, D. K. (1993). Blind variation, chance configurations, and creative genius. *Psychological Inquiries, 4,* 225–228.

Simpson, J.A., Rholes, W.S., & Phillips, D. (1996). Conflict in close relationships: An attachment perspective. *Journal of Personality and Social Psychology, 71* (5), 899–914.

Sims, J. M. (1996). The use of voice for assessment and intervention in couples therapy. *Women and Therapy, 19* (3), 61–77.

Skinner, B. F. (1938). *The behavior of organisms.* New York: Macmillan.

Skinner, B. F. (1953). *Science and human nature.* New York: Macmillan.

Skinner, B. F. (1968). *The technology of teaching.* New York: Appleton-Century-Crofts.

Skinner, B. F. (1971). *Beyond freedom and dignity.* New York: Knopf.

Skinner, B. F. (1974). *About behaviorism.* New York: Knopf.

Skinner, B. F. (1983). *A matter of consequences.* New York: Knopf.

Skinner, B. F. (1984). The shame of American Education. *American Psychologist* (September), 947–954.

Skinner, B. F. (1986). Some thoughts about the future. *Journal of the Experimental Analysis of Behavior* (March), 229–235.

Slaby, R. (1990, Spring). Gender concept development legacy. *New Directions for Psychology, 47,* 21–29.

Sleek, S. (1997). Weisel emphasizes need to thank elderly. *APA Monitor, 28* (10), 23.

Slomkowski, C. & Dunn, J. (1996). Young children's understanding of other people's beliefs and feelings and their connected communication with friends. *Developmental Psychology, 32* (3), 442–447.

Small, B. & Backman, L. (1997). Cognitive correlates of mortality. *Psychology and Aging, 12,* (2), 309–314.

Small, S. A. & Luster, T. (1994). An ecological, risk-factor approach to adolescent sexual activity. *Journal of Marriage and the Family, 56,* 181–192.

Smith, B. & Blass, E. (1996). Tast-mediated calming in premature, preterm, and full-term infants. *Developmental Psychology, 32* (6), 1084–1089.

Smith, B. K. (1989). *Grandparenting in today's world.* Austin, TX: Hogg Foundation for Mental Health.

Smith, D. W. E., Seibert, C. S., Jackson, F. W., & Snell, J. (1992). Pet ownership by elderly people: Two new issues. *International Journal of Aging and Human Development, 34* (3), 175–184.

Smith, R. (1990). *A theoretical framework for explaining the abuse of hyperactive children.* Unpublished doctoral dissertation, Boston College, Chestnut Hill, MA.

Smotherman, W. & Robinson, S. (1996). The development of behavior before birth. *Developmental Psychology, 33* (3), 425–434.

Snyder, H., Sickmund, M., & Poe-Yamagata, E. (1996). *Update on violence.* Washington, DC: Office of Justice.

South, S. J. (1993). Racial and ethnic differences in the desire to marry. *Journal of Marriage and the Family, 55,* 357–370.

Spence, A. (1989). *Biology of human aging.* Englewood Cliffs, NJ: Prentice-Hall.

Stambrook, M. & Parker, K. (1987). The development of the concept of death in childhood. *Merrill-Palmer Quarterly, 33,* 133–157.

Steefel, N.M. (1992). A divorce transition model. *Psychological Reports, 70,* 155–160.

Steers, W.N., Elliot, E., Nemiro, J., & Ditman, D. (1996). Health beliefs as predictors of HIV-preventive behavior and ethnic differences in prediction. *Journal of Social Psychology, 136* (1), 99–110.

Steinberg, L. (1990). Autonomy, conflict, and harmony in the family relationship. In S. Feldman & G. Elliot (Eds.), *At the threshold: The developing adolescent.* Cambridge, MA: Harvard University.

Stephens, M. & Townsend, A. (1997). Stress of parent care. *Psychology & Aging, 12* (2), 376–386.

Sternberg, R. (1986). *Intelligence applied.* New York: Harcourt Brace Jovanovich.

Sternberg, R. (1990). *Metaphors of mind: Conceptions of the nature of intelligence.* New York: Cambridge University Press.

Sternberg, R. (1996). *Successful intelligence.* New York: Simon & Schuster.

Sternberg, R. J. (1990). *Wisdom.* New York: Cambridge University Press.

Sternberg, R. J. (1986). The triangular theory of love. *Psychological Review, 93,* 129–135.

Sternberg, R. & Davidson, J. (1995). *The nature of insight.* Cambridge, MA: M. I. T. Press.

Sternberg, R. & Lubart, T. (1995). *Defying the crowd: Cultivating creativity in a culture of conformity.* New York: Free Press.

Sterns, H.L. & Miklos, S.M. (1995). The aging worker in a changing environment: Organizational and individual issues. *Journal of Vocational Behavior, 47,* 248–268.

Stevens, J. C. & Cain, W. S. (1987). Old-age deficits in the sense of smell as gauged by thresholds, magnitude matching, and odor identification. *Psychology and Aging, 2,* 36–42.

Stipek, D. & Ryan, R. (1997). Economically disadvantaged preschoolers: Ready to learn but further to go. *Developmental Psychology, 33* (4), 711–723.

St. Peters, M., Fitch, M., Huston, A., Wright, J., & Eakins, D. (1991). Television and families: What do young children watch with their parents? *Child Development, 62,* 1409–1423.

Stoller, E. P., Forster, L. E., & Duniho, T. S. (1992). Systems of parent care within sibling networks. *Research on Aging, 14* (1), 28–49.

Stossel, S. (May, 1997). The man who counts the killings. *Atlantic Monthly, 279* (5), 86–104.

Strawbridge, W. & Wallhagen, M. (1992). Is all in the family always best? *Journal of Aging Studies, 6* (1), 81–92.

Strough, J., Berg, C., & Sansone, C. (1996). Goals for solving everyday problems across the lifespan: Age and gender differences in the salience of interpersonal concerns. *Developmental Psychology, 32* (6), 1106–1115.

Subcommittee on Health and the Environment. (1987). *Incidence and control of chlamydia*. Washington, DC: U.S. Government Printing Office.

Sudnow, D. (1967). *Passing on*. Englewood Cliffs, NJ: Prentice-Hall.

Sue, S. & Sue, D.W. (1991). *Counseling the culturally different: Theory and practice*. New York: Wiley.

Sullivan, M. (1997). *The Boston College Chronicle*, Chestnut Hill, MA, pp. 1,5.

Sullivan, T. & Schneider, M. (1987). Development and identity issues in adolescent homosexuality. *Child and Adolescent Social Work Journal, 4* (1), 13–24.

Super, D. E. (1983). Assessment in career guidance: Toward truly developmental counseling. *Personnel and Guidance Journal, 61,* 555–562.

Super, D. E. (1990). A life-span, life-space approach to career development. In D. Brown, L. Brooks, & others (Eds.), *Career choice and development*. San Francisco: Jossey-Bass.

Swarr, A.E. & Richards, M.H. (1996). Longitudinal effects of adolescent girls' pubertal development, perceptions of pubertal timing, and parental relations on eating problems. *Developmental Psychology, 32* (4), 636–646.

Swedo, S., Rettew, D., Kuppenheimer, M., Lum, D., Dolan, S., & Goldberger, E. (1991). Can adolescent suicide-attempters be distinguished from at-risk adolescents? *Pediatrics, 88,* 620–629.

Tabourne, C. (1995). The effects of a life review program on disorientation, social interactions and self-esteem of nursing home residents. *International Journal of Aging & Human Development, 41,* 251–266.

Tada, W. & Stiles, J. (1997). Developmental changes in childrens' analysis of spatial patterns. *Developmental Psychology, 32* (5), 951–970.

Tanner, J. M. (1989). *Fetus into man*. Cambridge, MA: Harvard University Press.

Tate, D., Reppucci, N., & Mulvey, E. (1995). Violent juvenile delinquents. *American Psychologist, 50* (9), 777–781.

Taub, H. (1975). Effects of coding cues upon short-term memory. *Developmental Psychology, 11,* 254.

Tavalin, F. (1995). Context for creativity: Listening to voices, allowing a pause. *Journal of Creative Behavior, 29* (2), 133–142.

Taylor, M. (1996). The development of children's beliefs about social and biological aspects of gender. *Child Development, 67,* 1555–1571.

Taylor, N. (1995). Gay and lesbian youth. In DeCrescenzo, T. (Ed.), *Helping gay and lesbian youth*. New York: Haworth.

Taylor, R.D. (1996). Adolescents' perceptions of kinship support and family management practices: Association with adolescent adjustment in African American families. *Developmental Psychology, 32* (4), 687–695.

Taylor, R. D., Casten, R., Flickinger, S. M., Roberts, D., & Fulmore, C. D. (1994). Explaining the school performance of African-American adolescents. *Journal of Research on Adolescence, 4* (1), 21–44.

Temple, C. (1993). *The brain*. New York: Penguin.

Terman, L. M. (1925). *Genetic studies of genius*. Stanford, CA: Stanford University Press.

Thorndike, R., Hagan, E., & Satler, J. (1985). *The Stanford-Binet Intelligence Scale* (4th ed.). Chicago: Riverside.

Tingus, K.D., Heger, A.H., Foy, D.W., & Leskin, G.A. (1996). Factors associated with entry into therapy in children evaluated for sexual abuse. *Child Abuse and Neglect, 20* (1), 63–68.

Tirrito, T. (1996). Mental health problems and behavioral disruptions in nursing homes. *Journal of Gerontological Social Work, 27* (1/2), 73.

Todd, J., Friedman, A., & Karinki, P. (1990). Women growing stronger with age: The effect of status in the U.S. and Kenya. *Psychology of Women Quarterly, 14,* 567–577.

Tolbert, H. A. (1996). Psychoses in children and adolescents: A review. *Journal of Clinical Psychiatry, 57* (3), 4–8.

Tomada, G. & Schneider, B. (1997). Relational aggression, gender, and peer acceptance: Invariance across culture, stability overtime, and concordance among informants. *Developmental Psychology, 33* (4), 601–609.

Townsend, A. & Franks, M. (1995). Binding ties: Closeness and conflict in adult children's caregiving relationships. *Psychology & Aging, 10,* 343–350.

Travers, J., Elliott, S., & Kratochwill, T. (1993). *Educational psychology: Effective teaching, effective learning*. Dubuque, IA: Brown/Benchmark.

Tronick, E. (1989). Emotions and emotional communication in infants. *Child Development, 44,* 112–119.

Troumbley, P., Burman, K., Rinke, W., & Lenz, E. (1990). A comparison of the health risk, health status, self motivation, psychological symptomatic distress, and physical fitness of overweight and normal weight soldiers. *Military Medicine, 155* (9), 424–429.

Tully, T. & Yin, J.C. (1996). CREB and the formation of long-term memory. *Current Opinion on Neurobiology, 6* (2), 264–268.

Turner, J. S. & Helms, D. B. (1989). *Contemporary adulthood*. New York: Holt, Rinehart & Winston.

Twomey, L., Taylor, J., & Furiss, B. (1983). Age changes in the bone density and structure of the lumbar vertebral column. *Journal of Anatomy, 136,* 15–25.

Uhlenberg, P., Cooney, T., & Boyd, R. (1990). Divorce for women after midlife. *Journals of Gerontology, 45,* 3–11.

Unger, R. & Crawford, M. (1996). *Woman and gender: A feminist psychology*. New York: McGraw-Hill.

U.S. Bureau of the Census. (1992). *Vital statistics*. Washington, DC: U.S. Government Printing Office.

U. S. Bureau of the Census. (1995). *Statistical Abstract of the United States*. Washington, DC: Government Printing Office.

U. S. Bureau of the Census. (1996). *Statistical Abstract of the United States*. Washington, DC: Government Printing Office.

U.S. National Center for Health Statistics. (1986). *Advance data from vital and health statistics, No. 125*. DHHS Pub. No. (PHS) 86–1250. Hyattsville, MD: Public Health Service.

U.S. National Center for Health Statistics. (1992). *Aging in the eighties*. Washington, DC: U.S. Government Printing Office.

U. S. Public Health Service. (1995). *Monthly statistics report, 43*.

Uzgiris, U. & Raeff, C. (1995). Play in parent-child interactions. In M. Bornstein (Ed.), *Handbook of parenting*. Hillsdale, NJ: Erlbaum.

Vaillant, G. (1977). *Adaptation to life*. Boston: Little, Brown.

VanderZanden, J. (1989). *Human development* (4th ed.). New York: Knopf.

Vanfear, C., & Zietlow, P. (1991). Toward a contingency approach to marital interaction: An empirical integration of three approaches. *Communication Monographs.*

Vaughan, V. & Litt, I. (1990). *Child and adolescent development: Clinical implications.* Philadelphia, PA: W. B. Saunders.

Verbrugge, L.M. (1989). The twain meet: Empirical explanations of sex differences in health and mortality. *Journal of Health and Social Behavior, 30,* 282–304.

Vigil, J. D. (1996). Street baptism: Chicano gang initiation. *Human Organization, 55,* 149–153.

Vygotsky, L. S. (1978). *Mind in society.* Cambridge, MA: Harvard University Press.

Wachowiak, F. & Clements, R. (1997). *Emphasis art.* Reading, MA: Addison Wesley.

Wacks, V., Jr. (1994). Realizing our inner elder-child. *Journal of Humanistic Psychology, 34* (4), 78–100.

Wakschlag, L. Chase-Lansdale, P., & Brooks-Gunn, J. (1996). Not just "Ghosts in the Nursery": Contemporaneous intergenerational relationships and parenting in young African-American families. *Child Development, 67,* 2131–2147.

Wallace, J.B. (1992). Reconsidering the life review: The social construction of talk about the past. *The Gerontologist, 32* (1), 120–125.

Wallerstein, J. (1988). *Children of divorce.* Corte Modera, CA: Center for the Family in Transition.

Walther, R. R. & Harber, L. C. (1984). Expected skin complaints of the geriatric patient. *Geriatrics, 39,* 67.

Warabi, T., Kase, M., & Kato, T. (1984). Effect of aging on the accuracy of visually guided saccadic eye movement. *Annals of Neurology, 16,* 449–454.

Warren, S. B. (1992). Lower threshold for referral for pyschiatric treatment for adopted adolescents. *Journal of the American Academy of Child and Adolescent Psychiatry, 31,* 518–524.

Washington, A. E., Arno, P. S., & Brooks, M. A. (1986). The economic cost of pelvic inflammatory disease. *Journal of the American Medical Association, 225* (13), 1021–1033.

Watson, M. (1995). The relation between anxiety and pretend play. In A. Slade & D. Wolf (Eds.), *Children at play.* New York: Oxford University Press.

Weber, M. (1904). *The protestant ethic and the spirit of capitalism.* New York: Charles Scribner's Sons.

Wechsler, D. (1955). *Manual for the Wechsler adult intelligence test.* New York: Psychological Corp.

Wechsler, D. (1958). *The measurement and appraisal of adult intelligence.* Baltimore: Williams & Wilkins.

Wechsler, D. (1981) *Wechsler adult intelligence scale* (revised). New York: Psychological Corporation.

Wechsler, D. (1989). *Wechsler preschool and primary scale of intelligence* (revised). San Antonio, TX: Psychological Corporation.

Wechsler, D. (1991). *Wechsler intelligence scale for children* (3rd ed.). San Antonio, TX: Psychological Corporation.

Wechsler, H. (1996). Alcohol and the American college campus: A report from the Harvard School of Public Health. *Change, 7/8,* 20–25, 60–62.

Weiner, I. B. (1992). Psychological disturbance in adolescence (2nd Ed.) New York: Wiley.

Weeks, D. (1989). Death education for aspiring physicians, teachers, and the funeral directors. *Death Studies, 13,* 17–24.

Weinraub, M. & Gringlas, M. (1995). Single parenthood. In M. Bornstein (Ed.). *Handbook of parenting.* Vol. 3. Mahwah, NJ: Lawrence Erlbaum.

Weinrich, J. D. (1987). A new sociobiological theory of homosexuality applicable to societies with universal marriage. *Ethology and Sociobiology, 8* (1), 37–47.

Weiss, L., Farrar, E., & Petrie, H. (1989). *Dropouts from school: Issues, dilemmas, and solutions.* Albany, NY: State University of New York Press.

Weissbourd, R. (1996). *The vulnerable child.* Reading, MA: Addison Wesley.

Welte, J.W. & Mirand, A.L. (1995). Drinking, problem drinking and life stressors in the elderly general population. *Journal of Studies on Alcohol, 56* (1), 67–73.

Werner, E. & Smith, R. (1992). *Overcoming the odds: High risk children from birth to adulthood.* Ithaca: Cornell University Press.

Wertsch, J. & Tulviste, P. (1992). L.S. Vygotsky and contemporary developmental psychology. *Developmental Psychology, 28* (4), 548–557.

Whalen, C.K., Henker, B., Hollingshead, J., & Burgess, S. (1996). Parent-adolescent dialogues about AIDS. *Journal of Family Psychology, 10* (3), 343–357.

Whisett, D. & Land, H. (1992). Role strain, coping and marital satisfaction of stepparents. *Families in Society: The Journal of Contemporary Human Services,* 79–91.

Whitaker, R. & Dietz, W (1997). Predicting obesity in young adulthood from childhood and parental obesity. New England Journal of Medicine, 337 (13), 869–873.

Whitbeck, L. B., Simons, R. L., & Kao, M. (1994). The effects of divorced mothers' dating behaviors and sexual attitudes on the sexual attitudes and behaviors of their adolescent children. *Journal of Marriage and the Family, 56,* 615–621.

Whitbeck, L., Hoyt, D.R., & Huck, S.M. (1994). Early family relationships, intergenerational solidarity, and support provided to parents by their adult children. *Journal of Gerontology: Social Sciences, 49* (2), S85–S94.

Whitbeck, L.B. & Hoyt, D.R. (1991). Campus prestige and dating behaviors. *College Student Journal, 25* (4), 457–469.

White, D. (1997, October 15). The change that comes over men. Boston: *The Boston Globe,* p. D1.

White, L. (1992). The effect of parental divorce and remarriage on parental support for adult children. *Journal of Family Issues, 13* (2), 234–250.

White, M. (1994). *Stranger at the gate.* New York: Simon & Schuster.

White, N. & Cunningham, W. R. (1988). Is terminal drop pervasive or specific? *Journals of Gerontology, 43* (6), 141–144.

White, T. (1975). *Breach of faith.* NY: Atheneum.

Whitehead, A. & Mathews, A. (1986). Factors related to successful outcome in the treatment of sexually unresponsive women. *Psychological Medicine, 16* (2), 373–378.

Whiting, W.L. IV, & Smith, A.D. (1997). Differential age-related processing limitations in recall and recognition tasks. *Psychology and Aging, 12* (2) 216–224.

Who's Who Special Report. (1997). *What parents of top teens don't know about their kids.* Lake Forest, IL: Educational Communications.

Wickrama, K.A.S., Lorenz, F.O., Conger, R.D., & Elder, G.H. (1997). Marital quality and physical illness: A latent growth curve analysis. *Journal of Marriage and the Family, 59* (1), 143–155.

Wiederman, M.W., Pryor, T., & Morgan, C.D. (1996). The sexual experience of women diagnosed with anorexia nervosa or bulimia nervosa. *International Journal of Eating Disorders, 19* (2), 109–118.

Wierson, M., Long, P., & Forehand, R. (1993). Toward a new understanding of early menarche. *Adolescence 28* (112), 913–924.

William, G. & Wagner, W. (1996). Optimal development in adolescence: What is it and how can it be encouraged? *The Counseling Psychologist, 24* (3), 360–399.

Williams, K. & Bird, M. (1992). The aging mover: A preliminary report on constraints to action. *International Journal of Aging and Human Development, 34* (4), 271–297.

Willimon, W. & Naylor, T. (1995). *The abandoned generation*. Grand Rapids, MI: Eerdmans.

Willis, S. & Nesselroade, C. (1990). Long-term effects of fluid ability training in old-old age. *Developmental Psychology, 26* (6), 905–910.

Willis, S. & Schaie, K. W. (1986). Training the elderly on the ability factors of spatial orientation and inductive reasoning. *Psychology and Aging, 1* (3), 239–247.

Wilson, B. F. & Clarke, S. C. (1992). Remarriages: A demographic profile. *Journal of Family Issues, 13* (2), 123–141.

Wilson, E. O. (1978). *Sociobiology*. Cambridge, MA: Harvard University Press.

Wilson, J. (1993). *The moral sense*. New York: Free Press.

Wilson, S.M. & Medora, N.P. (1990). Gender comparisons of college students' attitudes toward sexual behavior. *Adolescence, 25* (99), 615–627.

Witter, F. (1993). Epidemiology of prematurity. In F. R. Witter & L. G. Keith (Eds.), *Textbook of prematurity: Antecedents, treatment, & outcome.* Boston: Little, Brown.

Woititz, J. (1990). *Adult children of alcoholics*. Lexington, MA: Health Communications, Inc.

Wolfe, D., O'Connor, D., & Crary, M. (1990). Transformations of life structure and personal paradigm during the midlife transition. *Human Relations, 43* (10), 957–973.

Wolford, B., McGee, T., Raque, T., & Coffey, O.D. (1996). Collaboration works for at-risk and delinquent youths. *Corrections Today* (August), 109–112.

Wolpert, L. (1991). *The triumph of the embryo*. New York: Oxford University Press.

Wolfson, M. (1989). *A review of the literature on feminist psychology*. Unpublished manuscript, Boston College, Chestnut Hill, MA.

Woodruff-Pak, D. (1988). *Psychology and aging*. Englewood Cliffs, NJ: Prentice-Hall.

Wortman, C. & Silver, R. (1989). The myths of coping with loss. *Journal of Consulting and Clinical Psychology, 57,* 349–357.

Wright, J., Huston, A., Reitz, A., & Piemyat, S. (1994). Young children's perceptions of television reality: Determinants and developmental differences. *Developmental psychology, 30* (2), 229–239.

Wyers, N. (1987). Homosexuality in the family: Lesbian and gay spouses. *Social Work, 32,* 143–148.

Yan, W. & Gaier, E. L. (1994). Causal attributions for college success and failure. *Journal of Cross-Cultural Psychology, 25* (1), 146–158.

Young, M. H., Miller, B.C., Norton, M. C., & Hill, E. J. (1995). The effect of parental supportive behaviors on life satisfaction of adolescent offspring. *The Journal of Marriage and the Family, 57* (3), 813–822.

Youngs, B. (1991). *The 6 vital ingredients of self-esteem and how to develop them in your child*. New York: Rawson Associates.

Yule, G. (1996). *The study of language*. Cambridge: Cambridge University Press.

Yuochi, S., Mischel, W., & Peake, P. (1990). Predicting adolescent cognitive and self-regulatory competencies from preschool delay of gratification. *Developmental Psychology, 26* (6), 978–986.

Zerbe, K.J. (1992). The Phoenix rises from eros, not ashes: Creative collaboration in the lives of five impressionist and postimpressionist women artists. *Journal of the American Academy of Psychoanalysis, 20* (2), 295–315.

Zippay, A. (1995). Exploring employment skills and social networks among teen mothers. *Child & Adolescent Social Work Journal, 12* (1), 51–69.

Zwillich, T. (1996a). Pregnant teens who work don't drop out. *Ob/Gyn. News,* (July), p. 17.

Zwillich, T. (1996b). Simple screen for alcohol use in pregnant teens. *Ob/Gyn. News* (July), p. 17.

LINE ART/TABLES

CHAPTER 1:

Fig. 1.1: From Developmental Psychology by R. Lerner, Vol. 27, 1991. Copyright © 1991 by the American Psychological Association. Reprinted with permission; Fig. 1.2: From John F. Travers, The Growing Child. Scott, Foresman and Company, Glenview, IL, 1982. Reprinted by permission of the author; Table 1.2: From John Dacey, Adolescents Today, 3d ed. Scott, Foresman and Company, Glenview, IL, 1986. Reprinted by permission of the author.

CHAPTER 2:

Fig. 2.1: Source: Data for diagram based on Hierarchy of Needs, in "A Theory of Human Motivation" in Motivation and Personality, 2d edition, by Abraham H. Maslow, 1970; Table 2.1: From John Dacey, Adolescents Today, 3d ed. Scott, Foresman and Company, Glenview, IL 1982. Reprinted by permission of the author; Table 2.2: From Childhood and Society by Erik. H. Erikson. Copyright 1960, © 1963 by W.W. Norton & Company, Inc., renewed © 1978, 1991 by Erik H. Erikson. Reprinted with permission of W.W. Norton & Company, Inc.

CHAPTER 3:

Fig. 3.1, Table 3.1, Fig. 3.2, Fig. 3.3, Table 3.4, Fig. 3.6: From John F. Travers, The Growing Child. Scott, Foresman and Company. Glenview, IL 1982. Reprinted by permission of the author.
Fig. 3.7: From Larue Allen and John W. Santrock, Psychology, The Contexts of Behavior. Copyright © 1993 Wm. C. Brown Communications, Inc., Dubuque, Iowa. All Rights Reserved. Reprinted by permission.

CHAPTER 4:

Fig. 4.5: Modified from K.L. Moore and T.V.N. Persaud, The Developing Human: Clinically Oriented Embryology, 5th ed. Copyright © 1993 W.B. Saunders Company, Philadelphia, PA. Reprinted by permission.

CHAPTER 5:

Fig. 5.1: From The Conscious Brain by Steven Rose. Copyright © 1973 by Steven Rose. Reprinted by permission of Alfred A. Knopf, Inc.
Table 5.1, Table 5.3, Table 5.4: From John F. Travers, The Growing Child. Scott,

Foresman and Company. Glenview, IL 1982. Reprinted by permission of the author.

CHAPTER 6:

Table 6.3: Source: From John Bowlby, "Attachment and Loss: Retrospect and Prospect" in American Journal of Orthopsychiatry, 52:664–678. Reprinted with permission from the American Journal of Orthopsychiatry. Copyright © 1982 by the American Orthopsychiatric Association, Inc.

CHAPTER 7:

Fig. 7.1, Table 7.1, Fig. 7.4: From John F. Travers, The Growing Child. Scott, Foresman and Company, Glenview, IL 1982. Reprinted by permission of the author.
Fig. 7.5: From John W. Santrock and Steve R. Yussen, Child Development: An Introduction, 4th ed. Copyright © 1989 Wm. C. Brown Communications, Inc., Dubuque, Iowa. All Rights Reserved. Reprinted by permission.

CHAPTER 8:

Table 8.7: From The Right Stuff for Children by M. Bronson. Reprinted with permission from the National Association for the Education of Young Children.
Table 8.8: Based on data from Rubin, Fein & Bandenberg.

CHAPTER 9:

Fig. 9.1, Table 9.1, Fig. 9.2: From John F. Travers, The Growing Child. Scott, Foresman and Company. Glenview, IL 1982. Reprinted by permission of the author.
Table 9.3: Source: Based on L. Kohlberg, "A Cognitive-Developmental Analysis of Children's Sex-Role Concepts and Attitudes" in The Development of Sex Differences, edited by E. Macoby, Stanford University Press. Stanford, CA. 1966.

CHAPTER 12:

Table 12.2: "Results from the National School-Based 1991 Youth Risk Behavior Survey and Progress Toward Achieving Related Health Objectives for the Nation" by L. Kann, W. Warren, J. L. Collins, J. Ross, B. Collins, and L.J. Kolbe from Public Health Reports, vol. 108, supp. 1, 1993, pages 47–55; Fig. 12.3: Source: Office of Technology Assessment, 1991. based on U.S. Department of Health and Human Services, Public Health Service, Centers for

Disease Control, National Center for Health Statistics, Division of Vital Statistics. Vital Statistics of the United States, Volume 1: Natality. U.S. Government Printing Office, Washington, D.C., various years; Table 12.6: Source: Adolescent Health (vol. 1–3). Office of Technology Assessment, Washington, D.C., 1991.

CHAPTER 13:

Table 13.1: Source: Bureau of the Census; Table 13.2: From John Dacey, Adult Development. Scott, Foresman and Company, Glenview, IL, 1982. Reprinted by permission of the author; Table 13.2: From Alexander P. Spence, Biology of Human Aging, © 1989, p. 8. Adapted by permission of Prentice-Hall, Inc., Englewood Cliffs, NJ.

CHAPTER 14:

Fig. 14.1: From The Seasons of a Man's Life by Daniel J. Levinson et al. Copyright © 1978 by Daniel J. Levinson. Reprinted by permission of Alfred A. Knopf, Inc.; Table 14.1: Source: From A. F. Saluter, "Marital Status and Living Arrangements: March 1991" in Current Population Reports, P-20 (No. 461). U.S. Bureau of the Census, Washington, D.C., 1991; Fig. 14.3: "Selected Sexual Practices" from The Social Organization of Sexuality. © 1994 by Edward O. Laumann, Robert T. Michael, CSG Enterprises, Inc., and Stuart Michaels. All rights reserved. Reprinted by permission of The University of Chicago Press.

CHAPTER 15:

Fig. 15.2: Source: From J. L.Horn, "Remodeling Old Models of Intelligence" in Handbook of Intelligence: Theories, Measurements, and Applications, edited by B. B. Wolman, Wiley & Sons, New York, 1985; Fig. 15.4: Source: Data from H. C. Lehman, Age and Achievement, Princeton University Press, Princeton, NJ, 1963; Fig. 15.5: Source: Data from W. Dennis, "Creative Productivity Between 20 and 80 Years" in Journal of Gerontology 21:1–8, 1966.

CHAPTER 16:

Table 16.2: From The Janus Report on Sexual Behavior by S. Janus and C. Janus. Copyright G 1993 Wiley & Sons, New York. Reprinted with permission of John Wiley & Sons, Inc.; Fig. 16.3; Source: U.S. Bureau of the Census; Fig. 16.4; From The Seasons of a Man's Life by Daniel J. Levinson et al. Copyright © 1978 by Daniel J. Levinson. Reprinted by permission of Alfred A. Knopf, Inc.; Fig. 16.5: From R. McCrae and P. Costa, Jr., Emerging Lives, Enduring Disposition: Personality in Adulthood. Copyright © 1984 Little, Brown and Company. Boston, MA. Reprinted by permission of the authors.

CHAPTER 17:

Fig. 17.1: Source: Social Security Administration; Table 17.1: Source: From Vital Statistics of the United States, U.S. National Center for Health Statistics, 1992; Table 17.2: From G. Jaquish and R. E. Ripple, "Cognitive Creative Abilities Across the Adult Life Span" in Human Development. Copyright © 1980 S. Karger AG, Basel, Switzerland. Reprinted by permission of the publisher; Fig. 17.3: Reprinted with the permission of Simon & Schuster from Developmental Physiology and Aging by Paola S. Timiras. Copyright © 1972 P.S. Timiras; Table 17.3: Reprinted with the permission of Lexington Books, an imprint of The Free Press, a Division of Simon & Schuster, Inc., from Fundamentals of Creative Thinking by John S. Dacey. Copyright © 1989 by Lexington Books; Table 17.4: From by R. J. Sternberg. Copyright © 1990. Cambridge University Press, New York. Reprinted with the permission of Cambridge University Press.

CHAPTER 18:

Fig. 18.1: From Robert Havighurst, "Perceived Life Space" in Contributions to Human Development 3:93–112 (1963). Copyright © 1963 S. Karger AG, Basel, Switzerland. Reprinted by permission of the publisher; Table 18.1: From "Sexual Interest and Behavior in Healthy 80- to 102-Year-Olds" by J. G. Bretschneider and N. L. McCoy in Archives of Sexual Behavior, 17(2): 117. Copyright © 1988 Plenum Press, New York, NY. Reprinted by permission.

CHAPTER 19:

Fig. 19.1: Source: From E. Kubler-Ross, On Death and Dying. Macmillan, New York: 1969; Fig. 19.2: Source: From Vital Statistics, U.S. Bureau of the Census, Washington D.C., 1992.

PHOTOS

PART OPENERS:

1: John Travers; 2: © John Fortunato/Tony Stone Images; 3: John Travers; 4: © H. Armstrong Roberts; 5: © Lori Adamski Peek/Tony Stone Images; 6: © Michelle Bridwell/PhotoEdit; 7: © Michael Newman/PhotoEdit; 8: © Michael/Newman/PhotoEdit; 9: © David Young-Wolff/PhotoEdit.

CHAPTER 1:

Page 4: Corbis-Bettmann; p. 6 a-e: Corbis-Bettmann; p. 14: © Jeff Greenberg/PhotoEdit.

CHAPTER 2:

Page 27 (top): Corbis-Bettmann; p. 27 (bottom): © Peter Dazeley/Tony Stone Images; p. 29: Corbis-Bettmann; p. 31: © Ulrike Welsch; p. 33: Courtesy of Andrew Schwebal; p. 36: Courtesy of James Wertsch; p. 40: © Christopher Johnson/Stock Boston.

CHAPTER 3:

Page 52a: © Walter/Dawn/Photo Researchers; p. 52b: © SIU/SPL/Photo Researchers; p. 62 (top): © Walter Hodges/Tony Stone Images; p. 62 (bottom): © A. Sieveking/Petit Format/Photo Researchers; p. 63: The Granger Collection.

CHAPTER 4:

Page 71 (top): © Nancy Durrell McKenna/Photo Researchers; p. 73 (top): © D.W. Fawcett/D. Phillips/Photo Researchers; p. 73 (bottom): © Omikron/Photo Researchers; p. 74: © Dr. C. Reather/Photo Researchers; p. 75 (top): © Petit Format/Nestle/SPL/Photo Researchers; Fig. 4.4, © Petit Format/Nestle/SPL/Photo Researchers; p. 81 (top): © Michael J. Oknoniewski/The Image Works; p. 81 (bottom): © John Griffin/The Image Works; p. 83: Courtesy of A.P. Streissguth, H.M. Barr, and D.C. Martin (1984); p. 86: © Will & Deni McIntyre/Photo Researchers; p. 90: © Bachmann/Photo Researchers; p. 91: © Eric Roth/The Picture Cube.

CHAPTER 5:

Page 99: © Tim Davis/Photo Researchers; p. 104: Courtesy Tiffany Field and Science, Fig. 2, Vol. 218, pages 179–81, 8 October 1982, Metzoff et al; p. 106, 107, 111: John Travers; p. 112: William Vandivert, Scientific American, April 1960; p. 114 (top): John Travers; p. 114 (bottom): © Barbara Rios/Photo Researchers.

CHAPTER 6:

Page 126: © Suzanne Szasz/Photo Researchers; p. 127: © Tony Latham/Tony Stone Images; p. 128: © Elizabeth Crews/The Image Works; p. 134: © Skjold Photographs; p. 136: © Sandra Johnson/The Picture Cube; p. 138: © Marjorie Nichols/The Picture Cube; p. 140: © Tony Stone Images; p. 143: © Julie O'Neil/The Picture Cube.

CHAPTER 7:

Page 151: © Dennis O'Clair/Tony Stone Images; p. 152, 154: John Travers; p. 156: © Tony Freeman/PhotoEdit; p. 157 (top): © Henry Horenstein/The Picture Cube; p. 157 (bottom): © Sharon L. Fox/The Picture Cube; p. 159: © Marjorie Nichols/The

Picture Cube; p. 166: © Robert Knowles/Black Star; p. 168: © Skjold Photographs.

CHAPTER 8:

Page 177: © Pedro Call/Stock Market; p. 178: © Alan Abramowitz/Tony Stone Images; p. 179: © Frank Herdoldt/Tony Stone Images; p. 183: © Lori Adamski Peek/Tony Stone Images; p. 189: © Jonathan Nourok/PhotoEdit; p. 191a: © Nancy Lutz/The Picture Cube; p. 191b: © Carol Palmer/The Picture Cube; p. 196: © Ulrike Welsch/Photo Researchers; p. 198: © Erika Stone/Photo Researchers; p. 202: © Elizabeth Crews/The Image Works.

CHAPTER 9:

Page 213: © Skjold Photographs; p. 216: © Alan Carey/The Image Works; p. 218: © Mimi Forsyth/Monkmeyer; p. 223: © James Carroll; p. 228: © Mary Kate Denny/Tony Stone Images; p. 229: © Myrleen Ferguson/PhotoEdit; p. 235: © Mary Kate Denny/PhotoEdit; p. 240: John Travers.

CHAPTER 10:

Page 245: © Tony Freeman/PhotoEdit; p. 252: © Richard Hutchings/Photo Researchers; p. 254: © Jack Spratt/The Image Works; p. 256: © Elizabeth Crews/The Image Works; p. 261: © Oscar Burriel/Latin Stock/SPL/Photo Researchers; p. 268: © Bob Kalman/The Image Works.

CHAPTER 11:

Page 279: © Elizabeth Crews/The Image Works; p. 280: Archives of the History of American Psychology, Akron, OH; p. 283: © Archiv/Photo Researchers; p. 287: © Giraudon/Art Resource, NY; p. 292: © David Young-Wolff/PhotoEdit; p. 294: Kansas City Star/Gamma Liaison; p. 297: © Susan Woog Wagner/Photo Researchers; p. 299: © Nourok/PhotoEdit; p. 302: © Tony Freeman/PhotoEdit; p. 303: The Granger Collection.

CHAPTER 12:

Page 314: © Myrleen Ferguson/PhotoEdit; p. 317: © Cleo Freelance Photography; p. 322: Corbis-Bettmann; p. 328: © John Griffin/The Image Works; p. 333: © Richard Hutchings/PhotoEdit; p. 337: © Phil McCarten/PhotoEdit.

CHAPTER 13:

Page 345: © Jason Laure; p. 347, p. 349: © Ellis Herwig/The Picture Cube; p. 363: © Amy C. Etra/PhotoEdit.

CHAPTER 14:

Page 372: Bobbi Carrey Collection/The Picture Cube; p. 375: © Mark Richards/PhotoEdit; p. 379: © Toni Michaels; p. 382: © Charles Gatewood/The Image Works; p. 383: © Bob Daemmrich/The Image Works; p. 384a: AP/Wide World; p.

384b: © Jaye R. Phillips/The Picture Cube; p. 386 (top): © Alan Carey/The Image Works; p. 386 (bottom): © Alan Carey/The Image Works; p. 389 (top): © Barbara Stitzer/PhotoEdit; p. 389 (bottom): © Spencer Grant/Stock Boston; p. 395: © Toni Michaels.

CHAPTER 15:

Page 405: © Ellis Herwig/The Picture Cube; p. 406: © Toni Michaels; p. 410: Courtesy of the News and Publication Service, Stanford University; p. 415: Corbis-Bettmann; p. 416: © Dion Ogust/The Image Works; p. 419: © Ellis Herwig/The Picture Cube; p. 422: © Toni Michaels.

CHAPTER 16:

Page 433: © 1994 Ulrike Welsch; p. 435: © Elizabeth Crews/The Image Works; p. 440, 443: © Toni Michaels; p. 445: © Toni Michaels/The Image Works; p. 448: © Nita Winter/The Image Works.

CHAPTER 17:

Page 457: © Topham/The Image Works; p. 460: © B. Grunzweig/Photo Researchers; Fig. 17.4, Fig. 17.5: University of Chicago Press; p. 466: © Toni Michaels; p. 468: © Barbara Rios/Photo Researchers; p. 474, 477, 479: © Toni Michaels.

CHAPTER 18:

Page 485: Corbis-Bettmann; p. 486: © Tony Freeman/PhotoEdit; p. 487: © Frank Siteman/The Picture Cube; p. 491: © David Young-Wolff/PhotoEdit; p. 498 (left): © FrankSiteman/The Picture Cube; p. 498 (right): © Toni Michaels; p. 499: The Museum of Modern Art Film Stills Archive.

CHAPTER 19:

Page 506: The Granger Collection; p. 508: © Toni Michaels; p. 509: © William Thompson/The Picture Cube; p. 512: © Michael J. Oknoniewski/The Image Works; p. 516: © Hank Morgan/SPL/Photo Researchers; p. 521: © A. Ramey/PhotoEdit; p. 523: © Paul Conklin/PhotoEdit; p. 525 (both): Keystone/The Image Works.

Name Index

Subject Index